❧ CATCH THE VISION OF ❧
The Well-Educated Heart

VOLUME TWO: METHODS & TOOLS

MARLENE PETERSON

Libraries of Hope

Catch the Vision of
The Well-Educated Heart

Volume Two: Methods/Tools

Cover Image: La Petite Jardiniere, by Daniel Ridgway Knight, (1887). In public domain, source Wikimedia Commons.

Libraries of Hope, Inc.
Appomattox, Virginia 24522

Website www.librariesofhope.com
Email: librariesofhope@gmail.com

Printed in the United States of America

Table of Contents

Methods

One Childhood

By Rachael Mulder

I want you to picture your child sitting in a modern-day classroom. Picture your child's days, month after month, year after year.

Now, close your eyes if you may, and in your mind's eye, I want you to remove the teacher lecturing in the front of the room. Remove the 25 other children the same age as your child. Remove the backpack full of textbooks, the tablet and learning apps. Remove the quizzes, tests, and standardized tests. Remove the monitored recesses and repetitive worksheets. Remove the government control and hours in front of a screen every day. Remove the waiting and the social insecurities. Remove the idea of falling behind or catching up. Remove the homework, the ringing bells, and the peer pressure. Remove the allotted times for individualized subjects. Remove the grade levels and benchmarks, the labels, and the desk. Now remove the building holding your child.

What's left? Your child, sitting outside with the blue sky above, an open mind and a whole world to explore. A whole person, capable of greatness. A person who has the potential to love reading and learning all their lives, to come to know God, to appreciate literature, nature, the arts, and history and have a firm understand of their world and society and how to find joy in it.

Earlier, we removed everything that makes a "school." But did we remove the possibility to receive an EDUCATION, or have we enabled it?

Now picture your child again. Add in siblings and friends of different ages, with ample time to interact and truly socialize, add endless unstructured hours in nature, time to think and ponder, and time to pursue passions and interests without a bell telling them time's up. Add a loving mother at their side, mentoring and guiding them as only a mother can. Add hundreds of classic stories and living books that teach them values, freedom, wisdom, bravery, and the joy of family. Imagine a place where God and morals are not prohibited, but spoken of freely and interwoven into subject of learning and aspect of life. Add in the freedom to pursue those things your family values, unencumbered by strict attendance rules and a school calendar. Add in ample time for prayer and pondering, scripture and family history study, meaningful discussions, music and poetry, all while cuddled up close on the couch. Add in more time to pursue hobbies like cooking, baking, gardening, skiing, painting, traveling, woodworking, whittling, knitting, biking, photography, imaginative play, caring for animals, starting a business, writing stories and plays, learning survival skills, playing music, road trips, and camping. Add in time for your child to dabble in a great many things, discovering their passions and what truly brings them joy. Add in long family discussions about the classic books you've read together, your feelings about them, and how they may relate to the current events of your country. Imagine a life where each subject is not separated and checked off, but where they are all interwoven and related to real life experiences, the books you excitedly read together, and the things your children are interested in. Add in the deep love and knowing of a family that is not separated all day, but that learns together, struggles and cries together, and encourages and grows together. Contemplate the gift we can give our children to know and be known, to love and be loved, not conditional on their performance.

What if instead of dry, fact-filled textbooks, our children learned from living books and directly from the great leaders and minds as they are motivated by Washington's courage, inspired and comforted by the journeyings of the apostle Paul, mentored by Martin Luther King, drawn to contemplation by Thoreau, and laugh and cry alongside Laura Ingalls Wilder.

Could it be that "school" as we know it might hinder a true education, while a true education may look nothing like what we expect?

Is it possible to receive an advanced degree but lack a true education? We live in a society full of skilled people with degrees, but are they receiving educations and raising up noble leaders who will have the wisdom, courage, and ability to be the leaders our future needs?

Before you worry too much over curriculum and schedules, I need to question everything you think your child's education and childhood should be. Question every aspect. Why do we do what we do? Listen to what the research says about academically-driven preschools and kindergartens, the loss of play, the effects of endless hours on screens, the essential role of time in nature, and true connection to their parents. Listen to what your heart says.

Could it be that the way we educate in our modern-world is outdated, and ineffective? Could it be that our busy schedules, shuffling from school to sports to homework is encumbering the ability for our children to play, to blossom, to think, and to know themselves and understand the world around them? Are we stuck in a system and societal pressures that are no longer serving us but we are too blinded to be able to jump off and create something different?

Are we weighed down and paralyzed by fears, unable to move forward and create a better way?

I've heard all the excuses, all the worries. I've heard them and I've had them. I've spent countless hours crying over my abilities, shortcomings and weaknesses, questioning everything again. And so has every other mother who has chosen to homeschool in spite of them.

But think about it. Who better equipped to teach a child than the one person on Earth who has been in tune with their needs and the inner workings of their soul from before they even took their first breath? Who better to lovingly nurture, guide, and counsel a child, modeling and encouraging as both the mother and child learn and grow together? No one is better equipped to be their teacher. No one is more dedicated to their success than you. If you feel called to homeschool, do not let fears take root in your heart. Fight them. Fight them with the passion and love only a mother has, open your eyes to a bright and beautiful future, take your child's hand, and begin this journey together.

Charlotte Mason: "Mothers work wonders once they are convinced wonders are required of them."

Keep Playing!

What is happening here at Well-Educated Heart is not 'what to learn' nearly as much as 'how to learn.' It goes against the normal way of doing things. And it's your heart that has to see it. Each heart has to create its own vision, and that requires many, many impressions and encounters with ideas, but once the heart sees clearly, you'll know for yourself what to do.

I often hear moms say they're looking for a curriculum that doesn't require any time on their part. They just want to open a book and everything's there. It would be easy for me to create something like that, telling you exactly what story to read on what day and questions to ask and what activity to do. But what will be missing is the connection to your child's personality, his aptitudes and interests; the dynamics of your relationship; your personal experience. What may be missing is your love for the topic and that magical flow of emotion from your heart to his won't happen. And the biggest piece that will be missing is the inspiration that shapes learning to the purpose, mission and calling of your child.

So here's what I'm going to try and say next time I'm asked the question, "How do you do this?" I'll answer that if you want to learn to play the piano, you have to start with the basics: Here is Middle C. If you want to educate the heart of your child, you also have to start with the basics: read more stories aloud together, share more poetry, sing more songs, listen to more music, seek out the best picture books to look at, spend more time out in nature and play more together.

And then keep warming your own heart. Take advantage of the study materials I've prepared for mothers, including the ongoing study at the Mother's University. There's something for everyone there. Take notes when something strikes you. I purposefully included some readings that may make you stretch. Stretching is good for our bodies and our hearts. Soon your heart will start filling up with impressions and ideas and visions. And as something impresses you, start practicing it. Just like the piano.

Yes, WEH requires more of you. But in the end, you'll feel greater peace and confidence in what you're doing. Because your heart will understand why you are doing what you are doing, you'll know what books to grab and what resources to turn to that will exactly fit your family and your circumstances.

As I present ideas, if you are asking yourself, "How am I going to get my kids to do this?" you are asking the wrong question. The right question is, "Is this something I want to do? Is this something I can see myself doing?" And if the answer is yes, I can guarantee your success because, even if your kids don't do it all, by engaging in these activities, you're going to be giving them the gift of a wise, warm-hearted mother with clear vision. You'll find yourself, quite effortlessly, saying things like the following: "I read something interesting today"; "Did you know that…?"; "I was thinking about…" And learning in your home will become a natural part of the day. And the chances are high that your kids, especially if they are younger, will do exactly what they see you do.

"Look at homeschooling as primarily an opportunity to educate yourself and bring the kids alongside."

So how will I answer the question, "How do I do this?" I'll try and answer: Start with Middle C. Be patient with yourself. Allow yourself time to learn and grow.

And keep playing.

"Everyday is a fresh beginning… Take heart with the day, and begin again." --Susan Coolidge

Thoughts from a Daughter

Krystal D'Abarno

I don't chime in much in discussions here because I don't have kids of my own, so I don't feel like I can have a meaningful opinion on this matter. But reading through comments here over the years and talking with my mom extensively on the issue, I have some thoughts that maybe someone might feel useful. So here you go. (And please forgive me in advance for my rambling.)

Marlene is my mother. I work with her, doing a lot of the nuts and bolts stuff of Libraries of Hope. But I have probably given her more push-back on the ideas of Well-Educated Heart than anyone else. (Sorry for all the grief I give you, mom!) I'm more of a pragmatic (mind) where she's clearly entrenched in heart. So for years we've debated the practicality of implementing her vision in today's world. She has struggled again and again with trying to find a way to help you mothers catch the vision of what's possible. And I've always argued that our society is so set on academics and making sure kids meet certain markers by certain deadlines, that you mothers are up against an entire world telling them that doing anything else will result in utter failure for your children. That's a really tough hurdle to surmount. And I know from personal experience that many of you get most of that pushback in your own home and families.

But here's how I've reconciled things in my own mind. This is not a curriculum. She has consistently pushed back against all the pressure to turn it into a curriculum. This is…something entirely different. It's a completely different way of looking at things. It's not about gaining an education to someday get into college and someday get a job. If that's your whole goal, I'm sure there are plenty of other wonderful programs out there. If, however, you want something that will bring life and light to you and your children's world, this is the place for you. She's creating a philosophy that will nourish parts of us that STEM alone won't.

However, if, like me, you have a hard time ignoring the pressures of the world (or your husband…), that doesn't mean you have to completely throw this out. The more my mom has developed and honed WEH, the more I've seen that it really is largely about you. It's about feeding your souls. And as you do that, as you implement more art and music and poetry and nature into your daily life, it will trickle down to your kids. Include them where you can and as they want to be included. Just give them the opportunity to experience life, rather than spend 15 years stressing out about academics. So if you can't bring yourself (or aren't allowed) to take your kids into the unknown, start with you. WEH wasn't a thing until after we'd all grown up and moved out of the house. But I've watched my mom spend years enriching her own life with these resources, and in turn my sisters, and in turn their children.

You know you and your children best. Just do what you can, at whatever level you're comfortable doing. Whether that's memorizing a new poem once a week or proverbially setting sail for a new route. But do something. Start somewhere.

One final note re: college/careers. I had an atypical education. I homeschooled for a lot of years, and got my high school diploma via an accredited distance learning course. Other than the distance learning course, which I ended up completing in a few months, I don't really remember much "formal" education. I was really worried about college because I hadn't done much formal schooling and I thought I would be so behind. But I got accepted to BYU, where I graduated summa cum laude and went on to get an MPA and a law degree. I attribute most of my success to knowing how to read and write…and to my parents not getting in my way. They never pushed me in any direction and never pressured me to do specific things. WEH will give your children that. They will learn how to read and write and think critically, and with time will teach them math and science, but more importantly, it will give them the desire to push themselves and learn to follow the path they want to live.

We never sat down at a specific time for lessons, though I think we did have to do "work" for a certain number of hours each day, just on our own schedule. And by "work," I mean it was basically reading and making notebook pages about what we read. She'd show us some books we could peruse, I assume based around our reading levels, and just let us have at it. For me, homeschooling started in middle school. So it wasn't all play and imagination. We did do math (I think we used Saxon) and had some textbook-like books for science (Abeka maybe?), though my mom would remember the source better than I did.

I don't think I'm alone when I say that I probably couldn't pinpoint many lessons I learned in school, public or otherwise, though I obviously did learn at both. I don't remember what I learned about Colorado history or the quadratic equation, and I can't remember what was on the historical timeline I made that wrapped around the walls of our entire schoolroom. But what homeschooling offered me that public school never could, was the opportunity to live at my own pace and do my own thing. We took "field trips" all the time. I got to volunteer at a children's museum once a week. We spent many, many hours outside riding our bikes on the canal trail near our house. When I turned 14 and was old enough to earn some money, I saved everything I had and went on a trip to Europe with my sister and a local school teacher who took students every year. And then went again two years later. I traveled with my dad who taught seminars all over the country. When I turned 18, instead of going straight to college, I went with another sister to Russia, where we volunteered as English teachers for a semester. I got to experience so much more of the world because I wasn't stuck in a desk from 7-3 every day.

I didn't live WEH, because it didn't exist yet. But my experience taught me that there's so much more to life than grades and tests. And I'm really grateful to my mom for letting me stay home.

How Do I Do This?

I receive many letters from moms who, after they hear about the philosophy of heart-based learning, tell me how excited they are to do this. And the question often turns to: "How do I do this?" They want to know which books to read to which child and how many books to read. They want to know how to do notebooking right…and what about math? And they want to know it now. Although I try and offer suggestions, I always say this is a process; to be patient, it will take time to unfold.

This is not a curriculum. This is a pattern for learning.

To borrow the words from someone else I heard, the truth is, I can teach you how to dance, but you have to feel the music for yourselves. And without the music, the dance steps aren't going to be very satisfying.

I can't make you feel the music. I can't transfer the vision of a well-educated heart directly from my heart to yours. The only way you'll see it is for your own heart to assemble hundreds of impressions into a whole picture for yourself. A masterpiece can only be painted one brush stroke at a time. A lot of those impressions will come from what you read or listen to or see. You'll find them in the lives of the great men and women you study; in literature; in poetry and in history. But you'll also find them in nature, art and music. They're buried like treasure—just like the pearl is hidden in the oyster shell deep on the ocean floor. It will require effort to find them. And slowly, over time, your heart will understand. You will see through new eyes and everything you do with your child will flow from that understanding heart.

This kind of learning is caught, not taught directly. It requires your diligence. It's fitting that the word 'diligence' comes from the root word *diligo*, meaning to 'love earnestly.' You can create beautiful notebooks and read a thousand books, but if there is no understanding why you're doing what you're doing—if there is no love in the process—they're just dance steps without music.

All the suggested readings in this introductory class and in the Mother's University are filled with pearls of ideas and impressions, waiting for your heart to mine them. It's an individualized and personal course of study, but you'll have help, for as Job said, "[T]here is a spirit in man, and the inspiration of the Almighty giveth them understanding."

I share 18th century educator Pestalozzi's desires as he wrote: "I wish to wrest education from …cheap, artificial teaching tricks, and entrust it to the eternal process of nature herself; to the light which God has kindled and kept alive in the hearts of fathers and mothers; to the interests of parents who desire that their children grow up in favour with God and with men…. [Love is] the sole and everlasting foundation in which to work. Without love, neither the physical nor the intellectual power will develop naturally."

Here are 5 distinguishing features of the Well-Educated Heart philosophy of learning.

Our objective is to prepare to live lives of maximum joy. Jobs and careers may be part of that, but they are not the end destination.

Our focus is on mothers, not on curriculum or method. There is a very natural occurrence in nature—the young offspring search for something to attach to and then they grow to be like that to which they have attached. Humans are no different. So our aim is to first develop rich personalities in moms who will in turn influence their children. Relationships matter a lot in the Well-Educated Heart. Dr. Gordon Neufelt wrote, "You cannot parent a child whose heart you do not have." And I would add: "You cannot teach a child whose heart you do not have." How a child feels when he is around you matters more than the words you say or what curriculum you use.

I often hear moms say they aren't qualified to teach their children because they were never trained; which usually translates to the fact that they never graduated from college or earned a teaching certificate. I am not aware of any university in any place or at any time that offered a degree in Motherhood. But's about time we have one. So you'll find the beginnings of a Mother's University at welleducatedheart.com. The tuition is affordable because it is free. It works into any schedule because you work at your own pace. The more you put into it, the more you'll get out of it. I've assembled the finest faculty of heart specialists that ever lived to mentor and train you. It's a minor detail that they're all dead—their spirit and their personalities live in their writings. And then we'll bring in the research of modern experts who are confirming by studies that what was taught 100 years ago is correct. I hope the combination of the two—past and present—will give you confidence because the world needs what only you can provide.

Learning around here is piece of cake. If your child is hungry, would you feed him a cup of flour, a spoonful of salt and baking soda or spoonfuls of vanilla and vinegar? Would you offer him a cube of butter to suck on? And even if they love sugar and chocolate, would you sit them down to a bowlful of sugar or a half a cup of unsweetened cocoa?

Of course not. But if you take all of those ingredients which are totally unappetizing individually, stir them all together in a 9x13 pan and bake them in the oven for 30 minutes, you'll have the most deliciously moist chocolate cake to serve them. And I guarantee they'll ask for more.

It's become the way of education to serve learning by individual ingredients: vocabulary, spelling, rules of grammar, facts to memorize. And it's making our young children lose their appetites. Serve them stories, songs, poetry, pictures and allow generous portions of play time, they're going to not only keep coming back for more, you're going to find their heart and your heart wrapping around and attaching to each other. If you become the one who administers the daily dose of vinegar, they're going to run when they see you coming.

We promote spiral learning here, not linear learning. Linear learning as I use the term is where you have a list of subjects to teach and assign a grade in which to teach them. If we were machines, linear learning may be perfect. Just download the programs on the hard drive and they won't go anywhere. But because we are human, it's a system of test and forget. Most of what is learned in this way is thrown away in the pile of "Who cares?"

We're not machines. Our minds and hearts are very complex and very selective about what is allowed in. Neural pathways need to be re-traveled multiple times and interlaced with other similar neural pathways, creating networks of thought and emotion. Just as our bodies require constant nourishment, so do our minds and hearts. You can't eat an apple once and expect to be supplied with its nutrients for the rest of your life.

Spiral learning is about a lifetime of learning line upon line, layer upon layer, here a little and there a little. It's a way of returning over and over again to similar and familiar things, deepening the understanding each time around.

Everything on our site is organized around a 12-month rotation schedule to facilitate spiral learning. Rather than 8 or 10 individual subjects, there are only two: A study of people and a study of nature.

We use history, biography, geography, cultural studies, literature, poetry, music and art to help us understand human nature and to learn the art of living well and of living together peacefully.

In the nature spiral, we begin by helping our children love the beautiful world they live in by giving them eyes to see and more importantly, hearts to feel. We strive to awaken a sense of wonder and curiosity. As their curiosity unfolds, we start to unfold the laws that science has discovered. As they see the perfect order, harmony and beauty of Nature, and the attention to the tiniest detail, they come to feel connected to the Designer and where they fit in His grand design. Nature is God's University.

There is great flexibility in this 12-month rotation. It's meant to be a servant to you, not a master. This 12-month rotation schedule allows multiple ages of children to study the same topics at different levels. Your job is to get the spiral going by serving cake and creating an appetite for more. As your children get older, you just need to get out of the way and let them do their own chewing because, after all, all the flavor is in the chewing.

I suggest a system of Notebooking for the Well-Educated Heart to help young hearts begin to hold on to things they care about and start making connections as they enter these spirals of learning. These notebooks can also help satisfy proof of work for those of you who have to report to school officials.

Finally, the distinguishing feature of the Well-Educated Heart is that "True education is between the child's soul and God." To take spiritual influences out of your child's learning is like attempting to garden without sunshine. As a child's heart attaches to a mother's, a mother can then help re-connect a child to God. Remember—we grow to be like that to which we are attached. A child will develop more of the character traits you hope he'll develop through a genuine feeling that he is a child of God than will ever happen by 1000 well-crafted lessons on specific character traits. But more importantly, God will begin to lead your child on a customized, individualized course of study.

The trend to start rigorous academics at younger and younger ages is hardening the hearts and deadening the souls of our children. It is a law of nature that that which is not used, atrophies from disuse. By abandoning the arts in childhood—music, poetry, pictures and story—that part of us that can feel the quiet whisperings of Deity remain dormant and undeveloped.

That's why we spend so much time in the Arts here—to provide fertile ground for the Spirit to work. Sometimes I hear from moms who say they don't feel anything when they read poetry or listen to classical music or read a piece of great literature. Unfortunately, that's a sad casualty of our Mind-focused culture. The remedy is to start using those dormant faculties. Gradually at first. If you've been out in the desert for days without food or water and sit down to a big meal of roast beef, mashed potatoes and gravy, hot buttered biscuits, and turtle pecan cheesecake, that food's not going to stay down. You have to start with sips of broth, a little jello and some apple juice to wake the system up. I can tell you I have also heard from moms who are doing just that—and they are excited at the new measure of joy that is filling their homes.

We are living in extraordinary times. No generation of mothers has been able to do what you are going to be able to do because no one has ever had the resources you have. If we want to see different results, we need to find new ways of doing things. You are among the pioneers who are blazing new trails for others to follow.

The world may never know your name, but the impact you will have as one who tends to a child's heart is incalculable.

Heart-Based Education Basics

Did you hear about the newly married husband whose bride always cut off the ends of the roast before she put it in the oven? Finally, he asked her why she did that, and she said it was because that's what her mom did. So next time he saw his mother-in-law, he asked her why she cut the ends off her roast and she said it was because that's what her mother did. As luck would have it, grandma was in town, so he asked her why she did it. And she said, "Oh, that's because my roasting pan was too small and the meat wouldn't fit otherwise."

When it comes to educating our children, just because something has been done a certain way for a long time doesn't mean it's necessarily the best or most effective way of doing it. The reasons certain methodologies and emphases were put into place may not even exist anymore. I think it's a really good thing that more and more people are questioning not just the *how*'s but the *why*'s of school and education because we are living in one of the most extraordinary times in the history of the world and we can't afford to be cutting the ends off the roast 'just because that's what mom did.'

Never before has there been a generation that can be offered the kind of education I am describing, primarily because of three reasons:

> It's taken thousands of years to develop the 'curriculum'—ours is the generation of the harvest.
>
> It requires today's technology to deliver it.
>
> It can only thrive in the oxygen of freedom, and freedom has been a rare commodity through the ages.

Unfortunately, in the very day mankind has the most sumptuous feast ever spread before him, he has no appetite to partake. As one of my storyteller friends described, we "crawl through life surrounded by all stirring things, unmoved." Ironically, our loss of appetite has been largely caused by the very technology that has made the feast possible.

Before photography, which is the technology that brings masterpieces of fine art to our homes, if you wanted to hold on to a moment and capture and preserve an image, you had to draw or sketch it. In the mid-1800s, John Ruskin warned people not to let the ease of taking pictures replace the habit of sketching; that our eyes would lose the capacity to see. He compared two people going out for a walk down a green lane; the one a good sketcher, the other having no taste of the kind. He said the non-sketcher will notice the trees are green, but not give it another thought. He may notice the sun is shining, but that's all.

But what will the sketcher see? Ruskin said, "His eye is accustomed to search into the cause of beauty, and penetrate the minutest parts of loveliness. He looks up, and observes how the showery and subdivide sunshine comes sprinkled down among the gleaming leaves overhead, till the air is filled with the emerald light. He will see here and there a bough emerging from the veil of leaves, he will see the jewel brightness of the emerald moss and the variegated and fantastic lichens, white and blue, purple and red, all mellowed and mingled into a single garment of beauty.

"Is this not worth seeing? Yet if you are not a sketcher you will pass along the green lane, and when you come home again, have nothing to say or to think about it, but that you went down such and such a lane."

Today we take hundreds of pictures, but how much do we really see?

Now consider the printing press that gave us books. By the end of the 1800s, children's books were plentiful and easy to come by. Before that time, values, lessons and histories were passed from generation to generation by the fireside as stories were shared heart to heart. When books came along, it was easier to pick up a book and read it, lessening the emotional impact on the heart. There was now a book between the reader and the listener with the reader sharing someone else's words, not the words filtered through his own heart. People no longer learned stories by heart because they didn't have to and consequently the stories didn't soak in as deeply.

By the early 1900s, a group of storytellers rose up to warn that we weren't going in a good direction; that, yes, books were good, but we needed to keep the art of storytelling alive to keep our hearts warm. We were losing depth of soul. They wrote dozens of books teaching mothers and teachers of young children how to do it and gave them hundreds of stories to tell.

Story groups were formed across the nation much like our book clubs, for the purpose of practicing the art. Sadly, today, few people can tell a single story by heart. We leave storytelling to the professionals. Gone are the days of story hours around the fire. Consequently, too many children are severely story deprived. Without a love of stories, there is little desire to read. So in an age when there are more books available than any other time in history, not only can Johnny not read them; he doesn't even want to.

And then think about what happened when films came along. Before movies, people went to plays that were close and intimate and produced a profound effect on the heart because they were so close to the actors. They drew people into the story—they lived it. The fear was that films were too passive and distant.

So in 1912, there was a Little Theatre movement to encourage people to keep plays alive in their neighborhoods. Props and costumes were simple. Stages were framed with boughs of trees in open fields. Putting on the plays had nothing to do with making money. It had everything to do with feeling. Brigham Young once said, "If I were placed on a cannibal island and given a task of civilizing its people, I should straightway build a theatre." And when he first got to the Salt Lake Valley, that's exactly what he did. Today, movies have not only displaced intimate plays, they've replaced the reading of books.

We're also losing the ability to express ourselves in writing. The technology that enables us to quickly type out our thoughts is making cursive handwriting obsolete, yet brain scans reveal the whole brain is engaged when writing cursive, which doesn't happen when we print or type.

Furthermore, neuroimaging reveals that ideas flow more freely when cursive handwriting is used.

We learned much about the people of the past through the letters they wrote to each other. Letter writing is also a thing of the past. We rely on instant communications of emails and texts. What are we leaving behind?

The technology that brings symphonies into our homes has made music a performing art, rather than a natural expression of our own hearts. We're losing the benefits of the musical vibrations within us. We don't have to sing; someone else can sing for us. And we can just listen, but in the process, we lose the joy that comes from singing our own songs. The national anthem is supposed to unite people as they join their voices singing the same song. Now, we hire people to perform it; we don't even know the words anymore.

As hearts grow a little colder, we feel a little emptier; unsatisfied; disconnected. Our souls long for authenticity; we tire of the artificial plastic.

Imagine if we were wise enough to realize our mistake. Imagine if we could hold on to the benefits of our technology, and yet put back into place those activities that keep our hearts warm so we have a greater capacity to enjoy all that technology is delivering. Imagine if we can give our children eyes to see, ears to hear, and hearts to feel.

That's what the Well-Educated Heart is all about—how to warm our hearts back up. Let me touch on a few heart-based learning basics.

Principle 1: Warm the heart first.

Our ultimate objective is to raise whole-brained children. Many of the problems of our world are caused by the fact that there are too many half-brained people running around! Emotion without reason is as problematic as reason without emotion. Scientists who have studied Einstein's brain tell us the secret behind his genius was because he had an extraordinary number of neural pathways connecting both sides of his brain.

The whole left-brain/right-brain theory of science has spawned all kinds of big business. Teaching companies help you determine if you have a left-brained or a right-brained child and then cater learning activities to that child. The left-brained person excuses himself from art and the right-brained person says he's just not a math person.

But in 2012 researchers at the University of Utah debunked the theory. Although they acknowledged the left- and right-brained regions, they claimed that new neural pathways connecting the two regions can be created clear into old age. What I take away from that is, if you're the art type, you should engage in more math and the connections between the two hemispheres will be greater. If you're the science guy, you ought to spend a little more time with poetry and literature. And you'll be happier for it.

One thing neuroscientists agree on—children develop emotionally before they develop intellectually. They tell us that they observe a first significant intellectual shift at around age 8 and another one at the onset of puberty, at around age 12-14. Although it's still being debated, some scientists argue that the brain isn't fully developed until our 20s and the region that doesn't develop until then is the part that connects consequences to actions, which would explain a lot of teenagers' actions.

What that means is that the first eight year of a child's life can best be served by making impressions on the heart while the heart is uncomplicated and open. It makes it possible for us to instill a love of all things good and beautiful and true. Hearts tend to harden the older we get, and if you spend too much time pushing academics and intellectual activities at too young of an age, you may miss a golden window of opportunity to reach the heart.

I'll say it again: Childhood is for warming the heart. And, as Plato said over 2000 years ago, "All learning has an emotional base." We want to first broaden the base to build upon. A strong emotional base will give life and meaning to the academics that come later.

Think about what happens when you plant a sunflower seed in the ground. The sun can shine all day on a seed planted in the middle of January and nothing is going to happen until the soil warms up. It's not the light of the sun that starts the growing process; it's its warmth. The warmth releases the life force that gets things growing. And then the seed starts building a strong root system that enables the developing plant to draw nutrients from the soil. It's not until it finally sprouts above ground and opens its leaves that it has something to catch the light. If it has a shallow root system, the sun will scorch the plant and it will wither and die. But if the roots are strong and deep, the plant will use the light to grow until it finally produces the flower.

The root growing process is underground. We can't see it. If we pull the plant up to check to make sure it's going well, we'll kill the plant. Likewise, we have to trust that the things we are doing to warm the hearts of our children at this young age are doing exactly what they're supposed to be doing. It's a preparatory time.

The tools we use for the heart are different than the ones we use for the mind. You inform the mind. You impress the heart. The mind feeds on facts and information—the language of words and numbers—while the heart favors images and feelings, patterns and shapes. To reach the heart, we primarily use Music, Pictures, Poetry and Story. We call these the Arts—you even find the word 'Art' in the word 'Heart.' 'Earth' without 'Art' is 'Eh.' The more you use these tools in early childhood, the greater will be your success.

Kate Douglas Wiggin, who wrote *Rebecca of Sunnybrook Farm* and is a personal inspiration, wrote of these younger years: "Those are the years that count the most. We learn much afterwards and much of the originality is lost in the process; we love, marry, accomplish a little, or a great deal, as the case may be, but the first ten years, in the stocking of our memories and the development of our imaginations, in the growing of all those long roots out of which springs real life, these do far more for us than all the rest."

Don't shortchange them.

Principle 2: Only the warm heart kindles warmth in another.

Warm your own heart first and everything will flow a lot more naturally. The fun thing about a heart-based education is you'll get to spend time doing things that are inherently enjoyable. If you missed out on nursery rhymes growing up, you'll get to enjoy them now. If you didn't get a lot of fairy tales when you were little, now you will. I have been amazed at how much my heart has opened up by doing 'childish' things. You can't rush the process going forward, but to a degree, you can pick up what you missed. And your heart will warm up in the process and will effortlessly and naturally spill to your children.

The important principle is that your children imitate what their hearts see played out in front of them. Albert Schweitzer noted that "example is not the main thing in influencing others. It is the only thing." Picture a mother duck with her little ducklings. They happily waddle along behind her, doing what they see her doing. Now picture that mother trying to drive her ducklings from behind. They'd scatter in every direction, not knowing what to do or where to go!

If you want your children to sing while they work, you sing while you work. They need to work beside you so they can see what you're doing. They don't instinctively know how to organize toys. If you want them to love beautiful music, let them see you loving beautiful music. If you want them to love reading, let them see you love reading. If you want them to keep a nature journal, let them see you keep a nature journal. You get the picture.

Show them. Don't tell them. Their hearts don't understand telling.

Feed your heart. I can't emphasize this enough. If you find your children lack motivation and they're not doing what you think they should be doing and you find yourself getting discouraged, take time to feed your own heart. It will keep you moving forward. It's like the oxygen masks on the airplane—we are instructed to put the mask over our own mouths before we attempt to place it over the mouth of our child. I encourage you to spend as much time as you can with the circle of storytellers and educators I keep telling you about who lived 100 years ago. I'll be showing you where you can find their writings. Take time to read the prefaces and forwards of a lot of these classic children's books—it's an education in itself! You'll find your heart growing warmer and warmer every day and it will quite naturally spill over to your children.

Principle 3: Force negates learning.

Plato knew it: "[K]nowledge which acquired under compulsion obtains no hold on the mind." Da Vinci knew it: "Study without desire spoils the memory and it retains nothing it takes in." And yet we're still reluctant to let go. We think that without force and pressure, without compulsory education, our children won't learn.

Today, scientists can watch what's happening in the brain when learning is going on. There's actually a little gateway in our brain that shuts down when information is forced. It's now a pure scientific fact: If a student is stressed out, the information is not going to make it to the higher centers of the brain where there's long-term storage and comprehension. Joy and enthusiasm are essential for learning to happen. Students learn what they care about; that which they love. It's the pleasure of the Arts that make it ideal for childhood learning and actually opens up the mind for future learning. As other information comes along, it finds an emotional base to attach to. And then the brain pays attention. I recommend googling 'learning and emotion' and read more about how the brain functions if you need more convincing.

Antoine de Saint-Exupery summed up the learning process quite nicely with this: "If you want to build a ship, don't drum up men to gather wood, divide the work, and give orders. Instead, teach them to yearn for the vast and endless sea."

The fear that is most often expressed by parents who choose to homeschool their children is they're terrified their child is going to 'get behind.' It's that fear of falling behind that makes us drive our children to work harder and harder. I know I was concerned about that when we were raising our children. And even some of my children felt the fear. It's part of our culture, I suppose. One of our daughters in Junior High was so worried that we suggested she go back to school and see for herself, which she did. It took her about a week to see that her two years at home "not doing much" hadn't made her miss a thing, and she chose to come back home a few months later.

The problem facing us is we have become a very academic-oriented culture where we measure and test and compare. It takes courage to trust this process of root building that can't be seen, especially when your neighbor or family members have children who are reading and writing and doing math at a level your child is not because you have been placing your focus on internal matters. It's always hard to go against the norm. But keep your eyes open for the increasing number of research studies that are coming out in favor of heart-based learning. It's out there.

For instance, I read this coming out from the University of Virginia: "Two major studies confirmed the value of play vs. teaching reading skills to young children. Both compared children who learned to read at 5 with those who learned at 7 and spent their early years in play-based activities. Those who read at 5 had no advantage. Those who learned to read later had better comprehension by age 11, because their early play experiences improved their language development.

I am not recommending something that has not been proven. As I spend time reading the biographies of many of the great men and women of history, I find the same pattern of childhood learning: lots of stories in childhood and an abundance of free time for imaginative play.

We talk about a rigorous education as though we can make it happen. The truth of the matter is, there is no greater taskmaster than the heart. Thomas Edison refused to learn in school, but as a young man, a friend recalled walking in his living room and seeing him with six feet of scientific volumes piled around him that he had sent for from around the world and within a matter of days, he had come up with ideas for over 2000 experiments to test his theories. Noah Webster learned 28 languages so that he could study the roots of all our words in the English language and define them in a dictionary. Read the story behind any great discovery or work, and you'll find a heart fueled by passion that's doing the driving. Not a heart that is being forced.

Let go of the fear of falling behind and work on inspiring your child's heart, and I promise, it will all work out fine and your child will make a contribution to the world that only he or she can make. Trying to force children to learn will work against you every single time. And remember, there's no such thing as falling behind when you're blazing your own trail.

Principle 4: Light the kindling first.

Have you ever tried to start a campfire by dropping a big log in the fire pit and lighting a match to it? Didn't go so well, did it? Of course, you know that you have to start the fire with kindling. At first, maybe you'll light pieces of paper that burn easily and then start feeding the fire with twigs and small branches, gradually building up to bigger pieces of wood. It's only after you've gotten the fire blazing that you can drop the log on, and then it will feed on the log for a very long time without any more help from you.

My daughter went to an education conference and told me of a father she talked to who was frustrated that his teenage daughter didn't love the classics he loved as a boy. His daughter had absolutely no interest in them. I also often hear the frustration of mothers who don't understand why their young children won't sit still while they're reading a book to them.

Maybe they're trying to drop the log before the fire's burning.

You have to build up attention spans and the capacity to sustain thought. A child who has never learned to create images from words or who was never exposed to rich language in younger years isn't likely to sit down with *War and Peace* or Shakespeare as a teenager. If an older child has no interest in reading history books, you may have to first peak interest by telling stories or reading shorter high-interest stories. You have to hold the interest of young children with shorter fairy tales before you can sit down and read *Little Women* to them.

Principle 5: The flavor is in the chewing.

Helping your child to love learning is like bringing your child to a buffet of the most delicious foods as far as your eyes can see and letting him dish up. What I see happening too much, today, though, is an education system that not only makes all the food selections for the child, it also chews up the food for them really, really well and then turns to the child and says, "OK—Open wide!" When the child closes his lips up tight and says, "unh unh, that's not coming in here," some well-intentioned educator may say, "Come on, Billy, open up. If you don't open up, you're never going to get into a good college and if you don't get into a good college, you'll never be a global worker in the global economy." So the child opens up just enough to swallow, but I can guarantee there's not much tasting going down.

Somewhere along the way, we've forgotten that all the flavor is in the chewing. By pre-digesting all the information and organizing it on worksheets with questions and assigned activities so that they're getting exactly what we think they need to get out of the learning activity, we take away the joy of self-discovery; we shortchange the ah-hah moments that come when they see connections for themselves or when they find answers to questions their own hearts have asked.

The textbook with carefully laid out learning objectives and a systematic way of unfolding the knowledge will be of use in certain subjects in later years after the heart is sufficiently warmed and it's time to train the mind. But if you give long lists of questions to a child who has no interest in the subject, the learning isn't going to stick anyway and may forever turn him off to ever want to taste it again.

Of course I'm not going to want my surgeon to have picked and chosen what he wants to learn; I will want to feel confident he knows the difference between my spleen and my appendix; I will want to make sure another competent surgeon has thoroughly trained him in all the details. The difference is, by the time a student enters that stage of learning and training, his heart wants to learn everything about the subject and will willingly do the assigned work to learn it, even if it's tedious work. Even the driest textbook comes to life to the warmed-up heart. Please, drill and test my doctor before you put a scalpel in his hand. But before he gets to that point, please be sure his heart has been fully equipped with compassion and integrity and thoroughness.

Childhood is the time to encourage questioning, not bombard him with questions we want him to answer. The ability to ask questions comes naturally. Anyone who has spent time around a 4-year-old knows that. Why is the sky blue? What is that? Why? Why? Why? When a question comes out of one's heart, it's the heart's way of saying that it has discovered a gap in understanding and has made room for and found a place for the answer. I find it telling that God waits for us to *ask*. He knows unless we're asking, we won't know what to do with the answer when it comes. How sad it is that we often squash that natural sense of wonder when children enter school by sending the message that the adult is now going to do the question asking. He soon learns to wait for someone else to ask the questions and the joy of learning dies.

In childhood, let him savor the learning moments at his own pace. Let him lead out with his own questions. Let him discover by experimenting. Let him do a lot of his own choosing and chewing because all the flavor is in the chewing. I don't think many of us would bother eating if we never got to taste the food. We can make suggestions, but don't be too quick to dish up his plate.

Principle 6: First impressions, then expression.

But what about writing?

John Milton who gave us *Paradise Lost*, rejected the idea of school compositions, calling it "forcing the empty wits of children to compose themes, verses and orations, which are the acts of ripest judgment, and the final work of a head filled by long reading and observing." I remember so well the stress of having to write papers in school when I didn't have anything to say. Then, to make matters worse, I was supposed to conform to rules that didn't make sense to me and I was going to get graded on how well I did. And to top it off, I dreaded the possibility that the teacher might read it out loud to the class for critique. Talk about writer's block.

That's called going against the natural order of things. Childhood is for filling the heart with impressions, and not forcing the child to express those ideas before he's ready. When the heart is full, it will seek an outlet. Then the rules of grammar and organization will be welcome. And because your child will have spent many, many hours immersed in examples of fine and elegant writing, the rules will connect to something already inside of him. He will have experienced them thousands of times already. When Lew Wallace, who wrote *Ben Hur*, finally arrived at the point that he wanted to write, he regretted that he hadn't learned the rules of grammar and he had to take time to learn them. But I suspect he learned them in a short period of time rather than spread out over years. His heart was hungry to know them at that point. And judging by the success of his book, he learned his rules well.

By spending too much time on activities for which the child may not be developmentally ready, you may be sacrificing something much more important. For example, President Garfield made this observation: "One half of the time which is now almost wholly wasted in district schools on English grammar attempted at too early an age, would be sufficient to teach our children to love the Republic and to become its loyal and life-long supporters."

You can find many natural ways to help children develop handwriting skills in preparation for the day they'll start expressing themselves, like copy work, writing letters to grandma or famous people or pen pals, and other means that don't force expression before a child is ready. Also, let a child be a storyteller before he's a story writer, and the writing process will come much easier. Let him see you write out the stories as he tells them and the process of writing will start to make sense to him in a natural way.

Principle 7: Let your home reflect what you value.

Is the most inviting room in your home the TV room or your library? What hangs on your walls? Are books something you check out from the library or are they worth owning? Your children will pick up on what you value by watching how you spend your money. Where your treasure is, there will be your heart also.

I want to spend a little time talking about what I believe is the most important room in the home of a well-educated heart—and that's your family library.

We live in a very temporary society. Many people prefer the convenience of a digital library and as wonderful as that portable library is, it's another technology that can have unintended consequences if we're not careful. "Out of sight, out of mind" applies to books. When I walk by my bookshelves, it's like walking by hundreds of old friends who continue to exert a quiet influence on me. As I touch each one, I remember how I felt while I was reading the book. Or I'll pull it off the shelf and open it and ideas come streaming back to me. A book stored on a Kindle doesn't do that. Nor can a book returned to the library do that. Someone once said that if a book isn't worth owning, it's probably not worth reading.

I think that may serve as a good criterion, especially today when we are overwhelmed with so many choices. I saw one figure that estimates 3000 new titles are published every single day. With print-on-demand technology, we've lost the gatekeepers who used to slow down the flow of books. Now, anyone can write a book today and have it up for sale tomorrow. Literally.

More than ever, our children need help selecting the best. Not all books are created equal. There's a lot more trash to wade through to find the treasure. One way we can help them is to let them taste the very best when they're young; literature that is satisfying; that is filled, as Kenneth Grahame who wrote *Wind in the Willows* said, "with divine spark of heavenly flame." If we give them that which tastes sweet and delicious to them when they're young, they're more likely to reject the vulgar and the shallow and the debasing when they're older.

That's why I would start with the classics. They have a proven track record. And if you value faith, family, freedom and virtuous living, you're especially going to need to build your own library of books for your children to feed from. We had our own cultural revolution in the 60s and the only way a culture of faith and family will be preserved is if you and I preserve it in our own homes.

Dr. Paul Vitz, Professor of Psychology at New York University, did a study of 90 of the most widely used reading and social studies texts used in our schools at the time. Keep in mind—this was back in 1986. In social studies, which was supposed to reflect American life to children in younger grades, not one of the texts examined—over 15,000 pages—had any reference to any word of any type of religious activity, such as attending church or worshiping or praying. Not one text mentioned marriage as a foundation of the family. Not one text used the words "marriage, husband, wife, homemaker."

In upper grades, there was not a single reference to any patriotic theme after the year 1780. Only one story focused on traditional male/female romantic love. No stories supported motherhood or showed any women or girl with a positive relationship with a baby, a young child or even a doll. However, stories of sex-roll reversal were common as well as stories of feminism.

If you value faith, family and freedom, look for books published before 1960 and hold on to them. You'll feel the difference. It's been a very long time since I've tasted strawberries like the ones my mother grew in our garden. I've just kind of come to expect that the strawberries I get at the store aren't going to have much flavor. So it really caught me off guard last week when I bought some strawberries and bit into one—and it actually tasted like a strawberry! It was juicy and sweet. Mmmmm. So delicious. If you haven't spent much time with the older children's books, I think you might have a similar experience. The word I hear most often that is used to describe these older books is that they feel 'warmer.' I would say they're delicious.

As we go along, I will show you where you can find books like these.

Emerson said, "You are what you think about all day long." Don't we want to give our children the 'best' thoughts to think about?

These are a few basics in heart-based learning. If you need something by which to measure your success, try this. In many shamanic societies, if you come to a medicine person complaining of being disheartened, dispirited, or depressed, they would ask one of four questions:

When did you stop dancing?

When did you stop singing?

When did you stop being enchanted by stories?

When did you stop finding comfort in the sweet territory of silence?

As we tend to our children's hearts through activities such as these, the end result will be a child whose countenance will reflect: I am really glad to be alive.

That's what I call a successful learning outcome in a heart-based education.

Practical Tips

I love the fresh start feeling that comes with the New Year and for some of you, using Well-Educated Heart principles is a new path. So I thought I'd have a little chat with you at the beginning of this new year and share some of the thoughts that have been going through my head the last few weeks.

I picked up a set of old books at a book sale not long ago—I know—big surprise! It was Elbert Hubbard's *Little Journeys to Homes of the Great* written between 1895 and 1910 and I want to read to you a few things from that. But before I do, I just have to take a little detour here because Elbert Hubbard left us a prime example of how the experiences of others plant ideas in our hearts and can shape the choices we make.

Hubbard wrote about the sinking of the Titanic in 1912 and singled out the story of Ida Strauss who refused to board a lifeboat and leave her husband and they both went down with the ship. Hubbard wrote:

> Mr. and Mrs. Straus, I envy you that legacy of love and loyalty left to your children and grandchildren. The calm courage that was yours all your long and useful career was your possession in death. You knew how to do three great things—you knew how to live, how to love and how to die… [T]o pass out as did Mr. and Mrs. Isador Straus is glorious. Few have such a privilege. Happy lovers, both. In life they were never separated and in death they are not divided.

Well, just 3 years later in 1915, Elbert Hubbard and his wife were on board the Lusitania when it was hit by German torpedoes just off the coast of Ireland. A survivor of the event left this account to his family:

> I cannot say specifically where your father and Mrs. Hubbard were when the torpedoes hit, but I can tell you just what happened after that. They emerged from their room, which was on the port side of the vessel, and came on to the boat-deck.
>
> Neither appeared perturbed in the least. Your father and Mrs. Hubbard linked arms—the fashion in which they always walked the deck—and stood apparently wondering what to do. I passed him with a baby which I was taking to a lifeboat when he said, 'Well, Jack, they have got us…'
>
> They did not move very far away from where they originally stood. As I moved to the other side of the ship, in preparation for a jump when the right moment came, I called to him, 'What are you going to do?' and he just shook his head, while Mrs. Hubbard smiled and said, 'There does not seem to be anything to do.'
>
> The expression seemed to produce action on the part of your father, for then he did one of the most dramatic things I ever saw done. He simply turned with Mrs. Hubbard and entered a room on the top deck, the door of which was open, and closed it behind him.

It was apparent that his idea was that they should die together, and not risk being parted on going into the water.

Do you think Ida Strauss planted that idea? I do. It's the power of stories in our lives.

Anyway, let me get back to where I was going. One of the *Little Journeys* volumes is all about Great Teachers and I found our friend, Pestalozzi, in there. So I want to open this chat with the reminder that what we're engaged in is not something new or something I have made up. It's just that the idea for educating hearts before minds has had a hard time taking hold over the last couple of hundred years. It's been a pretty bumpy road.

Hubbard gives us a good reminder of what heart education looks like as he described Pestalozzi's method:

> Pestalozzi educated by stealth. At first he took several boys and girls of eight, ten or twelve years of age, and had them work with him in the garden. They cared for fowls, looked after the sheep, milked the cows. The master worked with them, and as they worked they talked. Going to and from their duties, Pestalozzi would call their attention to the wild birds, and to the flowers, plants and weeds. They would draw pictures of things, make collections of leaves and flowers, and keep a record of their observations and discoveries. Through keeping these records–[notebooking]–they learned to read and write and acquired the use of simple mathematics… When work seemed to become irksome they would all stop and play games. At other times they would sit and just talk about what their work happened to suggest. If the weather was unpleasant, there was a shop where they made hoes and rakes and other tools they needed. They also built birdhouses and made simple pieces of furniture… [T]hey patched their shoes, mended their clothing, and at times prepared their own food.
>
> [T]o his own satisfaction, at least, he proved that children taught by his method surpassed those who were given the regular set courses of instruction.

Pestalozzi wrote accounts of his experiments and emphasized his belief that we should educate through the child's natural activities; also that all growth should be pleasurable. His shibboleth was, "From within, out."

That's a pretty good summary, I'd say.

I haven't talked as much about Friedrich Froebel, one of Pestalozzi's followers. So I'd like to take a couple of minutes and tell you more about him and read a little more from Hubbard's *Little Journeys*. Pestalozzi was 60 years old when Froebel came to study under him as a young man. "Pestalozzi had faced much opposition, ridicule and indifference, and had spent most of his little fortune in the fight, but he was still at it and resolved to die in the harness."

After working with Pestalozzi, Froebel went home to Germany to try and put into practice what he had learned. He was joined by two colleagues—Middendorf and Langenthal. Pastors advised parents to not entrust their darlings with the teaching experimenters. Froebel's argument that women were better natural teachers than men on account of the mother-instinct, brought forth a retort from a learned monk to the effect that it was indelicate if not sinful for an unmarried female, who was not a nun, to study the nature of children.

Despite disappointments, failures and opposition, none of these three men were willing to give up the fight for education by the natural methods. But how could they get the people on board?

The ah-hah moment came to Middendorf and Langenthal, at the same time–out on the mountainside! Begin with the children before the school age, and call it the Kindergarten!

Hurrah! They shouted for joy, and ran down the hill to tell Frau Froebel.

The schools they had started before had been called, "The Institution for Teaching According to the Pestalozzi Method and the Natural Activities of the Child," "Institution for the Encouragement and Development of the Spontaneous Activities of the Pupil," and "Friedrich Froebel's School for the Growth of the Creative Instinct Which Makes for a Useful Character."

Hubbard commented, "A school with such names, of course, failed." No one could remember it long enough to send his child there—it meant nothing to the mind not prepared for it.

There's a gem—Let me repeat that line: "It meant nothing to the mind not prepared for it." We're going to come back to that.

The translation of the word *kindergarten* is "child garden" and the idea took. It was to be a place where children could blossom. "Love was the keystone, and joy, unselfishness, and unswerving faith in the Natural or Divine impulses of humanity crowned the structure."

Froebel wrote: "The occupations pursued in the Kindergarten are the following: free play of a child by itself; free play of several children by themselves; associated play under the guidance of a teacher; gymnastic exercises; several sorts of handiwork suited to little children; going for walks; learning music, both instrumental and vocal; learning the repetition of poetry; storytelling; looking at really good pictures; aiding in domestic occupations; gardening." That sounds familiar, doesn't it?

But Froebel wrote, "It will take three generations to prove the truth of the Kindergarten idea." It was very clear to him that education must begin "a hundred years before the child is born." In other words, he knew it would take time to change the way people think and do things.

He knew it was the mothers and home he needed to reach, but "to reach and interest the mother in the problem of education was well-nigh impossible. Toil, deprivation, poverty, had killed all the romance and enthusiasm in her heart. She was the victim of arrested development."

But he noticed that it was the older girls in the family who took charge of the younger ones while the mother worked in the fields or toiled at her housework. This little other-mother was a child, impressionable and could be taught. So he told the little other-mothers to come to school and bring the babies with them. And then he set to work showing these girls how to amuse, divert and teach the babies. His plan was to reach the home and the mother through these children.

These girls went on to be teachers he called school-mothers, which later was shortened to school marms. They combined mother-love and the teaching instinct. Froebel utilized their service in teaching others in order that he might teach them. The years went by and the little mothers had children of their own, and these children were the ones that formed the first, actual kindergarten. Also, these were the mothers who formed the first mothers' clubs. And it was the success of these clubs that attracted the attention of the authorities, who could not imagine any other purpose for a club than to hatch a plot against the government.

Officials thought, "Here comes a man who thinks he knows more than all the priests and scholars who ever lived, and fills the heads of fool women with the idea that they are born to teach instead of to work in the fields and keep house and wait on men.

"Mein Gott in Himmel, the women know too much already! If this thing keeps on, men will have to get off the earth, and women and children will run the world, and do it by means of play! This thing has got to stop before Germany becomes the joke of mankind."

And so, in 1850, an interdict was placed on Friedrich Froebel, making the Kindergarten a crime, and causing the speedy death of one of the gentlest, noblest, purest men who have ever blessed this earth. His ideas were spreading—success, at last, was at the door; he had interested the women and proved the fitness of women to teach—his mothers' clubs were numerous— love was the watchword. And in the midst of this flowering time, the official order came, without warning, apology, or explanation, and from which there was no appeal. It crushed the life and broke the heart of Friederich Froebel.

The chapter ends with these words: "Men who govern should be those with a reasonable doubt concerning their own infallibility, and an earnest faith in men, women and children. To teach is better than to rule. We are all children in the Kindergarten of God."

I like that. So here we are again, trying to convince mothers that they possess God-given gifts to do what no one else can do better. And that learning is best begun in play, in poetry, story, picture, singing and music, and spending time in nature. Love and joy are vital ingredients. And it may yet take three more generations to get the idea firmly planted because it seems we have to keep starting over.

But this time around, we have so much the advantage. We're not starting from scratch. Much has been prepared for us. Women aren't toiling out in fields just trying to survive. We are blessed with labor-saving devices and technology has brought the finest learning resources into even the humblest home. Mothers can connect with other mothers and learn from each other and support each other. Mother's Clubs can be taken to a whole new level.

Pestalozzi said it may take 300 years to get his idea to take hold. Like I've said before, let us be the generation that finally gets it right.

So in that spirit, let me make three suggestions or offer three reminders as you move forward if this is the journey you want to take.

One: Become one who seeks knowledge and help your children do the same. The scriptures constantly remind us: "Seek and ye shall find." When God placed Adam and Eve on the earth, He didn't give them a study guide or manual. He simply placed them in a garden. And look what mankind has accomplished as we have questioned and wondered and searched and discovered.

Sadly, we've developed a system of schooling that squashes that natural desire to seek. We've learned to wait for our assignments; for someone to tell us what to read, what questions to answer, what we're supposed to get out of our learning. For the first 15 or 20 years of our lives, someone else is telling us what we are going to study. We don't trust ourselves to learn. Part of your challenge is to reawaken that desire to seek not only in your children, but in many cases, yourselves.

There's a reason why God repeatedly reminds us to Ask and Seek. Remember the gem I said we'll come back to?

"It meant nothing to the mind not prepared for it."

If I was given a dream or a vision with E=mc2 in it, what would I do with that? It would mean nothing to me. I am not prepared for it. But to an Einstein who had been searching and asking and pondering, when that simple equation came to him, it was a Eureka moment.

How many "E=mc2" are we forcing on our children? Things they're not prepared to take in?

You'll notice that the Mother's Study Guides in the Mother's University aren't very specific. I don't tell you which book to read first or what you need to get out of what you read or listen to. I just place them where you can access them, but you have to do the seeking. Some of you will only have time for a nibble here and there while others can sit down and feast. It doesn't matter how fast you work through it–only that you do something out of a desire to know and understand. There's so much you'll miss out on if you don't seek.

The same pattern of learning is laid out for your children. I have provided years' worth of study materials that just need a 'seeking' mind to search them out. The whole world is filled with hidden treasures waiting for inquisitive and seeking minds to discover them.

We hold on to that which we're ready to receive, but there is no finding if we're not seeking. Seek for inspiration; inquire of the Lord and ask for direction for *you* and for your children. He will help you.

So first reminder: SEEK. And it doesn't matter where you start...just start.

The second reminder is tied into the first one: Our bodies need constant nourishment and so do our hearts and souls. Repetition is key to learning.

Somehow, no matter how busy we are, we find time to eat every single day. We know our bodies won't last long without food. Well, hearts also need food every single day. If you aren't making time to read and study and ponder, you'll feel the effects. Sometimes a mom will write and ask, in essence, "Just tell me how to do this." In my mind, that's like someone asking me for the one meal they need to eat so that they don't have to bother with cooking anymore. There is no single meal. Eating every day will be going on for the rest of your life, but the good news is that, for most of us, eating is something we like to do. We look forward to it. So get into the habit of feeding your heart every single day. Find the time–where there's a will, there's a way. It doesn't have to be large meals. But if you want to have a well-educated heart and that's what you want

27

for your children, there is no other way. We need to constantly be learning and we need that learning to be refreshed and replenished or it grows stale. We need to be regularly reminded of things we have learned before. That's just the way it is. Repetition.

Which is why notebooking is so vital to this process. The more you write, the more you learn and the more you hold on to. We forget things so easily!

Also, avoid the tendency to checklist your learning. In other words, don't read one story about Thomas Jefferson and cross him off your list. Encourage your children to constantly seek to deepen their understanding. When you read additional books or even re-read the one you read, new facets of his personality will unfold as well as more details to bring him and the times he lived in to life. Sometimes you'll run into conflicting information which your mind will seek to resolve. That's how critical thinking is learned. Think broad and deep.

Stories can be read over and over again. The first time, you are usually looking to see what happens. But the next time, you read because you want to feel what you felt the first time, all over again. You want to find out if there's anything you missed the first time around. The next time, you may be better prepared to receive more that's in the story. That's the beauty of stories–we all connect at different levels. So don't worry that you read a story to your 10-year-old and now he might hear it again when you read it the next year or the year after that to his younger brother. Stories are often better the second time around. I've heard the story of Cinderella more than a hundred times and I never get tired of it.

Think constant nourishment, not one-time meals.

Third reminder that you've heard me say before: Tend to the kindling before you try and drop the log on the fire.

Sometimes I hear from moms who have lined their shelves with wonderful old books and their kids groan at the thought of reading them. Or moms are so excited to have all their kids do notebooking and they get the same reaction.

I'd call that dropping the log before the fire is burning strong. Drop it too early and the log will crush the fire and put it out.

Your job is to kindle desire so that eventually, your child will sustain his or her own learning. Once the log is burning, you no longer have to sit there and tend it. But you've got to get the fire burning strong first, and you start with little pieces of paper, little twigs, and gradually add larger pieces until the fire is strong enough to sustain burning the log.

So let's talk some kindling suggestions. And I might add, your little children will likely take to stories, pictures, songs, poetry and nature like a fish to water. It's usually not a problem. But sometimes older kids have created walls and barriers and can be more of a challenge. Hearts tend to harden as we age.

Most important thing: Avoid force at all costs. Neuroscientists have actually observed a little gateway in the brain that leads to long-term storage. It cannot be forced open, but can only be opened by a pleasurable experience. The Arts are inherently pleasurable and it's why love and joy are such a vital part of this kind of learning. Think of the contest between the wind and the sun to see which one of them could get the man to remove his coat. The harder the wind blew, the closer and tighter the man drew his coat around him. But when the sun shined its warmth, he easily removed his coat.

You're trying to shine warmth.

You can't force your way in. Sometimes we use force in innocent ways. You would think that creating a course of study around character traits, for example, would be a good thing. But remember that little gem–we only take in that which we're prepared for? If you choose Honesty, for instance, as a theme and try and find a story to drive that trait home and make a lesson of it, it can actually backfire on you. Little hearts know when they're being forced and will keep the gate closed. Most stories contain many lessons that the heart will gather out according to what it's prepared to receive. Let the process happen naturally. The same story may teach honesty to one child, love to another, and patience to another. And at a later time, that child will pull out a different lesson. That is the beauty of learning with stories. Don't short-circuit the process by forcing the lesson.

Think gradual. If your child has been living on a french-fry and milkshake diet, if one day you clear that all away and say from here on out, we're only eating healthy seaweed and kale chips, you're probably going to run into a little resistance. You want to gradually replace what they've been eating with better choices.

The kind of heart food we're trying to incorporate into our diets around here is very rich and nutrient-dense. Sometimes you need to offer a sip here and there–you know, the spoon full of sugar to make the medicine go down. Once they trust that it really does taste good, they'll be willing to take larger bites. What does that spoon full of sugar look like?

Start with short stories, especially stories that connect to something your child likes.

If they're reluctant, try something like saying, "I just read a story that I love. Can I read it to you while you're eating lunch (or breakfast or dinner)?"

Read stories by candlelight.

Read stories while they're engaged in an activity they like that uses their hands–drawing, handicrafts, Legos, learning to write cursive, and so forth.

Use audio stories in the car or let them listen to them in bed after the lights are off.

Ease into chapter books. If they balk at what you're reading, you know you've dropped the log prematurely. Set it aside and look for some kindling.

Offer choice wherever possible. For example, familiarize yourself with maybe three books and tell them about each one and ask which one they'd like to read. Would they like to read to themselves or read it aloud together?

Read a chapter or two aloud–make sure they're sucked into the story–and then set the book in a conspicuous place where it can be easily accessed–and somehow 'not have time to read it' so that they pick it up and finish it.

If you feel overwhelmed trying to fit in art and music and nature drawing, start introducing them gradually as well. Maybe start with a poetry tea time once a week or even once a month and read poetry and make poetry pages together. Then add in a day once a week where you look at a piece of art and tell a story about it, sketch it, play a memory game with it. Consider setting aside one afternoon a week or even every other week to work on notebooking pages for the story of the world history notebook or literature gems. Put some music of the month on in the background. Work on learning to sketch things in Nature once a week. Add in one cultural day where you make a craft or cook an ethnic food and play some traditional folk music from that country in the background.

Along the way, teach your children how to use all the resources available to them so when the fire's properly flaming, they can take off and you can get out of the way.

My daughter asked me the other day how anyone gets through all these books that I have listed. In the beginning, you may only read one book a month and that's okay. Just make sure it's an enjoyable and positive experience. Later, once the fire is burning stronger, it's not unusual for young people to read a book every single day. But even if that doesn't happen, you've laid a foundation for a lifetime of learning.

Think simple. Think kindling. This is the stage for fanning desires; it's not the time for mastery. Of course I want a doctor who can correctly identify every piece of my anatomy. But that task isn't the task of childhood.

I was talking to a mother yesterday who told me about her grandparents and how the stories just flowed out of them as she sat on their porch and listened. That was the education of her childhood and she told me what a force and power it had had in her life. Our generation is largely story depleted–that's why I say it might take a couple of generations before we really begin to see the results we hope to see because we have to fill our hearts back up so that the stories will just naturally flow out of our mouths and hearts. If we can re-learn the stories of the flowers and the stars, we can tell them while we're out on walks like Pestalozzi did and so many others I have bumped into in the reading of old books and open the joys of nature to our children's hearts. We can inspire hearts as they did when we re-learn the stories of legends and fairy tales and the stories of history. We have to re-learn how to look at fine art and how to hear the message of beautiful music. We have to acquire a taste to appreciate the rich language and imagery of poetry. This learning by heart is going to take some time.

But if we will seek, daily nourish our hearts and souls, and keep kindling the desire in our children, one day we will see a generation rise unlike any generation that has ever lived because their hearts will be filled with a rich inheritance. To accomplish this is our burden and our joy.

I pray for you mothers every morning and every night and in between. I keep seeking and constantly ask what more I can do to help–and ideas somehow keep coming.

Remember—nothing is required of you, but that you will, with the help of our Father in Heaven, be able to accomplish. Just keep moving forward, one step at a time. You can do this!

Raising Lifelong Learners

Keep in mind—we're trying to do a deeper layer of learning here and it looks different than what you may be used to. I know that having a curriculum to rely upon may feel like a much safer way to go and if you are brand new to homeschooling, maybe that's where you need to start while you learn more about the Well-Educated Heart methods. If I was going to choose a curriculum, I would, hands down, choose Jenny Phillip's Good and Beautiful. There are lots of wholesome lessons for the heart. Every day you'll know exactly what you need to cover. It's all laid out for you. It's a familiar way of learning. You'll feel more in control. Many moms are afraid that they'll forget to teach something or leave something out or that their children will fall behind. Curriculum calms that fear for moms who are afraid they're going to ruin their children's lives. But because you are here listening to me, I suspect that somewhere deep inside of you, you feel like something is missing. That there has to be a different way because for too many students, this way of learning kills their love of learning. They can hardly wait to graduate and put learning behind them. Sadly, far too many students, after graduation, will never choose to pick up a book and read it despite all our lessons in reading comprehension. How many adults write anything? Who spends evenings in deep conversation? Who chooses to spend their leisure hours studying science, history or literature?

One of the objectives of the Well-Educated Heart is to create lifelong learners. Childhood is for warming and opening hearts to that end. Most of what I talk about and the resources I share with you are for warming and opening their hearts, not mastering a subject. Mastering is the second step, not the first. Nor is it the end. We want learning that will bear fruit—learning that will serve a usefulness; learning that will bring joy into their lives and make the world better.

I keep trying to find ways to help you see how this kind of learning differs from the way we're all used to because the tendency is for moms to take the resources I've gathered and try to fit them into or organize them into a curriculum, where the mom is still in control of the learning. She's picking the books her children will read. She's deciding what people they'll learn about and when. She's still in charge. And it short circuits and defeats the whole process.

Let me try and illustrate it this way. My husband and I and a couple of our kids went to an Escape Room for the first time a couple of weeks ago. If you don't know what that is, there are usually 3 or 4 rooms you can choose from. You're given a scenario and then you have one hour to escape. We chose the Fire Escape and here was our scenario:

> The smell of smoke causes you and your family to evacuate your home. While outside, your father tells you his precious family heirlooms are going to be destroyed. Without thinking twice, you tap into your hero instincts and rush back into the house. Can you find all the items *and* escape before time runs out?

There was a list of about 18 items on the wall for us to look for. Now, we had no idea at all what this was going to look like. I can't give away any details, but I can tell you that the room we were in was very sparsely furnished—a bed, a couple dressers, a few pictures on the wall. At first glance, we thought, what on earth? What are we even looking for? None of those items were in plain sight.

So, we just started opening drawers and looking behind things and under things, looking for anything that might give us a clue and we started telling each other random things we were seeing, not knowing if they meant anything or not. Now, we were told that if we got stuck, we could call down to the desk two times and they'd give us a clue. After about 20 minutes of finding nothing, we decided we better ask and he said, "Did you find the such and such item" and told us where to look for it. Suddenly seeing that made us see how the clues fit together and it got us going. Now we understood what we were looking for and it started getting exciting as we scrambled to look for hidden clues and solved puzzles and there were all kinds of surprises along the way.

We finally got down to the last 5 minutes with one more heirloom to find. We had all these pieces of puzzles that didn't make any sense and didn't seem to fit together, and we thought, "Oh darn, after all that, we're not going to get out in time." We didn't think there was any square inch that we hadn't searched. Then my husband said, "Uh, guys, did any of you look here?" and he held up an item that suddenly brought all clues together and we frantically worked a combination and got out of the room with one minute to spare.

It was exhilarating! We were elated! We kept saying "We did it! We did it!" Afterwards we went to dinner and we kept reliving how the clues came together and how we solved the puzzles and all the unexpected surprises. We can hardly wait to do it again!

Now let's revisit the Escape Room curriculum style. First of all, you're not there by choice. Someone has compelled you to be there. You are usually not even given the reason why you're in the room; rather, you're handed a stack of tasks to be completed before the hour is over. And if you don't, you can't go out and play.

So the Fire Escape room, curriculum style, might look like this. Open the third drawer down in the dresser. You will find a locked box. Here is the combination to the box. When you open it, there is another assignment inside.

And now imagine reporting to the same room, day after day, with a new stack of tasks to be completed.

True, no child will be left behind. They will probably all eventually get out of the room. But at what cost? I guarantee, there would be no Escape Room franchises. Who would go back? There is no thrill.

But isn't that what learning by curriculum looks like? Every day we give our children a list of tasks to be completed. Define this word. Spell that word. Answer this question. Read this story. And tomorrow, we'll do it again. And the next day and the next day.

How many children do you hear out in the backyard saying, "That was so cool when we copied the definition of refraction." "Yeah! Hey! I can spell it!"

Designers of curriculum have already made all the connections. They have solved all the puzzles. Your job is to simply complete the tasks they give you. There is little room for the ah-hah moments when pieces come together. There are few Archimedes in the bathtub moments where he shouted "Eureka!" when he figured out a problem he had been working on.

It reminds me of a community I saw in China where everyone was given employment. Everyone had their meals provided for and their housing. They were given clothes to wear. All their needs were met. They finally had to seal off the balconies because too many were jumping to their death. What was the point of living?

We are designed and hard wired to learn by discovery and exploration. It's finding the clues and the patterns and making the connections for ourselves that keep us coming back for more.

My hope and my desire is that you, at some point, will have the courage to relinquish your role as taskmaster and embrace the fun of loading the rooms with clues and getting out of the way while your children explore and discover for themselves. It's up to you to tell the story and light the fire to get the process going. And just like the guy at the desk downstairs, you're there to answer questions when they get stuck. In the end, it makes life a whole lot easier for you because you are not burdened with a million facts you feel you need to hammer into your children. When your children learn by exploration and discovery, they'll keep coming back for more. And they'll find hidden treasures of knowledge you may not even know exists.

I think it was William Wordsworth who said one day that there was so much in life that he still wanted to learn, that if he lived 70 times 7 lifetimes, he couldn't get to all of it.

The friends of the great scientist Louis Agassiz wanted to gift him with a trip to Europe. He said, "How can I take time to go there when there is so much in my own backyard I have not yet discovered and learned about?" He stayed home and spent the next 9 months exploring every inch of his back yard and thrilled at all he learned.

Is this the love of learning you want to see in the hearts of your children? Then it will require that you let go and trust the process.

Does it help you if I remind you this is God's method of learning He uses with us? He created a beautiful world and loaded it with endless clues. But He has never assigned and compelled His children. His instructions are simply, "Seek. Ask. Knock." It didn't bother Him that it took us nearly 6000 years to discover electricity and put it to good use. It's been there the whole time. We only figured out flying a little over a hundred years ago.

He knew to not allow the explore and discover process of learning would be to deny us one of our greatest joys. As Dr. Alan Stockdale wrote: "God gave to man the challenge of raw materials, not the ease of finished things. He left pictures unpainted, music unsung, problems unsolved that man might know the joys and glories of creation."

That process of creation is to take matter unorganized and organize it into new ways. In our escape room, we organized pieces of information into a usefulness, and it was thrilling. Think of all the music that has been created from just 8 notes on a scale, all the art that has been painted from 3 primary colors, and all the works of literature written using 26 letters of an alphabet. And think of all that has yet to be created.

What a tragedy that we train our children to wait for instructions; that we rarely give them a chance to explore or discover something that excites them. As I said a moment ago, this "finish the tasks we assign" mentality is turning out generations of students who want nothing to do with learning once they have a diploma in hand. And many other students don't care enough about the diploma to even earn that.

Granted, there is risk involved. We checked and only about 30% make it out of the Fire Escape room on the first try. But even God knows the risk is worth it.

As a wise man said, "A child is ready to learn when a child is ready to learn. Not when we are ready to teach him." Here at the well-educated heart, I will constantly encourage you to let go of the job of taskmaster and embrace the fun of learning the way we were divinely designed to learn. I'm not asking you to do nothing—your job is going to be to set up the rooms of discovery and that's where I'll be going with the tools and resources I will be sharing, which is really nothing more than setting up rooms.

If you visit welleducatedheart.com, everything is set up for this kind of learning. For instance, when you go into the Mother's University, I don't give you an order of what you should read first or even tell you exactly what you should read or give you questions to answer. I don't even tell you what to do or what conclusions you should draw. Rather, I set up rooms that I know are loaded with clues for you to look around and discover and begin to piece things together for yourself, which is the same process I hope you'll allow your children. It's how I've been learning all the things I have been sharing with you about educating hearts of children. And the more I learn, the more I want to learn. My list grows bigger every day! It's an exciting and joyful way to live.

I had a mom write who said she went to the Simple Joy Conference because she wanted to learn how to do the Well-Educated Heart and she said she got really frustrated after the first couple of speakers because they weren't telling her what to do. Then, after a couple of more presentations, all of a sudden, the light went on and she could see for herself things she could do with her own children, even though those ideas weren't laid out directly.

There is no one-size-fits-all to learning, although there are too many people out there trying to make it so. Learning the way I am trying to describe to you allows for individual circumstances, personalities, capabilities, aptitudes and interests. It's a very personal journey.

The Rotation Schedule

I'm going to talk about the rotation schedule today which is a way to help you organize learning in your home and still allow for that freedom to choose and the creative process of learning.

A mom posted an experience in our Facebook group that is a perfect illustration of what I am trying to describe. She was inspired to start reading more classic literature but was overwhelmed with where to start. So she went to a thrift store and picked a couple of books off of the shelf and decided to start with Charles Dickens' *Great Expectations*.

Here's what she said:

> I was wondering what is the big deal during most of the book. I enjoyed reading it. I appreciated the interesting language and overall it was more of a diversion than a huge learning experience.
>
> And then by the very end...I was so touched by his homecoming, even when certain of his hopes were not as expected! His feeling of home was so deep and stayed with him through all of his trials and journeys (even though at the time of his childhood he seemed more tormented than loved).
>
> I cried and cried. I was just so touched. I want to build this feeling of home in my life and for my children. It is powerful and long-lasting!
>
> I was also touched on the way Pip measured his life in years or tens of years, when sometimes I am so caught up in what my kids are doing at the moment or for the day. It was a blessed lesson to me to mentally calm down and embrace and improve rather than be caught up in the race!
>
> I am on the lookout for more lessons to put into my heart!

How might this experience with the book be different if she had been given assignments of what to get out of the chapters and had study questions she had to answer? In fact, the true impact of the book on this mom's heart cannot be expressed in words. And the impact will be different for each and every person.

This is what I mean by bringing a child into a room and allowing the freedom to seek, ask and knock; to assemble the clues until you see something for yourself that can be applied and used.

When I talk about incorporating the rotation schedule in your home, I don't mean to imply that everything in your day needs to fit around this. It's just one part of the learning environment—there will be hobbies and music practice and chores and games and life. But it helps to bring a sense of order and rhythm to the learning going on. And by the way, you can still fully implement a heart-based way of learning in your home without utilizing the rotation schedule! It's simply a tool.

We are a very fact-and-information, test-and-measure culture and I want to spend a few minutes now trying to get you to think along different lines. The tendency is to look at the rotation schedule through the eyes of accumulating facts and information, but I'm aiming for a much loftier purpose. I hope I can bring this vision to life so you can see.

A couple of days ago in my scripture study, a phrase caught my attention. Here's the phrase: "he was entangled in the vanities of the world." I copied that down: entangled in the vanities of the world. When I want to get more insight into a word, I always turn to my 1828 Noah Webster's dictionary first. I love that book. Here's what I learned about the word *vanity*: it describes an emptiness, a want of substance to satisfy desire; inflation of mind upon slight grounds; and here's the definition that really struck me: fruitless desire or endeavor—trifling labor that produces no good.

Looking back over my school years, I regret that much of my learning and time was "entangled in the vanities of the world" or in other words, "trifling labor that produced no good." So much of the busy work left me feeling empty and it rarely connected to anything useful in my life. I hope your experience was different. But because of my experience, I'm always questioning why I do what I do. Will there be fruit to my labors?

Have you taken the time to really look hard at what you want the outcome of your children's education to be? Are you just trying to get your child to test well so he can get in a good college and get a high paying job? If that is what matters to you, then you may want to take a different path than what I'm about to lay out here. Although, nothing I promote would interfere with that. I know your kids need to know how to read and write and have a working knowledge of math. But I can tell you so many of the subjects we devote time to direct study like spelling and grammar and vocabulary will happen in a much more natural way as you engage in notebooking and other activities that we'll cover in the days ahead. I'll spend time in another place talking about satisfying testing requirements and doing the WEH in the backdrop of the realities of the world we are living in. I had to smile—my daughter just moved from a state that requires testing for homeschoolers and she panicked when she saw that her 8-year-old was three levels behind in some subjects. But then she said she took five minutes—literally *five* minutes—and caught her up. There were a few concepts she hadn't covered and it didn't take long to teach them. Sometimes it's a silly game we just have to play.

I've told you before what I have come to adopt as the purpose of education is to prepare children to live lives of maximum joy. I want to prepare them to live rich, abundant lives with all its variety of what that looks like. This is the loftier aim.

I think of the scripture where Jesus taught, "Strait is the gate and narrow is the way that leadeth unto life and few there be that find it." "Eye hath not seen, nor ear heard, neither hath entered into the heart of man, what great things are in store for those who do find it." There's no vanity or emptiness in this pursuit. Every teaching of Jesus is about how to be happy; how to have not just life, but that we might have it more abundantly. His whole focus was on building an inner kingdom, because He knew that out of the treasures of that inner kingdom, or the desires of the heart, the outer kingdom would be built.

But notice the risk—in spite of the fact that only a few would find it, he still simply invites us to Seek, Ask and Knock. There is no compulsion; no assignments. Rather He surrounds us with clues. They're in Nature. They're in the scriptures. They're in the words of inspired writers, the paintings of inspired artists, the music of inspired musicians, the lessons of history and of nations and in people's lives.

So, like the Escape Room I described yesterday, here is the room I find us gathered in. Let me give you the scenario as I see it.

Long ago, a wise and benevolent king sent His children into a far-away land in search of the secrets of rich and abundant living. He told them that at a distant time in the future, He would gather them together to share the treasures of their findings with each other, that all may be made wiser, for He intended to establish His Kingdom in that land.

Our task is to find and assemble the clues and the lessons that we may learn the secrets and take part in the establishment of that Kingdom.

Two words guide our study: understand and appreciate, which is really another way of saying *love*. I want each nation and people to have a chance to share their gifts and discoveries; to tell their stories. I would ask of them: What truths did you discover and apply? What have you taught us by your religion and its role in your lives, by your methods of education? What does your art, your stories, your lore and legends, your cultural celebrations, reveal about the hearts of your people? What mistakes have you made we can learn from? Tell us about your leaders and your forms of government. Tell us about your noble sons and daughters and your wayward ones. Tell us what role your geographical gifts played in your history; and how you overcame obstacles—I'm thinking of the Dutch holding back the ocean; or the Egyptians living by the rise of the Nile.

None of this can be taught in a one-time drive by. It will take years to gather clues—but in time, I begin to see why the French are who they are, the Russian, the North Korean. I understand the Muslim; I appreciate the devotion of the Buddhist. I am richer for knowing them. And I love them.

And then we have other rooms to spend time in to search for more secrets and lessons. We'll want to spend time in the Stars room, the Rocks room, the Birds, the Insects and the Flowers room. They, too, have lessons for the heart because Nature is God's University and there is no better way to get to know the Creator than through His Creations.

Would you rather spend your time dissecting sentence structure, spelling words, identifying nouns and verbs, analyzing the use of writing devices…or allowing the "solemnities of eternity" to sink deeply into the hearts of your children?

If we're looking for it, we'll see the teachings of Jesus and this strait and narrow gateway to life he talks of played out in the stories of nations and peoples. We'll see love work miracles and change lives; we'll watch hate and envy destroy. What happens when you bless those who despitefully use you, turn the other cheek, forgive someone who has wronged you; when you seek not your own, when you witness no greater love than this—that a man lays down his life for his friend. When a people learn the healer's art and lift the downtrodden and succor the weak. What happens when a society tends to the inner kingdom; when it seeks for that which is virtuous or lovely or of good report or praiseworthy—China has a wonderful story to tell us about that.

> The "gospel" of Confucius worked. According to Marcus Bach, "It worked so well for a short time in the state of Lu that people said, 'We have seen what paradise is like.' In that brief Confucian period, love was really love and justice was really just. There was a saying that theft ceased to exist among the people because it had been removed from people's hearts. An era of trust and mutual faith had been ushered in. The good of one was premised on the good of all. Anything lost on the highways was restored, and any wrong was righted because gentlemanliness was man's richest prize. In those days Confucius said, "The superior man understands what is right; the inferior man understands what will sell."

Can one person letting his light shine make a difference? History is filled with stories of the power and influence of the One.

At first glance, you may have no idea what you're looking for. But as you begin to collect and assemble the clues, you will begin to see the patterns, connections and lessons emerge for your use. We're going to have to spend time in many rooms looking for the clues and revisit the rooms over and over again to pick up what we missed in earlier visits. Each nation and people has a story to tell and gifts to offer from its heritage. It will take time to understand and appreciate what those gifts are. To tackle this great undertaking as a whole would be impossible. But by breaking the study down into nations, we can begin to unfold the secrets.

This is the reasoning behind the rotation schedule. Each month, you will lead your children into a room and let them look around and start gathering clues from a nation's literature, art, songs, histories, biographies, scientific discoveries, landmarks and cultural heritage. All the subjects are brought together under the umbrella of the study of a nation. In childhood, they may pick the imaginative tales of that land, the fairy tales and mythology. They may share in the celebrations of holidays, the enjoyment of their music and songs. An older child will begin to want to get to know some of the stories of the people in that land and will take interest in a study of events. A study of the great classic literature and poetry teach us much about a people. All ages can enjoy looking at the paintings and the architecture of the buildings, and in time, they will begin to see for themselves the lessons gifted from each nation.

You have heard me say it before. This is the great day of the harvest. I believe it is the time designated by the king who sent his children into far-away lands to come together and share their lessons with each other. We are the generation chosen to gather that which has been learned and discovered by those who came before us into one great whole of knowledge and understanding.

On the next page is a copy of the Rotation schedule and you'll find the resources on the website are organized around this schedule.

There are two rotations going on throughout the year—the first one is around people through a study of nations and the second is a study of nature, which is organized generally around the order of creation. The people rotation schedule is organized around America as the spine. You may be from another country and be inclined to use your home country as the spine. Of course you love your own country and you want your children to love it. But let me explain why I think you may want to reconsider keeping America as the spine.

There are many reasons why a study of America is worthwhile.

YEARLY ROTATION PLAN

MONTH 1	MONTH 2	MONTH 3	MONTH 4
1500s: Exploration	1600s: Colonies	1700s: Independence	George Washington
China/Asia India Scandinavia South Seas	Netherlands Spain Spanish Main/Pirates	England Scotland/Ireland/Wales	Greece Rome Italy
Stars	Ocean	Rocks	Plants/Trees
A Mother's Influence	Nature Study	Music	Art

MONTH 5	MONTH 6	MONTH 7	MONTH 8
American Revolution	A New Nation	1800s: Expansion	Abraham Lincoln African Americans/Slavery
France Switzerland Canada	Holy Land Ancient Civilizations	Arabia/Islam/Crusades	Africa Ancient Egypt
Gardening	Insects	Birds	Animals
Poetry	Storytelling	Imagination	History

MONTH 9	MONTH 10	MONTH 11	MONTH 12
Civil War	World Wars	American: Overview	American Biographies
Latin America	Germany Russia Eastern Europe	World: Overview	World Biographies
Human Body			
Writing	Math	Science	Joy

KEY
American History
World History
Nature
Mother's University

Figure 1: 12-Month Rotation Schedule

As you look at how long it has taken for freedom to find a home, America, conceived in liberty, is the culmination of centuries of strivings of people everywhere. The story of freedom is the most important story that can be told, because only in freedom can we obtain our highest potential and joy. America's story is the story of freedom. Already we see people trying to replace it with systems that have failed repeatedly throughout history. A study of nations will help your children see that. From America's earliest beginnings, the main facts were well established for us to study. There is no "dim twilight of myth and legend" such as you find in the majority of other nations. We can see its growth unfold line upon line from simple huts to complete vast networks of cities through a historical record that is complete, authentic and reliable.

And probably the most important reason to make America the spine of study is the fact that America's story is the combination of the stories of all nations. We are the children of England, of Scotland, China, France, Spain, India, Africa—each one weaving its heritage into the fabric we call America.

Because of our roots, the study of America easily lends itself to the study of all nations. So here is how they are connected. America's history is divided into 10 chronological monthly studies, with Months 11 and 12 left open for review and for revisiting favorite topics. Each of these monthly topics then tie into a nation or a geographic area.

For instance, in Month 1 when you study the early explorers like Columbus, it leads you into a study of China and India because that is where he was trying to go. The Vikings came from Scandinavia, so we want to know their story.

In month 2, when you study the Pilgrims, you can visit Holland because that's where they sought refuge before coming to America. And in learning Holland's story, you'll see its similarity to America's story. Just as we freed ourselves from England and set up a Republic, 200 years earlier, Holland fought to free itself from Spain's rule and set up a Republic. So you'll want to know Spain's story, too.

In Month 3, we are the colonies of the British, so we turn to a study of our Mother Country.

Month 4 takes a look at George Washington, who is likened to the great Roman leader Cincinnatus which leads us to a study of Rome which cannot be separated from a study of Greece.

In month 5, with the study of Lafayette, the young Frenchman who came to fight for liberty in our Revolution, it leads us back to France.

Month 6, the new nation of America is born, conceived in liberty and built upon the rock of the teachings of the Bible, which leads us to a study of the Holy Land and the early Hebrews and their neighbors.

Month 7 is for a study of the expanding American frontier, and is tied into the study of the expansion of another world frontier under the teachings of Islam.

The study of Lincoln and slavery in Month 8 leads us back to Africa.

Grant and Lee and the Civil War are the focus of Month 9. Both Grant and Lee fought in the fight against Mexico and so leads us into a study of Mexico and our neighbors down south in

South America.

Month 10 brings a study of World War I and leads us to take a look at Russia and Germany.

When you understand the Developmental Levels, which I will address later, the *why* behind the rotation schedule becomes a little more apparent. I know many people use some kind of rotation schedule. The most popular one is a four-year rotation schedule through history. My problem with that is that it doesn't take into account the difference in a child's capacity to grasp things from year to year. If a child goes through Greece, for example, as a 6-year-old, he can only take in what a 6-year-old mind can grasp, which isn't a lot yet. By the time he returns at age 10, so much time has passed by that he will have lost much of what he learned. And he'll miss out on what he could have learned as a 7, 8, or 9-year-old. Maybe that tour at 10 will be the last visit to Greece and he will have missed out on what his 11, 12, and 13-year-old mind can take in.

By switching to a 12-month rotation, there are fresh and new topics to visit every month. I've heard children complain when they have to spend long periods of time on one subject. They're inquisitive when they're young! It's not a time to go deep.

The 12-month rotation allows for lots of overlapping and repetition. For instance, you may discover some Spanish explorers in month one when you talk about explorers and then you'll see them again in month 2 in a study of Spain and again in month 9 when they're seen from a Latin America's point of view. In month 2, you see the Spanish Armada from Spain's point of view and in month 3, you see the Spanish Armada from England's point of view.

But—I hear it said—history needs to be laid out chronologically. Not so. This was clearly taught by the heart educators. Our minds and hearts have to sift through tons of information every single day. It has to be weighed out by importance and placed in a correct file in our brains. We are very equipped to do that. In the early years, we're simply giving them puzzle pieces that will come together over time. These puzzle pieces are going to be in the form of fine art and illustration, poetry, story and even music—all tools that are long lasting. Like Rudyard Kipling taught: "If history were told in the form of stories, it would never be forgotten." The more your children can see and feel history, the more they will want. Facts and information kill a love of history.

Most learning through curriculum is linear. It's presented as though a child just has to be taught a fact, tested to make sure he got it, and then you move on. Most learning that happens in this way goes into the pile of "Who cares?" and is forgotten. But for deep and lasting learning, I see a spiral—returning over and over to a topic, expanding and rising each time it's visited. Have you ever read a book and then read it again a few years later and it's like reading a new book? You see so many things you missed the first time around. It's not that the words on the pages have changed—but you have. You bring more to your reading. That's the same principle at work with the rotation schedule—a child returns to the same general topic every year—maybe even re-reads a book he read earlier, but the next time, it is seen with wider vision.

We have a huge subject on our hands! We want to learn about the whole world—not only of all the people who have lived here, but we want to understand the physical world in which we live. In fact, while we have many subjects we study—History, Science, Social Studies, Geography, Literature, Music, Art and so forth, I only see two subjects: a study of people and human nature and a study of nature.

We learn about people through literature, art, music, history and even geography. Where we live and how we build our homes and adapt our lives is very much tied into geography. The subject shouldn't be isolated. We learn about nature through science and math. So I have a 12-month rotation based on history, or more correctly, a study of people and one for nature, which is understanding the world in which we live. Eventually the two spirals start spiraling together into one whole.

Each month you'll lead your child into a 'room' which you have prepared with clues and let them look around and start gathering clues from a nation's literature, art, songs, fairy tales, histories, biographies, scientific discoveries, architecture, landmarks and cultural heritage. What they are drawn to will be according to their developmental level. And you can help facilitate that. All the subjects we typically study separately are drawn together under one history umbrella.

A young child may pick out the imaginative tales of the land, the fairy tales and mythology. They may enjoy sharing in that country's holiday celebrations or their music and songs. An older child will begin to want to get to know some of the stories of the people of that land and will take an interest in events. A study of the great classic literature and poetry teach us much about the hearts of the people we are studying. All ages can enjoy looking at the paintings and architecture of the buildings, and in time, they will begin to see for themselves the lessons gifted from each nation.

In this way, families can be studying the same general topic, but at different levels. It makes it possible for all family members, regardless of age, to join in the conversation. As you rotate back each year, older siblings will share favorite stories with younger ones. Maybe they'll even volunteer to read favorite books aloud to them—and they'll gain new insights their second time around.

Notebooking provides a way to start to sort and organize the clues they will find and even begins to lay the events out in chronological order. If they get to the end of the month and haven't covered all the books you had laid out, no worries. You'll be back around the next year and the year after that.

This rotation schedule is meant to be a servant, not a master. It brings a little order and rhythm to your learning so that you aren't trying to pull something out of the whole world every single day. If you get to the end of the month and you are in the middle of a great book or exploring a line of study, you don't have to abandon it just because a new month has started. There is plenty of room for flexibility and adjustment. You can even study in a different order. The only thing in an order is the American history spine, and really, the first half is colonial and the second half is post-Revolution, so you can rearrange easily.

It will take time to learn and apply the lessons. A lifetime, really. When you see your child walk across the stage in cap and gown, it's not called a Conclusion Ceremony. It's called a

Commencement. This is the Commencement of life but I also think of it as a Commencement to a lifetime of learning of which you have but laid a foundation. Remember the thrill when seemingly unrelated things suddenly start clicking and connecting and taking life? It will happen. If you don't interfere with the process and if you are a fellow traveler on the journey, delighting in your own discoveries and sharing them, all with a purpose of helping your children discover the rules for happy living, individually and as societies. You may still wonder what those lessons for the heart look like that I'm talking about. I hope those lessons will become clearer as we continue. As we tend to the inner kingdom of our children's hearts, it will be from the treasures there that they will begin to build a new world.

Now, you may be saying "Great! I'm on board! Now…how do I do it?" Well, I think you know what I'm going to say. This is your moment to seek for clues and apply the principles you are learning about the creative process of learning. To tell you exactly what to do would be to rob you of the joys of that creative process and would deny you that ah-hah moment when you see for yourself. It will look different in your home than in another home. And that King who has sent us here to seek is standing by, waiting for you to Ask Him for clues. Keep in mind, what we are attempting to do here has never been done before. Are you courageous enough to blaze new trails?

I know this is the stuff of dreams. A world without hate? A world of beauty and love and peace? My mind says it cannot be done. But my heart says, "Why not?" If mothers will rise and take their place as the nurturer of the heart of the next generation, in partnership with God, the King who has intended this all along, why can we not believe it will happen?

Weaving Stories with the Rotation Schedule

I listened to an interesting TED talk given by a young Nigerian woman on the danger of the single story. She illustrated it by telling of her experience as a college student in the U.S. Because of the single story her roommate had of the "African," her roommate wondered how this Nigerian has mastered English so well (it happens to be the official language of Nigeria), she wanted to listen to her tribal music, so was surprised when she pulled out Mariah Carey, and was shocked that she knew how to use a stove. She had no concept that her roommate from Nigeria could have a father who was a professor and mother who was an administrator.

There is a danger of attempting to tell a single story of the Pilgrims. The story of the spiritual leader, William Bradford is different than the story of the military leader, Miles Standish, which differs from the barrel maker, John Alden, which differs from the good-for-nothing first man to be hanged in America story of John Billington. If you were to make your judgment of the Pilgrims by hearing just one of their stories, your view will be distorted and incomplete, even though your story may be true. Only by weaving all of their stories together can you have a correct view. And the single story is especially dangerous if your one story doesn't even happen to be true.

The fact is, there were Native Americans who were brutally savage and Natives who were noble and good. There were white men who were brutally savage and white men who were noble and good. There is not a single story of the Founding Fathers, of slavery, of capitalists, or of Darwin. There is no single story of the Christian or the Muslim or the atheist. There is no single story of America. The only way to get a true and complete picture is to weave many stories together. And each heart must do his or her own weaving.

E pluribus unum—out of many, one. You cannot see the pattern of a tapestry from a single thread.

You see the same principle in the Four Gospels of the New Testament. Why are there four books that basically tell the same story? Well, Matthew wrote to convince the Jews so he pulled in some Old Testament prophecy. Mark wrote to convince the Gentiles, so his stories are very picturesque. Luke, the physician, had a Greek background that could appeal to the Greeks and John wrote to a people who already believed and so he spent more time deepening their beliefs with doctrines. Only by weaving all four accounts together can you gain a more complete picture.

Can you see why trying to find one history textbook will fall short?

And even within individuals, there is no single story. If the only story you know about me is that I stole candy from the grocery store when I was 4, you may never trust me with anything. You may shun me. But that single story hardly defines who I am. Never let the first story you give to a child be of the warts. Once the warts are pointed out, it can be hard to see past them. Start with the good! Inspire their hearts first. Warts can come later when their more mature minds can keep them I proper perspective.

Our schools have been a single-story system for a long time. Crashing and colliding stories are creating all kinds of divisions and conflicts, many of which could be resolved by teaching the art of weaving stories together.

Childhood is where we begin teaching that art. The process is enjoyable and satisfying as pictures and patterns begin to emerge from our threads. It's a lifetime process and our tapestries will become more intricate and beautiful as we gain experience. Along the way, we have to be willing to pull out the threads that we find out are not true. This art of weaving, in the end, will produce wise and understanding hearts.

Weaving many stories together requires a plan and a rhythm for order. There's a word for haphazard learning—the word is 'desultory' which means not having a plan or purpose; it means 'unconnected.' Desultory learning—winging it—isn't a good way to go. It makes me think of the weeks I don't make up a menu and shopping list. Those weeks are chaotic and stressful—5:00 rolls around every day and I'm scrambling to figure out something to cook and I have to run to the store because I don't have the ingredients and by 7:00 we order pizza.

We eat a lot better when I have a plan.

I think Sir Arthur Conan Doyle observed rightly: "Desultory readers are seldom remarkable for the exactness of their learning." It's a tiresome way to go over time.

But the other extreme isn't good, either, where learning is so structured and forced, the child is never allowed to follow his passions or interests or where there's never any room for the Spirit to work. I've been trying to find a good balance, and for me, the 12-Month Rotation has worked well.

Should We Ever Force Our Children to Learn?

I want to address a question that came up in the Facebook group. I had posted a wonderful article written by Jenny Phillips on what has happened to education in America. One of the moms in the Well-Educated Heart group wrote this comment:

"This article mentions that a love of learning can still be fostered, while at the same time requiring our children to do assignments they don't want to do, using curriculum in a structured way. I know I have heard you speak, and have emphasized that since learning cannot be forced, we should not require that our children do notebooking, assignments, reading, etc., if they aren't interested. Is it only if they are resistant? What about if they are just blah, and will do it if I insist, without resistance? Can you elaborate on these seemingly opposing thoughts for me? I'm currently in conflict over this particular aspect of 'school'…in my years of home educating my children, I have tried inspiring, I have tried requiring, and neither one has been successful. Trying to figure out if one of those philosophies is inherently flawed, or just my application of it. Perhaps I need a combination. I need to firmly know my approach going forward, so we can move along with confidence. So it's on my mind a lot lately, and her words in this article jumped out at me."

I believe many of you are trying to work through the same issue. So let me 'elaborate' my point of view as you find the right answers for yourself. The first question I would ask, though, is, when you say that neither method has been 'successful,' how are you defining success? Is it reflected in test scores? Is it in engagement level? Are you afraid your kids just aren't doing 'enough?' If success is to be determined by grade-level expectations and test scores, then you may be on a different path than the Well-Educated Heart path may lead you.

Also, while I understand the desire to firmly know your approach going forward, you may have to continue to experiment before you have the confidence that you're on the right path for you. I would never want you or anyone to just accept what I say because I say it.

I don't agree that one of the philosophies must be inherently flawed. I just think the two philosophies serve different purposes. The philosophy of require and compulsion has served masses of school students at a level of functionality for quite awhile. We generally have a population that can read and write at a functional level and that can hold down jobs. Most of us went through a system of structured curriculum and we might say that we're doing just fine so why topple the system?

In Jenny's defense, although I don't embrace the philosophy to force a child to do something he doesn't want to do, I don't think she's wrong to do what's she's doing. I have heard her say that she felt inspired to do what she is doing and I believe her. The reach of her influence is phenomenal. I think I read that she has reached over 350,000 students around the world. And that's in a matter of just a couple of years.

But I see her as a bridge, not a final destination. She is connecting to a system that is familiar and comfortable—going to where people are—and lifting them to a higher level by adding a layer of the good and the beautiful. Woven into the curriculum are the older stories and beautiful fine art that are filled with values and truths. I believe it is the warmth of these resources that is touching and awakening hearts and is the true secret of her success. Our souls are famished! And she is feeding them. If you took those parts out of her materials, it would be just another academic exercise and would lose the light and life of what she is accomplishing. That is my opinion. Force and compulsion have always had to be used to get kids to do academic exercises when the heart has not first been opened and warmed.

When you step back and look at the whole, though, what is this system of standardized curriculum and compulsory means costing us? Like Jenny said, 42% of our college graduates will never pick up another book after graduation and read for pleasure. Where are our Michelangelo's and our Shakespeares? Where are our great leaders? Where are our great writers? How is this vast knowledge being used? Is our world growing lighter or darker?

Although force may get results, I don't believe a child will ever rise to the height of his potential that way. His will must be engaged for that to happen and a will can never be forced. The art of sparking desire; of awakening the will is what we're trying to learn at the Well-Educated Heart so that you don't have to resort to force. It's not about doing nothing and hoping everything will just work out. It's about creating a proper learning environment. You are using example and story and music and experience to feed desire and open hearts. Your love for learning is an actual energy that is transferred from your heart to your child's.

And plus what learning is so urgent that we feel we have to force it? Where to place a comma in a sentence? The difference between a vertebrate and an invertebrate?

There is a big difference between being able to decode the word 'love' and understanding the layers of its meaning. Decoding is the easy part. But that's where most of the attention is focused. And when we put the outer wrappings on first, we tend to shut down the inner learning. It is causing us to have a generation that takes the literal meaning of all things and cannot see or understand the underlying lessons. There is a big difference between constructing a sentence and having a sentence worth constructing. What doth it profit a child if he can write a five paragraph essay but he has no love or reverence for life?

In a 1920 book I just finished on the power of music in our lives, in addressing how to teach music to children, the author wrote: "Many a person's real love for music has been blighted by having first been given the outer form just as the real consciousness of God is often spoiled by the outward form of learning the prayer book by heart. All studies should be based upon this law—from within, out."

That's the danger of our standardized curriculum. It goes from without and rarely makes it in. It allows for little to no individuality. It asks not what a child is interested in. It causes a child to rely on someone else to structure his learning, never awakening the tools for learning that are divinely gifted each child. Hence the reason for needing to resort to compulsion.

More from the book: "In the old method it was necessary for the pupil to depend eternally upon the teacher, so in most cases he grew bored and ceased to play at all. No one can remain really interested in a subject for any length of time unless there is a possibility of getting something to work out alone."

I am watching this in the life of a little 9-year-old boy I know. My grandson. He's been diagnosed as being on the autism spectrum. In first grade, he couldn't handle the pace and would often yell out to the teacher to slow down. His inability to control himself caused him to be the victim of bullying by other first graders—yes! 6-year-olds!—who would taunt him and set him up so that he would get in trouble. He came home in tears every single day.

His mother wisely brought him home, although she got the usual looks of disapproval from certain in-laws and associates who warned her that her son needed the socialization of school and would fall behind academically. Yet it was the socialization of school that was destroying him.

For the next two years he blossomed. She didn't follow any kind of structured curriculum. They live right across the freeway from Thanksgiving Point gardens and spent hours in the garden, museum and farm. He devoured books. He'd take a stack of books into his room and come out hours later detailing all the things he had learned from them. His memory was astounding. He loved all things outer space and comprehended complex topics. He loved science.

He had a harder time getting into fiction, but fell in love with the *Series of Unfortunate Events* books. His mom was just happy he was reading. But then something happened. This sweet kid started developing kind of a snotty attitude. As they talked, he realized he was acting out what he was reading in the books and *he* chose to quit reading them. Wow.

His math skills were amazing. He could solve problems in his head at 7 that I was trying to wrap my mind around. He *loved* math. He loved puzzles and solving things and would devour books with problems to solve.

And yet, the naysayers kept putting doubts and fears into my daughter's head. A few weeks ago, she was talking to another mom of an 8-year-old autistic boy who was attending a charter school not far from them and she said he was thriving there. So my daughter took her son for a visit and he was so excited he could hardly stand it. The thrill of being with other kids and the after-school space program and ballroom dancing and chess club and art and so many possibilities! They had an opening and a few days later, he started school again. And loves it.

But. He started struggling academically according to the system. Here was a kid who could devour a stack of books in one sitting and could tell you all about them and had an insatiable appetite to learn and yet in school was not able to read a paragraph and write out the five comprehension questions designed to help a student learn to increase his reading comprehension—something he previously had no problem with. He's finally settling into the system. But last night, his mom told me he no longer loves to read.

Just three weeks is all it took.

And he's starting to call out to the teacher to slow down again when he has to go at the same pace as the rest of the class.

He was having to bring home his math assignments because they weren't getting done in the allotted time at school. But here's an example of his difficulty. He was given a story problem. 4,260 people attended 5 concerts. Approximately how many people attended each concert? He was stuck. He agonized over the answer. But when he finally talked it out, he said, "Mom, 4000 divided by 5 is 800. 200 divided by 5 is 40. 60 divided by 5 is 12." Then he added those figures together in his head and came up with the correct answer of 852. "But mom," he said, "the question says, 'Approximately.' It's exact. 4,260 divided by 5 is exactly 852. I'm going to get the problem wrong."

This is the problem with curriculum. It's unbending. It's one size fits all. It doesn't allow for individual styles of learning. And it tends to shut down the whole process. Here's another quote from the music book I just told you about. She's talking about learning music, but I would say it applies to all subjects. "[I]t is certain that they have it in them and will do so, if we have patience coupled with the right attitude. Forcing is of no avail. It has to come through naturally, *and the function of the teacher is to awaken, not to instruct*…it is indeed better for children to grow up before they are given the old-fashioned teaching, if they are to have it at all. Some mothers have known this intuitively and have allowed their children to go without music lessons rather than be given the kind of teaching which…gives them a 'hate on music.' For this reason it is better not to have any lessons than to have mechanical, theoretical lessons: it is a kind of mentally blighting process."

Some kids will sail through the system. But many will leave it thinking they are stupid. And many of them will have to be forced all the way through.

I happen to believe there's another path, a path less traveled. I believe Jenny is a bridge to that path—like I said, starting where people are and introducing them to what it feels like to have their hearts warmed and opened through the abundant story, poetry, art and music included in the program.

The scripture that runs through my mind frequently is: "Strait is the gate and narrow the way that leads to life and few there be that find it." Of what value is an education if it doesn't lead us to an abundant and joyful life?

It's not that the gate and the path can't handle everyone; it's just that few will find it because it requires that they ask and seek and knock.

There was a beautiful stained-glass window in the front of the chapel in the church I went to when I was growing up. It depicted Jesus standing at a door and knocking. But there was no door handle on His side of the door. The door had to be opened from the other side.

There's a lesson for us who are seeking His path of learning and also to our children in their learning process. For true learning to happen, we have to learn the art of awakening their wills and opening their hearts and desires. That is God's way as I see it. I can find no evidence anywhere of His use of force. There are rewards and consequences. But He patiently knocks and waits for the invitation. He never barges in unwelcome.

Once we accept the invitation, the way becomes very structured and strict. The path is narrow, and He leads us by the hand. So it is with our children. Once their hearts are opened and the desire to learn is there, the way may become very structured and strict. But the pattern must be followed—heart first. Desire first.

So here we are back to the problem. You said you have tried to inspire. I would suggest you keep learning the art of inspiring. I believe it to be a true principle.

Here's an example of a learning technique our schools have abandoned. Music. Another quote from the book: "After listening quietly and hearing inwardly there comes an inner sense of harmony. The chaos of vagrant thoughts is calmed into repose; the mind is stilled to outside influences and becomes a reflector for the inner light which comes only through stillness.

"Thoughts become positive, ideas are born, and one dares to dream of great accomplishments, and through the stillness comes the thought, 'I can and I will.' Those things which seemed beyond reach come quite naturally within the realm of possibility. Faith in our own powers is built up when the chaotic thoughts of the outside world are stilled, and we believe in our own ability to be and to do what we will. Dreams and ideals which have been vague take on definite form, shaping themselves under the influence of that harmony which has been established through listening."

I am definitely promoting a path less traveled. It's a path on which travelers must depend upon and be partakers of a spiritual grace; where they are endowed with heavenly powers and light that organizes and orchestrates learning for the purpose of multiplying and replenishing the earth with the good, the beautiful and the true. It is not a path that can be systemized or standardized for the masses. It is individual. It is heaven directed and it cannot be forced.

A new way of learning isn't going to happen overnight. Our generation may only start making a shift or maybe we'll only manage to keep our foot in the door so that it doesn't slam shut completely. But we can begin to lay a foundation for a better way going forward; a way that doesn't have to rely upon force and compulsion.

It will require a new measure of success.

God never worries about numbers. He can do amazing things with even a few, should only a few find the path less traveled. I love these words of Newell Dwight Harris:

> Not all men are of equal value—not many Platos—only one, to whom a thousand lesser minds look up and learn and think. Not many Dantes; one, and a thousand poets tune their harps to his and repeat his notes. Not many Raphaels; one, and no second. But a thousand lesser artists looking up to him are lifted to his level. Happy that town blessed with a few great minds and a few great hearts. One such citizen will civilize an entire community.

I think the question you have to ask yourself is if you want to stay on the path with the masses, or take the risk and walk a path less traveled; a path few there be who find it. The path requires you let go of how the world teaches and cannot be traveled by compulsion in any form. The parable of the sower warns of those things that will take you from the path. You may recognize some in your own journey. Sometimes the seed—the idea—falls on stony ground. The idea of a heart-based education is received with gladness, but because it has no root within, it endures but for a time. When affliction or persecution arises, they are immediately offended, as the parable says. One of the definitions of offended is to be wounded or disturbed. When family members or friends or school officials look at what you are doing and question it and fill you with fears and doubts, it's easy to be 'wounded' and 'disturbed' and can cause you to step away.

Another problem is when the seed falls among the thorns or the cares of the world. There's just too much to do. Too many demands on our time. Sick babies. Sick mommies. Houses that need cleaning. Food that needs cooking. Not enough money. Too many cares. And so we return to comfortable, well-worn paths. Or, he says, there is the deceitfulness of riches. What if my child never gets into a good college? What if he is never successful by the world's standard? He's got to get a job! We've got to be practical here. Why 'deceitful?' Because we're told money buys happiness. But it really doesn't. Or the parable says we're pulled into the lusts of other things we desire more—which chokes the word and it becomes unfruitful.

But when the idea—Truth—falls on good ground, when it is heard and received and tended to and nurtured, it will bring forth fruit. And the fruit of this kind of learning is always the riches of eternity: increased joy, love, light, a more abundant life, in this life and the life to come—all the riches that cannot be measured. As the Lord said, "Not as the world giveth give I unto you."

But don't take my word. Experiment and prove these things for yourself. But you must set the standard by which you will measure your success and decide what matters the most. As Goethe wrote: "Things which matter most must never be at the mercy of things which matter least."

I probably haven't answered your question. But I hope I've given you some things to think about.

For now I want to close with the wisdom of Calvin Coolidge—Silent Cal he was called. He was a man of few words, but when he spoke, he was profound. And these are the things I think matter the most and which are the focus of learning at The Well-Educated Heart, none of which can be learned by compulsion.

We do not need more intellectual power, we need more moral power.

We do not need more knowledge, we need more character.

We do not need more government, we need more religion.

We do not need more of the things that are seen, we need more of the things that are unseen.

It is on that side of life that it is desirable to put the emphasis at the present time.

If that side is strengthened, the other side will take care of itself.

It is that side which is the foundation of all else. If the foundation be firm, the superstructure will stand.

More Thoughts on Inspire vs. Require

Here is the question I am addressing today. The mom wrote: "My question is about balancing the natural learning process with structure and discipline. Sure, you have to have a great love and exposure to music to become a musician, but are there very many musicians out there whose parents didn't make them practice at some point?" She goes on to describe a little school she's involved in that is trying to incorporate more well-educated heart principles, but she wrote, "I feel like I need a systematic way to teach writing skills."

First, I'll give the very simple answer and then I'll give you my long, drawn-out thought process—probably more than what you want to hear—for what it's worth.

The mom asking the question covered the first two parts of the Pattern for Learning I talk about a lot in the training videos. The first part of learning is for the heart—you expose children to great music and musicians to help them develop a love and desire for becoming a musician and appreciating beautiful music. And she's right—you have to have that love and desire to truly become a musician. The second part is the skills part, or what I would put into the Mind part. It's absolutely true—a musician cannot develop skills without practicing.

I was thinking about the combination of these first two parts in the Pattern and adding in the third part, which is the Spirit part or the inspiration part and how all three parts are necessary. If I have a great love for music, and I was inspired and given the most beautiful piano piece that has ever been heard—if that beautiful music played out in my head, how would I ever be able to share that with the world if my fingers had never been trained to play what I was hearing? It would be impossible, wouldn't it? What if I had no way to write down the notes because I didn't know the language of music?

On the other hand, if I had all the technical skills of playing scales and arpeggios, but there was no music in my heart, the chances of being inspired also are nil.

So of course, both are necessary. We want children who have writing skills, but we need them to have something in their hearts they want to write about. We want children with reading skills and comprehension, but we also want children who love to read. We need heart and mind to work hand in hand, but if you don't tend to the heart first, the child will balk at the hard work of practice because he doesn't yet see the point or the reason. You may get a little mileage from "Because I said so." But that child isn't likely to reach the same level of proficiency as the child who is motivated from desire.

I don't want to be misunderstood—there can be a place for a systematic way of teaching writing or reading or math. But if you force it before the heart is open and ready, you may do more damage than good.

So here comes the longer explanation because I want to address the part of the question where the mom asked, "Are there very many musicians out there whose parents didn't make them practice at some point?"

It's the 'make them' that I have the problem with. And this is an ongoing conversation I'm having within myself—should 'making them' ever be a part of the learning process? Does the end justify the means?

So I'm just going to share some of that thought process and see what you think.

I always go back to a story that is part of my faith. You don't have to accept or believe the story to get the point.

I believe that we are all spirit children of our Father in Heaven, or God and that we lived with Him before we came to earth. Knowing that it was essential that we be given a chance to learn by our own experience, an earth was to be created for us to gain mortal bodies. A great Council or meeting in heaven was called in which there were two plans presented. The first plan was the no-child-left-behind plan. The intention was good. Every child would make it back home to our Heavenly Father. It was going to require force—but the end justified the means. And by the way, all the glory for the success of that plan was to go to the one who was proposing it. He would make it happen.

The other plan involved choice. It was risky because some of us would choose poorly. Some may not make it Home. A vital part of that plan was that there would be a way provided to recover from those mistakes in the learning process.

The first plan was rejected, and a big war in heaven followed as we took sides. And if that's too much fantasy for you, then let's make it real as we see that same battle between force and choice playing out, still, here on the earth.

We still see those who don't trust us to do what we need to do and feel only force will make it happen. It's why freedom has been enjoyed by so relatively few peoples throughout the ages.

I think of some of the early church leaders who would not allow the members of their church to read the Bible on their own. What if the untrained laymen interpreted it wrong? What if they took it literally and plucked out their own eyes or cut off their hands when they offended them? The priests felt they needed to maintain the power and control over the lives of the people. They fought against those who tried to put the word of God directly in the hands of the people, such as William Tyndale who translated the Bible into English so that even the ploughboy would have access to it. His life was in constant danger for doing it. I had seen *A Man for All Seasons* that holds up Sir Thomas More for the hero he was in standing up to the King of England. Yet, he is the same man who relentlessly pursued William Tyndale to stop his work and as we know, eventually Tyndale was rewarded by being burned at the stake.

But burning him couldn't close the door that had been opened. Thousands who tasted that word of God chose to be burned at the stake themselves rather than give it up.

It was the spirit of that book that led families to a new world where, although life was hard and some failed, they could govern themselves. That is the spirit of America. Or at least was. My biggest worry is that we, as a people, are more interested in security and comfort than allowing the natural risks that come with being a self-governing people. There are do-gooders amongst us who want to make sure everyone has everything they need and they're willing to do it by force rather than choice. The ends justify the means. Man cannot be trusted. God also wants a world where there are no poor—where everyone is rich. When His kingdom is finally established, that's how it will be. But while man will force the rich man to share his wealth, God's way is to have a man choose to share his wealth because he loves his brother. Every system of force to spread the wealth that man has put into place has failed miserably and has caused massive death and destruction. Will we ever learn?

Speaking of do-gooders, Horace Mann realized that the success of our Republic and the maintenance of freedom depended upon an educated and informed citizenry. Because he feared for his country and saw too many parents neglecting the education of their children, he wore out his life trying to make sure that all children received an education. He is the seen as the father of compulsory education here in America. The parents couldn't be trusted to get the job done. Did the ends justify the means? I think you know why I have a problem with compulsory education. A couple of years ago, a state senator, I believe it was, proposed abolishing compulsory education in Utah. Wasn't he made to look like the fool! "No one will go to school if we don't make them," critics cried. Even though history has shown the greatest advancements have been made in an environment of freedom of choice—among them the great advancements of the Saracens—we still are afraid to let go.

And let's take a look at China not that many years ago. Chairman Mao saw problems. If he could just force all the people to see what he saw, he thought he could advance their civilization. He destroyed their antiquities, their monuments, their old traditions, their books and replaced them with a little red book. Did that book teach them to be horrible people? I was surprised to read what was in it. How many of these ideas do you have a problem with?

> It is important for a country to retain modesty, and shun arrogance.

> It is the duty of the Party to serve the people. Without the people's interests constantly at heart, their work is useless.

> China's road to modernization will be built on the principles of diligence and frugality.

> A communist must be selfless.

> The multiple burdens which women shoulder are to be eased.

> In order to get rid of blindness…we must…learn the method of analysis.

In talking about Russia, Rose Wilder Lane said this: "The Soviet government exists to do good to its people, whether they like it or not."

Does the end justify the means?

So let me just go back to where I started. Two plans were proposed. One was rejected. We're still battling it out in large arenas and in small ones, like your home. This I know: God will force no man to heaven. Am I ever justified in forcing my child to do what I think he must, even if it is for his own good? Given what I just shared, my conclusion is no. Force is never justified.

The ends do not justify the means. It damages relationships and keeps a child from ownership. Until ownership happens, a child will never reach the heights he could have. God knows that. I'm a little slower understanding. But I am beginning to understand why.

But we're back to the problem—my child needs to practice handwriting and he's not old enough to know that on his own. The words of a hymn I shared a couple of podcasts ago run through my mind: "Know this that every soul is free to choose his life and what he'll be, For this eternal truth is giv'n: That God will force no man to heav'n.

"He'll call, persuade, direct aright, And bless with wisdom, love and light, In nameless ways be good and kind, But never force the human mind."

So our task at hand is to look at how many ways can we call, persuade, direct aright, how can we be good and kind and bless with wisdom, love and light?

In other words, how can we inspire instead of require? It may be easier to just say, "Because I said so," but at what cost?

One way is to always think choice. My daughter has been looking for ways to get her young girls on board with reading more of the history books in the rotation schedule. So this is what she just proposed to her 9- and 12-year-olds. She asked her girls to choose a book from the Well-Educated Heart list for the country they're learning about. At the end of the month, anyone who finishes their book gets to go out for hot chocolate or ice cream and they'll have a little chat about what they learned and liked about what they read. She said they're both so excited and can't wait to start. And she added an idea from BraveWriter—as she listens, to take the time to write down something they say. "Ooh—that is so good! I've got to write that down so I don't forget it." That shows you value what they say and also becomes something to add to the notebook pages. And isn't that going to give them the incentive to keep reading and thinking and sharing?

That's a much different approach from assigning the book to read and requiring a book report at the end.

I don't have a problem working with incentives to help through those initial rough spots. Another little granddaughter was excited to read at first but kind of hit a plateau. So I offered to pay her a penny or so per page and my daughter found a list of engaging books that were right at her level and she took off! Next time I saw her, she was so excited to show me all the books she had read…and, you know, pay up, Grandma. Which I was happy to do. The practice made her a much more confident reader so that she's reading more on her own again. The incentive just helped her move off a plateau.

We know without practice, handwriting is going to be a big stumbling block for all the learning yet to come. Yes, you can force it. Or you can find the spoonful of sugar to make the medicine go down. After all, "In every job that must be done, there is an element of fun. You find the fun and snap! The job's a game."

How about this. "I've been noticing the way you're holding your pencil and I think you're grown up enough to start learning how to write! I'm so excited for you! You're going to be able to write stories and write down toys you want for your birthday and write a letter to grandma! Do you think you're grown up yet? Do you remember how hard it was to ride your bike at first and how you kept falling down? But now look at you! Look how easy it is for you! Well, learning to write is going to be just like that. At first, you might get frustrated, but if you keep trying and practicing, it will get easier for you, just like riding a bike.

"How much time a day do you think we should start with? Because we're going to want to practice every single day." Now you've set the expectation, but you're allowing ownership in the choice of how to get there. Even if they choose 30 seconds, that's better than nothing. Start there! "Shall we do it in the morning or after lunch? Great! You know what—I want to make my handwriting better so I'm going to practice too. Think about what you want to copy to practice your handwriting. I have some poems I want to copy. Do you have something or do you want me to help you find something?"

Practicing handwriting time can have a little fun music going on in the background and could even involve a plate of cookies on the table.

Maybe that sounds too much for you. But I'm trying to make the comparison of assigning practice sessions vs. involving your children in the process so they take ownership.

If your child refuses to come, you keep doing it consistently. Model it. And keep in mind— some things are resisted because the child is not developmentally ready. Just table it and come back later and keep watching for incentives.

Or how about: "I know if you memorize your arithmetic facts so you can say them without even thinking, you are going to be able to do so many things! When you get them all memorized, let's go out and celebrate" by whatever will be a fun incentive for that particular child. Keep it simple. And then you help break it down in manageable steps.

Everything worthwhile requires steady effort. Yes, the musician needs consistent practice. If you've been hiking and have felt those times you wanted to give up but kept pushing through, and how good it felt to make it to the top, you can draw upon that experience. If they're starting music lessons, for instance, acknowledge at the very beginning that at the beginning they'll be really excited, but then they'll hit those plateaus or those steep climbs and talk in advance, "What are you going to do when you reach those spots? Because you will. We all do. What would you like me to help you keep going?" And keep the conversation going.

I hope that sparks some ideas. I don't think incentives are bad for some of these tasks that are necessary but, in the beginning, unpleasant. Involve your children and find ways to help them have choices so they retain some ownership. Keep inspiring with the *why*'s and the desire. Know there will be hills, valleys and plateaus. But I really don't see force as justification as a means to an end.

Relationships always come first, I think. And love.

Try, Try Again
by T. H. Palmer

Tis a lesson you should heed,
Try, try again;
If at first you don't succeed,
Try, try again;

Then your courage should appear,
For, if you will persevere,
You will conquer, never fear.
Try, try again.

What About Socialization?

Remember that whole sense-impression thing Pestalozzi talked about? Well, here's a great example of how those sense-impressions work on us. My husband loved the social part of school. He had great friends and was involved in sports and overall has really happy memories. When he thinks socialization, that's what comes to his mind. And I suspect there are many of you moms and dads who also have happy memories and want your kids to experience what you experienced.

I had a completely different social experience. I was the gangly nerd with the sparkly pink wing-tipped glasses and braces who stood a head taller than my classmates. I was always the last one to be picked for teams and I heard the groans when a team had to accept me and was often made fun of because I was a brainiac. I still carry the scars of school socialization.

Independent of your experiences, what exactly is the socialization going on in school that people are so concerned about? Is it the six or so hours sitting at desks where you're told to not talk to your neighbors? Is it the very unnatural environment where you, for 12 or 13 years, interact only with kids your own age? Is it the part where you are daily compared and evaluated against those peers?

If there is socialization going on at school, most of it is happening in Drama class, PE, sports, music, art, debate, clubs. Every one of those activities is open to homeschoolers. In fact, because they don't have the six hours sitting in a classroom behind a desk, they actually have more time to participate and socialize.

My five little granddaughters—ages 3 to 12—go to karate a couple of days a week. What a great experience that has been as they have formed friendships in an environment where the instructor teaches them respect and discipline and service. They interact with children who are older than them and younger than them in the same class. In such an environment, bullying is less likely to happen. The big kids root and cheer for the little ones and the little ones have the big kids to look up to and be inspired by.

There's an endless list of ways children can get together with other children in wholesome environments and socialize. Dance, Community Theater, Community orchestras and choirs, Volunteering at museums or equestrian centers, or senior care centers, Sports, all kinds of recreational activities, art and craft classes. Church activities. They can sign up for enrichment classes. Many schools allow homeschoolers to enroll for one or more classes of their choosing. My son picked band and basketball. A couple of daughters picked choir. I had a daughter who wanted to play with her friends at the elementary school down the street during the lunch recess. The administration wouldn't let her because she wasn't a student. Well, I looked it up and the law defined a student as someone who was enrolled for at least one hour. So I enrolled her in recess. Recess wasn't quite an hour, but they were fine with her reading a book in the office for the last 20 minutes. They got money for her as a student, and my daughter got to play with her friends. The rest of the day we got to do other things.

We all hear about socially awkward homeschoolers. Well, guess what. I've met socially awkward public schoolers. I was one of them. Public school isn't a guarantee against social awkwardness.

The bigger issue isn't about a lack of opportunities to socialize our kids. The bigger issue is one addressed by Dr. Gordon Neufeld. If you haven't listened to the talk I posted online, I hope you will take the time do so. And if you're on board with homeschooling but you have a spouse that's holding back because of the socialization issue, invite him or her to listen with you.

He reminds us that attachment is a pre-eminent need for all creatures. We will hopefully attach ourselves to many things and many people throughout our lives. We need to feel connected. But Nature has designed that the primary attachment be to the parent who helps the young get his bearings; to teach what really matters, what's important, and instill good values. In his studies, he has determined a very noticeable shift in the 1960s to where those primary attachments are to peers rather than parents. In the name of socialization, we are attaching our children to other children who are not capable of teaching their peers how to act. And we are seeing the fallout. He explains it so eloquently and simply—I would be bold enough to say that watching this video may be a life-changer for you.

When you understand these attachments, you probably won't be so eager to socialize your little ones, but rather you'll want to strengthen the bonds and relationship with home and family first before sending them out into the world. It's a fact that children who gain a strong sense of identity and core values from home, are much more confident and less prone to be swayed by peers when they do start socializing more outside the home.

From the time our first daughter was born until our last one left home, we moved 13 different times. The one constant in my children's lives was family. While they developed friendships wherever we lived, the friendship that has remained is with siblings. When they moved to a new area, they had each other first. Today, their siblings are their best friends. When work or the world beats them up, it's to their siblings, home and family they turn.

I don't think that's a bad thing at all.

Home is Good

I love the story of Maria von Trapp from the Sound of Music. Here's a gem I copied down when I read her story:

> After supper came the most beautiful time of the day, the evenings spent together. A fire was lit in the fireplace. The older girls brought their knitting, the younger ones, their dolls; the boys and their father usually worked on wood, carving or whittling; and I, settling in a most comfortable chair, started to read aloud. It is most amazing how much literature you can cover during the long winter evenings. We read fairy tales and legends, historical novels and biographies, and the works of the great masters of prose and poetry.

And then they'd sing.

After you finish reading, tuck your children in bed with beautiful scriptural language floating through their heads and a prayer. And a sense that home is good. I love how it smells. I love how it feels. And I love my family. Life is good. Life is happy.

"There is only one way to improve the taste of a nation. It cannot be done in a hurry and it cannot be done by force. It can only be accomplished by exposing the people patiently to that which is truly "good"; to that which is truly "noble"... Try and persuade your children to make the good choice for themselves by exposing them just as much as possible to that which is a true product of divine inspiration and honest human craftmanship... In the end, those able to see and look for themselves will then make the right decisions and because they will do it of their own volition, it will be a lasting one."

--Hendrik Willem Van Loon

Developmental Levels

GROWING STRONG ROOT SYSTEMS IN THE HEART

16. 'The Beginning' of Learning
15. Classic Lit., i.e., The Great Books
14. Threads: Art, Music, Architecture, Religion, Science
13. Moral Heroes
12. Stories of Nations
11. History like Landmarks, Signature Biographies, etc.
10. Historical Fiction
9. Short Picturesque Stories
8. Epic and Legendary Heroes, i.e., King Arthur
HEROIC

7. Famous Childhoods, child life in far away lands
6. Children's Classics, i.e., The Secret Garden,
    A Little Princess
5. Fairy Tales, Mythology
IMAGINATIVE

4. Transitional Stories – part familiar, part imaginative,
    i.e., Raggedy Ann
3. Short Repetitive Stories, i.e., The Three Bears,
    also family/nature
2. Picture Books
1. Mother Goose
0. Lullabies
FAMILIAR

"In order to read the 'great' books of Plato, Aristotle, St. Augustine and St. Thomas, we need to replenish the cultural soul that has been depleted and create a place where these works can thrive by cultivating an imaginative ground saturated with fable, fairy tale, stories, rhymes and adventures — the thousand books of Grimm, Andersen, Dickens, Scott, Dumas and the rest. The one thing a great books education will not do is create a moral imagination where there is none."

— John Senior

Figure 2: Developmental Levels Chart

And now I'd like to talk about development levels. If you want to build a strong root system in a child's heart, the heart educators taught that a child must progress through three developmental stages, each one serving a specific purpose. To some extent, you can go back and pick up what was missed, but you can't rush the process going forward. Nor would you want to. As I go through this, you'll notice the layering process. Heart-based education is very much a line upon line, layer upon layer, here a little, there a little process, which is very different from acquiring facts and information.

The first step is the Familiar Stage and in the learning process, you always need to find or create a familiar link to build upon. My kids tease me because I still use AOL and Word Perfect. I know—I'm a dinosaur. They tell me there are much better options out there, but I resist them because AOL and Word Perfect are familiar to me and it's human nature to resist that which is not familiar to us. Little children demand the same story be read to them over and over again because of its familiarity and babies cling to mama because she is familiar. A child will resist a subject that has no familiar connections. Attention, desire, interest, and enjoyment all depend upon recognition of familiar qualities.

Let me illustrate…with a couple of stories, of course.

One December, my daughter's family was learning about George Washington and she suggested a couple of biographies to her oldest daughter. One book was about George and the other one was about Martha. The books sat unread. Then I took my granddaughter up to Mt. Vernon. It was just before Christmas so there weren't many people there and we rocked in the rocking chairs on the veranda and watched the boats out on the Potomac and our hearts knew why Washington loved the place so much. Then our tour guide took us to the second floor to Washington's bedroom—we saw the very bed he died in. She told us that, after he died, Martha was so broken hearted, she closed the door to the bedroom, locked it and never went in again. Then the guide took us to the third floor where visitors usually aren't allowed to go and showed us the little bedroom Martha spent her last few years in. Outside her bedroom was a small, round window—the day they buried her husband, the tour guide told us that she sat and looked out that very window because she couldn't bear to go down. As we looked out the window, we could see the vault where his body was originally laid and imagined the sorrowful scene. We did far more "feeling" than "talking."

My daughter told me later, without any urging on her part, that after my granddaughter got home, she had both biographies read by the next night and commented that she wished she had read them before she went to Mt. Vernon, and she now wanted to go back.

The is the attraction of the familiar.

My little 2-year-old grandson has been sick so he's been a bit cranky. A couple of nights ago, his daddy went to read him a bedtime story. "Do you want to hear the story of Mulan?" NO! "Do you want to hear the story of the Mouse and Cookies?" NO! "Do you want to hear the story of the Little Mermaid?" NO! "Do you want to hear the story of the little boy who could only say No?" Huh? And he listened attentively while his daddy made up a story of a little boy who could only say no.

He had connected to the familiar of the moment.

Your wonderful and enjoyable job as a mom is to make as many unfamiliar things familiar to your children as you can because then you've given them many connecting links for learning to take place. You can familiarize things by naming them, telling stories about them and bringing your child in contact with them. The first five years of a child's life are primarily for familiarizing your child with the immediate world he lives in. A toddler becomes familiar with the world he lives in by touching, tasting, hearing, smelling, and seeing and the more connections to the real world you give him, the stronger foundation for future learning you are laying. I've always found it interesting to watch how connected to true things children are. I can give a child a bright neon colored plastic toy to play with, and his attention lasts about three seconds. But if I put him next to mud or grass or water or sand, his attention is held for a very long time.

The first language you have to work with is music. Your lullabies to a newborn bring a sense of calm and comfort to his heart. Both the language of words and the language of music are acquired by exposure, so do play beautiful classical music in your home so it will become familiar to him. And sing songs.

There is also a music to spoken language. In the beginning, a child isn't listening for the meaning of words. He's listening to the music. One of the reasons preschoolers can effortlessly pick up several languages simultaneously is because he's not encumbered by verb conjugations and tenses; he's listening to the music of the language and mimicking it. The reason that reading aloud to your children is so important is because the music in your voice adds a layer of meaning that their hearts understand. Much of the deepest meaning of great literature is found in the music of the words and so you want to familiarize your little ones with beautiful language. There are few books in the English language that does this as perfectly as the King James Version of the Bible. Scholars tell us this was written at the peak of the English language. It's full of poetry, imagery and story. Feel the difference between these two passages of scripture. The first one is from the King James Version:

"And straightway coming up out of the water, he saw the heavens opened, and the Spirit like a dove descending upon him. And there came a voice from the heavens saying, 'Thou art my Beloved Son, in whom I am well pleased.'"

Now listen to a modern version:

"As he was climbing up the bank again, the sun shone through a gap in the clouds. At the same time a pigeon flew down and perched on him. Jesus took this as a sign that God's spirit was with him. A voice from overhead was heard saying, "That's my boy! You're doing fine!"

Could you feel the difference?

When you read scriptural language to little children, they're understanding it at a different level than you. I have found little children are drawn to scriptural language. My personal opinion is they're hearing a familiar language carried with them that has not yet been completely forgotten. Its familiarity is a heavenly music. Much of the meaning of literature they'll read later will come from the music of the words. Familiarizing them with beautiful language lays the groundwork.

It's the music of words that make Mother Goose so delightful to children. The words are mostly nonsense. That's not what they're listening for. You may not think it, but by giving your 1-year-old Mother Goose, you're preparing him to one day love Homer. And that's not as in Homer Simpsons. It's the other Homer. And rhyme begins to bring order to your baby's brain.

As you continue up this developmental ladder and begin to introduce your little ones to art, poetry and story, you want to apply this familiar principle to the subjects you choose. What's more familiar to a little child than family and home, nature and animals? I think it's worth paying attention to the fact that the Old Testament opens with a story of a family in a garden and the New Testament begins with a story of a family in a stable surrounded by animals. Familiar and Family have the same root words. And you will want to make all things family familiar to your little ones in these first five years. I'll also mention here, there is a heart-based way to learn Science, too, and stories of Nature begin to grow the root system for that.

The next language is pictures or images. Why do toddlers love picture books? Because they speak to their hearts; it's a language their hearts understand. You can help them acquire a taste for beautiful fine art by exposing and familiarizing them with it when they are young and allowing it to speak to their hearts. I was sitting behind a little 2-year-old girl on her daddy's lap at church and was watching her stare intently at a little book of fine art prints her mom had created for her. The pictures depicted Jesus' life and she had glued them on bright colored paper and put them in a little photo album that was just the right size for her little girl's hands. She stared at each picture for the longest time. I knew the pictures were speaking directly to her heart.

And I thought—you can do the same thing with fine art images of mommies and babies and kittens that are 'familiar' at this age. I picked up a little photo album for 97 cents at Walmart—it's just the right size for little hands. You can print out some fine art prints of mothers and babies and kittens and put them in a little picture book like that.

Learning by heart is a lot like eating cake. Estelle Hurll, an art educator from 100 years ago, wrote, "If you are giving a child a piece of cake, it adds nothing to his enjoyment to tell him that it contains certain ingredients and was made by certain rules or that it will contribute to his nourishment. If it is good, he eats it and wants more."

I gave my daughter a little picture book about how all the farmyard animals go to sleep at night. She called me one night and said, "Thanks a lot for the book…" Her little 18-month-old had just made her read it to her 17 times in a row. She finally got her to go outside to play with her sisters and my daughter hid the book in the bottom of a big pile of books. As soon as her little girl came back in the house, she dug through the pile of books until she found it again, and made her mom read it again.

We were trying to figure out why the fixation and then it dawned on us—we had just spent a week in Lancaster, Pennsylvania, in Amish country. Her little girl had been petting baby lambs and little ponies and watching the sunsets over barns and farms. We think this book recreated all those feelings that were still so fresh and familiar to her and she wanted to keep reliving them.

Again, the attraction of the familiar. Familiarity gives pleasure.

By age three, children are ready for stories. Look for stories with that familiar family element—the story of a mama bear, papa bear and little baby bear; stories of how mommy birds and mommy squirrels take care of their babies; stories of when daddy was a little boy; simple stories of family life. Play time allows them to process what they're learning as they pretend being mommies and daddies and taking care of little babies.

When they pick up a crayon and start to draw circles and squiggly lines, don't be too quick to say, "Look what you can do! You can draw a letter A!" There is nothing in the letter 'A" that is familiar or appealing to a 3-year-old. They want to draw sunshine and flowers, kittens and mommies—all with smiley faces. Let them improve their manual dexterity by drawing pictures, not letters. Once the heart sees a use for letters, writing will happen easily. No need to rush it.

By age four, they're transitioning into the imaginative years and they love to hear stories of familiar things in imaginative ways—like Raggedy Ann, a doll who comes to life, or Peter Cottontail. And the more they listen to stories they love, stories that make them feel something, their little hearts send a message to their brains; "Brain, mom doesn't have enough time to feed us as many stories as we want down here. I need you to learn how to read so I can get at more stories." And the brain gets to work. I have met many people who were raised in story-rich environments who had no recollection of being taught how to read. It happened as naturally as acquiring speech. I've seen research that backs it up.

Now we enter the prime years for Imagination, starting around age five when the heart longs to see familiar things from new angles. And the Imagination makes it possible by creating its own images of things the eyes have actually never seen. Don't rush or slight these years. This is the stuff upon which dreams are built, and as Laboulaye cautions: "Mothers who love your children: Do not set them too soon to the study of history; let them dream while they are young."

There are many reasons for cultivating imaginations. For instance, creativity is dependent upon imagination. Nothing in this world has ever been created that didn't first exist as an image in someone's mind. And Felix Adler wrote, "Much of the selfishness of the world is not due to actual hard-heartedness but to a lack of imaginative power…the faculty of putting one's self in the place of others." Plus, a vivid imagination is crucial in the study of history, because it is impossible to reproduce history except through the imagination.

Fairy tales and simple stories from mythology are the perfect foods for feeding the imagination. As your children listen to fairy tales, they are not only expanding their capacity to create pictures and images in their minds, their young, impressionable hearts are processing right and wrong, good and evil, justice and injustice in a way that could never be taught directly. They're going to need that as they start applying those lessons to the stories of history. As you tell them fairy tales and folk tales from around the world, you are also providing a layer of familiarity to names and cultures from other lands. A young child loves the music of names like Aphrodite,

Prometheus and Eurydice. They're difficult words to read, but when the music of their names is familiar, they'll be like old friends. And there is one more important benefit of introducing these fairy tales and myths. These Imaginative stories can connect your child's heart to the hearts and spirit of the families of historic times because the stories flowed out of their hearts and were passed from generation to generation, from mother to child, down to your child.

Figure 3: Mom's page

As you start to share these stories, you'll want to help your children begin to pay attention to those things that strike their hearts and help them hold on to them. For little children, it can be as simple as this. After my daughter read *The Frog Prince* to her little girls, she said, "I liked that story. I want to remember it." So she sat down and drew this picture and she wrote the gem from the story: "A promise is a promise." Her little 4-year-old said, "I want to do that." And her 10-year-old said, "I want to do that." And they did.

But I'll talk about that more in the Notebooking section.

A 6-year-old who is familiar with beautiful language and can create pictures in his head will love to have you read the wonderful children's classics aloud to him, like *Secret Garden*, *Treasure Island*, and *Heidi*. A child's listening comprehension at this age far exceeds his reading comp-

Figure 4: 4-year-old's page

rehension, so you can offer impressions to his heart that he couldn't yet get on his own. Even if he's a good reader, freeing him up to feel the music in your voice and create all the pictures in his heart without being bogged down in the mechanics of reading will make for long-lasting impressions.

Figure 5: 10-year-old's page

By age seven, you can start familiarizing your children with some of the great names of history by telling them stories of their childhoods, which provides the link of familiarity. They also like to hear stories of what it looked like to be a child living in a far-away land. These stories begin to make impressions of different cultures that is preparatory work to the study of nations that lies ahead. And around this time, the heart says to the brain, "Brain, I have stories in here that I want to remember. I need you to get working on and figure out all that writing and spelling stuff so that I can write them down." And the brain says, "But I don't know how to do that." And the heart says, "Well, maybe you just better go ask mom." And the brain gets to work.

Around the age of 8, the child is now prepared and ready to enter the Heroic years. He has strong image-ing capabilities. He has the beginnings of discernment between right and wrong. He has lots of familiar connection points. He's at home with stories. And he now, quite naturally, wants to hear about real people. At no other time in life will heroes make a deeper impression on the heart than between the ages of 8 to around 11. He wants his first heroes to be action heroes which make introductory stories to the great epic and legendary heroes a perfect choice. They provide a bridge between the Imaginative years and the Heroic years because they're partly grounded in fiction and partly in fact. These are the stories of King Arthur and Robin Hood, Roland and Siegfried, Beowulf and Hiawatha.

By age 9, children are interested in short, picturesque stories of the great men and women of history. This is the Plutarch approach to history which looks nothing like the school approach of facts and information. When Plutarch wrote his lives of great Greeks and Romans, he admitted that already the facts of their lives had been obscured. That didn't concern him and he covered himself by using a simple device, "So the story goes…" And he wrote, by "lodging these men one after the other in my house… I may see how to adjust and adorn my own life. Through daily living and associating with them I perceive all their qualities and select all those that are noblest and worthiest." And his bible for heroes is one of the most influential books of all time.

Help your children to now start doing the same thing—to lodge the great men and women of history one after another in their homes so they can see how to adjust and adorn their own lives. Nothing is more interesting to us than Life. Stories of people are what children's hearts are interested in. And while how we dress and what we eat may have changed throughout history, human nature has not. The ancient Greek has as much to teach your child's heart as the Knight in shining armor. Children care little for the dates and facts of history. Long ago is far more meaningful at this age than 600 BC. You can pique their interest in historical stories by looking for familiar elements. Does your child own a dog? Here's a good story:

> Did you ever hear the story of Newton and his little dog, Diamond? One day, when Newton was 50 years old, and had been hard at work more than 20 years studying the theory of light, he went out of his room, leaving his little dog asleep before the fire. On the table lay a heap of papers, containing all the discoveries which Newton had made during those twenty years. When his master was gone, up rose little Diamond, jumped upon the table, and overthrew the lighted candle. The papers immediately caught fire.

> Just as the destruction was completed, Newton opened the door, and saw that the labors of 20 years were reduced to a heap of ashes. There stood little Diamond, the author of all mischief.

Almost any other man would have flown into a rage, some even hurting their little dog. But Newton patted him on the head with his usual kindness, although grief was in his heart.

"O Diamond, Diamond," said he, "thou little knowest the mischief thou hast done!"

This incident affected his health and spirits for some time afterwards, but from the way he treated his little dog, you may judge what was the sweetness of his personality.

If you can find an illustration, paste it on a page like I did for Isaac Newton. Or a child can illustrate it.

Figure 6: Sample Notebook Page of Sir Isaac Newton

Historical fiction can increase familiarity with these men and women they're getting to know and familiarize the places and times in which they lived. As your children's reading skills improve, they'll do more independent reading to keep up with the desire to learn more.

By age 10 or 11, their hearts don't need to be fed as much with make believe—but there's no reason to leave it behind—and they want history delivered more directly. The Landmark Series from the 50s and 60s is an example of a good read for that age and they'll continue to meet new people through biographies and stories.

You can use fine art to bring stories of history to life an deepen impressions, like this:

391 AD

ROME

" It was the last fight at the Colosseum."

" He was a hermit ... one of those Holy men who tired of the wickedness of the world, had gone to live in the hills."

" He died, but his work was done. All that was best in Rome was stirred by the sight of the hermit slain in the midst of the great theater ...

... and there was no more slaughter in the theater."
(Young Folks Treasury, Vol. 7.
PP. 289-290)

Figure 7: Sample Notebook Page

In the proud days when Rome ruled the world, and the emperor lived in a palace of white marble, or in a house of pure gold, the Colosseum was the greatest theater ever known to be set up on the earth.

There to this day it stands, shattered and broken, but still, perhaps, the most impressive ruin in all the world. In its dark and shameful days, the great white Colosseum, rising story after story from the ground, with great galleries inside to hold forty thousand people, was a wondrous sight to see. Here came the gladiators, strong men trained to fight each other until one of them was killed. Here the Christians were thrown alive to the lions to make a Roman holiday. No place in the world has seen more cruel sights than this.

But slowly Christianity made its way, until the very emperor became a Christian. Then these shameful things ceased, and the Colosseum became only a circus. The Christians had been growing stronger and stronger for four hundred years, when there came a terrible day for Rome. Alaric, leader of the Goths came thundering outside Rome but a brave general set the Goths to flight.

Such rejoicing there was in Rome that day that the people flocked to the Colosseum, cheering their brave general. There was a wonderful performance, when suddenly came out of one of the narrow passages leading into the arena, a gladiator, with spears and swords. The rejoicing of the people knew no bounds.

Then happened a strange thing. Into the middle of the arena came an old man, bareheaded and barefooted, calling upon the people to prevent the shedding of blood. The crowd shrieked back at him to stop his preaching and to go away. The gladiators came forward and forced him aside, but still the old man came between them. A storm of stones fell upon him from the angry people. The gladiator struck him down, and the old man perished before the eyes of Rome.

He was a hermit, named Telemachus, one of those holy men who, tired of the wickedness of the world, had gone to live in the hills. Coming to Rome to visit the sacred shrines, he had seen the people flocking to the Colosseum, and, pitying them for their cruelty, had gone to stop it or die.

He died, but his work was done. All that was best in Rome was stirred by the sight of the hermit slain in the midst of the arena and there was no more slaughter in the great theater. It was the last fight at the Colosseum.

I found a picture of this by googling it and I glued it on a page with Telemachus written on the top along with when he lived in the right-hand corner. When I look at these pictures, my heart starts carrying on a conversation within itself like this: Can you imaging a people who are entertained by watching others being tortured and murdered? Well, take a look at the kind of movies people are flocking to these days. But what can I do about it? What can one person do? My heart asks. And then it reminds me of Telemachus… One man of virtue making a stand. And then my heart stops talking and leaves me to ponder.

By age 12 or 13, a student is ready to start putting pieces together. Find introductory stories of France, of Greece, of Germany, one nation at a time, so that his heart can begin to get a sense of the sweep of history and can begin to pick up patterns because the heart is always looking for patterns. He'll also be able to start fitting familiar names into their proper place in history. A student who has no understanding of the history of nations will be clueless as to what's going on in the world. It's like walking into the movie two hours late where you have no idea what's going on because you missed out on everything that happened before. As our world shrinks, our children need to be very aware of the underlying causes of world conflicts.

By age 14, the student's heart may have found topics that it wants to understand at a deeper level and he may choose to study a thread of art or music, architecture, religion or science through those nations.

By age 15, because he's comfortable with words and imagery and has a rich cultural background, he will gain much from the great works of classic literature like *Les Misérables* and *Tale of Two Cities* that will further deepen his understanding of historical events and from which he will continue to underline and extract gems of wisdom for his literature notebook.

By age 16, his heart, hungry for deeper understanding, may tackle books like Durant's *Story of Civilization* or other works of history. There are so many gaps to fill. He'll continue to read Dickens, Tolstoy, Austen and is well prepared to enter the ongoing conversation of the world's greats. This is not the end of his learning. This is only the beginning.

John Senior who wrote *The End of Christian Culture*, said, "In order to read the 'great' books of Plato, Aristotle, St. Augustine and St. Thomas, we need to replenish the cultural soil that has been depleted and create a place where those works can thrive by cultivating an imaginative ground saturated with fable, fairy tale, stories, rhymes, and adventure—the thousand books of Grimm, Andersen, Stevenson, Dickens, Scott, Dumas and the rest…"

This you will have done.

"The one thing a great books education will not do is create a moral imagination where there is none."

And now maybe your child has gone off to college and he's away from home for the first time. And he's homesick. His heart reminds him of a story he heard in childhood told by an Ancient Greek—Homer—a story of the longing for home. And now, because he's very comfortable in the music of poetry and imagery, his heart wants to feel the story at a deeper level and pulls it out in its poetic form. And, when he's done, maybe his heart will say, "Ah. I really love that. But, Brain, we want to feel it on a deeper level. We need you to learn us some Greek." And the brain, ever the obedient servant, says, "I'll get right on it." It's amazing how quickly and efficiently the brain learns hard things when the heart is in the driver's seat and how slow and painful and inefficient the process is when the heart is nowhere to be found.

As I have lodged the great men and women one at a time in my home, this progression of learning—the familiar to the imaginative to the heroic—is the pattern of learning I see in their lives. I see childhoods rich in story and experience, vivid imaginations and hearts that are always hungry to go deeper as they apply what they are learning to their own lives. As I have gone back, even with my older brain, and replenished the cultural soil of my own heart by reading more fairy tales, reciting more poetry aloud, listening to more classical music, looking at beautiful works of art and picking up works of great literature, especially the children's classics, my life has been enriched tremendously. When I see a sunset, I am sitting on the hillside beside the great French painter, Millet, and I hear his father whisper in my ear, too, "Son, that is God." When I see the daffodils, Wordsworth reminds me I can carry their beauty in my heart always. And my capacity for joy grows larger every day.

As to the formal study of history, I remember reading a well-respected historical scholar's opinion that a student isn't ready for a true study of history until he's 26. I just finished an article where a neuroscientist explained how a brain isn't fully developed until around age 24. Why do teenagers do stupid things? He said it's because the brain is not yet connected to where he can clearly see the consequences of his own actions. Yet, we expect that same teenager to analyze political and economic policies and their effects on historical events? The best he can do is parrot back what he hears. He is not yet ready to make such judgments. There are better ways to use his time.

We often make the study of history so dry and distasteful, that our children put aside their history books long before the age of 26 when they can actually begin a true study of history, which has enough interesting topics to fill a lifetime. As Marguerite Dickson wrote a hundred years ago, "A taste for historical reading is, after all, the valuable gift we can bestow upon our youthful student of history. Having given him that, we may safely leave the rest to him."

I also hear moms and educators say that they will only give their students original source documents because they want to be sure they only have the facts. I believe that is a flawed approach. How is it that two highly-trained scholars can read the identical source document of Christopher Columbus, and one will conclude Columbus is one of the most despicable men on the plant, and the other will conclude he is one of the bravest and noblest? The answer is, we all filter what we read through our own hearts and only a well-seasoned and mature heart can make proper judgments of history. That only comes with age and experience.

This developmental chart will help you further zero in on choices of what to read with your children. If you have a 6-year-old, look for fairy tales. If you have a 3-year-old, look for stories from nature or homes. If you haven't followed these levels, you haven't ruined your child! I'm creating new neural pathways every single day. Just look for familiar things to connect to, don't neglect imaginative readings and start feeding a desire to read more about great lives and history by offering short, high-interest stories in the beginning that have a connection to something in your child's world.

This is a general guideline. Don't try and make a curriculum out of it. Take in the whole picture of what it is trying to teach you.

The Pre-School Years

If you have preschoolers, I would encourage you to drop the notion that you need a curriculum to teach them. I see two primary learning objectives that should guide these years: Relationships and Impressions.

Let's look at Relationships first.

Have you listened to Dr. Gordon Neufeld's talk yet? Here are two vital takeaways from that talk:

First, the young seek for something to attach to, and once it attaches, it grows to become like that to which it attaches.

And second, you cannot parent a child whose heart you do not have.

The first one is a reminder to keep feeding your own heart. Your children are learning by your example which will speak way louder than the words you speak.

And the second one isn't really separate from the first one. The most important lessons you will teach your littles ones are that they are of great worth; they are cherished and they belong. Also, the feeling that home is safe and a good place to be. These impressions will be as an anchor to their souls their entire lives.

It's not your words that will communicate it. It will be through the music in your voice—is it always harsh and yelling, or is it sweet and soft? It will be through touch. It will be through eye to eye contact. It will be through you being totally present in the moment of contact. They will forget the details of the days. But they will carry with them for a lifetime the impressions that were made on their hearts.

I know life with pre-schoolers is hectic and messy and loud. Days rarely go as planned. You have to stay flexible and open. You will lose it from time to time. But if you can only manage one moment in every day to be completely present and connected, eye-to-eye—as a young mom puts it, you only have to be once-a-day-amazing—those moments will make deep and long-lasting impressions. It may be the walk around the neighborhood holding hands, the hug and the squeeze, and perhaps the most important moment of the day, tucking a child in at night. Aim to be at least once-a-day-amazing and then don't be hard on yourself for the rest of the day. I think the pre-school years were some of the most challenging for me. I remember being so tired. And it was a big adjustment to only having to watch out for myself to suddenly have all these little ones who demanded my attention 24 hours a day. Be kind to yourself! Enjoy it for what it is.

The primary teaching tools you have for the first years are rhymes, singing, music, pictures and nature. All of these activities are bonding activities.

Don't underestimate the value of Mother Goose rhymes. They're non-sensical to us. On purpose. Their value is in their rhythm and their rhyme, not in their meaning. Studies have shown that poetry, because of its rhythm and rhyme, help bring order to the chaotic brain. Little children love the familiar, so you get a lot of mileage even out of a few of them. If somehow you missed these rhymes as a child, you'll find a ton of them in the online library.

The reason little children pick up foreign languages so much easier than adults is because they're picking up the music of the language. Surround them with beautiful language even though they may not yet understand all that you say. In fact, don't worry about reading stories to them aloud even though they're not yet comprehending. That music of speech is going to be so important down the road.

Be a singing mom. It doesn't matter what the quality of your voice is. This is also another connecting moment. The Wee Sing Series has a lot of great tried and proven favorites. Never make it about "teaching" new songs. Let your children learn to sing by singing. Singing is one of the few activities you can do at the same time together and can be incredibly bonding.

Give them a taste for beautiful music. Play a variety of music in the background of your day, and especially include classical music so that it becomes a familiar language.

One of the important activities of toddlerhood is naming things. They naturally want to know everybody's name and the name of everything. Think of how chaotic your world would be if no one you knew had names; that you were known as the tall lady with blonde hair or you wanted to call a specific child, but they all had red hair. It would get pretty frustrating, wouldn't it? We have to name things. But don't buy vocabulary books. Name objects and people in the real world as your child comes in contact with them, although picture vocabulary books can be fun to test and reinforce that knowledge. Children delight with seeing familiar objects. I love that my father taught me names of flowers instead of just saying they were all flowers. From the time I was little I knew the hibiscus, the camellia, the hydrangea, the gardenia. And I loved them.

Naming things is a big deal. And you certainly don't need a curriculum for it. You don't need a worksheet to teach the color green. Just go outside on a summer day and exclaim, "Look how green the grass is!" Children learn best in context.

Toddlers love looking at pictures. Be aware of the images they are taking in. Expose them to beautiful art, but use subjects they can relate to such as children and families, animals and flowers. And look for ways to expose them to real life rather than just pictures in the book. Visit the fire station, the bank, introduce your child to the produce man at the grocery store. How many different scenes can you create for them to add to their stockpile of impressions, complete with sight, scent, sound, touch and even taste. So much better than just a picture in a book. And the memory of you taking them to such places is the big bonus.

Let your first stories be about familiar things as well. I cringe a little when I hear a mom ask for a suggestion for a book about the Civil War, for instance, for a 4-year-old. It's not the time.

There will be time later. In early childhood, you want to make impressions for that which is good and beautiful so that they will acquire a taste for that. Let there be innocence in childhood.

Their most favorite stories will be the stories you tell them of when you were a little girl or when grandpa was a little boy. They want stories they connect to. And your family stories will give them a sense of belonging.

Now, to the second part. Impressions.

Our friend Pestalozzi used the word Anschaaung which has proven difficult in finding a good translation. The one that has satisfied educators the most is sense-impressions. A little child learns about the world he is in through his senses—his sight, touch, smell, hearing and taste. These are the gateways. Allow a child the freedom to discover and explore, and he'll pick up a million lessons without you doing anything. Your primary role is to create a safe environment and be nearby to make sure he doesn't do serious harm to himself.

It's those sense-impressions that make Nature the perfect classroom. I have yet to see a child who doesn't prefer playing with water, sand and mud to plastic toys. In fact, this is my experience with toys. I used numerous systems to keep my kids' toys organized. And the way they played with them was consistent. I would spend hours putting them in proper bins on shelves and then they would come into the playroom with glee and proceed to dump out every bin on the floor, spread them around the room so that there was no empty space, and then go off to find something else to do.

I've noticed the same play activity with my grandchildren.

It only dawns on me now that I was fighting a losing battle. Children actually need very little in the way of toys. And if you're spending hours in chaos because of all the toys spread all over the house, maybe you need to reconsider their place in your home.

With toys, more is definitely less and less is more.

The gift my mother gave me was the gift of time and imagination, although I don't think she knew that's what she was doing. I remember hours of imaginative play in the flowers in the backyard. I remember creating cities out of the stones on our fireplace hearth. I'd use whatever I found around to create stories—I specifically remember marble families. I had paper dolls and one baby doll, although I didn't play with it much.

I think tablets and instant entertainment gratification is robbing our kids of their imaginative power. We're so quick to step in and entertain them. But let children be bored, and eventually they'll find something to occupy themselves.

Do feed them stories to feed their imagination. If I were to do it over again, I think I would have replaced all the plastic toys with a big box of good quality wooden blocks with different shapes and a bag of little wood people figures along with some toy cars. From those, they could have built their own dollhouses and cities and forts and castles and stories for hours of endless play. And clean up would have been easy. They would all go into one box and we'd be done.

Maybe in the beginning you have to get them started by playing with them. But once they begin to see the possibilities, children have wonderful imaginations with which to create.

Along with that is to have a box of dress-up toys and props.

Can you think of what else they would really need?

The same goes for outside. I took a few of my grandchildren to the park last summer and after they got tired of the swings and such, we were going to head home, but one of them got dirty hands. So we walked over to a little creek to wash them off, and that's when the real fun began. I sat on the grass and watched them dig in the mud with sticks and float things down the water and watch the dragonflies and create dams. It was by far the funnest part of the day.

Children like real things. They're smart that way. Think of all the sensory impressions being made. How many of the senses are being used with plastic toys?

I've watched Nature's effect on crying grandbabies. When nothing I can do will calm them down inside, almost without fail, taking them outside to the sway of the trees and the feel of the grass and the breeze on their faces has brought order back into their little systems.

It works for grown ups, too.

Nature's classroom is also conducive to running and jumping, spinning and twirling. Studies show the necessity of movement for connecting neural pathways in their bodies. Sedentary sitting at desks in classrooms is preventing those vital connections from being made. And there just isn't room inside a home for those large body movements! Throw in the fresh air and sunshine, not to mention the fact that when your children are playing outside, your house is staying clean—it's a win-win proposition. I just posted an article written by a woman who made it a point of taking her children out to play in nature for a couple of hours every day. She said they didn't have any temper tantrums for a year!

And shall I remind you that Nature is free if you're on a tight budget?

Home is also a natural classroom for life. Is it really more satisfying to pay a lot of money for an easy bake oven than it is to help mommy measure and stir and bake a real cake? Even household chores can feel like play to little children. They love to match socks with mommy and carry loads of towels to bathrooms. They love to squirt windows and wipe them off. My daughter said her little girls fought over who got to scrub the toilets with the toilet brush!

I read the autobiography of Kate Douglas Wiggin who wrote *Rebecca of Sunnybrook Farm* and was instrumental in bringing the kindergarten program to the United States. In her chapter where she shared memories of childhood, she wrote, "Life was by no means all play, but the idea never dawned upon us that there was anything wearisome or obnoxious about work. Our childish duties and cares were as many and as diverse (thank Heaven!) as our plays and pleasures. We 'helped' in everything, and divided the responsibilities of the household as if we belonged to the working class instead of being the children of a well-to-do physician."

So much has to do with our own attitudes that will rub off on our children. I wish I had known that lesson as a young mother. I think I spent way too much time worrying about trying to keep a clean house rather than building healthy relationships with work for my children. Although I have to admit, in spite of my shortcomings, each one of them, in their own way and time, have learned to keep nice homes. Which reminds me—children are very resilient and learn in many different ways! I see too many moms piling guilt on themselves that they are ruining their children!! I have two words for that…stop it!! Doing the best you can in the moment and in the circumstances you are in is enough. I put a lot of ideal living out there, but they're for directional pull. Not to make you feel like you're a failure.

If you want to include pre-schoolers with older siblings in the rotation schedule, the age-appropriate parts will be the music, songs, stories of children from other lands, stories of families in other lands, especially if they happen to be members of your own family tree, simple craft activities, scenes from countries, fine art such as you find in the My Book of Delights, a few words from their language, a game, occasionally a movie.

I won't take the time here to talk about all the advantages for later learning that will come as you fill their little preschool years with sense-impressions rather than trying to force academic ABCs on them. A sense of wonder which comes from their senses and a connection to you and family is far more important at this stage than anything else.

And now I'll close with a little poem for you. I'm not sure who wrote it.

Mother's Boys

Yes, I know there are stains on my carpet,
 The traces of small muddy boots;
And I see your fair tapestry glowing,
All spotless with flowers and fruit.

And I know that my walls are disfigured
With prints of small fingers and hands;
And that your own household most truly
In immaculate purity stands.

And I know that my parlor is littered
With many odd treasures and toys,
While your own is in daintiest order,
Unharmed by the presence of boys.

And I know that my room is invaded
Quite boldly all hours of the day;
While you sit in yours unmolested
And dream the soft quiet away.

Yes, I know there are four little bedsides
Where I must stand watchful each night,
While you may go out in your carriage,
And flash in your dresses so bright.

Now, I think I'm a neat little woman;

And I like my house orderly, too;
And I'm fond of all dainty belongings,
Yet I would not change places with you.

No! keep your fair home with its order,
Its freedom from bother and noise;
And keep your own fanciful leisure,
But give me my four splendid boys.

The High School Years

I have been asked several times what the Well-Educated Heart looks like in High School years. I can only give you a vision of possibilities because we're blazing new trails here.

My answer is that the principles still apply. Tend to the heart before you tend to the mind. Hopefully, by the time a child reaches high school age, you've created interest in many subjects through stories and experiences and he or she will be ready to engage in a lot of independent learning. High school will be a time to shift to the beginnings of a scholar phase of academic understanding. But no matter what subject you're learning, desire has to be awakened first. And desire comes from the Arts—from Story, Pictures, Poetry and Music. Remember, personal experiences are a form of story. So continue to find ways for your kids to engage in life. As High Schoolers prepare to take steps towards specific careers, see if you can facilitate shadow experiences in fields they show an interest. Let them follow a vet around or observe the work life of an architect. If you are homeschooling, you have a gift of time and flexibility that others may not have.

The other principle still in effect is that force still negates learning. You want to allow your High Schoolers to take ownership for their study because all true education is self-education. Sit down and have regular sincere conversations with them. Maybe plan a set time they look forward to like the first Sunday evening of the month. Let them know you are there to help them find those avenues that will take them where they want to go.

Help them to see the value of some structure to their day, but let them work out the details. For instance, maybe they want to block 4 hours off in the morning for reading and study, and then plan on a part time job in the afternoon or sports or classes with friends. Maybe they like to get up early or others may want to sleep late. If you don't let them begin to make their own choices and you keep micro-managing their lives, they'll never be able to manage themselves when they're no longer under your roof.

Like I said, High School is a time to begin scholarly work and learning mastery—but 'begin' is the operative word. At no other time in life will a person have the luxury of learning without the cares of life like a young person has. It's still a time of exploration and discovery. Many 'experts,' whatever that means, recommend that even college-bound students take a year to travel and experience the world before settling into a four-year degree. For what universities charge for tuition these days, that may be a cheaper Freshman option! And the different perspective may help your child see more clearly the role he wants to take on.

I know that High School is when parents panic about their child getting into college. If you have a child who is very clear on where he's heading, then find out what the requirements are for that particular school and work those requirements into the planning sessions. Many colleges are very supportive of homeschoolers and don't require any kind of high school transcript, but will rely heavily on an ACT or SAT score. If that's the case, working through many practice tests is great preparation. I haven't looked recently, but I could pick up old tests at the library and my kids practiced with those. My experience is that they test a child's ability to read a text and comprehend it as opposed to testing specific knowledge. A strong vocabulary is a big plus. If you are doing all the reading I recommend in the rotation schedule, that will come naturally.

If a college requires a transcript and lets you make one up, if you continue to follow the rotation schedule through high school, you'd have:

    4 years of American History
    4 years of World History
    1 semester of U.S. Government
    4 years of Literature and Composition
    2-4 years of Humanities

because literature and humanities are incorporated within the monthly studies of countries. If they're notebooking, writing is part of how they're learning.

If you continue with the Nature schedule, tying the study into scientific topics such as Month 1 to Physics and Light and Month 4 to Biology, you would have at least 2 years of Life Sciences and 2 years of Physical Sciences.

The fun thing is your child can create his own courses of study, which may include textbooks or a combination of living books, textbooks, nature journaling and real-life interaction. He may decide to seek out a course online, such as the Teaching Company or sign up for a class at school in science. Many of the elite universities such as Harvard, MIT and Stanford are offering their courses online for free. Your kids can experience them without the pressure of assignments and grades. Many school districts allow students to go part time. Most of my kids did that option. It gave them somewhere to go every day, yet gave them the freedom and flexibility for study. It was easier to take some of the math classes at the high school, for instance. But mostly they signed up for choir and band and classes of choice. Some of their friends didn't even know they were homeschooling.

Most colleges require at least two years of math. And there are a number of different ways to do that. I list some math curriculums in the Math section of the Mother's University.

Foreign languages can also be learned in different ways—tutor, programs like Duolingo or Rosetta Stone, or community learning courses. Just look around.

A college-bound student will need practice in writing papers in approved formats. Look for online tutorials. Isn't it nice if your child has a topic he loves so much that he'll look forward to research it in depth and write about it? Again, it's the stories and experiences that will feed the desire and interest. Nothing is more dreaded than being assigned a research paper with deadlines. Especially when you have nothing you want to write about.

What I'm trying to say is that I recognize, if your children are college bound, there are hoops you have to jump through. Your children need to find out what those hoops are, with your help. But there are a variety of ways of jumping through them. The most important preparation is a child who reads well and has a desire to learn. Let me repeat that. The most important preparation is a child who reads well and has a desire to learn. Who will read better? The student who works through one assigned book per semester, or the student who is allowed to create his own course of study and may read through a book a day? When you cut out all the busy work created in so many classrooms, many hours open up for reading. And the rotation schedule provides enough of a guideline that a student will have a broad exposure to many subjects. Add conversation to that, and you have the classroom of many of our greatest men and women of renown from the past. That's what I keep seeing. They read and read and read in their formative years and were given time and space to ponder, think and ask their own questions. And then they found someone to talk about what they read and to explore their questions.

High school credits become irrelevant to a lot of universities after a certain number of community college credits are earned, and community colleges usually have no entrance requirements. So that may be a different gateway. BYU Pathways is also providing another way to college.

I have even been reading that many prestigious universities are modifying their entrance requirements. They're seeing lots of perfect ACT scores, and they're realizing the folly of that. So they're looking more for life experiences and initiative, service, and personality. The WEH philosophy will serve you well for that.

And for goodness sake—not every child needs to go to college! There is no shame in vocational training. Our world needs a variety of skills.

Just a little detour—it seems everyone wants their son to grow up to be a lawyer. As I've read the stories of many of the great artists, musicians and writers, a goodly number of them had to go to law school to please their dads, and hated it. Thank goodness they finally worked up the courage to abandon what their fathers thought was so practical and developed the talents gifted them. What would our world be without them?

Each month, I'd set aside time to sit down with your high schooler and help him create a study schedule for himself for the month. Every student is at a different level and this allows for individuality, not one-sized fits all cookie cutter learning. Hopefully he is familiar with the benefits of notebooking and can work on that individually. At the end of the month, have him share what he's done. This way you're giving ownership yet allowing accountability.

That may make you nervous. But usually our nervousness comes because we have this pre-conceived time table. Get rid of that notion if you can. All our children graduated from universities, but each one did it in their own way, on their own time table. I never thought that one of my daughters would ever go to college in a million years. She decided to go to massage therapy school out of high school and got a good paying job doing that. Several years later, as she saw her sisters graduating from college, she said she didn't want to be the only one who didn't go. So she enrolled herself at the University of Utah and worked her way through. I was so proud of her! But more importantly, what a sense of accomplishment she had for herself. Her degree ended up putting her in a management position at a 5-star hotel. And now she's learning other things just for the sake of learning. She's independent and confident and does hard things every day.

Let your job be to inspire learning. Show your student all the different options for learning. And then get out of the way.

So do I think there are benefits to organizing classes for high school-aged students?

Yes—absolutely.

But my governing purpose would be to only do those things that require a group to do it. I personally think reserving morning hours is best for individual and private study. Those are prime hours when the mind isn't too cluttered. Then, if there are friends doing the same thing, bring them together in the afternoons for a couple of hours 3 or 4 days a week.

It requires friends to learn the art of conversation—a lost art that I would place in the top skills a young person needs to acquire. The ability to engage in conversation will open all kinds of doors of opportunity. I'm amazed at how many people cannot carry on a conversation. Plus it helps to clarify thought and expression. Oral expression precedes written expression. If informal, natural conversation can be facilitated, based on books and subjects of choice by the students, and not dictated by the teacher, wonderful learning will happen! Here is the joy of inspiring others and being inspired by them.

Here is the socialization part; how to get along with others outside the family. As I listen to the stories of my parents and my grandparents, we seem to have lost the wholesome social activities the youth of their day engaged in, which formed lifelong friendships. They'd hike and dance and do service together. They were engaged with each other, though. Not staring at video screens together. Funny how people argue against homeschooling because they say children won't be socialized. Yet how much socialization is going on inside the classroom where you can't talk to your neighbor most of the day. I grew up with the same large group of youth in my church, but because our only interaction was sitting together in a classroom, listening to a teacher, after nearly 18 years together, I still didn't know a single one of them!

If the students are reading much of the classic literature I recommend, the stories themselves will suggest activities and things to do. They were much more social back in the olden days, I think. Some of the social activities could be"

> Putting on informal plays together
> Forming choirs or instrumental ensembles
> Organizing service projects
> Going on nature outings and working on nature journaling together
> Working on notebooking pages together
> Practicing the art of storytelling
> Reciting poetry
> Folk and social dancing
> Sports and recreation.

They can form themselves into groups to work through the rotation schedule, focusing on specific threads, such as Paintings or Music, Architecture, World Religions, or Literature. Let them create their own course of study, don't tell them how to do it. Students can take turns sharing what they've learned about their artist of choice, for example, with the other group members. It gives them a chance to practice public speaking and presentations. Without grades and without the pressure.

Or how about creating a Delphian study group and creating a group with a variety of ages and people, not just high schoolers. Wouldn't that be awesome to engage in a conversation with wise mature adults, but as an equal?

None of these things are new or even so different from what you may see in a traditional High School. The difference is that it's student-led, not teacher directed. Which makes all the difference in the world.

For a long-extended project, I can envision a group of students forming a 'club' where they plan a trip to a foreign country together. They can fundraise together, learn about the landmarks they want to visit, the history of the country, the interesting historical people, study the language, sample the food and the culture, the music, learn about their holidays and traditions. Maybe they can make humanitarian service part of the service.

Of course this list is only meant to jog thoughts of possibilities.

I hope this is making sense. There's always such a gap between what I see and what I can say.

Now, what if you have a high school student who is totally turned off to learning?

Well, I can say that force and pressure are going to make the problem worse. I know it sounds scary, but you may need to allow time for the heart to heal—a sort of detox. Back way off. Go back to activities that build relationships. Spend time in nature, if possible. Find stories that will connect in some way to his or her personality and interests and will begin to inspire to action. Use audio books and stories if you have a reluctant reader.

And then keep feeding your own heart and praying for inspiration. Again, back off the notion your child is on a time table. Unless he or she is allowed to take ownership, you'll always be fighting a losing battle. Life has an endless variety of possibilities. Your unconditional love and the freedom to choose provides the right environment for a child to explore his or her purpose and plan. Get rid of the time table. Stop comparing. And if your child suddenly decides on a certain college path and has missed some classes like math or science, or grammar and writing, I have seen firsthand that a motivated child can accomplish much in a very short space of time.

So in short, what does the WEH look like in High School? It looks a lot like it does in the earlier years, only far more self-directed, with you as a trusted advisor and friend.

I believe every child has a purpose and a mission, and it will unfold to him in ways you cannot control, nor should you. Work on the love part and the relationship part. And trust the process.

"A commonplace life," we say as we sigh.
But why should we sigh as we say?
The commonplace sun in the commonplace sky

Makes up the commonplace day.
The moon and stars are commonplace things,
And the flowers that bloom and the bird that sings.
But dark were the world and sad our lot
If the flowers failed and the sun shone not.
And God, who studies each separate soul,
Out of commonplace lives makes His beautiful Whole.

Learning by Heart

There have been a lot of King Charles' in history—so many, in fact, they had to use descriptive words like Charles the Ugly and Charles the Fat. But how many of you have a picture or an impression come to your mind when I saw King Charles I of England? Let's see if we can bring him to life.

First, let's try and connect him to something familiar to you so we can set him in his proper place in history. You do know about the Mayflower Pilgrims, right? Can you remember what year they landed in Plymouth? 1620. Charles I was made king of England in 1623—just three years after they landed—when his father died. So let's link him to his father by linking him to something that is probably familiar to you. His father was King James as in the King James Bible. And you may be familiar with the story of his grandmother, poor Mary, Queen of Scots, who had her son, James, taken away from her when he was only ten months old and she never saw him again. And, you may remember, she later lost her head.

Now let's use a little artistry to give him some life. I'm going to combine a story written for little children with a lesson in fine art.

Once there lived a very beautiful queen and a very proud king. They had three beautiful children, whom they loved very dearly. They were very proud of these children, and gave them everything they could to make them happy. They had such a great number of toys they almost filled a large room. There were several servants who brought out the toys and put them away again, and who had nothing else to do but wait upon these children.

Figure 8: Children of Charles I of England
by Sir Anthony Van Dyck

The children had a fine large yard to play in, too. It was so large, they called it a park. Once day they were having a good time in the park when they were told their mother wanted them. They were to be dressed to go and have their pictures painted.

There were no cameras in those days, so instead, there was a great artist whose name was Sir Anthony Van Dyck. He painted beautiful pictures with oil paints.

The oldest child had already had his picture painted so many times he probably would not have cared to go it if had not been for the boat ride he knew he would have. You see, the king's palace and Sir Anthony Van Dyck's house both stood near the banks of the same river. Sir Anthony had a private boat landing made just for the king and queen and their children. The king liked so much to watch Sir Anthony Van Dyck paint that he used to visit him nearly every day.

It must have taken a long time before the children were dressed and ready to go. When at last they were all ready, the boats were waiting for them. It was a beautiful ride down the river to Sir Anthony Van Dyck's house. The great Van Dyck himself came out to meet them. He was glad to have three such lovely children to pain. He was very fond of children and he liked to have a great many people about him as he painted. The ladies wore beautiful dresses and the men, too, were dressed in velvets and silks, and carried shining swords. Van Dyck was very fond of music and always had some musicians playing while he painted. The children liked the music, too, and it made them forget they were standing still so long.

The child standing so straight with his hand on the dog's head is a boy, although he is dressed much like a girl. His name is Prince Charles. I don't see how he could run or even walk in such a long, heavy dress, do you? Van Dyck had a very large, fine dog, and as soon as the dog saw the children he came right up to them. He seemed to like Prince Charles the best, and sat beside him all the time his picture was being painted. He liked to feel the soft stroke of Prince Charles' kind hand.

Prince Charles grew up to be King Charles II. He did not like to do anything but have a good time, so people called him, "The Merry Monarch." He nearly always took a dog with him wherever he went, even to church. He seemed to like a certain very small dog best, and people named these dogs after him. They called them "King Charles spaniels." Have you ever seen a King Charles spaniel?

"Baby Stuart," as people loved to call little Prince James, wore blue silk, trimmed with lace. He looks a little shy as he stands there, holding his apple tight in his chubby little hands. Probably the queen mother gave Baby Stuart the big red apple. He was only two years old, and she thought he might get hungry or need something to play with. Baby Stuart grew up to be a great naval officer, who fought and won battles on a big boat at sea. When his brother died, he became king.

When you look at Baby Stuart you feel sure he will grow up to be a good king. But, do you know, he was not a good king. The people did not like him at all, and even drove him out of the country. But we like to think of him always as a pretty baby whose queen mother used to sing him to sleep just as other mothers do.

Their sister, Mary, must have held some roses in her hand and dropped them. Can you see them on the rug, in front of her? Van Dyck painted a curtain just back of the children, and through the window we see a rosebush which may be the one from which the little Princess Mary picked her roses.

When princess Mary was only ten years old, she was married to William, Prince of Orange, who was only fifteen years of age. But she lived in her own home until she grew up. When at last she did go to live in her husband's country every one was glad to see her, for she was such a good and wise princess. She often helped her brothers, too, for it seemed as if they were always in trouble.

The great artist Van Dyck painted many pictures of these three children, but the king and queen liked this one best of all.

My daughter told this story of the painting to her girls when they were little, and a couple years later she was reading a story about King Charles I, which I'm about to tell you, and her young daughter said, "Wait, mom, isn't that the father of those little children we saw in the painting?" Her little girl remembered and made the connection, which is the point of this little exercise.

So now I want to paint a scene in your heart. But first, let me give you a visual of King Charles, courtesy of Van Dyck. You can see him from some different angles here. And for a little perspective, he's only 5'4".

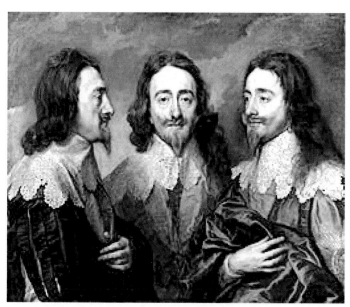

Figure 9: Charles I in Three Positions by Sir Anthony Van Dyck

Now a little background. Charles believed in the Divine Rights of kings. That's how he was raised. But it got him into trouble over the years because he kept disbanding Parliament when they got in his way. Oliver Cromwell thought he had a much better plan. And part of that plan meant getting King Charles out of the way. So charges of treason were brought against him. The year is now 1649. He's been ruling for about 26 years. Three more children have been born to him and the queen, a daughter aged 13, a son aged 8, and another daughter, aged 5.

And now let's paint the scene. (This scene is adapted from a Messner biography, *Death to the King* by Clifford Lindsey Alderman.)

It is still dark in London as the watchmen making their morning rounds bawled, "Past five o'clock on a cold, snow morning!" Bitterly cold it was on this 30th day of January, 1649. In his apartment in St. James Palace, the King was still sleeping quite peacefully. On a pallet beside his bed, his faithful servant Herbert was wakeful, however; indeed, he had scarcely closed an eye through a night that seemed endless.

At half past five the King awoke. "I will get up now," he said to his servant, "for I have a great work to do today." As the cold seeped into the chamber, the King chose the clothing he would wear with an eye to its warmth.

"I will not have the people see me shiver in the cold lest they think me afraid," he told Herbert. Dressing and the King's painstaking toilet lasted an hour. For a year he had allowed his beard to grow. His chestnut colored hair was beginning to turn white.

At about ten there was a gentle tap on the bedchamber door. "It is time to go to Whitehall, sir." Taking the bishop by the hand, he smiled and said, "Come, let us be going."

As they made their way, a deafening roll of drums began. Drawn up in a double line on each side of the path that ran across the park were companies of infantry armed with muskets. They were holding back the dense throng of spectators behind them.

The pace of the procession was slow. Now Whitehall Palace loomed ahead. Inside the palace grounds he was taken through the long passage known as the Stone Gallery. Here hung the King's collection of masterpieces by the celebrated painters of the time, for he was a great lover and patron of the art.

From the Stone Gallery, the King entered the building which housed the royal apartments. Here he was taken to await a summons. He hoped it would not be long in coming. A wooden platform had been built against the side of the Banqueting Hall. All around it a black cloth had been stretched. Behind the black cloth around the platform was the scaffold on which the King was to die.

In an outer room of the apartments, a guard approached. "There is a man outside who demands to see the King. He says it is most urgent and refused to go away."

The man was Henry Seymour, who had once been page of honor to the King. When he told his errand, he was brought straight to the royal apartments.

Entering the chamber where the King was, Seymour burst into a flood of tears. He knelt, kissed the King's hand and then clasped him about the legs in an agony of grief. Then he handed the King a letter from his son Charles, the heir to the English throne, who had sent this envoy from France with all possible speed.

The King read the letter slowly and carefully. For the first time his melancholy face was touched with a deeper sadness.

Enclosed with the letter was a sheet of paper. The only thing on it, at the very bottom, was the prince's signature.

Seymour then explained that a second copy of this paper had been given to the Puritan leaders who now controlled England. They could fill in whatever they wished on the paper above the signature, he said.

"Your son will do anything, anything," Seymour added. "He will even give up his right of succession to the throne."

The King's smile made his dour face radiant. He threw the paper with his son's signature into the fire. Then he gave Seymour a letter he had already written— a message to his beloved son.

Now was not the time to back down. At his trial, he had declared, "It is not my case alone. It is the freedom and liberty of the people of England. I must justly stand for these liberties. If power without law may make law, I do not know what subject in England can be assured of his life or anything he can call his own."

The previous night, two of his children, 13-year-old Elizabeth and 8-year-old Henry were brought to him; the others had escaped to safety. A Bishop witnessed the event. As the children wept, Charles told them they must not be too sad, for he was dying gloriously for law, liberty and the true Protestant religion.

He told the prince that the Puritans might try to make him King so that they could use him for their own purposes, and that he must not yield to them as long as his older brothers were alive.

"I will sooner be torn to pieces!" the little fellow cried.

Then the king divided some jewels between them and bid farewell.

The time of execution arrived. The King's step was firm and steady as he stepped out upon the platform. The King was allowed to speak and he spoke for some time. He said he was innocent of the crime with which he had been charged. Then he said, as his grandmother, Mary Queen of Scots, had said before him, "I have forgiven all the world, and even those in particular that have been the chief cause of my death."

And finally, "I die a Christian."

The King then spoke to one of the executioners. "I shall say but a short prayer," he said. "When I hold out my hands thus, strike."

The King then took the white cap from the Bishop and put it on. He tucked his long curls under it to leave his neck bare. Then he disappeared from the view of those in the courtyard as he lay down with his head on the block. They saw only the flash of the ax as the executioner brought it down.

A spectator later wrote: "At the instant when the blow was given there was such a dismal, universal groan among the people as I never heard before and desire I may never hear again."

King Charles I was dead. England had killed him. Rulers before him had been deposed from the throne or forced into exile. One who came after him would be ousted. But never before had an English king been executed—nor would another be afterwards.

What had caused England to rid itself of Charles I in this way? It was part of the struggle by the country's liberty-loving people for freedom, a struggle that had begun more than four centuries earlier.

You have just experience learning by heart. The next time you see King Charles I in a text, you are now going to have impressions and images that will instantly come as a flash in connection with that name. Of course, this is not a complete picture. It will take time to create a complete picture of who he was and his role in history. Was he a good king or a bad one? A good man or a bad one? Even scholars disagree. But, would you like to learn more? You now have something to build upon.

Rudyard Kipling wrote, "If history were taught in the form of stories, it would never be forgotten." I would expand that and say any subject taught by stories will not be forgotten. We say in one ear and out the other, but we don't say in one eye and out the other. Images stick. That's one reason pornography is so dangerous. It's nearly impossible to rid the mind of those images. And the reason stories stay with us is because they paint pictures on our hearts and stir our feelings.

Let's apply a little artistry to a study of the Civil War.

First a little music. The Battle Cry of Freedom was composed by George Frederick Root in 1862. The song was so popular that the music publisher had 14 printing presses going at one time and still could not keep up with demand. It is estimated that over 700,000 copies of this song were put in circulation. A soldier tells us this:

A glee club came down from Chicago, bringing with them the new song, "We'll rally 'round the flag, boys," and it ran through the camp like wildfire. The effect was little short of miraculous. It put as much spirit and cheer into the army as a victory. Day and night one could hear it by every camp fire and in every tent. I never shall forget how the men rolled out the line, "And although he may be poor, he shall never be a slave." I do not know whether Mr. Root knows what good work his song did for us there, but I hope so.

By listening to this song, and better yet, joining in singing it, you truly enter into the spirit of that day. Interestingly, the same song moved the hearts of the Confederate soldiers. They tweaked the words a bit, but my heart made a note when I heard that…both sides believed they were fighting for freedom?

Now let's combine a little illustration with some poetry. This is a N.C. Wyeth illustration of a poem, The Picket Guard. The usual headline had been, "All quiet on the Potomac." And then, one day in September, 1861, the headline simply read, "A

Figure 10: The Picket Guard by N.C. Wyeth

picket shot," which prompted this poem by Ethel Lyn Beers.

"All quiet along the Potomac," they say,
  "Except now and then a stray picket
Is shot, as he walks on his beat, to and fro,
  By a rifleman hid in the thicket.
'Tis nothing—a private or two, now and then,
  Will not count in the news of the battle;
Not an officer lost—only one of the men,
  Moaning out, all alone, the death rattle."

"All quiet along the Potomac tonight,
  Where the soldiers lie peacefully dreaming;
Their tents in the rays of clear autumn moon,
  Or the light of the watch fires, are gleaming.
A tremulous sigh, as the gentle night-wind,

Through the forest-leaves softly is creeping;
While stars up above, with their glittering eyes,
    Keep guard—for the army is sleeping.
There's only the sound of the lone sentry's tread,
    As he tramps from the rock to the fountain,
And thinks of the two in the low trundle bed
    Far away in the cot on the mountain.
His musket falls slack—his face, dark and grim,
    Grows gentle with memories tender,
As he mutters a prayer for the children asleep
    For their mother—may Heaven defend her!

The moon seems to shine just as brightly as then,
    That night, when the love yet unspoken,
Leaped up to his lips—when low-murmured vows
    Were pledged to be ever unbroken.
Then drawing his sleeve roughly over his eyes,
    He dashes off tears that are welling,
And gathers his gun closer up to its place
    As if to keep down the heart-swelling.

He passes the fountain, the blasted pine-tree
    The footstep is lagging and weary;
Yet onward he goes, through the broad belt of light,
    Toward the shades of the forest so dreary.
Hark! Was it the night-wind that rustled the leaves?
    Was it moonlight so wondrously flashing?
It looked like a rifle—"Ah! Mary, good-bye!"
    And the life-blood is ebbing and plashing.

All quiet along the Potomac tonight,
    No sound save the rush of the river;
While soft falls the dew on the face of the dead
    The picket's off duty forever.

Whoa. That reaches deep. Let's make another impression, same illustration:

The Picket's Song
Alice May Youse

Jesus, lover of my would,
    Let me to Thy bosom fly;
While the waters near me roll,
    While the tempest still is high.

It was on an ocean steamer,
   And one voice above the rest,
Beautiful, pure, rich and mellow,
   All the air with music blest.
Something more, a faint remembrance
   Broke upon the listener's ear
"Yes," he thought, "tis not the first time
   That sweet voice is mine to hear."

Silence followed. Then the stranger
   Stept up to the singer rare,
"Were you in the Civil War, sir?"
   "A Confederate, I was there."
Then a time, a place, were mentioned.
   "Were you?" "Yes, and strange to say
This same hymn was then my comfort,
   That you hear us sing today.

"Dark the night, so cold and dreary,
   And my boyish heart felt low,
Pacing there on sentry duty,
   Dangerously near the foe.
Midnight came, the darkness deepened,
   Thoughts of home foreboding brought.
So, for comfort, prayer and singing,
   Dissipated gloomy thought.

"'All my trust on Thee is stayed,
   All my hope from Thee I bring,
Cover my defenceless head
   With the shadow of Thy wing.'
Then a strange peace came upon me,
   No more fear and gloom that night,
Dawn came, heralding the morrow,
   Ere the first faint-streak of light.

Then the other told his story:
   "I, a Union soldier, true,
In those woods that very evening,
   With my scouts were passing through.

You were standing, and our rifles
   Covered you. We heard you sing:
'Cover my defenceless head
   With the shadow of Thy wing.'

"Twas enough, 'Boys,' I said,
'Come, Lower rifles; We'll go home.'"

Poetry combines the imagery of words with the rhythm of music to stir our feelings. It's a powerful heart tool.

Now let's pull out one more tool of the artist—probably the one most used—the Story. And let's see if we can begin to bring the two Generals of the war to life.

First, a little story about Robert E. Lee, the Confederate general, right after the battle of Gettysburg.

"I was badly wounded," says a private of the Army of the Potomac. "A ball had shattered my left leg. I lay on the ground not far from Cemetery Ridge, and as General Lee ordered his retreat, he and his officers rode near me. As he came alone I recognized him, and though faint from exposure and loss of blood, I raised up my hands, looked Lee in the face, and shouted as loud as I could, 'Hurrah for the Union.'

"The general heard me, looked, stopped his horse, dismounted, and came toward me. I confess I at first thought he meant to kill me. But as he came up, he looked down at me with such a sad expression on his face, that all fear left me, and I wondered what he was about. He extended his hand to me and grasping mine firmly, looking right into my eyes, said, 'My son, I hope you will soon be well.'

"If I live a thousand years, I will never forget the expression on General Lee's face. Here he was defeated, retiring from a field that cost him and his cause almost their last hope, and yet he stopped to say words like those to a wounded soldier of the opposition, who had taunted him as he passed by.

"As soon as the general had left me, I cried myself to sleep there upon the bloody ground."

Now let's turn to Ulysses S. Grant, the Union General. A little longer story.

Ulysses S. Grant was sixty years old; he was healthy, wealthy, and wise. It seemed as though nothing could disturb or molest him, and yet, at one blow, the old general was struck down, wounded in the tenderest of all places, his honor, his reputation—his word.

It was this way. In 1880 he had gone into business, investing a hundred thousand dollars in the banking business in which one of his sons was a partner, but General Grant was not an active partner in the business. At first the firm made lots of money. General Grant's name, of course, gave people confidence and one of the partners was such a sharp and shrewd business man that people called him the "Napoleon of finance."

On the morning of Tuesday, the sixth of May, 1884, General Grant was, as he thought, a millionaire. Before sunset that same day he knew he was ruined.

The bank had failed. The "Napoleon of finance" whom everyone thought so smart a business man, had been too smart. He had speculated and lost everything. Worse than this, he had lied and stolen. He had used the name and fame of General Grant to back up wicked schemes and dishonorable transactions; he had used up all the money put into the business by General Grant and Mrs. Grant and the others who had gladly put in the money because of General Grant's name, and he had so turned and twisted and handled things that not a dollar was left in the business.

General Grant and his sons were ruined; their good names apparently, were disgraced by being mixed up with the affairs and wickednesses of their bad and bold partner, who, as soon as he saw the truth was out ran away, like the thief and coward he was.

Every one was surprised. More than this, they were so startled that, for a time, even the great name of Grant seemed beclouded, and thoughtless people, cruel, people, the folks who like to talk and to say things without thinking of the consequences, said mean and hateful and wicked and untruthful things about this great and noble soldier who never in his life had done a dishonorable act, or said a mean or unkind thing… It was hard, was it not?

It was especially hard on such a man as General Grant. He never complained, he never spoke of the treatment to his friends; but it hurt terribly.

It made him sick and he developed a terrible trouble in his throat—cancer—that brought him months of suffering, of torture, and of agony.

He sent to work to do something to earn money. At first he was discouraged. For, as he looked at the wreck of his fortune made by the dreadful business failure, and knew that he was a sick man, no longer able to work or make his own living, a future looked very dark and he could not see how he could make things better for his wife or the boys he so dearly loved.

Then it was that he determined to write, as did Julius Caesar, the story of his life, his battles and campaigns. He saw a way out of his difficulties; he determined to try. Then the world saw one of the most remarkable things in all its long history—a sick man, without experience or training, deliberately sitting down to write the story of his life, fighting off death with all the might and strength of his giant will, in order to save his name from dishonor and leave something for his wife and children after the death that he knew was not far away.

Writing or dictating, sometimes four, sometimes six, sometimes eight hours a day, so the months went on. It was a tremendous effort. In the eight weeks that followed the first of May, he did more work, in writing his book, than in any other eight weeks of his life. As an army in battle sometimes gathers up all its strength for a final charge or for a last stand against the foe, so the old general, weakened by disease, worried by anxiety, but determined to win, actually held death at bay until the work he had set himself to do was accomplished.

At last, the work was done. The book was finished. On the first day of July, 1885, his preface was dated and signed. Just 3 weeks later, on the morning of the twenty-third of July, 1885, the tired hand dropped limply within that of a patient, faithful wife. The last fight was over; the last victory had been won.

The book he wrote and completed under those fearful conditions is one of the world's notable books, while its success more than met the desires of the writer and placed his family again in comfort and security.

To the last, the great soldier's thoughts were all for peace. He had seen battles. He knew the horrors of war. He knew the beauty of peace.

"Let us have peace" is what he used to say.

We tend to teach the facts of history which are swept into the dustpans of our minds because we can't find a use for them. The fact that the war lasted from 1861-1865 and a list of key battles or players does little for us. But as the fox said in *The Little Prince*, "Only the heart sees rightly. What is essential is invisible to the eye." As we use the tools of the heart, and apply our hearts to understanding, here are a few of the lessons taught to my heart from just these few stories and poems: Duty, Integrity, Honor, Reputation, Compassion, Sacrifice, Courage, Forgiveness, Love, the power of hymns and prayer to comfort the heart in dark nights, the power of music to stir the soul. As I read the stories of the two generals—both honorable men—my heart was reminded that two honorable people can have different points of view. Wow. Isn't that a badly needed lesson for today?

Although the details may fade with time, the impressions will stay with me for a very long time, maybe even forever. When I see the name Robert E. Lee or Ulysses S. Grant, these impressions will instantly connect to their names in a flash. When I see the picture of the Picket later, all those feelings that were stirred will instantly connect to it.

Repetition is a vital key to learning. None of us can comprehend or hold onto the whole of anything at once. So I have a notebook that gives me a chance to review and remember. It's loaded with pictures of people and events because a picture is worth 700,000 words and I can review many things very quickly. I'll jot down enough of a story to jog my memory and write down the reference so I can go back and read it again, if I want the details, although the impression of the story will happen immediately. I'll copy quotes that touched my heart or principles I've learned from a life.

Here's Charles I and his children. As you see the picture, what impressions come to you from the story I told earlier? I placed his page in the book chronologically according to the year he was born.

King Charles I

1600 - 1649

ENGLAND

Only King of England to be executed.

"It is not my case alone. It is the freedom and liberty of the people of England. I must justly stand for these liberties. If power without law may make law, I do not know what subject in England can be assured of his life or anything else he can call his own."

Prince Charles, Princess Mary, Baby 'Stuart'

Favorite Van Dyck painting of 3 older children

Figure 11: Sample Notebook Page of King Charles I

And look—I notice William Bradford was born ten years earlier.

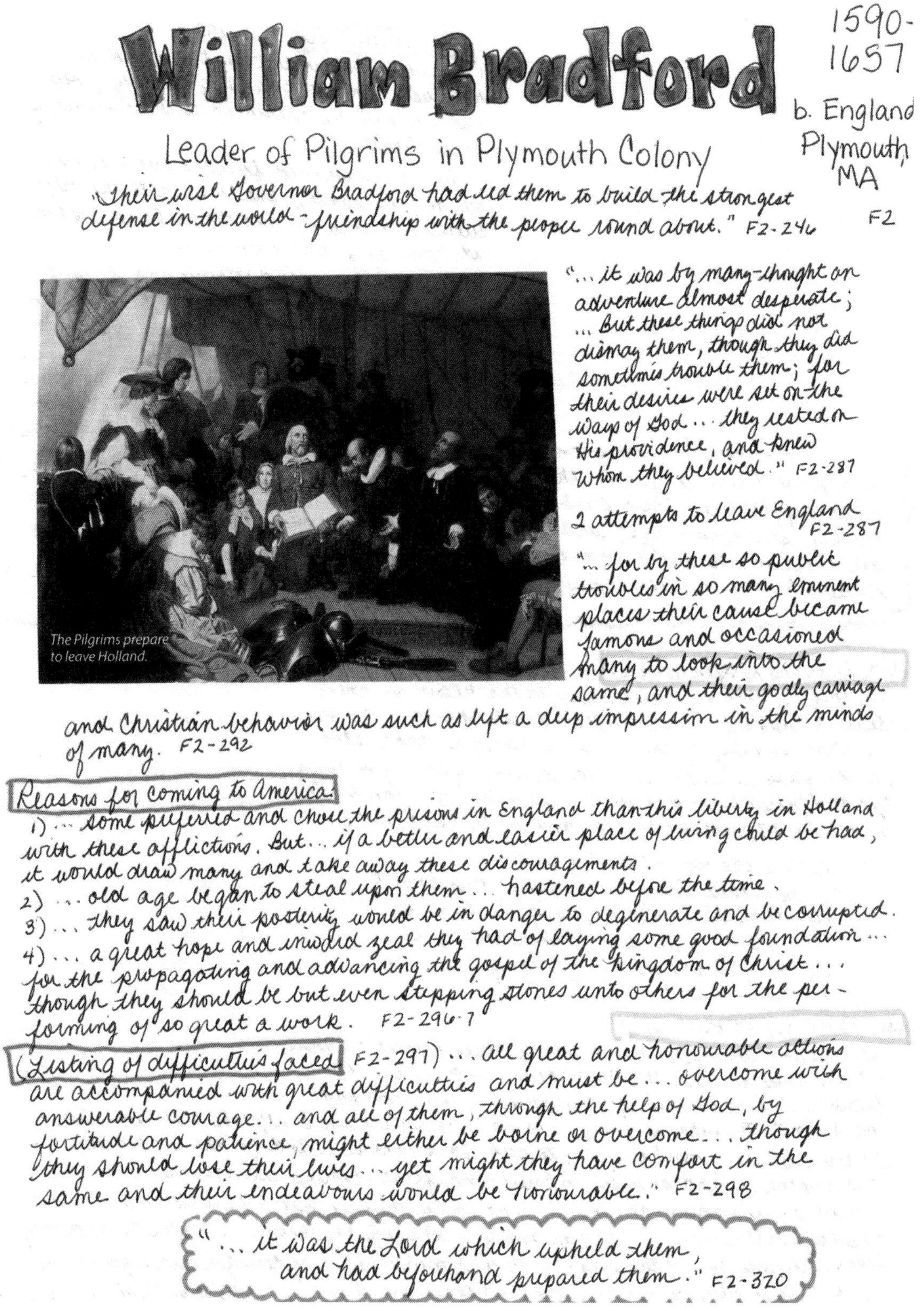

William Bradford

1590-1657

b. England
Plymouth, MA

F2

Leader of Pilgrims in Plymouth Colony

"Their wise Governor Bradford had led them to build the strongest defense in the world - friendship with the people round about." F2-246

The Pilgrims prepare to leave Holland.

"... it was by many thought on adventure almost desperate; ... But these things did not dismay them, though they did sometimes trouble them; for their desires were set on the ways of God ... they rested on His providence, and knew Whom they believed." F2-287

2 attempts to leave England F2-287

"... for by these so public troubles in so many eminent places their cause became famous and occasioned many to look into the same, and their godly carriage

and Christian behavior was such as left a deep impression in the minds of many. F2-292

Reasons for coming to America:
1) ... some preferred and chose the prisons in England than this liberty in Holland with these afflictions. But ... if a better and easier place of living could be had, it would draw many and take away these discouragements.
2) ... old age began to steal upon them ... hastened before the time.
3) ... they saw their posterity would be in danger to degenerate and be corrupted.
4) ... a great hope and inward zeal they had of laying some good foundation ... for the propagating and advancing the gospel of the kingdom of Christ ... though they should be but even stepping stones unto others for the performing of so great a work. F2-296.7

(Listing of difficulties faced F2-297) ... All great and honourable actions are accompanied with great difficulties and must be ... overcome with answerable courage ... and all of them, through the help of God, by fortitude and patience, might either be borne or overcome ... though they should lose their lives ... yet might they have comfort in the same and their endeavours would be honourable." F2-298

"... it was the Lord which upheld them, and had beforehand prepared them." F2-320

Figure 12: Sample Notebook page for William Bradford

Henry Hudson was out looking for the Northwest Passage when Charles was born.

Henry Hudson

1560?
1611
b. England
Holland

English sea explorer searching for Northwest Passage to China. Laid foundation for Dutch colonization.

The Dutch sent Henry Hudson to find a shortcut to Asia.

For nearly 150 years after Columbus the elusive passage was to preoccupy the minds of Europe's greatest geographers, map makers, and explorers... It remained out of man's reach fr the simple reason that it never existed in the first place.

F1-(6)-11
F1(9)

> BUT IN THE COURSE OF THE SEARCH, MAN ADDED GREATLY TO HIS STORE OF KNOWLEDGE.

The passage which was not there inspired a surge of exploration and discovery unparalleled in history.
F1(9)-7

> They were men who knew IT TOOK MANY FAILURES TO BRING SUCCESS. F(9)-36

A strange wind "we had not found common on this voyage." - The escape was so narrow and the coming of the wind from a new direction so fortuitous that Hudson could only attribute his good fortune to GOD'S INTERVENTION.
F(9)-34

← Maybe Hudson survived? by befriending them

Mermaid sightings??
F(9)-42

Eskimo in middle of nowhere??
150
The un-sung hero:
The keeper of the ship's log.
F(9)75

REASON FOR THE DUTCH GOLDEN AGE: Spanish cruelty had driven many wealthy and intelligent men from Spain, Portugal and Belgium ... others came for Holland's respect for freedom of thought and religion. THE INFLUX BROUGHT AN AMAZING AMOUNT OF TALENT. F(9)-61

A desire for learning swept the nation.
F(9)62

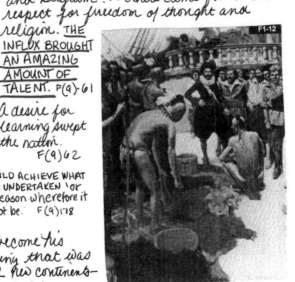

HE WOULD ACHIEVE WHAT HE HAD UNDERTAKEN 'or give reason wherefore it will not be. F(9)178

HUDSON'S so-called FAILURE would become his greatest TRIUMPH — in seeking something that was not there, the explorers discovered 2 new continents— a greater prize than a short passage to Asia 177

Figure 13: Sample Notebook Page of Henry Hudson

Here's Robert E. Lee. Queen Victoria was born not long after him and she was just a year older than Florence Nightingale.

And my heart begins to see the flow of history. By creating a page for interesting people I want to remember, I now have a landing page or place to add new stories and quotes and information all along the way.

A friend said her 14-year-old son was holding his notebook one day and he said, "Mom, if people knew what was in this notebook, they would know it's a treasure of great worth."

To awaken that desire in the hearts of your children—to help them Learn by Heart—is your great calling and privilege.

Tools

Enjoying the Grand Buffet

I am now going to start sharing the tools and resources you have to work with found at welleducatedheart.com. Don't let them overwhelm you!

Have you ever started a diet that required you to eat completely different foods than what you're used to eating? I have. And it didn't end well. Well, mostly, it just ended, really fast.

We've been a mind-based culture for a very long time. We're used to testing and academics and milestones and grade levels. We're comfortable with curriculum where someone tells us what to teach, how to teach it and when to introduce it. It's systematic, controllable and predictable. Many curriculum companies pride themselves on the fact that you don't have to do anything to prepare. Just open the book and say exactly what it says to say and do exactly what it says to do.

A heart-based learning environment is not like that at all. True, it's going to require more from you in the beginning. But in the end, and even during the journey, it will be far more satisfying and enjoyable. It requires a different mindset; a different way of thinking. Which is why I brought up the diet scenario. If you try and implement all this in one day, I'm not sure how it will go over. The most effective diets are those where small changes are made gradually over time and they become a way of life.

The Well-Educated Heart is not a curriculum. I cannot even begin to suggest a one-size fits all scenario. There are as many different personalities as there are people. Each home and each family has a different feel to it. There are varying levels of abilities and talents; aptitudes and interests. To prescribe an exact 'curriculum' that would fit every personality would be impossible. And not very wise.

What I am offering is a Pattern of Learning—First Heart, Then Mind and then allowing the Spirit to do its work.

And I can give you quality tools and resources to work with. I hope you'll take the time to familiarize yourself with them, and then customize their use for the needs of your own family and circumstances. There is a LOT to choose from! No one will likely use them all.

This is about feeding your heart first. That doesn't mean your children will be on hold while you're learning. Remember what I said about gradual changes? Just start by reading a few more stories together, aloud, listening to a little more music, singing more, taking more time for poetry, spending more time in nature, playing more games, looking at more masterpieces of art, learning handicrafts like knitting and crocheting—yes, even the boys. Leave large blocks of time open where your kids have to find ways to amuse themselves. Boredom can be a great gift to get the imagination flowing. TURN OFF THE ELECTRONICS. They will work against you in a big way.

If you have older self-motivated learners, introduce them to the tools and resources and let them go. For other ages, focus on warming their hearts with the activities I just listed while you're warming your own heart. I promise they're not going to fall behind in anything that matters. Trust the process. As you gradually start incorporating the ideas you are learning about into your home, I suspect by the end of one year, your home life will look much different than it did at the beginning.

Maybe, for awhile, to get out of any ruts you may be in, try switching your daily schedule around to reflect the pattern of learning—first heart, then mind. Instead of starting every day off with a list of chores, get in the habit of putting your house to bed at night so that when you wake up, you can start 'playing.' Of course, keep the basics like making beds, getting dressed and brushing teeth. But I was inspired by an incident written by the daughter of Julia Ward Howe who wrote The Battle Hymn of the Republic. One of her fond memories was of early morning walks with her parents. There's something magical about nature first thing in the morning. I wish I had thought of that when my children were young. I wish I had done much more enjoying life with them and much less worry about getting the house clean. When the order is work first before you play, sometimes you never get around to the play. But if you play first, maybe you'll find your children more willing to join in the work? Those happy memories together help bond hearts, and I hope you remember from Section 1 how important that is. Besides, is there a rule that says work always has to come before play?

Do simplify your life wherever you can so you have more time to enjoy the buffet. Get rid of stuff. One idea for putting the house to bed at night is to set the timer for five minutes after dinner where kids can put away anything that means something to them. If it's left out after that, it's gobbled up in a big bag or basket and put in a closet. They won't see any of those items again until Saturday when they're all dumped out again. Those toys or items the kids have a place for and value enough to 'save' will survive. The rest can be given new homes. It's one way to keep purging your house of too much stuff and maintaining a little order during the week. Save the deep cleaning for family chores on Saturday morning.

Don't worry about how you're going to get all this into your children. Focus on warming your own heart first— the rest will start flowing naturally.

Be a light…not a hammer.

And now, let the tasting and sampling begin.

What is Libraries of Hope?

Libraries of Hope is just what its name implies—it's about libraries of books, fine art, music and other resources to inspire the hearts of young people with hope. Hope for better things is what keeps us moving forward and reaching higher. Our world doesn't seem to be offering much hope these days.

I frequently hear from mothers who tell me they no longer feel comfortable allowing their children to bring books home from their public library. They are shocked at what even their youngest children are being exposed to. The classics are vanishing from the bookshelves. The history selections for children are growing smaller. It's almost impossible to find books that reflect faith, family and freedom and that inspire the heart with goodness, love and beauty. In many libraries, the books are being removed all together and are being replaced with computer screens. And during our Covid crisis, public libraries have been closed altogether. What I have tried to do is give you another choice, another library you can turn to.

The central library at librariesofhope.com is an online library. Most of the books offered here are free and can be read immediately on electronic devices or printed out. But the intention is that, through the resources you will find here, you will become acquainted with books that you will want to include in a library of hope in your own home. Which is why I call it Libraries of Hope instead of Library of Hope. As these family libraries grow, maybe you will want to do as other families are doing and turn them into lending libraries for your community of neighbors and friends. As you do this, you are being a part of a cultural uplift to our world.

So you may be asking how I selected the books for this library. My main intention was to look for living books. If you love Charlotte Mason like I do, living books is a familiar term. You also know the difference between a living book and twaddle. One definition I like is this: "Living Books are those which have worthy thoughts, inspiring tales, inspiring ideas or pictures of life, and with fit and beautiful expression." Living books help learning come alive and fill us with ideas and ideals, which fulfills the purpose of creating a library that will fill young people with hope.

I've spent many years searching for books with which to fill this library. My initial search led me to books written before 1923; books that were in the public domain. When Libraries of Hope began, Internet Archive had just started digitizing old books and placing them on the internet for all of us to read. I made note of the books that were being recommended by educators back in their day and I soon came to find my own personal favorites as well and organized the library around these very old wonderful children's books. They didn't hide their reasons for writing the books they did. They definitely had an agenda. They wrote to help children understand how to remain free. They wrote to help children learn how to live happy, fruitful lives. The books are packed full with gems of wisdom.

While I provide links to the digitized copies, Internet Archive makes it very easy to push a button and print them out if you prefer paper in hand. In that way I was able to add many books to my library. It only costs a couple of dollars for me to print them out at home.

And then I started to learn about children's books written after 1923. I studied the writings and recommendations of May Hill Arbuthnot, starting with her 1947 edition of *Children and Books*. I dug through hundreds of bins of old books, looking for the treasures to rescue. It became a favorite hobby and my personal library swelled to several thousand books. I was always looking for the best of the best. I poured through book recommendations of fellow book lovers whose opinions I came to value and trust—Elizabeth Wilson and her *Books Children Love*, Lisa Ripperton and her monumental work at the Baldwin Project, Valerie's Living Book list, my friends at Reshelving Alexandria, William Kirkpatrick's *Books That Build Character*, Jenny Phillips' Good and Beautiful booklist, and Jan Bloom's *Who Should We Then Read* volumes and many others along the way. Not every book they recommended went into my library. But I paid particular attention to titles and authors that came up repeatedly and made sure to place them in the library. I wanted to be sure and include books for all reading levels and that would appeal to different interests and then tried to organize it in a way that you can find just what you are looking for. At first, there were no copies of these books to read online, so I provided links to Amazon where you could almost always find a used copy.

But then I watched something sad happen along the way. These wonderful older children's books have become the hottest selling items in today's bookselling market. Titles that I used to be able to pick up for a dollar or two now sell for $50, $100 even $200 and more IF you can even find them. How can I recommend a book to you if you have no way to read it?

Can you imagine how excited I was when I learned that Internet Archive has recently started digitizing these out of print but still in copyright books and making them available for us to borrow? While you sometimes have to join a waitlist and wait, it makes it possible for you to read books you can't read otherwise. As interest grows, the availability of these titles will undoubtedly grow as well. I have been busy linking hundreds of these hard to come by titles into the library.

When you enter the library, you will have a choice of accessing the books through categories or a rotation schedule. You can easily access either in the menu bar. If you choose categories, you'll find the books are sorted according to American History by chronological order, stories of nations and regions arranged alphabetically, biographies by types of stories such as great scientists or great artists, and so forth, nature and a miscellaneous other category. You will also see the topics of the Mother's University arranged alphabetically. It's a way to find what you are looking for very quickly.

The rotation access is for those of you who want to follow the rotation schedule as explained earlier. This rotation schedule makes it possible for your family to study the whole world together, adapting it to the ages and interests of individual family members. Understanding layers in year after year and can go on indefinitely! It's a lot of fun.

If you select a country or American history topic, it will take you to what I call a landing page. It gives you ideas of things to study that month and I highlight a few books, just like all good librarians do. You can see I post my podcasts on these landing pages that tie into that particular study to awaken interest in a variety of topics. You will also notice an option to print out a booklist for all the books related to that topic which gives you a quick reference.

The enrichment button will take you to a page that has craft and food ideas, plays, movies, fine art and classical music. Many of the art and music selections have stories attached to them. I will talk about these resources in the Enrichment section.

Now for the books. They are sorted by Elementary, Middle School and High School. These categories don't necessarily mean reading level. It's a general guideline. A High Schooler may find many engaging and satisfying books in the Elementary level, but an Elementary Age student is not likely to like the complexity of the High School books. And just because it's in Elementary doesn't mean an Elementary student may be able to read it on his own. It's there because the subject matter is appealing to a younger mind and can be used as a read-aloud. The best thing to do is to do what you do in a library—take a book off the shelf, open it up and read a few paragraphs and see if it's a good fit for your child.

Each page is then broken down into sub-categories such as picture books, beginning readers, imaginative, Epic/Legendary heroes, cultural, history, fiction, historical fiction, classic literature and biographies.

Let me walk you through the symbols and colors you'll see on the pages. *Notice you will click on the icon to open the books, not the titles themselves.*

The little red arrow that looks like a play button links you to an audio version of the book. These are free audios with the exception of the Jim Weiss audios, which are noted, although you may want to check for copies in your local library.

A heart leads you to books that can be read immediately online through Internet Archive. They have a heart because we love these books—most of them have beautiful rich language and you will probably want to begin to use them as read-alouds until your children are more comfortable with the language. These books are in the public domain and can be printed out if you want.

A diamond leads you to the borrowed books on Internet Archive. They have a diamond because they are often like rare jewels and you may have to wait to read them. You can only keep them for two weeks and they may not be printed out. It's an imperfect system, but without it, there would be no hope of reading many of these books.

A dollar sign leads you to where a copy of the book can be purchased. Most of them link to Amazon. But it also gives you a place to learn more about the book and to read what other people say about them. The dollar sign is also usually associated with books that may be available through your public library—either in stock or through interlibrary loans.

If all these choices are overwhelming to begin with, you may want to focus on the colored block sections at first, especially if you are someone who wants a book in hand.

The blue sections refer to the Forgotten Classics Family Library. These are the books I originally compiled from pre-1923 children's stories. When I created this library, the tablet had not yet been invented and I couldn't picture moms gathering their kids around the desktop computer. So I searched for favorites to reprint and to make available to purchase as hard copies. But I have also provided free digital copies you can read online. It's like a Harvard Classics for children—the challenge I gave myself was how much could I fit into 5 feet of books that would provide a well-rounded education. If you click on the blue Forgotten Classics Family Library box at the bottom of any page, it will take you to a page where you can quickly access all the books in the Forgotten Classics library.

The peach sections refer to selections from the 1971 edition of *My Book House*. While there is a copy online, you will probably be on a waitlist forever. My recommendation is, if you want to purchase a set of books that you will get a lot of mileage from, look for a used set of these books on eBay or other booksellers. Very worthwhile. You may run across *My Book House* sets that were published in other years. They are great sets—the pages just won't correspond with what I have listed. I only chose the 1971 edition because I thought it would be the easiest for you to find.

The purple sections refer you to selections from Grolier's 1962 edition of *Junior Classics*. This set will also give you a lot of mileage and they have not been too hard to come by. I selected the 1962 edition because it is the easiest to come by. Earlier sets have wonderful stories, but they won't correspond with the stories I have listed. Buy both *My Book House* and *Junior Classics* if you can, or start with just one set.

The yellow sections refer you to the Delphian Course readings I have talked about elsewhere.

There's a lot to explore when you get inside the library. Notice at the bottom of each page is a search field. If you are out and about and come across a book and want to know if it's one of the books in the library, you can quickly find out by entering the title and author in the search field.

If you are saying to yourself, well, this is all fine and wonderful but my kids aren't going to read books like that, then I encourage you to visit the Well-Educated Heart side of this website if you haven't already. You will learn all about the tools to begin to open up their hearts. You can access it in the menu bar.

So you may be wondering how much it costs to use this Library. Libraries of Hope is a labor of love. I charge nothing to use the Library or any of its resources. You can help move the work forward simply by sharing these resources with your family and friends. Build your family library and share your books. The more families that are involved, the greater the influence. But the greatest contribution you will make is every story, or poem or work of fine art or music you plant in the heart of the next generation. I truly hope you will take full advantage of all the resources that have been gathered for you and your family. Don't tiptoe around...dive in!

We are living in extraordinary times. It is the best of times and the worst of times. As is said, "'As childhood goes, so goes the world." Within your homes and within your children's hearts are the solutions to a kinder, more beautiful world.

We each have a part to play. I happen to love books and stories and all things pertaining to the heart. I love my work here with Libraries of Hope. I hope these efforts can be a blessing to you and your family.

Forgotten Classics Family Library

When I first started Libraries of Hope, I fell in love with the pre-1923 children's literature I was finding that was all in the public domain which meant I was free to do anything I wanted with it. Since I couldn't picture moms gathering their children around their big desktop computer, I wanted to find a way to get the stories in their hands with a printed copy and the idea for the Forgotten Classics Family Library was born.

I was inspired by Charles Eliot's five feet shelf of books—the *Harvard Classics*. My governing thought was, if a family only had this little library of books, how much could I cram into them? The original library ended up with 76 volumes, organized into six different series.

The first series I created was the Freedom Series, which was a collection of American History stories. Each book is unique. Some books are comprised of 2 or 3 complete books, others are a collection of stories from multiple resources. I always tried to include something for younger minds and something for older minds and I looked for some original source material to include in each volume. I made the decision to not include illustrations because I wanted to fit as many stories in as I could. The books are between 300 and 400 pages—they are designed more as a read-aloud than for a child to read straight through them.

The Freedom Series begins with the stories of Columbus and America's history unfolds with each successive volume. When you get to the final volume, I included a couple of sweep books, meaning you get an overview of the history so you can better fit the pieces together. The Stories of Great Americans has a lot of shorter high-interest stories to introduce some of America's key players and is arranged chronologically.

It's called the Freedom Series because these writers wrote to instill in young people the principles they need to understand to remain free. These principles are woven into the stories and they are loaded! If you are familiar with the book *The 5000 Year Leap* by Cleon Skousen, he identified 28 principles of liberty from the founders' writings. This book had been sitting on my desk but I hadn't had time to read it while I was creating the Freedom Series. When I was all done with it, I picked it up and started going through the principles and I thought to myself—I remember which story that one was taught in and I was satisfied that all 28 principles were woven into these stories.

You will find a lot of overlapping and a lot of layering for better comprehension. I would suggest age 8 as an appropriate age to begin reading from the Freedom Series. Keep in mind, for the most part, they're not meant to be read cover to cover.

The next series I'll talk about is the World History Series. Each nation in the world has a story to tell and I tried to find the most appealing book I could find among the options available to me to unfold that story to young people. It dawned on me that each book in the Freedom Series could connect with a country or countries, so the World History library was organized in that way. The story of Columbus tied into a study of China and India because that's where he was trying to go and he was inspired by Marco Polo who wrote of his visits to China. So stories of China and India became book one in the World History Series. I talk more about the connecting links for each book on the landing pages of the website.

I would recommend that these books be read by children 12 and older. It's not that younger children can't grasp them. It's just that history is full of a lot of cruelty—killings and beheadings and treachery. The story can't be told without those unsavory details, and I would rather a child be older before being exposed to it. But you can do a lot of preparatory reading by reading biographies and fairy tales and cultural stories of the countries so that they will bring a lot of impressions of the countries with them.

I also created the Great Lives series where I sorted stories of great souls into categories such as great artists or great humanitarians or great scientists. Most of the books in this series are organized chronologically. Most of these stories will appeal to older children, but you will see the ones that will appeal to younger ones referenced in the online library. Every story that is in there is in there because it contains a gem of wisdom to teach your children lessons in life and living. None of them are a mere recounting of a life. They're intended to be inspirational stories. Stories of Great Spiritual Leaders includes a look at all the major religions of the world and the leaders associated with them.

The Nature, Art and Music series has eight books about nature. They are generally arranged according to the story of creation, starting with the physical creation and then the life creation from tiniest creatures to the largest. These stories will plant all kinds of ideas in your children's hearts of things to look for when they are out in nature. And they also are tied back to practical lessons for living. Whenever I could find them, the first stories in the books are the familiar ones—meaning pertaining to family. I included stories of mommies taking care of their children and the kinds of homes they built. I also threw in poetry in most of the books. The books will appeal to children—and adults—of all ages.

I needed a place for a little Art and Music, so I put them in this series. The History of Music and Art takes you on a tour of the history of music and art arranged by country. This would be best appreciated by an older student who has had some introductory stories of musicians and artists. Stories of Hymns is arranged chronologically and gives you background stories on some of our most endearing hymns. Stories from Operas are light stories that will appeal to all ages, including your little ones.

The Story Hour series was created because I didn't have a place yet for Literature. And I wanted to have stories that would be especially appealing to children under the age of 8 because the history is intended for the older children. So in the story hour series, you will find fairy tales, myths, introductory stories to Shakespeare, Dante, Chaucer, Plato, first stories of epic and legendary heroes like King Arthur and Odysseus. You'll find Bible stories—just the narrative without doctrinal issues. There are heartwarming stories for Christmas, and a volume sorted by character traits—Stories That Teach Values. I also included Nature stories just for little ones and simple high interest stories aimed at younger listeners or even older listeners who have not yet developed a taste for biography and history in the Great Lives and History volumes. You will also find a volume with stories of great art to help you do picture talks with your younger children. But in the back, there is a wonderful reprint of a book that will deepen your understanding and appreciation of the tools artists use to create their art. Finally, there is a book for the youngest of the young—Mother Goose arranged developmentally, poems for the very young and stories for that familiar, repetitive loving toddler age. And I threw in a little *Raggedy Ann* and *Uncle Wiggily*, bridges between the familiar and the imaginative.

There are four bonus books to the library. Mara Pratt's *American History Stories* has been a favorite among homeschoolers. Some of her volumes have been reprinted under the name *American History Stories You Never Learned in School*. I included all four of her volumes in one book and it is actually a very good beginning introductory book to American history.

Poetry for the Well-Educated Heart is a collection of poetry I took from multiple poetry collections. It's arranged so that the first section is the Familiar section—poetry for little children that has to do with home and family and that is followed by a section for the Imagination. The next section is poetry for nature study arranged by the topics in the Nature Series—Stars, Ocean, Rocks, etc. That is followed by a section organized by the 10 monthly rotation history topics. And finally, the last section is poetry with wisdom for happy living.

The third book is *Restoring the Art of Storytelling in the Home*. When I first learned about the storytelling revival in the early 1900s, I printed out every book I could find that was written by the storytellers of that era. There were over 25 of them. I read them all and then, gleaning from their wisdom, created this manual for a new generation of storytellers in the home. I open the books with my own understanding of what I had learned from them, and then include a section where I organize their own words so you could hear from them directly. Finally, the bulk of the book is stories they suggested to use for telling. They were written by them. I organized them by Familiar, Imaginative and Historical. I spent the earlier years of this Libraries of Hope journey trying to get moms on board relearning this lost art because I came to understand and still understand the most powerful interchange between a mother and her child will be in the stories she tells from her heart, with no written words between them. But I have come to see that our story reservoirs have been so depleted, that's a step that's off in the future. We've got to put the stories in first. Although I hope there will be some of you who will pick up the torch and relearn this ageless and beautiful art.

Finally, here is the *Story Bible*. This was actually the very first book in the library we created. If the only book you owned was a Bible, you could give your child a superior education. It is loaded with languages of the heart—Story, Pictures, Poetry and even Music. In fact, the words of the King James Version are intended to be read aloud because of the music within the words. In the early years of America, everyone read. And they learned to read from their Bible. I believe with all my heart the Bible is a lamp to the soul and children, from the days of their birth, will benefit from that beautiful scriptural language being read to them.

They will understand something that is deeper than the words.

The problem I saw was that after you get through Genesis, you get stuck. Leviticus and Deuteronomy are pretty tough to get through with all their begats and laws. So my husband

and I created a Story Bible where we kept the language of the King James Version, but divided the reading out by story. We took off all the extra markings on the page, used a larger font and kept a lot of white space on the pages.

The effect has been that we have heard from so many people who said that this version has drawn either them or their children into the Bible where there was no interest before. One young woman said she was reading it on the plane next to her father who had lost all interest in religious things. As he started reading over her shoulder, he said he would like to read that book. Another woman said her 20-year-old son who had been resisting church and all things related took an interest and was drawn into it. I watched my little 6-year-old granddaughter read it and feel the stories as she went to bed each night. The rich and beautiful language will open up a deeper place of comprehension for all reading that follows.

It certainly is not meant to be a replacement of the Bible itself. Just a gateway. We also created a *Stories of Jesus* version that isn't quite so big and would be a perfect beginning reader and would serve to connect little hearts to Jesus Christ. There are even pictures of fine art for them to paste into the book.

One other comment—the two deepest impressions that were made on my heart while working on this book were that God wants His children to know that with Him, nothing is impossible and that Righteousness exalteth a nation. All the stories lead to these two great truths.

Also, as I made my way through the Bible, certain verses would grab my attention and I would jot them down. When I was done with the stories, as I went back through the book, I placed the verses where they seemed to connect with the story. These little gems are a great copywork activity, by the way. When we were all finished with the book, I noticed something that I had not planned.

The very first scripture gem that was placed in the book reads: "The Spirit beareth witness with our Spirit, that we are children of God." And the scripture verse in the very last chapter reads: "I have said: all of you are children of the most High" and I thought to myself—that is the most important message of all and it opens and closes the book.

The final series in the original library is the Mother's Learning Library. This is where I compiled the favorite writings of the heart educators so they can teach you directly. The Mother's University is organized around these writings.

There are additional series that have been added to this library, including the *Our Little Cousins and Twins* series, Eva March Tappan's *The World's Story*, and *My Book of Delights*, which is full of fine art, poems and simple stories for little ones.

The following series are in various stages of production. I feel when these are completed the Forgotten Classics Family Library will be complete:

- Fairy tales, sorted by rotation
- Epic and legendary heroes and mythology, by rotation
- Another world history series including the writings of H.E. Marshall, Mary MacGregor, Charles Coffin and John Haaren

- A Great Lives Series for young readers, organized by rotation
- A Great Lives Series for older readers, organized by rotation
- The Sunshine Series, comprised of harder to find titles that embody a WEH learning lifestyle
- Classic literature for young readers, to introduce works of Shakespeare, John Bunyan, Chaucer, Homer, etc.
- An Appreciation Series for High Schoolers that will deepen their understanding of literature, poetry, art and music
- Possibly a science series
- and possibly a History Through the Fine Arts Series, with stories attached to works of fine art that represent historical scenes.

I have been asked how I could possibly put together a library of this magnitude in such a short time by myself. The simple answer is I have had a lot of help. My son, husband and daughters have spent countless hours formatting books for me. I never could have done it without their help. But I give most credit to those Unseen Hands I keep referring to. I am not smart enough or knowledgeable enough to have done this on my own. I have had key words come to my mind that led me to books I never would have found on my own or books that randomly appeared on my way to look for something else. I have been given impressions of what I am looking for and gnawing feelings that something wasn't right—either that I had not yet found something that needed to go into the library or that something was in there that shouldn't be there. I would be ungrateful and entirely wrong to take credit for the creation of this library.

All the books in the library are available as free digital reads. The digital copies are found on a page that includes links to all of the Forgotten Classics. It can be accessed through the free app, or simply click on the blue Forgotten Classics box on the bottom of any page in the website. If you want hard copies, they are available in our store. Books may be purchased individually or as series. But the most popular way is as a monthly subscription.

We have worked with a number of individuals who work with charter schools and have been able to be reimbursed through those programs. None of them are able to pay for religious books, so when we send you the receipt, the receipt reflects only the secular titles.

So there you have it. This is the Forgotten Classics Family Library. I hope your families enjoy reading these stories as much as I have enjoyed putting this library together.

Forgotten Classics Family Library

For children 8 and under:

My Book of Delights
Story Hour Series
Nature Bundle and Nature Series
Stories of Jesus, Story Bible
Poetry for the Well-Educated Heart
Great Lives for Young Readers
Our Little Cousins/Twin Series
Some of the Sunshine Series
Imaginative Tales Series

For children 8 and older:

Freedom Series
Mara Pratt's American History Stories
Epic and Legendary Heroes
Our Little Cousins/Twin Series
Sunshine Series
Introduction to Classic Literature Series

For children 12 and older:

World History Series
The World's Story in Art, Poetry and Story
World Freedom Series
Great Lives Series

High School and Mothers:

Music, Art, Poetry and Literature Appreciation Series
Delphian Series
Mothers' Learning Library
Restoring the Art of Storytelling

Quotes for Book Lovers

"I cannot live without books." --Thomas Jefferson

"My early and invincible love of reading, I would not exchange for the treasures of India."
--Edward Gibbons

"The reading of all good books is like a conversation with the finest men of past centuries."
--Descartes

"What I want to know is in books, and my best friend is the one who will get me a book I haven't read." --Abraham Lincoln

"Books are a delightful society. If you go into a room filled with books, even without taking them down from their shelves, they seem to speak to you, to welcome you."
--William Gladstone

"A little library, growing every year, is an honorable part of a man's history. It is a man's duty to have books. A library is not a luxury, but one of the necessaries of life. Be certain that your house is adequately and properly furnished—with books rather than furniture. Both if you can, but books at any rate." --Henry Ward Beecher

"I am the product of long corridors, empty sunlit rooms, upstairs indoor silences, attics explored in solitude, distant noises of gurgling cisterns and pipes, and the noise of wind under the tiles. Also, of endless books. My father bought all the books he read and never got rid of any of them. There were books in the study, books in the drawing room, books in the cloakroom, books— two deep—in the great books case on the landing, books piled as high as my shoulder in the cistern attic, books of all kinds reflecting every transient stage of my parents' interest, books readable and unreadable, books suitable for a child and books most emphatically not. Nothing was forbidden me. In the seemingly endless rainy afternoons I took volume after volume from the shelves. I had always the same certainty of finding a book that was new to me as a man who walks into a field has of finding a new blade of grass." --C.S. Lewis

"At Sagamore Hill we love a great many things—birds and trees and books and all things beautiful, children and gardens and hard work and the joy of life. The place puts me in the mood for a good story. Of course, I am always in the mood for a good story. Perhaps that is why I am rather more apt to read old books than new ones. And perhaps that is why I surround myself with reminders of stories, long ago told, or those yet to be told. Life ought to be redolent with the stuff of life from which the stories of life inevitably spring." --Theodore Roosevelt

"The familiar faces of my books welcomed me. I threw myself into my reading chair and gazed around me with pleasure. All my friends present—there in spirit, ready to talk with me at any moment, when I was in the mood, making no claim upon my attention when I was not."
--George MacDonald

"I love to lose myself in other men's minds." --Charles Lamb

"All that mankind has done, thought or been: it is lying as in magic preservation in the pages of books." --Thomas Carlyle

"When I get a little money, I buy books; and if there is any left, I buy food and clothes."
--Erasmus

"Reading feeds the brain. It is evident that most minds are starving to death."
--Benjamin Franklin

"No man can be called friendless who has God and the companionship of good books."
--Elizabeth Barrett Browning

"You may perhaps be brought to acknowledge that it is very worthwhile to be tormented for two or three years of one's life, for the sake of being able to read all the rest of it."
--Jane Austen

"Men give me credit for genius. All the genius I have lies just in this: When I have a subject in mind, I study it profoundly. Day and night it is before me. I explore it in all its bearings. My mind becomes pervaded with it. Then the effort which I make the people are pleased to all the fruit of genius. It is the fruit of study and labor." --Alexander Hamilton

"There is nothing more wonderful than a book. It may be a message to us from the dead, from human souls we never saw who lived perhaps thousands of miles away. And yet these little pieces of paper speak to us, arouse us, teach us, open our hearts, and in turn open their hearts

to us like brothers. Without books, God is silent, justice dormant, philosophy lame."
--Charles Kingsley

"My father had left a small collection of books in a little room upstairs, to which I had access (for it adjoined my own) and which nobody else in our house ever troubled. From that blessed little room, Roderick Random, Peregrine Pickle, Humphrey Clinker, Tom Jones, the Vicar of Wakefield, Don Quixote, Gil Blas, and Robinson Crusoe came out, a glorious host, to keep my company. They kept alive my fancy, and my hope of something beyond that place and time— they, and the Arabian Nights and the Tales of the Genii—and did me no harm; for whatever harm was in some of them was not there for me; I knew nothing of it. It is astonishing to me now, how I found them, in the midst of my porings and blunderings over heavier themes, to read those books as I did. This was my only and my constant comfort. When I think of it, the picture rises in my mind, of a summer evening, the boys at play in the churchyard, and I sitting on my bed reading as if for life." --Charles Dickens

"A small breakfast-room adjoined the drawing room, I slipped in there. It contained a bookcase. I soon possessed myself of a volume, taking care that it should be one stocked with pictures. I mounted into the window-seat; gathering up my feet, I sat cross-legged, like a Turk; and, having drawn the red moreen curtain nearly closed, I was shrined in double retirement. Folds of scarlet drapery shut in my view to the right hand; to the left were the clear panes of glass, protecting, but not separating me from the drear November day. At intervals while turning the leaves of my book, I studied the aspect of that winter afternoon. After, it offered a pale blank of mist and cloud; near a scene of wet lawn and storm-beat shrub, with ceaseless rain sweeping away wildly before a long and lamentable blast." --Charlotte Bronte

Confessions of a Book Sale Junkie

My family has been aware of my addiction for some time now, although I don't think some of my grown children realized how out of control it had become until they visited me in Virginia and saw the thousands of books that now line my walls downstairs in the basement. Our bookshelves have always been the focal point of our décor. Whenever we moved…and we moved a lot…it never felt like home until the books were back on the shelves.

We had a respectably sized collection, until I discovered the Friends of the Library book sale. That's when I lost control. And here on the East Coast, I'm not limited to *the* annual books sale at one local library. Oh, no. I can find one almost every weekend.

M poor husband comes with me—a somewhat willing partner in crime—as I pass off book bag after book bag loaded with books he gets to lug to the car. How can I leave behind a 1912 set of Young Folks' Treasury when they're 25 cents a book? It doesn't matter that I have ten other equally valuable sets I have rescued.

"Rescued."

That's why this has become such a problem. I see a culture vanishing before my eyes and I've become a one-woman crusade to rescue it; a culture of refinement and decency and faith and family and love of liberty. I know I'm probably chasing windmills, but I can't help myself. I don't see the replacement culture as a good thing. If the pattern of history continues to repeat itself, the direction we're heading doesn't end well for us.

Several decades ago, two men wrote two books with visions of the future. In *Brave New World*, people quit reading because they no longer cared about reading. In *1984*, people quit reading because the books were destroyed. Today, in 2013, we are seeing both visions playing out.

IKEA recently announced discontinuing the sale of bookshelves because they're not in demand anymore. They said in the future they will have a narrower design so they can be used to display knick-knacks. A school district in Utah threw away all their Charles Dickens books because the sentences were too long and the words were too hard for the students to understand.

But that's not the worst of it. I have been heartsick to read of book murderers out there. Just a warning if you continue to read…if you are a fellow book lover, you'll be horrified by these shocking true accounts.

Back in August of 2008, following the scare when lead was found in toys shipped from China, Congress hastily passed the Consumer Product Safety Improvement Act requiring that anyone who sold items for use by children under the age of 12 would need to have certification that the product was lead free. Included in the list of suspect products were children's books printed before 1985 because they claimed there was lead in the printer's ink before that time. Even though a child would have to literally consume the entire book and there has never been a single case of that ever happening, and even though Congress was petitioned to exclude books from the law, the law went into effect February 1, 2009. By the way, the cost of testing a single book runs between $300 to $600. At the last minute, the penalty was increased from $5000 per incident violation to $100,000 per incident and potential imprisonment.

Needless to say, thrift store owners couldn't take the risk. And on that February 1st, reports like this came in from all over the country:

"I just came back from my local thrift store with tears in my eyes! I watched as boxes and boxes of children's books were thrown in the garbage. Every book they had on the shelves prior to 1985 was destroyed!"

Fortunately, three years later, Congress finally exempted books from the Act, but you can't bring back what's already been destroyed. Books published after 1923 are in copyright protection, which many, many of these old books likely won't see the light of day in our lifetime. Publishers who hold the copyrights aren't interested in re-publishing books for a market that apparently doesn't exist anymore.

And as if that isn't horrifying enough, I was checking into Amazon's new bookseller program. (The agreement with my family is that I can keep my book fix if I sell at least as many books as I keep.) For a small shipping fee, I can ship books I want to sell to a giant Amazon warehouse where they'll store them, box them and ship them for me for just a small fee. It sounded like a good deal until I got to the part where I read about what happens to the books that don't sell. If I get to the point I no longer want to pay the storage fee, they'll ship them back to me for $3.00 a book. Let me rephrase that. *Three dollars a book* OR they'll destroy them for 50 cents a book. That's the word they use. *Destroy.*

Suddenly I'm picturing book scavengers like myself snatching up the old children's books, sending them off to an Amazon warehouse, and, not realizing their actual value is what's written inside, will opt for the DESTROY option when they don't sell. And by so doing, will not only kill the books, but kill our culture as well.

(*Note: I don't believe that is the policy in 2020.)

So, yes, on the outside I'm an out-of-control book sale junkie. But really, I'm on a crusade. My kids ask me what I'm going to do with all those old, dusty books downstairs. I tell them I'm not sure. But inside my heart, I envision a young girl in some future day who looks just like a girl I read about in a book. The book was a true story written by a young Chinese woman who lived through Chairman Mao's Cultural Revolution; a time when culture was changed, in part, by destroying books. She was one of the lucky few assigned to learn English and it just so happened a small collection of books had escaped destruction because they were written in English and were hidden away in a library attic. I'll let this young Chinese woman speak for herself:

> Louisa May Alcott's *Little Women* was the first novel I read in English… My joy at the sensation of my mind opening up and expanding was way beyond description.

> Being alone in the library was heaven for me. My heart would leap as I approached it, usually at dusk, anticipating the pleasure of solitude with my books, the outside world ceasing to exist. As I hurried up the flight of stairs…the smell of old books long stored

in airless rooms would give me tremors of excitement, and I would hate the stairs for being too long.

...I became acquainted with Longfellow, Walt Whitman, and American history. I memorized the whole of the Declaration of Independence, and my heart swelled at the words, "We hold these truths to be self-evident, that all men are created equal," and those about men's "unalienable Rights," among them "Liberty and the pursuit of Happiness." These concepts were unheard of in China, and opened up a marvelous new world for me. My notebooks...were full of passages like these, passionately and tearfully copied out.

Book junkie by day. Caped crusader at night.

I can live with that.

(*The book is *Wild Swans* by Jung Chang. Highly recommended.)

Why We Need the Bible and Thoughts on Faith

There are many reasons why I linked the study of the Holy Land to our study of America as a new nation with its constitution written to keep a people free. One of the reasons is because the Bible, with its history and teachings, is so intertwined with us as a free people under God. What other people in the history of the world have ever made that claim? I would be so bold as to say had there been no Bible, there would have been no America. And if we lose the influence of the Bible as a people, America as we know it will cease to exist. I happen to be in good company in that belief, starting with George Washington, the Father of our country: "It is impossible to rightly govern the world without God and the Bible."

Listen to the words of a number of our other presidents:

Thomas Jefferson:

> I always have said, and always will say, that the studious perusal of the sacred volume will make better citizens, better fathers, and better husbands.

John Quincy Adams:

> I have for many years made it a practice to read through the Bible once a year... The earlier my children begin to read it, the more confident will be my hopes that they will prove useful citizens of their country and respectable members of society.

Andrew Jackson:

> The Bible is the rock on which our Republic rests.

Abraham Lincoln:

> In regard to the Great Book, I have only to say that it is the best Book which God has given to men.

Ulysses S. Grant:

> Hold fast to the Bible as the...anchor of your liberties. Write its precepts on your hearts and practice them in your lives. To the influence of this book we are indebted for all the progress made in true civilization, and to this we must look as our guide in the future.

Benjamin Harrison:

> If you take out of your statutes, your constitutions, your family life all that is taken from the Sacred Book, what would there be left to bind society together?

William McKinley:

> The teachings of the Bible are so interwoven and entwined with our whole civic and social life that it would be literally—I do not mean figuratively, I mean literally—

impossible for us to figure to ourselves what this life would be if these teachings were removed.

The more profoundly we study this wonderful book...the higher will be our destiny as a nation.

Theodore Roosevelt:

No other book of any kind ever written has ever so affected the whole life of a people as...the scriptures.

Woodrow Wilson:

I have a very simple thing to ask of you. I ask of every man and woman in this audience that from this night on they will realize that part of the destiny of America lies in their daily perusal of this great book of revelations—that if they would see America free and pure, they will make their own spirits free and pure by this baptism of the Holy Scripture.

Warren G. Harding:

Both as literature and as inspiration, the Bible has a value with which no other work can be compared.

William Gladstone who served for many years as Prime Minister of England wrote:

If I am asked what is the remedy for the sorrows of the heart...I must point to the old, old Book which is the greatest and best gift ever given to mankind.

I have known ninety-five great men of the world in my time, and of those eighty-seven were all followers of the Bible... My only hope for the world is in bringing the human mind into contact with Divine Revelation.

Daniel Webster:

If we abide by the principles taught in the Bible our country will go on prospering and to prosper, but if we and our posterity neglect its instructions and authority no man can tell how sudden a catastrophe may overwhelm us and bury our glory in profound obscurity.

He also wrote: "We cannot divorce education from religion, and sustain the Republic."

Charles Fairbanks, former VP:

The more the Bible is put into the minds and hearts and daily lives of the people, the less concern we may have with respect to our political laws. Take out of our lives the Scriptures and you would strike an irreparable blow to our national progress.

Thomas Marshall, VP:

If I were to have my way, I would take the torch out of the hand of the Statue of Liberty...and in its stead place an open Bible.

General Robert E. Lee:

The Bible is a book...which in all my perplexities and distresses has never failed to give me light and strength.

General Pershing, commander in chief in World War:

I am glad to see that every man in the Army is to have a Testament. Its teachings will fortify us for our great work.

John Ruskin:

All that I have taught of Art, everything that I have written, whatever greatness there has been in any thought of mine, whatever I have done in my life, has simply been due to the fact that, when I was a child, my mother daily read with me a part of the Bible, and daily made me learn a part of it by heart. Read your Bible—make it your daily business to obey it in all you understand. To my early knowledge of the Bible I owe the best part of my taste in literature.

Immanuel Kant, German philosopher;

The existence of the Bible as a book for the people is the greatest benefit which the human race has ever experienced.

Charles Dickens:

It is the best book that ever was or will be known in the world...

Count Leo Tolstoy:

Without the Bible the education of the child in the present state of society is impossible.

Jacob Gould Schurman, former President of Cornell University:

The Bible is the most important document in the world's history. No man can be wholly uneducated who really knows the Bible, nor can anyone be considered a truly educated man who is ignorant of it.

Yet, the Supreme Court in a series of three decisions in 1962 and 1963 removed the Bible and prayer from our public schools. This battle to get it out of our schools has been going on for a very long time—I ran across a book written in 1854 called *The Right of the Bible in Our Public Schools*. At that time, it was the Catholic church that was putting the pressure to have it removed. But no matter—the object of the book was as a warning of what would happen if any group finally achieved their end. It has been over 50 years since it was removed. Was he right? Here are few highlights:

1. The exclusion of the Bible and of all religious bias would be followed inevitably by a fear and jealousy of all religious teaching, and by and by, when any allusion be made by the teacher to God, Christ and religious motives...there would be an instinctive repulsion, as if this were trenching on forbidden ground.

2. There will be such an accumulation of...despotic element, that loves the darkness and hates that light, that it will be as much as a man's life is worth, even to examine it;

it has been so in other countries, and some day, if we let it work successfully against the Bible in our schools, it will make an explosion that will shatter our whole system.

3. God will have men and nations governed; and they must be governed by one of two instruments—an open Bible, with its hallowed influences, or a standing army. One is the product of God's wisdom, the other, of man's folly; and that nation or people that dare discard, or will not yield to the moral power of the one, must submit to the brute force of the other.

4. What God has united man may not separate without peril…to separate the head from the heart, to cultivate the one, and neglect the other, is a divorce as unnatural…as perilous. The child whose hand is educated in elegant and exact penmanship may yet try his acquired art and skill at counterfeiting and forgery, unless his conscience is duly educated.

5. If we…get the Bible and religion effectually out of our schools, ignoring it, or legalizing its exclusion…another generation will not be likely to restore it to its rightful place, or to redeem themselves from the fetters of this dreadful mistake. More and more the affections of the people will be alienated from the common schools, if we take the Bible out from them. Respectable, and religious, and well-informed parents, will cease to send their children to them; conscience itself would destroy the school system.

6. Take from us the open Bible, and like Sampson shorn of his locks, we should become as weak as any people. Take away the Bible, and we would need a despot on a throne, and a standing army…to keep the populace in subjection.

7. If the school teacher should neglect moral and religious instruction entirely, that very neglect might be an influence on the minds of many children against religion.

8. The State appoints the formality of an oath to be taken on the Bible…it is a mockery, if the State, having appointed this form of oath by law…do not provide the means of understanding it. I will add—Is there any story written that impresses more forcefully the binding nature of an oath than the story of Jepthah who made a rash vow that cost him the life of his innocent and beautiful daughter?

9. Our whole possibility of safety and prosperity as a country is founded on habit and influences of religious self-control, and yet, the only book that teaches such control without sectarianism is forbidden in the FREE public schools. Language cannot state strongly enough the greatness of the danger from such a course.

10. In our country, the foundation of power in the individual and liberty in the masses is self-government founded on religious belief and conscience—if these be lost or corrupted, our expiring anguish will surpass that of any nation that ever lived.

Look around and see what is happening in our country where God's laws have been replaced by man's confidence that his reasoning abilities can develop a new, more practical moral code. How is that working out for us? To see anyone applaud the termination of a baby's life is about as repulsive as anything I can possibly imagine.

I don't believe we can get the Bible back into our public schools in the near future—but we can make it a part of our children's lives right now, today, in our homes. If you did nothing else but plant a love of the Bible in the hearts of your children, you not only will have given them the greatest gift you can give, you will be taking the most important step I can see to secure the liberty of our nation.

Now let's revisit a Margaret Eggleston story I shared elsewhere:

> One day I went into a class of boys of sixteen years of age. They were boys from the lower part of the city. Their teacher was a young man who was earnest and sincere, but who did not understand the adolescent boy. In the course of the lesson the question had arisen, "Is there a God?" and boy-like, one had asked the teacher, "How do you know?" He had been battling with the question in the light of Moses, and Ezra, and Jesus, and the flowers, and the sunsets, and the Psalms—every way he knew, but still the boys insisted that that was no proof. "Did anyone know that there was a God?" It was plainly to be seen that he was glad to see me when I appeared. "The boys want to know how we know there is a God," said he. "They don't seem to think I have a proof."
>
> I looked about the group, their faces showing that they thought they had won a victory, and said quietly, "Yes, boys, I know there is a God. But it is closing time. If you will all be here next Sunday, I will tell how I know. But I assure you that I do know." On the following Sunday they were all there when I entered the room, and two boys whom I had not seen for a long time were there with them. Knowing they lived in the house with the boy who had asked the question, I was sure why they had come. And this is the story I told them—and the results.
>
> Away up in the hills of Maine there is a little lake named after the Indian word for the West Wind—"Keewaydin"—and on the lake in a dear little tent of three rooms I had lived for four summers. All around us there were mountains, and the birds and chipmunks played right around the door. It might be very hot in the city, but at night the little breezes played about the waters of the lake and cooled the tent so that we could sleep. The woods were full of flowers and berries were plentiful on the hills. One could hardly find a more beautiful place to live.
>
> But this summer we were not very happy, for in the springtime the father of our little family had been taken very ill and the doctors had ordered me to take the little girl of seven and the sick father and go to camp for months where all was quiet. No one was to visit us. We must stay alone with the beautiful things about us. So there we were, just the three of us with strength gradually coming to the sick one.
>
> But there came a dreadful day when a worse sickness came and we were so worried. In the morning the doctor came from the town nearly twenty miles away, shook his head, left some medicine and went away. But the day went much better than we had expected, and at night we were all asleep when there came a sound at the tent door and I found the doctor there. Calling me to one side, he told me that analysis had found poison all through the system of the sick one and that the medicine which he had left was not the

126

best, that he had come with all speed when he had found the poison. A little while the doctor stayed, but he had other very sick patients and had to go. He could leave me no word as to what the morning might find. The patient might be alive but he might go in a flash. I must give him the medicine every fifteen minutes during the night and hope for the best.

No neighbors could be called, though they would gladly have come had they known. He must be absolutely quiet and have no worry. And so I stood at the door of the tent and watched the little light disappear through the trees to the road, and then I was alone with the little girl, the one who was fighting death and the darkness.

How should I spend the time? I would write to his mother, but when I tried my hand shook so that I could not hold the pen. I would read, but I could not see. The whole night was before me. The whip-poor-will and the owl were both behind in the trees and the frogs were making noises in the swamps. The stillness was so oppressive, and for the first time in my life I began to be afraid.

After about two hours had gone by and I had given the medicine over and over, I walked to the flap of the tent before me. Just at the front of the tent, was the lake so still in the moonlight, and beyond a fine mountain, rearing its peak to the sky. To steady myself, I had to hold to the tent pole with both my hands, but the breeze was comforting. Something was there if it was only a breeze.

Suddenly there came into my heart a message—the same one that came into the heart life of the Psalmist:

"I will lift up mine eyes unto the hills from whence cometh my help. My help cometh from the Lord who made heaven and earth. He will not suffer thy foot to be moved. He that keepeth thee will not slumber. Behold, he that keepeth Israel will not slumber nor sleep. The Lord is thy keeper. The Lord is thy shade upon thy right hand. The sun shall not smite thee by day nor the moon by night. The Lord shall preserve thee from all evil; the Lord shall preserve thy soul. The Lord shall preserve thy going out and thy coming in from this time forth and even forever more."

A second time I heard the message through, but this time I repeated it softly aloud. Then I turned to the tent. The fear was all gone, the weakness was all gone, and I was ready to face the hard thing with God. But God had spoken to me and I knew that though the night was hard and lonely, yet God was right there. "He that keepeth thee will not slumber."

I knew there was a God.

The night passed, the letters were written, the dawn broke red over the sky and the death angel had passed by for the time.

God had spoken, I had heard, and he had kept his promise, and had preserved me from all evil while the rest of the world slumbered.

So I know there is a God.

There was silence when I had finished and, though the hour was not over, I dismissed the boys and watched them go their own way home. Each boy was thinking as he went.

The following Sunday morning I found a group of older boys from the street in the hallway—more than half a dozen of them. With them was the boy who had first asked the question. I went up to welcome them and asked my boy if he had found them and brought them to the school. "Oh, no," he answered, "they go to all sorts of churches but they all live around here. I told them your story and they said they would like to see a woman who really knew there was a God, and so I knew you would like to see them 'cause they were boys who wanted to know, so I brought them. Now, boys, you see I told you the truth. It was a real story." A little while we talked and I invited them to come whenever they felt like it, for we wanted to be friends with the boys in the neighborhood. Then they went their way. Occasionally I would meet one of them in the street, and always there was the same glad smile as they stopped to speak to me. Always I knew what they were thinking of, and always it reminded me of the statement made to me by my old professor: "Boys long to feel God, to know God and to love God, but the trouble is, they do not like the God we have chosen to show them. Some day we will show the boy's ideal of God and then we shall win them, for we shall tell them the stories that show that kind of God. They are waiting for that person and how gladly they will follow some day."

Under the white cross in France, the little newsboy who came with that group is sleeping. Often I have wondered if God was there on the battlefield to help him as he helped me. I only hope he, too, heard the voice that said, "The Lord is thy keeper."

To the skeptics who may hear that story, they may still dismiss it and say that's no proof—that's just a feeling. They will still demand evidence they can see with their eyes and handle in their hands and measure with their measuring tools. Yet, for those who have felt the spirit of God, they know of its existence. They need no further proof. It's real and tangible. The skeptic who needs proof of unseen powers needs merely to place his hands on the wire of a hot electric fence. The energy that shocks his body will never be seen with his eyes. He will never be able to catch hold of it. But I dare him to deny its existence.

We cannot see an electrical current, but we can see it lighting up lightbulbs and our computer screens or flashing in a bolt of lightning. We cannot see the wind either, yet we know it's there because we see it rustling the leaves of a tree or feel it blowing against our faces. We cannot see the Spirit of God, but we can see it manifest in the lives of those who feel it and learn from them about its operations until we experience it for ourselves.

Our world today seeks to completely secularize education; to separate it from any spiritual connection. To me, that makes as much sense as turning off the electrical current and going back to reading by candle light and making dinner over the fire in the hearth because to believe in the existence of a power that cannot be seen is nonsense.

The educators of the early 20th century recognized the children they taught not only possessed heart and mind, but spirit as well. It wasn't unusual for them to talk about it freely and matter-of-factly. They didn't remove it from the stories of the great lives they wrote about like we do. So we get to read, in the old books, Samuel Morse's reason why the first words transmitted through the telegraph were 'What God hath wrought'; he humbly acknowledged God as the Author of the invention. He should know.

We tell children how courageous Harriet Tubman was as she rescued slaves in the Underground Railroad. But today we leave out the part of the story that tells why she was so brave. When asked how it was possible she wasn't afraid to go into town with a tremendous bounty on her head, she always answered, "t'want me, 'twas de Lord! I always tole him, 'I trust to you. I don't know where to go or what to do, but I expect you to lead me, 'n' he always did" —and I will add, in exact detail; when to turn left, when to leave the road, when to cross the stream, where to go. Yet, even when confronted with the evidence of her own words, skeptics attribute it to a head injury she suffered as a child.

Julia Ward Howe didn't struggle over the immortal words of The Battle Hymn of the Republic. After having her heart deeply touched by spending a day out on the Civil War battlefield, she rose in the middle of the night to write down the words as if by dictation. She'll tell you who actually wrote the song.

Uncle Tom's Cabin's Harriet Beecher Stowe said her book was given to her as a vision in response to a heartfelt prayer to be able to do something to help the plight of the slave.

Columbus, although trained as a sailor and a navigator, wrote, "It was the Lord who put into my mind (I could feel his hand upon me) the fact that it would be possible to sail from here to the Indies… There is no question that the inspiration was from the Holy Spirit, because he comforted me with rays of marvelous illumination… For the execution of the journey to the Indies I did not make use of intelligence, mathematics or maps. It is simply the fulfillment of what Isaiah had prophesied."

Even the great Michelangelo declared:

> My unassisted heart is barren clay,
> That of its native self can nothing feel.
> Of good and pious works Thou art the seed,
> That quickens only where Thou sayest it may;
> Unless Thou show to us Thine own true way,
> No man can find it. Father! Thou must lead!
> Thou then breathe those thoughts into my mind,
> By which such virtue may in me be bred,
> That in Thy holy footsteps I may tred.

I could go on. I have pages and pages of evidence.

Isn't it time to enter the subject of spirituality back into our conversation when we talk about the problems of education? I continually refer to these words from Charlotte Mason's writings that express it best: True education is between a child's soul and God.

We need to gather the bricks and the boards; we should learn to drive nails and mix cement, but only God has the vision of how to turn those raw materials into palaces and the palaces into a magnificent Kingdom. At the end of our school days, most of us just leave behind our pile of knowledge bricks. They're never made into anything useful or beautiful because it's the spirit that breathes life into everything and gives it purpose and meaning. The Spirit is a power of Creation. We live in the day Paul saw in vision, where men are ever learning, but never coming to a knowledge of the Truth. Truth is synonymous with Spirit and Light.

We've not only removed the heart, we've removed the soul from learning as well.

And the Bible is the connecting link to put it back in place.

The Bible teaches us on many levels. One day, as I stepped back and took a look at it from a distance as opposed to zooming in on just the words, I recognized the pattern of learning I have been trying to describe. I noticed that both the Old and New Testaments are front-end loaded with stories to warm and open up the heart. The familiar stories we tell most often are found either in the book of Genesis or in the Four Gospels. They're teachings for the heart. The next sections in both Old and New present rules, laws, doctrines, principles and teachings for the mind. Whether we're talking about art, music, grammar, nature, or happiness, we see rules that must be followed, or it all falls apart. Children a hundred years ago were taught our liberty was in law. Today, our children gleefully mimic Elsa's word: "No right or wrong, no rules for me, I'm free! Let it go, Let it go."

And the disintegration is setting in.

The books of the Old and New Testaments that are probably least read are at the end. These back-end books often leave us scratching our heads and yet they provide the final piece in this pattern of learning. The meaning of these books is completely hidden to the literal and factual mind. They're filled with imagery and symbolism and require a much higher level of learning. To the mind and heart that are prepared to study them, they reveal multi-faceted layers of meaning that are rich and satisfying. To gain any kind of understanding requires much preparatory study and experience, but even then, much of the meaning remains hidden. Its true meaning requires that 'Spirit which giveth understanding' that Job talked about. The truth of it can only be revealed spirit to spirit, which is the soul part of learning I am now going to attempt to describe.

The Artists that relearn the secrets and rules the master artists knew; the musicians that relearn the secrets of the master musicians; and the writers who relearn the secrets of literary devices and beautiful language will still be powerless to move the human heart without the divine spark of Spirit lighting up their work.

Our job is to prepare our children's hearts to be inspired.

Everything we do is preparatory for this final phase of learning. The knowledge we help our children gain is of little use without the Spirit which gives it life, usefulness and purpose. We saw the transformation of our world when, after nearly 6000 years of it being undetected, man finally discovered electricity. It was always there. We just didn't know it nor know how to use it. Imagine the giant leap forward of mankind if we now harnessed the power of spiritual light and quit walking around in darkness while the noonday sun is shining.

We need help navigating through this explosion of knowledge that has hit our world. Let me try and offer a little perspective. One week's worth of the New York Times contains more information than a person was likely to come across in a lifetime in the 1700s. It is estimated that there will be 40 exabytes or 4×10 to the 19th power of unique information generated worldwide this year. That's more than the previous 5,000 years in just one year. I can't even begin to wrap my mind around that number. People much smarter than me estimate that the sum of all human knowledge will soon double every 72 hours.

I previously mentioned it is estimated that 3,000 new books are now published every single day. Emerson, almost 200 years ago, said, at that time, "There [were] 850,000 volumes in the Imperial Library at Paris. If a man were to read industriously from dawn to dark for sixty years, he would die in the first alcove."

We don't need help in finding something new to learn. We need help in learning how to select what's of the greatest use to each of us, personally. And I'm pretty sure we're not smart enough figure that out on our own.

The scholar among us, studying from morning to night, at best will draw out his little cup of water of knowledge by the end of his life, still leaving an entire ocean of learning untouched. Sir Isaac Newton said, "I was like a boy playing on the seashore, and diverting myself now and then finding a prettier shell than the ordinary, whilst the great ocean of truth lay all undiscovered before me."

What a tragedy that our current educational mindset is bent on determining which common cup of knowledge every child should drink from. Wouldn't we be much better served by allowing individual hearts to contribute that which their hearts love and where spiritual light directs? Has the Creator of our Universe not given us sufficient proof that He knows how to organize and fit a multitude of parts together into one great magnificent whole? Imagine what He who knows our individual talents and gifts could do if we let Him. Having the Spirit reveal to our spirit what our unique contribution and our particular mission and place in the world is makes for one of life's most meaningful and joyful journeys.

How many Michelangelos are crunching numbers behind an accountants desk? How many Beethovens became computer programmers instead of composers of symphonic masterpieces?

A heart-based education prepares our children to tap into a spiritual light that can lead them along a personalized course of individual learning and help them navigate their way through the tsunami wave of knowledge that has crashed upon our world.

This light can even lead us to hidden treasures of knowledge. I have experienced this for myself as I have been learning the things I am sharing with you. For instance, when I was serving on the Executive Board of HomeMakers for America (now MomsforAmerica), I was helping to put together a little book to articulate our message. I had had an impression working on my heart and although the idea has become more mainstream today, at the time, I never heard anyone suggesting what I was suggesting. I felt pressed to finish the book, but I was seeking validation that what I was saying was correct. I wanted someone much smarter than me to back me up; that this wasn't just a fluffy ideal.

My desk is a mess. I usually have piles of books and notebooks and papers all around me. One of my notebooks had been opened to a particular page for a few days. I was just writing on papers over it, not paying attention to it. This particular day, feeling the need to finish up, I closed my eyes and prayed for that validation. As I opened my eyes, I looked down and noticed that somewhere along the way, I had highlighted the title of a book: *The Story of Stones* by David Starr Jordan and the feeling came to look for it, which I did. I had never heard of David Starr Jordan, but as the list of books he wrote came up, it was immediately apparent that he was a scientist. I later found out he was not only a brilliant scientist, he was the first president of Stanford University—definitely qualified as someone much smarter than me.

As I scrolled down the books he had written, one of them stood out because it was different than the rest. It was called *The Care and Culture of Man*. As I opened the book, within the first few pages was the validation I was seeking. I gasped out loud and thought how incredible it was that I could be led from a book about stones to a quote I never would have found on my own in a million years. I felt deeply humbled and grateful.

This spiritual light is not reserved only for those who we might call the 'greats,' it's there for ordinary people like me. Because, really, in God's eyes, there is no such thing as an ordinary person. I have no doubt there are many hidden treasures of knowledge and records He is anxious to reveal to the mind and heart of he or she who is seeking for them. And the world will rejoice in their discovery.

The Bible contains the rule book by which we can learn how to tap into and be conduits of this spiritual Light. The words of the Bible speak directly from God to the soul—I've heard them referred to as 'letters from home.' God has no need for an interpreter or middleman. Through the spirit of its words, we feel the love of a Heavenly Father and a purpose for our existence. It answers the questions the philosophers have agonized over for thousands of years, in a way a child of two can understand: Who am I? I am a child of God. Where am I going? Home. Why am I here? To learn to love. These answers have resonated in countless hearts as pure Truth.

While statistics tell us many of our youth are leaving organized religion, they also tell us their quest for spirituality and meaning remains high. We are living in the day described by the prophet Amos: "Behold, the days come, saith the Lord God, that I will send a famine in the land, not a famine of bread, nor a thirst for water, but of hearing the words of the Lord; And they shall wander from sea to sea, and from the north even to the east, they shall run to and fro to seek the word of the Lord, and shall not find it. In that day shall the fair virgins and young men faint for thirst."

Mothers and fathers are in a unique position to quench that thirst.

Reading the Bible aloud together as families would restore more power and strength to our world than any other single act. Our children will once again be connected to a light of which millions of people from nations throughout the world, across the span of hundreds and thousands of years can attest; a light that has comforted weary hearts, guided explorers and inspired kings. To read the words of the Bible, pure and undiluted, is to share the same experience as the greatest minds that have ever lived.

But it's not just the mechanical, check-it-off-the list kind of reading that will restore that power and light to our world. It's possible to read the Bible just as words and have it mean nothing. Just as we've seen with all our other studies, love is the force that binds us to that which we study. When we 'love' art, we want to be close to it and study it. When we 'love' science, we spend a great deal of time with it. A person who 'loves' music will find ways to listen to and express it.

Similarly, love unlocks the spirit and power of the Bible. And that's why we should start by telling the stories of Jesus. I don't know a lot about electricity, but I do know it has something to do with positive charges attracting negative and neutral charges which cling to it. Think of what happens when you rub two balloons together and place them on a wall. Jesus Christ is a source of light and we, who are negatively charged or neutral, are drawn to him through his stories of pure love, kindness and sacrifice for us. Little children, especially, are drawn to him in stories. As we hear his stories, we feel something in our hearts. It feels like being wrapped in a warm blanket; it's a comforting and peaceful feeling and you long to stay there. Although I would start familiarizing little children with the language of the King James Version of the Bible from infancy, as soon as they understand stories, I would start telling them the stories of Jesus; not showing them the cartoon Jesus we often show them, but telling the stories so their own hearts create the visual image. In that way, he becomes real.

Little children love Jesus.

The Bible then becomes a welcome 'rule book,' teaching us how to keep that light flowing that we're feeling. Spiritual power comes not just from knowing, but doing; experimenting with and applying the rules as they are learned.

As I zoom out again and try to further take in the pattern of learning I see in the Bible, I learn something else. The Old Testament is the study of a people who are given a long list of rules to follow, but they don't first have an object of love. The rules are detailed and exact—how many steps they can take on the Sabbath, what they can and can't eat and how and when that food must be prepared, and so forth. The bulk of the Old Testament gives us a case study of a people who struggle to live those rules without first a base of love. When they do follow the rules, they prosper. God protects them from their enemies in miraculous ways. But in the end, they just can't manage to live all those rules and they fall apart. Their society disintegrates to the point that those who aren't killed outright are scattered or carried off to Babylon in captivity.

Now Jesus Christ comes to the earth. He says those laws have served their purpose. He now gives a new law encompassed in one word: Love, first God and then each other. And then he not only tells us what love looks like, he shows us. We see him loving his enemies and doing good to those who despitefully use him. We see him doing alms in secret; of laying up treasures in heaven rather than on earth where moth and dust doth corrupt. He is meek. He is merciful. He is a peacemaker. He forgives. He lets his light shine. He teaches us, "No greater love than this…that a man should lay down his life for his friend."

Be as a little child, he says, for little children's hearts understand these things. They 'feel' them. And once their hearts are drawn to him, the rules become the means of keeping that light flowing.

The New Testament gives us a case study in the Apostle Paul of this new law in action. Paul was a Jew raised as a Roman citizen. Tarsus, his boyhood home, was the seat of all learning. He was classically trained. He learned to reason. Yet, reason alone failed him as he willingly stood by and watched an innocent man, Stephen—a man without guile and a pillar of his community—be stoned to death. It was on the road to Damascus that his heart, "breathing out threatenings and slaughter against the disciples of the Lord," came in contact with the Light.

And everything, for him, changed. Instantly. Later, he wrote:

> Who shall separate us from the love of Christ? Shall tribulation, or distress, or persecution, or famine, or nakedness, or peril, or sword?

> Thrice was I beaten with rods, once was I stoned, thrice I suffered shipwreck, a night and a day I have been in the deep;

> In journeyings often, in perils of water, in perils of robbers, in perils by mine own countrymen, in perils by the heathen, in perils in the city, in perils in the wilderness, in perils in the sea, in perils among false brethren;

> In weariness and painfulness, in watchings often, in hunger and thirst, in fastings often, in cold and nakedness.

> I am persuaded, that neither death, nor life, nor angels, nor principalities, nor powers, nor things present, nor things to come,

> Nor height, nor depth, nor any other creature, shall be able to separate us from the love of God, which is in Christ Jesus our Lord.

A third of the writings of the New Testament are written by Paul as he shares the rules for abiding in this love.

You might say the Old Testament is about living the letter of the law; the New Testament is about living the spirit of the law. To me, one demonstrates what happens when you give laws and rules before warming the heart. The other, what happens when laws and rules are given because the heart is looking to learn how to hold on to that which it has already felt. I believe we see the mass exodus from religion by our young people because our churches are attempting to lay down the law before their hearts have experienced the fruits of the spirit, which are joy, love, gentleness, peace and hope. Change the order, and we'll see our churches fill back up.

The New Testament ends with a vision of the new world that will come when this law is realized and lived, which should give us all great hope. Despite how dark and chaotic our world often looks like today, somehow, we're going to get from here to there. And we're right in the middle of the story. The many case studies given in the Old Testament aren't found in the New because I believe ours are the lives that will be studied. No one before has had free access to the Bible like we have. For hundreds of years, the Bible and its connection with spiritual light was hidden in monasteries and away from the common man. It's not coincidence that we call those years the Dark Ages. Church services were given in Latin and the Bible's teachings were interpreted through the Priests. The people were not allowed direct contact with the Light of the Bible. The first book printed on Gutenberg's press in 1456 was a Bible. Within a hundred years, William Tyndale, with a "fire burning in his bones" translated the Bible into a language that the poorest of the poor could understand. He was thanked by being burned at the stake. But it was too late.

The light was released and those who tasted it were as unwilling to part with it as we would be to turn off the power grid. Hundreds of thousands followed Tyndale as martyrs. They would rather die than give up their Bible.

The enemies of the Bible are still the ones who crave the power to rule over the lives of people and who understand that "where the Spirit of the Lord is, there is Liberty." Those who live by the Spirit allow no man to rule over them. Tyrants hate that.

Sadly, today, the average home has three copies of the Bible, but it's rarely opened. The word that is the lamp unto our feet and the light to our path goes unnoticed.

But we can change that.

The Bible belongs to all of us, Methodist and Baptist, Mormon and Presbyterian, Catholic and Lutheran. It is the one book capable of uniting us as a people because no one group can claim ownership of it. Its marvel is that it is not the work of one man, but a collection of writings over hundreds of years from prophets, herdsmen, kings, physicians, tax collectors, and fishermen, all being acted upon by the same sublime Spirit of Truth and delivering the same hopeful message: that life has purpose and meaning and there is a guiding power. We are not left alone to muddle our way through.

Its universal message of the fatherhood of God and the brotherhood of man touches the hearts of the poor and the rich, the scholar and the unlearned, those in captivity and those who are free. Its wisdom is valued by the Hindu, the Muslim and even the atheist. It needs no commentary to be understood. It offers ideas so simple a little child can grasp them, and yet scholars can spend a lifetime attempting to uncover the depth of their meaning. One simple phrase from its pages, on many occasions, has changed the course of a life and even the course of nations.

The most deeply moving music that has ever been composed, the most inspiring art that has ever been painted, and the most exquisite words that have ever been written, have found their inspiration in the Bible.

As Lincoln exclaimed, the Bible is simply the greatest gift God has given to mankind.

No heart can be well educated without it.

The Enrichment Page

The purpose of the enrichment page is to enrich the learning. That's simple, huh? You can access the enrichment pages from the Landing pages of each World History and American History topics. The enrichment button is the one on the far right. You will also find some enrichment activities on the bottom of each Nature page. Let me walk through what you'll find and give you some ideas for using these resources that use different languages of the heart.

The first thing you will see are a couple of links to Pinterest pages. The first one takes you to craft ideas. Some of you love to do crafts and others don't. Do what suits you. It's not that the crafts are necessarily instructive in themselves, but sometimes they provide a cultural connecting link. What they do provide is a way to keep little hands busy so that you can engage their hearts. They may not be willing to sit down and listen to some classical music, but they may not mind if it's going on in the background if they are doing something else and in that way you will help familiarize them with it. Or they may be more willing to listen to you read longer stories when their hands are engaged. Waldorf schools teach kindergarteners to knit for that reason. The knitting keeps their hands engaged in a rhythmic way so that they can listen to the stories.

You'll find a variety of crafts. I tried to find ideas for the very young up to older teens. If possible, I tied them into something that has to do with the culture of that country or a holiday celebration that provides another connecting point. I don't think I could handle a craft every single day. Maybe you'll set aside one afternoon a week for a craft time or even once or twice a month. Do what works for you.

And do take a picture of you and your kids and the crafts and put them in your planning books or in a cultural notebook that I talk about elsewhere. The memory of the time shared together is worth even more than the craft itself.

The other Pinterest page is of food ideas to go along with the study. Again, this provides a fun way of connecting to another culture and trying new tastes. You might decide to set aside one night a month to have a cultural celebration. Have your kids help cook the meal. Put some music on in the background from that country—a little French café music or an Italian accordion serenader, which you will find in the music section on the enrichment page. Take some pictures! And be sure and have someone practice handwriting skills and copy the recipes for family or individual cultural books. While you're eating, talk about favorite things members of the family have learned from their reading. Keep it light and fun. Or just try out different recipes throughout the month. Your choice.

Next you will find some plays if I could find something to go with the topic. Plays are a wonderful way to make the impressions go deeper by having the music in their voices reflect the emotion in their heart. Let me share a little introduction from one of the play books:

I have often been asked questions of the sort:

How do you teach your children to speak so well? Their pronunciation is correct, their enunciation is clear, and their voices well-modulated and truly expressive.

Why is it that the boys and girls talk so intelligently in the classroom during a history, or geography, or English literature and composition period?

How do you train your children to be so self-contained and at ease when meeting strangers;

Why is it that in none of your classes does there seem to be any of the old drill in facts, and forms, but rather that there is always a happy, pleasing spirit of interest and enthusiasm which makes the lesson periods fly fast?

And the answers all have to do with the attention placed on dramatics—on plays. Every subject taught becomes alive and interesting when children are engaged in living out what they are studying through plays.

A famous teacher, after watching a group of children act out a play from history, said to another standing there, "You have seen today the difference between formal teaching and real education of a child; e-duco-means I lead forth, that which is within. The dramatic instinct that is in every child is one of the greatest powers in helping a mother educate her children.

These plays can involve the whole family—even dad. Everyone gets a part. Invite other families to join in or double up on parts. Use simple props. From time to time your children may want to actually memorize the parts and put on a performance, but it doesn't have to be that involved.

Print out the plays. There's a pdf option on the plays I have linked to and you can print out just the pages you need rather than the whole book. Let everyone mark his own part and practice on his own saying his own part so that the voice reflects the emotion. Is it tender and sweet or rough and gruff? And then come together and let it unfold.

Chances are, your kids will want to start writing their own plays. This was a favorite pastime of the children you read about in the old books like Louisa May Alcott and others. I'm still adding plays as I find them. And you may want to note that I generally organize them on this page so that the first plays are for younger children and on up. Use your imaginations as to how you might be able to incorporate plays into your homelife. Puppets maybe? Making a video of them? Or just a reader's theater? Have fun with them.

You may want to give them several days to practice. Give your littlest ones the shortest parts and help them rehearse their lines so they feel like they are part of it. There is some wonderful flowery language in a lot of these plays which is part of the benefit in familiarizing your children with a richer language than what we are used to. And like I said, invite dad to participate! It can be a family bonding experience. Since most of these plays are scenes from history or from classical literature, it will leave a long-lasting connection to these people and events. You will find scenes from fairy tales as well. I organized them, generally speaking, from the simpler plays to the more complex when you go to select what is right fit for your family.

Another related activity is something Karla Huntsman taught us at the storytelling workshop. From time to time, create tableaus. This is where all the members of your family choose a particular scene from a book you've been reading or an event from history you've been studying or even a movie you watched. Each member chooses the character he or she wants to be and you all arrange yourself in the scene. And then you freeze for a moment. Then, let each member tell what is going through his or her head. I hope that makes sense. It allows them to become that character for a moment and feel what he or she is feeling. And, again, it leaves a long-lasting impression and connection to that character.

Of course, you don't need a script to put on a play. Little children can re-enact fairy tales and older children can make up their own scenes from books they are reading. Community theater was a big deal in older days. They weren't elaborate productions. But it provided a bonding experience and was a cultural uplift. Brigham Young once said, "'If I were placed on a cannibal island and given a task of civilizing its people, I should straightway build a theatre." And, "On the stage of a theatre can be represented in character evil and its consequences, good and its happy results and rewards, the weaknesses and follies of man and the magnanimity of the virtuous life." Plays can be an ennobling experience. And of course—take your children to the best of plays you can afford to take them to!

Next on the page, you will find some movie suggestions. Just a caution—I have not previewed every single movie I have linked. But I have linked each one to IMDB so you can learn about the movie for yourself and decide if it's appropriate for your family to watch. Pay particular attention to the Parental Advisory section.

You'll notice a lot of old movie classics. Some of them aren't great movies, but they do serve to bring to life different eras of history in helping the heart to paint the pictures. Many of them were filmed on location. So maybe you'll only watch parts of movies. Movies can be used to awaken an interest or to deepen the impression. Many movies will spark conversation. "Hey— that isn't how it went!" Or you can compare different versions of movies and talk about what you liked and didn't like about the different versions. I find it very difficult to watch a lot of the movies today because they have replaced storyline with non-stop action shots. I agree with the person who said a lot of movies look like they were filmed by a monkey on someone's back. There is little character development. The camera doesn't give me time to study emotion in the faces. These older movies serve to slow things down. If your kids have a steady diet of action, they may find some of these movies boring—at least at first. But if movies are a treat in your house, they may give them a chance. I tried to find a variety. I have to admit some are downright corny, but that's part of their charm. Most of these movies can be streamed online, or you can check with your public library.

And now we come to art. I'm still building this section. If you used the old website and wonder where all the art from art renewal went, much of it went here on the enrichment pages. Some wonderful volunteers divided all the art images by nation, either by the nationality of the artist or where the scene takes place. Furthermore, they divided them by family scenes and historical scenes, making it possible to focus on a few at a time. One reason art doesn't appeal to some children is there is nothing in it that is familiar to them or that connects to them. That's why these family scenes are a good start for younger children and for even older children who haven't had much exposure to art. You can pick a few art pieces to print out and hang on your walls or even refrigerator during the month. Or have your children pick a favorite they want to study and place on the gallery in their heart. If they are making a notebook of art that speaks to their own heart, have them choose what they want to go in there. If printing isn't an option, let them view them full screen on a tablet or even project them on your TV screen.

The historical scenes are perfect for printing out to go in their story of the world or great souls notebooks, which I talk about in the notebooking section. Or just for studying, again, to make a deep, long-lasting impression of the events of history. Most of these art images are from Art Renewal who give permission to print them out for your personal use and study, but to use them for any other purpose, you need to contact their licensing department. The other images I include come from Wikimedia Commons. This is not an all-inclusive selection—just enough to whet the appetite to search for more on your own.

I am also adding art images that have stories connected to them. You'll find the link to the story underneath the art image. This gives you an easy art appreciation lesson, either about the artist or about the work itself.

You might also check out the art on simplejoyart.com which is all linked to Wikimedia Commons where it can easily be printed out.

Of course, these art images do not have the impact that the original work of art has. Do take advantage of art museums whenever you can. And as your children become familiar with these great works of art, when they see them in a room, they will run to them like an old friend.

The final section is music. Again, I looked for variety. I included a nation's national anthem—there's a lesson right there. I looked for background music that you can use to play while you are notebooking or working on crafts or having a cultural dinner like I suggested earlier. If a nation had an instrument that was unusual, I included that so you'll see a Russian balalaika orchestra or unusual instruments played up close. You'll see familiar pieces played by symphony orchestras all over the world, showing there is music that is loved by people everywhere. You'll see famed conductors like Leonard Bernstein and famed musicians such as Itzhak Pehrlman. You'll see ballets performed by the Boshoi Ballet and operatic numbers performed by the Metropolitan Opera. You'll even see or hear music performed by the composers themselves—Debussy playing Claire de Lune and Grieg playing his compositions. Some moms like to make playlists of the month's music. Project some of them on your TV if you can and watch. Some have fine art images, others show the instruments up close.

Also, there is a section called Music and Story. These are typically pieces that aren't too long to introduce children to classical music. There is a link to a story right beneath them. Many of these stories link to the program notes put together by the North Carolina Symphony Orchestra for their series of children's concerts over the last 70 years, so it highlights things about the composer or the music that will appeal to children. They are short and sweet and give you an easy music appreciation lesson.

So there you have it! And remember—this isn't check off the list stuff. Just because you listen to a piece of music doesn't mean you check it off and never listen again. It's meant to return to over and over again because you enjoy how it makes you feel. Have fun!

Notebooking for the Well-Educated Heart

When I was a newlywed, my husband and I were both students at Brigham Young University. And it was my good fortune to be asked to serve on a committee that organized a special meeting for the women with Freda Joan Lee as our special speaker. Her husband was Harold B. Lee who had passed away just a few months earlier. Now, I know not all of you are of my faith—so I'll explain that Harold B. Lee was the president of our church. He was revered as a prophet just as there were prophets in Old Testament days. To be able to meet his wife was a great honor.

It fell on my husband and I to drive to Salt Lake from Provo and pick her up at her home and drive her down to the event, and then take her back home again. So I got to go into her home and spend the day with the wonderful woman in a very close and private way. She shared so many personal experiences and had such profound words of wisdom. I kept meaning to write them down, but I thought, "How could I ever forget these things?"

But time passed. And I did forget them. All of them. I remember my husband got to wind President Lee's grandfather clock and I remember Sister Lee fell asleep on my shoulder in the car. I remember how I felt when I was near her and how I felt when I was in her home. But the rest is all gone.

Not writing down the things I learned from her is one of the big regrets of my life. And no matter how hard I try to retrieve them from my memory, I simply cannot.

That which is not written down is easily forgotten. Through books, your children are going to spend time with some of the greatest, noblest, wisest men and women who have ever walked the earth who are going to teach them priceless lessons about life and living. Notebooking is a way for them to capture and remember those lessons and experiences so that they're not forgotten.

Knowledge of whole civilizations has vanished where they left no written records. And much of our learning washes away when we don't take time to write. In fact, the more we write, the more we learn. Very few of us retain much at all of what we read or study. One of my biggest frustrations is when I remember reading a story or an idea and I can't for the life of me remember where I read it. There are a couple of incidents I read about that have been bugging me for months now because I cannot find them again anywhere. I can't remember what books I read them in. I've been wanting to find them because I can't remember all the details. I kick myself that I didn't record them somewhere where I can find them again.

That's when I knew I had to develop a different system because as I have read more, it has become harder and harder to go back and find what I am looking for. I have filled dozens of notebooks with quotes and ideas from my reading and it has become unruly. Sometimes moms ask if they can just make one notebook—why do there need to be so many? Well, you can. And if that works for you, go for it. I can tell you Thomas Jefferson kept a Commons Book and as far as I can tell, he wrote as he went along. That worked for me for awhile, but I can no longer keep track of things anymore like that. From the *Life of Emerson*, it reads: "[Emerson] went out early to hunt a thought as a boy might hunt a butterfly, and, successful, pinned the prize in his cabinet by entering it in his 'Thought Book.'" Abraham Lincoln wrote things down on a piece of board with charcoal from the fire. His system worked because he didn't erase what he wrote down until he retained it in his memory. Some people have wonderful memories like that. I don't.

That's why I created so many different notebooks. It helps me organize my learning. I hear from a lot of moms who are confused about or are reluctant to start Notebooking. They're not sure what's supposed to go inside and the idea feels overwhelming. I look at my notebooks as books of remembrance—a place to write down those things that I want to remember. If you have not yet found something you want to hold on to, then there's not really a need to start a notebook. The same goes for your children. And by the way, once you assign notebooking, you've killed the spirit of it. Instead, feed the desire in your children by letting your children see you notebook for yourself.

Our minds can't hold on to everything we read or hear, nor would we want to! We are bombarded with information. A secret to the art of living well is learning the art of consistently choosing that which is of greatest worth—of holding on to the kernel of wheat and letting the chaff blow away in the wind. The notebooking I'm talking about is all about digging for priceless gems and jewels—that which will nourish our hearts and our souls.

I like to think of these notebooks as scrapbooking wisdom. As I have looked at other notebooking systems, I see a great emphasis on facts and information. There may have been a time when memorizing capitals of states and names of presidents was useful because people didn't have easy access to information. They had to draw upon that which was in their memories. We no longer live in that age and can put our attention on higher matters. I have yet to find a fact that I can't access instantly on my phone: What is the capital of Maine? Who was the 17th president? What year did Napoleon die? It's a modern-day technological miracle. With our explosion of instant information available to us, it makes no sense to fill my notebooking pages with trivia. I'm going for the gold.

I'm going for those things Mr. Rogers taught: I want to be more concerned with a sense of wonder than with information. I want to place a higher value on those things that are not seen than those things that are seen. He taught that everything that really matters isn't found in the words on a page—they're found in the white spaces between the words; the white spaces between the lines. They are the ah-hah moments when the light goes on and we get flashes of pure inspiration. Notebooking as I am about to describe is designed for lots of white space learning.

I'm all for simple. We get so overwhelmed with the number of subjects we think we have to be teaching our children: History, English, Geography, Science, Math, Grammar, Spelling, Writing, Art, Music. Juggling it all makes us feel inadequate. And the nagging doubt is, what if I forget to teach something?

And so we spend hours every day trying to get information to stick and the sad truth is, at the end of all those years, your child, by some estimations, will forget 90-98% of what you tried so hard to teach them. There just has to be a better way to spend our time, doesn't there?

This isn't a new realization. Leonardo da Vinci understood hundreds of years ago: "Study without desire spoils the memory, and it retains nothing it takes in."

And Plato got it hundreds of years before that: "Knowledge which is acquired under compulsion obtains no hold on the mind."

Unless we care about something or find a use for it, it's likely going to wash away with time. Creating a desire and use for knowledge is the task of childhood.

So a vital key of Notebooking for the Heart is an abundance of freedom to choose and nurturing desires rather than assigning topics.

Like I just said. I'm all for simple. I believe there are only two subjects we need to be teaching our children: People and Nature.

The tools we're going to use to understand people are History, Biography, Literature, Geography, Cultural Studies, Language Arts, Poetry, Art, and Music. All of these subjects reveal human hearts and human nature. We study history, not because we need to understand people of the past so much as we need them to help us understand ourselves. From all these sources, we learn about how to live abundant lives and how to get along with others who are different than ourselves; how to understand and empathize with others; how to love. We begin to learn the laws and principles upon which human happiness is based and as we apply them, we become wise and we become more civilized. Wisdom is of far more worth than mere knowledge.

The main tool we'll use to understand Nature is our eyes. Our textbooks are going to be the Stars and the Ocean, the Rocks, Plants, Trees, Insects, Birds and Animals. As we study them the science of nature will be revealed—the laws upon which all the Universe operates. And in time, the two subjects—People and Nature—will blend together into one great whole as nature reveals lessons to human hearts that cannot be taught more effectively in any other way; lessons like: We reap what we sow. Spring always follows winter. Diamonds are formed under great pressure. As we use our eyes, we begin to see the perfect and majestic order—the Math—by which the universe operates.

Nature is God's University and brings us face-to-face with our Creator wherein we begin to gain a sense of our worth in His eyes and the effect is pure joy which is the ultimate objective of a heart-based education.

Louisa May Alcott recorded this in her notebook:

> I had an early run in the woods before the dew was off the grass. The moss was like velvet, and as I ran under the arch of yellow and red leaves I sang for joy, my heart was so bright and the world so beautiful. I stopped at the end of the walk and saw the sunshine out over the wide 'Virginia meadows.'

It seemed like going through a dark life or grave into heaven beyond. A very strange and solemn feeling came over me as I stood there, with no sound but the rustle of the pines, no one near me, and the sun so glorious, as for me alone. It seemed as if I felt God as I never did before, and I prayed in my heart that I might keep that happy sense of nearness all my life.

To that entry there is a note added, years later: "I have, for I most sincerely think that the little girl 'got religion' that day in the wood, when dear Mother Nature led her to God."

No informational textbook can teach that. This is white space learning.

I'm going to make suggestions for notebooking that I'm using, but there's no reason for you to not adapt the ideas to your circumstances and personalities of your children. And if you're asking, "How do I get my kids to do this?" you're asking the wrong question. The right question is, "Do I want to do this?" Because the best way to teach Notebooking for the Heart is to lead by example.

I'm going to start with Nature. A Nature Journal or a Nature Notebook is primarily drawing what your eyes see. It's that simple. You may say, "But I can't draw," and that just isn't true. There are very few people who can't learn to draw. But it takes time and practice, just like when you first learned to write letters.

Why does drawing matter? As was said in an 1880 art text for children, "Why do we wish to learn to draw? ...In order to develop in us those nobler faculties which God has given for the appreciation of His works in nature..."

"Drawing produces an exactness of thought."

Drawing gives us eyes with which to see. As Charles Kingsley wrote, "So it is. One man walks through the world with his eyes open, another with his eyes shut; and upon this difference depends all the superiority of knowledge which one man acquires over another."

I just got home after spending several weeks with my 95-year-old mother. She's still very independent, but we feel for her comfort and safety, it is best to move her into an Independent Living facility which has been a very emotional transition. There are so many memories tied into her home and neighborhood. As I crawled into bed one night, I pulled out a sketch pad and tried to sketch the scene from her back yard from memory and I couldn't do it. There were so many gaps in my mind even though I've been in her backyard hundreds of times. So the next morning, I went out and attempted to sketch what I saw and I noticed details I didn't notice before. It doesn't matter that this sketch is out of proportion—what was imprinting as I did it were the orange pyracantha berries, the quakies to the side of the fence, the weeping willow and the poplar at the back of the horse pasture. I hadn't before noticed the little green bird feeder on the side of the storage shed or the pink rose bushes. I made special note of the little gate that led to the pasture and the tree behind it. Somehow in that little exercise, it has left a much more vivid impression and scene on my heart because I want to remember it long after I can no longer go and physically see it with my eyes.

My mother's backyard in Salt Lake City, Utah
September 11, 2016

Figure 14: Drawing of my mother's backyard

Louis Agassiz was a legendary professor of science at Harvard University—a contemporary of Charles Darwin. He was known to place a single fish scale in front of his students, leave for a couple of hours, and then come back and ask each student what he saw. Or he would put a fish in front of them and leave them to themselves for a couple of weeks and allowed them their own discoveries. He taught that's how we learn about Nature—we use our eyes and ask ourselves questions. Textbooks were not the first step in learning.

I love a little book I found written in 1904 by Edward Bigelow: *How Nature Should Be Taught.* He said Nature Study is emotional while Science is intellectual. The emotion needs to come before the intellect—we need to raise children who love nature if we wish to raise scientists. And that love comes by direct contact; by spending time with her.

With a little tongue in cheek, he offered this:

> Oh, no, some scientific appreciator of a mother may say, that is crude; it flavors of the Middle Ages, of the amateur, of those who love their mother from the heart. This is an age of scientific spirit, an age of the intellect rather than of the affections.

> Do nothing so simple as that; learn really to know your mother, and then you can love her with solid, intellectual appreciation.

> First collect some pictures and drawings of all the mothers you can find; arrange them side by side and compare your mother to them. That will add to your knowledge of the comparative merits of your mother's personal appearance.

Devote a half-hour at a certain time every day to the study of mothers. Draw pictures of them;

Make a detailed list of color of hair, number of eyes, nostrils, ears; length of chin, height, weight, number of fingers on each hand; state the age, past history and a hundred or more other facts. Arrange these details under a few heads, draw a bracket around each, and collocate these in line under one big brace, with the word Mother written in capital letters.

Make a drawing of your own mother standing erect, and also bending down to kiss you as you start for school in the morning. Sketch in detail her eyes, fingers and nose.

Write a list of nouns, adjectives, verbs and adverbs that will apply to your own mother, and from these compose ten sentences each day from 10:15 to 10:45 am, in connection with your drawing work, and if the task is completed before the time has expired, we will fold our arms and sing about our mothers. Bear in mind that you must never really go to see your mother for the enjoyment of seeing her, nor only for the enjoyment of her loving presence, but you must learn to love her, and to let her influence permeate every fiber of your life, by noting down with pad and pencil, all possible details of her physical structure.

And then he added: "Too much detail, too much method, too much correlating kills a love of nature."

He went on to tell of a contest where he was asked to judge the best nature journal. He received a nicely tied up bundle of beautiful nature journals. The penmanship was perfect. The pictures were drawn just so. And they all looked exactly alike.

He continued:

Next I picked up an unattractive letter written on the leaves of a pocket note-book. The drawing that accompanied it was crude and the paper was soiled by finger marks. With difficulty I read it, but was fascinated as I deciphered the story of a boy's seaside investigation of the fiddler crab. He wanted to know how they lived underground; what they did; what food they ate; what kind of quarters they occupied. He made inquiries of the fishermen. No one knew. He said, "I'll find out if it takes a week." He borrowed pick, shovel, and crowbar. He went to work and he found out. Then he wrote the story, as he sat beside the hole that he had dug after several hours' hard work. He made the drawing after careful watching of the living object. He wrote the article on the field of battle, where the weapon was a spade, the enemy a crab. I was sorry that I had not a basketful of prizes to give that boy, because he wrote his letter for the love of it, and not for a reward, of which he knew nothing.

That reminds me of the drawings I got on the back of a letter recently from my 11-year-old granddaughter. She loves bugs and slugs and all things nature and recently she's been searching and collecting caterpillar eggs and growing caterpillars. This is what she sent me. Can you feel the love?

When your little ones first pick up a pencil, don't be so quick to teach them to draw the letter A. Help them strengthen those fine motor skills by drawing pictures of kittens and suns and flowers. Let them learn by watching you. Pick up a book like Watch Me Draw or Draw Write Now. You'll find drawing books all start with noticing the shapes within an object. Transferring those circle and line skills to letters won't be hard at all when the time is right.

I read a biography of Beatrix Potter and it said that "writing came easily, for Beatrix could copy shapes of letters as quickly as she copied leaves and flowers."

Pestalozzi utilized this method. "They would draw pictures of things, make collections of leaves and flowers, and keep a record of their observations and discoveries. Through keeping these records they learned to read and write."

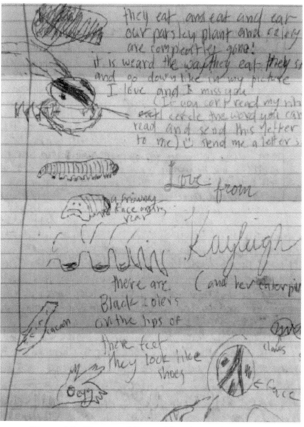

Figure 15: 11-year-old granddaughter's letter to me

Experiment with watercolors in your nature sketching and journaling. Recreating the colors your eyes see is half the fun and it's hard to do with pencils. This is a new field for me—I always avoided watercolor because I ended up with a big mess of colors that ran together into various shades of gray. I've been learning the secret is to make sure you buy a good quality of watercolor paper so that the water can soak into the page and not puddle on top.

There are some awesome free videos online done by John Muir Laws on how to draw from nature. He also just published a new book. I highly recommend him. And the thing I love about him is he absolutely loves what he does. It's contagious.

Be sure and leave room on your pages to add poems or quotes you may come across later, like Edith Holden did in her *Country Diary of an Edwardian Lady*. Wouldn't that be fun sometime to do what she did? But no matter if you never get there...there are satisfying rewards all along the way.

Figure 16: Sample page from Country Diary of an Edwardian Lady

Stories add to the sense of wonder. If you've spent any time with me, you know my love for the books written in a Golden Age of Children's Literature between the years of around 1880 to 1920 which you can find on my website. The Nature books of this era are a wonderful blend of heart and mind and you'll find so many things to add interest to your nature walks. For instance, can you draw a dandelion leaf from memory? Did you know dandelion means tooth of a lion? Can you now see the lion's teeth in the leaf? I bet you'll never forget that. And I was reading a story about apple blossoms. I love apple blossoms in the spring. And the writer went through what happened over the course of summer and fall when apples are produced. And where did the apple blossom go? It's right inside the apple! I couldn't believe it so I went and cut an apple in half myself, and sure enough, there's an imprint of an apple blossom inside.

Nature is full of such surprises to spark wonder. Nature journaling helps you preserve it.

I was talking with a mom in our group who told me of a young woman she knew who had decided to pursue a course of study in college that required science. She was nervous because she had never taken a formal science class before—she had just drawn in a nature journal. But the first semester she called home:

"Guess what, Mom? I'm doing better than anyone in my Biology class because I can see what the professor is describing."

Now let's move over to the People side. Children are naturally curious and ask a lot of questions. A question is the heart's way of saying, "There's a gap in here I need to fill," and when the answer comes, the heart knows exactly where to fit it in. Even God waits for us to Ask. But think what our current system of education does when a child enters school: The teacher says I'll ask the questions around here and you answer the questions I tell you to answer. For the next 12+ years, a child will be given little to no choice in what he learns. His days will be assigned and structured and tested, with no regard as to whether or not he cares about what he is learning. By the time many children leave school, they've lost their desire to learn anything. I've even talked to people who have to rely upon someone else to tell them if they liked a book or a movie. They don't have the capacity to judge for themselves.

You can change that. A big part of notebooking for the heart is allowing a child to connect to those feelings within. What do they like? What do they want to learn more about? You can increase those desires by offering a wide variety of stories and experiences, but allowing them the freedom to say "I like that" or "I don't like that" is vital to the learning process in childhood.

A very first notebooking experience for preschoolers can be to let them cut out pictures from a magazine and choosing favorite things to glue into a little notebook of their own. My daughter has been picking up fine art books from used book sales and she recently let her girls go through and cut out their favorites and glue them in a book.

Pictures and Poetry will then be the next step in our People study.

A couple of summers ago while I was helping my daughter with a new baby—her fifth little girl—I pulled out a sheet of blank white paper and said to 6-year-old Madison, "Madison, what's your favorite Mother Goose rhyme?" She thought for a minute and said, "Hey diddle diddle."

Figure 17: Hey Diddle Diddle page

"OK. Where do you want me to write it?" Right there. Her heart was getting a little writing and reading lesson while she watched me form letters and write left to right. We read it together and then she drew a picture of the cow jumping over the moon and the dish running away with the spoon. We three-hold punched it and put it in a notebook.

The next day, "Grandma, can we do another one?" Sure. Which one? Twinkle, Twinkle Little Star. Where do you want me to write it? Right there. Then she ran off to draw her picture.

Figure 18: Twinkle, Twinkle Little Star page

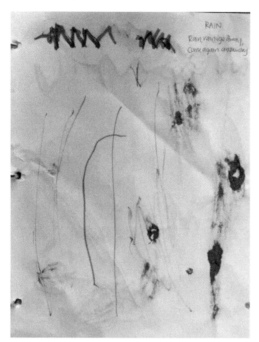

Figure 19: Rain, Rain, Go Away page

4-year-old Emma had been watching. "Grandma, I want to do that." OK. What's your favorite poem? Hmmm. Little Bo Peep. Same thing. 3-year-old Andi said, I want to do that. Rain, rain go away. 9-year-old Kayleigh was watching and said, I want to do that. But she did her own writing and drawing.

We didn't do it every day, but after I left, my daughter said one day Madison got a little impatient waiting for her to finish feeding the baby, so she said, "That's OK, mom, I'll just write it." Madison had been a somewhat reluctant writer, but she went and pulled out the Mother Goose book, found the picture of the poem she was looking for, and copied it. Hickory Dickory Dock.

I wish I had paid closer attention at the time, but one of our daughters had a First Grade teacher who taught the children to read through poetry. Each week she would read a new poem aloud and then the children said it aloud with her. Then she would hand it out in print where they read it together and illustrated the page and put it in a special notebook. Reading happened so naturally in that class. I think it's because poetry has such fantastic ordering properties for our brains and creates so many visual images, not to mention the connection to feelings.

Why do we study poetry?

I like this answer by Newell Dwight Hillis: "The soldier fights for his native land, but the poet touches that land with the charm that makes it worth fighting for... The statesman enlarges and orders liberty in the State, but the poet fosters the love of liberty in the heart of the citizen." Simple poems learned in childhood may last a lifetime.

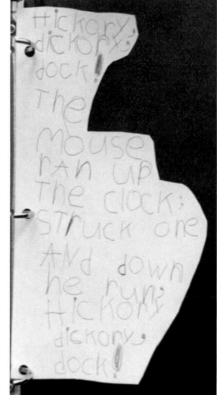

Figure 20: Hickory Dickory Dock page

The best way to kill a love of poetry in the beginning is to analyze it. The best way to help your children to love poetry is to love poetry yourself and read it aloud to them. Compile an anthology of your favorite poems to share with your children and then encourage them to build their own collection of favorites, which is the purpose of the Poetry/Memory Gems notebook. Those poems we love the most we will naturally want to commit to memory.

Copying and illustrating poetry pages can be part of a weekly Poetry Teatime where you gather with simple refreshments and share your favorites. Copying poetry is a good way to help a child practice his handwriting skills. And do teach them cursive— brain scans show that the entire brain lights up when a person writes in cursive, which doesn't happen when they print or type the words.

Around age 4, which is when children enter a prime age for Imaginative stories, you might consider a Favorite Fairy Tales book in preparation for the Literature Gems book which is to come later. I wouldn't make a child draw every story you read—but here again, you can lead by example. My daughter had finished reading the story of the Frog Prince and she said something like, "I like that story. I want to remember it." So she drew a picture and added a Gem: A promise is a promise. And then her girls all wanted to draw one, too. You can do these on sheets of paper and put them in a notebook, or, for the sake of space, create a My Favorite Fairy Tales book from a Bare Book and include the illustrations in one volume. If you fill it up, start a new one. Here are their illustrations from A Real Princess.

Figure 21: "A Real Princess" illustration page samples

Then, from time to time, sit down one-on-one and have a conversation like this: "Oh, how did that story go again?" And let your child retell the story or part of the story. Verbal expression precedes written expression and this is a natural way to help kids begin to narrate. I suggest as you find lesser known fairy tales, you make a note on the page where you found the story. I hear from moms who tell me of a favorite story they heard as a child and they've looked and looked for it and can't find it again.

As you start reading some of the popular children's classic literature, like *Treasure Island* and *Secret Garden*, I suggest creating a Literature Gems notebook. I like the word 'gem' because it's something that's small but extremely valuable, long lasting, and it sparkles. A Literature Gems notebook is where you can copy the gems you mine from your reading. The difference between the Literature Gems notebook and the Great Lives notebook is the characters are fictional.

Here's how I would create a page: Write the title on the top of the page and underneath who the book was written by. Include where and when the story took place and, when you know it, add a one line synopsis of the story. In the beginning, let the page mostly be pictures to remind children of the story. They can either illustrate it themselves or shrink the illustrations down from the book and glue them on a page.

Figure 22: Secret Garden Gem pages

THOUGHTS ARE AS POWERFUL AS
ELECTRIC BATTERIES. p. 287

When new beautiful thoughts began to
push out the old hideous ones
→ LIFE began to come
back to him. p. 288

He'd be at home in
Buckingham Palace or
at the bottom of a
coal mine. p. 210

❀ sometimes the immense quiet of the dark
blue at night with millions of stars waiting
and watching makes one sure

❀ sometimes a sound of far-off music
makes it true

❀ sometimes a look in someone's eyes.

❀ One of the strange things about living in
the world is that it is only now and then
one is quite sure one is going to live forever
and ever . . . one knows it sometimes when
one stands by oneself in a wood at sunset and
the mysterious deep gold stillness slanting
through and under the branches seems to be
saying slowly again and again something one
cannot quite hear, however much one tries.
p. 218

I SHALL LIVE FOREVER AND EVER
AND EVER ! p. 216

The springtime . . . I was thinking
that I've never really seen it
before. I scarcely went out
and when I did I never
looked at it. p. 212

Figure 23: Secret Garden Gem pages (cont.)

I organize the book titles alphabetically in my notebook. Do you have your child make a page for every single book he reads? No. Only the books that have something in them he wants to hold on to and remember. And if they read a lot of books with nothing worth holding on to, they may realize for themselves maybe there are some better choices out there for them.

In the beginning, use pictures to help jog your child's memories as they tell the story from the pictures. But the real value of this notebook is when they are able to start adding the gems they're gleaning from their reading, which, they'll learn to do by watching you.

When I'm reading along, I often come to something that just grabs hold of me—that sets me to thinking—something that I say to myself, I want to remember that. I use little post it tabs to mark the place. And then when I'm done with the book, I go back and re-evaluate. Do I care about this enough to actually copy it down? If the answer is yes, it goes on my page. Sometimes, if the passage is long, I just write enough to remind me and I always write the page number of the book down so I can find it again.

Here are the kinds of gems I hold on to. This is from *A Little Princess*:

Figure 24: Little Princess Gem pages

154

" Have you never pretended things? ...
It's so easy that when you begin you
can't stop. You just go on and on and
doing it always. AND IT'S BEAUTIFUL." p.35

STORIES BELONG TO EVERYBODY. p.56

"If Nature has made you a giver, your hands
are born open, and so is your heart; and though
there may be times when your hands are empty,
your heart is always full, and you can give
things out of that — warm things, kind things,
sweet things — help and comfort and laughter —
and sometimes kind laughter is the best help of all."
p. 80

"...soldiers — even brave ones — don't
really LIKE going into battle." p 6

If I'm a princess — when they were
poor and driven from their thrones —
they always shared — with the populace —
if they met one poorer and hungrier
than themselves. p. 204

Anyone who is kind wants to know when
people have even made them happy. They care
for that more than for being thanked. p.278

Perhaps you can feel if you can't hear...
Perhaps kind thoughts reach people
somehow through windows and doors
and walls. Perhaps you feel a little
warm and comforted, and don't know
why, when I am standing here in
the cold and hoping you will get well
and happy again. p.187

Figure 25: Little Princess Gem pages (cont.)

Perhaps to be able to learn things quickly isn't everything. To be kind is worth a great deal to other people.

She had not learned French exactly… Her papa loved it, and she loved it because he did.

When people are insulting you, there is nothing so good for them as not to say a word—

155

just to look at them and think…when you will not fly into a passion, people know you are stronger than they are.

If Nature has made you a giver, your hands are born open, and so is your heart; and though there may be times when your hands are empty, your heart is always full, and you can give things out of that—warm things, kind things, sweet things—help and comfort and laughter—and sometimes kind laughter is the best help of all.

Perhaps kind thoughts reach people somehow through windows and doors and walls. Perhaps you feel a little warm and comforted, and don't know why, when I am standing here in the cold and hoping you will get well and happy again.

These gem pages are never finished. When you read the book again, you may find new gems to add.

Pages don't have to be illustrated. Here's a page from *A Lantern in Her Hand* and I just added a few splashes of color here and there. But you don't even have to do that! Here a few gems:

Figure 26: Lantern in Her Hand Gem pages

You have to dream things out. It keeps a kind of an ideal before you… If you want a garden, why, I guess you've got to dream a garden.

Because the road was steep and long,
And through a dark and lonely land,
God set upon my lips a song
And put a lantern in my hand.

On the next page:

That is what LOVE is to a woman…a lantern in her hand.

It takes Faith and Courage and Love and Prayer and Work and a little Singing to keep up your spirits.

Afterwards they went out on the porch and Abbie held the little girl on her lap. She cuddled her up and put her wrinkled cheek against the child's firm one. Oh why didn't mothers do it more when they had the chance?

Figure 27: Lantern in Her Hand Gem pages (cont.)

As these gems are copied, a lot of white space learning about writing is going on. Master artists learned to paint masterpieces by copying the masterpieces. Master writers did the same thing.

They copied the writing of masterful writers. As your children copy beautiful words written by masters of writing, writing lessons are being impressed on their hearts that cannot be taught directly. As they read them aloud, they're getting the best of lessons in grammar. A study was done where one group was taught grammar by the typical direct worksheet approach. The other learned through literature like I am describing. At the end of the study, both groups had the same level of grammar comprehension, but the first group had developed a distaste for the whole subject.

I'm now going to move into the notebooks that are connected to a study of history, but I want to help you visualize the kind of learning that is going to take place. Most learning I see in schools and typical curriculum is linear learning. There is a shopping list of subjects to teach—you teach them and move on. If we were machines, learning like this would work perfectly. But we're not machines. Most learning in this way gets thrown away in the big pile of "who cares."

What I'm looking for are ways to accommodate Spiral learning, which is where learning happens line upon line, layer upon layer, here a little and there a little. Which is why I have created a 12-month rotation schedule. It's built around a study of American History with the major nations of the world tied into the monthly American History topics. I explain it in more detail in other places and I don't want to take the time here to go into it. But basically, if, for instance, it's Month 5 which includes a study of France, I'll draw from literature written by French writers or which takes place in France, music by French composers or with a French theme, art by French artists, history, biographies and cultural studies about France and French people.

An 8-year-old may hear a very basic story of Joan of Arc, but as that child returns as a 12-year-old and a 14-year-old and even a 20-year-old, new insights and discoveries will deepen and expand his understanding of her, the circumstances around her story, and the role it played in what followed. Learning will layer in over time and could never happen in one shot.

As you start to rotate through the countries, it's fun to start with the culture and create a world culture notebook. I call mine 'Around the World.' Each child can have his or her own, but if you have a lot of kids, you may want to have a family notebook for everyone to share. I have dividers for the countries listed in the rotation schedule, arranged alphabetically.

What kinds of pages go in this book? If you eat some French food, take a picture of it, preferably with family members, glue it on a page and have one of your kids copy the recipe. If you make a craft, take a picture of your kids making it or enjoying it. If there's a story behind it, such as using it in connection with a holiday, let one of your children add that to the page. Or learn a game from that country, take a picture of you playing it, and write down the instructions. I keep maps in this notebook so that when you hear a story, you can find and place it on the map as you go. Map work without stories is easily forgotten. As you learn about interesting places to visit, print out a picture of the place, paste it on a page called "Places We'd Like to Visit Some Day." Let a child tell reasons why it would be interesting to visit there; what happened there;

what's something you'll want to look for.

Now let's look at the Story of the World Notebook or sometimes I think of it as my Great Lives notebook. Two things are going into this notebook: Real people and events. The way I'm going to grow this notebook is by creating what I call landing pages and it doesn't matter where you start. I call it a landing page because, over the years, I'm going to be drawing from a lot of different resources. Maybe I'll hear of an anecdote or an interesting piece of information about someone or a quote or a story that I want to remember and I need a place for it to land. When you create a page, it's not intended for you to finish it in one sitting. It's a very open-ended project. And if you should fill up a page, just start another one. If you fill up a notebook, start another one.

Here is how I create a 'landing page.' I write the name of the person at the top of the page. I like to use color, but it's not necessary! Then I either go to Wikipedia or simply ask my phone when that person was born. I put the year in the upper right-hand corner. I'm going to organize the book chronologically according to birth year, so it's important that I see it easily.

Figure 28: Sample Landing Page of Carolus Linnaeus

159

Underneath, I'll write the year that person died. Then I write the country where that person was born and if he or she was primarily connected with a different country in later life, I'll note that. Then I'll check with Wikipedia and write a brief statement of what that person was noted for. That's it. I've created a landing page. For children, even this much begins to familiarize names.

Then I do a Google search for images, shrink it to fit on my notebook page, and glue them on the page. Or sometimes I find wonderful illustrations in the old books on Internet Archive and I use those illustrations. I usually look for images that remind me of a story I have learned about that person and try to include a portrait painting to have a visual of what the person looked like.

The King of Sweden wrote:

His life was noble and true. He loved the study of plants, and when rich he worked just as hard to find and classify them. It was a pleasure to him to help his students, who remembered him with the greatest respect and love. When he became famous and rich he lived in the simplest and most frugal manner until his death.

Botanists have given the twin-flower the scientific family name of Linnaea. This dainty plant, with its nodding pink or white fragrant bell-shaped flowers, was a great favorite with the noted botanist.

Thriving as it does in poor soil and under rugged alpine conditions, it is a type of the wonderful life of the man for whom it is named – the man whom poverty and the most adverse circumstances could not keep from becoming truly great...

the man who was a success because HE FOLLOWED A COURSE WHICH WAS ONE OF THE GREATEST POSSIBLE INTEREST TO HIM.

Figure 29: Back side of Carolus Linnaeus page

Here are some of my landing pages.

James Russell Miller

1840 – 1912
Pennsylvania

'J.R.' "Jesus and ♥ are Friends"

OUR HEARTS MAKE OUR WORLD FOR US.

The Life of Dr. J. R. Miller
by John T. Faris (1912)
• Music was solace
• The poets were his great delight.
• It was his habit to memorize
   sentences and paragraphs
   that impressed him.
• Fond of illustrations "that
   would be like windows through
   which the visions of the soul
   might become real to others.
• Took delight in studying the
   book of Nature.

LONG WALKS IN THE COUNTRY INCREASED
HIS LOVE FOR GOD AND GOD'S WORLD AND ALL
MANKIND.

When he gifted a Bible to his brother:
   "Read this Book as a letter from the dearest
         of all friends."

PICTURES IN THE HEART (1880)
   Story of Niebuhr : His HEART was his world, and there
            was no darkness there.'

It is not so much the OUTWARD in life that we need
to have changed – as the spirit of the INNER life.

GET THE SONG IN YOUR HEART –
         AND YOU WILL HEAR SONGS ALL ABOUT YOU.

BOOKS: • A Gentle Heart   • The Garden of the Heart   • Home-Making

Figure 30: Landing Page for James Russell Miller

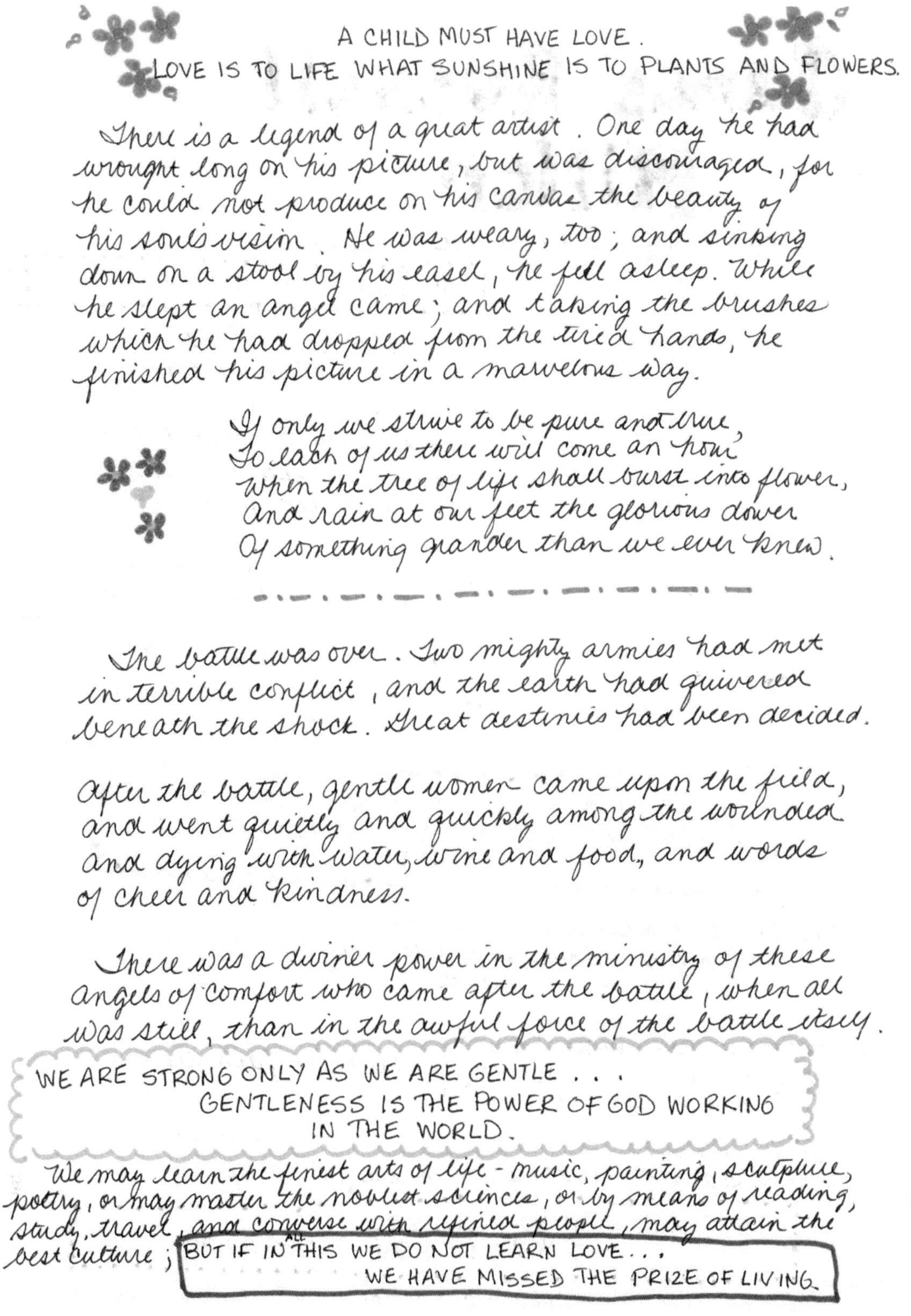

A CHILD MUST HAVE LOVE.
LOVE IS TO LIFE WHAT SUNSHINE IS TO PLANTS AND FLOWERS.

There is a legend of a great artist. One day he had wrought long on his picture, but was discouraged, for he could not produce on his canvas the beauty of his soul's vision. He was weary, too; and sinking down on a stool by his easel, he fell asleep. While he slept an angel came; and taking the brushes which he had dropped from the tired hands, he finished his picture in a marvelous way.

If only we strive to be pure and true,
To each of us there will come an hour
When the tree of life shall burst into flower,
And rain at our feet the glorious dower
Of something grander than we ever knew.

The battle was over. Two mighty armies had met in terrible conflict, and the earth had quivered beneath the shock. Great destinies had been decided.

After the battle, gentle women came upon the field, and went quietly and quickly among the wounded and dying with water, wine and food, and words of cheer and kindness.

There was a diviner power in the ministry of these angels of comfort who came after the battle, when all was still, than in the awful force of the battle itself.

WE ARE STRONG ONLY AS WE ARE GENTLE . . .
GENTLENESS IS THE POWER OF GOD WORKING
IN THE WORLD.

We may learn the finest arts of life – music, painting, sculpture, poetry, or may master the noblest sciences, or by means of reading, study, travel, and converse with refined people, may attain the best culture; BUT IF IN ALL THIS WE DO NOT LEARN LOVE...
WE HAVE MISSED THE PRIZE OF LIVING.

Figure 31: Back page of James Russell Miller

Corrie ten Boom

1892–1983

Author 'The Hiding Place'
Hid Jews in Dutch home during
Nazi occupation.

Netherlands

BETSIE   NOLLIE   PAPA   WILLEM   MAMA   CORRIE

HAPPINESS ISN'T SOMETHING THAT DEPENDS ON OUR SURROUNDINGS.
IT'S SOMETHING WE MAKE INSIDE OURSELVES.   W2 (i) - 37

LOVE is the strongest force in the world, and when it is blocked that means of PAIN p. 48

My job was simply to follow His leading one step at a time, holding every decision up to Him in PRAYER. p. 86

THERE IS NO PIT SO
DEEP THAT HE
IS NOT DEEPER STILL.

MIRACLES:
• the fleas
• keeping a Bible
• released, not executed
• right people at right places
• the house ... with flowers

THE WATCH SHOP

Figure 32: Landing Page of Corrie Ten Boom

THE 'ROOM'

I discovered that it is not on our forgiveness any more than on our goodness that the world's healing hinges, but on HIS. When He tells us to love our enemies, He gives, along with the command, THE LOVE ITSELF.
p. 231

❋ ❋ ❋ ❋ ❋

NEVER BE AFRAID TO TRUST AN UNKNOWN FUTURE TO A KNOWN GOD

I know that the experiences of our lives, when we let God use them, become the mysterious and perfect preparation for the work he will give us to do.

IF THE DEVIL CANNOT MAKE US BAD, HE WILL MAKE US BUSY.

There is no panic in Heaven!

God never measures the MIND.... He always puts His tape measure in the HE♥RT.

Don't bother to give God instructions, JUST REPORT TO DUTY.

"It's such a beautiful house, Corrie! The floors are inlaid wood, statues set in the walls, and a broad staircase. And gardens! Gardens all around it where they can plant flowers. It will do them such good to care for flowers."
– 206

PEOPLE CAN LEARN TO LOVE, FROM FLOWERS.... p. 210

And we'll need bright yellow-green paint - the color of things coming up new in the spring.

Betsie

Figure 33: Back page of Corrie Ten Boom

William Penn

Quaker founder of Pennsylvania

1644-1718
b. England
PENNSYLVAN

Said to be most accurate likeness.

* When William was ten, his highly decorated father was thrown into the Tower of London, although innocent. He had a younger sister and a baby brother. It was a frightening time. He spent hours each day reading his Bible, and meditating until he was "ravished by joy and dissolved into tears." One day, alone in his room, he was "suddenly surprised with an inward comfort and ... an external glory" that convinced him not only that God existed but also that
- he could communicate with Him
- could know His will
- feel His peace.

"THERE CAN BE NO FRIENDSHIP WHERE THERE IS NO **FREEDOM.** FREEDOM LOVES A FREE AIR, AND WILL NOT BE PENNED UP IN STRAIGHT AND NARROW ENCLOSURES."

" [NATURE] IS BOTH THE PHILOSOPHER'S GARDEN AND HIS LIBRARY, IN WHICH HE READS AND CONTEM- PLATES THE POWER, WISDOM AND GOODNESS OF GOD."

* WILLIAM PENN: QUAKER COLONIST
by Kieran Doherty

by Benjamin West

Figure 34: Landing Page for William Penn

"We meet on the pathway of good faith and good will. No advantage shall be taken on either side, but all shall be openness and love.

• I will not call you children, for parents sometimes chide their children too severely

• Nor brothers only, for brothers differ

• The friendship between me and you I will not compare to a chain, for that the rains might rust or the falling tree might break.

WE ARE THE SAME AS IF ONE MAN'S BODY WERE TO BE DIVIDED INTO TWO PARTS; WE ARE ALL ONE FLESH AND BLOOD.

NOT A DROP OF QUAKER BLOOD WAS EVER SHED BY AN INDIAN

" If the people want of me anything that would make them happier, I should readily grant it. "

♥ HIS FAREWELL ♥

" My love and my life are to you and with you, and no water can quench it nor distance bring it to an end. I have been with you, cared over you, and served you with unfeigned love; and you are beloved of me and dear to me beyond utterance. You are come to a quiet land;

LIBERTY AND AUTHORITY ARE IN YOUR HANDS.

♥ Dear friends, my love salutes you all.

(F3-62)

Figure 35: Back page of William Penn

As I flip through the book, my heart starts noticing who lived around the same time; what order things happened. It's like a timeline in a book. The pictures help provide instant recall. Pictures are worth thousands of words.

I'm not going to fill these pages with facts and trivia. I'm looking for wisdom. And stories. And quotes. And ideas. And questions I want to answer. Just like in the Literature Gems book, I don't have to copy entire passages. I just need enough so that I can retrieve it again. One thing I'll mention here—if you rely on recent books, you may not find a lot of gems. That's because recent historical books have become very informational or entertaining, but there's not much for inspiring hearts. Turn to the older books and you'll find gems all over the place.

A young child can start landing pages by drawing his or her own pictures. Here are some pages my granddaughters made about Balboa. It's interesting how they all had the same impression

Figure 36: Sample Balboa pages from granddaughters

from the story they were read that he was a mean man. In a few years, they'll hopefully revisit him with another point of view. I just finished a book: *The Honor of Balboa* and this is what this book said about him: "…unlike many of his ruthless compatriots, Balboa could not bring himself to senselessly slaughter and brutally enslave the native population. This humanitarian instinct was both his greatest source of strength and his fatal weakness."

Was he mean or wasn't he? This is the makings of critical thinking skills. Research has proven that trying to directly teach critical thinking doesn't work. What works is immersing young people in rich content where they bump into conflicting information and they have to learn to sort it out. It takes time and experience but we do them no favors by constantly only feeding them what we think is the 'correct' story. Encourage them to read widely and always be open to learning new things. Truth has a way of working its way to the top.

I like to create landing pages for my own ancestors and place them in the story of the world.

Here's a page for my Grandma Johnson from Sweden. She was a woman of incredible patience.

Esther Marie
Grandma
Lanzen
Johnson

1887-
1968
b. Sweden
Idaho

"Next time it will
be better ..."

Young Ester Lanzen - about ⌐

Ester Maria Lanzen & her father, Carl Johan Lanzen
About 1897

Ester with friend in Swedish national dress.

Figure 37: Notebook Page of my Grandmother, Esther Johnson

The other kind of page that goes in here is an Event page, but I don't have nearly as many of them. I look for key events such as the Landing of the Mayflower or the Civil War. If I think it's very significant, I'll create it on a Divider Tab like this. You'll notice there aren't a lot of

Figure 38: Sample Divider Tab

'have tos' in this because you want to allow your children to create notebooks that are meaningful to them.

As they become familiar with the lives of history, maybe they'd like to create a special book of personal heroes where they tell the stories of some of their favorites. What a great writing

169

activity. In the beginning, have them dictate the story to you. Or encourage them to create individual books of the lives they found the most interesting using Bare Books—their own Story of Joan of Arc, for example. Let them illustrate it themselves or help them do a search for Google images to add another layer to the text. As they read a variety of books reflecting different points of view, you'll recognize the beginnings of research skills. And these books they create can become real keepsakes. So much better than being assigned a report. When I visit my grandchildren, they run to bring me their books and show me what they've been learning.

Later, when they begin a formal study of history, the names will have personalities and the men and women of history will come to life, even becoming teachers, mentors and friends.

For instance, a couple of weeks ago, for some reason, my website started acting squirrely and I couldn't publish new content. We contacted support and the more they worked on it, the worse it got. Chunks of the website started disappearing until it was completely gone.

Several days later, we were told that it looked like a lower level support person had accidentally deleted all our content and there was apparently no back up.

I was devastated. I had spent hundreds if not thousands of hours over several years putting together the content. There were over 3,000 books I had personally hunted for, selected and reviewed, organized and linked. I had found many of them in obscure, round about ways and I didn't think I could ever find them again. And there were hundreds of other links to music and other resources that would be impossible to duplicate.

I couldn't imagine starting over again. I was heartsick. And, yes, tears were involved. And I found myself thinking of just walking away from it all. It was too overwhelming to begin again. (That moment of crisis has happened more than once!) In the middle of my pity party, Thomas Carlyle stepped into a room in my heart and pulled up a chair. "Oh, Marlene," he said, "I know how you feel." He had spent months of hard labor and painstaking research on a book about the French Revolution. He and his wife were destitute and they were counting on the sale of the book to pay some way overdue bills. He gave his only manuscript to a friend to look it over before sending it off to a publisher. When he didn't hear from his friend for quite some time, he stopped by his house only to discover the housekeeper thought the manuscript was rubbish and had been using it to light the fire. It was gone and Carlyle had already destroyed his notes.

Sir Isaac Newton got wind of our conversation and stopped by, too. "Ah, yes, he said, I remember well…" He had stacks of papers on his desk containing years of observations and data. His favorite little dog accidentally knocked over his lamp and the papers went up in flames.

Then John Audubon pulled up a chair, shaking his head in sympathy. He had spent years tramping out in the wilds in search of rare and unusual birds and had painted detailed drawings of them. He had over 200 of them. He had to travel East for a time, but when he got home to Kentucky, he found the rats had eaten them all.

And then a new friend of mine stopped by—Orison Swett Marden. I knew what a hard life he'd had. As he overcame his challenges, he wanted to help other people who were discouraged and down on their luck. So he had spent years gathering stories and anecdotes to compile into a book. One night as he stayed in a hotel, someone yelled, "Fire." He made it outside with just the clothes on his back. But all his hard work went up in flames.

They understood what I was feeling all right. But then, one by one, they reminded me how they picked themselves up out of their depression and began again. This time, Carlyle wrote straight from his heart. Critics say no one has ever brought the French Revolution to life as Carlyle did. The book has never been out of print since the day it was published and it even inspired Dickens to write his *Tale of Two Cities*.

After weeks of deep depression, Audubon determined he would begin again and this time make his drawings even better. No one has brought the bird world up close and personal like Audubon. Marden, too, began collecting new stories. It was said that Marden, a hundred years ago, was personally responsible for inspiring millions of people around the world who were down on their luck to pick themselves up and try again.

William Bradford, leader of the Mayflower Pilgrims, was a little late to the conversation, but he stopped by to remind me, "Marlene, all great and honorable actions are accompanied with great difficulties, and must be overcome with answerable courage." When half of the 106 pilgrims lost their lives that first winter, with most of the survivors among the 39 children, it took great courage to turn down the Mayflower captain who offered to take them home to England. Thank goodness, for us, they stayed.

My friends from history lifted me up and encouraged me to start again if I had to. And before they left, I promised them I would.

Fortunately, in this case, I had a much easier outcome than they had. A few days later, someone higher up in the support chain was able to get to the bottom of the problem and restore everything. But I thought to myself—this is the blessing of studying the lives of the men and women of history.

No matter what you are facing, no matter what your children will face, there is someone from the pages of history or from the pages of literature to show the way through. The child—or grown up—whose reservoir of stories is broad and deep will more likely possess a heart that will not fail. Faces, alone, cannot do that.

A mom in our group said her 14-year-old son had a copy of his Story of the World notebook in his hands one day, and, looking at it, he said, "If people knew what was inside of this, they would know this is a priceless treasure."

And so it is.

Which brings me to the final notebook and probably the most important one. The Alcott children were encouraged to keep diaries from the time they were little in which they wrote down their thoughts and feelings and fancies—Louisa called her's her Heart Journal. My experience I just shared will go into my Heart Journal as well as other times I find my life influenced by my friends from History and Literature. But that's not all. Orison Swett Marden wrote:

Where do writers find all those interesting things they write about? They find them because they are always on the lookout for them... Just think how many curious, interesting things you have forgotten or lost in your life simply because you did not make them permanently yours by taking the pains to jot them down... Even if you never become a writer, the notebook habit would enrich your life wonderfully, and make you a much fuller, a more complete, more worthwhile man or woman.

In a different book, Marden wrote of a certain aged woman who always had an air of serenity about her and was approached by a woman who was weighed down with life's troubles and cares and wanted to know her secret of calm. The aged woman replied:

I keep a Pleasure Book. Long ago I learned that there is no day so dark and gloomy that it does not contain some ray of light, and I have made it one business of my life to write down the little things which mean so much to a woman. I have a book marked for every day for every year since I left school. It is but a little thing: the new gown, the chat with a friend, the thoughtfulness of my husband, a flower, a book, a walk in the field, a letter, a concert, or a drive; but it all goes into my Pleasure Book, and when I am inclined to fret, I read but a few pages to see what a happy, blessed woman I am. You may see my treasure if you will.

The fretful woman glanced through it, even noticing the entry: "He died with his hand in mine and my name upon his lips." Laced throughout were bits of verses and lines from her daily reading, making its pages a storehouse of truth and beauty.

"He gets the most out of life who realizes the latent treasures invisible to most eyes; who sees beauties and graces where others see only ugliness, deformity."

What a simple but far-reaching habit—to sit down with a young child at the end of each day and jot down even one small thing that brought him or her joy that day in the beginnings of that child's heart journal. By such a simple means, great lives are formed.

So, in summary:

For your preschoolers, start by helping them making notebooks with pictures of favorite things.

Teach them to draw before you teach them to form letters. Draw from nature whenever possible. Be sure your preschoolers get to watch you.

Around age 4, start poetry books, beginning with Mother Goose rhymes, in preparation for creating anthologies of favorite poetry.

At 5, create Favorite Fairy Tale books in preparation for creating notebooks for Literature Gems. By 6 or 7, include children in a World Cultures notebook, either personal or family, with maps, recipes, holiday celebrations, games and places you hope to visit.

By 8, set up Story of the World notebooks with landing pages for people and events.

Finally, encourage the keeping of a Heart Journal.

If you live in a school district that requires proof of subjects taught, your Literature Gems and

Heart Journal reflects a correct usage of grammar, spelling, writing and a study of literature.

Your World Cultures notebook and Story of the World reflects the study of Geography, Social Science and History as well as Art and Music, critical thinking and research skills. Your Nature Journals demonstrate a study of scientific topics.

Keep track of the books you have read as further proof of learning. I guarantee it will far exceed the number of books read in a traditional classroom.

There are many, many free resources for you to use to accomplish all the things I've been talking about at welleducatedheart.com. It may feel overwhelming when you first get there and even moms who have been using our site for awhile will say to me, "I had no idea that was there!" The Take 5s will further orient you to the resources available to you.

I'll close with this poem from a 13th Century Persian poet:

> If, of thy mortal goods, thou art bereft,
> And from thy slender store two loaves alone to thee are left,
> Sell one and from the dole,
> Buy Hyacinths to feed the soul.

As you Notebook for your heart, may you and your children find many "Hyacinths to feed your souls."

Using the Planner

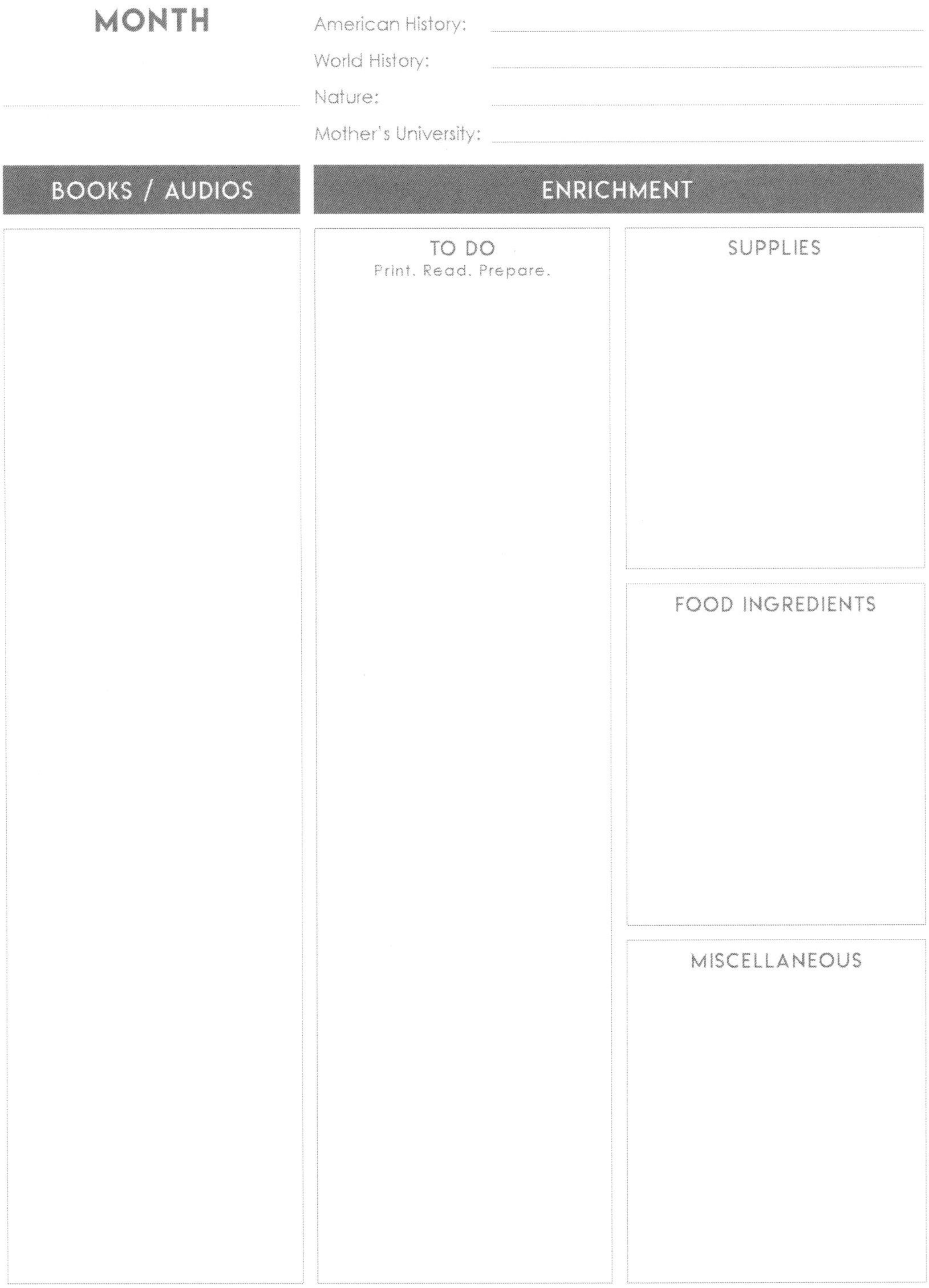

MONTH

American History: ....

World History: ....

Nature: ....

Mother's University: ....

....

BOOKS / AUDIOS	ENRICHMENT	
	TO DO Print. Read. Prepare.	**SUPPLIES**
		FOOD INGREDIENTS
		MISCELLANEOUS

Figure 39: Sample Monthly Planner Page from the WEH Planner

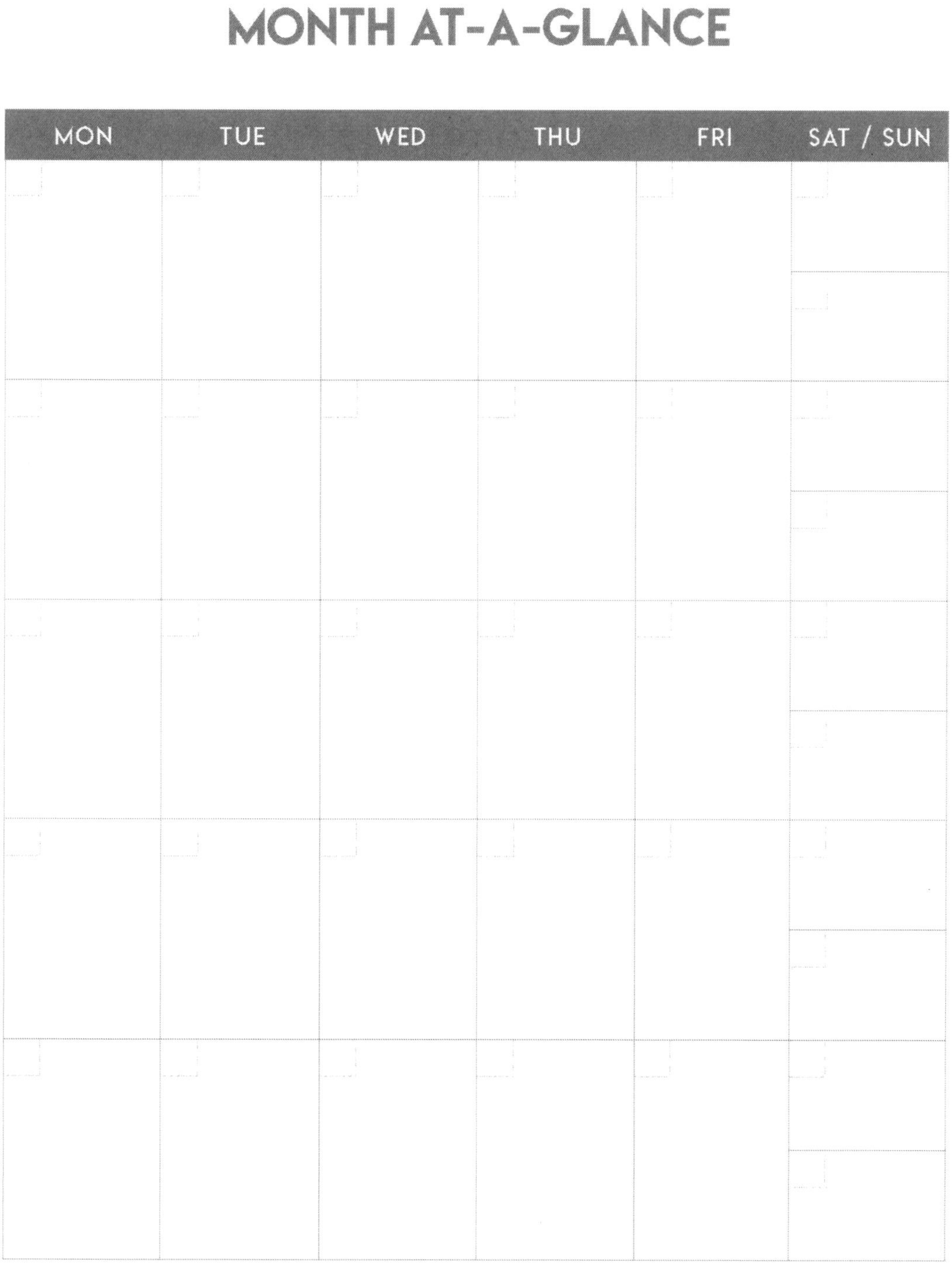

MONTH AT-A-GLANCE

MON	TUE	WED	THU	FRI	SAT / SUN

Figure 40: Sample Month-at-a-Glance Page from the WFH Planner

Notes:

Figure 41: Notes Page from the WEH Planner

WEEK 1

Ⓜ Music Ⓐ Art Ⓟ Poetry Ⓢ Stories Ⓝ Nature

MONDAY Ⓜ Ⓐ Ⓟ Ⓢ Ⓝ

TUESDAY Ⓜ Ⓐ Ⓟ Ⓢ Ⓝ

WEDNESDAY Ⓜ Ⓐ Ⓟ Ⓢ Ⓝ

THURSDAY Ⓜ Ⓐ Ⓟ Ⓢ Ⓝ

FRIDAY Ⓜ Ⓐ Ⓟ Ⓢ Ⓝ

SATURDAY	SUNDAY

Figure 42: Sample Weekly Planner Page from the WEH Planner

177

Over the years I have used a number of systems to manage meal planning in our family. There was a time there were 11 of us around the dinner table. I'll tell you what didn't work. Having no plan. I would have dinner weighing over me all day, wondering what we were going to eat that night. Finally 5:00 would roll around when I finally had time to pull out the recipes—I had a million recipe books—and after I finally decided on something, I'd have to run to the store to get the ingredients and when I got home, I still had the cooking ahead. By then everyone was starving and we'd order pizza.

What has worked the very best—and it's what I use today—is to sit down once a week to plan. Rather than pulling out a million recipe books, I made a couple of recipe books that have all our family favorites. I know anything I choose from these books, the family will like. I still like to try out new recipes, so I keep them together so when I feel like getting adventurous, I maybe pull out one to work into the weekly menu. And if it's a hit, it will eventually go into my main cookbook.

I make out my shopping list and shop for the week and write down the meals on a whiteboard on my fridge. Now there's no worrying about what we are going to eat. There's flexibility in the system because I can choose anything from the seven meals on any given day. So if it's been a hectic day, I'll pick a simple prep one. Or if I'm going to be gone all day, I'll choose the crockpot meal. And when I choose the meals, I keep a variety in mind in that way—quick fixes, crockpots, and so forth.

And then there's one more thing—I go for color. Have you ever noticed that everything man makes ends up being brown or gray? We make brown cookies, brown bread, brown casseroles, brown brownies. We make gray houses and gray buildings and gray streets. But everything God makes is full of color! The blue sky and the green grass and the pink roses. Same with His food—purple grapes, orange oranges, bright yellow lemons, red peppers, green artichokes. The more we put color into a meal, the healthier our meals are. It's that simple. Granted, ketchup might fit that bill, but the base of it is still God's—the red tomatoes. So I fill my shopping cart with color to fit around my menu choices and the goal is always how much color can I fit into my meal? If I make a green salad, instead of just lettuce and tomatoes, I'll add carrots or radishes or purple cabbage. All the real nutrients of a meal are in the color. And isn't it interesting that the most nutrient dense foods of all are fruits? I think God made them sweet so that we will eat them. Some people tell us to avoid them because of the sugar content. They would keep us gnawing on kale chips all day—not that kale isn't healthy. But by avoiding the fruit, we miss out on all the health benefits.

I hope you can see the connection—the most nutrient dense type of learning you will feed your children and your own heart are the Arts and they taste the sweetest. They add the color to all your learning.

Now my meal planning is done for the week. We still go out to eat on the spur of the moment sometimes, but it's not nearly as often as before I used this system. And we are eating so much healthier. I can now go about doing the other things I need to do without worrying about what's for dinner. I know I have what I need.

This is the reasoning behind the planner. You may have your own system—go with it. But if you are looking for a way to manage these things you're learning, you might want to give this a try. It was designed to be adaptable to many different personality types. If you are one who needs detailed schedules, you can use it for that. It can be used to plan in advance or can be used as a record of what you did. And while I am suggesting ways for use in a homeschooling family, a woman can use this to fit jewels into the lives of her family if they are in public school or private school or if you have no children, it can be used to plan for your own personal study each month.

I've included some sample blank pages here for a visual. You can print out planning sheets for free (look in Section 5 of the intro course) or my daughter has designed a lovely colorful planner with watercolor floral designs in the background, if you like pretty, that can be purchased in our store. There is also a less expensive black and white version if you want to buy several for your children rather than print them out yourself. They are available in the store. You may want to spiral bind them after you get them. But it's not necessary.

While you will probably be the main planner in the beginning, your goal is to help your children do their own planning of their months as soon as they are ready to be more independent. Plan together for awhile until they get used to it. Make a date night of it if you want where you can talk about what was learned in the previous month and where they want to go next.

This learning lifestyle is meant to integrate into life, not to be separate. I hope you can let go of the idea that you need to block off a time for school and that school is some painful thing you just have to do. If it becomes something you need a break from, I would say you need to re-evaluate what you are doing. Learning and life go seamlessly together. And it tastes sweet.

The first thing you want to do is put all the things on your month at a glance calendar that you know are happening—doctor appointments, music lessons, classes, church activities—whatever there is. Now you can put your mind at ease—they are planned for—no surprises. You know what you have to work around.

Next, choose your topics for the month. Even if you are using the rotation schedule, you can fit it into your year however you want. The only part that is in an order is American History and actually the first half is mostly colonial times and the second half is after we were formed as a nation. The American history topic does tie into a world history topic, though. The only advantage of following it by the months I designated is that when I do podcasts or recommend things or others in the group recommend ideas, it will likely be from the month that is designated.

Now you are going to go shopping for all the ingredients you'll need for the month so that you're not always scrambling to figure out what you're going to do. You'll have all the craft supplies, all the art prints, all the ingredients for the food, etc. on hand.

So let's go on a sample shopping trip. Let's shop for France. Going to the online library is like going to the family favorite recipe books I created. These books are there because they are consistently the favorites. You won't go wrong with whatever you choose. Although, of course your children have different tastes and if they don't like something after they've tried a few bites, pull out something different. You'll want to select more than you will probably get through just to allow for adjusting to individual tastes. Along the way, you'll find books that aren't on this list. Jot them down in the month they'll apply to and when you get to that month, there they are. You can work them into your schedule.

If you haven't listened to the developmental ages presentations, you might want to do that. It, too, helps to narrow down choices. I'm going to say that I have a preschooler, so I'm going to pick some books out of the picture book section. Just a heads up—although I preview the books, just because it's a picture book doesn't necessarily mean a pre-schooler will like it. So stay flexible. Some I may want to see if my library has them, so I'm going to put an L next to the books I list in the Books section on the planning page. This is really my shopping list. So now I can see which books I need to pick up from the library. Other titles I really think I want to buy and keep in my library so I make a note of those titles and put a little dollar sign next to them. We have created a pdf list of all the titles you will find in my library. You can find a free pdf by topic on the landing pages. Or you can buy a complete book list in the store. You'll want to have this reference nearby as well. Go through your personal library and see if you already have books in the list and mark them in the box. That's an easy way to see what you have on hand. As you read the books, just highlight them with a colored highlighter so when you come around next year, you can remember quickly what you have already read. Your older children will want to have their own individual book lists to keep track of their reading. This replaces the reading logs I used to suggest. There is plenty of white space on the pages to add books that aren't on the list.

I'm going to say I also have a child in the imaginative age, so I want to be sure and include some French fairy tales, but I know all my kids will enjoy those. Now I go through and select some books for my older children—and if they're old enough, I have them help narrow the choices. Would you like to read this book about such and such or do you think you'd rather do this one? The more you give them ownership, the more motivated they'll be. The main thing at this stage is just to make sure you have the books on hand, whether they need to be borrowed from the library or bought or pulled from your own shelves. Go for color and variety—a little fiction, a little biography, a little history, a little nature, a little culture. I think my 7-year-old will like *Our Little French Cousin*. My teen is ready for an overall history of France and Mary MacGregor's looks like a good one. I think we'll do a family classic for an evening family read-aloud. When I create my menus, I go for variety. I don't want a whole week of chicken or a whole week of Mexican food. I like to mix it all up.

Now you can turn to the enrichment page. If you are a crafting family, then pick out a few crafts you want to do at some point in the month. The main thing right now is to write down the supplies you need so that you are sure you have everything on hand. The same for the food. If you're going to have a cultural night, pick a night and plan it on your calendar and now you can transfer the ingredients you need from this shopping list to your main shopping list.

Take a look at the plays. Is there one that will work for your family? Print it out so that you have the parts for everyone. Make a note in your to-do section.

Take a look at the art—you can choose a couple to print out and display and study or have your kids help you. Same with the music. The thing about the art and the music is it can be spontaneous or you can plan specifically for which one you want to do and when you want to do it. Art goes on the planning page if you want to have a printed copy of it. In the music section, there are some selections that have a story connected to them. They are short and sweet. I suggest previewing a couple and seeing which ones you think will appeal the most to your children and jot those down. The rest of the music can be spontaneous.

Also, plan for family movie times. Pick out the movies that look interesting—check them out at IMDB to make sure they're appropriate for your family, and note whether you will be able to stream them or if you need to track down a copy. Put that on your to-do list.

Now you know you have on hand what you need for the month. And you won't be scrambling every day to figure something out. It's like you have loaded your pockets with jewels and you're like the fairy godmother watching for opportunities to gift them. These jewels are the Arts—Music, Pictures, Poetry and Story. They provide the nutrient-dense color to your day. And they are sweet to eat.

It's common among homeschool moms to constantly feel like life is getting in the way of school. I'd like to make the suggestion that you reverse that and make sure school isn't getting in the way of life.

Now you can turn to your week-at-a-glance page and you can either roughly plan things out, or you can develop a sort of rhythm to your day. But a gentle reminder—don't get so structured that there is no room for inspiration. Maybe connect breakfast with a story of a great life or lunch with a nature story. Allow time for free reading. Take time to read individually and as a family. But your day isn't going to be all reading. Your younger children needs lots of time for free unstructured imaginative play. You want to get outside as much as possible. You want variety to your day.

The little letters you see—m a p s n—are gentle reminders to work a little music, a little art, a little poetry, a story, some nature—in every day. When you do, just put an x through the letter. If you go for several days without any poetry, you may make it a higher priority to do some poetry on the next day. Or if you've missed music for awhile, or art, this reminds you. It's not a chore lord! Just a simple way to keep track and make it a mindful effort.

Back to establishing a rhythm to your day. Maybe you'll choose to practice handwriting after lunch. Put some music on from the month's selection as a background or an audio story to listen to. Little ones can draw circles and lines or pictures to help develop those fine motor skills. In fact, the more things you find to keep your children's hands busy, the more read-aloud time you'll be able to engage them in. Teach them to knit—even the boys. That's a part of the Waldorf schools. Let them color. Even build with legos. Or combine their crafts with music or audio stories.

I have tried to make the resources as spontaneous as possible for you to fit into the flow of your day, if that's your personality. If you have *My Book House* or *Junior Classics*, or Forgotten Classics, when you are first starting out, you may want to lean more heavily on those stories.

And like I said, if little hands are busy, if your children's attention spans are short, it will help to stretch them. These stories provide a quick grab and go. Just highlight them in your book list after you read them.

Don't stress about fitting into the developmental schedule. It's a general guideline. Kids have a way of self-selecting. If you start reading a story to your whole family and it's above the head of a younger child, he or she will likely wander off. Let them. But often they'll take in more than you expect. Listening level far exceeds reading level.

On your weekly calendar, jot down when you want to have a poetry tea time. You can even plan on adding a little music appreciation or art appreciation in connection with your poetry tea time. In the beginning, maybe plan just one afternoon a week for notebooking. You can plan for it in your week-at-a-glance page. Eventually, your children will do it far more often, but this gets them started. Make it an event! Put on some music. Put some cookies or some kind of treat on the table and colored markers and stickers and pictures. Be sure you work on notebooking pages, too.

Jot down on your calendar when you want to have a cultural night. Maybe they have crafted some decorations. Let them help cook the food and plan the night. Maybe it will be in connection with your cultural night that you perform your play—or just do your read-aloud theater if it's just your family. Talk about the things you've been learning about—or your favorite things you've done.

I left a full page blank in the calendar each week and in other places in the planner to adapt it to your needs. Some of you like to do bullet point journaling. The blank note page gives you a place to do it. Some of you may want to use it as a record of what you have done. You could take pictures of your cultural night or crafting or outings and print them out and glue them on a page. So this planning journal could become a remembrance journal as well. If you have to report what you are doing, this gives you the reference to go back to.

Or the blank page can be where you jot down ideas you come across. Maybe you're in the France month and you come across a fun idea or resource for Germany—jot it down on the Germany page so that when you get to that month, you can remember you want to work it in.

In the back of the deluxe colored planner from our store are pages for notes from your monthly Mother's University study if you're doing that. And if you are part of a Mothers of Influence group, you can put contact info on that page. The black and white planners in the store do not have this section as it will more likely be used by your children.

I hope you can catch the vision of this. You've already selected the books. What might I take along to the doctor's office to read while we're waiting? What might we listen to in the car on the way to music lessons? My daily goal is to gift my children with at least a few lines of a poem, some music, a story and something beautiful to look at—Goethe's 4 jewels for happy living. It's all the colors added to the meals of your life. Just one story, one poem a day becomes thousands of stories and poems stored up in a child's heart before he leaves home. If I at least did that much, I'm doing something lasting and worthwhile. These jewels can fit into the busiest of schedules—if you have the ingredients on hand.

Let me try and unfold how this may all look like in the course of a day. Well, we always eat breakfast and lunch, so I'm going to attach a story to each one. I think I'll attach a fairy tale to breakfast. It's primarily for my Imaginative age child, but everyone can listen. My toddler may wander away, and that's OK. My teen will probably stick around because no one is too old to enjoy a well-told fairy tale. In fact, I may see if my teenager wants to take a turn reading one.

With the fairy tale fresh in their minds, my imaginative kids will run off for free play time. They may want to draw the fairy tale or maybe they'll play dress up and act it out or maybe they'll pull out the blocks and create a fairy castle and re-enact the story. Don't assign it for heaven's sake! Force always kills the fun. But you can light the desire to draw the fairy tale, for instance, by you drawing it. With an imagination stored with stories, imaginative play is the natural course of action. It's how a child digests the story. Play is the work of childhood —unstructured, free, wonderful play. Don't get in the way, although in the beginning, you may need to play with them just to show them. But usually kids figure it out for themselves.

While they're off playing, older children will engage in their projects. Maybe this is when you can work in some math or writing projects. Or I may see my 8-year-old playing with Legos or invite him to play with Legos and ask him if I can read a story to him? And read him the story of Roland. Or maybe that's when I'll let him listen to the story of Lafayette. Or we'll put on some music and work on notebooking, whether it's copying poetry, writing out recipes, copying passages from books we've read for our great souls notebook or our literature keepsakes.

Maybe I'll ask a child to read to me while I'm fixing lunch or I'll ask if they want me to read to them while they're cleaning their room or folding their clothes. And we'll definitely want to sing while we work! That used to be so common for families to sing while they worked. It adds the sparkle to what they're doing. The work around home doesn't have to be a dreaded chore that has to get done before we can do anything else. It's part of life—teaching children the art of making a home is one of the great life gifts you can offer them and it is happening throughout the day. Making a bed may be a chore; running outside and picking a flower to put next to it turns it into an art.

When I'm nursing the baby, I can see if my 4-year-old wants to sit next to me and we'll watch one of the music videos together on my tablet after I read the story that goes with it. If I've stocked my house with games and creative and appealing learning materials, mostly I need to get out of the way.

I've watched this with my daughter's little girls. The 6-year-old will pull some books out and start copying the words because her heart saw others doing it and she wants to do it, too. Or her 4-year-old came to her mom and asked, "Will you teach me to read?" That's a whole different scenario than mom saying, "OK, you're four, I'm now going to teach you how to read." I can tell you how that would go over.

Boredom is the friend of imagination and initiative. And I can tell you with 100% confidence— electronic devices can be your worst enemy. You have to restrict their use in your house or they will wreak havoc. Don't take the role of entertainer and cruise director. Avoid structuring every moment. It is healthy for children to feel some control over their lives. Don't constantly feel like you need to ask them questions about what they're reading—silence is often the best teacher. But do engage in spontaneous conversation.

Continuing on with the day…I know we're going to eat lunch every day, so I'm going to add a story about nature to lunch most days. Just one story is good—then I'll sent them out to play and digest it. If you happen to notice the dandelions springing up in the grass, let that story be about a dandelion. Don't assign them to go out and find a dandelion and write up a report— just send them on their way. And you'll likely hear, "Mom! Guess what! We found a dandelion—and look!" And they'll re-tell you the things they just heard in the story.

Or maybe you told them a story about ants, and they'll find an ant hill and lie down on their stomachs and watch it for a long time because you've given their hearts something to watch for. And now they'll really remember it because they are seeing it with their own eyes.

Older kids may stay inside and read something that's interesting to them or work on math or whatever they have planned for themselves. When the younger kids come back inside, some will hopefully take a nap, or you can establish a time for quiet activities. Every day will probably look different. Life is like that—full of variety. And you know what they say—variety IS the spice of life. Going grocery shopping with you and watching how you engage with the grocer and other people is school. Helping you cook is school. Helping you do laundry is school. Helping you plant flowers is school. Starting hobbies is school. Making and taking cookies to the widow down the street is school. Sitting and being quiet sometimes is school. Because life is school in childhood. And in some magical way that nature has provided for, all those childhood academics that you're tearing your hair out trying to get your kids to do, will naturally happen, all along the way. I am watching it happen with my grandchildren. And they each are doing it on their own timetables and in their own ways. Individual personalities and gifts are manifesting themselves because there is freedom for that to happen.

And now I want to suggest one more thing—the golden hour of the day. If there is one hour in the day that is worth all the others to reclaim in your life, it's the family story hour just before bedtime. Do whatever you can to protect it. And if you only had this family story hour, it can compensate for a LOT of what else happened in the day. This is the hour I reserve in my imaginary scenario here for the family classics—I'm going to choose books like *Heidi* and *The Secret Garden* and *Understood Betsy* and *Swiss Family Robinson* because these books will impress upon children's hearts what strong family relationships look like; how loving families treat each other. The books don't all start out that way, but in the end, strong bonds of love overcome all challenges and difficulties. These families all look different—some are with a grandparent or an aunt and uncle. Many of the families are in crisis—but the underlying spirit of the story is always bonds of love will see it through. And these stories begin to suggest to children's hearts ways to spend their time—they show children what life looks like. They start to paint a picture what a Well-Educated Heart learning style looks like. And then you can add in other works of literature as your children get older.

No one is ever too old for read-aloud time. It's that voice thing.

I love the story of Maria von Trapp from *The Sound of Music*. Here's a gem I copied down when

I read her story:

> After supper came the most beautiful time of the day, the evenings spent together. A fire was lit in the fireplace. The older girls brought their knitting, the younger ones, their dolls; the boys and their father usually worked on wood, carving or whittling; and I, settling in a most comfortable chair, started to read aloud. It is most amazing how much literature you can cover during the long winter evenings. We read fairy tales and legends, historical novels and biographies, and the works of the great masters of prose and poetry.

And then they'd sing.

After you finish reading, tuck your children in bed with beautiful scriptural language floating through their heads and a prayer. And a sense that home is good. I love how it smells. I love how it feels. And I love my family. Life is good. Life is happy.

And so go our days and our month is over. You may still have jewels in your pocket that never got handed out. That's OK. Because you're going to be back again next year and the year after and the year after that. No worries. It's a journey, not a destination.

This journey will look different for every one of you. I'm sure I've stirred up more questions than answers. I cannot begin to prescribe what will fit with your family and style. I've just tried to paint some possibilities. And do I think your days will be all sunshine and rainbows? Of course not! There will be noises and messes and some days, pure chaos. But no one ever climbed higher by reaching beneath them. Just giving you an ideal to reach upwards towards.

Some mothers say I just don't have time to do these things. Well, there is a law of the harvest. You cannot reap what you do not sow. Start simple. Even one tiny seed will eventually give you a flower. Plant what you can.

Use the planner to make it work for you. Knowing you have whatever you need will take a huge weight off your shoulders and you'll learn by doing. Let me stress again. If you are thinking grade level, you are thinking like a technician. These are general guidelines. If you have a 13-year-old who missed all the developmental stages I talked about, you haven't ruined his life. Think Familiar first—what's familiar to him that you can connect to and build from. Or maybe you need to familiarize him with more things with short, high-interest stories. And just because age 8 is a good age to introduce King Arthur doesn't mean that you'll never read King Arthur at any other age. It's just that a 4-year-old probably isn't going to be interested. Yet. Neither can you hand a book of history to a 14-year-old and expect him to care about it if you don't pick up some shorter, engaging stories to kindle the desire first and if he has no imagination to picture what he is reading about.

I hope that makes sense.

This planner helps you plan the learning you will do, but also provides a record of what you have done so that next year, when you plan again, you can refer to what you already did. Make it something memorable! Include pictures!

I can only offer a glimpse of this path less traveled, but if heart-based learning resonates in your heart and you want to incorporate it in your home, I suggest a gradual change while you are learning. The hardest diet for me to maintain is the one where I throw out all the familiar foods in my kitchen and try to incorporate a whole new eating lifestyle at once. That's a recipe for disaster. Gradual works best. Start adding in the jewels to your day as you feel comfortable and it feels familiar to you—read a little more, play a little more classical music. Memorize a few lines of poetry. Spend more time in nature. Play more games together. And use the summer months to declutter and simplify your life by clearing out the junk if that's a problem and keep warming your own heart. The more jewels in your heart, the more they will flow out naturally and effortlessly.

I hope this planner will help create a little order to your day.

Take 5s

Take 5.1—Welcome

(There is a short YouTube connected with this Take 5 you will want to watch.)

I used to get frustrated when someone would tell me that they had gone through the entire Catch the Vision course, and then they'd ask me a question that would make me think, "What?? You made it all the way through and you have no idea that there is a library of 4,000 books you can read for free online? You don't know that you need to click on the little heart to open the book up? You don't know there are music suggestions? You have no idea there are Pinterest pages of craft ideas or planners or any number of details that somehow got missed?"

And I'd wonder how can this be?

Well, I believe it's this gorilla factor. Our brains can't take the whole of anything in the first round. Advertisers know that—they know a potential customer has to hear, on average, an ad seven times before it sinks in. Furthermore, we tend to look for that which we are most interested in or that we connect to or have a need to know and automatically tune the other things out. Maybe you just weren't ready for some of the details yet. Which, by the way, is the same for our children as they learn. We can't explain something once and expect them to grasp and hold on to the whole of it.

So my purpose in creating this little supplemental course is to go back now and do some freeze frames. Look—the gorilla is walking across the stage. Look—the curtain just changed color. Because once you are made aware of those things, you will likely never miss the gorilla or curtain change again.

I am assuming you have gone through the Catch the Vision course and you have a desire to learn more. If you haven't gone through it, I encourage you to still do that, but you can do it while you are going through these Take 5 activities. The purpose of that class was exactly what it says—it was intended to help you Catch the Vision of what a heart-based education is all about. But I knew it wouldn't answer all your questions.

There is a layering process in learning that as you layer in line upon line, one day it seems like the understanding suddenly pops. It's like the light goes on. I have a friend who I met about four years ago, and we have spent a lot of time talking about educational philosophies. She's been trying to wrap her mind around what I am teaching. Well, she attended the class I taught in Logan a couple of weeks ago, and afterwards she called me—with tears—"I get it! I finally get it! And it is so beautiful!" What had happened was she experienced something she had never experienced before and it was like a whole new world—a whole new facet of learning opened up to her and she was so excited.

That is what I want for you. And even if the light has gone on, I want to make sure that you have as many tools in your toolbox as I can possibly give you.

I'm going to plant some seeds of ideas in you and if you give them a chance to take root, one day I hope they will bear some delicious fruit in your life. Nothing here is rocket science—you can 'know' it pretty quickly, but that isn't the same as understanding and applying. It's best to take just a couple of minutes every day so we can do some freeze frames and isolate just one little thing. And then try it on for size and see if it fits. You have to experience this kind of learning to really understand.

So here is the promise. I'll keep the sessions short. "Take 5" means 5 minutes. And then I'll give you something to do on most days. Something to try out. Something to add to your toolbox.

To make this habit easier, I have an app you can download to your phone. It's free. From this app, you will be able to quickly access your daily Take 5 activity as well as new announcements, inspiring quotes, the navigation page on the website, podcasts, the mother's university, catch the vision, the Facebook group, the store and other things. Go to Google Play or iTunes to download the app. Search for well-educated heart or libraries of hope and you will see a little apple heart icon. So if you are waiting in line at the store, or sitting in the car waiting to pick up one of your kids and have a couple of minutes, just click on the app and come spend a couple of minutes with me.

Take 5.2—Paint by Number

This week I want to make sure you have a few basic tools in place. Then, starting next week, the first day will cover a general topic or principle. Then day two will be music. Day three, art. Day four, poetry. Day five, story and day six, nature. I'm not suggesting to you that this is how you should organize your learning and your life. But in the beginning, it may provide just enough structure to ensure that you're getting a well-rounded view of this process of educating hearts.

Before we go any further, although most people who come to the well-educated heart are homeschool parents, these things I teach are not exclusively for homeschoolers. Your children may be in public school or private school now or in the future. Or maybe they're all grown up. Or maybe you've never had children. The principles and resources still apply and will be useful. Everything you learn will bless and enrich your own life as well as your relationships. So I don't want you to feel excluded, even though I may lean more heavily on the homeschool side. I trust you to have the maturity to sift through that which will be of most value to you in your personal circumstances.

Let me try again to find a way to illustrate the difference between what we are doing here versus traditional curriculums. Do you remember doing a paint-by-numbers kit? As a kid, you got a set of pre-mixed paints with numbers on them and a picture divided out by sections with corresponding numbers.

All you had to do was paint all the number one areas with the number one, paint the number two areas with the number to paint and so forth. It actually can be very satisfying to watch the picture start to come together. And in the end your painting matches the painting on the cover. You don't need an artistic bone in your body to do it. Anyone can do it.

Taking over responsibility for the education of your child can be very scary and a risky proposition. I totally understand why a mom often searches for a paint-by-number curriculum. She's very busy and often feels inadequate. She just wants something that, every day, she can just open it up and all the learning is all laid out for her. So, what's the downside? Well, to me, the downside is you have painted someone else's picture, someone else's vision. Someone who doesn't have any idea what your child's unique talents, abilities, personality or even divine mission is. It takes no account of your personal circumstances or home life. Everyone who picks up the same paint by number kit will end up with the same picture at the end. Unfortunately, you won't learn any creative artistic skills along the way. You will be dependent on purchasing paint-by-number kits in the future for all your learning needs.

I frequently hear conversations between moms—So what curriculum are you using? What method are you using? And she might respond: Jenny Phillips' Good and Beautiful or Sonlight or Beautiful Feet or Gentle Feast. All wonderful curriculums. In fact, someone may say she follows Charlotte Mason's method or the Waldorf or the Montessori method, which are all heart-based methods, by the way.

But really what that often means is that they have found someone who has put together a Charlotte Mason paint by number kit or a Montessori paint by number kit. Someone else has interpreted the method and put together the books you should read and the activities you should do, taking the pressure off of you to organize the learning yourself.

I won't fault anyone for using them. It may be exactly what you need to get started, but I suspect you are here because you feel like you are missing out on something. And in the beginning, you may come hoping to find the well-educated heart paint-by-number kit and you may leave because you won't find it. That's because my desire and intention is to train you to be an educational artist and not just an ordinary artist, a master artist, someone with the confidence and skills and vision to paint a masterpiece that is uniquely yours. When someone asks you what curriculum or what methods you are using, I want you to be able to say with confidence and without apology that you were using the 'fill in your own name in the blank' method of education. And ultimately, my hope is that your children will become apprentices to you and learn the tools and tips of the trade so they can be educational artists too. Heaven forbid that you ever say I am using Marlene Peterson's curriculum or even the well-educated heart curriculum. That would be a knife in my heart.

When aspiring artists of the Renaissance wanted to develop their skills, they flocked to Italy to learn from the Masters. They imitated what they were doing as part of the learning process. But the immortal artists were the ones who eventually found their own style. I can recognize a painting by Van Gogh or Rembrandt or Monet, and I bet you can, too. I believe I have discovered a community of master artists of heart education, our own Italy, if you will. And most of what I have been doing is trying to find a way for you to gather to them and learn from them based on their recommendations. I have been pulling together the brushes and paints and resources, but you must develop the heart of an artist to use them to full effect. Even these resources can be turned into a paint-by-number kit. Resisting the urge to do so is one of the biggest challenges you are going to face.

Now, I realize this all must sound very vague and likely intimidating, but let me assure you, the process flows naturally. Once you think like an artist, you will act like an artist from the very first brush strokes; from the very first paint you apply to a canvas that is entirely your own. The process will be enjoyable and you will look forward to new discoveries every single day. I won't even ask you to give up your paint-by-number in the beginning, but I have a feeling once you experience that creative expression of an artistic heart, you'll never be satisfied with anything else again.

Are you still on board?

Take 5.3—Printers

I hope that by not requiring you to buy any curriculum from me, your budget will allow you to buy a good color laser printer. This is worth gold in a heart-based learning environment. You may have heard me quote Dr. Rich Melheim who said that a picture is not worth a thousand words; it's worth seven hundred and fifty thousand words. We're going to use a lot of fine art and illustrations and note booking because of the instant feelings and recall they provide.

If every time you find a picture you want to print out, you have to wait until you make a trip to Staples, it probably won't happen. And a lot of the permanence you were looking for in your learning will be lost. Also, your own printer will make it possible for you to print out many of the books that are in public domain. I read a lot of the books on my computer or tablet, but sometimes I just want to hold some paper in my hands and underline and highlight and add my own notes and questions.

When I print out a book from Internet Archive, I typically reduce the size of the page to save on ink and print double-sided. We buy paper by the case at Wal-Mart and I can print out most books for less than $5. I trust you to do your own search to find the best quality printer at a price you can afford. Anything I recommend here will likely be obsolete in a few months from now.

Definitely order your ink online. We get our ink through Amazon Prime, which has saved us a ton of money. All you have to do is enter in the serial number of your printer. Then it will take you to the ink at the cheapest prices. It's a fraction of what you'll pay in the store and it's usually delivered very quickly. We have a black and white laser printer as well as a color printer, but, of course, that is not necessary for most families. There are many advantages to getting a laser with double-sided printing capability. WiFi is a must for us, but you can save money if you don't need that feature.

There are also printing services like the Home-school Printing Company. If your budget just won't allow buying a printer, this can be an alternate choice. But you have that waiting factor and it's so much easier to strike when the fire's hot. Or maybe you have some friends that you can all go in together and share a printer. For those of you who are part of homeschool charter schools that provide funding, I've been told that many of them will let you use your funds to buy a printer.

If you don't know how to copy and print images from the internet, there is a little video my husband put together in Section 5 of Catch the Vision you may want to watch. It's so simple, even I can do it. And that says a lot. I'm definitely technologically challenged.

Printing out a book from Internet Archive is also easy. If you are accessing a book from the Libraries of Hope library, remember—only the books with a heart icon are in the public domain and can be freely printed for any use. The diamond books are still in copyright and cannot be printed.

To print a book, scroll down the page and notice there are a number of download options. Select PDF. Once the book downloads, you can click on the print option and print the book out. You can even select certain pages to print out if you don't want the whole thing. Be sure you go by the page counter in the PDF display and not the actual page numbers in the book. I may have had to learn the hard way…

Take 5.4—Planners

Now I want to talk about planners. I probably should call this something other than a planner, because so much of the learning in this way can be spontaneous and random or tied into what is happening in the experiences of your life or current interests. If you become too much of a planner and create rigid schedules for yourself, it can turn this whole experience into a paint-by-number and also, quite possibly, a nightmare. On the other hand, if you leave everything to the spur of the moment, you may not get the results you're hoping for because you'll always be scrambling to find a copy of the right book or looking for craft supplies or tracking down a movie. I offer some ideas for using a planner in section five of the Catch the Vision course to get you thinking of the best way you can use a planner in your life. I know I'm talking to a bunch of individualists and finding a one-size-fits-all planner is a bit of a tall order, so you'll find a lot of flexibility in the use of this particular one that we designed. Mostly what you're looking for is a place to put your brain on paper. This is brain central. You're going to come across a ton of ideas and resources and you want a place to jot down the ones that are most appealing to you and you want to put them somewhere where you can find them again. Many of the ideas will be for future reference.

For instance, you may read about a great book about Germany, which is month 10, but maybe you're in month three. This planner gives you a place to jot it down so that when you get to month 10, you'll have a reminder. It can also provide an instant portfolio and record of work you've done in case you live somewhere where you have to report it or it provides a nice record of learning to refer back to when review each year as you revisit monthly topics in the rotation schedule. Maybe when you come around in the rotation again, you may have jotted down people or topics you want to explore more deeply the next time around and your previous year planner gives you a quick reference tool. Actually, you could just pick up a spiral notebook, add a few divider tabs and you're good to go.

If you want to try out ours, go to Section 5 of Catch the Vision and print out a few sample months from the PDF you will see there in the planner section. See if it works for you. If you like fancier, we have a full color download with soft watercolor floral backgrounds or you can buy a printed version from our store. I took mine to Xpdex and had them spiral bind it and I found cute []avender polka dot divider tabs at Walmart. They're reusable, so I don't have to buy new ones every year. There's also a section in the back of the planner where you'll find pages to jot down ideas and notes as you move through the Mother's University topics.

Or if you want a basic black and white version that's already printed out for half the price of the color one, you'll find it in the store as well.

Ultimately, you want to lead your children to the place where they're mapping out their own learning. Desire + what they are willing to do = their curriculum. So teach them to use a planner where they can plan for their monthly learning as well as record what they did. It's going to take a lot of pressure off of you.

The black and white student planner would be just right for your kids. It doesn't have the Mother's University pages in the back. Spiral binding will make it much easier to use.

So take a minute and look at the sample pages and decide how you want to proceed. You're likely to modify it along the way. We learn as we go, don't we? Don't put it off. Having some kind of planner is crucial as you move forward.

Take 5.5—Internet Archive Library Card

Sometimes we put off doing the unknown. I want to make sure you have signed up for a library card at Internet Archive. It will take you about 30 seconds. It's free and it's going to open up a whole world of possibilities before I give you instructions and send you on your way. Let me explain some things about this particular group of books in Internet Archive, which have only been added fairly recently. By the way, the books that require the use of a library card are the ones with the diamond icon. These books are often out of print, but still in copyright. If this service was not offered to us, most of us would never be able to read these books. And there are some wonderful titles in there. For those of you who recognize the shortage of wholesome, inspiring books for our kids, many of these were written by the best of the best authors for children. I have watched books like these that used to sell for a couple of dollars on Amazon, now selling for $50, $100, even $200—if you can even find them. Your library card is going to give you access, free access to many of them. Just another reminder. Unlike the books marked with a heart, these books marked by a diamond cannot be printed out. That option is blocked. You can, however, download them to a device. But the book will expire in two weeks, which is how long you have to read the book. You cannot renew it if there is a wait list.

Simply click on the button and there will be another button for you to click on to add you to the wait list. When the book is available, you'll be notified by email and then you'll have 48 hours to access it or you'll forfeit it. You can only put yourself on the wait list for five books, so if you don't yet have a library card, let's do it now. I've given you a direct link to one of my library pages. When you get there, look for one of the little diamonds to the left of a title and click on it when the page opens. There will be a book that either says borrow or wait list. Either way, click on the button. If you don't have a card, you can now select the option to sign up. All you have to do is enter your email address. Select a username and a password. Don't forget to write down your username and your password in your planner somewhere. If you keep signed in, you usually won't have to bother with this very often, but sometimes you may have to enter it again. It is so very easy to borrow books in Internet Archive. When you're done reading them, simply click the return button.

Simple, huh? Now go do it. Remember, look for a diamond and click on it.

(*Please note: Internet Archive recently had legal action brought against them for opening the library up during the Covid crisis. Their policies are changing as they work things out. At the time of this writing, they give us an option to borrow the book for one hour at a time, but there is no waiting period. That may change in the future.)

Take 5.6—Rotation

Remember *Mission: Impossible?* Your mission, should you choose to accept it, is to teach your children about the whole world, past, present and future and everything in it and make it relevant to their lives. Good luck. This tape will self-destruct in five seconds.

To borrow from someone more clever than me, how on earth are you going to do it for heaven's sake?

Well, I think the process isn't unlike the exactly one painting I've painted in my life. I attended a three- or four-day painting workshop with Jon McNaughton several years ago, and what I learned applies exactly to our discussion here. First, an artist needs a subject in mind—a general idea of what he wants to paint. And this was sketched very roughly on the painting surface. Next, we added a layer of what he called scumbling that covered the whole surface and gave us a foundation to now build upon. Then we started filling in more details of the painting. I painted trees and irises and lilac bushes, a little path, a cottage and a bench focusing on one thing at a time. But I have to admit, I wasn't very happy with my work. In fact, I was tempted to not show up the last day because I was so embarrassed. They kept telling us to not give up; that we were going to be amazed at what would happen on the last day. On that last day, he taught us about jewels where we would mix white with various colours and apply them around the painting.

As we did it, it's like the painting came to life. Suddenly I could feel myself in the scene with the cool breezes and the glow of the summer sunset. It's something I cannot even explain. It has to be experienced.

The rotation schedule I've created allows for this kind of learning. You may want to go back and review details in my presentation on the rotation schedule in Section 5 of Catch the Vision. But I hope this illustration will help you catch the why if you're still reluctant to give it a try. We are trying to allow learning to layer in and to add details one at a time according to our children's developmental abilities. This is a process that can last a lifetime. It's not a "check it off the list" learning exercise. This is not learn, test and forget. This is learn, apply and enlarge.

One of the most frequent objections I hear is that it doesn't make sense to unfold history that is not in a chronological order. I will just say that is your grown-up, adult mind speaking that tends to require systems in order. Your children are in a different stage of development. They are in the scumbling stage. Details will be added over time. Eventually they'll have the whole picture, all the pieces, that will fit together nicely, I promise.

I will say it one more time. This rotation schedule is your servant, not your master. If your family is going to France in month 2, by all means, don't wait until month 5 to study France or if you find something you love and want to study more deeply for a while longer, yes! Do it! You want that to happen. Or if you had a baby in February and life was chaotic, just keep going. You'll be back around many, many times. Also, remember, you have two months in the summer you can use to go in more depth or if you missed a month along the way or for whatever reason. There's a lot of flexibility in the schedule, but the truth is there is no getting behind or catching up in this way of learning. The rotation schedule is a way I came up with to provide just enough structure and rhythm to learning so that you can cover the whole world and everything in it and you have an entire lifetime to do it. Just keep layering up and adding fresh details to your painting until you have created a masterpiece. You may come up with your own plan. It's not the plan that matters. It's the principles. But be cautious. You don't want to get so rigid and structured in your plan that you shut down the learning process.

All the resources I provide can be accessed on the rotation navigation page from your app. So take a moment to open it up and see what's there. And that's all I'll say for now. But we'll fill in more details as we layer up.

Take 5.7—Why Focus on Arts?

If you're still wondering why I spend so much time focusing on the arts, let me try and explain again. And if you missed it, when I refer to the arts, I'm referring to music, pictures or imagery, poetry and story. I know your children need to learn to read and to write and to do math. There are tests out there and requirements for college, admission standards and all that stuff. I'm not your one-stop shopping center. I'm not your best resource to find the best science textbook in high school or the best calculus course. What I am trying to do is fill a learning gap in childhood. I define childhood generally as the first 12-14 years of life. If your children are older than that, it's a little more challenging to make up for what may have been missed along the way. But it is never too late! As we move along, I'll offer suggestions and ideas for doing that. What the arts do is give your child eyes to see, ears to hear and hearts to feel. The arts light up desires in their hearts, which is vital because all our actions flow from the desires of our hearts. I recently heard someone say the arts tenderize our hearts. When the arts are the foundation of all learning, there is a depth and richness to learning that cannot happen in any other way.

Academic lessons are woven into many of the activities we do, lessons that are usually separated out. Because of the context, it is actually a much more effective way to learn things like vocabulary, spelling, grammar, even facts and information. For instance, when you read a story aloud, you are building a huge vocabulary. Naturally, you're instilling a sense of writing with a beginning, a climax and a satisfying conclusion. You were enlarging a child's capacity to create images from the words which is vital for reading comprehension. The music in your voice adds a layer of understanding. A child's listening comprehension far exceeds his reading comprehension in early childhood, so you are expanding his mind for future learning as well as building character, igniting curiosity and planting ideas. When you have your children copy a passage from a book in their notebooks, you're teaching that sentences begin with capital letters and end with a punctuation point. You are teaching them, through experience, correct grammar and correct use of punctuation. You are teaching them spelling as they visualize the words they are copying. They're learning sentence structure. And if it is used for practicing cursive handwriting, they are lighting up their entire brain.

Many of the great writers developed their writing styles by copying passages of master writers. Style is not something that can be taught directly, but through their copy work, your children are absorbing lessons in styling.

When you teach children to draw what they are seeing, you are teaching them exactness of thought; the habit of attention and to detail. A mom told me when her daughter decided on her career in nursing and realized she needed to take college-level science courses and had not studied any formal science in her high school years, she panicked. While she hadn't done much textbook learning, she had been a nature journalist. She called home in her first semester and said she was at the top of her biology class and attributed it to the fact that when the teacher explained something, she could see it because her brain had been trained in that way while her classmates struggled to see what the professor was talking about.

When you listen to music, you are listening to math in motion. Through music, you can develop a habit of attention and instill harmony in order and thinking. A brilliant professor had a stroke and lost his memory, but through music it ordered his thinking again so he could access what was still stored in his brain but had become inaccessible.

When you have your children memorize poetry, you're strengthening their memory muscle. Our memories have gotten so flabby over the years. It's incredible what people used to be able to hold on to through their memories. We can all use a good memory workout which poetry can offer in a pleasant way.

Beauty, love and goodness are revealed through the arts. Each art reveals a unique facet of learning that can be delivered in no other way. By divine design, we respond to arts naturally in childhood. They are our first languages. They are enjoyable. Children are drawn to them like ducks to water. When a Hebrew child was first taught to read, the parent would place honey on a child's finger so that after he traced a letter, he would lick his finger and associate sweetness with learning. Scientists have observed that there is a little gateway into the brain where higher learning takes place, and it requires a pleasurable experience to open that gateway. The arts provide that pleasurable experience and adds all the sweetness to our learning.

One young boy who started attending public school after having homeschooled found himself getting more and more depressed. One day he told his mother he felt like something had gone missing. A little while later, she found him reading a French story and listening to some music which met that longing in his heart. He instinctively knew where to turn.

I'm now going to start sharing resources and offering ideas for incorporating more art into your lives and in the learning process. The writings in the mother's university will deepen the experiences you will have with all these languages of the heart. You will begin to find your favorite activities and resources and the right fit for your family as you begin to apply the brush strokes to your personal masterpiece. Keep your planner nearby so that you can jot down ideas as they strike you. I'm going to give you a lot of information and you'll want to have a way to retrieve what you need. Above all, enjoy the process.

Take 5.8—Make Fine Music Familiar

The more I learn of the power of music in our lives, the more I realize how much we are missing out. Music is healing in so many ways as well as transformative. Yet we tend to stay locked in a "See Spot Run" level of appreciation and never experience the beauty on a Shakespearean level.

Older children, especially, can be resistant to classical music if they haven't had much exposure. Or maybe that is even you. I cannot stress enough the importance of understanding the powerful draw to the familiar. There's a wonderful music book I will refer to later, but one of the concepts it teaches is that one of the most important ways to awaken this language of the heart is to make the rich classical music the familiar music of childhood.

Just start. You don't need to make a lesson out of it. Just play it in the background or while you're driving in the car. If your kids balk, tell them you want to listen for you. They don't have to listen. My daughter started playing the music while she was doing the dishes. Inevitably, one of the kids would come running from somewhere in the house: "What is that song? I love it." It had struck a familiar chord for that child. As the music becomes more and more familiar, they will find more to love about it. There are other things you can do, but we'll talk about them as we go along. One mother in our Facebook group wrote: "I've never really connected to music before. I've heard songs I like but never found it healing in any way, although I know many people find music healing. I've been doing some inner healing work and suddenly I'm finding myself drawn to music and can feel its healing influence. Currently, I can't get enough of the Mulan soundtrack. Something in it speaks so deeply to me. It's amazing. I've never experienced this feeling before. It was almost like I had previously been numb to the effect of music."

You may well have your own favorites, of course. Play those. But if you'd like some suggestions, I've collected some popular pieces that go along with the rotation schedule, meaning either the composer is from a certain country or the subject ties into the country or American history topic. Or maybe it has to do with the nature topic. Some moms like to make a playlist of the month songs and play it in the background like we talked about. Or you can play it while your children are doing something else like handicrafts, playing with Legos, doing copy work, driving in the car and so forth. There are some YouTubes that are an hour or longer, especially folk songs, that give a cultural feel for a country that I've placed in the enrichment section. Play one of those while you're working on a craft or doing a cultural night dinner, which we'll talk about later. Or even while everyone is cleaning the house. This is definitely one of those times having some kind of a speaker you connect to will be a big plus. Or you can just pull up a YouTube and find a moment to sit down with a child in his room with you, maybe while you're at a doctor appointment or you just find yourself with a minute waiting for dinner to finish cooking.

If you have just one child listening, let them listen with headphones to surround them with the sound and make the experience even more wonderful. I tried to include a variety of presentations and include orchestras from around the world. Isn't it amazing to see musicians from China, Germany, South America all playing and loving the same music? Music really is a universal language. Some have unique instruments that are unfamiliar to us, like the beautiful balalaika orchestra from Russia. Some are fun to watch because it shows the various instruments up close. Some are old recordings that may include an original composer performing the piece. Some have artwork or scenes from that particular country. If you're able to project the YouTube on your large TV screen, that can add some interest. This isn't an activity where you say, OK, we watched that one. All done with that. Check it off the list. The more you repeat the listening, the more familiar it becomes.

I leave it to you to find ways to incorporate more music in the environment of your home. Find somewhere today to play something. And of course, you're not limited to what I provide. To find the classical music and the different musical pieces I've found, I'm going to link you to the rotation page on the website, but you can certainly access it through your app.

Some tablets only display sideways, so if you have a problem going through your app, you may want to just go to welleducatedheart.com directly and pull up the rotation navigation page.

I want to help you to become familiar in navigating your way around the library. Let's start with month 1. Click on 1500s exploration. It's going to pull up what I call a landing page. On that landing page, you will see four buttons. The last button is enrichment. Click on that. Scroll down the page until you start seeing music videos. I found some sailor music because this is the month about sailors exploring the world. The first one the Russian sailor dances is incredibly fun to watch. I've watched it over and over. You even get a glimpse of Putin in the audience. Of course, just click on the little square in the bottom corner to make it full screen or play one of the sailors hornpipe versions. If you or your kids happen to find yourself wanting to get up and dance or clap your hands, do it. I even included a fun little sailor song your kids can sing to. Let me mention that when you pull up any of the nature topics from the rotation schedule, you will find the musical YouTubes directly on the bottom of those pages. You won't have to go through a landing page to get to those.

Now, find some way to add a little music in your day today!

Take 5.9—Home and Family Art

Several years ago, when one of my granddaughters was about 18 months old, I bought her a little picture book called *Sleepy Night at the Farm*. My daughter called and said, "Thanks a lot, mom. She just made me read it to her 18 times in a row." When her little girl ran off to play with her sisters, my daughter hid the book under a pile of books, but when she came back into the room, her little girl dug into the pile of books, found it, pulled it out, and demanded that it be read to her again and again. We were trying to figure out the attraction, and then it dawned on us. We had just come back from a family trip to Lancaster, Pennsylvania, the heart of Amish farm country. We had spent time visiting farms and petting lambs and going into barns and watching the sunset over the fields. This book captured the experiences we had just had, and I think her little girl was drawn to all those wonderful feelings she'd had and wanted to experience them over and over again.

I saw for myself the draw of familiarity when I visited the Louvre in Paris. I posted a picture in this section of how close I was willing to get to the Mona Lisa. I couldn't believe the crowds in the line for that one little painting that has a room all to itself.

I asked someone who is well versed in art history, "Why?" She explained a bit of the history of the painting and why it is the most recognizable piece of art in the world. And that is the draw. It is familiar. Whenever I go to an art museum, as I look around the room, I first go to those paintings that I recognize.

I'm going to keep coming back to this concept of looking for the familiar when you're trying to awaken an interest in a subject. But for now, let's apply it to art. Everyone responds to art differently. What connects to me may not connect to you and to me, the first most important step to help a child love art is to allow him to recognize the connections being made in his own heart. How often do we give a child a piece of art to study that is beyond anything they can yet relate to? And to make things worse, we teach him to analyze the elements of the painting rather than allowing the painting to do its quiet work upon the heart. A lot of people grow up thinking they hate art for that reason. So, as Julie Andrews sang, let's start at the very beginning, a very good place to start. We want to find art that is a familiar subject to children. Well, really, all of us. Doesn't it make more sense to expose them in the beginning to art about families, babies, mothers, fathers, children playing kittens, ducks, flowers, all things in nature rather than teaching them: This is a Picasso or a Rembrandt or a Monet.

My heart-educator friends taught one of the most important gifts of art is it gives us eyes to see the beauty in everything. According to a study done years ago, on average, by the time a child is 18, he will have viewed over 200,000 acts of violence and 14,000 murders. My question to you is how many images of beauty, love, kindness will he have stored up? In fact, another study of schoolbooks back in the 80s revealed that children weren't being exposed to a single story of a mother or baby in the home at school. And things have only gotten worse since then. I have created a page to begin to remedy that. You can access it from your app. Just select fine art images. Or if you want to go directly from the website, in the search field at the bottom of any page, simply enter 'art, home and family' and it will take you to the same place. Please make a note. We're working on a way to get these fine art images into a more accessible gallery for you to view. But for now, they are sorted in Pinterest pages. You may need to sign up for Pinterest to fully access them. The majority of these paintings have been taken from the art renewal center that I've talked about in other places.

Another place we are gathering and organizing art like this is on our sister site, simplejoyart.com. These fine art images are linked to Wikimedia Commons where you can print them out and use them as you would like. The images are sorted by family themes, like I have been describing, as well as nature and historical subjects. It's a work in progress—keep checking back for new art.

A child cannot store up too many pictures that reflect beauty and goodness. So do find a variety of ways to get them in front of them. Using the pictures can be as simple as saying to your children, or even better yet, to an individual child, "Shall we look at some pictures?" Of course, she'll want to make them full size on your phone or tablet or laptop. Some tablets only display horizontally from the app and we've not found a way to remedy that. So you may just want to go directly into the page through the website. If you have the ability to project the fine art on your TV screen, even better. But I would show them with an objective in mind—we're looking for our favorites, which is another way of saying which of these works of art resonates in your heart the most? What is connecting to that child? So you might say something like, "I've been thinking, I'd like to add a painting on this wall. Will you help me choose one?"

When you find it, print it out and put it in a little frame and hang it up. "Or would you like to find a painting we can put in this little frame next to your bed or on a bulletin board in your room or even posted on the fridge?" I think you get the idea. And tell your children you'll change it frequently.

Another option is to help them create a book of their favorite art. I've talked about bare books elsewhere. I'll give you the link again here. I suggest keeping a supply of different sizes on hand because there are so many ways to use them. In this case, let them start gluing in prints of their favorite pictures. Do one a week or one a day, or when the right times strikes. They could make different books if they want. For little children: maybe one will be my book of animals or my book of flowers or my book of babies. If they're learning the alphabet, they could make their own ABC book. Let's look for a picture that has something that starts with the letter A or as you go through the pictures. If you're ambitious, you could create your own ABC book from fine art to share with them.

If you have older children, let them help their little brothers and sisters go through the pictures. They'll be picking it up at the same time. If there are no little brothers and sisters left in the house, you might tell them about what I said about the draw to the familiar, and maybe suggest they create some books that they can use when they have children.

I'm just trying to get the creative juices flowing and finding what works for you. Over the coming weeks, we'll talk about ways to deepen and broaden their appreciation for art. This is just a first step. Before I end, I noticed that many of the direct links in art renewal from the Pinterest pages are no longer working. So you may need to write down the name of the art piece and the name of the artist and do a direct search in the Art Renewal Museum. When you're ready to print it out, to be able to access all the high-resolution images, you'll need to become a member. But I hope you'll consider supporting the important work they're doing.

Take a minute and go to find art images on your app or enter "Art, Home and Family" in the search field in the website and then make a decision. How do you want to approach this with your own children? If you need to buy some frames at the dollar store, jot it down in your planner so next time you're at the store, you can have them on hand. Better yet, let your kids pick out the frames in the anticipation that they're going to find a picture to fill it. The important thing is that you try something. You can modify it as you go.

Take 5.10—Finding Poetry Books

I've spent time elsewhere talking about the importance, the gift and blessing of poetry in our lives. If you've had a bad experience with poetry, I hope you'll give it a fresh chance. Let me step up on my soapbox again and preach the power of familiarity, which, by the way, if you recall the developmental steps I talked about in Section 5, familiar is the first stage, and that doesn't just apply to little children. If you have a reluctant 16-year-old, you're going to want to find that familiar connection for him. You're going to hit your head against the wall if you try to get him to read books that do not have that familiar tie somewhere in them. Part of your skill as an artist is to make the unfamiliar, become familiar. But that's a topic for another day. For now, let's apply it to poetry. If you want your children to grow up loving poetry, let it be a language they associate pleasant memories with. Poetry is meant to be read aloud for its musical qualities and beautiful imagery. In fact, your littlest children are listening to the music more than the meaning of the words. So don't be afraid to read poetry that is over their heads from time to time. Today's task is to make sure you have some quality poetry books on hand to start reading from.

Let me first direct you to a collection of poetry I put together: *Poetry for the Well-Educated Heart*. I went through probably 50 poetry books looking for poems that go along with our rotation schedule. The first section includes poems for that familiar connection. They are poems about families and family relationships. Then there is a section where you'll find poems that connect to each of the nature topics. The next section has poems that fit in with the monthly rotation history topics, and the final section has poems with ideas for happy and meaningful living. You can buy a hard copy of the book in the store or there is a free digital copy online. I'll just mention it's one of the free gifts if you sign up to receive the monthly forgotten classics bundle. Let me walk you through where you will find the free digital copy rather than direct link it because a lot of people don't know this link is available. If you go to the bottom of any page in the website, you will see a blue block that says "Forgotten Classics" in it. Click on it and it will take you to a page where you will find links to free digital copies of all the forgotten classics. You'll find the poetry book towards the bottom of the page.

Another place to find a treasure trove of poetry books is on the Categories navigation page. If you click on rotation from your app, you will see an option at the top of the page to switch to categories. I'll let you scroll through that just to help you become familiar with what's there until you find a section called 'other.' Now look for poetry. It's in alphabetical order. Click on it. The first section that comes up gives you a variety of mother goose and nursery rhymes that we'll talk about next week. Then there's a section of books with poetry in the public domain. The last section gives you some books you can view online or better yet, purchase so that you can start building a library of poetry books for your children to freely search through. My personal favorite, if I was going to start with one book that's still in print, is Helen Ferris's *Favorite Poetry Old and New Selected for Boys and Girls*.

I always visit the poetry section at used book sales and have found some beautifully illustrated poetry books. Building your collection is half the fun. You can't start reading poetry if you don't have a book to read it from. So pick a book and start reading aloud.

Take 5.11—Sunshine Stories

If you did nothing else but read a quality story to your children every day, you'd be surprised at what you will have accomplished by the time your children leave home. If you think about it, one story a day is three hundred and sixty five stories a year. And if you read a story a day from age 5 to age fifteen, that is three thousand six hundred and fifty stories. That is a significant number of seeds you planted. Many children grow up with only a handful of stories in their hearts. And if you understand the power that stories have on our lives, you will see what a tragedy that is.

If you have young children, you're going to want to look for familiar stories, which means stories of families, animals, nature, things they are in contact with. Sometimes I will see a mom ask for an appropriate Civil War story or something like that for her 4- or 5-year-old. And I ask myself why? Childhood is not the time for such stories. Also, young children love the familiarity of repetitive stories, so they love to hear the same stories over and over, or listen to stories with repetitive words or phrases in them. One of the most important things you can do to help your children catch the vision of the kind of learning we're trying to accomplish here is to have a family read-aloud of families living this kind of learning lifestyle.

I call them my Sunshine Books, and although they are written for children, your older children and even adults will enjoy them. They inspire hearts and build vision. So many of the books written for young people today are full of sarcasm, attitude, vulgarity, selfishness, snarkiness. I look for books that demonstrate wholesome relationships and activities. I'm going to list a number of the books I have found here in this section. Although there are strong family values in them, many of the families are in crisis. Mother has died. Father has died. Mother is sick. Mother and father have died. But what the books demonstrate is how to find joy, even in hard circumstances and through the strength of relationships. They teach self-education through books, through observation, through nature, through music, story and poetry, and art, all the principles we are learning. I started recording some of them and placing them in BelMonde, which I'm going to talk about another day. For now, I'll mention that you will find them by looking for the pale green title blocks within that site.

Let me share a book. You may want to start with this book. It is nearly impossible to come by. I keep checking for used copies online and the very few that are available start at about 90 dollars. I lucked out and found a copy at a thrift store and recorded it for you and put it in BelMonde. It was written in 1955, but according to all my searches, the text has fallen into public domain for reasons you probably don't need to hear about right now. Anyway, the book is called *The Golden Name Day* by Jennie Lindquist. It was actually up for the Newbery Award the year it was published. But *Carry On, Mr. Bowditch* took the honor instead. If you are in month one where we talk about Scandinavian countries, this would be a perfect book to begin with because it shares a Scandinavian tradition of celebrating name days. It's just a sweet story of warm relationships, and even though it's simple, I love it as an adult. There are two sequels that are even more difficult to come by and are under copyright protection, so I'm not sure how I can get them to you. But if there's a way I will do it. To find the audio version, go to Scandinavia Literature at mybelmonde.com.

I have listed and linked other Sunshine books on the Take 5 page for this section. We also have created a Sunshine Series in our Forgotten Classics collection if you would like to have hard copies.

Take 5.12—Playing in Nature

As I studied the lives of the great souls of history, one thing I found in common with so many of them was their love of nature. Many of them spent their childhoods roaming forest, field and meadow—a love they carried throughout their lives. As adults, they would return to nature to calm their minds and inspire their thoughts.

Nature is a child's best and most important classroom. If you are lucky enough to live with a big yard and trees or have a park nearby, spend as much time there as you can, letting your kids explore and discover on their own. Play is the work of childhood. It may look like they aren't learning anything, but believe me, they are. As they run and jump and climb, they are connecting vital neural pathways. A bonus for you if they're playing outside, they're not messing up your house. If you don't have a yard, see if there's some kind of garden or park in your community not far away that you can take your kids to regularly. If none of these are options, YouTube has wonderful nature videos, many of them with calming music or sounds of nature that you can have playing in the background on your TV. Of course, you don't get the sense of smell or the touch, but it's better than nothing.

If you haven't listened to the nature presentation in Catch the Vision, take a few minutes and listen to it today. I shared parts of a wonderful book I came across that was all about how to help your children fall in love with nature, which is the simple and foremost objective here. Science is going to be a natural outgrowth of that love and curiosity.

Charlotte Mason wrote that our objective in allowing children to spend time in nature is "…to give the child delightful glimpses into the world of wonder he lives in, to reveal the sort of things to be seen by curious eyes and to fill him with desire to make discoveries for himself." As we take a heart-based approach, nature is going to reveal wonderful life lessons to their hearts. We'll talk more about that as we go along. For today, think about how you can spend more time with your children in nature and plan for it. And no guilt because your kids are playing so much and not doing worksheets inside. There will be a time and a place for academic learning, but childhood is not that time.

Take 5.13—Math

Let's talk about math right now here at the beginning, because it seems to be a number one concern on the minds of moms who are attempting to teach their own children. I can't think of another subject that gives mothers more worry and concern than finding the right math curriculum. It's been ingrained in us that somehow proficiency in math is the golden ticket to all that is good and important in life.

Math is important. It is a beautiful and useful language to learn. But it is being used as a measuring stick of success that reflects on how good of a job you are doing. We define a child's intellect according to whether he falls above or below level in math for his age. And that part frustrates me so much. I was a guest at a Mothers of Influence meeting recently and one of the moms attended for the first time. She came because the topic was math that night. And by the way, she wasn't familiar with any of the well-educated heart philosophies. So I don't fault her at all. She was a teacher and was clearly passionate about math and its importance in our lives. She talked about how vital it is to cover certain concepts at each level, starting with the first grade and how we must insist on mastery at each grade level. She was so pleased at how her daughter was doing calculus in the ninth grade, and then she casually mentioned that that same daughter came home after her first year away at college and announced that she was a communist.

She had been persuaded this was the way of compassion and justice in our society. By the way, she was attending a university in Utah. That is not typically thought of as a liberal university. It made me think of a quote by President James Garfield: "One half of the time, which is now almost wholly wasted in district schools on English grammar attempted at too early an age would be sufficient to teach our children to love the republic and to become its loyal and lifelong supporters."

I don't focus on math in the early years because I believe we have much more important matters to attend to, and I happen to not buy into the idea that success in math is our most important accomplishment. Still, I know some of you are under state requirements and you have to render unto Caesar that which is Caesar's, but as a heart-based educator, please put math in its proper perspective.

I've posted a number of interesting articles and talks that for many moms have been eye opening. You'll find them in the math section of the Mothers University. I encourage you to take the time to go through them and then make your own determination of the right course for your family.

Please don't misunderstand me. Math is important. It's a beautiful language and that is why we study it. I especially like the TED talk by a high school math teacher. He said the only ones who are using high-level math in their careers are—drumroll—math teachers. Another mother, who was at our Mothers of Influence meeting called her three brothers. One is a doctor. One is a high-level accountant, and one is an engineer. She asked them how much math they needed in their careers. They said arithmetic, basic adding, subtracting, multiplying and dividing for a couple of them. A little bit of beginning algebra. And the doctor said maybe a little bit of geometry.

An engineer that put a man on the moon said he had never even heard of the word calculus before he went to college, but he had learned to think and observe and draw conclusions about what he saw. Which are all things that we're concerned about here. Some of you may be counting on high math scores for scholarships. That's a whole different subject and you need to do what you need to do. Some children take to math like a duck to water—let them swim! But other children are gifted in other ways and should not be made to feel stupid because they don't get math as it is taught. And you shouldn't feel like a failure if your child is not scoring three levels higher for his age on math tests.

At the very least, consider the fact that children are more developmentally ready for math concepts when they are ten and older than they are at age five or six. An interesting experiment was run that you will also find in the Mother's University math section, where one group of children delayed a formal study of math until the fifth or sixth grade, while the other group, the second group, did the normal drilling of math skills. Starting in the first grade, the first group had rich experiences in language, in discussing ideas. When formal math instruction was finally introduced, the first group learned in one year what the second group had been working on for five or six years, and the first group soon surpassed the second group.

I do include several resources that will provide a strong, heart-based foundation for math in those younger years and ideas you can incorporate that teach math in a more natural way. Learning to count by playing games, learning fractions by cooking, cutting pizza into six pieces and giving one-sixth to each person and so forth. So what I'm trying to say is make an informed decision about what importance you place on math in your own home. But I won't be talking much about it at all because I am more concerned with other things.

Take 5.14—NC Youth Symphony

If you've been listening to some of the music selections on the enrichment pages, you may have noticed a section just below it that has links underneath the YouTubes. The section heading is Music Plus Story. Let me tell you what that is. The North Carolina Symphony Orchestra has been doing concerts for young people for decades and I happened to find many of the old programs posted in Internet Archive. I thought these program notes could give you a quick and easy music appreciation lesson to throw in here and there. And the selections were specifically made for young ears. They're usually not very long. The notes may have a simple story about the composer that you can read to your kids, or you can offer a brief synopsis to increase interest in the piece they'll be listening to. Or it might give them ideas of things to listen for.

Simply click on the link underneath the YouTube for the program notes and it will take you directly to the page that coincides with that particular musical selection. And then you can go back and look at the YouTube. I looked for performances by musicians around the world. Sometimes I was able to find a performance by the composer himself, such as Debussy playing Golliwogs Cakewalk that you'll find on the France Enrichment page. I've linked about half of the program notes so far. I'm still working away at it. So look for new selections as you circle back through the rotation. Look at it as one more tool in your toolbox to increase a love and appreciation for fine music. It's something you can easily reach for in a spontaneous moment.

Take 5.15—My Book of Delights

My oldest daughter, Shannon, has been implementing the Well-Educated Heart philosophy and resources for many years now. If you haven't found her Facebook page yet, it's called One Hundred Days of WEH and she shares what they're doing in their home. You might say her home has in large measure been my laboratory. She's taken a little break as she gets ready to welcome baby number six. But there are a lot of archived ideas. Each month, her girls pick out books that go along with the rotation schedule, topics they want to read. And last year, her 6-going on 7-year-old said, "Mom, where's a book just for me?" She was a beginning reader. The chapter books were still a bit beyond her as a personal read, although she listened to them as read-alouds. And she felt a little old for just picture books. That got me to thinking. I wanted a book just for Andi. So, I first did a search on Internet Archive looking for every level one and two beginning readers in the public domain I could find. I settled on about 50 of them. Then I went through each one looking for simple stories and poems that would fit in with the rotation schedule. Finally, I went on a treasure hunt for fine art that would fit in with each month's topics that would be appealing to young children. I looked for artists from those particular countries or artists that recreated scenes from those countries. I especially looked for family scenes. What I ended up with is a book filled with full color, beautiful fine art, poetry and beginning stories; stories like fairy tales or stories of great lives that will appeal to young children like Andi. Of course, Andi was my boss. It had to have her seal of approval and she gave it a thumbs up. She loved it and so did her sisters. So my next dilemma was what to call it. I called on my Alaskan team for ideas, and the clear winner was My Book of Delights. There are twelve books in this series, one for each of the 10 main months of the rotation schedule and two books that cover 'Around the World and Through the Year.' There are about 90 to 100 pages in each one and they're loaded with full-color art prints, poems and a few stories suitable for Level 1 and 2 readers. One final touch—Kayleigh is Andi's oldest sister and is an aspiring illustrator. So I asked if she would create some illustrations for my title pages. I love what she's come up with! There is a link to digital copies of the books on the Forgotten Classics Library page or you can buy hard copies in the store.

I created it for 6- or 7-year-olds. But guess what? Your whole family will find something to delight in. For example, you can use it with a preschooler. Let him enjoy the pictures and read the poetry aloud to him when he comes back a year or two later. The poems, because of their familiarity, will become enjoyable first reading experiences. Or you can use the art in ways I'll describe over the coming weeks.

Take 5.16—Poetry Tea Time

Poetry tea times are growing in popularity and they're a wonderful way to increase the love of poetry in your family. The basic idea is to set aside a time, often once a week, or even once a month is good, and come together for a poetry tea time. Some families like to make it an event and put a tablecloth on the table, a few fresh flowers in the center and pull out a pretty tea set. It's been fun for me to shop for a pretty tea sets in the Facebook marketplace or antique and thrift stores just for poetry tea times. It's a nice touch, but you don't have to. Of course, you may not drink tea. So, use hot chocolate or juice or lemonade, whatever your family likes. Add some snacks, cookies, crackers, fruits, whatever you like. Then come together and share the poetry that each of you loves. Maybe one child will bring a book to the table and share his poem for another child. Maybe he's been working on memorizing a poem and will recite it from memory. Or maybe you'll take the time to read from a poetry book while your children are enjoying the refreshments. You might leave time for them to each create a poetry page for their notebooks, or to copy poems in their personal anthology of favorite poems. Play some beautiful music in the background from the month's rotation schedule while they work or drink the tea with a little music appreciation lesson.

I had some mothers of boys who said no way would their rough-and-tumble boys enjoy an activity like that, but they were blown away when it became a highly anticipated event. A few years ago, I started a story group for adults, and one of the things we did to break the ice was to share a favorite poem or story. There was one man in the group who was usually very quiet and reserved. I knew he had a love of all things having to do with planes in aviation, and he recited from memory a poem his father had taught him about flying, and it was one of the most moving experiences I've ever had. He gave me a deeper appreciation for him and his passion. So please don't ever think poetry is a girl thing. And need I remind you most of the immortal poets were men. For Mother's Day a couple of years ago, my family bought me a beautiful tea set and gave me a book of poems with fine art images. They compiled for me something for every month of the year. It is a cherished gift.

Take 5.17—Forgotten Classics Library

I want to differentiate between the Forgotten Classics Family Library and the Libraries of Hope online library. I've had some people write and ask if the Forgotten Classics we offer in the store include all the books in the library. The answer is they do not. There are over 4,000 books available to you and the library as free online reads. I did not condense 4,000 books down to 76 volumes.

The Forgotten Classics Family Library is my personal collection of some of my favorite stories and books. On the Forgotten Classics page is a video that explains all about what went in there and why. Do I think a child would get a wonderful education if these are the only books they ever read? I do. I think they would come away with a more rounded understanding of the world we live in than many college graduates have. Do I think these are the only books a child should ever read? Definitely not. They are just one of your tools.

If you lived on a desert island and could only take a 5-foot shelf of books, they would be a great choice. But thankfully, we're not living on desert islands and we want to take advantage of all kinds of books and resources, don't we?

Another thing that is confusing to some people is that not all of the books are numbered to fit into the rotation schedule. The numbering on the Freedom series, which is American history, the World History Series, and the first eight volumes of the Nature series coincide with the rotation schedule.

The Story Hour series and the Great Lives series are not numbered according to the rotation schedule. However, I've divided the stories out in the online library pages, which is what I want to direct your attention to now.

If you go to any page in the library, notice the blue blocks as you scroll down the page. All those selections in the blue blocks are suggested Forgotten Classics stories. You'll see a letter and a number in front of them. The letter S is story. The F is freedom and N is nature and so forth. I can't directly link these books at this point because the digital version we use won't allow us to link to a specific page. However, if you scroll down to the bottom of any page in our web site, you will see a blue box in the footer that says Forgotten Classics Family Library. If you click on it, it will take you to a page that links all of our Forgotten Classics to a free digital copy. For example, you will see "S3-[#]." The S tells you it is from the Story Hour Series. The 3 tells you which volume, and the number after the dash is the page number. Many people like to have the hard copies of the books and the references in the blue boxes will give you a heads up of which stories go along with that month's topic. You can just pull the right book off your shelf and read.

The books are also divided out according to general age appeal on the online library pages. But if you don't have the hard copies, just go to the Forgotten Classics page where you can find the free digital reads.

By the way, I'd start with the elementary age stories, even with a high schooler. I heard a respected well-seasoned Professor say he always started any new study by finding a children's book on the topic. It always gives a clear foundation of essentials to build upon. In fact, if you were part of the James Holzhauer frenzy on Jeopardy, he said he spent his time reading children's books. That's how he stored up so much information in preparation for his phenomenal winning streak on Jeopardy! So don't pass over the elementary books with your middle and high schoolers. Even though these stories are written for children, they are rich and loaded with ideas that are satisfying even to adult minds.

Do check out the Forgotten Classics Family Library page by clicking on the blue box at the bottom of any page. There is also a link to the store on that page if you would like to purchase hard copies. The monthly bundle option is the most cost effective and if you choose that option, you will receive the mother's learning library as well as four bonus books for free.

Take 5.18—Thornton Burgess Books

Nature stories are the stories of choice for young children, along with stories of families and familiar things. Some of the most beloved stories about nature were written by Thornton Burgess. What makes him so outstanding? He wrote from personal observation of what he saw while he was growing up. He loved the beauty of nature in all its living creatures. You can feel the love. His father died when he was a baby, and so he grew up in humble circumstances, exploring the wildlife all around him. His stories are accurate and not only reveal nature to the hearts of children, he teaches lessons about life to be learned and instills good character values.

I picked up Burgess's autobiography and he closes the book with these words: "Peter Rabbit's oft repeated advice to the children the world over who know and love him is '…with open mind, go on your way, and add to knowledge every day.' That is most easily and effectively done through the story. I think I have proved it." Burgess wrote over 170 books and 15,000 stories for his daily newspaper columns. The first book he wrote was called *Mother West Wind*, which was followed by *Mother West Winds' Children* and then *Animal Friends and Neighbors*. In these books, he introduces the animal characters that will appear in the stories that follow. We have compiled these early books into one volume if you want a hard copy.

His first wife, Nina, died in childbirth a year after they were married, leaving him to raise his son alone. So, every night when his little boy got a little older, he told a story to his son when he tucked him in bed, which were later written down and became the Bedtime Story Books. These have been favorite nature stories of young children for generations. The only problem with them is he's always ending a chapter in an exciting spot. So you may get a plea to please keep reading. Dover sells a nice set of these books at a reasonable price, or I have linked free online versions that will give you a chance to try them out. You can also search for them from your local public library. I wouldn't worry about fitting the books in the rotation schedule at this age. You can read them aloud to children as young as 3 and 4 years old, and children can read them on their own by the second or third grade.

Later, some more informative field guide books were written for children, although they still were story-based and included character lessons. One was all about birds, another about animals, one about flowers and then one about the seashore. I will link those as well. These would be great books to include in your nature rotation schedule as your kids get a little older.

You might want to make a note in your planner that there is a link to a YouTube playlist of the birds Burgess talks about in the bird book. I'll link it for you. As you read stories like these to your children, you are giving them things to watch for and discover when they're out in nature.

There are some other excellent children's nature books I'll tell you about another time. If you don't have any young ones left at home, read them for yourself. Or if you have older children, see if they'll read them to younger brothers and sisters. If there are no younger brothers and sisters, encourage them to read them so they're familiar enough with them that they can share them with their children when they become parents.

Take 5.19—Booklists

I was reluctant to create a booklist for several reasons. First of all, there are over 4,000 titles and it seemed a bit unwieldy for a list. The entire Libraries of Hope part of the website is basically a booklist. Plus, the list is very fluid. I am constantly on the lookout for new titles to add and I am frequently changing where I place the title, moving some from Elementary to Middle School and so forth.

But my daughter convinced me that having a quick reference would be useful. So, it may not be perfect, but if it will be of use, do take advantage of it.

You will find free PDFs of each month's topic at the top of each landing page. What I call a landing page is the page that shows up when you click on one of the countries or U.S. topics from the general navigation page. From there, you navigate to Elementary, Middle, or High School or the Enrichment pages. You'll also find suggestions for study as well as podcasts. Anyway, look for Booklist PDF and click on it and you can print the page out for that particular topic. Or, if you are at a book sale or at the library and want to quickly check on titles, just bring that list up on your phone.

If you don't want to print out the individual pages yourself, you can also buy a complete list in the store. There are two options. If you are following the rotation schedule, you will probably want to buy that one. If you are looking for a list organized by nation alphabetically or U.S. History chronologically, you will want the categories edition. They both contain the same books, they are just organized differently.

The books are listed alphabetically by title, but organized by Elementary, Middle and High School. There is room on each page to add your own books to the list or to add any new titles you may come across that I have added after this list was created.

I am finding people are using this list in various ways. Let me offer some suggestions. For those of you who are building a substantial family library, it is easy to lose track of which books you already own. I envisioned being able to use this list as an inventory checker. Go through your library and put an "x" in the box in front of each title of the books you own. That way, when you are planning for the month, you have a quick reference to see what you have on hand. As you learn about titles, you could also use the list to create a dream list of books you want to own. Create a system that works for you—maybe pencil in a heart in the square next to a title to remind yourself of books you want to buy.

I also see it as a way of keeping track of what you read. In the past I created reading logs to write in the books you read. That may still work for some of you. But I found for many of you, taking the time to write in the book just didn't happen. So I thought it would be easier to simply highlight the title on your list with a highlighter and then you can quickly glance at what you've already read. Some moms jot a date down after the title if they have to report it somewhere. Having each child have his own booklist would be helpful so he can keep track of his own reading. A child might write the date in the little box or maybe he can create his own rating system and give the book a number from 1 to 10 as to how much he liked the book and put that number in the little box. Or maybe he didn't finish a book and wants to come back in the next rotation. So he can pencil in a reminder to himself, maybe what page he got to.

You will also find all the Forgotten Classics selections as well as My Book House and Junior Classics on the list. It's easy to forget what you've already read, so this can help you keep track. Just use a highlighter and mark it. Having said that, the thing about stories and good books is you don't want to read them just once. You always pull out something new or you re-read something so you can feel all those wonderful feelings again. So just because it's checked off the list doesn't mean there is any harm in reading it again! In fact, the list can serve as a reminder of those stories that you want to go back and read again. Put a star by those selections if you want.

Of course, you are free to use the booklists any way you want, or not use them at all! But now you know where they are and some possible ways to use them.

Take 5.20—Singing

A song is a wonderful kind of thing, so lift up your voice and sing.

I have talked elsewhere about the importance of voice. The voice is the great connector of mind and heart and when you sing, your whole brain is lighting up and sending feel-good endorphins and working all kinds of amazing physical and emotional magic. It's a great connector to others and enlarges the capacity for creativity.

The Greeks understood the importance of the voice and their great abilities in writing are attributed to their focus on oral expression in childhood.

My husband had a family reunion in Hawaii recently and for the first time in decades, all his siblings gathered together with their nearly 90-year-old mother. His mother suffers from Alzheimer's and she doesn't know who any of her children are or have any memory of their lives growing up. It's difficult for her to speak even the simplest words or phrases. But when they pulled out the old-time songs and hymns, she joined in singing every single word. It was incredible to see it for myself. Song can often retrieve old memories.

But what if you don't have any songs to remember?

I don't have time in this little 5 minutes to talk about all the benefits. I'll just encourage you to find more ways to get your kids singing and using their voices. There is a wonderful TED talk out of Australia I posted in the Music section of the Mother's University that will give you goosebumps as the presenter talks about how she has used song to bless lives if you want some inspiration.

How many lullabies do you know to sing to your baby? There are so many fun songs for children to sing. I've linked to the Wee Sing Series that has lots of options if you need some ideas. They even have a book for folk songs around the world you can incorporate into the rotation schedule. I've also linked a children's song book that my church uses. If you are of another faith, there are some songs that have particular doctrine, but there are many songs that are universal. One thing that's nice is there are recordings of the songs to help you become familiar with them and they are provided in languages all over the world if you want to use them as part of your rotation study.

Search for folk songs and the stories behind them as you move through the rotation. I'll be sharing some resources in the future that can help with that. Singing hymns together as a family can bring a spirit into your home that can't happen in any other way. Use songs to learn facts—there are a lot of possibilities out there.

So the take away from this 5 minutes: sing! Sing in the morning, sing at night, sing in the car, sing while you are working and playing together. And see what happens.

Reading aloud is a form of expressing music in the voice—maybe start with having them read aloud more often. And of course, you are the example.

I linked a song to sing today—whether or not you're good enough for anyone else to hear. Just sing…sing a song.

Take 5.21—Drawing

From the time young children first pick up a pencil, it seems we are so anxious to teach them to write letters. But letters aren't nearly as exciting as pictures and we stop the process of learning to draw before it has a chance to begin to develop. When you think about it, if you trace back the history of letters and numbers, they originated as pictures. The Hebrew alphabet is especially rich in picture meaning.

In order for a child to write fluently, he needs good manual dexterity and that only comes from practice. You are much more likely that a child will practice more when he is drawing something he enjoys rather than copying a row of A's.

Drawing has so many benefits that I'll keep talking about, and it's not that there are those of us who cannot learn to draw, there are only those of us who have never taken the time to learn how to draw.

I love a series of books called *Draw Write Now* that I will link in the section. It helps a child begin to see the shapes in all the objects around them which is where drawing starts. It can help to build their confidence.

Having said that, in my experience, little children aren't inhibited by a lack of drawing skills. They freely express themselves in their drawing and you want to encourage that.

As they get older, there are many drawing programs out there. One that I particularly like is Mona Brooks' *Drawing With Children* that I will link for you.

Nature journaling is also a way to practice drawing. How many ways can you find to incorporate drawing in your days?

Take 5.22—Mother Goose

It has been said, if you want your children to love Homer, give them Mother Goose. No one knows exactly how long Mother Goose rhymes have been around, but some researchers have traced origins to the mother of Charlemagne way back in the 8th century. There are reasons for their tremendous staying power.

After traveling all this way through time, I am surprised at how many young mothers today are not familiar with Mother Goose rhymes. And you cannot give to your children what you don't have inside yourself. I don't know when or how I learned them—my mother must have read them to me—but I know dozens of them by heart. And I'm sure most of you do, too. But how often are you using them?

Studies have shown that nursery rhymes have wonderful organizational properties for young developing brains. And children delight in them. They aren't looking for meaning, yet there are snippets of truth being planted in their little hearts. Many of them are pure nonsense. But they love the music of them and they delight to repeat them.

If you are among those who missed this phase of growing up, if you go to the Poetry section of the Categories navigation page, you will find a lot of books to choose from. I especially love looking at all the different illustrations. You will also find a good collection in *Stories and Rhymes for Young People* in the Story Hour Series. These happen to be laid out developmentally. The first rhymes are filled with lots of fun sounds and made up words:

Dancy diddly poppity pin,
This is the way the farmers ride-hobbledy hoy, hobbledoy hoy

and things that are familiar to little babies.

Hushaby, don't you cry.

The next section expands to rhymes about animals:

Bow wow says the dog, mew mew says the cat.

Then we move on to rhymes about other children:

Jack and Jill went up the hill.

Now a little feeding of the mind with facts, days of the week and such:

Monday's child is fair of face.
How many days has my baby to play!
Sunday, Monday, Tuesday and so forth.

Next come games and riddles and counting:

Here we go round the mulberry bush,

London Bridge is falling down.

Then stories and experience rhymes:

Old King Cole was a merry old soul and a merry old soul was he.

I'm not suggesting you have to unfold Mother Goose this way. But if you have a baby and you aren't familiar with them, this may be a fun way to start learning and sharing them.

They are probably the easiest rhymes to memorize on the planet. A child can store up dozens with little effort and enjoy repeating them. It's a way of activating their voice. As they experience this joy of saying rhymes by heart, they will be more open to memorizing other poetry down the road. So sprinkle them throughout the day just for fun.

And then, these Mother Goose rhymes can be used for a first favorite poetry anthology that I'll talk about more later. Pull out a piece of paper or a bare book and ask, "What poem shall we write down today? Where do you want me to write it on the page?" And then let them recite it while they watch you write it down. And then run your fingers under the words while you say it back to them. It can become a favorite first reading book, too. Then let them illustrate it any way they want. Or you could even print out some of the illustrations from the old Mother Goose books you'll find online and glue them into the book.

So what if your older children have missed out? Let them help the little ones do these activities. Explain why they matter and have them learn them so they'll all be stored up in memory for when they are parents or favorite aunts or uncles.

Or put a big piece of paper on the wall and have them see how many Mother Goose rhymes they already know by memory. Let them write the first line on the chart and see how long they can make the list.

You can also find a lot of Mother Goose rhymes put to song. You can get singing and rhymes in one shot. It shouldn't be hard to find songs like that.

So don't neglect Mother Goose in your house. As one teacher wrote, "Without the poetry of the nursery, every other poetic mode and philosophic instinct can be left undeveloped, resulting in education itself becoming a crippled thing. Mother Goose prepares the way for other educational journeys. In the end, Mother Goose matters because she is a beginning."

Take 5.23—Picture Books

You may have older kids and wonder when I'm going to get around to them. There is a reason for the order of these Take 5s. I am unfolding these ideas and resources developmentally. So much of what I talk about will apply to older children who may have bypassed some of these foundational things. Singing, drawing, connecting to familiar things apply to all ages. So I hope you won't skip over them.

Today I want to talk about Picture Books. I heard an Oxford trained professor say that whenever he wants to learn anything new, he always starts with a children's book because he knows the topic will be explained clearly and simply, usually with lots of illustrations, and then he can build upon it. And if you followed the incredible winning streak of James Holzauer on Jeopardy recently, he said that he read tons of children's books to prepare for his stint on the show.

So don't necessarily bypass the Picture section on the Elementary section of the website if you have older children. My daughters usually make a list of picture books they want from the library and their libraries have been really good to order books in for them. Then they pick them all up at once and put them in a basket in their living room. Now they have books to grab and read all month long and my daughter with a teenager even finds her teen sitting down and going through them.

Picture books are short enough that many of them will be read multiple times before they're returned. And as you borrow them, you'll start to find your family favorites that you can now look for copies online to use in building your own family library. It's often the picture books that older people look back to which stir fond memories of home and these picture books become treasured keepsakes.

I especially like to own beautifully illustrated fairy tales. I've included several of my favorites in the Picture Book list.

Picture books are how you can include even little children in the monthly study and they provide just enough of an introduction to familiarize names or events.

Let your older children read picture books to younger siblings and they'll both benefit.

The picture book section is the section where you will likely find the most additions in the coming months as I find more and more wonderful reads that fit into the rotation. One of my daughters just created a PDF list of the picture books listed online right now, organized by the monthly rotation, so that you can carry a quick reference with you if you are picture book shopping at your library. I'll provide the link in this section. But keep in mind more titles will be added in as we go along.

Illustrated picture books is definitely one area of book publication that has improved over the years and so you will find many more recent titles in this section, which is why you are more likely to find picture books in your library as opposed to many of the chapter books I have listed.

Take 5.24—Nature Journaling and Three Tools for Learning

You don't need to know how to draw to start nature journaling. Just start where you are and you can learn skills as you go along. But let me back up and address again why nature journaling is so important. One of our objectives as teachers of children is to help them truly see. When you attempt to draw what you are seeing, you are increasing exactness of thought. You begin to see details you wouldn't see otherwise, and the images have more permanence in your memory.

One of my biggest inspirations for nature journaling is John Muir Laws and I talk about him all the time. I'm a big fan. I even convinced him to come to Salt Lake and do two days of workshops. He isn't willing to travel much because he is a dedicated family man and doesn't like to be away from his young children. But he came and taught about 300 of us! And I think all who came will agree it was a life-changing experience.

I've linked a brief 2-minute video so you can begin to catch his passion for what he does. If you go to his site, which is also linked, you will find free videos to not only motivate you, but also to teach you drawing skills. He says anyone can learn to draw and that if you will commit to just 15 minutes a day, at the end of the year you will be astonished at what you can draw.

Let me pass along three simple tools to help open your eyes as you nature journal. They are: "I notice," "I wonder," and "that reminds me of." If you watch one of his introductory videos, he will explain in detail what that means. I find myself applying them to all my learning and I'll demonstrate again how I apply them when I look at fine art in a future Take 5.

I would caution you about assigning them things to look for. Let them explore and discover for themselves.

To get started, it can be as simple as picking up a sketch pad and some color pencils. Find something that catches your interest and sit down and take the time to pay attention to it by attempting to draw it. It is the process, not the final product you need to focus on. Let your children see you doing it. I have watched this process with my grandchildren with some as young as four years old. As they watched their mothers, it wasn't long before they wanted their own sketch pad and pencils to draw what they were seeing.

Later, you can add poetry or comments or ah-hah moments or facts you learn about what you are seeing. Nature journals are a very personal expression and a perfect place to record that which you 'notice,' you 'wonder about' or what it 'reminds you of.'

And as with all things, the proof is in the trying it out.

Take 5.25—Landing Pages and Podcasts

Today let's talk about the landing pages and podcasts. If you click on any of the U.S. History topics or any of the countries on the main navigation pages to the library, you will be taken to what I call a 'landing page.'

From this page, you will be able to narrow down where you want to go next. There are four tabs at the top of the page: Elementary, Middle School, High School and Enrichment. If you are looking for books for younger readers, you will likely want to go to the Elementary section. But don't discount these books for your older children. They may be a perfect place to start, like I've talked about previously. Also, keep in mind that these Elementary books may still be above the level of your young readers to read on their own, but work well as read-alouds. Treat it like a library—take a book off a shelf, read a page or two and see if it is a good fit. If not, close it and move on until you find what you want.

There is also an Enrichment button. This will take you to movies, plays, crafts, cooking, music, and art. I'll keep referring to this section as we go along.

Please note: the nature topics do not have a landing page. When you click on a Nature topic, all the Elementary, Middle and High School books are on one page as well as all the nature enrichment activities.

You will also find the PDFs of booklists for that particular topic as I mentioned in a previous Take 5. Look for the link near the top of the page.

If you are overwhelmed with all the choices, look to the landing page for some suggestions to get started. You know how the librarian will regularly go through the shelves and place some on top so it calls attention to them? That's what I've done on the landing page. I'll highlight a few suggestions of books to start with.

I also give some foundational thoughts on the study of the topic as well as remind you of the connecting points between the nation and the United States topic.

One more thing you will find on the landing pages are the archived Podcasts. The purpose of the Podcasts is to awaken interests in your heart and I often share samples from books so that you can become acquainted with them. They give you little tastes, which is the same process of learning you'll go through with your kids. There are over 175 podcasts now. Please don't feel like you need to start at #1 and make your way through all of them. The first 5 or 10 cover general topics and a lot of people have said they have been really helpful to catch the vision of heart-based learning. But I have incorporated most of what is said in them in the Catch the Vision course. After that, most of the podcasts tie into the monthly topics in the rotation schedule. So I'd just work your way through them as you move through the rotation. I'll continue to add to them on the landing pages as we go along. They are another way of sharing books I love. I know you won't get through all the suggestions in a single month. Jot down people or books you want to revisit in your planner as a reminder in coming years.

All of the podcasts are archived on the podcast page as well and can be accessed through the Podcast button in the menu bar of the main site or from the app. I will link a PDF of all the podcasts to date in this section that you can reference if you are looking for a particular topic.

Take 5.26—Finding the Melody

I really enjoyed an article I found in an old Reader's Digest magazine from the 1950s. It told of a man who hated listening to classical music, but found himself one night sitting next to Albert Einstein at a musical performance in someone's home, and dreading it. He tells how Einstein took him by the hand and led him upstairs to another room where he opened his heart to love the music.

You'll find a link to the whole article in the Music section of the Mother's University, but what I found interesting was that he simply taught the man to listen for the melody.

If you want to help your children love music, I want to tell you about a book that I hope at some point you'll take the time to read. It has been added to the Music volume of the Mother's

Learning Library, but I will also link it in this section. It completely changed my outlook on the best way to go about teaching music to children. We tend to look for a music teacher when we think our children are old enough for music lessons. And the teacher then begins to teach music by teaching them to read musical notation. This approach has a tremendous rate of failure, by the way.

Bad idea, according to this book. I would say teaching music that way is out of line with the Pattern for Learning which requires Heart first. There is so much you can and should do first. And mothers are best suited for this job.

As I read this book, I recognized that the very method Einstein used with this man I just mentioned is what is suggested in this book—help a child pay attention to melody and you will open an inner world where music can have a powerful influence on their lives.

The book is called *What Music Can Do For You* by Harriet Seymour and it will inspire you to want to bring more music into your lives. At least it did me.

Let me share an excerpt:

> Listening forces us to look within, to seek and know ourselves. The inner world is the real world… You will not only hear the end of the tune and the fundamental chords, but you will learn that by stilling your mind you will be able to get the right answer to your problems. Follow this inner listening with action and you have a perfectly balanced philosophic basis for both music and life.
>
> From within out, this is the process, this is education, this is the road to…happiness.

And this concept may sound familiar by now:

> You cannot force children to learn anything, but you can so present a thing to them that you will arouse their interest and cause them to undertake the subject of their own free will. At first they may seem uninterested, but give them a chance to act on their own impulse, have faith in the child and his unerring feeling for beauty and truth, and this will pass.
>
> So having aroused the child's interest in music, leave him alone.

By the way, I've been collecting quite a few books to help you appreciate music more. They are all on one page in the website and to get to them, select the Categories navigation page. Look for that 'other' category, and then look for Music Appreciation.

Take 5.27—Crafts and Creativity

If you haven't yet found the crafts section, go to the Enrichment button on one of the Landing pages and click on it. At the top of the page you will find a link to a Pinterest page full of craft ideas.

The purpose of these crafts isn't necessarily instructive. Rather, it's an activity to allow your children to experience the joy of creating. There is something wonderfully satisfying about gathering materials and creating something with them.

Some of you aren't crafty. That's OK. You don't have to do them. Some of you may do crafts once a month, some once a week, some of you may have ongoing crafts going on in your house. Do what works for you.

One of their benefits is that when your children's hands are occupied, they may be willing to do things they wouldn't ordinarily be open to such as listening to the music or to stories. Or you might find more conversations going on while their hands are busy. Crafts are a fun activity to invite friends over to enjoy with you or to incorporate into a co-op.

I tried to find a variety of crafts and looked for activities for preschoolers through high schoolers. Many of them tie into traditions and cultures of the countries you are studying which provides another connection as your children learn about them.

I suggest including your kids in choosing what they want to create during the month and then gather the supplies you have on hand. Or make a note in your shopping list in your planner so that you can pick them up when you are at the store so that they are easy to access when it's time to create. If you don't get to them during the month, put them in a bag and set them aside for next year.

One warning—it's very difficult to keep Pinterest pages current. Websites are constantly changing or being taken down, so you may click for instructions and find the link is no longer working. That's frustrating. I understand. But that's where you can be even more creative! Take the idea you see and make your own creation based on the idea.

By the way, a big thanks to my daughter Anna-lee who is trying to keep the Pinterest pages refreshed and current for you.

And what are you going to do with all those crafts? I'd take a picture of your child and his friends, if they've joined in the fun, with their crafts and keep it in your World Cultures book, which I talked about in Catch the Vision. I'll talk about it more in a future Take 5. And then, after a comfortable amount of time for you, dispose of most of them. Or find a box for storing the crafts and let your children go through at the end of the year and decide what they want to keep and let the rest go. It's not so much the craft itself that is important, but the happy memory of working together and creating it that is worth preserving.

Take 5.28—Personal Poetry Anthology

As I perused the old books looking for ways to help children fall in love with poetry, the suggestion I came across the most often was to start by creating a personal anthology of the poems you love and then share them with your children. As they watch you do that, there's a good chance they are going to want to create their own book of favorites. If you started with Mother Goose rhymes, it's a natural next step.

The thing about poetry is that poetry touches us in an individual way. A poem that moves me to tears may do nothing for you. And vice versa. Allowing your children to listen to that inner voice of connection rather than always assigning poems is a wonderful gift you can offer them.

So I followed their suggestion and picked up a nice journal at the craft store and every time I come across a poem that touches my heart in some way, I take the time to copy it into my poem journal. I've started accumulating quite a few now and I love sitting down from time to time and reading through them.

Let your children pick out their poetry journal or even start with a 3-ring binder and add individual pages as you go along. You can use poetry tea times for your kids to copy poems or let them do it whenever they are looking for something to do. By the way, copying poetry is a great way for them to practice handwriting skills. Put a little music on in the background, and it can make the activity even sweeter. Let them illustrate or decorate their pages if they'd like.

This poetry anthology will become a treasured keepsake. Imagine your great, great grand-children reading the poems you loved in your very own handwriting! It's one way you can bond their hearts to yours even when you are long gone.

Take 5.29—My Book House/Junior Classics

On many of the Elementary pages, and sometimes on the Middle School pages, you will see orange and lavender blocks. These refer to stories from *My Book House* and *Junior Classics*. Although there are copies that can be borrowed in Internet Archive, borrowing them may not be practical because there are so few copies available and you may or may not have immediate access.

My Book House and *Junior Classics* are collections of stories that are out of print. But for those of you who like to have a book in hand to read, you will get a lot of mileage from the money spent to acquire one or both of these sets. There are several other similar sets that are wonder-ful, as well, but I have found these two are easier to find used copies to buy at an affordable price.

If you want to use the selections I reference in the rotation schedule, you'll want to look for the 1971 edition of *My Book House*, which is the white set and the 1962 edition of *Junior Classics*. The older editions are excellent, too, but they just won't line up with the pages and selections I have referenced in the rotation schedule. Which may or may not matter to you.

Your kids may not yet have the attention span to listen to full chapter books, so the selections you find in these books are short and sweet and just the right size for helping them develop a taste for stories. In fact, if, in your first year of working through the rotation schedule and getting more comfortable with heart-based learning, you mainly relied on either of these sets, you would be laying a wonderful foundation for future learning. These are easy grab-and-read stories. By the way, the stories are also listed in the booklists I talked about previously. As you read a story, I suggest just highlighting it on the booklist page so that you can see what you have already read.

You will notice the sets are organized developmentally, like we've been talking about. The first volumes of both sets include nursery rhymes, poetry for young children and simple familiar stories. Then they move into Imaginative tales—the fairy tales and myths. Then you will find stories of children and stories of legendary heroes, great lives and stories from history and from all around the world as well as stories from nature. You will find a lot of classic stories, too, from Shakespeare and Chaucer and other great writers, adapted for children. Once you realize these books are organized to advance with age, you will know to grab the lower numbers for your younger ones and the higher-numbered volumes for your older children, older children meaning probably upper elementary.

Junior Classics has a lot of chapters from books to whet their appetites. If I was able to find a copy of the book online, I linked it in the library so that you can read the whole book when you find something that especially grabs your interest.

I'm not suggesting everyone has to have these books. They are just another option in your tool chest. For copies, I'd keep my eyes open for them in eBay or used book sales. Or shop some of the used book sites like Amazon or Abe Books. But the best deals I've seen have been in eBay or used book sales and thrift shops.

Take 5.30—Clara Dillingham Pierson

I was really reluctant to put Nature into the Rotation Schedule because nature is best taken in as a whole and there is something going on in nature all year long. When your kids go out for a walk, they see clouds and dragonflies and squirrels and bluebirds. I would never want you to reserve looking at a tree only in month four when there are so many wonderful changes to observe through Spring, Summer, Fall and Winter. Nor should you only go look at the Stars in September.

But as I thought about it more, I could see value in having a systematic plan to make sure you are covering all the parts. By spending a little time focusing on a certain aspect of nature each month, you are helping your children store up ideas and wonderful things to look for every time your children are out in nature. As you follow the nature rotation, you are moving through the process of creation every single year. First is the physical creation—the Light, the water, the rocks, and the soil all necessary for sustaining life. Then the plants and the living creatures, starting with tiny insects then the birds and finally the animals and God's crowning creation, Man.

As you move into science topics, you'll find that roughly the first half of each year are the Physical Sciences and the last half, the Life Sciences. So you can continue to build and layer upon the foundation you are building in Nature.

What I want to talk about today, though, is to highlight another writer who will help your children fall in love with the world around them: Clara Dillingham Pierson. She wrote a series of books called *Among the People*: Among the Meadow, Forest, Night, Farmyard, Pond, and Dooryard People. Her stories will plant a lot of ideas in their hearts. And many of her stories contain a moral truth. She was a leading nature-story author of her day.

The Thornton Burgess readers are a perfect start for your youngest children and I would say Clara's books are the next step up. If I were to put an age, I'd say five years old and up. Because they don't align with monthly topics, you may choose to read them over the summer months or there is absolutely nothing wrong with reading them all along the way.

I've provided links to free digital versions in this section, but if you like a hard copy in hand, we combined all six books into two volumes and they would be a very worthwhile addition to your family library. And yes, we kept all the wonderful illustrations.

Let me tell you a little more about Clara. For starters, she was homeschooled and later went through kindergarten teacher training in Chicago. She married and she and her husband had a little baby who died shortly after birth, but they later adopted and raised two sons.

One of her grandchildren said: "Grandfather was a good man, he turned the money he made into good for his friends and neighbors. His wife loved nature so much she would tiptoe into the kitchen late at night to feed mice that came into her house and would even coax them with bits of cheese."

In her first letter to the children in her first book, she wrote, "I have been asked if I am acquainted with the little creatures about whom I tell you, and I want you to know that I am very well acquainted indeed."

Let me give you a little taste of her personality by sharing the opening letter in her *Among the Night People* book.

My Dear Little Friends—You can never guess how much I have enjoyed writing these stories of the nighttime, and I must tell you how I first came to think of doing so. I once knew a girl—and she was not a very little girl, either—who was afraid of the dark. And I have known three boys who were as brave as could be by daylight, but who would not run on an errand alone after the lamps were lighted. They never seemed to think what a beautiful, restful, growing time the night is for plants and animals, and even for themselves. I thought that if they knew more of what happens between sunset and sunrise they would love the night as well as I...

I think I ought to tell you that I have not been alone when writing these stories. I have often been in the meadow and the forest at night, and have seen and heard many interesting things, but my good Cat, Silvertip, has known far more than I of the night-doings of the out-of-door people. He has been beside me at my desk, and although at times he has shut his eyes and taken Catnaps while I wrote, there have been many other times when he has taken the pen right out of my hand. He has even tried running the typewriter with his dainty white paws, and he has gone over every story I have written. I do not say that he has written any himself, but you can see that he has been very careful what I wrote, and I have learned a great deal from him that I never knew before. He is a very good and clever Cat, and if you like these stories I am sure it must partly because he had a paw in the writing of them.

Your friend,
Clara D. Pierson

Stanton, Michigan
April 15, 1901.

I hope you enjoy them!

Take 5.31—Knowing vs. Being

I've been thinking a lot lately about the difference between knowing and being. For a long time, school has been concerned about the knowing part. But I am hearing more and more people raise their voices in favor of a shift in education towards being. They say we are operating on a system that was created for another time. Today, with a literal explosion of available knowledge, we no longer can be served well by devoting so much time to pouring bits of knowledge and information into the minds of our children. There is just too much out there. And we are experiencing a fallout of our lack of attention on 'being.'

Technology makes it possible for us to focus on more important things. Any time I need a piece of information, it's as simple as: "Alexa what year was Columbus born. Alexa what is the capital of Arkansas. Alexa how far is it to the sun." I can immediately get answers to factual questions in the moment that I am needing it. And if I don't have a use for the facts, it really isn't serving me well to spend so much time cramming them into my head for a test. They are going to fade away anyway. I can't count how many times in school I had to put the planets in order and I still can't do it from memory. But if I ever need to know which is further away—Saturn or Jupiter—I know where to get an immediate answer.

On the other hand, how much more value is there in being creative, being curious, being compassionate, being diligent, being honest, being loyal, being thorough, being trustworthy, being happy…the list goes on.

So, my suggestion for you today is to become aware at how much time you are devoting to knowing and how much to being. The more time you spend in the older books—I'm talking about the ones before 1960 but especially before 1923—the more you are going to find lessons on being. My focus with the activities I suggest here in the Well-Educated Heart all have to do with being. It's the unseen, unmeasurable side of learning. There will be a time when facts and information will be crucial as a child settles in on a career. But in these formative years of life, there are much more important lessons to be tended to, in my opinion.

Take 5.32—Hazel Kinscella

Today I want to show you another resource for helping your children appreciate fine music. I came across a little set of books from the 1920s that were written by Hazel Gertrude Kinscella and fell in love with her storytelling. Yes, they are out of print and I only found a couple of the books from the series online as digital reads so I can't link all of them for you. Instead I went in search of hard copies of the books and was so happy to track them down! They are hard to find.

So now the next problem was how to share them with you. It appears some of the copyrights were renewed, but not all so I can share much from them. At first I thought of reprinting what I could of the books, but then I had another idea. What if I could sort the stories out according to the rotation schedule and attach a YouTube of the musical number suggested by the story so that you can listen.

So that is what I've settled on—at least for now. This gives you another grab-and-go simple music appreciation session.

You will find them in the Music and Art sections of the BelMonde audio library. It will take me time to get them all recorded so I am starting with Month 1 and will work my way through. You can find the first ones in the Scandinavia section and I will give you a direct link here in this section. The stories are very short and sweet, so give it a try.

Take 5.33—Art Tableaus

The habit of attention is one of the habits we are trying to build into our children. It's possible to look at a piece of art and never notice most of the details. Creating art tableaus is one fun way to help children begin to notice and remember all the details of paintings.

My daughter has been having fun doing these with her girls. They don't do it very often, but it's another tool to add to your tool chest.

What you do is look for a painting the you can re-create. If you need to invite a few friends to play along, it's a great activity for a group. Look for a painting that has the same number of people in it as you have and then each person chooses who he or she wants to be. Involve dad if he's willing! Gather or make a few props and then pose yourselves just as they are in the painting. Participants will need to pay close attention to facial expression, the pose of the body, the relationship of the subjects to each other. As they engage in this activity, the painting itself will leave a more lasting impression on their minds. Hold the pose or the tableau for a minute or two. Have someone take a picture.

Then talk about it if you want. But don't make it a chore. Ask questions like, "What do you think you were thinking about or looking at when the artist painted you into the picture." "What are you feeling?"

You can make a little keepsake book of the tableaus using a bare book or other blank journal. Be sure and copy a picture of the original painting and display it next to your creation. Add whatever comments you want to the page, including the date you created the tableau.

These tableaus can also work to bring history to life as you look for paintings of historical characters.

Take 5.34—Poetry Memorization

Now that you have started collecting your favorite poems in your personal poetry anthology, let's talk about memorizing poetry. Is it worth the effort? I think so.

When you make the effort to memorize poetry, you are training your brain to remember things. Our brains have gotten pretty flabby overall and just like you need to exercise your muscles to make them stronger, you need to exercise your brain. You need a working memory in order to learn and to make connections and to comprehend what you are learning. I am astonished at what people in history have been able to retain in their memories. Before there was written language, all stories and histories had to be learned by heart and passed from storyteller to storyteller.

I may have mentioned it before—the entrance exam to get into a Turkish university was to prove the entire Koran had been memorized. We generally don't begin to tap our brain's capacity to retain things.

With our shrinking attention spans, memorizing a poem encourages the habit of attention and teaches our children to focus.

And of special interest to me is that memorizing poetry has been shown to delay typical cognitive decline in old age.

The recitation of poetry by heart can be a first step in building confidence in public speaking. And according to a 1902 handbook, it says, memorizing poetry "stocks the mind with the priceless treasure of the noblest thoughts and feelings that have been uttered by the race." It is the cheapest, most durable tool of moral and emotional education.

According to a well-respected spiritual leader in a private setting, he said that when God didn't have prophets to speak through, He spoke through the hearts of poets. They have much Truth to teach us and through poetry, we find kindred spirits across the centuries.

One day this well-stocked mind of poetry may be a lifeline. Other people have found themselves in desperate isolated situations and found peace and strength by drawing upon the words stored up in their hearts. Often these words will come floating to our remembrance at just the right time.

So how can we best go about memorizing poetry?

First, love the poem. Don't waste time trying to memorize something you don't like at all. Turning to your personal anthology is a good place to look for a poem worth memorizing.

Say the entire poem through out loud several times as you take in the rhythm and the rhyme, which are going to be your helpers to hold on to it. Remember—poetry comes from an oral, not a written, tradition. It is meant to be spoken and heard. Be theatrical in your recitation; let the music in your voice reflect the meaning of the words. Always recite by phrase, not by line. Don't chop a thought in half.

Look up any words that may be giving you trouble, either for meaning or for pronunciation.

If the poem has a story to it, briefly narrate that story to yourself so that you can follow the order.

Now take the time to copy the poem again on an index card so that you can carry it around with you. The very act of copying it in cursive will make another imprint and activates the whole brain. Focus on one stanza at a time if the poem is long. Tape it to your mirror while you're getting ready in the morning or carry it in your purse or your pocket so you can take advantage of those moments here and there to work on it.

In the Mother's University in the Poetry month, you'll find a presentation that La Dawn Jacob gave at our Simple Joy conference. She brought many of her children and grandchildren and inspired us all with possibilities and she has lots of suggestions she uses for memorizing poems.

Do find a place to share it. Poetry Tea Times can be a perfect place. Frequently review the poems that you are adding to your repertoire. Memorizing poetry gives your brain a good and beautiful thing to work on and keep you company and is a wonderful pastime to introduce to your children. I read of one senator who was able to entertain himself on a 12-hour road trip by reciting 12 hours of poetry he had committed to memory.

Hmmm…maybe more of our senators would do well to occupy their minds with such a worthy activity. But that is a topic for another day.

Take 5.35—Our Little Cousins Series

As we continue talking about the Familiar stage of development, I want to tell you about a series of books that are a nice lead into the study of history and enables your younger children to participate at a level they are ready for.

They are called the Our Little Cousins and the Twin Series. Young children—and I'm thinking maybe ages 6 to 7 if you are reading the books aloud or 8 to 9 and older if they are reading the books to themselves—enjoy hearing about other children and these little books will begin to teach them about various cultures around the world with a good amount of history thrown in that they can start building upon.

Keep in mind, some of the information will be out of date because these books were written a hundred years ago. But that can give you a teaching moment to show how times have changed. As you continue to layer deeper in the rotation, many of those ideas will correct naturally over time. Sometimes you may read something that is kind of jarring. They had viewpoints that were much different than ours or used words that are not comfortable to us today—like referring to a group of people as savages. Use it as a lesson. Or replace the words if you are doing a read-aloud.

Racism has become a hot topic today. There are things in these books that can lead to important discussions.

You'll also get a good introduction to new words in other languages. You'll want to look up pronunciations on the internet to help you pronounce the words correctly. But that is so simple to do these days.

The Our Little Cousins Series was introduced at the beginning of the last century as a way to help children make friends with children all over the world. Travel and means of communication were shrinking the world, and learning about cultures all over the world is even more important and relevant today as we easily engage with each other. We need to learn and understand each other's stories.

The publishers of this series engaged the best children's writers of the day. Some are better than others, of course. But give them a try. We have started reprinting all the books that are in public domain that we can get hold of. There are free digital reads online, but many of the books are only found on Gutenberg and if you've tried to read Gutenberg texts, they're a little more tricky. Those books weren't photocopied from original text but rather were typed out. So you have long passages of typed text to read in the Gutenberg versions.

We have reformatted the books and retained all the illustrations. We are always budget conscious, so we are combining two or three books into single volumes to cut down on the cost of owning these books. We're releasing them in line with the rotation schedule and bunching the books together according to the monthly topics. For instance, the Month 2 book will include *Our Little Dutch Cousin*, *Our Little Belgian Cousin* and *Our Little Spanish Cousin*.

We laid the text out with lots of white space so that it will appeal to your beginning readers if they want to pick the books up on their own.

When you get to Month 4, you'll find reprints of a series that were all written by a favorite storyteller of mine, Julia Darrow Cowles and takes a look at life in Ancient Greece and Ancient Rome. In Part 2 of the Series, you will find additional stories of children from Ancient Times.

There are so many books, we couldn't get them to all fit into 12 volumes, so in the second part, you will find stories on countries we missed the first time around and also will be adding in text of another wonderful series, the Twin Series, written by Lucy Fitch Perkins whose intention was the same—to bring enough of an understanding of the culture and history of the countries that a child will become familiar and will want to know more.

Like I said, these are great read-alouds or I know my 9-year-old granddaughter has thoroughly looked forward to reading them on her own each month.

You can subscribe to the series in our store or we will be posting them in the Forgotten Classics library.

Here is a sample from the Preface to *Our Little Norwegian Cousin*:

> Long before Columbus discovered America, there were brave men in the north of Europe who dared to sail farther out upon the unknown waters of the Atlantic than any other people in the world. These daring seamen were called Vikings. Their home was the peninsula of Scandinavia, now ruled over by one king, although divided into two distinct countries, Norway and Sweden.

[Pause. My wondering mind asks if that is still true. I'll have to look it up.]

It was along the shores of Norway, with rugged mountains fringing its deep bays, that the Vikings learned command of their curious, high-prowed ships, and overcame all fear of wind and storm. Their strong nature shows itself today in the people of Norway, who patiently endure many hardships while trying to get a living on the rough mountain-sides or along the rocky coasts.

Many of our Norwegian cousins have come to America to make a home for themselves where the sun shines warmly and the winds blow less keenly. Their fair-haired children are growing up amongst us, showing us the qualities their parents most admire.

Be brave, be honest, be kind to all creatures, be faithful to every little duty—these are the lessons they have been taught from babyhood, as well as their brothers and sisters who have not as yet ventured far from the land they love so well—the land of rapid-flowing rivers, deep, dark bays and narrow valleys.

Come with me today to the home of one of these blue-eyed cousins and join her for a while in her work and play.

One thing I love about such a study is you come to appreciate that, as much as we love America, other people love their countries just as much and for good reason. That is an important lesson to instill if we are going to get along in the world.

Take 5.36—Mother's University Nature Book

Today I thought I would reference the Mother's Learning library. I hope you have found it by now. All of them are linked in their respective topics in the Mother's University. What I did was gather some of my favorite writings from the heart educators of a hundred years ago so that you can read some of the same books I have been reading and get a feel for all of this firsthand and deepen your understanding. If you didn't catch it, if you purchase 5 or more of our series, either by monthly subscription or all at once, you get all 12 volumes of the Mother's Learning Library for free as well as 5 bonus books. But, like I said, you can also read digital copies of all of them for free, either from the Forgotten Classics page or in the respective topics in the Mother's University.

In the Nature Study volume, I included sections from a wonderful little book called *How Nature Study Should Be Taught: Inspiring Talks to Teachers* by Edward Bigelow. I've shared a few pieces of the book here and there in different presentations, but here is where you can expand upon those ideas.

Here is an idea to start with, taken in the introduction:

Formerly, the question was, What does a man need to know? Now the question is being asked, What does he need to be? It is the emphasis upon this question, in the minds of the leaders of educational thought, which is making it clearer and clearer that we need a knowledge of nature, not only because we want to be able to talk with one another across the ocean…but because we want to be men.

I talked about the difference between knowing and being earlier this week.

And here is the difference between a study of science and the study of nature.

> ...the primary purpose of elementary science is the imparting of scientific knowledge, and the development of habits of scientific thinking, while the primary purpose of nature study is the development of a love of nature. Of course knowing cannot take place apart from feeling, nor feeling apart from knowing. But the cold love of truth, the feeling that the teaching of science seems to awaken, is a vastly different experience from the feeling of love or of admiration for an animal, or an object, which the teaching of nature study seeks to awaken.

Maybe jot a note down in your planner to spend a little time with Dr. Bigelow in Month 2 when the Mother's University topic is Nature Study.

The second half of the book is not a book designed to be read straight through. It's called *Type Lessons for Primary Teachers in the study of Nature, Literature and Art* by Anna McGovern. The book is arranged by the four seasons and I included it because it has a wonderful treasury of poetry and ideas you can use with your children when you're out in nature to open their eyes. I'd take this book in tiny sips—a place to come when you are searching for an idea of something to share in nature—and revisit it often as the seasons change.

Take 5.37—Reading

"But what about reading?" I am frequently asked. "Don't we need to be teaching our children to read?"

Of course!

But this is what I know about learning to read.

Some children will learn to read at three and some won't be reading until age 11 or older. Some children will begin reading as naturally as they learned to speak. Other children will benefit from more formal instruction. Some children have eye disorders that need to be evaluated and treated. Some children are dyslexic. Some children will never be able to read fluently, but will learn through other means—audio books, direct observation and discussion, drawing.

All of these things are perfectly normal. Which is why I never promote a one-size-fits-all approach to learning to read.

There are some things that appear to apply to all children, however. Well, most children. If you have a child who cannot hear or see, of course you have to have a different approach. And I only recently learned of a disorder called misophonia which literally means "hatred of sound." So I suppose I can never use the word "all."

So most all children benefit tremendously by having books read aloud to them, even before they understand words. Their vocabulary will grow in this way. They will learn to form pictures in their minds without the clutter of letters. They learn the structure of a story very naturally—

the grabber in the beginning, the sense of "what happens next" leading to the satisfying conclusion.

I referenced previously a kindergarten in New York that was largely made up of non-English speaking children. Rather than using basal readers (textbooks broken down by reading level with carefully selected words and skill sets), they used rich, beautiful literature. Nearly all the children were reading by the end of the year.

Children who listen to the music of language have better reading comprehension later on. They develop a habit of attention, not to mention the bond created between reader and listener.

Forcing a child to learn to read before he is developmentally ready can sometimes set him back for years. If you are getting a lot of resistance and push back, back off for awhile. A love of stories and a desire to get at more of them will fuel a child's desire to figure out this whole decoding of words thing. Decoding words by itself will not make your child a reader. I think our problem is not, "Why can't Johnny read?", it's "Why doesn't Johnny want to read?" You will be way ahead by spending more time loving stories together than worrying about teaching names of letters and their sounds in childhood.

Waldorf schools don't introduce any formal instruction in reading before age 7. Before that time, they engage little hands with knitting while they listen to a wealth of stories. Finland does no formal academic instruction until after age 7 and they are listed consistently as the number 1 schools in the world.

"But my child is 3 and is begging to learn to know his letters." Then follow his lead! By all means, feed his desire. But also don't panic if your child is 11 or 13 and still struggling. Keep feeding his heart. I know a man—one of the most brilliant and gentle men I have ever known. He was nearly out of high school before he could read and he became a voracious reader with a very distinguished career after that.

There are any number of phonics and learn-to-read programs out there. If you go to the Language Arts section of the Mother's University, you will find just a couple of popular resources I've listed that you can check out. One is a free phonics program that I tested on a granddaughter. I picked up a little white board at the store and she had fun drawing pictures to go with the words we were creating. But look around. You know your child best. Pick what works for you.

I'm not an expert in that field. But I do know you will benefit greatly by reading aloud a variety of books with your young ones. And since strengthening the imagination, creating visuals and desire in hearts, is one of the primary aims of the well-educated heart, that is my focus where reading is concerned. That applies to everyone, well with the few exceptions I already mentioned.

One other thing you will find in the Mother's University section is that I have linked you to some of the most popular readers from a hundred years ago that are broken down by reading level. These are generally high interest stories and may work well as worthy books for your beginning readers to read.

Take 5.38—Childhoods of Composers

Going along with our topic of connecting to the familiar, one of the ways of increasing a love of fine music is to help your children get to know the great composers. A young child isn't ready to dive into a full biography, but sharing stories of when the composer was a child is a great connecting point to start.

Many of the stories of great composers I share in the Stories of Great Musicians book contain stories of their childhoods. If you refer to the blue blocks on the online library pages in the Elementary section, you will likely be taken to a story that contains something about his childhood.

But I want to share another resource for you. Thomas Tapper created a set of little books just for children called *Child's Own Book of Great Musicians*. You'll see links to them in the Music Appreciation section I've talked about earlier, but I'll give you a direct link to the page in this section. By the way, if you've been reading the Mother's University book on Music, Tapper wrote *Music Talks With Children* that is the first selection. Very inspiring.

The idea behind these books was to offer a simple story and then there were little blank squares for children to glue in pictures, like what I did in the Stories of Jesus book. The downside is not all of the books I link have a PDF option, so it's a little trickier to get usable copies. I'ts on my to-do list of projects I'd like to tackle and I own a couple of books that aren't available in Gutenberg that I hope to create PDFs for and I'll add them to the list. I have Brahms, Mendelssohn and MacDowell.

But I also want to call attention to a member of our Well-Educated Heart group who has created books you can buy. They are only $5.00 each and contain three composers in each book. I'll give you a link to her site because she also offers lessons in singing that look really interesting! I think it's worth checking out. If you scroll down the page, you'll see a link to where you can buy the books. She does not have the three books I mentioned so I better get busy, huh? I'll add them to the Music Appreciation page and provide links to the PDFs when they are ready.

Here is a little sample from the book about Mendelssohn. It's called *The Story of a Happy Brother and Sister Who Loved to Make Music*.

> It is always pleasant to see people do beautiful things: like writing books, making music, doing kindnesses and making other people happy.

> And, of course, just to try to make others happy makes us happy too.

> Perhaps it was because Mendelssohn's father and mother knew their boy would make happiness for others that they named him Felix, which in Latin means 'happy.' His full name was Jakob Ludwig Felix Mendelssohn, but everybody called him Felix for short.

> Here is a picture of Felix as a boy.

I think that gives you a feeling for the writing.

After your children take time to look at the pictures and listen to the story, Mendelssohn will seem like a new friend and when they later hear his music, they will more likely be willing to open their ears to hear what he is trying to tell them.

Take 5.39—Childhoods of Artists

What I said about sharing stories of the childhoods of great composers applies to helping your children gain an appreciation of the great artists. I hope you are beginning to get a sense of this layering process as children move through the rotation schedule over the years. When they are four, five, or six, in those familiar and imaginative years of development, stories of children are what will appeal to them. Then they have names and connections to someone to start deepening their relationship with them as they mature.

The same thing also applies to the Forgotten Classics books that I mentioned about Musicians, especially the Stories of Great Artists. If I listed a story in the Elementary section, it is usually because it contains something of their childhoods. Look for the blue boxes in the Biography section.

Today let me highlight one book I took quite a few stories from, but you can go to the original book to get the rest.

It's called *Stories of Great Artists* by Olive Browne Horne and Kathrine Lois Scobey, published in 1903. By the way, if you look at the list of books on the copyright page of Stories of Great Artists in the Forgotten Classics Library, you will see a number of books that highlight childhoods: *Little People Who Became Great, Boyhood Stories of Famous Men, When They Were Children*. I drew heavily from these books when compiling the great lives series, but I didn't use all the stories. So do check them out for more stories.

Here's a sample from the story of Raphael.

> Far away across the sea lies the sunny land of Italy. Blue are the sparkling waters of its seas. Still more blue is the cloudless sky. Nestling among the mountains are many little villages. Urbino is one of these. The gray stone houses can scarcely be seen against the background of trees. From a window of one of these houses one may see the valleys with their beautiful vineyards. Here the dark-eyed Italian children are picking purple grapes.
>
> About four hundred years ago, in a beautiful house in Urbino, lived Giovanni Sanzio. His wife was an Italian woman. She had soft, dark eyes and a low, musical voice. Very much like her was their little son Raphael. They loved him so dearly they gave him the name of an angel. His eyes were deepest blue. They were thoughtful and dreamy. His brown hair floated lightly over his shoulders. In his little blue cap and suit, he was beautiful as an angel.
>
> Raphael's father was an artist. Let us visit his home…
>
> When a very small boy, Raphael loved to play in his father's studio. There were many little tasks that he could do to help his father. There were brushes to be washed and palettes to be cleaned. Oh, there was work in plenty for little Raphael! Giovanni Sanzio

painted beautiful angels and holy Madonnas. His little son was often at his side as the work was going on.

In Italy, one loves to be out of doors. Raphael spent much of his time in the bright, sunshiny air. There was much to be seen in those olden times, if one used his eyes.

Don't you just love the pictures these writers from this Golden age of children's literature create? They appeal to all the senses. A child can relate to helping his father. And look—a well-educated heart principle—spending time in the bright, sunshiny air, seeing much *if* one used his eyes.

And I'll mention it again—if you have older children, use them to read these stories to their younger siblings if they are willing.

I'm going to be moving into the next Developmental stage next week, so let me just mention one more group of books that bring to life childhoods in this Familiar stage before I move on. They are the *Childhoods of Famous Americans* and *Childhoods of World Figures* series of books. A lot of children, especially beginning readers, love these books. I link some of them in the library. I wish I had a way to give you access to the older books that are out of print. If I could find them in Internet Archive, I linked them. If you are a used book sale shopper, keep your eyes open for them. They are worth holding on to. You will likely find many of them in your library. But if you can't find them, there are other options open to you.

Take 5.40—Poetry for Young People Series

Going along with our theme of making the unfamiliar become familiar, you don't have to wait until a child is older to begin to acquaint him with the great poets. Of course, there is much they won't understand, but children are listening more to the music of the poems than the words. So share the music of the great poets with them even in childhood so their voices become familiar.

To help you do this, there is a wonderful series of books that is in print now and that you may well find copies of in your public library. It's called the *Poetry for Young People* Series. I've linked all the books I could find to Amazon if you want to start collecting them. I've listed them all together on the Poetry page and I'll link you to that page in this section. I probably should spread them out in the rotation schedule as well. When I do, I'll include them in the Cultural section on the Elementary pages. I can't find them in Internet Archive to borrow yet. But, like I said, check your library, as well.

What I love about these poetry books is they are filled with beautiful illustrations. You'll find just enough about the poet to get to know him. And then they selected stanzas from the longer works to help to give children a taste for the poetry without firehosing them. They explain a little about what the poem is about and clarify words that may give trouble.

They are still in print and reasonably priced at around $7.00 for new books.

Take 5.41—Family Stories

Nothing creates emotional bonds between generations like sharing family stories. Simplified versions of these stories are perfect for the young familiar years of development.

When I first started this work many years ago, my message was restoring the art of storytelling in the home. But I found that was too much of a leap. I didn't realize how story depleted we are. So I have focused on filling up story reservoirs, but I haven't abandoned my belief that a generation of storytelling mothers would transform the world. Yes, reading stories from a book is really good. But oh! The magic that happens when you put the book down and tell a story by heart.

One way we can move towards becoming storytellers again is to start with stories that are most familiar with us—the stories from our lives. We know them. They flow naturally out of our hearts.

In the first section of Catch the Vision, I share a presentation by Dr. Gordon Neufeld, that, in its essence, says that the young seek for something to attach to and once it attaches, it seeks to become like that to which it is attached. Telling your stories and the stories of your family—your ancestors—is a powerful way of attaching.

There are skills you can learn, of course, and I'll talk about that another day. If you get bogged down in details or go off on a million detours, you'll lose the emotional flow of the story. But you'll find that out for yourself, if storytelling is new to you.

For today, I want to direct you to a place where you can find some story joggers. You may be thinking, "I have no idea what I can tell." I will link you to a site that has all kinds of ideas. And do encourage your children to start telling their own stories. If you find that day after day and week after week goes by and absolutely nothing has happened in your life that can be told in a story, you have some re-examining to do. You may have gotten caught in a rut of just existing. If every day looks the same—we got up at 7:00. Ate breakfast. Did math until 10. Writing to 11. Lunch at noon. Quiet reading until 3. Played with Legos. Ate dinner. Went to bed…. There isn't much of a story to tell. Although rigid schedules may help you keep your sanity, they can also be a killer of joy and rob you of life! Those days that can't be translated into a story will fade away from memory.

It may be time to be spontaneous and head out on an adventure. I remember a few times of walking to the bus stop, loading my kids into a bus, even though we had a car, and heading downtown because you always see interesting people on the bus, for good or bad, and riding the bus was out of the ordinary. And we'd go see new sights and hear new sounds. Now there's a story to tell dad when he gets home from work.

And I've found disaster + time often turns to laughter. A favorite story around my house is told by my son. When he was in second grade, I gave each of the kids a brown bag to decorate and some Andes mints and post-it notes to give to their teachers for Christmas. On the way to school, he ate all the mints, so the bag just had wrappers in them. Well, not all teachers open their presents in front of the class. But his did that year. And he watched as she got closer and closer to his present and he was just dying inside. Finally, when she almost got to his present, he quickly raised his hand and said, "I've got to go to the bathroom," and ran out of the classroom. Well, he actually walked very, very slowly once he got outside the room. And took his sweet time, trying to make sure that the class had moved on to other things. When he finally walked back in, the teacher said, "Oh, Michael! We wanted to wait until you got back to open your present."

Maybe it's because we all love Michael's personality, but that story makes us laugh every single time. And we tell it over and over again. As an adult, one Christmas he gave us all a present that we all got the meaning of—we each got a brown lunch bag filled with Andes mint wrappers.

These are the simple life events that bring us together.

One more suggestion. When I was about 3 years old back in the 50s, my dad bought one of those reel-to-reel recorders. You'll have to Google them if you have no idea what I'm talking about. But my grandma and grandpa were visiting us in California and my dad took the time to record some of their stories and a little interchange with us kids. I can hear my little 3-year-old voice on the recording. And then he recorded my grandpa singing a Swedish folk song.

I loved my grandpa. He died when I was fourteen—fifty years ago! But when I turn that song on, I am filled with his presence and his love.

Such a simple thing to do. It only took a few minutes. But priceless to me.

What are you leaving behind?

By the way, reel-to-reel recorders aren't easy to come across these days. But I found that the university by us had a media center and they took my reel-to-reels and were able to transfer them to CDs. I'm not sure what the next step is in media. I worry about everything being stored in Clouds, but I'll have to find a way to keep preserving it and passing it down the line. And you'll have to do the same.

Take 5.42—Using the Forgotten Classics Nature Series

I can only imagine the visual stack of books in your mind you are feeling like you need to get through. Let me give you another gentle reminder—not every book is going to be a right fit for you. And what doesn't work for you now may very well work later. Or not at all ever. My job is to familiarize you with possibilities. And then let you choose. You have a lifetime to explore. And so do your children. Children's books don't have to be read in childhood, you know.

So I have talked about Burgess and Clara Dillingham Pierson nature books that are wonderful to read to young children. And if I haven't mentioned it, I need to: in those younger years before 8 years old, I would lean more heavily on nature stories rather than the history side of the rotation. There are things your little ones can be involved in that begin to give them awareness of the nations of the world—the crafts, the music, the art, the folk and fairy tales, the stories of children. I don't mean read exclusively nature stories, but this is a wonderful age to help them love the world of nature that surrounds them so I would lean more heavily on the nature side of things.

I don't picture The Nature Series in the Forgotten Classics Family Library as something you would read straight through to your children. I see them as something to refer to as they interact in nature. I suggest that you use the nature side of the rotation schedule the first year to familiarize yourself with what is in the books, not necessarily read them cover to cover. Notice that in some of the books in the very beginning, I included stories, if I could find them, for the familiar years where it talks about how mommy birds and mommy animals and even mommy plants take care of their babies. That is something a little child can understand. Some of the books have poetry at the back of them. Each book has a little different flavor to it.

There is nothing wrong with reading them straight through to your kids, unless they start groaning because it is too much information being thrown at them that they do not yet have a use for. It would be much better to take them a little at a time. And then try and find what you read about out in nature and learn by first-hand observation.

You will notice on the Nature pages that the Enrichment activities are on the bottom of the main page. Use some of the craft ideas to keep little hands busy while you read, if you want. Or listen to the music suggestions while you do crafts.

If you have time to read them yourself, you'll begin to store up a lot of ideas that you can talk about when you are out in nature with your kids. If you have older readers, by all means, encourage them to read them on their own, a little here and a little there.

And I'll say it again—explore all of nature all year round. Just because I talk about trees in December in Month 4 doesn't mean you shouldn't be watching all the changes that take place from winter to spring to summer and to fall. The only purpose for having a rotation schedule in nature is to help you devote a little time each year to studying a certain aspect of nature that can then be observed and applied year round.

Take 5.43—Imagination

I have now spent several weeks in the Familiar Stage of Development. I cannot stress enough the attraction and pull to the familiar. So take advantage of that as you try and plant many familiar points to build upon and also as you tie into familiar things to awaken interest in new things.

But now it's time to turn to the next stage of Development—the Imaginative Stage. In little children, this kicks in around age 4 or 5. Prior to this time, you have been helping them make sense of what they are seeing and experiencing in the real world around them. Now it's time to help them see things with their inner eye; things that may not even exist in the real world.

You don't have to teach a child to have an imagination. They come equipped with it. But it is possible to kill it or have it slowly atrophy with disuse. In our age of science and academics, we are raising a generation that is unable to see past a literal level of understanding. Symbolism is difficult to grasp. A lack of imagination is behind a lack of empathy; of seeing what others are seeing. Without an imagination, there is no dreaming, no hope, no creativity. There is no heaven or God or faith. A lack of imagination makes a life of dull grays. Imagination sees beauty and loveliness. Dr. Curry calls imagination "the thinking of the heart."

John Senior, who wrote *The End of Christian Culture*, said, "In order to read the 'great' books of Plato, Aristotle, St. Augustine and St. Thomas, we need to replenish the cultural soul that has been depleted and create a place where these works can thrive by cultivating an imaginative ground saturated with fable, fairy tale, stories, rhymes, and adventure—the thousand books of Grimm, Andersen, Stevenson, Dickens, Scott, Dumas and the rest. The one thing a great books education will not do is create a moral imagination where there is none."

If you need more reminders of why you want to allow plenty of time to facilitate the growing of the imagination, you might want to revisit talk #7 in Catch the Vision called Romancing the Heart.

If your child is well past the Imaginative years, there is nothing we will talk about over the next several sessions that won't still apply to them. We are told we are capable of growing new neural pathways well into old age. It's not too late.

Take 5.44—Opera

I have a confession to make. I love music, but it is only recently that I have started acquiring a taste for Opera. It has been way too rich for my liking. But two things are opening it up to me: learning the stories and familiarizing myself with the music, a little here and a little there.

So why does it matter? Plenty of people get through life perfectly fine without loving Opera.

I think I can best answer that question by sharing an experience of a granddaughter that I have shared before. When she was maybe 4 or 5 years old, her mother turned on an old 1950-ish black and white recording of an opera written for children—Amahl and the Night Visitors—for her to watch on a computer screen. The image was grainy and there were no spoken words. Just music. My daughter didn't expect that her little girl would watch for more than a few minutes. But half an hour later, there she was, glued to the screen.

My daughter asked her if she was liking it and she said, "Oh yes! It's like the music is telling me stories."

I would add it was feeding her imagination.

And that's why opera matters. It speaks to a deeper place in our hearts than words alone. It doesn't matter if the opera is in Italian or German, it's the music that will speak to your heart. Opera opens another door into the heart.

So what can you do to open this art up to your children—and to you, if you're not a fan? I would suggest share the stories and familiarize yourself with the music, a little at a time. Hum the melody like we've talked about before.

I will continue to add opera selections on the Enrichments pages. And you'll find stories of operas in the Nature, Art and Music series. These are great stories even if you don't add the music, by the way. I'm not sure Wagner is where I'd start, but the version of the story of the Rhine Gold I included in that volume is a good one. By the way, Tolkien says his Lord of the Rings has nothing to do with Wagner's work, but they sure carry a similar theme.

Not all opera storylines are suitable for little children, of course.

Humperdinck's Hansel and Gretel has some memorable children's music—like Now I Lay Me Down to Sleep and Won't You Come and Dance With Me. Pirates of Penzance is also a really fun one that children will enjoy—a perfect one to go with the Month 2 study or H.M.S. Pinafore, which I included the story in the opera book.

The Magic Flute is also a good beginning children's opera, but you will likely want to break it down into small introductory pieces.

You will find several books on the Music Appreciation page that include introductory stories of operas, as well.

Dolores Bacon reminds us in her *Operas Every Child Should Know* book, "We go to opera…to hear music and see beautiful scenic effects… Music is first of all something to be felt."

Don't forget the scenic effects! Some of the most magnificent scenery is found at the Metropolitan Opera and you can have front row seats…for free. What an amazing age we live in!

Take 5.45—Imaginative Gem Pages

Notebooking is a great way to hold on to what you are learning, and so, as we go along, I'll suggest different ways of notebooking.

I'll be talking about fairy tales in a couple of days, but let me suggest something you can do in connection with reading a fairy tale. I would never make this an assignment, but sometime when you read a fairy tale, say, "I want to remember that." And then pull out a piece of paper and draw something from the fairy tale. It doesn't matter if you know how to draw or not—the very act of attempting to draw what you saw in the story is going to work wonders for you. And there's a good chance your children will want to pull out their own piece of paper and draw something. Write down the name of the fairy tale and if there is a gem you can connect to it, add that to the page.

For instance, from the Frog Prince, it might be: A promise is a promise.

Research has shown that drawing is the fastest and most effective way to learn. So drawing scenes from fairy tales is a great way to make drawing a natural thing to do. Little children aren't as inhibited as grown-ups. Have you ever had a toddler explain their scribbles? They know exactly what they have in mind.

A group of volunteers were asked to memorize a list of words or definitions. Half of them were instructed to repeatedly write them down. The others were told to draw them in order to memorize them. The doodlers won, hands-down. And it didn't matter in the slightest if the participants showed any artistic ability. The report of one study said: "After just 40 seconds of low-quality sketching, subjects not only remembered significantly more, they also recalled more detail and context about the words and ideas they were studying. In short, they learned more, faster."

Why is drawing such a powerful way to study? To figure this out, the researchers tried to narrow down what exactly about drawing was so effective. Would tracing an existing drawing of an idea have the same effect? Would looking at someone else's visual representation? While both of these approaches were better than just reading over a word or concept, the act of drawing beat them all.

The researchers hypothesized the reason why drawing is so effective is because drawing gives your brain so many different ways to engage with new material—you have to figure out how to draw it by imagining it in detail in your mind; you experience the physical feeling of rendering that idea, and then, in the end, you look at a visual representation of it.

So you can see there will be more applications of using drawing for learning as we move forward. This is a fun start and can also serve as a beginning literature gems notebook. You can draw on individual pages, 3-hole punch them and keep them in a notebook, or dedicate a bare book to drawings from fairy tales.

Just another way to expand the image-ination of a child.

Take 5.46—A Child's Garden of Verses

Robert Louis Stevenson was a sickly boy who spent much of his childhood in bed. But he was blessed to have a beloved nurse—Cummie—who filled his boyhood heart with endless stories to fire up his imagination. Among the gifts of his imagination to the world was one of the most popular children's classics of all time, *Treasure Island*. And from that same imaginative heart came an endearing poetry collection of childhood memories, *A Child's Garden of Verses*, which, by the way, was written when he was an adult convalescing in a hospital room.

> When I was sick and lay a-bed,
> I had two pillows at my head,
> And all my toys beside me lay
> To keep me happy all the day.
>
> And sometimes for an hour or so
> I watched my leaden soldiers go,
> With different uniforms and drills
> Among the bed-clothes, through the hills;
>
> And sometimes sent my ships in fleets
> All up and down among the sheets;
> Or brought my trees and houses out,

And planted cities all about.

I was the giant great and still
That sits upon the pillow hill.
And sees before him, dale and plain,
The pleasant land of Counterpane.

Or who has not heard:

I have a little shadow that goes in and out with me
And what can be the use of him is more than I can see...

Or:

When at home alone I sit
And am very tired of it,
I have just to shut my eyes
To go sailing through the skies!
To go sailing far away
To the pleasant Land of Play.

His *Child's Garden of Verses* is one of the most illustrated collection of children's poetry out there. I regularly keep my eyes open for new versions. Among my favorite illustrators of his poems are Jessie Willcox Smith, Florence Edith Storer, Tasha Tudor and Gyo Fukiyama. If you go to the Poetry page that I have taken you to before, you will find links to several versions of the book. I also included the poems in the Story Hour Series volume, Stories and Rhymes for Young Children. Why not have your children create their own illustrated volume of his poems?

He dedicated the book to his nurse with this poem found in the beginning:

To Alison Cunningham, From Her Boy
For the long nights you lay awake
   And watched for my unworthy sake:
For your most comfortable hand
   That led me through the uneven land:
For all the story-books you read:
   For all the pains you comforted:
For all you pitied, all you bore,
   In sad and happy days of yore: -
My second Mother, my first Wife,
   The angel of my infant life –
From the sick child, now well and old,
   Take, nurse, the little book you hold!
And grant it, Heaven, that all who read
   May find as dear a nurse at need,
And every child who lists my rhyme,
   In the bright, fireside, nursery clime,

May hear it in as kind a voice
  As made my childish days rejoice!

This gem of a poetry book reminds us:

  The world is so full of a number of things
  I think we all should be as happy as kings.

Take 5.47—Fairy tales

Let me quote Albert Einstein one more time: "If you want your child to be intelligent, read him fairy tales. If you want him to be more intelligent, read him more fairy tales."

I am seeing a trend among mothers who want to keep their children grounded in the real; the factual. They don't want any of this fairy land stuff in their children's lives. I don't think they realize the damage they are doing because the fairy tales that have been handed down to us over centuries are some of the most nutrient dense foods for the imagination that we have. And these fairy tales are how concepts of right and wrong, good and evil, justice and injustice were passed down over hundreds of generations. The heart educators taught that the secret of their endurance is because they contained kernels of Truth and Truth is everlasting.

I am so grateful for those great souls who felt a call to visit distant lands and visited the villages and homes of peasants to gather these time-worn tales and write them down, thereby preserving them for us. A generation or two later, they would have all likely disappeared as storytelling traditions were replaced by hectic lifestyles and other forms of media.

I'm not suggesting every fairy tale or folk tale is right to tell your children. Originally, they were not intended for children's ears. But over time, they have been adapted and rough edges knocked off.

Many of the storytellers in the Golden Age of Children's Literature in the late 1800s and early 1920s as well as later gave us wonderful versions we can use with our families. You will find a good number of them linked in the Imaginative sections of the different nations on the Elementary pages in the library. I still suggest previewing the stories, though, because you know the sensitivities of your own children and you might come across some pretty gruesome things. My daughter was reading a fairy tale from Russia to her little girls and suddenly the little sister was axed by her brother in the forest. She came back to life later, but my daughter didn't exactly want that image planted in their minds, so she quickly ended the story and bypassed that scene.

But I would never say that none of you should read that. I have a friend you had a terrible childhood and was bounced from foster home to foster home. She lived for fairy tales and, for her, somehow even those gruesome ones helped her through her ordeals. And I will mention she is one of the most creative and warm-hearted souls I have ever known.

Another place you will find a great selection of fairy tales is on the Mother's University Imagination page. I linked all of Andrew Lang's *Color Fairy Tale* books there as well as some others. You will find some good articles on why Fairy Tales matter on that page as well.

I plan on recording fairy tales and posting them on the BelMonde site, so watch for fairy tales there, too.

One more mention—I love to collect beautifully illustrated fairy tales. I'm always looking for them. I have linked some of my favorite illustrated versions in the Picture Book sections of the Elementary pages.

Don't overdose—one fairy tale a day, I think, is sufficient. But do what works for you.

Take 5.48—Nature Fairy Lands

One idea for feeding the imagination in nature is to create a mini magical fairy garden. If you do a Google search of how to create a fairy garden, you will find lots of ideas to help you imagine what you want your own garden to look like. This little garden can be created outdoors, but if it's the middle of winter, build one in a pot inside. It can be simple or be an ongoing project.

I have linked you to a basic tutorial in this section to get you started. So much funner and satisfying to play in than plastic.

Take 5.49—Imaginative Play

Ok. Confession time. Remember the definition of insanity? Doing the same thing over and over again and expecting a different result? By that definition, I was an insane mother. I dreamed of this wonderfully fully stocked playroom for our children. At one time, we had 8 children under the age of 11. So I was always looking for just the right way to organize all the toys and whenever possible, we designated one room as the play room.

Bins! That's what we needed. So we built some shelves and I sorted all the toys in colorful bins on the shelves at child level. Then my kids would walk into the room, dump them all out in the middle of the room, and leave. And then there were tears and tears trying to get them to help me pick them up.

Bags! That's what we needed. Something so that they couldn't dump them out easily. So I sewed colorful bags with drawstrings and hung them on a peg board on the wall. The kids came in, dumped the toys all out in the middle of the room, and left.

Big baskets! That's what we needed. Something that we could just hurry and throw all the toys into. The baskets were loaded. The kids came into the playroom, dumped all the toys out in the middle of the room and left.

Well, the toys didn't all make it to the middle of the room. My children were determined to evenly distribute them all over the house. And I was always annoyed that the house was a mess and so I entered the next round of insanity—what we needed was a good chore chart. I found chore charts had about a one-week lifespan, if I was lucky. And then I had to find a new gimmick.

What I didn't understand was that the problem wasn't that I hadn't yet found the right solution for organizing and cleaning up the toys. The problem was we had way too many toys. Less is more in childhood.

They had way too much stuff. Way too many choices for a little child brain to process. I was constantly stressing them out! A study was set up where one group of children were given four toys to play with, the other group with 16. The children with fewer toys played much longer in more varied ways than the children with more toys. Kim Payne, who studied the effect of the number of toys on a child's wellbeing, wrote:

> Many of today's behavioral issues come from children having too much stuff and living a life that is too fast.

> As you decrease the quantity of your children's toys and clutter, you increase their attention and their capacity for deep play. Too much stuff leads to too little time and too little depth in the way kids see and explore their worlds.

How I wish I had understood this concept when my children were little. As I watch my grandchildren now, I watch them play for hours when they are given open ended toys with which they can use their imagination. It really doesn't take much. They can do more with a few sticks and rocks and a little grass and mud in the backyard than with all my carefully organized bins of colorful toys. The plastic toys and toys with batteries only served one purpose—the pleasure of dumping them out on the floor.

So take inventory of your toys. A good set of wooden blocks with a few wooden peg figures is far better than a roomful of toys. Look for toys that tap into their imagination. A basket of dress-up clothes is pure gold in childhood. Thrift stores, especially at Halloween time, usually keep an extra stock of imaginative costumes.

If you are a mom who thinks it is up to you to entertain your children all day long, you are going to experience major burnout. Let boredom do its work on your children to your advantage and then remember that play is the work of childhood. Allow for long stretches of imaginative play. By so doing, you are increasing their capacity for creativity and problem solving and self-regulation. Book learning is not the only way we learn.

You may need to prime the pump a little. Fairy tales awaken the imagination so take a fairy tale you have read and see if you can build a little setting with blocks to recreate the story they have just heard, and then let them help you act it out with the little play figures. They'll get the idea. You don't want them to be dependent on you for play, nor should you feel like you should be playing with them all day. A child with a rich imagination and a few open-ended toys can be a wonderful blessing to a busy mother.

I read an article awhile ago that said that workshops were being set up to teach children how to play again, because they don't know how. Too many academics in childhood, too many electronics, too little unstructured time alone is robbing them of this vital developmental milestone.

Let's stop the insanity.

Take 5.50—Leonard Bernstein

So we've been talking a lot about just listening and enjoying music. But when you are ready to take your understanding to a deeper level, I want to tell you about Leonard Bernstein's Young People's Concerts. He loved doing these concerts for young people and considered his educational mission among his most highly prized activities of his life as he introduced a whole generation to the joys of classical music.

His first concert was conducted just two weeks after being named as Musical Director of the New York Philharmonic Orchestra back in 1958. He led the programs until 1972, completing 53 programs in all. I remember when they were aired on Prime Time CBS. His programs were an event! The prime viewing hour happened because a TV executive was bemoaning the vast wasteland on TV at the time. Can you imagine what he would say today? The concerts were broadcast live so there was no chance to edit for mistakes. Leonard Bernstein was so charismatic and made music come alive.

I realize the fact that they are in black and white and are definitely old recordings may make your kids think they are boring, but you never know! Why not give them a try! Especially if you pick a program where the music is already somewhat familiar. I promise you will gain much musical understanding by watching. And by the way, as I write this, we are in Month 1 where we are studying the Stars. His final program in 1972 focused on Gustav Holst's The Planets, which you will find on the Stars enrichment section.

I will link to a site that has links to the 25 of the 53 episodes that are on YouTube. There may be more now; just do a search. DVD versions can be purchased or your library may even have access to them.

You'll notice I selected a lot of the musical YouTubes in the enrichment sections with Leonard Bernstein conducting. I love his facial expressions, and if you spend time watching these Young People's Concerts, he'll become like an old friend. He was truly a legendary conductor.

Take 5.51—Digital Art

Today's Take 5 is very brief. I just want to pass along an idea a mom made in the Facebook group that I think is worth sharing. As you try and find ways to expose your children to more Fine Art, thereby making it familiar, this mom suggested loading art that goes along with whatever you are studying, into a digital art frame—the ones where people generally load rotating pictures of their family.

Depending on your budget, you can buy a large frame to hang on your wall with changing images, or even a small one on a coffee table will work. I can certainly see my grandkids picking one up and looking at the changing images.

There is so much more I hope to be able to do to bring art that is relevant to the monthly studies to you in a way that is easy to access. Of course, there is no reason you can't do your own Google searches. But I know you don't always have a lot of time to do that.

You may have noticed that in the Art for Home and Family library, my daughter has started taking the art off of the Pinterest pages and creating new galleries that are much easier to click through and view. Evidently when Art Renewal redid their site, most of the Pinterest links I had were broken. If you want to see if a higher resolution image is available in Art Renewal, just do a search for the name of the art that you will find just below each picture.

She'll start working through the monthly Enrichment pages over time and there is a lot of art I hope to add to those pages as well. So do keep checking back.

Also, we have created a sister site, simplejoyart.com, where we are organizing and lining fine art to Wikimedia Commons where you can easily access digital images.

If your budget allows it, I am blown away at the simplicity of the Skylight digital frame. The images are instantly loaded by sending them to an email address. My children gave me one for my birthday and are giving me a steady feed of pictures of my grandchildren. I absolutely love it!! No reason why some fine art images can't be sent the same way.

As you create your own gallery of art to view for the month, I hope some of these suggestions will get you started. The possibilities are endless!

Take 5.52—Shakespeare

My son-in-law is in the Army and his next assignment is to teach Shakespeare and poetry to the Freshman cadets at West Point starting next year. In preparation for that assignment, he has been immersed in a Master's level study of Shakespeare. When I was visiting with him not long ago, he said, "You know, Shakespeare really is for adults." And it's true—there is a lot in Shakespeare plays that just isn't appropriate for children or that children are not mature enough to process.

But it made me think of my own experience with Shakespeare. My first introduction to Shakespeare was in Junior High where I was somehow expected to write an essay comparing *Romeo and Juliet* with *West Side Story*. It wasn't that I didn't see the connection. I just had no idea how to translate it into an essay and I remember how much I hated the assignment, even though *West Side Story* was a movie I loved.

Then in High School English, I was thrown into full Shakespeare plays and the language was so difficult for me and, not knowing what the storylines were, I struggled to make sense of what was even going on. On top of that, I was supposed to write essays on themes I was clueless about. I muddled through the assignments with some Cliff notes and the whole Shakespeare thing left a sour taste in my mouth.

It was years later when I watched a wonderful production of *A Midsummer Night's Dream* that I was even willing to entertain the thought that Shakespeare might not be all bad. I really enjoyed it. And decades later, I am finally opening the door to him.

So do I think Shakespeare is worth studying?

Yes!

I am coming to appreciate that he is the most masterful storyteller and poet of all time. His stories are rich and his characters are compelling and complex. I'm sorry I missed out on him for so many years. We owe so many of the phrases we commonly use to Shakespeare.

Phrases like:

> All that glitters is not gold
> All's well that ends well
> Bated breath
> Be-all and the end-all (Macbeth)
> Neither a borrower nor a lender be (Hamlet)
> Brave new world (The Tempest)
> Break the ice (The Taming of the Shrew)
> Dead as a doornail (2 Henry VI)
> A dish fit for the gods (Julius Caesar)

If you want your children to appreciate him as adults, there are many things you can do in childhood.

Follow the Pattern for Learning.

First, acquaint them with the stories. Start with the Comedies. I would personally leave the Tragedies to at least Junior High if not High School age. You will find collections of Shakespeare stories retold on the Elementary page of England under Classical Literature. But I will also link them here in this section. I start with the book that I think has the simplest retelling for your younger children and will go up from there. Of course, you don't have to settle on just one—each version will layer in a little bit more understanding of the story.

I also sorted many of the stories by the rotation schedule according to the setting of the play. No need to only study Shakespeare when you are studying England. You'll find a few of them in the Stories of Great Literature volume of the Story Hour Series.

Then turn to the music of the voice. Shakespeare is not meant to be read silently. It was written to be performed. Take advantage of the many Shakespeare festivals located around the country and watch it performed to make the language familiar.

Another way to familiarize the language is to read selections of it aloud as a reader's theater. Invite another family or two over if you need more players. You'll notice on the Enrichment pages, some of the months have a Shakespeare play that has been adapted for young people. The words are the same, but they are just shorter.

And then add pictures to the study.

In the Mother's Learning Library Art book, this suggestion is given:

> Pupils studying Shakespeare should be encouraged to collect pictorial Shakespeariana, a pursuit which may become so engrossing that they will follow it all their lives. The making of the Shakespeare scrapbook will work both ways, to fix the characters and plots in the memory, and cultivate artistic discrimination.

So do a Google Image search of characters from Shakespeare plays or the plays themselves and print out fine art that can be collected in notebooks, like we've talked about. Or go to Internet Archive and look for the plays and see if there are illustrations you can copy and print out. You could add pages to Literature Gems pages with favorite quotes from the plays and fine art scenes. Or use BareBooks to make personal booklets of the plays. The Art book suggests: "It is a worthy ambition to stimulate in young people to be possessed of an entire set of single-play volumes, each one the basis of a picture collection."

I hope that gives you a few suggestions to get started. My 5 minutes are up, so I'll leave you with this thought:

> Young men and women cannot learn too early in life how the study of Shakespeare's work may, in a far higher degree than the study of other literature, strengthen them in virtue, withdraw them from selfish and mercenary thoughts. Life will bring them no better instructor in the doing of sweet and honourable action, no better teacher of courtesy, benignity, generosity, humanity; for of both stories and characters proferring the counsel to seek what is good and true and to shun what is bad and false Shakespeare's pages are full.

Take 5.53—Mythology

I've talked elsewhere on why we should study mythology. Let me just recap. Myths provide more food for the moral imagination. They were used to teach people right from wrong. The heroes are heroes, the monsters are monsters. My husband was just telling me about a new movie coming out about the Joker in which the bad guys are the good guys. Isn't that happening all around us? These myths made no mistakes. There is a very clear line between righteous and immoral behavior.

Beyond that, our language is especially steeped in Greek mythology. You will miss so much of the deeper meanings if you are ignorant of it—words such as arachnophobia, narcissism, what it means to be struck in your Achilles' heel or opening a Pandora's box. The Constellations all have stories connected to them drawn from Greek mythology. Fine art is loaded with allusions to Greek myths.

They teach us about human nature and help our children explore virtue.

Don't skip them because they are fantasy. You can still teach your children about one true God and not confuse them with these other deities.

There are definitely many levels of mythology books out there. Many are not suitable for young children at all. But there are some really wonderful ones adapted for children that were written in the Golden Age of Children's Literature that I link in the Imaginative sections on the Elementary pages, particularly when you get to Ancient Greece. Take time and test them out to find the ones you like the best for the ages of your children. The D'Aulaire mythology books are loaded with beautiful illustrations and are still in print and would be a great addition to your home library. I provided sample stories from a number of the older writings in the Greek

Mythology book in the Story Hour Series, by the way. That may be an easy place for you to start.

These stories will appeal to young and old alike.

And like the suggestion for Shakespeare, gather fine art of mythological scenes and characters. The Mother's Learning Library Art book says:

> The domain of classic mythology is contiguous both to literature and to history. It is a fairyland of dreams and visions beloved by children of every age. Not all subjects lend themselves to art, but some have been beautifully illustrated, and such works are of immense interest in the schoolroom… One must make the selections carefully, avoiding a certain line of subjects, like the amorous adventures of the gods, which are quite unsuited for use. It is through antique marbles that we get our highest conception of Greek divinities… Like the portraits of sovereigns, as a background of history, these sculptured figures form the background of our mythological lore, and should be made familiar to school children of higher grades either in plastic reproductions or in photographs of the originals.

Of course, you can do Google image searches of the different characters and stories, but I'm sure you will quickly see you will likely want to preview the pictures if nudity in art is something you are not comfortable sharing with your children. Still, there are many options out there that can be collected by your children and added to their notebooks. After all, a picture is worth 750,000 words.

Take 5.54—Dallas Lore Sharpe

And now I want to tell you about another nature writer, Dallas Lore Sharp. What I love about him is that he understands there is more to learn in nature than what the eye sees. I'll share more about that in a minute. Among his writings are four books—Spring, Summer, Fall and Winter—where he takes you out to explore nature through all the seasons. There is never a time in the year where there isn't something wonderful to see. We have reprinted all four books in one volume called *The Whole Year Round*. It is part of a special Nature bundle that also includes Thornton Burgess's first *Mother West Wind* books and all six of Clara Dillingham Pierson's *Among the People* books I have been sharing with you. There is one more book in the series I'll tell you about next week. Of course, we always make a free digital version available to you.

Let me give you a taste of his personality by sharing from the intro to this book:

> While I have tried to be accurate throughout these books, still it has not been my object chiefly to write a natural history—volumes of outdoor facts; but to quicken the imaginations behind the sharp eyes, behind the keen ears and the eager souls of the multitude of children who go to school, as I used to go to school, through an open, stirring, beckoning world of living things that I longed to range and understand.

The best thing that I can do as writer, that you can do as teacher, if I may quote from the last paragraph—the keynote of these volumes—is to "go into the fields and woods, go deep and far and frequently, with eyes and ears and all your souls alert."

Mullein Hill,
May, 1912

Take 5.55—Knitting

I included a section on knitting on the Imagination page of the Mother's University. You may be wondering what on earth does knitting have to do with Imagination?

Well, a lot more than you may realize. At a basic level, occupied hands generally make for more open ears. Your children may be willing to listen to more stories or music if their hands are engaged in an enjoyable activity, thereby increasing their imaginative capacity. And there is something wonderfully calming about the rhythm of knitting and the ordering properties it has on our brains.

But it goes much deeper than that. The Waldorf schools teach children to knit starting in Kindergarten. They don't even attempt to start teaching reading skills until the second grade, if my memory serves me right. What knitting does is provide an activity that crosses both spheres of the brain. It helps them master a fine motor skill known as "crossing the midline." This is an important developmental skill that connects the right and left brains and it's required for overall coordination and everyday tasks such as writing, putting on socks or hitting a ball with a bat.

Knitting improves hand-eye coordination, builds habits and improves focus, reduces anxiety and fatigue, and builds self-esteem as your child creates something with his very own hands. Creativity is a wonderfully satisfying activity.

After Einstein died and they studied his brain, they saw an extraordinarily well-developed corpus collosum which are the nerve fibers that connect the two hemispheres. It was his constant crossing over and utilizing both hemispheres of his brain that made him so brilliant. So anything you can do to strengthen the connections between both sides is of great benefit.

And knitting does that.

It combines mathematics and artistry. From another Waldorf site:

> Counting is required in knitting. Students must count stitching and rows often in complicated ways. There are different colors and different row lengths based on what's being created, which force children to think flexibly about patterns that emerge and transform.

> Those patterns and pattern thinking impressed electrical engineering professor, Dr. Karen Shoop, of Queen Mary University in London. When she took her first knitting class, she immediately saw a connection between computer coding and knitting.

"We 'code' in our outside world. Computers ultimately started off partially inspired by weaving and the Jacquard loom. Knitting instructions are largely binary [and] read just like regular expressions [of code], used for string matching and manipulation."

It's not just coding, according to mathematics professor, Sarah Jensen at Carthage College. It's geometry at its most complex. As she reports in her article in Smithsonian Magazine, *What Knitting Can Teach You About Math*, the abstract, spatial oriented, concept of rubber sheet geometry is perfectly illustrated through knitting.

"One way of knitting objects that are round—like hats or gloves—is with special knitting needles called double pointed needles. While being made, the hat is shaped by three needles, making it look triangular. Then, once it comes off the needles, the stretchy yarn relaxes into a circle, making a much more typical hat. This is the concept that rubber sheet geometry is trying to capture. All polygons become circles in this field of study."

She says knitting also teaches abstract algebra and topology typically reserved for math majors in their junior and senior years of college. Yet the philosophies of these subjects are very accessible, given the right mediums.

Last, but not least, the simple act of working with hands in math results in better learning outcomes. Studies show that using physical materials, or manipulatives as they call them, improve math skills and learning.

So I should maybe also include a section on knitting on the math page, too.

Waldorf starts with knitting because it uses both hands. Then they move on to crocheting and then on to needlework.

Do a Google search and you can find all kinds of YouTube tutorials and patterns and helps to get you started. Or better yet, ask around and find a friend who knows how to knit if you don't, and have her help you. Finger knitting is a good place to start for kindergartners.

Take 5.56—Mini Concerts

Playing a musical instrument has so many benefits. Of course, everyone should start with the voice. And then, wherever possible, I'd have some kind of a keyboard in the house. I'm astonished at how many free pianos go through my Facebook marketplace every single week. I wouldn't start by finding a music teacher who will likely teach a child to play by reading notes. Rather, I would encourage a child to pick out familiar melodies on the piano. Children love to work at that, generally. In time, teach some basic chords for the left hand and let his ear begin to help him find the ones that work in harmony with the melody. In that way, he is making music work from the inside out. He is first feeling and expressing music before he starts reading it.

The music book I talked about earlier, Harriet Seymour's book that is in the revised Mother's Learning Library Music volume, talks more about doing that. Our traditional piano lessons that start with notation have a tremendous failure rate. Yet, children love to play the piano and make music at it and they can easily learn to accompany themselves on the piano while they sing. The piano, because you can create your own harmonies, is a complete instrument.

But what I want to talk about today is encouraging children to also pick up another instrument of choice to study. There is something wonderful about bringing your instrument and joining others in a school or community orchestra and making music that is grander as a whole than as an individual instrument.

I'm not talking about forcing the choice, but rather inspiring a choice by bringing in performers of different instruments into your home where your children can see and feel the instrument played up close and personal. I would think just about any university with a music program would have students who would love a chance to perform in front of an appreciative audience. And may even get credit for it. Offer them a nice home cooked meal or some yummy refreshments and then invite a few friends over. Teach your children concert manners as they listen. Ask the student to keep it short and simple—you just want to give your children a taste. It will even be more meaningful if you know ahead of time what they will be playing so that you can make it familiar to your children ahead of time. And then allow time for your children to ask the performer questions or to let them talk about their instrument with the children.

Cultural get-togethers like these used to be quite common. Now that we have recordings, we don't make the effort. But to hear an instrument performed live is so much more satisfying than a recording, don't you think?

If your house is too small, see if there is a meeting room in the library you can use.

And who knows? Perhaps you will have entertained in your home a future world class performer!

Take 5.57—Art Memory Game

Attention and love connect us to things, ideas and people. When you find a painting you love, by finding ways to pay attention to the details, you can store the painting away in the Imagination where you can recall it on demand and, again, feel its message to your heart, even though the physical painting isn't in front of your eyes.

One way you can help your children to notice details are through some simple memory games. I'm not suggesting you should use these all the time. But pull the idea out from time to time and help them pay more attention to what they are seeing because it is so easy to look and not really see. We do that all the time.

The first idea is to have family members—or invite some friends over—look at a painting together. Make it part of poetry tea time if you want. Did you ever play a game where you bring out a tray loaded with objects and everyone looks at it for a couple of minutes, then it's covered up again and each person makes a list of everything he can remember? The winner in one version is the one who remembered the most objects.

You can adapt it to a painting. Everyone studies the same painting for a minute or two, then you turn it over, and each person makes a list of every detail he can remember. The winner names the most details.

A variation is to play it like Scattergories, where you are looking for the details others may miss. After you each make your list of details, you share your list, and if someone else has the same item on your list, you don't get a point for it. You only get a point for every item you list that no one else found. The one who wins is the one who wrote down the most details that no one else saw.

Another variation doesn't really have a winner. It's just for fun. You study a painting, turn it over so that you can't see it, and then sketch the painting from memory. This is a fast sketch where you mostly are placing objects or people on a page and as you do this, it is making a deeper impression upon the Imagination for storage. Turn the painting over after a bit and see what you got right and what you missed. Or you can even do it as a group painting, where family members contribute parts of the painting from memory that someone else may have missed.

You may come up with your own variations. If it becomes a chore, by all means, stop. But I expect that as you do this a few times, your children will begin to automatically look for more details in the painting and become more aware of the painting's composition.

Take 5.58—The Bible/Poets

The prophets of the Old Testament were all poets-they didn't use plain language, which is why I am including the Bible in the poetry category this week. These prophets said what they wanted to say in pictures and literal minds have difficulty making sense of it.

The scriptures are said to be a lamp to light our feet. There is a music to the King James Version of the Bible that can only be heard when it is read aloud and adds to this light. Back in the days when the Bible was the only book found in many homes, it was regularly read aloud and little babies became familiar with rich scriptural language that way. They may not understand the words, but they felt the music. And then, by the time they started to read words, the text was familiar. It is astonishing what children were reading by age six or seven 150 years ago compared to what they are reading today. And I can't help but wonder if the imagery and poetry and music of the Bible laid the foundation for that to happen.

One of the first books created for our Library of Hope was the *Story Bible*. Because I understood the importance of connecting children to the spiritual light of the scriptures at a young age, I wanted to provide something that would help families do that. Using the Pattern for Learning, stories and pictures as well as that scriptural music are the first go to's. Reading Genesis isn't too hard because it's all familiar stories. But once you hit the begats and all the laws of Leviticus and Deuteronomy, the reading bogs down a bit. Plus the stories don't flow after that. You read stories in Kings that are repeated in Chronicles and it gets confusing.

So the *Story Bible* is simply stories taken from the King James Version of the Bible. Instead of chapters, they are offered as small story segments, identified with a title that will help a child understand what is going on. The stories are arranged chronologically, as much as possible, to keep a flow of events going. No one knows exactly where Job fits in, by the way, so he is included in a place that disrupted the flow of story the least.

When you get to the New Testament, I combined elements of the stories that were spread out among the four gospels into one narrative, but you will see I reference where the pieces came from.

I envision that this *Story Bible* can be used as a first reader for a child learning to read. We chose a large font and kept a lot of white space on the pages, without all the extra references and notations that are usually found and that can be distracting to a child. There are a lot of simple words that are repeated, and a child can feel very grown up to be able to read from text with the whole family, especially if the text has been made familiar because he has been hearing it for a long time already.

Awhile ago, we took a section of the *Story Bible* and created a smaller book focusing on just the stories of Jesus and added Fine Art to it. The pictures are available as a separate print out for children to cut out and glue into the book, adding a little anticipation of seeing what the next picture is going to be. It is hoped by engaging in this little activity, they will take more time to notice the details of the pictures and that it will add another layer of deepening the impressions on the heart.

We have done the same for the Old Testament stories.

Also you will notice little blocks of scriptures sprinkled throughout the text. These little 'gems' work well as something to memorize or as copy work text.

By the way, the complete *Story Bible* is one of the free gifts you receive if you subscribe to five or more series from our store, or there is a free digital version on the Forgotten Classics page. Of course, it is not intended that it should replace the full Bible, but rather lead your children to it.

You can also deepen impressions into the Imagination by sharing many versions of the stories to bring details to life. You will find a good number of options in the Month 6 Holy Land section.

Without a working knowledge of these Bible stories, much of the meaning of the world's greatest fine art, music, poetry, and literature will be closed off to your children.

Everything you can do to help your children visualize these stories and store them in their Imaginations is going to yield good fruit down the road.

Take 5.59—Plays

Brigham Young is said to have said, "If I were placed on an island and given a task of civilizing its people, I should straightway build a theatre."

There is something about being in an intimate setting, watching a story unfold, that makes a deep impression on the heart. And you'll take that impression even deeper if you assume a role and speak the thoughts of that character. Remember—the voice is the great connector of heart and mind.

Little children quite naturally improvise stories in their play and assume the roles of different people. Some of the earliest play involves: You be the mommy and I'll be the daddy and you often hear them repeating what they heard you say. Which keeps us mommies on our toes, huh?

With some simple dress up props, they can have a lot of fun acting out simple fairy tales they are learning. Or create puppets and let them act the stories out that way.

But let me call attention to one more resource you have available to you. On the Enrichment pages, you will see a section called Plays. Here are some scripted plays you can use in a number of ways. By the way, I arranged them, generally, from plays that are shorter and simpler for younger children to those that are more mature for your older children.

You can easily print these plays out. There is no need to print out the entire book, just select the pages of the plays. Involve the whole family—even dad—in assigning parts. Or invite another family or two to join you so that you have enough actors for the parts. Or you can even double up on parts. Use different voices to differentiate the roles.

Although you can do a full production and memorize the lines and actually perform a play, the easier thing is to simply use it as a reader's theater for your own enjoyment. Let each person highlight his part and practice it before coming together. That means that he or she will need to figure out who their character is and let it come out in the music of their voice. Is the character loud and gruff, or soft and sweet? What is that character feeling? Those feelings are conveyed through the voice.

Even a beginning reader can take part by practicing his lines and making sure he can read all the words before adding his part to the group.

You will find plays depicting fairy tales and imaginative stories, but you will also find a lot of historical scenes. What a great way to bring familiarize the people of history and bring them to life and engage in what they must have been thinking and experiencing in some of these pivotal events of history.

A lot of the language used in these plays is richer than we use today, but it can also be fun to perform. But if it's too much, have your children adapt it. That can be a worthwhile experience, too.

In fact, let them bring history and great literature to life by writing their own plays of their favorite scenes.

Remember the March girls in *Little Women*? A favorite pastime was putting on plays for themselves. Your kids can have a lot of fun doing the same.

Take 5.60—Arabella Buckley

I've been telling you about several nature books that are wonderful for opening up the world of nature to young children that will make up the Nature Bundle, or they are available separately. Today I want to tell you about the final book in that series, a book called *Eyes and No Eyes* by Arabella Buckley. I want to talk about her here while we are talking about Imagination because she takes children into Nature through the realm of Imagination. Let me show you what I mean by sharing excerpts from a first chapter in a different book she wrote called *The Fairy Land of Science*.

I have promised to introduce you today to the fairy-land of science—a somewhat bold promise, seeing that most of you probably look upon science as a bundle of dry facts, while fairy-land is all that is beautiful, and full of poetry and imagination. But I thoroughly believe myself, and hope to prove to you, that science is full of beautiful pictures, of real poetry, and of wonder-working fairies; and what is more, I promise you they shall be true fairies, whom you will love just as much when you are old and greyheaded as when you are young; for you will be able to call them up wherever you wander by land or by sea, through meadow or through wood, through water or through air; and though they themselves will always remain invisible, yet you will see their wonderful power at work everywhere around you....

There are forces around us, and among us, which I shall ask you to allow me to call fairies, and these are ten thousand times more wonderful, more magical, and more beautiful in their work, than those of the old fairy tales. They, too, are invisible, and many people live and die without ever seeing them or caring to see them. These people go about with their eyes shut, either because they will not open them, or because no one has taught them how to see. They fret and worry over their own little work and their own petty troubles, and do not know how to rest and refresh themselves, by letting the fairies open their eyes and show them the calm sweet pictures of nature....

How can we see them?

Just go out into the country, and sit down quietly and watch nature at work. Listen to the wind as it blows, look at the clouds rolling overhead, and the waves rippling on the pond at your feet. Hearken to the brook as it flows by, watch the flower-buds opening one by one, and then ask yourself, "How all this is done?" ...Look at the vivid flashes of lightning in a storm, and listen to the pealing thunder: and then tell me, by what machinery is all this wonderful work done? Man does none of it, neither could he stop it if he were to try; for it is all the work of those invisible forces of fairies whose acquaintance I wish you to make. Day and night, summer and winter, storm or calm, these fairies are at work, and we may hear them and know them, and make friends of them if we will.

There is only one gift we must have before we can learn to know them—we must have imagination...the power of making pictures or images in our mind, of that which is, though it is invisible to us. Most children have this glorious gift, and love to picture to themselves all that is told them, and to hear the same tale over and over again till they see every bit of it as if it were real. This is why they are sure to love science if its tales are told them aright; and I, for one, hope the day may never come when we may lose that childish clearness of vision, which enables us through the temporal things which are seen, to realize those eternal truths which are unseen.

Take 5.61—Recap

Well, we're about halfway through the Take 5s—maybe not quite. I'll finish when I finish. But I wanted to take a minute and review where we've been. It's true that many of the activities I've been talking about are aimed at younger children. That's because I am walking you through Developmental Levels. As you understand these developmental levels, you'll better be able to target what kind of stories you need to look for to awaken interest in your children. If you have a preschooler, the stories he will love the most are the ones that have something familiar to him. And the same thing goes for a teenager. If you have an older child that can't seem to find anything interesting to read, look for a familiar connecting link. What are his interests? What is going on in his life? That's what you target. There are ways to expand that familiar base, which I try to model with my podcasts by introducing you to stories of people and things I love. You can do the same.

Then came the Imaginative stage. The ability to see pictures with the inner eye is crucial for faith and creativity and even reading comprehension. So imaginative stories are good for young and old and reading aloud, even after a child can read to himself, is one way of building those imaginative powers.

Next week we are going to move on to the Heroic years. We'll begin to move into it this week as I talk about epic and legendary heroes which are partially based in the imaginative realm and partially on fact. If you have laid the foundations, a child is going to carry his moral imagination into making sense of the stories of great lives and history. A child with no imagination isn't going to be able to picture historical scenes and events. And his understanding of the world in which he lives will be dwarfed.

When we first started these Take 5s, I told you to not skip ahead and to make a daily habit of listening. I hope that is working for some of you. But my concern is that if you are just listening and not applying; if you aren't experimenting with the suggestions and trying out the tools, by now you've got a lot of lumber stored up in your brain and I'm not sure there is enough room for the workshop. So if you feel overloaded, make sure you are not just storing up ideas. Spend more time trying them out and then come visit these Take 5s when you are looking for some fresh ideas. I hope you understand what I am trying to do here. Because heart-based learning looks differently from traditional curriculums, I'm trying to suggest ways by which learning takes place. I frequently have moms ask me what heart-based learning looks like and I'm trying to show you. There are no worksheets or daily assignments. Adopt what works for you and shelf the ideas that aren't a good fit. But this is not an exhaustive list. I hope it will be more suggestive and that many of the ideas will inspire new creative ways of your own. It isn't enough to know about the tools—you've got to start using them. As you do, you'll find learning is just a way of life, not something you schedule into your day.

I compare traditional learning to climbing a tower. There is a destination in mind, usually graduation day or college. You can measure where you are on that journey. This kind of learning is not like that. Think of a rose. A rose blooms because the pressure of its inner fulness pushes the petals outward. As you fill the heart, you are creating an inner fulness that will naturally bloom outward forever. There is no moment of arrival. Learning layers and expands and it is such a joyful and satisfying journey.

Towers and roses work against each other. One is pushing from the outside in, the other from the inside out. The question at hand is which way do you choose?

Take 5.62—Folk Songs

The heart educators suggested that you don't start a study of history before the age of 8. And even then, it should be unfolded through stories of lives and scenes from history rather than a facts and information approach. But part of the foundation of that study is engaging in cultural studies and activities. So I've suggested crafts and celebrations of different nations, listening to their music, cooking ethnic food and even reading stories of Our Little Cousins so a child's heart can be introduced to life in other countries. It provides a familiar connecting point.

Another layer to add in is to become familiar with their folk songs. Folk songs have no known composers. They flowed directly out of the hearts of common everyday people who made the songs up while they worked and while they played and in connection with their religious activities. They didn't have the luxury of recorded music or sheet music. They learned the songs by singing them and they were passed down from generation to generation, often changing them along the way.

Manual laborers sang songs to reduce the boredom of repetitive tasks, it kept the rhythm during synchronized pushes and pulls, and it set the pace of many of the activities they were engaged in, such as planting, weeding, reaping, threshing, weaving, and so forth.

In leisure time, singing was how they entertained themselves and how they told and preserved their history. As you sing the same songs that sprang out of their hearts in their everyday lives, you are connecting with them at an even deeper level.

So by adding in the singing of folk songs into the study of nations, you are going to layer in a whole new facet of understanding of these people you are studying. I think how our national American spirit could be revived by our singing the songs of our fathers. You may have heard me speak elsewhere of the Singing Revolution. The tiny Eastern European country of Estonia, who had a rich heritage of folk songs, was under Communist rule for fifty years. During that time, the people were forbidden to sing their songs. But then, beginning in the late 1980s, they systematically and repeatedly gathered in public places to sing their forbidden songs. If you ever saw the scene in Casablanca where the French patrons sang La Marseillaise in defiance of the Germans and then multiply the scene by thousands, you begin to get a sense of the force behind the Singing Revolution.

In the end, the Communists could not remain in power against a hundred thousand voices united in a song of the heart. They withdrew without shedding a single drop of blood.

"You cannot defeat a singing nation."

How many of our folk songs do our children know? I'll list some folk song books to get started, but I am always keeping my eyes open for folk song books that contain the stories behind the songs. These songs would be a wonderful addition to your study, especially of American history. And learning the folk songs of other nations will add a richness to understanding the hearts of our neighbors around the world, as well.

Let me read you the intro to one of those books. She says it much better than I do.

> When I was a little girl I was always fascinated by the magic carpet about which I read in fairy tales and wanted to sit on one and be wafted around the world. If you were to take a trip around the world today, you would want to go…high into the air and rush at great speed from England to France, Germany, Spain, Italy, Russia, Japan, China, then ever so quickly to Honolulu, California, and across the United States to New York and then back to Europe… Now because you traveled so fast and because you did not stay long enough in each city, you did not learn very much about the different people, how they lived, what costumes they wore, and how they sang. How they sang about the things they loved, the things with which they were familiar. How they sang when they were sad as well as when they were happy.

> But if you traveled slowly you would have time to hear these songs and to hear how the songs of one country differ from those of another country and how often-times the songs are quite alike just as costumes of one country resemble those of another, differing in only a headdress or an apron.

> These songs that come from the hearts of the people are called Folk Songs and they are like the seeds that come from the hearts of flowers. You know that the wind will carry seeds of certain flowers to an entirely different country where they will take root and remain for all time.

> Songs traveled from one country to another; no one really knows how… Perhaps like the seeds the songs were blown across a border through the air; no one really knows. The important thing is that the songs are there, but we have to find them. We will travel as people did many years ago when they had more time and traveled more slowly.

> From Around the World in Song by Dorothy Gordon

Take 5.63—Starting Starting Literature Gems Notebooks

Dr. Rich Melheim taught that the human ear can process up to 10,000 bits of information per second, but the human eye can process up to 7 billion bits of information per second. I have no idea how someone measured that, but basically what that means is that a picture is not worth a thousand words, it's worth 700,000 words.

If a book I am reading has illustrations—and I like to read lots of children's books, which almost always have pictures—I like to copy and print out the illustrations for my notebooks. The reason is that the picture will instantly refresh my memory about what the book was about. Teachers for decades have required children to write book reports, which I think has done more to kill a love of reading than just about anything. But if you keep in mind that oral precedes written language, creating pages for a notebook with illustrations from the book can be a good way to generate a conversation about the book without subjecting them to the tedious task of a book report, for which they may not be developmentally ready.

A literature gems notebook is like a book of remembrance of books that have been visited. As you, from time to time, sit down with them and open their literature gems notebook and notice the illustrations, you might ask questions like, "What was going on here again, do you remember?" "Oh, that was so…happy, sad, scary, you fill in the blank." And then talk about how the story made you feel. Or from time to time, pull out this literature gems notebook and invite your child to tell the story from the pictures. Or just let the pictures quietly act upon his heart as your child recalls the impressions that were made as he heard the story the first time.

Are you getting the picture?

Beginning a literary gem notebook is as simple as taking a piece of paper, writing the title of the book and the author at the top, and pasting illustrations from the book on to the page. This is different from my Great Lives notebook where I'm notebooking about real people. Because most of the books I recommend are classics, you can find copies in Internet Archive and it is simple to click on Copy page and paste it to a blank page in Word and print them out. I like to arrange my Literature Gems notebook in alphabetical order by title. An older child can begin to copy gems on those pages—this is a process that teaches a child to pay attention to those parts of the book that grabs his heart and makes him say, "I love that. I want to hold on to that." If a beloved passage is too long to copy, just copy enough to trigger the recall and then note what page it can be found on again.

And by the way, copying the writing of great writers is how many of the great writers learned to write! But that is a topic for another day.

Take 5.64—Epic and Legendary Heroes

I mentioned in the first Take 5 this week that we are going to start bridging into the Heroic years and today I want to talk about Epic and Legendary heroes who provide a perfect bridge. I am talking about them in the poetry section because the stories were first preserved in rhyme and song and handed down orally generation after generation, each generation adding and adjusting as the stories traveled through time.

By around age 8, a child becomes especially interested in Action heroes, not the moral hero yet. And these epic and legendary heroes fit the bill. They are on exciting adventures and an important layer is being layered into a child's heart in the process—they are beginning to absorb the hero's journey.

Joseph Campbell was an American College Professor who has done much to define this hero's journey, especially as it appears in the stories of epic and legendary heroes.

The hero of the story comes to a time when he leaves that which is comfortable and familiar and sets out on an adventure to an unknown place. Now the hero must face a series of trials and tribulations. The hero's journey isn't safe. The hero is tested in battle, skill, and conflict. The hero may not succeed in each action but must press on. Along the way, the hero meets allies, enemies and mentors, often with supernatural aid. Having endured the trials and hardships of the adventure, the hero returns home. But the hero is no longer the same. An internal transformation has taken place through the processes of the experiences. And he is ready to serve the world around him in even greater ways.

A hero is someone who has given his or her life to something bigger than oneself. Are you willing to take the hero's journey? Do we not want to prepare our children to make such a journey in life?

Campbell wrote:

> We must be willing to get rid of the life we've planned, so as to have the life that is waiting for us. The privilege of a lifetime is being who you are. The cave you fear to enter holds the treasure you seek. The big question is whether you are going to be able to say a hearty yes to your adventure.

Almost every nation has a story of an epic or legendary hero. I'm afraid America isn't letting one even slightly begin to emerge because we are so focused on facts and an epic hero is never born in mere facts. For the Greeks, it was Odysseus. France has her Roland. England her Beowulf. Germany her Siegfried. So we'll have to borrow theirs in the meantime. You will notice a section in the online library for Epic and Legendary Heroes. I looked for the simplest retellings for the Elementary pages and that is a good place to start. As your children become familiar with the Heroes' Journey, they will not only begin to recognize it in the great lives they will now begin to study, they will begin to recognize it in their own lives. And it can be a way to help them push through hard obstacles and challenges.

I remember reading of a young boy who was battling cancer. It was an article on storytelling and it said what that young boy needs is not a story of another young boy battling cancer, he needs the story of a Hercules who can show his young heart courage to do hard things in a big way.

Let your children make friends with the great epic and legendary heroes of the ages and you will provide a layer of strength and resolve that has largely gone missing in our day.

Give them the courage for them to set out on their own adventure—their own hero's journey.

Take 5.65—Children's Classics

If you have got the kindling fire burning by sharing short, high-interest stories, such as fairy tales, you are ready to move into longer chapter books. You have helped your children to develop a habit of attention and increased their capacity to create images in their minds while they listen to you read. Certainly, by ages six or seven, a child is ready to start listening to the great children's classic books. Remember their listening comprehension far exceeds their reading comprehension. So do introduce books like *Treasure Island*, *The Secret Garden*, *A Little Princess*, *The Princess and the Goblin*, *The Lion, the Witch and the Wardrobe*—the list is long. The wonderful thing about these classic books is that they will likely revisit them several times while they are growing up and each time they will discover new layers of meaning. If they are not quite ready to take on the whole book, some people are opposed to giving introductory abridged readings, but I am not. I think it's perfectly fine to introduce a child to characters and a story line at a simpler level if that is all they can take in. Then visit the full version later.

It's nice to always have a classic story going on as a family read-aloud. You will find suggestions in the Elementary classic Literature sections on the various pages. And if I found a Librivox recording, I put an arrow next to it. Let me mention here—Librivox is kind of a hit and miss. Some readers are definitely better than others. I searched for the most popular readers if I recommended a Librivox book. But just because I don't have a link to a recording doesn't mean it doesn't exist. So do your own search. Although your voice is the preferred one, if you can.

These classic children's book are filled with lessons on living life that can't be taught directly, but your children will catch them. The universal truths and principles contained within them gives them their staying power. Generations after they were originally written, they are still connecting to hearts of children. Truth endures. Do make them a memorable part of their childhoods.

Take 5.66—Nature Collages

Today's tip is short and sweet—a simple idea from someone in the group. They took a walk out in nature and collected stems and seeds and flowers and leaves and whatever else they could find, took them home and spread them out on the middle of the table and then created pictures out of the objects. I'll post some pictures for you to see. What a great imaginative idea connected to nature!

Take 5.67—Moving Into the Heroic Stage

Now that your children have experienced stories and found them to be enjoyable and desirable, and you have strengthened their imaginative powers so they have the ability to create scenes and pictures from words, we are now ready to enter the Heroic years at around age 8, which actually will last the rest of their lives and draws much upon the stories of history. With the aid of fairy tales and myths in childhood, you have begun to lay a foundation of a moral imagination—the ability to discern right from wrong, good from evil, the ugly from the beautiful which will now begin to be applied to real life.

Neuroscientists have observed an actual intellectual shift in the brain of children where, at around age 8, they can begin to reason for themselves. Interestingly, the brain will not fully develop until their early 20s and one of the last parts to develop is the region that allows them to actually see the consequences of their actions. When we look at decisions teenagers make and say, "What are they thinking?," the answer is, they aren't...yet. They can't yet see the consequences of their actions and so they do things that are completely unreasonable to us.

That's why a well-respected historian suggested a serious study of history can't even begin until around age 26. We expect younger students to begin to analyze cause and effect of history prematurely. All they can do at that point is memorize and relate back someone else's conclusions. And the danger of that that I see is they think they are wise, but they do not yet have the experience or perspective to be wise.

If you are following the rotation schedule, you will see a huge emphasis on stories from history and great lives. We are not trying to produce Jeopardy trivia champs. Our purpose is to raise up a generation that is wise. And to be wise, they must see life through 1,000 different eyes, not just through the limited and narrow view of their own experiences.

That's why I don't worry about chronology yet. But if you adapt some kind of notebooking system like I suggest, you'll find the chronology naturally weaves into the process. I don't even worry about facts yet. I'm not nearly as worried about something being True as I am that it relays Truth. And as you focus on life lessons rather than on dry facts, you'll find, in time, that the lessons of Nature and the lessons of History start intertwining.

As you immerse your children in the stories of history and the story of lives, they will begin to see patterns for themselves. They will begin to recognize the Hero's Journey and most importantly, begin to see their own place in the world's story and their personal hero adventure.

At least that is the experience I am having as I read the older history books and biographies. As connections are made and patterns discovered, I get those little flashes of light and surges of dopamine that makes learning so enjoyable.

There truly is a light in the older books you won't find in modern history textbooks. Textbooks remove the stories and leave you with facts and information. It's part of our mind culture. But shall I remind you we call facts cold and hard? Another thing you will notice in Biographies is that around 100 years ago, they quit writing to inspire hearts and instead starting writing to expose all the warts, faults and the weaknesses. They want to make sure we know these people are just like us. But in the process, they've taken away that which will lift us to higher ground.

An artist doesn't see things as they are. He sees things as they can be. The writers of the Golden Age were artists.

And now to those of you who are panicking at what I am saying, who are thinking children must be given facts and only that which can be verified as authentic and true, after all you don't want to have to unteach your kids—let me ask the question: Where has history come from? Do you realize we are trying to piece together a 10,000 piece puzzle and we've only dug up about 63 pieces and we're not even sure those 63 pieces actually belong to the puzzle? Much of the history we teach has come from ballads and rhyme, embellished with grandeur and sparkle over time. Nobody kept a history of the world with nothing but authentic and true facts. Take just one day; no, let's narrow it down to one minute in the world today and try and document it for posterity. Where would you begin? And this notion that we'll be safe if we keep to original sources has no foundation of truth for me. None of us read anything without filtering it through our worldview. Two people can read the identical letter of Christopher Columbus and one will pronounce him a vulgar and loathsome man and the other one a faithful and inspired soul.

My take on the study of history is not that it is a subject to be learned and mastered. It can't be. My take is that history and the story of lives is the main tool we have to draw upon to teach us about life and how to live together in this world in harmony and love and that there is no end of discoveries to be made. So give it to me in movies and historical fiction and literature and art and music and a variety of histories and stories written from a variety of points of view, and I'm going to take a lifetime to make sense of it all.

We are fascinated by stories of people. Why else are there a dozen magazines at the checkout, all about people and their lives. I love reading biographies! And I'll even throw in a textbook here and there to help me with a little order. But I will never be done. In fact, the more I know, the more I realize I don't know and the more I want to know.

Here are two guiding principles as you venture into these Heroic and Historical years. The first from Marguerite Dickson:

> A taste for historical reading, is, after all, the valuable gift we can bestow upon our youthful student of history. Having given him that, we may safely leave the rest to him.

And Rudyard Kipling:

> If history were taught in the form of stories, it would never be forgotten.

Oh, how I dream of a generation of students who spend most of their study time in high school years freely digging and digging and reading and reading the stories of history.

Take 5.68—Opal Wheeler Music Biographies

Since we are talking about the heroic years now, now is the time to begin to delve deeper into the lives and biographies of the great music masters. Maybe you've introduced them earlier through childhood experiences and helped make their names familiar. Now keep adding to that understanding.

There is a wonderful series of books written for young people by Opal Wheeler that can add a new layer of appreciation. The books have been reprinted recently so you should be able to find hard copies. But I have also linked copies found in Internet Archive. Some of them have to be borrowed, but you will also find some of them are in public domain and so you can freely access them any time and even print them out yourself if you'd like. I've linked them on the Great Musicians page and also you'll find them sprinkled throughout the rotation schedule under Biographies on the Elementary pages.

Why do I think it's so important to know the music masters? Because one of their primary objectives was to reveal to the human heart the very glory of God. These are men worth hanging around. If our children can become familiar with the language of music, they will experience an even deeper layer of connection to God and His mighty works.

There has been much work in recent years to paint these music masters in unfavorable light; movies that portray them as idiots or womanizing, vulgar human beings. There is a great book called *The Spiritual Lives of Great Composers* written by Steven Kavanaugh that will give you fresh perspective. The book is linked in the Music Appreciation section. While these men may not be perfect, we are not being given the whole story. Your high schoolers might enjoy using this book as a study, listening to some of the works referenced as they work their way through. If they are going through the Rotation schedule, suggest they study the composers in their respective months. But I will say you will find Month 10 the most heavily loaded. Which begs the question—why did Germany and Eastern Europe and even Russia produce so many inspired musicians? I don't know the answer yet, but I am curious to find out. Can one of you shed some light on the subject for me?

Take 5.69—I Notice, I Wonder, That Reminds Me Of

I've talked about John Muir Laws elsewhere and how, when he teaches students how to nature journal, he gives them three tools to help open their eyes: I notice, I wonder and that reminds me of. I use these three tools not only in nature but in fine art and in everything I read. I demonstrate using it in art in Section five of the Catch the Vision course. If you haven't watched it yet, I hope you'll take a few minutes to watch. Look for 'Using the Enrichment Page' starting at about the 10-minute mark or the 27-minute mark in Podcast #173.

Now as you move into a study of history, use Fine Art to drive home lessons and impressions. It is really hard to hold on to history long enough to make sense of it without a picture in the mind. With the Google Image search engine, it is easy to find paintings depicting the very people or events you are studying. Use these tools: 'I notice,' 'I wonder,' and 'that reminds me of' to bring the painting to life and see details that may go unnoticed at first glance otherwise. It gives you a way to talk about the painting in front of you.

Later I'm going to talk about art appreciation resources that will take the appreciation of art to an even deeper level, but these tools can easily be applied without that understanding.

As we start getting into notebooking, do use fine art images of historical scenes and people abundantly on notebooking pages. It is so easy to copy the images and size them down to a workable notebook size and print them out. Also, you will find wonderful sketches and detailed drawings in the old history books in Internet Archive. I frequently copy and print those pictures out for notebooking as well.

Take 5.70—Get to Know the Lives of Great Poets

Carrying on the theme of studying the lives of great people, do include a study of the lives of the poets. Spencer Kimball said, "When God didn't have prophets to speak through, he spoke through the hearts of poets."

I came across a little book that is a simple introduction to some of the great poets by taking a look at their homes. The book is called *The Poet's Corner, or Haunts and Homes of the Poets* by Alice Corkran, written in 1892. This could be a perfect study for your high schoolers. Its light reading, just a few pages per poet, including Chaucer, Shakespeare, Milton, Tennyson, Wordsworth and Longfellow.

The book opens with this poem:

The Poets' Corner

Where are the mighty poets gone?
Where are their burning spirits fled?
Is it beyond the stars and sun,
And do they sleep among the dead?
Or who will wake their songs again,
Or strike their silent harps once more,
And sing, in these sad days, a strain
Of chivalry and love of yore?

Take 5.71—Teaching Character

Let's talk for a couple of minutes about teaching character. Teaching character is a good thing. But one thing I have come to realize is that the more you try and teach it directly, the less effective it is. Character is one of those lessons better caught than taught. Which is why stories are the perfect medium for delivering the lessons. The listener will take in what he is ready to take in. A story allows the heart to actually see and feel the character trait in action. And once the heart truly desires something, it's going to happen.

I generally resist the idea of creating study plans around character traits. For instance, if you say October is the month for studying Honesty, you might find a number of stories to drive home the point. But maybe you have a child who has found being dishonest is serving a valuable purpose in his life at the moment. In other words, being dishonest is getting something that he wants more than being honest. If you are telling the story by calling attention to the fact that you are trying to teach honesty, the child may tune the story out and completely miss out on another aspect of the story that he might be ready for—maybe that story will also be conveying a lesson in kindness or courage that he is receptive to. You wouldn't want to miss the opportunity by redirecting attention. I don't see a need to make them into formal lessons that tend to settle more on the mind than the heart.

Usually those formal lessons involve definitions and explanations, food for the mind. A person can understand with his brain what it means to be honest, but until his heart desires to be honest, he will not act as an honest person. Defining and explaining honesty isn't going to get it into the heart.

This isn't just my opinion. Let me call attention again to a page you can access on the Categories navigation page in the Other section. Select Character Traits and on that page, you'll see a link to an audio page where I share chapters from a book called *How to Teach Children Through Stories*. It was a guide that went along with Eva March Tappan's *Children's Hour* Series. There is great wisdom in this little book on using stories to build character in your children. And I learned much of what I am saying here from this little book. And from experience.

Enrich your child's heart with a steady diet of a variety of stories, and you'll revisit many character traits time and time again, seen through different lenses and you'll increase the chances of finding a connection to your child's heart at just the right time.

Sometimes I will see a mom post the question in our group, "Where can I find character-building stories?" And my response is: all the stories and books I include in the Libraries of Hope library are character-building stories. These writers of the older books didn't hide their intention to inspire children to live happier lives, which is the result of acquiring desirable character traits.

If you are interested in finding stories by character trait—and there may well be times when you feel inspired to share such a story—I posted some books that have stories sorted by character trait in that Character Trait section I just referred you to. Also, check out *Stories That Teach Values* in the Story Hour Series and William Bennett's *Books of Virtue* are also great resources for you.

Take 5.72—Early Morning Walk

As I study great lives, I have noticed how often daily walks in nature are a vital part of their lives. We talk about getting outside for recreation. Recreation is re-creating; it re-creates our perspective and restores our souls and helps clarify our lives. Nature is so healing to our hearts. Let me share a little sampling.

Anne Frank wrote: "The best remedy for those who are afraid, lonely or unhappy is to go outside, somewhere where they can be quite alone with the heavens, nature and God. Because only then does one feel that all is as it should be and that God wishes to see people happy, amidst the simple beauty of nature. As longs as this exists, and it certainly always will, I know that then there will always be comfort for every sorrow, whatever the circumstances may be. And I firmly believe that nature brings solace in all troubles."

John Muir: "Climb the mountains and get their good tidings. Nature's peace will flow into you as sunshine flows into trees. The winds will blow their own freshness into you, and the storms their energy, while cares will drop away from you like the leaves of Autumn."

Charlotte Bronte: "We know that God is everywhere; but certainly we feel His presence most when His works are on the grandest scale spread before us; and it is in the unclouded night-sky, where His worlds wheel their silent course, that we read clearest His infinitude, His omnipotence, His omnipresence."

There is a pleasure in the pathless woods,
There is a rapture on the lonely shore,
There is society, where none intrudes,
By the deep Sea, and music in its roar:
I love not Man the less, but Nature more,
From these our interviews, in which I steal
From all I may be, or have been before,
To mingle with the Universe, and feel
What I can ne'er express, yet cannot all conceal.

Lord Byron, Childe Harold's Pilgrimage

"Those who contemplate the beauty of the earth find reserves of strength that will endure as long as life lasts." --Rachel Carson, *The Sense of Wonder*

Hans Christian Andersen: "Just living is not enough. One must have sunshine, freedom and a little flower."

Jesus loved to walk on the seashore, teach on the hillside, retire to the mount. He used the lessons of nature to teach the people: faith the size of a mustard seed, consider the lilies of the field, even a sparrow cannot fall unnoticed.

I hear moms say they don't have time to go outside and do nothing. I say if you make it a point to go outside—get away as frequently as you can in nature—you will find more time to do the things that actually matter.

And you will be living the life of the greats.

I love this little poem from Elizabeth Barrett Browning:

The Little Cares
by Elizabeth Barrett Browning

The little cares that fretted me,
I lost them yesterday
Among the fields above the sea,
Among the winds at play;
Among the lowing of the herds,
The rustling of the trees,
Among the singing of the birds,
The humming of the bees.

The foolish fears of what may happen—
I cast them all away
Among the clover-scented grass,
Among the new-mown hay;
Among the husking of the corn
Where drowsy poppies nod,

268

Where ill thoughts die and good are born,
Out in the fields with God.

Try and mix things up. Don't save the walk for the end of the day when the work is done. Wake your kids up early one morning just to go for a walk. There is something about the early morning sun and early songs of birds that can't be duplicated by any other experience. Don't make a lesson of it—just soak it all in and enjoy.

Take 5.73—Handwriting

I probably should have brought up today's topic earlier. Sometimes people think I am anti-academics—not at all! It's just an order thing. So we've talked about teaching children to read and how letting them listen to stories and building their imagination and increasing their experiences will increase their reading comprehension but more importantly their desire to read. And we've talked about math—the importance of not starting formal instruction before a child is developmentally ready, but filling their lives with math in the real world such as counting in games and measuring while cooking and so forth. So now let's turn to the 3rd "R" of the three R's–which is ironic because only one of the three R's actually begins with the letter R—writing.

Specifically, the skill of handwriting.

Like many, if not most of you, I learned how to print before I learned how to do cursive. Actually, many of you may never have learned to do cursive because a lot of schools have discontinued teaching it. Keyboarding is more efficient and practical is the argument.

But many studies are showing that technology is increasingly adding to our illiteracy. Neuroscientists can watch what is going on in the brain during certain activities and they can see that a person that is writing in cursive is lighting up the whole brain—both the right and left hemispheres. Printing and keyboarding do not do that.

I think you'll know why I liked this little quote: The debate between cursive and printing "is a little like comparing the act of printing vs. cursive to dot-to-dot painting by numbers vs. the flowing rhythmic brush strokes of true artists."

In olden days, a child was never taught to print. He started with cursive and look at the masterpieces that flowed out of the hearts of the great artists through their pens. I read, "the speed and efficiency of writing in cursive allowed the student to focus on the cohesion of idea."

Well, I cannot cover everything about the advantages of teaching cursive in a 5-minute Take 5, but I hope I can pique your interest to look into it further. I've linked a couple of resources that will give you a pretty thorough search into the topic.

At first glance, it makes perfect sense. When you think about forming letters in print, a child has to keep picking up his pencil and placing it in a whole variety of places to form letters. With cursive, the pencil is placed in one place at the beginning of the word and isn't picked up again until the end. They say it is helpful for dyslexics because the movement is left to right.

There are no directional changes.

So from a heart based point of view, the focus on drawing in childhood is going to increase their manual dexterity in preparation for writing. But as they learn to write in cursive, there are no shortcuts—they have to practice daily. What you can do to make the sessions more pleasant is to add a 15- or 20-minute session—or even 5 minutes in the beginning—into the rhythm of the day so that it isn't thrown on them unexpectedly. Maybe set aside time right after breakfast or lunch. Have everyone sit down together—including you! If possible. Since much of the mastery of penmanship has to do with the rhythmic flow of the pen, in the beginning, it will look like lines of swirls and curls. You can make the time go by more pleasantly by letting them listen to a story or some music while they are practicing. The skills of handwriting can be performed automatically without having to focus on them. Or so I have been told.

I'm not an expert in this field, but I am intrigued by the research and since I am trying to bring ways to you to open the hearts of your children and to help them express that which is in their hearts, calling attention to the benefits of cursive handwriting seems to be in order.

Start wherever you are. If your children already learned to print, just move into cursive. If they haven't yet started to write, take a look at the resources and consider diving right in.

Beautiful penmanship is so rare today. Truly a lost art.

Take 5.74—National Anthems and Map Work

Most studies in history take the world as a whole and work through it chronologically. I have really enjoyed taking it a nation at a time and learning each story and getting to know the hearts of the people. One of the great revealers to me was taking the time to listen to the words of each of their national anthems. I think you can learn a lot about a country by listening to the anthem they have chosen for themselves. We are seeing a shift going on in our own country and it is being reflected in how we view our anthem. Do we still believe:

Oh! thus be it ever, when freemen shall stand
Between their loved home and the war's desolation!
Blest with victory and peace, may the heav'n rescued land
Praise the Power that hath made and preserved us a nation.
Then conquer we must, when our cause it is just,
And this be our motto: "In God is our trust."
And the star-spangled banner in triumph shall wave
O'er the land of the free and the home of the brave!

I fear to think what new anthem may arise when I see what is happening around me. On the other hand, if more of the younger generation were taught this anthem with their hearts filled with the stories behind it–the stories of what made us a nation–would their united voices slow the tide?

Our national anthem is not meant to be performed. It is meant to unify as a nation by combining our voices in singing a song from the heart. Part of our disintegration as a nation—and I do feel like that is happening—was when we quit singing our songs together as a people, starting in the classroom.

If you notice in the music section of each of the nation's enrichment pages, I included a YouTube of their national anthem and if I could find one with the lyrics, I posted it. I think that little exercise alone does much to curb a spirit of nationalism which can be harmful as children see that other children love their countries as much as we love ours. And we see how often we are more alike in what we cherish than we are different.

Just one more note in this Take 5 about geography. Some people wonder where geography is in our studies. I would say it is meant to be integrated all along the way. Do have your children find every country they study on the world globe or map. Whenever you hear of a country or a region in your stories, take the time to identify on the map so that they begin to get a clear picture in their heads of countries in relation to other countries as well as land forms that play into the story; why access to water is so important; how mountains provided natural protection. The first time through the rotation, take the time to print out some blank outline maps and add them to their notebooks. Then when you read about an event or a person, take the time to locate it. Do a Google search–it's fast and immediate. And then have your kids mark it on their maps. They will retain the information far longer than separate map studies that are not connected to any stories or people.

Take 5.75—Art Appreciation

At some point, you will likely start feeling an urge to dig a little deeper in appreciating art. I want to direct you to a few books and resources that I have really enjoyed. One of them is called First Steps in the Enjoyment of Pictures by Maude Oliver and you will find it in the last half of the Story of Paintings in the Story Hour Series. While it is aimed at a young audience, you may enjoy it as a sort of self-taught art appreciation course that you can in turn find ways to share with your kids as you go along. I only included black and white replicas of the paintings that are talked about, but I found color versions of almost all of them by using a Google search. So either take the time and print them out as you go along to study, or just pull them up on your laptop or tablet.

In the preface, the writer says: "If this tool be presented by sympathetic parents to young people, a general concept of the artist's message may be acquired at an early age, the basic structure for an appreciation of the fine arts will be formed, and the capacity for enjoyment increased."

Another great resource are the Sister Wendy lectures on the *Story of Painting* that I have included on the Mother's University Art page. You can feel her passion for art.

Do check out the last two volumes of the Nature Series where I included a great text of the history of the arts by country. I've divided them out over the rotation on the guide.

And finally, go to the Art Appreciation section in the Other section on the Categories page.

As your understanding increases, go back and visit favorite paintings and see what new layers you can discover.

Take 5.76—Example of Historical Poetry

As your children mature and make friends with poetry, adding historical poetry into your studies will add another meaningful layer. So many of the events of history have been captured by the poet's pen. Feeling the galloping horses in Longfellow's Paul Revere's ride is so much more fun than a straight telling of the story.

I collected a few poems to go along with each month in the rotation schedule in Poetry for the Well-Educated Heart, but it's just a very meager start to what is available. One book that I have really enjoyed that has a lot of poems that are arranged chronologically according to America's story is called *Poems of American Patriotism* by Brander Matthews. I included several of the poems found here in the *Poetry for Well-Educated Heart* book. Each poem includes a date and the event associated with it. I'll link the full book here in this section, but it is also linked in the Elementary section of A New Nation. A wonderful bonus are many colorful illustrations by N.C. Wyeth.

Statistics can give a sense of numbers lost in a battle. But only the poet can show the heart its cost. You may have heard me share this poem before. I don't think I need to say anything more for you to understand its value to the heart.

The Picket Guard
by Ethel Lynn Beers

"All quiet along the Potomac," they say,
    "Except now and then a stray picket
Is shot, as he walks on his beat, to and fro,
    By a rifleman hid in the thicket.
'Tis nothing—a private or two, now and then,
    Will not count in the news of the battle;
Not an officer lost—only one of the men,
    Moaning out, all alone, the death rattle."

"All quiet along the Potomac tonight,
    Where the soldiers lie peacefully dreaming;
Their tents in the rays of clear autumn moon,
    Or the light of the watch fires, are gleaming.
A tremulous sigh, as the gentle night-wind,
    Through the forest-leaves softly is creeping;
While stars up above, with their glittering eyes,
    Keep guard—for the army is sleeping.

There's only the sound of the lone sentry's tread,

As he tramps from the rock to the fountain,
And thinks of the two in the low trundle bed
   Far away in the cot on the mountain.
His musket falls slack—his face, dark and grim,
   Grows gentle with memories tender,
As he mutters a prayer for the children asleep
   For their mother—may Heaven defend her!

The moon seems to shine just as brightly as then,
   That night, when the love yet unspoken,
Leaped up to his lips—when low-murmured vows
   Were pledged to be ever unbroken.
Then drawing his sleeve roughly over his eyes,
   He dashes off tears that are welling,
And gathers his gun closer up to its place
   As if to keep down the heart-swelling.

He passes the fountain, the blasted pine-tree
   The footstep is lagging and weary;
Yet onward he goes, through the broad belt of light,
   Toward the shades of the forest so dreary.
Hark! Was it the night-wind that rustled the leaves?
   Was it moonlight so wondrously flashing?
It looked like a rifle—"Ah! Mary, good-bye!"
   And the life-blood is ebbing and plashing.

All quiet along the Potomac tonight,
   No sound save the rush of the river;
While soft falls the dew on the face of the dead
   The picket's off duty forever.

Take 5.77—Relative Finder

One of the funnest connecting points to something familiar in history is to find out where your ancestors are from and then helping your children realize that these people they are studying included their great-great-great-grandparents and family members. They will look at the events through different eyes! And if you know stories of your ancestors, include them as you come around to the various monthly topics as part of your study. Create notebooking pages for them and place them in a chronological order in the notebook so that they can see what was going on in the world when that relative was alive. Making connections are so much fun and bring learning to life.

I've mentioned elsewhere that several years ago when we were studying the Pilgrims, we kept bumping into the stories of a loud, obnoxious, good for nothing family named the Billingtons. Their mischievous son almost blew up the Mayflower. He later got lost and got taken in by the Indians. The father was the first man to be hanged in America. They were about the only family who didn't lose a family member that first winter. I said it was probably because they stole food and blankets from everyone else.

Well, my husband kept telling our kids they had ancestors on the Mayflower, and I asked what their names were. So he looked them up. Sure enough. It was the Billingtons.

I told my kids the good news was they had ancestors on the Mayflower. The bad news was they should probably keep it to themselves.

Of course, I was kidding. And they love to tell people about their ancestors. Fortunately, my husband is also related to William Bradford and John Alden, so we'll keep him around.

Whenever I tell that story, it is so fun to hear from so many people who also had ancestors on the Mayflower. There are millions of us. Isn't that remarkable? Especially when you consider that, after that first winter, only half of them survived and most of them were children. A handful of people.

What stories are in your past?

familysearch.org and relativefinder.org will make your search easier.

Take 5.78—Stories of Scientists: Experimenting

I have spent a lot of time now talking about the value of spending time in nature and learning the stories and lessons of nature. But what about science, you may be asking. Don't our kids need to know about science?

Of course. But what people refer to when they talk about science is more textbook science, not entering into the true scientific mind of wonder and questioning and experimenting and finding answers. The science that we force on a child's mind that doesn't care seems like a giant waste of time to me because that mind will retain little or even none of it. Warm the fires of desire first and it will pay big dividends later.

So, to me, an important part of the layering process is to share many stories of scientists so that children can take to heart that passion the true scientist felt to find answers to his questions. Let them live the life of a scientist through their stories and hopefully capture a portion of the same spirit of inquiry and willingness to do hard things to find answers to their questions.

One of the Great Lives Series books is a collection of stories about scientists and inventors. There is also a section in the website I haven't talked about a lot yet because I haven't had a chance to develop it as fully as I'd like to. If you go to the Categories navigation page, one of the sections is Great Lives and you will see a link to Scientists. I have just a few books there right now, but in time, I hope to give you many more options. There are also biographies of scientists sprinkled throughout all the pages in the library under the Biography section.

And then let them start to engage in experiments and seeing things with their own eyes. If you have been nature journaling with your kids, you have been training their eyes to pay attention to details and to see things that ordinarily may have been missed.

Take 5.79—Notebooking

I can't go into a lot of details about notebooking in five minutes and I've spent quite a bit of time talking about it elsewhere. But what I can do is try, again, to help you catch a vision of possibilities. I see notebooking as a way to hold on to all that I am loving learning about. They are scrapbooks of favorite things. So I've talked about a little book of favorite art prints for a young child, a collection of favorite poems, creating a page of favorite gems you pull from books of literature as well as illustrations when possible and nature journaling as a form of notebooking.

One of my favorite notebooks is my book of great lives which is really a study of history. I load mine with fine art prints and illustrations because it saves me from a lot of words and as I look through it, I am reminded of many things instantly. I don't load mine up with lots of facts because facts are so easily accessible now. "Alexa, when was King George born? Alexa, what is the capital of Syria?"

I was visiting my little granddaughter who is just learning how to write and she gave me a letter she had just written. I said, "Wow! This is wonderful! How did you learn to spell all these words already? Did your mom help you?" And she said, "No, when I got to a word I didn't know how to spell, I just asked Alexa."

What an amazing age we live in!

So, there may be some facts that are meaningful to you that you want to hold on to, but I don't see a need to create notebooks full of facts and information, which is what typical notebooking activities look like.

Rather, I use my notebook to jot down a story I want to remember and where I can find it again. Or a quote. Or a question that comes to mind. Or an idea I want to remember.

I often hear a mom say that her kids refuse to notebook. I would guess it's being used as an assignment and you're getting that resistance that comes from compulsion. My suggestion is for you to work on your own notebook. I see it happen all the time—a child watches and says, "Hey! I want to do that!" Let it be their own creation. Maybe it will be nothing but pictures in the beginning. I try and create notebook size pictures for you anytime I can to make things easier on you. As I grow BelMonde, if there are pictures that go with the audio stories, you will see a PDF of them by the title. Easy, easy way to start. For instance, I just recorded stories from a couple of books about the children of English history. There are wonderful illustrations to go along with the stories that can go on a notebooking page. Just write the name of the person at the top, do a quick Google search for the year he was born and died and put it in the upper right hand corner, and then make a reference to the country he is from. Let a child either dictate to you what he wants to remember from the story, or even let him describe what is going on in the picture, or let him write whatever he wants.

If you keep forgetting to notebook, maybe designate Friday afternoon as notebooking day and pull out pens, markers and pages, put on some music, and start working on yours. Eventually, hopefully, your children will find keeping these notebooks as desirable and they will just do it on their own. It's how they can demonstrate what they have learned and will become a keepsake of these years of learning.

A cultural notebook can be where you keep the blank maps to mark as your learn about where stories take place. You can take pictures of crafts that you make and create pages in a notebook with tabs for each country. Especially including the people making the crafts in the pictures which becomes happy memories of growing up. Include recipes and pictures of cultural dinners together. Make note of holidays and customs. You can even create Places I Want to Visit Someday and print out pictures and highlight a few things about that place so that when you visit, you know the stories behind the place.

My notebooks inspire my heart. And for those of you worried about putting the pieces of history together because we aren't moving through chronologically, when you place the pages in the notebook chronologically by birth, you start seeing who were contemporaries, who lived before and after who. And do add your own family members in there! As your notebook fills up, just pull out half the pages and put them in another notebook and keep growing. If you fill up a notebook page and find something else interesting about that person, just insert another page. That's why I use individual sheets and 3-ring binders. I can keep growing and adjusting.

You don't need anything fancy. Just blank paper, lined paper if you want or you can use blank white paper and put a lined template behind it for your beginning writers.

Out of sight, out of mind is a real thing. Notebooking keeps our learning refreshed.

There is no wrong or right way to do this. Only your way. And you will likely find yourself adjusting what that looks like over time. I know it does for me.

What I do know is that I am so sad for the times I didn't take time to notebook a story or a person and I cannot for the life of me find it again. Also, I am amazed at all I forget and when I go back through, I am reminded of wonderful people and lessons.

Just begin. Make it as simple or elaborate as you want. Notebooking replaces the myriad of worksheets that are usually tossed anyway. And you get to choose what goes in them! Have fun with it! It's not a chore. I promise.

Take 5.80—Story Hour Series

I'm going to divert a bit from how the past weeks have been structured. I've tried to include something for Music, a little art, a little poetry, something for story and nature. But I have quite a few resources to cover that you can draw from as you share stories for the Heroic years, so I'm going to spend the rest of the week highlighting some of these resources, starting with the Story Hour Series in the Forgotten Classics.

After I finished the Freedom Series and looked to the other series I was creating, I realized I didn't have stories for children younger than eight years old. Plus, there wasn't a place to introduce stories from literature. So I created the Story Hour Series to fill that gap. The stories are meant to be read aloud and the intention was to aim them at listeners under the age of 8. There are a couple of exceptions to that. For example, I included retellings of a couple of Shakespeare's Tragedies and I definitely would not tell those to a child under 8 years old.

The second volume, *Stories and Rhymes for Young Children*, is a volume created for your preschoolers. Also, the *Stories of Paintings* have some beginning art appreciation studies that will appeal to an older child. But I mostly had you in mind when I included it. I wanted to give you a way to start introducing elements of art to your children. Do a Google search for the black and white images that are in the book.

In the Story Hour series, you will find fairy tales, Greek mythology, introductory stories to legendary and epic heroes, narrative stories of the Bible, stories about nature for little children, some beginning stories to begin to whet the appetite for stories from history and great lives, a book with stories divided by values and a Christmas book. Also, the volume of stories from great literature will give your children a simple introduction to Chaucer, Plato, Dante, Spencer, Cervantes and Shakespeare.

Like all the other stories in the Forgotten Classics, you can find free digital reads on the Forgotten Classics page and I have sorted them out according to the rotation schedule. Look for the S in the blue boxes—S for Story Hour Series.

And remember—just because they are created for young listeners in mind, the stories are rich enough to appeal to older listeners. So do encourage your older children to read them.

Take 5.81—Freedom Series

I could have called the Freedom Series the American History Series, but Freedom Series seemed more descriptive because all of these stories and books included in this series were written by great storytellers who didn't hide the fact that they had an agenda. And their agenda was to teach children how to hold on to the freedom that had so recently been won. So they loaded their writings with principles of liberty and freedom. But it's not the in-your-face kind of teaching. They land softly and you just might find yourself pausing from time to time because they have said something that makes you think.

I had a copy of Cleon Skousen's *5000 Year Leap* sitting on the desk next to my computer while I was putting together the Freedom Series, but I hadn't had time to read it. If you don't know what that book was, Dr. Skousen took years to carefully go through the writings of the Founding Fathers and discovered 28 principles of freedom that he discusses in the book. Well, one day after I finished the Freedom Series, I glanced over at the book and the thought came into my mind, "Did you know all the principles in that book are found in the stories you just included in the Freedom Series?"

And I thought, "Really?" And as went through the principles, I thought—yes—that was included in that story and I read that one in another story and so forth. In fact, I had somehow assimilated all of them into my thinking just from the stories that were selected to go into the series.

Each book is unique. Some of the volumes are comprised of a number of stories included from multiple sources. Other volumes have one or two complete books in them. When I could, I looked for a book that would appeal to a younger listener and then added another book they can come back to in a few years to refresh what they learned and layer a little deeper. Also, you will find original sources in most of the volumes, such as excerpts from William Bradford's diary or quotes from Abraham Lincoln.

As you go through the books, you will begin to get a sweep of American history. One of the final volumes is a what I call a concentrated sweep of history so that those events can begin to find an order in your memory and fall into place. Another book that does that is the Mara Pratt *American History Stories* book that is offered as one of the free gifts. Mara Pratt's story has been a favorite among homeschoolers for years. It has also appeared under the title, American History Stories You Never Learned in School. It typically comes in four volumes, but we combined all four volumes into one.

If I were to name an age that I would begin to share the stories from this series, I would say around age 8, not because a younger child can't understand, but because, developmentally, there are more important stories to prepare a child for stories of history. But if you are reading it aloud to your family, your little ones will self-select. They may pick up more than you think, even though they may not seem interested.

I shared these books with my 85-year-old history buff uncle and he couldn't believe how much he learned that he didn't know. These are children's books, but they are not childish.

Look for them on the Forgotten Classics page. And if you missed it, each book ties into a World History topic so that you can use American History as a spine to tie all your studies together. I talked about the details of that in the Intro course. A little here and a little there all along the way will soon add up.

Take 5.82—World History Series

When I was creating the World History Series, I was looking for books that gave a good overall sweep of each nation's history in an engaging way. I compared all the books I could find written for young people and made a selection—which wasn't easy! That's why you have an online library to go to as well because there are other great options there, too. Unlike the Freedom Series, the World Series selections are complete books and are written at a little higher level than the Freedom Series. If I were to suggest an age for these books, I would say maybe 11 or 12 as a read-aloud, depending on how much foundation work you have done. But certainly a 14-year-old or older could read these books on his or her own. A younger child may be able to follow what is going on, but history is not pretty and there were many cruel things that happened. I just don't think younger children have to be exposed to that too soon. I would spend more time reading stories like *Our Little Cousins*, imaginative stories, short high-interest stories of people, quality literature and historical fiction and cultural stories before the age of 12 for world history.

Of course, you know your children and every child is different. So do go take a look and decide for yourself if your child is ready.

The final book in the series is a sweep of the story of the whole world. It will take many stories to weave together a picture. For those of you who like a book in hand, we are creating some other world history series to continue to build that picture. I'll talk about Tappan's *World Story* in a future Take 5 as well as another World History series that will include outstanding writers of children's history like Henriette Marshall, Mary MacGregor, Helene Guerber, John Haaren and Charles Coffin. These gifted writers help you see and feel history.

Take 5.83—G.A. Henty/Historical Fiction

First a word on historical fiction—I love it! The one complaint I hear from moms is that they worry that it may not be factual. Which is true, hence the word fiction. The authors are using their imaginations to help paint a picture of how an event may have played out. But most historical fiction writers do massive research before unfolding the story and there is much you can learn from their writings. If you are choosing only one book to teach history, then, yes, choosing historical fiction as that one book is a problem. But if you haven't picked it up by now, I am a believer in the weaving of many stories and as you read about events from numerous points of view, you naturally bump into conflicting information which makes you go, huh? What's the truth here? And sends you on a rabbit trail to try and discover it. That's when learning gets exciting. As long as you are building a desire to read widely, truth is going to eventually come to light. At least the truth that really matters. There are many facts in history that we may never know.

Historical fiction can light the flame of desire to know more about a subject that may be unattractive at first. I remember having no interest in the Civil War in school. But I picked up *Gone With the Wind* on my own and it brought faces and lives to life, even though most of them were fictional. I could see the cost of the war through new eyes and I became deeply interested in the study of the Civil War. Historical fiction helps us to see and to feel.

You will find Historical Fiction sections on each library page. It wasn't easy for me, though, to determine the fine line between an historical writing and a fictional one. In other words, you can have a book where the characters are all real and the events described are based on factual occurrences. What the author might add is an imaginary conversation between characters. So technically it puts it on the Fiction side, but I may have included it in History or Biography.

Most of the historical fiction books include imaginary characters woven into the story.

One of the great historical fiction writers was G.A. Henty who wrote 122 books for young people. I found copies of most of his books in Internet Archive and have them linked and sorted by country in the online library. You will find them on the Middle School pages. Jim Weiss has recorded several abridged versions and I have linked those with a red arrow.

So who was Henty?

Henty was an Englishman who was a sickly child and had to spend a lot of time in bed. So, he became an avid reader and developed a wide range of interests. He left his university studies in Cambridge early to go to Crimea, where war was raging, and there he saw for himself the appalling conditions under which the British soldier had to fight. His letters that he wrote home were filled with such vivid descriptions, his father sent them to the newspaper which printed them. He went on to become a war correspondent and travelled around the world, including Palestine, Russia, and India, meeting many fascinating characters along the way.

His storytelling skills grew as he related the tales of what he saw to his children around the table after dinner. These stories grew into the 122 books that were very popular reading in his day. Before writing the books, he would order several books on the subject he was writing on from libraries. Many of the books were of events that he had witnessed for himself, so he adds details from those first-hand experiences.

The fictional character around whom the story revolves was typically a boy or a young man living in troubled times. These boys are intelligent, courageous, honest and resourceful, yet modest, which is one reason these books have become popular with homeschoolers today. But the books are not without their drawbacks. Some critics say the stories become formulaic after awhile. And they can occasionally be seen as racist, which is really another snapshot of the times and is something you'll want to talk about. He loves England. That is apparent.

But the general effect of the books is to light a fire of interest in learning more about the events described in the book. Give them a try. A lot of people have loved them.

Take 5.84—Messner/Landmarks

In today's Take 5, I want to make sure you know about a couple of excellent series of books that will greatly enrich your history studies. The first series is called the Landmark Books.

Let me share parts of an article written by David Spear, a professor of history at Furman University where he tells the story of Landmark books.

> Once there was a history book series that was so successful, it lured an entire generation of young readers to the discipline, including many of today's professional historians. The publisher hired the absolute best authors of the day, which might account for a small but dedicated audience in the present. Random House's Landmark Books Series ran from 1950 to 1970 and ultimately generated 180 volumes.
>
> Bennett Cerf, the magisterial publisher who helped found Random House, invented the Landmark series in 1948. While vacationing with his family on Cape Cod, he went to buy a book about the Pilgrims for his young son. The proprietor of the local bookstore told Cerf that there were no juvenile books in print on that topic. Cerf thereupon decided to fill the gap. And fill it he did. In short order, James Daugherty, winner of the

Newbery Medal, completed the book about the Pilgrims.

Cerf set the pattern for the series by persuading celebrated novelist Dorothy Canfield Fisher to write two of the early volumes—one on Paul Revere and the other called *Our Independence and Constitution*. Her name added a certain gravitas to a new series directed at teens, especially since rival series relied on professional children's book authors. 35 out of the 114 writers were women, a high proportion for the day. (Many authors contributed more than one title.) Some of the books were biographies, and some were more traditional histories.

Not a single author was an academic. Cerf clearly preferred skilled wordsmiths, the more famous the better, who could engage a general audience. The early years of the series relied on such literati as war correspondent Quentin Reynolds, Pulitzer Prize winner MacKinlay Kantor, double Pulitzer Prize recipient Robert Penn Warren, and Nobel Prize winner Pearl Buck. C.S. Forester, author of *The African Queen* and inventor of the Horatio Hornblower novels of adventure on the high seas, penned *The Barbary Pirates* for the series...

One or two of the books were explicitly racist. But many displayed a wonderful magnanimity of spirit—as, for example, in MacKinlay Kantor's capacious treatment of Lee and Grant's dramatic surrender ceremony at Appomattox. Moreover, the series included 15 books with female subjects, not the least of which was Women of Courage. Seven of the books dealt exclusively or largely with Native Americans, including sympathetic biographies of Geronimo and Sequoyah. And one of my personal favorites was George Washington Carver: it made me want to be a botanist.

If the titles from the 1950s focused mostly on colonial history, the American West, pirates, and inventors, the 1960s highlighted the events of World War II. Most of these were written by actual war correspondents, such as Bruce Bliven, Richard Tregaskis, and John Toland. In some instances, these were adult best sellers simplified for younger readers. William Shirer published his mammoth *The Rise and Fall of the Third Reich* in 1960. The next year, his *Rise and Fall of Adolf Hitler* appeared in the Landmark series.

Bennett Cerf had phoned Shirer, asking for the Landmark biography of Hitler. "It was not so easy as he assured me it would be.... How did you write for young people? You couldn't be condescending. You had to respect them. But you had to keep it simple enough for them to understand," Shirer recalled in his memoir.... His comment goes to the heart of the success of the Landmark series. The authors had no in-house guide to follow, no formula for how many words of four syllables were allowed. Each author was given absolute freedom to craft the subject matter as he or she saw fit. Most took their task very seriously.

Cerf's hunch was correct: for young readers it was more important to tell a good story and to tell it in a simple but urbane way. In that regard, it would be hard to find prose more challenging and engaging to a juvenile than Shirer's closing words: "The remembrance of the grisly world nightmare [Hitler] provoked, of the millions of innocent beings he slaughtered, of the hurt he did to the human spirit, lingers on. The memory fades but slowly as the years pass and mankind resumes its ages-old effort to make the world a more decent place in which to live."

About 10 of the titles have been reissued, but in paperback, with different illustrations, with the type completely reset and with tiny margins—noble, but altogether less inviting—by Sterling Point Books. And since so many copies of the original series were printed, they are still to be found in used bookstores and online.

It would be a shame if this icon of American history were forgotten.

So there you have it. You will find Landmark books highlighted in the online library, not because I can always link you to a copy, but because, if you can get hold of a copy, either by finding one at a used book sale or through an interlibrary loan, it's worth reading. If I'm at a used book sale, I always grab the ones I find. You'll come to recognize them if you don't already. Unfortunately, the prices for used copies have skyrocketed recently. But because they were so popular, many can still be found through interlibrary loans.

The other series of books I want to highlight are the Messner biographies. These are a little harder to spot and are rarer to find, but, oh my goodness, they are so good. At least all the ones I have read. I would say most of them are at a higher reading level than the Landmarks, but not all. But for ease in finding them in the online library, I always put them on the high school pages and designate that they are a Messner title. Because they are so difficult to find, I mostly limited it to titles that I can link you to titles in Internet Archive.

If you are out in the book shopping wild, you will begin to recognize them by their size and if you open to the title page, look for Julian Messner as the publisher. Reshelving Alexandria has a complete list if you are interested.

Take 5.85—Building a Family Library

I am really sad what I see happening in our public libraries, not the least of which is that the books are disappearing and being replaced with screens! Many mothers no longer feel confident leaving their kids to pick out their books. There is much that is vulgar and inappropriate for children.

I have tried to offer you a free digital alternative in my Library of Hope. There are over 4,000 books you can access there. But I'm not confident we will always have that option open to us. We already are seeing censorship happening in the public square and denying access to certain topics on the internet.

I would feel much more confident that the ideals we are trying to secure of faith, family and freedom will have more chance of surviving if many families will take the time to build home libraries and fill them with books that will give our children and grandchildren hope for the future—that is why they are Libraries of Hope.

Plus, I, like you, prefer to hold a book in hand. Thankfully, many companies are bringing older out-of-print books back into print. I'm afraid these older used books have become used booksellers highest ticket items and titles I used to be able to get for a dollar now can be over a hundred dollars, *if* I can find them. So I am grateful more publishers are doing the work necessary to make them available.

I will link several of the publishers I am aware of in this section where you can buy these wonderful older living books. Jenny Phillips with her Good and Beautiful program is publishing many titles. I started linking them in the website but need to update it. Also, Yesterday's Classics is another wonderful source as well as Purple House Press and Living Books.

And, of course, we are trying to bring many back into print as well. I try to pack as much as I can in one volume to save you money, so you will find lots of collections in our offering. I'm mindful of the work of these other groups and I'm trying not to duplicate efforts, but offer you something they are not.

You can still find bargains if you shop thrift stores and, especially, check the Friends of the Library sales in your area. Or go to booksalefinder.com to find sales that may be worth traveling to. I have built most of my library from Friends of the Library sales.

Also, Abe Books is a great source and of course Amazon and eBay.

I have organized my library around the 12-month rotation schedule. Most of my books fall within the rotation. I do keep certain sets together and I have my "pretty books" upstairs in my living room. So, for instance, in Month 1, I have a shelf for Asia, one for India, one for Explorers, one for Scandinavia, one for South Seas, one for Stars—my nature topic and then because the Mother's University topic is A Mother's Influence, that's where I keep books about home organization and family traditions and such. Keep in mind this doesn't have to be an exact science. I usually will put a book in a certain month because the story takes place in that country. But other times I put a book in a certain month because the author is from that country. All the books that take place in America are also placed in certain months. So if I have a story that takes place in the 1800s in America, it goes in Month 7 on a shelf. If a story takes places in 20th century America, it goes in Month 10.

I don't arrange the books in any particular order on the shelf. It doesn't take long to look through a shelf of books to see what I am looking for as I make my way through the rotation each year. Having them organized this way narrows down my choices each month.

I also have a separate shelf for picture books, because many of them don't fit in a particular month. But if they do, I'll put it on the rotation shelf. So my illustrated fairy tales are usually on rotation shelves, for instance.

I also keep all my Forgotten Classics, My Book House and Junior Classics sets on shelves in my office because I access them frequently and they don't necessarily fit into a certain month.

Adapt it to what works for you. Maybe you need to spread shelves throughout your house rather than having them in one room. It can still work.

Building a family library is a fun hobby! And you have no idea the impact it may have on the generations that follow you.

Take 5.86—Movies/Musicals

On the Enrichment pages, you will find a lot of movies. A lot of them are old movies, and your children, if they are used to lots of action, may not like them. But don't write them off immediately. There is much to be gained from them, especially from a historical standpoint.

Many of these movies were filmed on location so it helps your children to paint clearer pictures in their minds of what events may have looked like. If they lose interest, don't make them sit through the whole thing. Take whatever you can from the movie.

If movie night is a special treat and not a steady diet, you may find they are more willing to give some of these old movies a chance. There is definitely a different feel to them, as the camera allows time for you to read character from facial expressions and to develop storylines.

Our recent movies are terribly lacking in storylines and character development. They try and make up for it with noise and non-stop action and special effects. By going back to some of these older movies, you'll be doing your kids' hearts a favor.

But they're not all old movies. By the way, I haven't watched all of them. I'm always on the prowl for recommended movies and when I find something that fits with something in the Rotation Schedule, I add it in. But I leave it to you to do your homework. The movies are all linked to IMDB where there is a parental advisory section and reviews and you can determine if this is a movie you want to watch with your family.

I am not a fan of R rated movies, but our rating system is also very broken. A movie like *The Mission* in Month 9 is rated PG, but it is hardly a movie for children. It's powerful and I enjoyed it, but there are scenes that make you wince and look away. There are also excellent movies that are rated R, but I try and find a cleaned-up version. That's my preference. All I'm trying to say with that is: do your homework. There are a couple of rated R movies like *Schindler's List* or *The Last Emperor* in the list, so just be aware of that. It is not a Good and Beautiful approved list of movies, if that makes sense to some of you.

Also, you will find lots of musicals. Watching these fun musicals is another way of bringing wholesome music into the hearts of your children. It is a taste worth acquiring.

Take 5.87—Symbols in Art

If your kids have made friends with art and found looking at art to be an enjoyable activity, by the time they are in their Heroic years, particularly Middle School and High School, they may be interested in taking their understanding to a deeper level, especially as they encounter art painted in earlier eras, particularly Christian art.

I want to highlight a book you can find in the Art Appreciation section called *A Handbook of Christian Symbols: Stories of the Saints as Illustrated in Art* by Clara Erskine Waters.

In the book, she explains that the first object of Christian art was to teach. The people weren't readers. They relied on pictures, so the paintings were filled with symbolism, certain figures and even color to relay meaning and if you don't understand this language they used, the art is really quite meaningless.

As you familiarize your children with these symbols and the stories behind the many Saints in these paintings, it almost becomes like a game to identify the clues and find their deeper meanings, which gives the paintings their power and depth of expression.

The fish, the cross, the lamb, the lion, the pelicans, peacocks, unicorns all have a meaning. I think it's interesting to learn, as we realize our role as nurturers of hearts, that the dove, from ancient times, has been used as a symbol of the divine feminine, of the influence of the Spirit, and was found abundantly on early Christian churches, temples and cathedrals, and they knew its meaning.

Colors also had their meaning. For example, blue represented heavenly love. Green was the color of spring, signifying hope.

I was especially interested in the Cedar of Lebanon which is the symbol we have chosen to represent Mothers of Influence. Waters said: "by its height, perfumery, healing qualities and its incorruptible substance, it symbolizes the greatness, goodness, and beauty of the Virgin." I think that applies to the intent of Mothers of Influence very nicely.

You will also find brief summaries of the stories of each of the Saints that appear in paintings. These stories were not meant to be taken as fact. The stories were embellished and exaggerated over the years. But she said that only the ignorant would have taken the stories literally. Rather the stories were used to teach some moral lesson, much like Christ did with His parables.

You will also find a companion book she wrote, highlighting the same things in Mythological art and paintings.

I am only beginning to learn this, but I'm enjoying it so much. I hope you do, too.

Take 5.88—Tappan's World Story

Another of our World Story Series is Eva March Tappan's *The World's Story in Art, Poetry and Story*. I love this series of books and have wanted to bring it back into print for a long time. We have regrouped it, though, to follow the rotation schedule. You will get everything in the original series, but just grouped differently. Hers unfolded in a more chronological way, and if you want to study it that way, it's not difficult to find how the books were originally ordered and you can certainly study it that way.

But I see it as a beautiful supplement to the stories of the nations you are learning as you keep cycling through, year after year. So we are releasing the books to align with the rotation study.

If you read her introductory section, she acknowledges that it isn't the facts that reveal the heart of any people. It's the poetry they write, the stories they tell and the art they left behind that help us to connect with them and understand them so we can learn from them.

Although the stories may work as a read aloud for a Junior High student, I think it is mostly your High Schoolers that will enjoy what they find in these books. I have links to the digital versions in all the High School sections of the website. You'll find them under the Cultural heading.

But if you have little ones who aren't ready, do read them for yourself and deepen your own understanding of the world we live in. There are so many fascinating stories to enrich your studies and you will likely find yourself just naturally sharing what you are learning.

Do notice the fine art on the covers of the books we are reprinting. They bring to life some story found in that particular volume.

By the way, she had two volumes of American History. We spread the contents of those two volumes in the corresponding monthly study according to the rotation. She had 15 volumes. We are offering 24 volumes—a little 'lighter' reading, literally. You can spread it out over two years or receive two books a month and receive all of them in one year. Or you can order the entire 24-volume set.

Take 5.89—Great Lives Series

About a hundred years ago, there was a definite shift in how biographers approached their subjects. They generally went from writing stories to inspire the reader to exposing all the faults and warts of their subjects. They seem to want to pull of them off their pedestals and say, "See? They are just like us."

When I read the story of someone's life, I want to be inspired. I want to see how they overcame weaknesses and challenges. They help me see life and all its possibilities through hundreds of eyes, not just through the narrow view of my own experiences.

So I love the older biographies, especially those written before 1923 because they do inspire and lift me.

The Great Lives Series was created because I wanted to share the stories I was finding, and I thought it would be helpful to you if I organized all the writers in one volume, the musicians in another, the scientists in another and so forth. I would say this is another series that will appeal more to older children, maybe as young as 8 years old as read alouds, but mostly to Junior High and High School students, which are the Heroic years after all.

I sorted them according to country in the online library and give you a general guideline as to the age of the appeal of their stories. Look for the blue boxes for the selections that start with a G for Great Lives. But, again, just because it is in the Elementary section doesn't mean that your High Schooler won't enjoy the story. It does mean that the vocabulary and subject matter in the High School section probably won't appeal to a younger child.

Let me highlight a couple of volumes. *The Stories of Great Greeks and Romans* is a collection of Plutarch's lives. I searched for all the various versions and chose the one I felt was aimed at the youngest reader. I see it as an introduction to Plutarch. These stories have influenced countless people over the centuries. It has been called a bible for heroes. I did a podcast on it in the Greek section.

I mostly had you, the mothers, in mind when I collected the *Stories of Great Wives and Mothers*. My son formatted the book for me and when he was done, he said he had a problem with it. I said, "Oh yeah? What's that?" And he said, with a smile, it made him want to be a mother! So when you need a little inspiration for yourself, here is some great company for you to surround yourself with.

The Stories of Great Philanthropists were chosen because they highlighted people who mostly used their wealth to bless the lives of other people. And they model behaviors of diligence, hard work and honesty.

If you want to inspire your children with lives of others who sacrificed much to serve others, who loved people, spend some time with the great Humanitarians and Missionaries.

The Great Writers books have many accounts of the stories behind what brought the writers to write the books they did. And their stories show that they often had many rejections before they found acceptance for their work.

The Great Spiritual Leaders is actually a great introductory study to all the major religions of the world. Not only do I include a story of the various leaders, I found a wonderful book called *Had You Been Born in Another Faith* which I included in this volume. Whether Hindu, Muslim, Parsi, Catholic or Protestant, you will see how much we actually have in common with each other. Our outward rituals may be different, but the hearts of each one are so similar. I see that as evidence of a loving God who loves all His children. I hope you aren't afraid, as your children get older, to let them visit and experience other churches and faiths. Shouldn't we seek to understand one another? There are so many misconceptions and way too much fear. Can we not teach our children respect for others who are different than us?

I mentioned it earlier, but I'll mention it again. On the Categories navigation page in the website, there is a Great Lives section. I have only begun to start building this part of the library, but that's where you will be able to find stories that align with how the Great Lives Series is organized. So if you have a budding musician or scientist on your hands, you might want to visit that section to introduce him around to some great friends worth having.

I also encourage you to create pages for each of the lives you touch upon like I've described before. Write their name at the top. Write down the year that person was born in the right-hand corner and the year he died just below it. I like to note what country that person is from just below that. Then do a Google search for some pictures and put a few on the page. Right below the name, I often write the major accomplishment that person is noted for. Then I write down what I learned from that person; experiences and stories I want to remember. I don't write the whole story out, just enough to jog my memory and then where I can find it again. I copy down quotes I want to remember or little gems from my reading.

It's a wonderful scrapbook of ideas and ideals. And these people really do become daily companions to me in this way. I love reading the stories of great lives—one of my favorite things to do. And the Great Lives Series gives you a great place to start!

Take 5.90—Experiments/Science

What about Science? Don't our kids need to learn Science? Of course.

But in my mind, there is a true spirit of science and then there's textbook science. I'm not a big fan of textbook science in childhood. Too much of that information and many of those facts go in and out.

The true spirit of science is all about wondering and questioning and curiosity; experimenting, finding out how things work. It has much to do with observation.

So when you are nature journaling, using the tools I Notice, I Wonder and That Reminds Me Of, you are nurturing the heart of a true scientist. Also, as you share stories of scientists, you are helping their hearts to see and to capture the excitement a true scientist feels as he explores and discovers. They see how much patience they have to have and how not everything can be solved in 23 minutes.

When you teach textbook science, it's as though everything has already been solved. A true scientist questions everything, doesn't he?

By high school, if a student is ready for a more structured study of science, there are tons of science programs out there. If they have had a lot of experience in the real world, the things they learn through a textbook will add to their appreciation of things they have already observed. They will pick up necessary terms and vocabulary to deepen their understanding and keep moving forward. It is a subject that will never be mastered! There is a lifetime of discovery possible.

If you apply the Pattern for Learning, use those pre-high school years for exposure and creating a desire to want to know the rules and laws upon which everything operates. You will notice, if you follow the nature rotation schedule, roughly the first half of the year is for Earth Sciences—Physics, Light, Chemistry, Geology. The second half are the Life Sciences—Biology, Botany and so forth. So start incorporating experiments that go along with their study. A lot of people like the Janice Van Cleave books that I have linked in the Science section of the Mother's University. But the internet is so amazing—there are no end of resources out there if you search.

Better yet is if your child designs his own experiments to test his own theories.

So the question you have to answer for yourself: Do you want to grow the heart of a scientist or do you want someone who can answer questions on a test? I can't answer that for you. But if you want the first, you have to leave lots of room for exploration and discovery along the way.

Take 5.91—Grammar

Let's talk about grammar today. I'm not anti-formal grammar lessons. But, again, it's following the Pattern for Learning. First, let the heart see and understand before you try and teach the rules. I don't believe early childhood is the time for formal grammar lessons.

In the Language Arts section of the Mother's University is an article entitled *The Wrong Way to Teach Grammar* that brings up some valid points worth considering. Let me recap:

A century of research shows that traditional grammar lessons—those hours spent diagramming sentences and memorizing parts of speech—don't help and may even hinder students' efforts to become better writers. For example, in one well-regarded study, students from 9th to 11th grades were grouped into three groups: one group had traditional rule-bound lessons, a second received an alternative approach to grammar instruction, and a third received no grammar lessons at all, just more literature and creative writing. The result: no significant differences among the three groups, except that both of the first two groups emerged with a strong dislike to the study of English.

The writer of the article worked with adult students and found that they became so focused on grammatically correct writing, that it never gave them a chance to explore their ideas or ways of expressing those ideas. It shut down the process of writing.

She said there is a mistaken belief that grammar lessons must come before writing, rather than grammar being something that is best learned through writing. Just as we teach children how to ride bikes by putting them on a bicycle, we need to teach students how to write grammatically by letting them write. Once students get ideas they care about onto the page, they are ready for instruction that will help communicate those ideas. When approached this way, surprisingly little formal grammar instruction is needed.

I would add that as you have your children read aloud from excellent writing as well as listen to great literature, and as they copy passages like we have talked about, they are internalizing lessons in a natural way.

You can read more about the studies yourself in the article, but let me share one more quote from it. In 1984, George Hillocks, a renowned professor of English and Education at the University of Chicago, published an analysis of the research on teaching writing. He concluded that, "School boards, administrators, and teachers who impose the systematic study of traditional school grammar on their students over lengthy periods of time in the name of teaching writing do them a gross disservice that should not be tolerated by anyone concerned with the effective teaching of good writing."

And there is another problem with spending too much time in childhood on the study of grammar. When you choose to spend time studying one subject, you are taking away the time that could be spent on teaching something that may be even more important and long lasting. President Garfield observed, "One half of the time which is now wholly wasted in district schools, on English grammar attempted at too early an age, would be sufficient to teach our children to love the Republic and to become its loyal and life-long supporters."

There are gentler ways to introduce parts of speech than worksheets. I included a little book called *Grammarland* in the Language Arts books of the Mother's Learning Library. This is a fun way to introduce terms such as nouns, verbs and adverbs in a way children will remember.

The rules of grammar can be learned very quickly if introduced at the right time. I think of the examples of Lew Wallace who wrote *Ben-Hur* and Abraham Lincoln. Both men read widely while growing up and when each felt a desire to write, they realized their deficiencies in grammar and found grammar books that caught them up pretty quickly. I think you'll agree they did all right for themselves.

Take 5.92—Symphony Stories

Today I want to add a couple of more tools to your toolboxes to help your older children refine their musical listening ear even more. In the Music Appreciation section of the library that I have directed to you before, there is a book called *Some Famous Symphonies and How to Understand Them*, also *Stories of Symphonic Music*, both found in the High School section. You might consider suggesting a thread of study for your High Schoolers for one of their rotations where they pick a symphony each month to listen to in greater depth, using these resources to deepen their understanding. Or make it a study for yourself. Take a few minutes and sort the composers out according to the monthly rotation and you are ready to go. Because there are so many composers from Germany, Austria and Russia, which are Month 10, you'll have to spread those out into the summer months and also you can study them in months 7, 8 and 9 when there isn't a composer directly tied into those months. I put Mozart's Jupiter in Month 1 because of the tie in to Stars. I put Mendelssohn in Month 6 because of his Jewish roots. Cesar Franck was born in Belgium, so he is Month 2. Stanford wrote the Irish Symphony that ties into month 3.

Let me give you just a little taste, starting with Beethoven's most famous Symphony No. 5: ta ta ta dum.

> Before attempting any description of this symphony, a certain fine point has to be considered. The work is of a specified quality known as 'pure' or 'absolute' music. This means that it possesses no literary description and must therefore be listened to purely as music. This particular quality is the opposite to 'programme' music, which has a literary description furnished or indicated by the composer. The absolute music composer leaves to the music to suggest its own message to the hearer.

> Music at its best is essentially spiritual, and should therefore convey some sort of message or even picture to the hearer's mind. The hearer is quite at liberty to supply his own meaning of the work, although it is certainly an outpouring of Beethoven's soul and can be best understood by considering the aspects of his life at the period of the symphony's composition.

> Beethoven's growing deafness was at this time an increasing tragedy in his whole outlook. Add to this the pathetically recurring thoughts of a woman he hoped would prove to be his 'eternal beloved one,' and the always stormy aspect of his innermost nature, and we may then form some idea of the mighty struggle of feelings undoubtedly

expressed in this symphony.

Few people possessing a real love of music can fail to be thrilled by Beethoven's Fifth Symphony. Its appeal can never be confined merely to the initiated; nor would Beethoven have wished this. His recognition by the people gave him more genuine delight than did the appreciation of the connoisseurs.

Those three short notes followed by a longer one dominates the whole first movement. Schindler once asked Beethoven as to the meaning of those notes and Beethoven replied: Thus fate knocks at the door.

For me, that one simple understanding made me listen through entirely different ears! Go back and listen to it for yourself and see if you cannot feel that inner turmoil and conflict going on in Beethoven's great soul as fate knocks on the door.

And then look at what follows his Fifth Symphony—his Sixth Symphony is known as the Pastoral symphony.

Here's an excerpt from the book:

The Sixth, Pastoral Symphony of Beethoven was composed almost at the same time as his wonderful 'story of the soul,' the 5th C minor Symphony. Together they present a wonderful contrast, each perfect in itself. In the Fifth we have the spiritual conflict, and an ultimate triumph over fate that thrills the hearer. In the Sixth, fate no longer 'knocks at the door.' The spiritual conflict is stilled, and the fiery, suffering temperament of Beethoven finds peace in the contemplation of nature, which he loved above all things.

Wagner said that Beethoven turned from the inner struggles of the Fifth Symphony to the fellowship and consolation of nature and the simpler folk who lived in communion with her. I often think that the 'Pastoral' is a truer expression of the inner soul of Beethoven than any other of his nine symphonies; it shows the real joy and content for which he longed. He once said, when complaining that he could see no trees from the window of a lodging offered him: "I love a tree better than a man." How he must have loved the associations and inspirations of his 'Pastoral' Symphony! Indeed, we know what it meant to him from the testimony of his friends, and from his own letters and notebooks:

"It is as though every tree in the country said to me: 'Holy, holy,'" he wrote. "O God, in such a forest, on the heights, is found peace for Thy service."

What a powerful lesson for the Well-Educated heart. What other lessons are buried within the messages of the great composers? Wouldn't you like to find out?

Take 5.93—Architecture

Another possible thread of study for High Schoolers is the study of Architecture. Let me share a number of books I have found and posted that could easily be sorted out by country and studied through a year of the rotation.

You will find them in the Art Appreciation section under High School and you will see them all grouped together with the word Architecture in front of them.

Let me give you a little sample:

> Architecture seems to me to be the most wonderful of all the arts. We may not love it as much as others, when we are young perhaps we cannot do so, because it is so great and so grand; but at any time of life one can see that in Architecture some of the most marvelous achievements of men are displayed. The principal reason for saying this is that Architecture is not an imitative art, like Painting and Sculpture. The first picture that was ever painted was a portrait or an imitation of something that the painter had seen…but in architecture this was not true. No temples or tombs or palaces existed until they had first taken form in the mind and imagination of the builders, and were created out of space and nothingness, so to speak…"

From another book:

> Architecture, sculpture and Painting share the distinctive title of the Fine Arts, or, as the Italians and French more fitly call them, the beautiful Arts; the arts, that is to say, of beautiful design. They are known by their beauty.
>
> By their beauty they appeal to the eye and through the eye to the mind, stirring in us emotions or feelings of pleasure—a higher kind of pleasure than that which is derived solely from the gratification of the senses…

When I traveled to Europe earlier this year and saw…or rather I should say felt…the beautiful architecture of the cathedrals and other magnificent buildings. I felt for myself, by comparison, what we have lost in our modern day of practicality. Our buildings are largely uninteresting— tall rectangular shapes, commonly built with mirrored windows, that do little to inspire the heart. How many of those buildings will be standing a few hundred years from now?

The buildings of the past tell us so many stories of the people who built them; their values and their beliefs. I am inspired by the decades of diligent effort and sacrifice, their attention to the tiniest of details, and I can't help but hope that the desire will be planted in the architects of the future to learn from these architects of the past and, as is said in one of the introductions, "that they may be led to demand for themselves buildings which shall declare to future generations all that is best in the religious, civic and domestic life of the present day."

As your older students—and you—learn about these beautiful buildings, consider making notebooking pages to put in your cultural notebook that highlights many of the features you are learning about so that one day, when you visit the world—which I hope you will find a way to do—you can read these 'sermons in stone' left for us to read and learn from.

Take 5.94—Personal Journal/Gratitude Journal

Most of the time when we plant seeds in the ground, we are anticipating the time when we get to eat good fruit or pick bouquets of flowers. Most people wouldn't go to the effort of all the work just to grow some stems.

Likewise, learning without some kind of fruit is pretty pointless. And notice, it is only in the fruit or the flower that seeds are found to continue multiplying and replenishing going forward.

Have you ever stopped to think what the fruit of the learning is that you hope to see for all your efforts?

When we eat too much food, we get indigestion. We need to allow time for the body to break down the food and make use of it. Likewise, if we are constantly feeding our children with mind and even heart food, but not giving them proper time to digest it, it can cause indigestion as well.

One of the ways to help them digest is to encourage time to reflect on what they are learning and helping them find ways to use and apply that learning in the real world, especially in a way to make the world a better place.

Since we spend so much time learning life lessons from history and from nature, keeping a personal journal of their thoughts and experiences not only will help them become better writers, it helps them to see the fruit of their learning. For example, maybe they experienced a failure in something, and they remembered the story of someone else who also failed at something who taught them how to navigate through it, and they write it down in their journal. It is so beneficial to take the time to preserve the experience. Our memories are so unreliable.

For a younger child, taking time at the end of the day to reflect on even one thing they are grateful for begins the process. My daughter does that with her 6-year-old, and she showed me her little diary of daily things she is grateful for last time I was at her house. She loves doing that.

I read this in a book about Louisa May Alcott: "The Alcott children were encouraged to keep diaries in which they wrote down their thoughts and feelings and fancies, and even at [a] very early age Louisa's journal was a record of deep feelings and of a child's sacred emotions."

And in a Beatrix Potter book: "If you really want to write, why don't you start with a journal?"

Keeping a personal journal is another method to teach writing in a natural, meaningful way. And a way to take time to notice the fruit of one's learning.

Take 5.95—Restoring the Art of Storytelling

It was a storyteller who introduced me to all of her friends who have mentored and taught me in the education of the heart. When I first started giving presentations, I promoted the idea of putting the book down and telling stories by heart. "Storytelling is an ageless and beautiful art. When the lights are low and your child is in a quiet, reflective mood, the stories told him will never be forgotten and their influence will follow him the rest of his life." I still believe that if we restored that single art as mothers, we would see a new world emerge. But as I presented the idea, I came to realize how story depleted we are. And we've got to work on filling up the reservoir of stories in our hearts first. Which is the focus of my work now.

But I've never abandoned the idea of the importance of becoming storytellers. One of the first books I put together was a manual in *Restoring the Art of Storytelling in the Home*. You can find a free digital copy on the Forgotten Classics page. It's also one of the free bonus books for those of you who have subscribed to at least five of the Forgotten Classics series. Or you can purchase it separately.

It was Margaret Eggleston who first helped me to discover the revival in the art of storytelling among mothers in the early 1900s. By the way, if you haven't heard her story, check out *A Strand of Pearls* in Section 3 of Catch the Vision. She, truly, is like a dear friend to me. And I know as you get to know her and her circle of storytelling friends, they will feel like friends to you, too. They are great people to hang out with.

When I first learned of this revival in storytelling, I searched for and printed out every book on storytelling I could find that was part of the movement. I found over 25 books and read and underlined and digested all 25 of them. Much of what I teach you came from them, especially pertaining to the developmental levels of children.

And then I tried to condense it down to deliver the basics of storytelling to you. It has little to do with character voices or costumes or instruments or even 'skills' per se. The best stories are told in candlelit rooms or firesides where the storyteller carries the listeners to faraway places and the storyteller fades away. Storytelling has everything to do with what is in your own heart.

So after a brief introduction of my own observations of the benefits, I gathered the wisdom of these storytellers so you can read their own words as they guide you through the process. And then the bulk of the book is short, classic stories that they created specifically for storytelling for you to practice your storytelling art with. I divided them out by the Familiar, the Imaginative and the Heroic ages of development.

At the back of the book is a list of all the books I consulted that are all found in Internet Archive. You will also find a substantial list of collections of stories they recommended for telling, also found on Internet Archive.

If you are ready to put the book down and to learn the art of telling stories by heart, I hope this little manual for storytelling will get you started. Maybe you will enjoy gathering some friends and starting a Storytelling Club like you will read about. Or maybe your Mothers of Influence group will, at some point, take on the study. Think of the good you could take out into the community as a teller of stories. And can you imagine the influence of a small army of storytelling grandmas and grandpas? That thought makes my heart happy.

I wholeheartedly agree with one of my storytelling friends: "I would rather be a teller of stories to children than be the Queen's favorite or serve in the King's court."

Take 5.96—Collections

I happened upon a wonderful article written by Melissa of Melissa and Doug toys on the benefits of making collections. Let me highlight parts of it for you:

It takes focus, faith and patience
To find treasures in the sand
When so many have been ravaged
By the ocean's mighty hand
And requires scanning thousands
To unearth a precious few
But that separates explorers
From those racing right on through.

She identifies five ways collecting prepares us for life.

#1 Collecting promotes optimism.

Collectors are eternal optimists—certain wondrous treasures are ever waiting—just needing to be painstakingly unearthed by curious and deliberate investigators. It's that sense of optimism and faith in the power of possibility compelling collectors to return to the same stretch of beach day in and day out believing extraordinary finds are just waiting to be rescued.

I would say that certainly applies to me and collecting old children's books. I can't tell you how many thousands of books I've sifted through, looking for the treasure. It is the thrill of the hunt and that can happen for so many things. Maybe your child will start a leaf collection and is always on the lookout for a leaf he has never yet seen to add to the collection. My brother collects rocks. Every rock in his yard has a story attached to it and his favorite thing is to go out in the Arizona desert and find the new rock he hasn't seen before and learn about it. Or maybe stamp collecting will be a thing.

As Melissa says, "...nature collections are free, abundant, ever-changing, and require one to spend time outdoors in all seasons." Maybe your children will collect photographs of birds or bugs or wildflowers if you can't pick them. But a collection of pressed wildflowers would be a lot more fun, wouldn't it? Or you can even sort the collection by colors.

#2 Collecting promotes persistence

Collecting rewards those who keep at it, who keep searching in the face of obstacles. It's truly a lesson in resilience because not every search results in a find. But it's the thrill of the hunt and its possibility motivating explorers to keep blazing new trails and searching with rabid curiosity to discover what mysteries lie ahead.

She then suggests to challenge your child to come up with a specific treasure to discover—a rock with a bit of red in it or a twig that looks like the letter Y, a nest, a feather, or a four-leaf clover. If they don't find it on their first search, encourage them to keep on trying, since explorers never give up.

#3 Collecting promotes focus

Beachcombing is not for multi-taskers or those seeking continual dopamine hits and adrenaline rushes. It takes tremendous focus and acute powers of concentration to suppress the noise of the world. For it is only when we tune out that noise that we can blissfully comb through thousands of dull, ordinary looking shells to perhaps reveal just a few precious gems. The ability to focus lets us hone in on what's truly relevant and essential, ignoring the superfluous, and ultimately unearthing the most profound insights.

Then she says to try this: Go on a nature collecting expedition leaving phones and devices at home. Encourage your child to use all their sense in the adventure. Consider creating a sensory collection. Look for items that shine and sparkle. Search for different textures. Or even different scents you detect, recorded on a nature journal page.

#4 Collecting promotes patience

"Perhaps the most essential quality in collecting and in life is patience. And that may be the most elusive one of all in today's frenetic world of instant gratification. Collecting is not an activity delivering immediate rewards. There are surely days brimming with bounty, but more of them coming up empty. But collectors know they are engaged in a marathon not a sprint, and revel in the painstaking and deliberate nature of the practice. For they already know the secret that the best things in life take hard work and patience."

Her suggestion for this one is: One of the best ways to teach patience is to model it. If your child seems to be getting frustrated on their search for an elusive object, acknowledge their feeling, but also assure them that good things come to those who wait. And look on the bright side—even a seashell-less beachcombing excursion is still a walk by the ocean with a loved one! Note that it takes time to discover true marvels and that is what makes them so special!

And finally, #5: Collecting promotes creativity

Collecting helps one develop an eye for detail and hone an aesthetic sense for what makes something beautiful and worth possessing. It also helps define what is most pleasing to each of us specifically. Sifting through dozens of so-so seashells to find the one that speaks to something in your soul is an exercise in creative vision and discovering what truly makes your own heart sing.

So she suggests to have your child explain why their collection speaks to why they are as a person. Find creative ways to display the collection—a shoebox, a pretty container.

Collecting and exploring cannot ever be about racing to a finish line or rapidly amassing riches. They have a mindset of just generally opening oneself up to wonder, never knowing where it might lead you. And the not knowing should be the most exciting part of the experience. Because with pure intent to seek wonder everywhere and no pressure to 'succeed,' the irony is before long we *will* inadvertently amass a lifetime of treasures—each with its own tale of discovery and intrigue.

Collecting is only intoxicating *because* its results are so unpredictable. How analagous is this to life in needing to have patience and allowing it to gently unfold before us instead of planning out each and every move we make? For we must continually take risks in order to find our passions before rushing to the finish line prior to discovering who we truly are.

If we can attack each day with the skills and mentality of a collector, our lives will be an adventure full of possibility and potential. And in my humble opinion, that's the only way to truly live.

I love the way she thinks! Now the only question—where do you want to start?

Take 5.97—High School

This week I want to talk about High School and beyond options and what the Well-Educated Heart looks like for your older kids. I'm going to throw out a bunch of ideas, but there are two questions you and your child will have to answer for yourselves:

Where are you going and where have you been?

Remember Alice's encounter with the Cheshire cat when she wanted to know which path to take? He said if she didn't know where she was going, it didn't really matter which path she chose. So of course you need to take time to figure out the destination point. Are you focused on education as a means to a career or do you care most about the learning?

As usual, there is no one-size-fits-all answer, although our current school culture places all children on the same college prep path. It's ingrained in us to pay attention to five-paragraph essays, grades, ACT and SAT scores, and putting together a transcript of classes. But I encourage you to step back and explore all the possibilities! There are so many paths open to your children. If your child has his or her sites on a particular college, of course it's important you find out what that college requires and design your high school plan accordingly. That child may need to work hard to get high test scores. Also, if you will need to use financial aid, there are certain requirements for that as well. But if your child has dreams of learning a trade or going an entrepreneurial route, those things may not matter.

As we work through this week of Take 5s, let me throw out some other possibilities, especially in light of the fact that you are listening to this because you are interested in a different way. I am frequently asked how to do Well-Educated Heart in the High School years and I can tell you what I think that looks like, but implementing that vision will depend on your answer to the second question: Where have you been? Or in other words, what have you been doing?

At the heart of the Well-Educated Heart is freedom and choice; it's familiarity with all the languages of the heart: Music, Art, Poetry and Story. If you have a High Schooler who has never been given freedom in learning, he will likely flounder if he is suddenly given a blank page and allowed to design his own study, especially if he has never developed any interests along the way. And he may resist—maybe traditional courses with tests and measurements and assignments are comfortable to him. Maybe that's how his friends are learning and he doesn't want to be the odd man out. He doesn't want to venture into an unknown world.

It's a different world for the child who has been raised in a Well-Educated Heart environment vs. that student who is entering it as a High Schooler. Do you remember the John Senior quote I shared? "In order to read the 'great' books of Plato, Aristotle, St. Augustine and St. Thomas, we need to replenish the cultural soul that has been depleted and create a place where these works can thrive by cultivating an imaginative ground saturated with fable, fairy tale, stories, rhymes, and adventure—the thousand books of Grimm, Andersen, Stevenson, Dickens, Scott, Dumas and the rest. The one thing a great books education will not do is create a moral imagination where there is none."

Of course, you can't go back and change the past, but you can start where you are and change the ending, like C.S. Lewis wrote. If you have missed out on these things, and your High Schooler is on board with replenishing that cultural soul, then you can use High School years to cultivate that imaginative ground to move forward in preparation for a life time of learning. But I would in no way force that on a student who is set on a different course.

But no matter which path you choose, one truth applies to everyone. The happier you are on the inside, the less you need on the outside.

If you are of the mindset that success and happiness is equated by a high salary and that is driving your decisions for what comes next, I invite you to consider the life of one of the happiest men I have ever met. He is car mechanic and he owns his own little shop. We love him because we absolutely trust him. He is fair and honest and knows what he's doing. And did I mention happy and pleasant? He doesn't live in a big house, but his house is clean and inviting. There are flowers in the yard with big shady trees. He travels with his family. He reads. In his spare time, he uses his knowledge to fix up old cars and provides them to refugee and immigrant families, single mothers and others who have no means of transportation. He finds joy in that service. He loves to help them.

I know another man. He is wildly successful financially and has held many positions of prominence and importance. I visited him one day in his mansion; with his white marble floors and pillared staircases. Yet, he was heartbroken—he was estranged from his children. Some suffered from drug addictions and had broken families. Some of his own children refused to talk to him. He was mistrustful of intentions…it seemed everyone wanted his money. For all that he had, for all that he had accomplished, I wouldn't call him happy or contented. He was a driven man.

So what I am trying to say is:

Tend the hearts of your children, and they will be rich on any income.

Neglect their hearts, and they will be poor no matter how much money they make.

Teach your children to live on less than they earn, and they will sleep at night. That should open the door on possibilities you may not currently be considering.

So let's start talking about those possibilities, starting with tomorrow's Take 5.

Take 5.98—College Bound

So let's start with the familiar path. Let's talk about getting into college, if that's the path you choose. Every college is different, so of course you want to narrow down the choices and find out exactly what is required and plan accordingly. Pretty basic common sense, huh. Sometimes you just have to render to Caesar that which is Caesar's.

But do be aware that times are a changing. In the past, the focus has been on ACT/SAT scores, GPA, number of AP classes taken and so forth. If you could score high enough, you were guaranteed admission.

But many universities are realizing that those indicators don't necessarily translate into good students. Often they get students who have learned to play the system and aren't exactly motivated to learn. Plus all the students were beginning to look the same—all over achievers. So instead they are looking for personality, passions, life experience—which is perfect for homeschoolers who may not have traditional looking qualifications. I'm not talking little colleges; I'm talking Ivy League colleges, who evidently love homeschoolers. And as the ACT/SAT testing program has undergone changes, some colleges are throwing test scores out all together.

One of my daughters is the academic advisor for the Kennedy Center at BYU and she told me the admissions process has undergone similar changes at BYU in the last couple of years. Perfect ACT scores and GPAs will no longer get you in and that has shaken up a lot of people. There is much more emphasis on the essay and the admissions committees are looking at the whole person.

While you may be worrying about preparing transcripts for courses, the college you are interested in may not even look at that.

Also, be mindful that if your student attends a community college for a year—and most community colleges are open enrollment—then they can apply as a transfer student and you bypass the whole high school transcript thing anyway.

Several of my kids earned their High School diplomas through American School which is an accredited distance learning program. That simplified the process for us. The thing I liked is that it didn't take much of their time so they were free to do other things. We were fortunate to live in a school district that allowed us to attend part time. So my kids took things like choir, drama, participated in sports, band—whatever they wanted. A couple of my kids preferred to take their math classes at the high school. Many of their friends didn't even know they were homeschooling because they saw them around school and just assumed they were there all day like them.

Explore and discover your options! Williamsburg Academy is also a good experience for many students if you are worried about getting an accredited degree. Or maybe you will opt for a GED. My understanding is that certain financial aid programs require a GED or accredited high school diploma, so those are things you need to check out.

One of the most exciting things I see for those of you who have kids who don't need that on-campus experience but who want a degree in hand is the BYU Pathways program which is now open for everyone—members of The Church of Jesus Christ of Latter-day Saints and non-members. There is a prep class to get them up to speed for college work and ACT/SAT scores are not required. I like the way that it is skill stacked; they are given marketable job skills at the very beginning and earn certificates along the way. A student can now earn their full Bachelor's degree through the program and the entire cost for the four years is under $9000, last time I checked. And is eligible for Pell grants.

We do live in an age where that piece of paper opens doors. It's the render to Caesar thing. And I see this as a great way to earn that piece of paper while still pursuing opportunities like I'm about to share over the next few days. It's a way to allow you to rest easy that a college degree is not closed to your children if you should choose to do the unconventional way of learning I keep trying to describe to you.

While I am grateful for the BYU experience I had, I can honestly say the most meaningful learning began after I graduated and gets more exciting to me every single day. I do hope you can begin to build within the vision of your children that college is not a destination and a conclusion to learning but that you are truly laying a foundation for a lifetime of learning.

And don't discount Vocational schools! They are a perfect option for many of your children. I'm thankful to many women who opened hair salons in their basements and helped provide for their family that way. Where would we be without someone skilled in cutting our hair! When we went to the induction ceremony for my daughter after she passed the Bar Exam, there were 1,500 new lawyers in that one room. Statistically only half of them would find jobs. And sadder yet, statistically, a majority of them will hate their job. Why is it everyone thinks being a lawyer is the answer to life? As I read the stories of some of our greatest artists, musicians, writers, I can't believe how often they had to go against their father's wishes that they become a lawyer! On the other hand, if you have a child with a passion to become a lawyer, run with it!

We would survive with a lot fewer lawyers but heaven help us if we no longer have plumbers and air conditioning repairmen and construction workers to build our homes and to fix our roads and build our bridges. There is no shame in working with one's hands.

I don't know if it's like this where you live, but it is nearly impossible to find anyone to come do work where we are. It took weeks to get someone to come look at my dishwasher and he didn't really know what he was doing. He told me he thought I had 'a engine problem.' My solution? I bought a new dishwasher. It took me weeks to find a builder who would come give us a bid on our basement. We are still looking for someone to help us landscape our yard. Not only is there a shortage of workers, but their work ethic is non-existent. We joke that we are going to open a business and our slogan is going to be "We show up!" I think we'll be able to corner the market on whatever we choose to do! Granted, we live out in the country, but my daughters who live in the city are having the same problem with workers. They simply don't show up or do the job they say they will do.

Which is actually symptomatic of heart troubles. Raise your children to be honest, dependable, thorough, compassionate and they will shine no matter what they choose to do.

And for all your careful career planning for your children, the truth is life has a way of presenting surprises and detours. My son-in-law joined the Army years ago as an officer. He's adventurous and daring. He was thrilled to jump out of planes. He started out intending to be a lawyer, and now he is finishing up a Masters in English Literature—as per his current military orders—which will have him teaching Shakespeare and Poetry to Freshmen cadets at West Point Academy. He never would have imagined that's what he would be doing when he made that decision to join the Army, but he is loving it.

One of my daughters had no desire to go to college. I never could imagine her going to college. She decided to go to Massage Therapy school instead, which we fully supported. As she watched her siblings all get their college degrees, she said, "Hey—I don't want to be the only one without one." So she enrolled at the University of Utah and graduated in Communications. She put herself through by doing massages. She showed up to work. She was a hard worker and got along with people. She was pleasant and went the extra mile—all heart things. Today she is the Corporate Spa Director for Stein Erikson Lodges, a 5-diamond resort in Park City, Utah. And by the way—she no longer does any massages.

Another daughter graduated from BYU in Family Studies. She had an assignment in one of her classes to prepare a job resume for her dream job. She said her dream job was to be a wife and a mother. The teacher took her out in the hall and told her that was unacceptable. My daughter laid the case that it fit the requirements for the assignment and that was her dream job. Again, the teacher questioned why she was even at college! What a waste of time. My daughter stood her ground and said it's because she wanted to be a better mother. She later married an occupational therapist. She decided to go back to school and get her licensing as an assistant OT. That gives her a chance to earn a little extra income and also provides a skill she can fall back on if she needs to. And by the way—she is living her dream job, with her fourth little one on the way.

I'm watching my granddaughters begin to pursue their passions. One of them loves animals and horses and her mother found a horse farm who was willing to let her come volunteer a couple of days a week. She showed up and worked hard and was willing to scoop poop without complaint. The owner of the horse farm said she had never had anyone work so hard and so cheerfully. The owner started giving her horseback riding lessons and now she regularly gets to go and ride the horses. She's in heaven. She's my illustrator for the title pages of the Books of Delight. I was recently telling her about someone I met who went to a two-year program at an estate in Pennsylvania where she learned all about growing things. Not only did the program include free room and board, they paid their students who were learning through experience in this beautiful place. She said in the summer they traveled to Europe to study the beautiful estate gardens there. I don't know that my granddaughter will choose to go there, but the point is there are so many opportunities out there! College is just one way.

I have heard there are high schools in Utah that have to hire extra counselors to come to the schools the week admissions letters to BYU are sent out because the suicide rates jump. Please don't set your kids up for a one option only life!! That is tragic.

Take 5.99—Free Learning Sources/Light a Fire

I stumbled upon a book that has generated a lot of pondering in me. It was written by Laura Ingalls Wilder's daughter Rose. Yes-the Laura of *Little House on the Prairie* fame. It's called *The Discovery of Freedom* and she first introduced the Saracens to me, who I had never in all my life or all my schooling had even heard the name.

Let me share a bit of that book:

> During the stagnation of Europe that is called the Dark Ages, the world was actually bright with an energetic, brilliant civilization, more akin to American civilization and more fruitful today for everyone alive, than any other in the past.

> Millions upon millions of human beings, thirty generations, believing that all men are equal and free, created that civilization and kept on creating it for eight hundred years.

> To them the world owes modern science, mathematics, astronomy, navigation, modern medicine and surgery, scientific agriculture.

> To them the world directly owes the discovery and the exploration of America.

> These men were of all races and colors and classes and all former cultures and many religions; by no means all of them were Moslems. They were former subjects or descendants of subjects of all former empires. There is no one name that applies to them all. Europeans called them Saracens.

> Their own records of the eight hundred years of their civilization, its institutions, and the causes of its collapse, are largely locked in the Arabic language. Since American scholars and intellectuals in general are European-minded, an American can get only glimpses of the Saracen world, seen through European indifference or hatred.

She talks a bit of their history and then let me start again where she talks about their universities.

> The refugee scientists in Persia were popular now—respected, admired, listened to. No Authority suppressed them;… They opened their schools; from Baghdad to Granada, their schools were crowded with students. In two centuries, there were great universities, the world's first universities.

> For hundreds of years, these universities grew. The University of Cairo was more than a thousand years old and still had forty thousand students, when I was there.

> These universities had no organization whatever. (Mohammed said that organization corrupts knowledge.) A Saracen university had no programs, no curriculum, no departments, no rules, no examinations; it gave no degrees nor diplomas. It was simply an institution of learning. Not of teaching, but of learning. A man, young or old, went to a university to learn what he wanted to know, just as an American goes to a grocery to get the food he wants.

> Men who knew (or thought they knew) something, and wanted to teach it, opened a

school to sell their knowledge. Success depended upon the demand for the knowledge they had…

The teachers lectured in open classrooms. Anyone was welcome to listen. An incoming student wandered about, listening. When he decided upon the teacher he wanted, they discussed privately whatever he wanted to learn and needed to study, and agreed upon fees. Then he joined the class regularly. If he was not satisfied, he could quit at any time and find another teacher. When he had learned what he wanted to know, he left the university to use his knowledge…

A thousand years after the Saracens built these universities, far away in time and on a continent that they never knew existed, a revolutionary leader, Thomas Jefferson—who knew little or nothing about the Saracens—realized the dream of his life when he created the University of Virginia. His dream was a new kind of education.

Proudly, almost bragging a little, he wrote to a friend in the medieval-university system of Harvard, "We shall give all them [the students] uncontrolled choice in the lectures they shall choose to attend. Our institution will proceed on the principle…of letting everyone come and listen to whatever he thinks may improve the condition of his min."

For more than nine hundred years the University of Cairo proceeded on precisely that principle. Until the end of the 19th century, Europeans were not able to impose upon that university any tinge of the European belief that minds acquire knowledge, not by actively seeking to know, but by passively being taught whatever Authority decides that they should know.

What a shock the Crusaders had when they entered the Saracen world. The Crusaders whose castles were rude stone walls and floors of earth or damp stone covered thick with rotting reeds, came into rooms like jewels, the floors tiled, the walls and ceiling of mosaic. Delicate lattice-work covered the windows. They did not know how to deal with the draperies, carpets, cushions, the silks, linens, leathers, the unknown metals. The fabrics seemed magical; chiffons that clung like cobwebs to fingers.

Everywhere there were fountains of flowing water. They were taught that a clean body was essential to a clear mind and a pure spirit. The people bathed several times a day…hence all the fountains of water.

What an impression was left on them from this Saracen world.

Can you see why I get so excited about the possibilities open to us today if we will have the courage to leave behind our broken systems of higher education and learn from the past? What if education can be about learning instead of teaching?

Already, there is so much available to our students if we will just open our eyes and look around and take advantage of it. The Saracens would look upon us in envy! Do you know about the Great Courses, formerly the Teaching Company? Some enterprising person started looking for the most popular teachers in universities all over the country and recorded their courses and made them available to anyone. For about $15 a month, you can choose from hundreds of topics, taught at a college level. Come and go as you want. There are no tests. There are no requirements. Just learning pure and simple.

Many of our greatest universities are posting many of their classes for free—of course you don't get credit, but you get to learn! MIT, Harvard, Stanford, Hillsdale.

One of my daughters who is an aspiring writer told me a couple of nights ago she has signed up for a writing class from Master Classes and is loving it. She holds a Masters degree; she was thinking of going back to school, but then thought why? What she wanted to do was learn. And now she is learning to write from one of today's top writers. And guess what it costs her? Fifteen dollars a month. She can do it when *she* wants. Have you looked at Master Classes? It's the one where you learn acting from Helen Mirren, comedy from Steve Martin, photography from Annie Liebowitz.

As such opportunities continue to expand through technology, think of the uplift of civilization that can come out of it!

I was tending my 6-year-old granddaughter over the holidays. We saw a squirrel outside and she wanted to draw it. She didn't know how; without any prompting from me, I watched her find a tutorial online that walked her through the steps of drawing the squirrel and what she did was amazing! She knows she can find anything she wants to know on the internet. And she is 6! She had just barely started to write when I got a beautiful letter from her. And I said, Esha! How did you get to be such a good speller so fast! And she said that when she didn't know how to spell a word, she just asked Alexa.

Oh! How I wish I could help more people let go of their fears and embrace the possibilities by letting go of old expectations and old ways of doing things. To the child in whose heart a fire of desire has been lit, the height of learning that child can reach is staggering.

How I wish more parents would let their High Schoolers not get bogged down with college admissions requirements and allow them the freedom to learn and learn without tests and assignments. It may be the one last time in their life when they have the luxury of time to do so.

Let them work through the Rotation schedule, soaking in the history overviews, spending time with Great People through their biographies, reading great literature. Encourage them to follow threads through the rotation; one time studying the architecture of the different countries. Another time the art. Another time the music. Another time the literature. Don't create curriculums for them—allow them that blessed experience of exploration and discovery and making their own connections. Some of the greatest minds the world has ever seen were self-taught or who sought out mentors to learn that which their hearts were on fire to know.

"All true education is self-education."

Do it to whatever degree you can. Like I said in the beginning, a child who has never been given that freedom may flounder. In my mind, it's an ideal to strive towards, but it may take us a couple of generations to get there.

Invite your daughters to join your MOI groups—let them start dabbling in the Delphian course and the Mother's University.

I'm afraid my experience in school taught me that when there was something I wanted to learn, the last place I should have looked was school. The assignments and the way it was taught almost, without exception, killed a love of the subject for me. Freedom to learn is the life and light of education.

The world has already proven it. But each generation seems to have to learn the hard way. Will you be part of the change our world desperately needs?

Take 5.100—Travel

Continuing on talking about possibilities for learning, keep in mind that learning from books is only one way to learn. Direct observation and experience are priceless ways to learn. If you aren't spending a hundred thousand dollars to put a child through traditional college, think of the travel experiences that could happen! Your children will learn so much from seeing the world first-hand.

And even if getting that college degree is still vital to you, there are options to make that happen that won't make you go broke—like the BYU Pathways program I talked about a couple of days ago—and will allow for flexibility of location.

A couple of my daughters taught English to kindergartners in Veronezh, Russia, through the ILP program—International Language Program. They lived with Russian families. What an eye-opening experience! One daughter said there was no trash pick-up, so the family learned to use and reuse everything until it was all used up. At the end of the week, the mother might carry one small brown bag to be burned. Can you imagine? And what book could relay the feeling they had while standing with a group watching a parade go by where they were chanting "Death to the Americans?" Yet, they lived with Russians who cared about them and loved that they were there teaching their children. They learned for themselves there is no single story of a people.

One of those daughters did the same thing in Japan with her husband for the first six months of their marriage. He had served a mission in Japan and had a chance to share a love for Japanese culture and people that is being passed on to their children.

My daughters worked and saved up money to travel to Europe. If your kids are homeschooling, they have chances to work while the other kids are in school. They didn't work full time, just a few hours. And that work experience was part of their education. One has climbed to Machu Picchu; another got to spend a semester in Jerusalem. My youngest daughter lived in Ireland for several years. She earned her Masters there. This is what I know about travel—if there is a will, there is a way.

There are humanitarian opportunities out there. One daughter who was working on her MPA was taken under the wings of a non-profit mentor in college who traveled with her to Cambodia and Asia and other places before sending her to do research in Mexico (where she met her husband at a university), Ghana and other African countries where she lived for weeks at a time. We loved hearing stories of all the interesting people she met. Her home has now become a magnet for drawing people together of many cultures and faiths. I just talked to her a few days ago—her Christmas dinner table included an atheist couple, a Muslim couple and a couple from the Netherlands. They live in Provo, by the way. A place not exactly known for its diversity.

Prepare your children to see the world by creating cultural notebooks where they post pictures of places they want to visit and the stories behind them. Let them dream of travel. When we were in Ireland earlier this year, we went to the hill where St. Patrick built the fire in defiance of the pagan king. My daughter brought an Irish friend with her and I asked her what she knew about St. Patrick. She said they weren't taught anything about him in school; she just knew he was an excuse to get drunk. Isn't that sad? So I told the story of what took place on that green mound and suddenly the imagination took hold of what took place on those very grounds hundreds of years earlier. And I hope you know what that feels like.

And how lucky if your kids have friends who are excited to learn and experience with them—what a great project to plan together and save for together and dream of together. There are plenty of organized student trips and opportunities if going solo makes you nervous. On my dream list of future projects is to bring students together from the Well-Educated Heart community and facilitate trips—both foreign and domestic, complete with stories to listen to from the Golden Age of Literature as they visit places. Wouldn't that be fun?

Take 5.101—Life Learning

Schools as we now know them are a modern development. Learning and life used to take place together. As I read about the education of the past, there were many more opportunities to interact with people of all ages and that learning by experience and observation was valued and encouraged. So when you look at what High School looks like Well-Educated Heart style, I hope you can see that it encompasses far more than what your children will learn from reading and books.

You want to allow time for practical knowledge—learning to make simple repairs around the house and even the car. How to check the oil and change a tire. How to manage their money. And how we have lost the Art of Homemaking! I'm not talking the chores of keeping a house clean. I'm talking about the Art of making a home. Like Orison Swett Marden wrote: "The highest civilizations have scarcely as yet glimpsed the possibilities of home."

Over a hundred years ago, Herbert Spencer imagined someone from the future trying to piece together who we were from our school books. He wrote: "I see here an elaborate preparation for many things; but I find no reference whatever to the bringing up of children. They could not have been so absurd as to omit all training for this gravest of responsibilities."

Evidently we have been so absurd! But you can correct that going forward. Let your High

Schoolers practice with other littles in the house if you are so blessed. So yes! Caring for your home is a part of High School studies.

High Schoolers can also engage in Apprenticeships and shadowing opportunities to help them see up close and personal what careers look like that they might be interested in. I know one mom whose freshmen son was crazy about science and they went to the local university who allowed him to hang around the labs and now as a freshman at the same university, is immersed in exactly what he wants to do.

High School is a time to encourage starting hobbies if they don't yet have one. Hobbies will be a tremendous source of joy and relaxation when they start engaging in the rigors of life and career. Encourage learning a musical instrument and allow time to practice.

And do find ways to serve others. Anything without an outlet will begin to stagnate and even begin to stink. And that includes knowledge. Always look for outlets for learning—how can the things you are learning be used to make the world a better place and to serve others? How have the things you have learned made you a better person? Made you happier? More useful?

Keeping a Journal in High School allows for reflective time. Don't let your High Schooler become so busy, there is no time to process and reflect on life. Help them find balance and joy in the journey. Help them take time for gratitude.

Take 5.102—Socialization

But what about Socialization? Isn't that always the question that comes up? Depending on your own experience, High School was either the perfect place to socialize or the worst place. And I suspect your experience will influence your biases towards the level of involvement you want your own kids to have.

We moved around a lot while my kids were growing up and I felt badly that many of our children didn't get to have best friends growing up. But time has given me perspective and I can now see clearly that friends come and go, but family is forever. Why do we spend so much time worrying that our kids develop strong relationships outside the family when it's the family that can be the stabilizing force of our lives? Are there any other relationships that are more important to build?

My kids best friends are their siblings. They go to each others' parties and hang out for Sunday dinner and go places together. Is there anything wrong with having a brother or a sister for a best friend?

But I know that isn't feasible for everyone.

To me, putting kids in same age groups is the most unnatural way of socializing. There are so many better ways. Let them get involved in community plays, sports, community orchestras. Let them interact with kids of many ages.

And if they need that friend, even one good friend is all it takes. I often felt alone in my own high school class of hundreds. My best friend went to another school. But that one friendship was all I needed because we shared so many interests in common. I had all brothers and we weren't close in age, so I needed that outside friendship and she was like a sister to me.

And I've seen families where there is an only child and the parents are like best friends to that child. Who says that a best friend has to be someone your own age?

In my ideal High School, I would like to see more students make best friends from the people of history and of literature—to have that luxury of time when they can hang out with them without intruding assignments and probing questions.

And if you are fortunate enough to find a group of High Schoolers who are in love with learning, in that ideal High School experience in my dreams, I see them getting together and having conversations and deep discussions about ideas and ideals; freely pouring out of their hearts, not contrived by assignment. I bump into friendships like that in literature and history books.

We are so disconnected and have lost the art of conversation. It's rare to find anyone who thinks about anything anymore. What a gift to nurture that in a group of High Schoolers.

I think of the stories my parents tell of the wholesome activities their friends would engage in—they loved trips to the mountains and the lakes and singing and laughing and carrying on conversations. Real things. Not phone screens and video screens. Things like planning activities and even doing service together and getting together and playing games and simple things like going on walks.

Is that a nostalgic relic of the past, or can we begin to restore these lost arts of sociability?

I know that for some of you who are looking for ideas for your High Schoolers, I may be leaving you a bit disappointed. The truth is, I can't tell you what a Well-Educated Heart High School experience will look like for your child. Because your child is unique. But I hope I have set you to thinking about possibilities. Do engage your High Schooler in the process. I don't understand a parent of a child that age doing all the planning for that child. The Arts will still serve as the way to create desires in their hearts to learn. The rotation schedule can still serve you throughout the High School years and beyond. High Schoolers will be ready to take on more academic learning. I never said academics don't have a place. It's the order thing—build the desire first, then teach the rules and the skills. Find balance. Enjoy the journey. And understand your influence and the process of learning does not end at the age of 18. It's just the beginning. There are lots of opportunities for course correcting.

Take 5.103—Mother First

This week, I'm going to focus on you—the mother. Which actually brings us right back to where we started. I frequently get letters that go like this:

I can't get my kids to do notebooking. I can't get my kids to read. I can't get my kids to nature journal. And so forth.

My immediate thought is: I don't know how to do that either. But are you notebooking? Are you reading? Are you nature journaling?

If you have no desire to do these things, can you blame your kids? And if you are doing these things, are you feeling the benefit for yourself? You know, you are a child at heart, too. And you deserve the opportunity to learn, too.

Be a light, not a hammer. Almost without exception, when a child is pushing back, the parent is driving them somewhere they don't want to go. So it's back to creating the desire, and often that desire comes from watching you engaging in an activity you are enjoying. I see that happening all the time. But having said that, you haven't failed if they don't jump in and do it.

I'm serious here. Your first job is to fill your own heart. Which, of course, is a journey, not a destination. You only need to be a couple of steps ahead of your kids. Because as you fill your own heart, you are going to see things much more clearly. And you are going to radiate something that isn't tangible or measurable, but it's real. So if your kids won't read the history books, you read them. And you will find yourself naturally sharing interesting things that you are learning. I have heard from so many moms who tell me that when they started notebooking, their kids wanted to do it, too. Not all. And that's OK. And maybe not in the beginning. And that's OK too.

Remember the wisdom of Dr. Gordon Neufeld—the young seek to attach to something, and once it attaches, grows to be like that to which it is attached.

That is why so much of the work I do is aimed at you, the mother.

For all the worry and anxiety you have over building lesson plans and curriculums and fitting everything in, years from now, your children will remember very, very little of that. But they will remember how they felt when they were around you; how home felt. And so much of that depends on what is going on inside your own heart. It's not about doing more on the outside. It's about being more on the inside.

And remember—your influence as a mother doesn't end when your child turns 18! You don't have a deadline of completion. Your child is going to go out into the world and be influenced by things over which you have no control. And that is how it is all designed. They are meant to go on a hero's journey—you are simply preparing them for that journey. He is going to learn by his own experiences to choose the good over the bad. If you have given him a lot of 'good' to experience, he will have that to compare to. And if you have a prodigal son, make sure he knows he always has home to return to; that someone will always be there to welcome him with open arms.

The story isn't over. Ever. There is always a sequel.

I hope you are more concerned with your relationship with your children than their high school portfolios or test scores. Because the latter two will fade in importance real fast; but that relationship—that is priceless and forever.

So be kind and patient with yourself. Keeping human beings alive is a pretty big deal.

In the next few days, I'll highlight some of the resources to feed your heart.

Take 5.104—Mothers of Influence Groups

I posted an article in Month one of the Mother's University written by a mom, Beth Barry, and I think it perfectly captures what many of us have felt or are feeling.

Basically, she reminds us that you aren't meant to do this mom thing alone. She wrote:

> Since the beginning of time (and until very recently) mothers have borne life's burdens together. We scrubbed our clothes in the streams while laughing at splashing toddlers and mourning the latest loss of love or life. We wove, sewed, picked, tidied, or mended while swapping stories and minding our aging grandmothers. We tended one another's wounds (both physical and emotional), relied on one another for strength when times were tough, and sought counsel from our community's wise, experienced and cherished elders…. We're supposed to be crying, celebrating, falling down, and rising together.
>
> We're supposed to have grandmothers and aunts and neighbors and cousins sharing the everyday moments, guiding us, and helping us see the sacredness in the insanity.
>
> We're supposed to be nurtured for months postpartum, cared for when we're sick, held while we mourn, and supported during challenging transitions.
>
> In other words, it takes a village, but there are no villages.
>
> In the absence of the village…enormous pressure is put on parents as we try to make up for what entire communities used to provide. Our priorities become distorted and unclear as we attempt to meet so many conflicting needs at once. We feel less safe and more anxious without the known boundaries, expectations and support of a well-known group of people with whom to grow. We're forced to create our tribes during seasons of our life when we have the least time and energy to do so. Our children's natural way of being is compromised, as most neighborhoods and communities no longer contain packs of roaming children with whom to explore, create, and nurture their curiosity.
>
> We run around like crazy trying to make up for the interaction, stimulation and learning opportunities that were once within walking distance. We forget what 'normal' looks and feels like, which leaves us feeling as if we're not doing enough, or enough of the 'right' things. Depression and anxiety skyrocket, particularly during seasons of our lives when we instinctively know we need more support than ever but don't have the energy to find it.
>
> We feel disempowered by the many responsibilities and pressure we're trying so hard to keep up with. We spend money we don't have on things we don't need in an attempt to fill the voids we feel. We rely heavily on social media for a sense of connection, which often leads us to feel even more isolated and inadequate.
>
> We feel lonely and unseen, even when we're surrounded by people. We feel frequently judged and misunderstood. We feel guilty for just about everything: not wanting or having time to be our children's primary playmates, not working enough, working too much, allowing too much screen time in order to keep up with our million perceived

responsibilities, etc.

Joy, lightness and fun feel hard to access.

We think we're supposed to be independent, and feel ashamed of our need for others.

It's causing us to feel that our inadequacies are to blame for our struggles, which further perpetuates the feeling that we must do even more to make up for them.

In the absence of the village, we're disadvantaged like never before. We may have more freedoms than our foremothers, but our burden remains disproportionately, oppressively heavy.

So then she poses the question: "How does an entire nation of mothers shift a storyline this massive while individually and collectively weakened by the absence of the very thing we so desperately need?"

I loved her answer...it may ring a little familiar:

We can buy into, make peace with, and conform to the way things are, or exercise the freedoms our foremothers and fathers won for us and commit to doing our unique and essential part in creating change, starting within us and working our way out.

Inside out. It starts with deep roots, upward growth and an encircling reach.

You are a Mother of Influence. Have you considered gathering your tribe; your village? You plus one more person is all you need to begin. And then grow from there.

You might begin by sharing this article I just shared with you with others to let them know what you are hoping to accomplish. Do include multi-generations and people who are different than you. You don't need to make it a homeschooling group. Look for commonalities among diversity. As we learn to come together in small ways, it will grow into mighty ways. There is no other way to change the world.

I spoke with one mother whose eight siblings left the faith they had all grown up in. Their family had grown divided and no longer seemed to have anything to talk about. When she heard about Mothers of Influence groups, it sparked an idea and she invited her family to join a Families of Influence group where the topic of discussion were the Arts. She said the Arts have brought them back together.

A simple effective way to begin is to invite the mothers to bring a story, a picture, a song, a poem that has meaning to them to share with the group. It's amazing how quickly these languages of the heart help us to see into each other's hearts and begin to bond. You design and customize your group according to the personalities and needs of your members, but as a Mothers of Influence group, we ask you to keep in mind our purpose, which is to learn to cultivate hearts through the arts. We are learning to open eyes to see the 'unseen' and hearts that feel. That's a universal course of study that touches you whether married or single, whether homeschooling or public schooling, whether Catholic or Protestant or undecided. There are many options to choose from in the Mother's University and the Catch the Vision course and other resources provided for you.

I just saw an article that said there is a new program back East where people who are guilty of minor crimes have an option to have the charges dropped if they are willing to go through an art appreciation class at the Museum. The results have been promising—with far fewer repeat offenders. Another prison has inmates growing rose gardens, with similar results. Another, knitting classes. Another Shakespeare classes. If the arts can free and transform the lives of the incarcerated, they can free and transform us all.

And in the absence of being able to gather a tribe near you, for whatever reason, I hope you will find friends and support through our Facebook groups and other online chats that are available. My daughter, Shannon, has a FB group called 100 days of WEH. Here you will find pictures of mothers in the trenches. She also hosts online discussions through Zoom.

When Jesus carried the burden of Gethsemane, an angel stood by to minister, comfort and strengthen him.

None of us are meant to go this journey alone. I hope Mothers of Influence can bless your life.

Take 5.105—Mother's University/Catch the Vision

I'm sure you have found it by now, but since I'm trying to touch on all the resources available to you, let me touch on the Mother's University and the Catch the Vision course. The Catch the Vision course was designed to do exactly that—to help you catch the vision of what it looks like to educate the heart.

I remember hearing from a mom after the Simple Joy Conference. She had come to it hoping to learn exactly what to do with her children. As the day wore on, she was getting increasingly frustrated because she wasn't getting what she was looking for. But then, as if by magic, suddenly a vision of what could be, opened to her heart and she knew exactly what the next steps were for her own family.

I expect the same things with this Catch the Vision course. It's not a paint-by-number experience. It's preparing you to paint your own masterpiece. It's the first step in the Pattern for Learning—to increase desire and to begin to have a vision of what you want for your family. (*The course online is audio. You are reading the written version which is heavily supplemented with other presentations and writings.) Then came these Take 5s—the mind part. The nuts and bolts. These are your paint brushes and paints; your canvases; the medium you will begin to work with. And then as you begin your work, you can expect inspiration to add flashes of light and continued direction, and often surprises.

The Spirit needs something to work with. The more you study, the more connections the Spirit can make. So the Mother's University is designed to give you something to continue feeding upon and to deepen your understanding of the languages of the heart. It's designed for exploration and discovery. If you only have time to take a few sips, then do that and when you come back by the next year, take a few more sips. At some point, you will likely be ready to start taking deeper gulps. It will be there patiently waiting for you, like the dutiful servant it is.

I haven't gathered everything there is by any stretch. What I have gathered is only meant to prime the pump. Who knows where your own journey of discovery will take you!

I will share another dream, though. My daughters have said, "Oh, mom, we wish we could have learned these things before we became mothers." It's so hard when you have the demands of little ones around you. Wouldn't be fun if we could actually create a real Mother's University somewhere—a place where young women can come and immerse themselves in the books and understanding and build a tribe? Maybe a year between high school and college. Ideally, in generations to come, the training will happen where it was always meant to happen—in the home. But in the transition from where we are to the ideal of what we hope to be, I can see real value in such a place and then, like scattered seeds, these mothers, whether or not they ever have children of their own, will bloom where they are planted and continue to scatter the seeds.

In the meantime, do invite your High School daughters to join your Mothers of Influence groups if they have the desire and let them start going through the Mother's University that way.

I love the prophecy of Joel: "...upon the handmaids in those days will I pour out my spirit."

That day is ours. He saw you. He saw your daughters. There is much that is expected. Do your part, and the Spirit will magnify it.

Take 5.106—Delphian Course/Doing the Rotation Yourself

I talk about the Delphian Course in Section 5 of Catch the Vision so I won't repeat the details here other than to say this was a college level course in the humanities created especially for busy women and mothers in the early 1900s. They knew moms couldn't leave home to go away to study, but they also knew the more educated a woman was, the greater her uplift was to society. They were inspired by Charles Eliot who had recently created the Five-Foot Shelf of Books—the Harvard Classics—and claimed that "anyone can get all the elements of a liberal education by reading for 15 minutes a day for one year from a collection of books that could fit on a five-foot bookshelf."

They made the same appeal to women. Here is a liberal arts education even if you only have 15 minutes a day. They encouraged the formation of Delphian chapters so that women could get together once a month and discuss the ideas they were learning. Based on their recommendations, a woman could expect to get through all ten volumes in four years.

We have reprinted all ten volumes and I searched for all the study guides I could get my hands on—they are pretty rare—and compiled them in a Study Guide that you can see as a PDF with the rest of the online digital versions or you can buy a hard copy in our store. The Delphian Course can be part of a subscription or you can order the whole thing at once. Or do keep your eyes on eBay and used book sites. 1913 editions occasionally pop up, although most people don't like to mark up old books like that, and you are likely going to want to do a lot of underlining and notes in margins. So getting a new version may be more practical.

My daughter started an online chat and they get together once a month to discuss what they are reading and you are welcome to jump in. I'll provide a link in the notes. Or some Mothers of Influence groups have chosen to incorporate the Delphian study in their groups. Some of your moms may not be ready yet…do what works best for your particular group. I wouldn't worry about starting in Volume 1 and working through. In fact, if you want to coordinate the study with the rotation schedule, on the High School pages as well as some Mother's University pages, there are yellow blocks that indicate what pages in the Delphian study go along with that month's topics. It can be a way for you to supplement what you are learning with your kids.

And speaking of the rotation, I hope you are dabbling in the reading yourself, as much as you are able to. Just because your kids may not be old enough for certain books doesn't mean you aren't. And the more you have stored up inside of you, the more it will naturally spill out and the better guide and mentor you can be.

If you are having a hard time choosing, I suggest starting with the Forgotten Classics. I compared a lot of options side by side and chose the ones, at the time, that I thought brought the events to life the most. I pictured reading them aloud and if they got too bogged down in detail, they didn't make the final cut.

You will be surprised how much understanding you will pick up as you make your way through these children's books.

Take 5.107—The Art of Homemaking/Family Retreats

C.S. Lewis wrote: "The homemaker has the ultimate career. All other careers exist for one purpose only, and that is to support the ultimate career."

And I'll come back to an Orison Swett Marden quote: "The highest civilizations have scarcely as yet glimpsed the possibilities of home."

Today I want to talk about the art of homemaking. I'm not talking the home from Good Housekeeping magazine. I'm talking about the home like Sally Clarkson describes in her *Life-Giving Home* book:

"In our deepest hearts, we want home to be a place where our spirits are filled. A lifegiving haven of warmth, rest, and joy that will encourage everyone who enters it; a welcoming respite in an isolated culture; a life giving home 'creating a place of belonging and becoming.'"

In the education of the heart, environment is everything. But it doesn't require a lot of money. It does require an eye for beauty and order. And those are two qualities we are seeking to develop in ourselves.

I have known people who have thrown their *Life Giving Home* book across the room because it made them mad. It was so far from their reality of barely getting paper plates thrown on the table and a hot dog microwaved for dinner. Candles on the dinner table? A tablecloth? Who can do that?

If you have a lot of little ones running around, life is going to feel messy and chaotic. But what

I would encourage you to do is to always have an ideal in your heart—something that makes you reach upward. And constantly causes you to be aware of little things you can do here and there to make your home a haven of rest, warmth and joy.

If you haven't read or listened to When Queens Go By, I encourage you to do so. Little things make a difference. I'll link it in the notes.

As we are planning the upcoming family retreats which will focus on the languages of the heart, we are already talking about sister retreats that will focus more on this art of homemaking and will have classes in decluttering and organizing, streamlined cleaning, cooking healthy meals, decorating on a shoestring, finding a rhythm, simple natural remedies, family traditions and making memories—ways to create the home environment that will be the outward expression of what is inside our hearts. I know many of you have talents and knowledge in these fields and I'd love to have you drop me a note so that we can begin to gather the pool of talent and make these retreats happen as well.

(**NOTE: At this time of writing, all the retreats have been placed on indefinite hold due to Covid restrictions.)

Take 5.108—A Vision of WEH Schools/Mothers Supporting Each Other

I am often asked if I see a place for schools in the Well-Educated Heart model and I do, but, of course, not in the traditional way. I see them growing the same way as learning unfolds within the individual—inside out.

In other words, a school can start with just two families getting together and doing those things that work best with more people, and then growing from there. I met someone whose community grew to about 50 or 100 families and they pooled their resources and built themselves a wonderful building to use, with family members actually doing a lot of the work. It was a school that love built.

I love that because then there is ownership in the school. They have an investment to take care of it.

I would rather see 50 one-million-dollar schools or 100 half-a-million-dollar schools than one 50-million-dollar school. The larger the institution, the more the education of the individual disappears. A secret of the success would be proximity. I see it as a gathering place where families would come and go and that has to be not too far away from home. It can vary in size according to the needs of local families.

Another advantage of growing it this way is that, if you start with a strong core vision of the purpose of your school, and then draw like-minded people to the vision, you will avoid many of the problems that come when an individual opens a school and opens it to everyone at once. You see power struggles in that kind of vision. And people who have stepped outside the traditional model are very independent minded.

It makes me think of the time you may have heard me talk about when I asked my family what they wanted for dessert. One of them said, "Coconut dessert!" And everyone said, "Yeah! Coconut dessert!" So I made coconut dessert. And when I served it, we found out that every single one of us had a different coconut dessert in mind.

So you may say you are opening a Well-Educated Heart school and soon find that everyone had something different in mind.

Having a strong core vision and adding gradually outward can avoid some of those problems, if that makes sense to you.

Inside out.

I see these Well-Educated Heart schools as home-centered school-supported learning. In fact, rather than calling them a school, I see them as family gathering centers or family learning centers. Which also has the advantage that they don't come under the scrutiny of government oversight which comes if you actually open a school.

I see them as a place to inspire hearts and to give moms a break—to share out the responsibility of inspiring hearts. The environment still has to be that of individual choice and freedom, not the top-down authority model of our schools. You may offer to teach a particular subject that you have a passion for, but it would be offered in a spirit of learning rather than teaching, such as I described in a previous Take 5 when I talked about the Saracen model.

I don't see kids grouped together by age, which is so unnatural. And much of what would go on in this school would be involving the kids in activities that happen best in numbers. A choir of one is a different experience than a choir of 50. An orchestra of one violin is not the same as an orchestra with a variety of instruments. Kids can get together to act in plays or impromptu reader's theaters. Families can come together for dances. Notebooking sessions. Poetry tea times. Making crafts. Listening to stories. Telling stories. Talent shows. Instruction in drawing and painting, knitting, nature journaling. Even writing workshops. Math tutors. Writing tutors. Book discussions. Game playing. Organized service activities. Planning trips together and raising money together for worthy causes. Planting gardens.

In my ideal school, the rotation schedule would be a glue that can tie activities together. Much of the reading and study may happen at home, but the school feeds the fire of desire to want to learn, especially as kids see other kids studying the same things as they are.

I see them as a way of making friendships in wholesome ways.

I see it as a way for moms to get together and talk and support each other.

The school may well look like a home. One of my favorite stories as a little girl was that of Jane Addams. Sometimes she would travel with her father to his work and they would pass through a very poor part of town where she saw trash in the yards, children in ragged, dirty clothes, screen doors hanging on their hinges. She asked her father why the people lived that way. And he replied they didn't know any better.

So when she grew up, she bought a big home right in the middle of a poor section of Chicago where she was surrounded by many poor immigrant families. She hung fine art on the walls.

Brought in music, books, and lots of love. As the neighbors came to this home, they were lifted up and had new visions of possibilities and would go home and begin to clean up their own homes.

I see the same spirit in these schools—a place for lighting visions of desire for all the finer things of life—the riches of the heart—the riches of eternity.

Take 5.109—Announcements

Facebook is a best of worlds and a worst of worlds. It can be a huge time waster. It can be used to compare ourselves with unrealistic expectations and has been used to bully others. It has proven to be a disseminator of false information.

But it has also been a tremendous blessing to me. I can think of no other way that I could have connected with thousands of moms and families all over the world and to connect them with each other. Facebook is the lifeline to my 98-year-old mother who feels so isolated, and yet in our family Facebook group, she is able to enjoy what's going on in our lives and to see pictures of grandkids and family activities. She panics when something happens to disrupt that connection. And I love that I can instantly communicate with my kids who are spread out from Alaska to North Carolina.

In spite of its convenience, I understand why some of you feel like you need to get off of Facebook. We have tried to come up with an alternative to stay connected, but nothing yet has had the convenience of Facebook. But we do have some things in place to keep you connected with some of the things happening with Well-Educated Heart.

Hopefully you have downloaded the app and you can easily access these things from the app. Or if you go to our main website page, they are in the menu bar. Notice Announcements. If you want to be made aware of new books that we are publishing or upcoming workshops or conferences or other happenings, or new recordings in BelMonde, you will find them in the Announcements. If you check once a week or every couple of weeks, you should be able to stay on top of new developments. We are constantly adding new things.

Also, you'll see a link to Podcasts where you can check to see if anything new has been added recently. Podcasts are also archived on individual landing pages when they fit in with a monthly topic.

Many of you are enjoying the quotes and fine art that I regularly post in the Facebook group. These can also be accessed through Quotes on the app or on the menu bar. They are also eventually being posted through our Instagram account. Because we are a private Facebook group, those quotes can't be easily shared, although you can copy and paste. But if you do a search on Facebook, I also have a Libraries of Hope page. This page is totally public and I have started posting memes there of the quotes and fine art that you can share on Facebook. This is one way you can help spread the message of WEH and add a little light to the world

You will notice there are options for comments on many of these options and so, while it may not generate the conversation you might get in the FB group, it may generate a conversation or give you a place to ask a question or make a comment and stay connected that way.

Of course, you can always email me through the contact page.

And remember—you can easily choose what Facebook notifications you receive. Some moms block everything but notifications from our group. If that works for you, that's another option.

I do hope you will find a way to stay connected if you choose to leave Facebook. I have no plans of shutting down the group because I love the interactions that are going on there. They are positive and supportive and it's a wonderful group to hang out with. But if you aren't on Facebook, let's stay connected!

Take 5.110—Electronics

Almost, without exception, when I get a letter from a mom who tells me her child just isn't interested in anything no matter what she does, eventually the conversation reveals that the child has a problem with electronics.

Electronics generally is another love-hate affair. I love everything that electronics has opened up to us. And in their right-use, they are a tremendous blessing.

But I have seen for myself what they do, especially to the developing brain. They may be a great babysitter, but it's not without consequences. I am a guilty grandmother! I have one game on my phone—Temple Run. I don't even know how it got there. But when I visit grandkids, that's what they want to play. Maybe you saw the meme I saw where the grandmother is lying dead in her casket and the little grandchild leans over and whispers: "Grandma, can I play on your phone?"

Electronic games are instantly addictive, and kids get so crabby afterwards and all they want is another chance to play. That's all they can think about.

An article in Psychology today crossed my feed this morning entitled: Screentime is making kids moody, crazy and lazy.

And the cure requires "methodically eliminating all electronics use for several weeks to allow the nervous system to 'reset.'"

The article continues: "If done correctly, this intervention can produce deeper sleep, a brighter and more even mood, better focus and organization, and an increase in physical activity. The ability to tolerate stress improves, so meltdowns diminish in both frequency and severity. The child begins to enjoy the things they used to, is more drawn to nature, and imaginary or creative play returns. In teens and young adults, an increase in self-directed behavior is observed—the exact opposite of apathy and hopelessness."

It's a beautiful thing.

I don't have time in five minutes to explore the subject, but I'm sure you know there is a ton of information available to you online. If a child is deeply addicted, it can be a tricky thing to navigate them through. But if you think electronics aren't wreaking havoc on your child's brain, you are sadly mistaken, I'm afraid.

The good news is that the real things you are feeding their hearts with—the Arts—also provide rushes of feel good hormones without the hangover. As you continue to lead them down that path, the less drawn they will be to the instant fix.

Take 5.111—Games

One more time. Play is the work of childhood. There is so much children are learning through play. I posted several articles about it in the Catch the Vision course which I hope you were able to read.

So today I just want to remind you that incorporating lots of games in your day is a good strategy for a Well-Educated Heart. Little children pick up concepts like colors and counting (think Candy Land) but also more important lessons like learning to play by the rules, that cheaters ruin the game, taking turns, being gracious winners and not sore losers. A lot of games open up conversations and give another way for parents to bond with their children. Laughing together is wonderful glue that holds family members together and I know when we play games as a family, somehow or other, laughter is involved.

I'll list some of our favorite games on the Take 5 page. But I'm sure you have your favorites, too.

And not all games have to come in a box! Some of the old-fashioned ones are still favorites like Charades and what we called the Dictionary game where you divide into two teams and find obscure words in the dictionary. If there are four people on your team, for example, one of you will give the correct definition and the other three will make up a convincible fake definition. The other team has to figure out who is telling the truth. We've had lots of fun with that.

Electronics are robbing us of games where we actually connect with each other.

Don't let these 'real' games become dinosaurs!

Take 5.112—Hymns

I was reading the history of Music in the Mother's Learning Library volume on Music, and it struck me again how it was in the churches that music grew and developed. When Martin Luther wanted to share a message, he wrote hymns to get it out there. The Wesley brothers did the same thing to share the message of the Methodists. They took their meetings to the open air and wrote thousands of hymns to sing.

I don't think we fully appreciate the power of hymns in our live to connect our souls to God and to heaven. As you read the stories behind them, you almost always discover that, especially the most beloved ones, came to the writer like a gift. It flowed through them.

Many Christian denominations sing the same hymns, furthering a feeling of the brotherhood of man and the fatherhood of God.

In the preface to the hymn book I sing from, it says "The hymns invite the Spirit of the Lord, create a feeling of reverence, unify us as members, and provide a way for us to offer praises to the Lord…. The hymns can bring families a spirit of beauty and peace and can inspire love and unity among family members."

We are encouraged to sing them as we work, as we play, as we travel together; to sing hymns as lullabies.

I was talking to a friend one day—a biblical scholar—and she asked me if I knew why Psalms resonate in so many hearts as pure truth. And why they were preserved in their purity where so many of the other writings were corrupted. Of course I didn't know, but she said she believes it is because these were the lullabies the mothers sang to their children.

I have reason to believe that is true.

Remember how the Greeks and the Hebrews first lessons were oral? The voice is the grand connector of heart and mind. And hymns speak to the heart divine truths.

Often telling the stories behind the hymns will deepen their meaning. I've tried to give you a few stories to start with in the *Stories of Great Hymns* in the Story Hour series, but dig around—they aren't hard to find.

I've been making my way through a book that you might be able to find a used copy of online called *Light From Many Lamps* by Lillian Eichler Watson and I just finished a section that talked about the stories behind a few of the hymns and the effect it had on people.

Here is one of the stories: (Story of Henry Francis Lyte, Light From Many Lamps p. 36)

I Triumph Still, If Thou Abide With Me

Slowly the Reverend Henry Francis Lyte walked into his study. His heart was sad and burdened. This had been another Sunday like so many other Sundays in the long years behind him. A half-empty church. Tight hard faces listening without hearing, minds far away, hearts locked against the meaning of his words.

He had accomplished so little, so very little, here in Brixham! He had tried to bring these people closer to God, had tried to teach them the meaning of love and faith, of tolerance and kindness.

But he had failed. He knew by the hatred and cruelties, by the fueds between neighbors, the greed and petty jealousies, how bitterly he had failed.

He was an old man now, near the end of the journey. He was tired and ill. The doctor had told him he had only a few months to live. He thumbed the well-worn Bible on his desk, and it fell open at one of his favorite passage: "Abide with us; for it is toward evening and the day is far spent." In the quiet of his curtained study, he read and reread those familiar comforting words.

And all at once he was no longer old and tired! All at once he was no longer sad and burdened, no longer discouraged! Words sang through his mind; and he put them down on paper; and in less than an hour he had written one of the most beautiful and inspiring hymns of all time:

> Abide with me; fast falls the eventide;
> The darkness deepens; Lord, with me abide;
> When other helpers fail, and comforts flee,
> Help of the helpless, oh abide with me.
>
> Swift to its close ebbs our life's little day;
> Earth's joys grow dim, its glories pass away;
> Change and decay in all around I see;
> O Thou who changest not, abide with me.
>
> I need Thy presence every passing hour;
> What but Thy grace can foil the tempter's power?
> Who like Thyself my guide and stay can be?
> Through cloud and sunshine, Lord, abide with me.
>
> I fear no foe with Thee at hand to bless;
> Ills have no weight, and tears no bitterness;
> Where is death's sting? Where, grave, thy victory?
> I triumph still, if Thou abide with me.
>
> Hold then Thy cross before my closing eyes;
> Shine through the gloom, and point me to the skies;
> Heaven's morning breaks, and earth's vain shadows flee;
> In life, in death, O Lord, abide with me.

Few people today know the name of Henry Francis Lyte. But the soul-stirring hymn he wrote in less than an hour, a hundred years ago, is known and loved all over the world—has given comfort and courage to millions.

When the famous nurse, Edith Cavell, went before a German firing squad, she whispered the words of "Abide With Me." When the R.M.S. Stella was sinking with one hundred and five victims during the Second World War, a woman—one of the noble unidentified of the world—stood on the bridge and sang "Abide With Me" until the others were singing with her, and they went down bravely. Countless other stories could be told of people all over the world.

So out of a great heart came a great hymn. At the end of life, in a moment of shining faith and inspiration, Henry Francis Lyte created a sentiment that lives on and on—words of enduring power and influence.

Hymns are doctrine wrapped in poetry. Can there by more worthy songs to learn by heart?

Take 5.113—Finding a Rhythm

I feel like I need to go on record one more time. I am not against academics. Children do need to learn to read and to write. There are academic subjects to learn. But, to me, it is an order thing. Tend to the desire first, and then to the skill.

A heart full of music that has no skills with which to express itself will keep its song hidden forever from the world. But the skilled fingers and notation writers that have nothing flowing out of the heart to perform will also fall short.

Heart and Mind work together.

Finnish schools and Waldorf schools, with their top performing students, are showing that delaying the formal instruction of academics until a child is 7 or 8 years old is the way to go. Prior to that, give them real world experiences. Immerse them in the Living Waters of the Arts. Let them play and explore and discover.

Then, as you begin to work in academic instruction, keep in mind every child is unique. Don't force. Observe. Test the waters. And then find a rhythm to your day to work them in. Maybe you can put some music on after lunch and all sit down together to practice penmanship. Maybe the time after breakfast is reserved for a few minutes of a phonics lesson or a math lesson. In the beginning, take it slow. And keep feeding the desire.

And remember how important it is that children move! Movement is vital for connecting neural pathways. Making them sit and study for long stretches of time will work against them.

I love a book written by Dr. Rich Melheim that you can buy on his site—*Rich Learning*. It gives you the Science behind an Arts-based education. He teaches, "You gotta open the kid before you open the book"

He wrote:

> Moving your body while learning a lesson or language or while trying to solve a particularly difficult math equation floods your brain with both oxygen and glucose. The higher the oxygen level, the more the brain can focus and stay alert. The higher the glucose level, the more efficiently the cells of the brain can fire, wire, grow and connect. What happens to learning when you flood both oxygen and glucose into the brain through employing movement in your teaching environment? Attention and retention.

> You want to get children paying attention, learning faster and remembering longer? It's actually quite simple and it doesn't cost a cent. Exercise supercharges mental circuits, beats stress, lifts mood, boosts memory and enhances both attention and long-term retention. According to Dr. Ratey, exercise improves learning on at least four levels:

> 1. Optimizes mindset to improve alertness, attention and motivation

> 2. Prepares and encourages nerve cells to bind to one another

> 3. Spurs development of new nerve cells from stem cells in the hippocampus and

> 4. Improves cognitive flexibility—the ability to brainstorm creative thoughts.

Dr. Melheim adds as a little note on the page: "Throw away your desks and chairs. Get out of those mind-numbing seats. No, really! And move! Move! Move!"

When I was staying with my daughter a few weeks ago, I watched her do Cosmic Yoga with her little kids and they loved it. That's one way to start your morning! Add it to the rhythm of your day to get those little brains ready to learn!

And it wouldn't hurt to take some random dance breaks all day long, right? Or go outside and run, climb, slide, twirl. It's all part of the learning process and part of the rhythm of your day.

Take 5.114—Joy

Every year when we go through the rotation schedule, by the time we get to Joy in August, I think we're all out playing with our families. I know I take a bit of a break. So I never talk about it. Maybe I should make Joy the first month! Because Joy is what we are all about. It's the objective of our learning. We want to prepare our children to live lives of maximum Joy.

Let me highlight a couple of resources to bring more Joy into your life. If you haven't started reading the Joy volume in the mother's learning library, it's one you can just kind of take in a little here and a little there. I loved the book I found because it pretty much sums up what we have learned for the rest of the year of how Music, Art, Poetry, Story and Nature bring Joy into our lives. And he gives lots of examples of how it has been applied in people's lives throughout history.

At the back of that book is a thought for everyday of the year that pertains to happiness. If you want some copy work, that could work as one of your sources—to copy a thought a day about being happy from some of the greatest minds who have ever lived.

Maybe you could pick up a little Bare Book for each of your kids who are writing and let them create their own little book of happy thoughts, using these as copy work exercises. Maybe throw in some fine art here and there to glue on the pages or just decorate pages with stickers? Or their own designs? I'm just throwing out ideas.

As a side note for beginning writers, if you haven't noticed them, there are some dark-line templates available through Bare Books that show through the blank pages if your kids have a hard time writing on blank paper. There are varying widths.

Or have them start a gratitude journal, but I think we talked about that elsewhere.

If you haven't visited the Joy page in the Mother's University, do take a look. I have elsewhere told the story of Orison Swett Marden who was orphaned as a little boy, but whose life hanged as he read the stories of great men and women. He went on to write books to inspire people all over the world. I've listed many of his books on that page as well as other inspirational writers who help us think like happy people should think. Check it out.

Take 5.115—Recap: Five Things

Here we are at the last week of the Take 5s, at least the planned ones. I won't say that I'll never add another one because if there is something I forgot or something new I want to share, I'll create some more.

We've spent a lot of time now, zooming in on the pixels of the Well-Educated Heart as we've talked about tools and ideas for using them. But like a photograph, if you stay focused on the pixels and don't zoom out far enough to take in the whole picture, you'll lose the vision of what we are trying to accomplish.

So in this final week, I'd like to zoom out and go back to vision—the why. Then you can start customizing the what.

I notice from comments in the Facebook group there is a wide variety of understanding what The Well-Educated Heart is. Some people may think it's the rotation schedule or the books. So when they say they are doing Well-Educated Heart, that means they are following the rotation schedule or reading books from the site. But the rotation schedule is simply a tool, as are all the resources in Libraries of Hope. You can follow the philosophy of the Well-Educated Heart without utilizing any of those things. It's not a curriculum—it is a philosophy not just of education, but of life.

There are five things that are in my mind when I talk about The Well-Educated Heart. Let me summarize them. But first, a reminder of the objective.

The objective is joy. While college and career choices may add to that joy, they are not my primary focus. I believe Joy is a gift of the Spirit, like Paul talks about. Spirit and Truth and Light are all synonymous words for me and my belief is the Source of that Light is Jesus Christ. So really what we are doing is directly connected to increasing our capacity for Light, and thereby, increased Joy.

So now the five things to keep in mind.

1. *Freedom.* True and lasting learning requires an environment of freedom and choice. There is great joy in exploration and discovery. When you structure the learning so tightly, which most curriculums do, you deny so many of those wonderful ah-hah moments when connections are made and your child discovers a truth on his own. It has been said all true education is self-education and self-education demands freedom to explore.

2. *Mothers.* Mothers are divinely gifted with attributes and qualities for nurturing the heart, where all lasting learning begins. Mothers are a child's best first teacher. You cannot teach a child whose heart you do not have, so a loving relationship is vital. The child looks for something to which it can attach, and once it attaches, becomes like that to which it has attached.

Therefore, the force of a mother's personality is much more important than her specific teaching skills or methods.

3. *The Arts.* The keys a mother uses to awaken desires in the heart are the Arts—Music, Art or Imagery, Poetry and Story. A young child understands these languages of the heart. The Arts are like Living Water to a young child's soul, and the mother who immerses her child in

these languages in childhood will grow deep roots that will later yield good fruit the rest of their lives.

4. *Balance.* Educating the heart without educating the mind is no education at all. There is a Pattern for Learning—if you start with the Heart through the Arts, then a student is ready to master the skills, the rules, the facts of the mind. Heart and Mind together become an inspired creative force. And the fruit of this heaven-directed kind of learning is that, through creation—the culminating action of their learning, they will multiply Joy, Love and Light in the world.

5. *Inside out.* The world works outside in, God works inside out. The world is always looking for something to measure. God values that which cannot be measured. True education is between a child's soul and God who will teach that which the world cannot teach. While the world focuses on that which is Seen, these things are temporal and temporary. Heaven is concerned with the Unseen things—Beauty, Love, Peace—and these riches are forever. They are Eternal. The world may teach a child to identify the parts of the rose; Heaven will help a child to feel its beauty. The world may teach that a figure from history was born on a certain date, heaven inspires the soul with the lessons of life that person left behind and those lessons almost always have to do with happiness. The world may teach mathematical facts; heaven teaches sacred geometry that reveals the presence and care of a Divine Creator everywhere.

A rose blooms outward from the pressure of an inside fulness. When God is the teacher, the direction is inward out.

I've taught these five things in greater depth in other places—and I will keep teaching these five things in every way I can—this is just the summary.

But if you want five reminders on your fingertips of what I see when I talk about The Well-Educated Heart, here are the five key words: Freedom, Mother, Arts, Balance, Inside Out.

I truly believe that if enough mothers will take these five things to heart, we will change the world.

Take 5.116—Music

If we only understand the power of music to bring harmony and order and desire into the lives of individuals and thereby the world, we would find ways to fill our lives with music. The vibrational qualities of music interact with us at our deepest levels.

I really like this paragraph from the Delphian course:

> Of all the arts, music is the most potent. Its subject matter—sound—is capable of more delicate gradations than the material of any other art. It can appeal to more people and move their emotions more strongly than any known human means of expression. It is able to bring about subtle shades of feeling which the most carefully selected words are powerless to convey. And it can lead the hearts and minds of men to regions far removed from everyday life.

Music is the first language a baby understands. He has formed and developed to the rhythmic beat of his mother's heart. Outside the womb, that rhythmic beat is still what will bring him the greatest comfort. A mother who sings to a baby within her womb, will find herself with a baby who recognizes her voice and is more readily comforted by her voice outside the womb.

A baby is disturbed by dissonance and relaxes to the harmonious sounds of a lullaby. We feel sad or reflective at a minor chord, anticipatory at a 7th, and only feel satisfied when the music has brought us safely to the home chord.

These vibrational sounds of music don't have to pass through our ears to affect us. Helen Keller was once interviewed for a magazine and brought her interviewer into her sitting room where she turned on her radio to listen to music. She placed her hand on the radio receiver and said, "Ahh. Beethoven's Moonlight Sonata. Isn't that amazing—a deaf composer composing music so that a blind girl could see the moonlight?"

It is only in modern times that music has been used primarily for entertainment. Throughout history, music has been used as a healing power—physical, emotional and spiritual.

If we tap into the power of music, we can change the environment of our homes and the dispositions of our children. From the mother's learning library book on music, I gleaned these two thoughts: "The Hindus have a morning song, a song for noon, an evening song, and a song for midnight. They have songs of praise, songs of love, songs of joy, songs of peace and many others. To them the home is a sacred temple and the parents, the priest and priestess of the actual presence of God, who is acknowledged and rejoiced in with every homely event of the day."

And, "An hour of good music at bedtime will so harmonize the child's consciousness that he will go to sleep happy and serene. Those thoughts will do their unfailing work of rebuilding, physically, mentally, and spiritually, all through the night, and the child will awaken in the morning in the same happy, healthy frame of mind."

Use music in your home to set the tone and the mood. Keep in mind that strong, repetitive beat dulls the senses and shuts down feeling.

The voice is the grand connector of heart and mind. Find ways to sing throughout your day. Folk songs originated in the hearts of the common folk; children likewise naturally respond to them and will love to sing them and dance to them! Movement is vital to their developing nervous systems and little children love to dance.

Sing together as a family, eventually harmonizing together. As you read the books in the Mother's University, your appreciation for music will grow and you will help to refine the musical tastes of your children. Make friends with the great music masters—they discovered the secrets of music that would reveal the very glory of God to human hearts—if the heart has been sufficiently awakened to hear.

In the Take 5s, I've shown where you can find stories of the music masters as children, stories to go with some of their masterpieces, books for music appreciation, and I've given you a repertoire of music to listen to. While I've given you music to start with, I have not even scratched the surface of possibilities! How many ways can you weave music into the fabric of your lives?

Take 5.117—Visual Arts

To come to appreciate fine art is to appreciate and find beauty everywhere. When I am referring to fine art here, I'm talking about the visual arts—the paintings and the sculptures. You may remember the quote of John Van Dyke:

"You must look at pictures studiously, earnestly, honestly. It will take years before you come to a full appreciation of art; but when at last you have it, you will be possessed of one of the purest, loftiest, and most ennobling pleasures that the civilized world can offer you."

And how do we do this? Estelle Hurll reminds us:

> Pictures are primarily intended for pure aesthetic joy, and it is a thousand pities to assume a didactic tone in showing them to children. Let them be, like the stories we tell, among their dearest delights. Above all things else we must avoid mechanical methods of instruction as the most deadly blight to the imagination. We cannot be too careful lest the child's perception be dulled by prosaic influence, or his taste vitiated by unworthy material. For the imagination is the key by which we unlock the doors of beauty. While the divine gift is still unspoiled, the child is most keenly alive to the joys of life.

In other words, seek out paintings that will give your children joy in the beginning—things they can relate to—children playing in the sunshine among the flowers, families enjoying each other's company. You can do much to counter the thousands of negative images our world is currently offering by making the looking at fine art an enjoyable pastime and helping your children to store up those beautiful images. Don't ever start by analyzing the techniques or the composition. That can come later—and will be welcomed at the right time when a child is ready to layer deeper.

I have tried to give you some artwork to begin with which I showed you how to access in the website. I will continue to work to bring more suitable art to your children.

We talked about different ways to help them look at the pictures in more meaningful ways— by finding the stories in the pictures, using the tools "I notice," "I wonder," and "That reminds me of;" looking for the details, even sketching what we are seeing.

Use fine art in the teaching of history and in creating their keepsake volumes of the stories of history and its people that they are learning. A picture is worth 700,000 words.

Don't be too quick to teach forming letters—let him strengthen his manual dexterity by drawing pictures and eventually painting. Drawing produces exactness of thought and will enable him to see things that he will never see without developing that skill. And almost everyone can develop that skill. Teaching cursive handwriting is part of that art process of the heart.

Introduce your children to the lives of the great artists. I gave you stories of their childhoods and other stories and books to deepen your appreciation of art. The more you understand, the more naturally that love and understanding will spill out into your children.

Visit art museums. As grateful as I am for art images, nothing surpasses the actual work of art. The more you expose your children to the great artists and their works, the more familiar friends they will find when they visit the museums. Let them find the art that speaks to their own hearts. Don't ask probing questions and make them describe how the art makes them feel in words. The deepest work of the heart has no words—that's why there is art.

As their eye for art becomes refined, so will their capacity to see beauty all around them increase.

Orison Swett Marden wrote:

> A great scientist tells us that there is no natural object in the universe which, if seen as the Master see it, coupled with all its infinite meaning, its utility and purpose, is not beautiful. Beauty is God's handwriting.

> Just as the most disgusting object, if put under a magnifying glass of sufficient power, would reveal beauties undreamed of, so even the most unlovely environment, the most cruel conditions, will, when viewed through the glass of a trained and disciplined mind, show something of the beautiful and the hopeful. A Life that has been rightly trained will extract sweetness from everything; it will see beauty everywhere.

That's where we are headed with our study of art: to help our children—and ourselves—see beauty everywhere.

Take 5.118—Poetry

How can poetry not impact our lives when you realize it takes all the power of music and combines it with beautiful imagery?

The poets through the ages have changed the course of history.

Helping your child acquire a taste for poetry is as simple as sharing Mother Goose rhymes in early childhood and reading poetry together aloud as they grow up. Mother Goose rhymes have wonderful ordering properties for young developing minds. The killer of poetry is forcing them to analyze it too early. Or assigning poetry to them. We each respond to things differently.

What resonates in my heart may not resonate in yours. So allow them the freedom to love the poems they love! And share with them the poems you love! Create your personal anthology of favorites and you will have a keepsake that may just be passed down for generations because it will speak to them of who you were and what you loved.

Inspire your children to create their own anthologies. Add fine art if you want. Make friends with the poets. They will see you through life's inevitable storms. As Louisa May Alcott wrote, "I am not afraid of storms, for I am learning how to sail my ship." The poets are there to help you steer. And do exercise your memory muscle to memorize those poems that resonate the most with you.

Take 5.119—Story

Stories help us to see and to feel. If you are looking for a way to light a fire of desire in your child to learn something, the story can be your best friend. The Golden Age of Children's Literature from around 1880 to 1920 yielded us a treasure trove of stories about history, nature, people, literature—everything on the planet. They wrote to inspire children's hearts. If you have not yet discovered the books of this era, please, please, give them a chance. It's true—the vocabulary is greater, the sentence structure is richer, than what you may be used to. But as you dive in, it will become familiar. These stories almost beg to be read aloud. If the choices in the Libraries of Hope library are too overwhelming, start with the ones I picked in the Forgotten Classics library. They are noted in the blue boxes on the pages.

Or start with the stories in My Book House or the Junior Classics volumes. The whole Libraries of Hope library is made up of the best books. Just pick one and start reading. If it isn't working, put it back on the shelf and try another. Don't overthink this! And don't worry about coming up with study questions—just read and let the stories do the teaching. Let conversation flow in natural ways.

These stories will teach your children things you cannot teach them directly.

I talked about developmental levels—to always start by finding the stories that will connect to something familiar in your child's heart. For your youngest children, that means stories of family and puppies and flowers. And then give them stories to build their imaginations—the great myths and fairy tales and legends that have been preserved and passed down through the ages. Then give them action heroes before you give them moral heroes and the stories of history.

Remember the quote by John Senior?

> In order to read the 'great' books of Plato, Aristotle, St. Augustine and St. Thomas, we need to replenish the cultural soul that has been depleted and create a place where these works can thrive by cultivating an imaginative ground saturated with fable, fairy tale, stories, rhymes, and adventure—the thousand books of Grimm, Andersen, Stevenson, Dickens, Scott, Dumas and the rest. The one thing a great books education will not do is create a moral imagination where there is none.

As you light a fire of desire to get at more stories, your children will start reading and searching out books independently. You can help guide them.

The rotation schedule provides a way to take in the whole world of its nations and peoples as well as nature. It allows your whole family to study the same general topic, but at their individual developmental level of understanding. Everyone can join in the conversation and have something to bring. It allows learning to layer in gradually and for connections to be made through a natural process.

It can be challenging to have a houseful of kids at various ages—that's one reason I created the BelMonde audio site. When you need to have children listen to different stories or you don't want to read the same book over again to a child who has become of age for the book, send them over to "grandma's house." I'm happy to read to them for awhile! Or look for other audio versions of the stories for them to listen to while they engage in activities for their hands.

Writing is best learned by letting them first tell oral stories to you and then you writing them down. As they begin to write, let them learn to write by writing. You can layer in the periods and capital letters over time.

Notebooking is not only a way to help them learn language art skills, it is a way to help them hold on to those pieces of truth and wisdom that strikes their own hearts. Their notebooks can become treasured keepsakes of their learning.

And when you are ready, if you haven't already discovered it, practice the art of storytelling. I've given you some guidelines to begin and even stories to practice with. It's amazing what happens when you put the book down, and share a story by heart.

Take 5.120—Nature

One more time. Nature is God's University. It is not one of the arts, but it is the greatest source of inspiration for all the arts. To the child with eyes to see and ears to hear and hearts to feel, nature is filled with music, beautiful imagery, poetry and story. Allowing a young child to run and play and explore in the sunshine or the rain in childhood is the most wonderful learning experience and classroom you can possibly give him.

We recreate in nature. But really, we re-create because we are surrounded by all the languages of the heart that heal us and help us put our lives in harmony and order. It is an immersion experience.

The stories you tell about nature, the poems you share, the music and the paintings will all serve to make all of nature even more wonderful. I gave you many resources you can use to give your children eyes, and ears and wonderment.

Like George Washington Carver said, "Anything will give up its secrets, if you love it long enough. "

John Muir Laws teaches, love is attention. As you teach a child to draw what he is seeing through nature journaling, it is developing a habit of attention and thereby love.

And as one of our heart educators said, "If the trees and flowers, the clouds and the wind, all tell wonderful stories to the child he has sources of happiness of which no power can deprive him.

As I have studied the lives of great men and women, I see a common thread of daily walks outside in nature to clear their thoughts, inspire their minds, and calm their souls.

This is our objective for Nature Study.

Concluding Thoughts

Corragio! You are Stronger Than You Imagine

While visiting the National Portrait Gallery in Washington, D.C., in one of the rooms, I happened upon a sculpture of a little girl—*La Petite Pensee*—that so captured my heart, I couldn't stop looking at her. What she was telling me, I have no words to describe. But I didn't want to leave her.

When I got home, I couldn't stop thinking about her. I wondered who the artist was who could have created such an exquisite work of art. His name was Thomas Ball and I found an autobiography of him online. At the end of his book was advice that he gave to young artist friends and as I read it, I thought, these words are for you, too, because I see you as artists—creators of children's hearts, caregivers of their inner kingdoms. And sometimes the work is discouraging. We feel ordinary and inadequate. We feel like we aren't doing a very good job. The work isn't turning out the way we hoped it would. So let me repeat his words:

My most bitter tears have been shed at the completion of some work, when I felt that I had done all I could do, and yet found it so far from what I had hoped to make it, and that it must go out to the world with all its imperfections. Falling upon my knees in agony, praying for comfort and faith to believe the present disappointment to be for my ultimate good, I have arisen comforted and strengthened in the hope that perhaps I had worked better than I knew.... Imperfect and unsatisfactory as all my work seems to me, I shudder when I think of what they might have been, and what I might have been, without the firm belief that He was ever at my right hand as long as I was true to myself—to bear me up when I would have fainted; to help me when my strength left me.

I write this for the encouragement of my young brothers in art; not those arrogant and proud ones who believe in nothing but their own strength and will, jealous of even a hint of assistance from a higher power.... But to the sensitive, retiring one who shrinks from the sound of approbation—to him I would say Corragio! [Courage] You are stronger than you imagine; be but sincere and conscientious in your efforts; work away with all your might. Strive to live a pure and clean life, and to improve the talents God has given you, and leave the rest to Him. He will not let you fail. Keep up a good heart; cultivate a cheery disposition.

Concluding Thoughts

Finally, here we are at the last talk. Whew. If you've listened to all the other ones, we've spent several hours together. Thank you for taking time to listen. Maybe in the beginning you started listening because you wanted to pick up a few tips or ideas to use in your homeschool or to supplement what your children are learning in public school. Or maybe you love the arts as I do and you were looking for ways to cultivate your own heart. I hope you found something you were looking for.

But if you made it through all these little talks, you may have picked up an underlying message; the real desire in my heart that drives me to spend hours every day looking for ways I can help you. The last thing I'm interested in is developing curriculum I can market. I have bigger problems on my mind that are best expressed in these words I copied down from the introduction to an old book about the fifteenth-century world of Henry V:

"Old faiths had lost their inspiration. Old forms of government were breaking down. The very fabric of society seemed to be on the point of dissolution."

Does that sound familiar?

Our children are growing up in a world on the verge of economic collapse. Terrorism and senseless killing are no longer something that happens in lands far away. It happens in our schools and our shopping malls. Hateful rhetoric as well as sleaze and vulgarity fill our air waves. Corruption is rampant. Faith is under attack. Families are falling apart. Men's hearts are failing them.

Not that we're the first generation to face these things. Every generation has had troubles of their own, but listen to the words of hope that follow the statement from Henry V I just read:

"It is, however, part of the irony of history that a great ideal too often attains its finest expression only when the period of decline has already commenced."

And then it continues:

"...the remedy for present evils was sought not in the creation of a new order but rather in the restoration of an old ideal. To bring back the Golden Past must be the work of a hero who could revive in his own person its virtues.

"Henry of Monmouth, deriving his inspiration from the past, was the champion of unity against the forces of disintegration."

There you have it. My husband and I do everything we do here at Libraries of Hope because we're hoping that from your home, 'champions of unity against the forces of disintegration' will emerge; that in your home will be found heroes who can 'revive in their own persons' the Golden ideals of the past: Faith, Family, Freedom and Virtue. I can't stop terrorists from killing. I'm not smart enough to fix our economy. I can't reform corrupt politicians. But there is something I can do and so can you. As Confucius says:

To put the world right in order
we must first put the nation in order;

To put the nation in order,
we must first put the family in order,

To put the family in order,
we must first cultivate our personal life, we must first set our hearts right.

Well-educated hearts. That *is* the solution to a world spinning out of control. "By small and simple means are great things accomplished." Many people are working hard to make sure our children have well-trained minds. That is good. But who is tending to their hearts?

These are the differences between mind and heart as I now understand them:

The mind is informed.
The heart is inspired.

The mind feeds on facts.
The heart feeds on Truth.

The mind asks, "Why?"
The heart wonders, "Why not?"

The mind is molded through questioning.
The heart asks its own questions.

The mind is verbose.
The heart relishes brevity.

The mind seeks pleasure, which is usually temporal and temporary.
The heart seeks joy, which is spiritual and eternal.

The mind clings to reason.
The heart clings to faith.

The mind often feels superior because of its vast knowledge.
The heart often feels humbled by all it doesn't yet understand.

The mind is critical.
The heart is compassionate.

The mind thinks.
The heart feels.

The mind seeks to be understood.
The heart longs to understand.

The mind is knowledgeable.
The heart is wise.

I have noticed a growing interest in classical education with its trivium of grammar, logic and rhetoric. The sponge of the young child's mind is used for memorizing facts. And then, students are taught to use those facts to logic and reason and finally, the highest stage is rhetoric where a student is taught to write persuasively so that he can convince others of the truth he has arrived at by means of his carefully trained logic and reason.

I would be more sold on the process if mankind hadn't demonstrated such a proneness to err in his calculations. I find few minds more narrow or less open to change than the mind that has arrived at a perceived point of truth by a process of reason and logic alone. Much of the contention in our world arises from opposing viewpoints, with both sides confident of their correctness. It seems our world would benefit by a little less persuading and a whole lot more seeking to understand the other's viewpoint, which is the function of the heart.

There is another way to persuade others of Truth, as demonstrated by One who has successfully influenced and led more people to Truth than anyone else. And He never wrote a single persuasive paper that we're aware of. His method for spreading Truth was very simple: He let his light shine and commended to us that we do the same. Our life, He taught, is the open book for all to read. How a person feels in our presence will be remembered long after our words have been forgotten.

The pathway for this kind of learning also has three parts: Faith, Hope and Charity. As I have said, our role as parents is to prepare our children's hearts to be inspired, give them good things to hope for, and teach them the right-use of all things in love. Everything I have presented to you have these three things in mind.

The rest we can safely leave in the hands of a Heavenly Parent, for true education, as noted before, is between a child's soul and God.

I know I'm a dreamer. But I'm hoping you're a dreamer, too. I copied these words about dreamers in my notes:

> [Dreamers] are the chosen few—the Blazers of the way—who never wear doubt's bandage on their eyes—who starve and chill and hurt, but hold to courage and to hope, because they know that there is always proof of truth for them who try—that only cowardice and lack of faith can keep the seeker from his chosen goal, but if his heart be strong and if he dream enough and dream it hard enough, he can attain, no matter where men failed before.

> Walls crumble and the empires fall. The tidal wave sweeps from the sea and tears a fortress from its rocks. The rotting nations drop from off Time's bough, and only things the dreamers make live on.

So it only seems fitting to leave you with a dream I had that sums up what I've been trying to say. But it's the kind of dream that it's not really about me. It's about you, too, and I hope you'll place yourself in the dream. Only your heart will understand it.

I dreamed I was in a large, noisy hall filled with people. There were long rows of cafeteria style tables throughout the hall and my sense was life revolved around set feeding times throughout the day. At certain times, we were all expected to sit down and eat what was placed in front of us and we all ate the same thing. It didn't feel like a bad thing. It's just how it was.

In my dream, I noticed a door I evidently hadn't noticed before. There were no windows in this hall, so I didn't know what was on the other side. Curious, I slipped over to the door, looked around to make sure no one was watching me, turned the knob and stepped outside into a thick fog. I could hear the sound of horse hooves coming closer, and soon a horse-drawn carriage broke through the fog and a tall, lanky man stepped out. He beckoned me to follow him, and I did. I had to practically run to keep up with him, but I remember how drawn I was to the features of his face. He smiled at me and his eyes were so warm, I didn't feel afraid at all. At first, he didn't say anything to me, but after awhile he introduced himself. He said he was Hans Christian Andersen. Just then the fog broke and I found he had led me to the most glorious meadow you can ever imagine! Everywhere, as far as the eye could see, were flowers of every color. White billowy clouds floated across a deep blue sky and I felt the warmth of the sun on my face. Butterflies fluttered among the flowers and the breezes carried the songs of hundreds of birds. I could barely breathe, it was so beautiful.

My friend held out his hand and motioned for me to lead the way along the path that now meandered through this glorious meadow. At first, I was anxious—I was going to miss my 2:30 feeding time. What would my peers say? But soon, the joys of the meadow so filled my heart, I didn't care what they said.

The two of us spent all afternoon in the meadow. My friend patiently waited while I stopped to take in every new site and discovery at every bend in the path. Then, just as the path ended, he said that he had to leave me. We were standing in a grove of tall trees and I told him that I didn't know where to go from there. He simply smiled and looked heavenward: "God directs."

Suddenly the scene changed and I was back in the noisy, crowded feeding hall. Immediately I was surrounded by angry peers. Where had I been? Didn't I know I had missed my 2:30 feeding time? I told them I had just spent the entire afternoon in the most glorious meadow with Hans Christian Andersen himself. I wanted to tell them more, but they rolled their eyes at me in disbelief and left me to myself.

But it didn't matter. All the joy of the meadow was stored in my heart—and I knew it would remain with me, always.

The dream ended and I woke up.

Maybe it was just coincidence, but a day or two later at a library used book sale, I happened to walk by a shelf of books and one title caught my eye: it was *The Fairy Tale Story of My Life* by Hans Christian Andersen. I didn't know anything about his life. I had only read his fairy tales and I don't remember having previously seen his picture, but there on the cover was an image of the friend of my dreams. I opened the book to read the first page, and at the end of the first paragraph, he had written, "The history of my life will say to the world what it says to me— There is a loving God, who directs all things for the best."

I, too, believe in a God who directs all things for the best. And as you turn to Him, He will direct and guide you as you lead your children through this glorious meadow of learning that has been prepared for us. May the ideas I've presented help to bring you closer to Him, that you, with your family, may live happily and joyfully ever after.

What Has Been Done Before, Can Be Done Again

Two thousand years ago, the Jews—a chosen people—were anxiously watching for their deliverer; the one who would make everything right for them; the one who would free them from their tyrannical rulers. Some of them hoped it was the carpenter from Galilee, but they were disappointed when, rather than tackling the problem at hand—the Government—He talked about a Kingdom within; of tending to the treasure within one's heart. When that was right, He taught, everything else would take care of itself.

They rejected His teachings. And they self-destructed.

Two thousand years later, another favored people are watching for their deliverer. Electing a new President will solve the problems, they hope; a new Congress will turn the ship of State around.

Will it?

History's pages say, 'No.'

Real change can only take place in individual hearts. I found a page in history that proves it is possible.

Six hundred years before Jesus, Confucius was teaching the same message in China—only his hearers listened and applied the teachings. It worked so well for a short time, the people said, "We have seen what Paradise looks like."

According to Marcus Bach, "In that brief Confucian period, love was really love, and justice was really just. There was a saying that theft ceased to exist among the people because it had been removed from people's hearts. An era of trust and mutual faith had been ushered in. The good of one was premised on the good of all. Anything lost on the highways was restored, and any wrong was righted because gentlemanliness was man's richest prize. In those days, Confucius said, "The superior man understands what is right; the inferior man understands what will sell."

Unfortunately, it didn't last because the neighboring ruler was afraid all his subjects would move over to that land of peace because it was such a desirable place to live. So he sent over the one thing that he knew would be their undoing—he sent a harem of beautiful dancing girls.

And the rest is history.

Still, what has been done can be done again. And you mothers are the ones who can make it happen as you raise a new generation where 'gentlemanliness' is the richest prize.

Maybe this time we'll be wise.

The Song is Never Ended

(From *My Garden of Memories* by Kate Douglas Wiggin)

In childhood, whenever I read Hans Christian Andersen's fairy-tales—which was all too seldom, for we had but one copy of the book—I always turned first to the story of the Flax; and as my sister and I grew older and were incessantly telling or reading stories to children, it exerted a great satisfaction, indeed a great influence, over me. It seemed a little piece of religion, and in some way a philosophy of life.

Do you remember how the Flax said to itself one fine summer morning?—"I am strong and tall. I am in full bloom; and every day something delightful happens to me. Oh! This is a beautiful world!"

A Hedge-Stake, near by, you know, overheard the Flax and grumbled: "It takes those who have knots in their stems to know the world!" –and he creaked out a mournful song:

Snip, snap, snurre,
Basse lurre:
The song is ended!

"Oh, no!" cried the Flax: "the song is not ended, it is hardly begun. Every day the sunshine gladdens, or the rain refreshes me. I know that I am growing. I know that I am in full blossom. I am the happiest of all creatures."

I used to feel even then that the Hedge-Stake was wrong in his philosophy of existence; but very soon in the story of the Flax, now full-grown, was pulled up by the roots, laid in water till it was almost drowned, and set by the fire until it was almost roasted.

"One must not complain," said the Flax. "If I've suffered something, I'm being made into something." And when it was put upon the wheel and spun into thread, and the thread woven into a web, still it sang its song of content as the wheel whirred and the shuttle shot to and fro. (I think two little girls, sitting by an open fire, with a few tears falling on the page of the beloved book, learned something just then—not through the head, but the heart!)

Then the Flax was spread upon the grass as a long piece of white linen, the finest in the parish, and there were many changes after that—snipping and cutting and making into garments— and the Flax said: "See how the little Hedge-Stake knew when he told me the song was ended: look what I have become! This was my destiny. Now I shall be of some use in the world. I am the happiest of all creatures."

At last the garments were worn quite to rags; and then they were cut into smaller bits and softened and boiled till they became white paper.

"What a glorious surprise!" cried the Flax. "Now perhaps a poet may come and write his thoughts upon me. See how I am led from glory to glory—I who was only a little blue flower growing in the fields. Ah! The poor Hedge-Stake, how little he knew about life!"

And truly a poet did come and write beautiful thoughts on the shining white leaves, and they were sent to the printers and made into books.

"This is the best of all!" said the Flax. "Now I shall sit at home, like an honored grandfather, and my books will travel over all lands. How happy I am! Each time I think the song is ended, it begins again in a more beautiful way!"

But now the paper was thrust into a barrel and sold to a grocer for wrapping his butter and sugar.

"I had not thought of this!" said the Flax (though the two little girls had, and a hundred readings could not prevent momentary tears). "But, after all, it is better, for I have been so hurried from one stage of my life to another that I have never had time to think! After work, it is well to rest. Now I can reflect on my real condition."

But it did not happen as the Flax had thought, for the grocer's children were fond of burning paper on the hearth. They liked the flash of the flames up the chimney, the gray ashes below and the red sparks careening here and there, and they often danced and sang when the fire was flashing its brightest; so they pulled all the paper from the barrel one day and set it afire.

Whis-sh! Went the blaze up the chimney. It soared higher than the Flax had ever lifted its blue flowers, and glistened as the white linen had never glistened.

"Now I'm mounting straight up to the sun!" cried a voice far above the chimney, and, more delicate than the flames, invisible to human eyes, a myriad of tiny beings floated in the air above, many, many more than there had been blossoms on the Flax.

Down below, the children sang the rhyme of the Hedge-Stake over the dead ashes:

> Snip, snap, snurre,
> Basse lurre;
> The song is ended!

But the little invisible beings in the air above them sang together, as clearly as if there had been a thousand voices in unison: "The song is ended; the most beautiful is yet to come; we know it, and therefore we are the happiest of all."

"THE SONG IS NEVER ENDED;
THE MOST *Beautiful* IS YET TO COME;
WE KNOW IT, AND THEREFORE
WE ARE THE *Happiest* OF ALL!"

Rotation Booklist

1500s: AGE OF EXPLORATION

ELEMENTARY	MIDDLE SCHOOL	HIGH SCHOOL
A World Explorer: John Smith, Graves	A Book of Famous Explorers	Adventures of the Chevalier de la Salle, Abbott
Adventures of Columbus, Humphrey	Amerigo Vespucci, Syme	Admiral Byrd of Antarctica, Noble
Adventures of Early Discoverers, Humphrey	Balboa: Swordsman and Conquistador	Christopher Columbus, Abbott
Amerigo Vespucci, Knoop	By Star and Compass, Wallace	Christopher Columbus, Ryan
Brendan the Navigator, Fritz	Captain Cook, Syme	Christopher Columbus, Young
Camp and Trail in Early American History, Dickson	Captain John Smith, Leighton	Columbus: The Catholic
Christopher Columbus, Judson	Cartier: Finder of the St. Lawrence, Symer	Explorers and Travellers, Greely
Christopher Columbus, Kaufman	Children's Stories in American History, Wight	Ferdinand de Soto, Abbott
Christopher Columbus, Krensky	Chistopher Columbus, Stapley	Heroes of Discovery in America, Morris
Christopher Columbus: Sailor and Dreamer, Bailey	Columbus, Syme	Man Against the Elements: Adolphus W. Greely, Werstein
Columbus, d'Aulaire	Columbus and Magellan, Lawler	Story of Christopher Columbus, Moore
De Soto: Child of the Sun, Steele	Days of the Discoverers, Lamprey	The Sea King: Sir Francis Drake, Marrin
Discovers and Explorers, Shaw	DeSoto, Syme	The Sword and the Compass, Leighton
Elfwyn's Saga, Wisniewski	Discovers of the New World, Berger	Voyages of Christopher Columbus, Columbus
Famous Discoverers and Explorers of America, Johnson	Explorers and Settlers, Barstow	Young Folks' Book of American Explorers, Higginson
Great Explorers, Buckley	Ferdinand Magellan	
Henry the Explorer, Taylor	George M. Towle Heroes of History	**Forgotten Classics:**
History with a Match, van Loon	Drake	F1-125 Columbus From His Own Letters and Journals
John Smith, Graves	Magellan	
Leif the Lucky, Berry	Pizarro	
Leif the Lucky, d'Aulaire	Raleigh	
Leif the Lucky: Discoverer of America, Berry	Vasco de Gama	
Matthew Henson: Arctic Hero, Ripley	Great Adventures that Changed the World	
Pocahontas and the Strangers, Bulla	Indian Sketches: Pere Marquette, Hulst	
Pocahontas: Young Peacemaker, Gourse	Into the Unknown, Henson	
Ponce de Leon, Blassingame	John Cabot and His Son Sebastian, Syme	
Sir Francis Drake, Foster	John Smith of Virginia, Syme	
Story of Christopher Columbus for Little Children, Harrison	Juan Ponce de Leon, Baker	
The Conquest of the Atlantic, d'Aulaire	Magellan, Syme	
The Double Life of Pocahontas, Fritz	Magellan: First Around the World, Syme	
The Magic Fountain, Lowitz	Pioneer Spaniards in N. America, Johnson	
The Men Who Found America, Hutchinson	Pioneers on Land and Sea, McMurry	
The Story of Pocahontas and Captain John Smith, Smith	Pocahontas and Captain John Smith	
The True Story of Columbus, Brooks	Sir Walter Raleigh, Baker	
The World of Captain John Smith, Foster	Story of the Discovery of the New World, Saunder	
The World of Columbus and Sons, Foster	The Life of Christopher Columbus, Hale	
Viking Adventure, Bulla	The Life of Chris. Columbus, Crompton	
Viking Tales, Hall	The Sea King: Sir Francis Drake, Marrin	
Where Do You Think You're Going, Christopher Columbus?, Fritz	The Story of Columbus, Seelye	
Year of Columbus 1492, Foster	The Story of Sir Francis Drake, Elton	
	The Story of Sir Walter Raleigh, Kelly	
Forgotten Classics:	The Story of the Vikings, MacGregor	
The True Story of Columbus, Brooks	The Voyages of Christopher Columbus	
F11-20 Balboa and Magellan	The Voyages of Henry Hudson	
F11-1 Christopher Columbus	Travellers and Explorers, Peary	
	Vancouver, Syme	
	Vasco de Gama, Syme	
	Walter Raleigh, Syme	
	Forgotten Classics:	
	W11-321 A New World	

1500s: AGE OF EXPLORATION		
ELEMENTARY	**MIDDLE SCHOOL**	**HIGH SCHOOL**
☐ F11-36 Jacques Carter	☐ W11-329 Christopher Columbus	
☐ F11-11 John Cabot Americus Vespucius		
☐ F11-41 Sir Walter Raleigh		
☐ F11-32 Ponce de Leon de Soto		
☐ F11-38 Sir Francis Drake		
My Book House:		
☐ 5-112 Columbus-Poems		
Junior Classics:		
☐ 6-260 Columbus Looks for China and Finds America		

1500s: AGE OF EXPLORATION		
ADDITIONAL BOOKS		
ELEMENTARY	**MIDDLE SCHOOL**	**HIGH SCHOOL**

CHINA / ASIA

ELEMENTARY	MIDDLE SCHOOL	HIGH SCHOOL
8000 Stones, Wolkstein	A Boy of Old Japan, Van Bergen	A Little History of China, Brebner
A Chinese Wonder Book, Pitman	A Single Shard, Park	America's First Trained Nurse, Baker
A Grain of Rice, Pittman	Adventures of Two Youths in a Journey	Anna and the King of Siam, Landon
A Time of Golden Dragons, Zhang	to Japan and China, Knox	China's Story in Myth, Legend, Art and
A Treasury of Wisdom	Children of China, Brown	Annals, Griffis
All the Way to Lhasa	China's Long March, Fritz	Fifty-Five Days of Terror, Hirschfield
Beautiful Warrior, McCully	Clipper Ship Days, Jennings	First They Killed My Father, Ung
Children of Cathay, Beckingsale	Confucius: The Golden Rule, Freedman	Genghis Khan, Abbott
Chinese Children's Favorite Stories, Yip	Genghis Khan and the Mongo Horde, Lamb	Historical Tales: Japan/China, Morris
Chinese Fables and Folk Stories, Davis	Gladys Aylward, Aylward	Keys of the Kingdom, Cronin
Chinese Fairy Tales, Giles	He Went with March Polo, Kent	I Was There…, White
Chinese Fairy Tales, Goulden	Homesick, Fritz	In the Mikado's Service, Griffis
Chinese Folk-lore Tales, MacGowan	House of 60 Fathers, deJong	Mao Tse-Tung and His China, Marrin
Crow Boy, Yashima	Marco Polo, Komroff	Marco Polo, Komroff
Dream-of-Jade, Alexander	No Mountain Too High, Grant	Our Boys in China, French
Favorite Fairy Tales Told in Japan,	Pageant of Chinese History, Seeger	Our Oriental Heritage, Duran
Haviland	Red Scarf Girl, Ji-Li-Jiang	Peeps Into China, Phillips
Folk Tales from Tibet, O'Connor	The Adventures and Discoveries of	Stories and Myths of Eight Immortals
Grandfather Tang's Story, Tomperl	Marco Polo, Walsh	The Earth is the Lord's, Caldwell
He Went With Marco Polo, Kent	The Adventures of Marco Polo, Atherton	The Good Earth, Buck
Homesick: My Own Story, Fritz	The Adventures of Marco Polo, Freedman	The Making of Modern China, Lattimor
Japanese Fairy Tales, Hearn	The Man Who Changed China, Buck	The Rent Collector, Wright
Japanese Fairy Tales, Williston	The Remarkable Journey of Prince Jen,	The Small Woman, Burgess
Japanese Fairy World, Griffis	Alexander	The Story of China, Douglas
Japanese Folk Stories, Nixon-Roulet	The Samurai's Tale, Haugaard	The Story of Japan, Murray
Li Lun: Lad of Courage, Treffinger	The Story of China, Van Bergen	The Story of Marco Polo, Brooks
Little Pear, Lattimore	The Travels of Marco Polo for Boys	The Travels of Marco Polo, Komroff
Little Plum, Godden	and Girls, Knox	The Vigil of a Nation, Yutang
Little Silk, Ayer	When I Was Boy in Japan, Shioya	The World's Story, Tappan
Marco Polo, Ceserani	Young Fu of the Upper Yangtze, Lewis	Warriors of Old Japan, Ozaki
Marco Polo, Weir	Young People's Story of the Orient, Hillyer	Wild Swans, Chang
Ming-Lo Moves the Mountain, Lobel		
Miss Happiness and Miss Flower, Godd	**Forgotten Classics:**	**Forgotten Classics:**
Our Little Chinese Cousin, Headland	W1-1 Adventures of Marco Polo	G9-110 Had You Been Born a
Starry River by the Sky, Lin	W11-541 Story of China and Japan	Confucionist
Tales from Cultures Near and Far		G9-139 Had You Been Born a Shintoist
The Cat Who Went to Heaven,	**Junior Classics:**	N9-12 Chinese Music
Coatsworth	9-22 Service at the Point of a Rifle	W12-277 Confucius
The Chi'i-Lin Purse, Fang		
The Children of China, Zhang		
The Emperor and the Kite, Yolen		
The Five Chinese Brothers, Bishop		
The Honorable Crimson Tree, Ferris		
The Last Dragon, Nunes		
The Magic Wings, Wolkstein		
The Nightingale, Andersen		
The Nightingale, Pinckney		
The Picture Story of China, Hahn		
The Story of Ping, Flack		
The Tale of the Mandarin Ducks, Paterson		
The Tale of the Shining Princess		
The Warrior and the Wiseman,		
Wiskniewski		
Three Strong Women, Stamm		
Tikki-Tikki-Tembo, Mosel		

CHINA / ASIA		
ELEMENTARY	**MIDDLE SCHOOL**	**HIGH SCHOOL**
☐ Wah Sing, Campbell		
☐ When I was a Boy in China, Lee		
☐ Where the Mountains Meet the Moon, Lin		
☐ Yen-Foh, a Chinese Boy, Eldridge		
Forgotten Classics:		
☐ S3-217 The Fisher Boy		
☐ S3-213 The Stone-Cutter		
☐ S6-169 The King and His Hawk		
My Book House:		
☐ 1-76 Chiense Nursery Rhymes		
☐ 1-78 Japanese Lullaby		
☐ 3-164 Little Maid of Far Japan		
☐ 3-165 The Tongue-Cut Sparrow		
☐ 4-137 The Girl Who Used Her Wits		
☐ 6-191 Pigling and Her Proud Sister		
☐ 6-222 The Moon Maiden		
Junior Classics:		
☐ 1-270 The Five Chinese Brothers		
☐ 1-298 How Little Pear Went to the Fair		
☐ 2-178 Yi-Chang and the Haunted House		
☐ 2-191 The Tongue-Cut Sparrow		
☐ 2-198 Chop-Sticks		
☐ 4-163 Li Lun Lad of Courage		
☐ 4-205 The Big Wave		
☐ 4-310 Wild Elephant Raid from Burma Boy		

CHINA / ASIA		
ADDITIONAL BOOKS		
ELEMENTARY	MIDDLE SCHOOL	HIGH SCHOOL

INDIA

ELEMENTARY	MIDDLE SCHOOL	HIGH SCHOOL
A Little Princess, Burnett	Adventures of Two Young in a Journey to Ceylon and India, Knox	Freedom's Battles, Gandhi
Balarama: The Royal Elephant, Lewin	Amy Carmichael, Wellman	Gandhi, Coolidge
Ceylon, Clark	At the Point of Bayonet, Henty	Gandhi: An Autobiography
Cradle Tales of Hinduism	Cobras Cows and Courage, Bothwell	India, Steele
Fairy Tales of India, Turnbull	Daughter of the Mountains, Rankin	India Through the Ages, Steele
Gift of the Forest, Singh	Exploring the Himalaya, Douglas	Kim, Kipling
Home Life in India, Finnemore	Gandhi: Fighter Without a Sword, Eaton	Mahatma Gandhi, Faber
India, Finnemore	Gandhi: Peaceful Fighter, Montgomery	Mooltiki, Godden
Indian Fairy Tales, Jacobs	In Times of Peril, Henty	Our Oriental Heritage, Durant
Indian Fairy Tales, Thornhill	India, Surridge	Some Great Lives of Modern India, Turnball
Indian Fairy Tales, Stokes	Kim, Kipling	The Animal World of India, Bothwell
Jataka Tales Retold, Babbitt	Kipling: Storyteller of East & West, Kamen	The Orphan Keeper, Wright
Just So Stories, Kipling	Mother Teresa, Wellman	The Rising Temper of the East, Hunt
Kari the Elephant, Mukerji	Omen for a Princess, Bothwell	The Story of British India, Frazer
Little Black Sambo, Brannerman	Rujub the Juggle, Henty	The Story of Buddhist India, David
Little Flute Player, Bothwell	Tales from India, Gray	The Story of India, Boulger
Manjhi Moves a Mountain, Churnin	Teresa of Calcutta, Wilson	The Story of Medieval India, Lane-Poo
Once a Mouse, Brown	The First Book of Pakistan, Bothwell	The Story of Vedic India, Ragozin
One Grain of Rice, Demi	The Lost Heir, Henty	
Our Little Hindu Cousin, McManus	The Promise of a Rose, Bothwell	**Forgotten Classics:**
Rikki-Tivvi-Tavi, Kipling	The Story of Lord Clive, Lang	G9-7 Had You Been Born a Hindu
River Boy of Kashmir, Bothwell	The Tiger of Mysore, Henty	G9-79 Had You Been Born a Buddhist
Sacred River, Lewin	Through the Sikh War, Henty	W12-285 Prince Siddartha
Search for a Golden Bird, Bothwell	Two Under the Indian Sun, Godden	
Star of India, Bothwell	With Clive in India, Henty	
Tales of the Punjab, Steele		
The Blind Man and the Elephant		
The Hidden Treasure, Bothwell	**Forgotten Classics:**	
The Holy Man's Secret, Bothwell	G9-63 Buddha	
The Jungle Book, Kipling	N11-17 All Hail the Power	
The Secret Garden, Burnett	S10-4 The Gift of Poesy	
The Stonecutter, Newton	W1-235 India's Story	
Three Bags of Gold, Kunhappa	W11-429 The Story of India	

Forgotten Classics:
- S3-227 The Timid Hare
- S3-231 Faithful Prince
- S3-241 The Ruby Prince
- S5-99 The King Who Saw Truth
- S6-230 William Makepeace Thackery
- S9-8 The Story of Kablu
- S11-72 Red Thread of Courage
- S11-82 The Quails
- S11-263 A Lesson for Kings

Junior Classics:
- 8-38 Fighter Without a Sword: Ghandi

My Book House:
- 1-79 East Indian Rhymes
- 2-118 Rama and the Tigers
- 2-178 The Turtle Who Could Not Stop Talking
- 3-76 The Foolish Timid Little Hare
- 5-182 Mowgli's Brothers
- 9-129 The Ballad of East and West by Kipling

INDIA		
ELEMENTARY	**MIDDLE SCHOOL**	**HIGH SCHOOL**
☐ 10-175 The Exile of Rama From the Ramayana		
Junior Classics:		
☐ 2-15 Jataka Tales		
☐ 2-212 The Gold-Giving Serpent		
☐ 2-349 The Elephant's Child		
☐ 4-23 Gift of the Forest		

SCANDINAVIA

ELEMENTARY	MIDDLE SCHOOL	HIGH SCHOOL
Baldur and Mistletoe, Hodges	A Slave's Tale, Haugaard	Champion of World Peace, Levine
Children of Northlights, d'Aulaire	Denmark, Thomson	Finland a Little Land, Gray
D'Aulaire's Book of Norse Myths	Doctor's Boy, Anckarsvard	Heroic Finland, Hinshaw
D'Aulaire's Trolls	Door to the North, Coatsworth	Historical Tales: Scandinavia, Morris
East o' the Sun, Thorne-Thomson	Everyday Life in Viking Times, Martell	Myths of the Norsemen, Guerber
East o' the Sun, Asbjornsen	Finland, Thomson	Papa's Wife, Bjorn
Fairy Tales from the Swedish, Djurklo	Hakon of Rogen's Saga, Haugaard	Roald Amundsen, Kugelmass
Favorite Fairy Tales - Denmark, Haviland	Hans Christian Andersen, Montgomery	The Heroes of Asgard, Keary
Favorite Fairy Tales - Norway, Haviland	Iceland, Leith	The Story of Norway, Boyesen
Favorite Fairy Tales - Sweden, Haviland	Jenny Lind Sang Here, Kielty	The World's Story 8, Tappan
Flicka Ricka and Dicka, Lindman	Norse Stories Retold, Mabie	
Further Adventures of Nils, Lagerlof	Norway, Mockler-Ferryman	**Forgotten Classics:**
Hans Christian Andersen 1, Stickney	Soldier of Peace, Hershey	N10-328 Edvard Grieg
Hans Christian Anderse 2, Stickney	Sweden, Liddle	N11-243 Song Sung
Hans Christian Andersen Fairy Tales	The Boy Travellers in N. Europe, Knox	W12-88 Ole Bull
Heroes in Mythology	The Picture Story of Denmark, O'Neill	
In the Days of Giants, Brown	The Story of Norway, Sidgwick	**Delphian Course:**
Jolly Calle, Nyblom	The Swedish Nightingale, Kyle	5:177-200 Norse Stories
Little Greta of Denmark, Bailey		7:297-316 Norwegian Drama
Little Mermaids and Ugly Ducklings, Sp	**Forgotten Classics:**	
Might Mikko, Fillmore	G10-62 Jacob Riis	
Norse Tales Retold, Freeman	G12-76 Hans Christian Andersen	
Ola, d'Aulaire	W11-215 Days of the Northmen	
Our Little Norwegian Cousin, Wade	W12-228 Jacob Riis	
Pelle's New Suit, Bestow		
Pippi Longstocking, Lindgren		
Princess and the Pea		
Scandinavian Folk/Fairy Tales, Booss		
Snow Treasure, McSwigan		
Snipp Snapp Snurr, Lindman		
Stories from Hans Andersen, Dulac		
Stories from Old Germany, Pratt		
Stories of Norse Heroes, Wilmot-Buxton		
Tales from a Finnish Tupa, Bowman		
The Art Work of Carl Larsson		
A Family		
A Home		
A Farm		
The Children of Odin, Colum		
The Danish Fairy Book, Stoebe		
The Diamond Bird, Wahlenberg		
The Emperor's New Clothes, Andersen		
The Land of Enchantment, Rackham		
The Legend of Christmas Rose, Lagerlof		
The Little Match Girl, Andersen		
The Little Match Girl, Pinkney		
The Little Silver House, Lindquist		
The Nightingale, Andersen		
The Nightingale, Ibatoulline		
The Nightingale, Pinkney		
The Saucepan Journey, Unnerstad		
The Snow Queen, Andersen		
The Snow Queen, Ibatoulline		
The Snow Queen, Lynch		
The Steadfast Tin Soldier, Andersen		

SCANDINAVIA		
ELEMENTARY	MIDDLE SCHOOL	HIGH SCHOOL
☐ The Swedish Fairy Book, Stoebe		
☐ The Three Billy Goats Gruff, Brown		
☐ The Ugly Duckling, Andersen		
☐ The Value of Fantasy, Johnson		
☐ The Wonderful Adventures of Nils, Lagerlof		
☐ The Young Hans Andersen, Spink		
☐ Thumbelina, Andersen		
☐ Thumbelina, Ibatoulline		

Forgotten Classics:

☐ G2-293 Thorvaldsen		
☐ G8-318 Jenny Lind		
☐ S3-167 Scandinavian Fairy Tales		
☐ S5-103 The Story of Beowulf		
☐ S5-285 Frithiof		
☐ S6-6 Jenny Lind		
☐ S6-135 King Canute and the Seashore		
☐ S6-156 The Ungrateful Soldier		
☐ S12-49 Life & Adventures of Santa Claus		

My Book House:

☐ 1-60 Norse Nursery Rhymes		
☐ 1-74 Swedish Rhymes		
☐ 1-144 Rhymes of Finland		
☐ 1-151 Kalevala Land of Heroes		
☐ 1-168 The Little Girls and the New Dress		
☐ 1-206 The Children and the Beart		
☐ 2-26 Old Shut-Eyes the Sandman		
☐ 2-30 Little Gustava		
☐ 2-47 Johnny and the Three Goats		
☐ 2-131 The Ugly Duckling		
☐ 2-141 A Swedish Evening		
☐ 2-145 The Sheep and the Pig That Made a Home		
☐ 3-12 The Cap That Mother Made		
☐ 3-137 Oeyvind and Marit		
☐ 3-204 The Doll Under the Briar Rosebush		
☐ 4-24 Doll i' the Grass		
☐ 4-45 Else and the Ten Elves		
☐ 5-144 Why the Sea Is Salt		
☐ 5-157 Boots and His Brothers		
☐ 6-80 The Princess on the Glass Hill		
☐ 6-98 The Squire's Bride		
☐ 7-48 The Snow Queen		
☐ 7-31 East o' the Sun and West o' the Moon		
☐ 9-164 Thor's Journey to Jotunheim		
☐ 9-172 The Stealing of Iduna		
☐ 10-130 Frithjof the Viking		

Junior Classics:

☐ 1-45 Three Billy Goats Gruff		

SCANDINAVIA		
ELEMENTARY	MIDDLE SCHOOL	HIGH SCHOOL
☐ 4-48 The Saucepan Journey		
☐ 4-142 Eskimo Boy		
☐ 4-323 Snow Treasure		
☐ 7-161 Thunder of the Gods		
☐ 7-180 The Last Adventure		
☐ 8-197 The Great Adventure: Fridtjof Nansen		

SOUTH SEAS / AUSTRALIA

ELEMENTARY	MIDDLE SCHOOL	HIGH SCHOOL
Ajax the Golden Dog, Patchett	A Final Reckoning, Henty	As I Have Loved You, de Ruyter
Australasia, Pratt	Call It Courage, Sperry	Cannibal Adventure, Price
Call It Courage, Sperry	Captain Cook, Syme	Giant of the Atom, McKown
Last Queen of Hawaii, Wilson	Hawaii Gem of the Pacific, Lewis	Hawaii's Queen, Stone
Our Little Australian Cousin, Nixon-Roulet	Healing Warrior, Crofford	Kon-Tiki, Heyerdahl
	Last Queen of Hawaii, Wilson	South Sea Adventure, Price
Forgotten Classics:	Maori and Settler, Henty	The Early Settlers, Strang
G4-230 James Chalmers	She Never looked Back, Epstein	The Story of Australasia, Tregarthen
	The Story of Australia, Day	The World's Story, Tappan
My Book House:	The Story of Captain Cook, Lang	Underwater Adventure, Price
2-176 A Boy in the Island of Bali	The Story of Hawaii, Alexander	Volcano Adventures, Price
3-59 The Battle of the Firefly & the Apes	The Story of Jon G. Paton	
3-81 The Right Time to Laugh		
6-202 Aruman A Hero of Java	**Forgotten Classics:**	
7-26 The Trial by Fire	G4-175 John G. Paton	
	G4-236 Chalmers the Friend	
Junior Classics:		
4-1 Ajax the Golden Dog		
9-306 Call It Courage		

SOUTH SEAS / AUSTRALIA		
ADDITIONAL BOOKS		
ELEMENTARY	MIDDLE SCHOOL	HIGH SCHOOL

STARS		
ELEMENTARY	**MIDDLE SCHOOL**	**HIGH SCHOOL**
☐ All About the Stars, White	☐ Our Starland, Wylie	☐ Astronomy for Young Folks, Lewis
☐ Conquest of the Sky	☐ Secrets of the Stars, McFee	☐ Comets, Elson
☐ Find the Constellations, Rey	☐ The Friendly Stars, Martin	☐ Curiosities of the Sky, Serviss
☐ Galileo and the Stargazers	☐ The Handbook of Nature Study, Comstock	☐ Star-land, Ball
☐ Good Night Moon, Brown	☐ The Stars, Rey	☐ Stars in Song and Legend, Porter
☐ Many Moons, Thurber	☐ The Stars and Their Stories, Griffith	☐ Sunshine, Johnson
☐ Maria Mitchell Stargazer, Wilkies	☐ The Young Folks' Astronomy, Champlain	☐ The Book of Stars, Collins
☐ Maria's Comet, Hopkinson	☐ This Wonderful Universe, Giberne	☐ The Star Pocket Book, Weatherhead
☐ Starry Messenger, Sis	☐ Wonder Stories, Miller	☐ The Wonder Book of the Atmosphere, Houston
☐ The Children's Book of Stars, Mitton		
☐ The Little Prince, de Saint-Exupery		
☐ The Storyland of Stars, Pratt		
☐ The Young Astronomer, Carlisle		

Forgotten Classics:
☐ Stories of the Stars

My Book House:
☐ 2-40 Moon So Round and Yellow
☐ 2-83 The Star

Junior Classics:
☐ 9-355 Circum and Terra

SETTLING THE 13 COLONIES		
ELEMENTARY	**MIDDLE SCHOOL**	**HIGH SCHOOL**
☐ A Little Maid of Massachusetts Colony, Curtis	Colonial Living, Tunis	☐ Bradford's History 'Of Plymouth Plantation'
☐ A Little Maid of Old Maine, Curtis	Days of the Colonists, Lamprey	☐ Colonial Folkways, Andrews
☐ A Little Maid of Philadelphia, Turner	Fifty Photographic Views of Plymouth	☐ Georgia History Stories, Chappell
☐ A Little Maid of PrinceTown, Curtis	John Smith of Virginia, Syme	☐ James Oglethorpe, Cooper
☐ A Little Maid of Virginia, Curtis	Life in Colonial America, Speare	☐ Miles Standish, Abbott
☐ A Lion to Guard Us, Bulla	Life in the 18th Century, Eggleston	☐ New Light on the Pilgrim Story, Mason
☐ Arthur and the Golden Guinea, Berwick	Mary of the Mayflower, Stone	☐ Peter Stuyvesant, Abbott
☐ Boy on the Mayflower, Vinton	Maryland Adventure, Long	☐ Rock of Freedom, Gerson
☐ Calvert of Maryland, Otis	Peter Stuyvesant of Old NY, Crouse	☐ Saints and Strangers, Willison
☐ Child Life in the Colonies, Baker	Roanoke, Levitin	☐ Stories of New Jersey, Stockton
☐ Finding Providence, Avi	Sea Venture, Doherty	☐ Story of the Pilgrim Fathers, Arber
☐ Getting to Know Virginia, Sutton	Stories of Georgia, Harris	☐ The Courtship of Miles Standish, Longfellow
☐ Heroes of Early Amer. History, Rowland	Stories of Pennsylvania, Walton	
☐ Huckleberry Hill, Gemming	Stories of the Old Dominion, Cooke	☐ The Devil's Shadow, Alderman
☐ If You Lived in Colonial Times, McGovern	☐ The Argonauts of Faith, Mathews	☐ The Making of Virginia, Drake
☐ If You Sailed on Mayflower, McGovern	☐ The First Year, Meadowcroft	☐ The Scarlet Letter, Hawthorne
☐ John Alden: Steadfast Pilgrim, Edwards	☐ The Landing of the Pilgrims, Daugherty	☐ The Story of Roger Williams, Leighton
☐ John Billington, Bulla	☐ The Pilot of the Mayflower, Butterworth	☐ The Story of the Pilgrim Family, Alden
☐ Letters from Colonial Children, Tappan	☐ The Story of Connecticut, Mills	☐ The Tree That Saved Connecticut
☐ Little John of New England, Brandeis	☐ The Story of the Thirteenth Colonies, Alderman	☐ William Penn, Holland
☐ Mary of Plymouth, Otis	☐ The Witch of Blackbird Pond, Speare	
☐ Maryland: Stories of Her People, Passano	☐ The Witchcraft of Salem Village, Jackson	**Forgotten Classics:**
☐ N.C. Wyeth's Pilgrims	☐ William Bradford, Doherty	☐ F2-283 'Of Plymouth Plantation'
☐ New Amsterdam, Emerson	☐ William Penn: Quaker Colonist, Doherty	
☐ Once Upon a Time in Connecticut, Newton	☐ William Penn's Dream House, Peare	
	☐ Young Folks History Boston, Butterworth	
☐ On Plymouth Rock, Drake	☐ Zeke and the Fisher Cat, Voight	
☐ Once Upon a Time in Delaware, Pyle		
☐ Palmetto Stories, Means	**Forgotten Classics:**	
☐ Peter of Amsterdam, Otis	☐ F2-101 Argonauts of Faith	
☐ Pilgrim Stories, Pumphrey	☐ F12-18 Words of Comfort	
☐ Pilgrims and Puritans, Tiffany	☐ W11-391 The Pilgrim Fathers	
☐ Richard of Jamestown, Otis		
☐ Rip Van Winkle, Irving		
☐ Roger Williams, Peterson		
☐ Roger Williams: Defender, Edwards		
☐ Ruth of Boston, Otis		
☐ Settlers on a Strange Shore, McCall		
☐ Slumps Grunts & Snickerdoodles, Perl		
☐ Squanto and the Miracle of Thanksgiving, Metaxas		
☐ Squanto Friend of the Pilgrims, Bulla		
☐ Squanto Indian Adventurer, Graff		
☐ Stephen of Philadelphia, Otis		
☐ Stories from Virginia History, Magill		
☐ Stories of Colonial Children, Pratt		
☐ Stories of the Old Bay State, Brooks		
☐ Stories of the Pilgrims, Usher		
☐ The Boy Who Fell Off the Mayflower, Lynch		
☐ The Courage of Sarah Noble, Dagliesh		
☐ The First Thanksgiving, George		
☐ The First Thanksgiving, Hayward		
☐ The Legend of Sleepy Hollow, Irving		

SETTLING THE 13 COLONIES		
ELEMENTARY	**MIDDLE SCHOOL**	**HIGH SCHOOL**
☐ The Lost Colony of Roanoke, Fritz		
☐ The Silver Mace, Petersham		
☐ The Skippack School, de Angeli		
☐ The Story of Pocahontas, Smith		
☐ The Story of the Empire State, Southworth		
☐ The Story of the Mayflower Compact, Richards		
☐ The Story of the New England Whalers, Stein		
☐ The Story of New Netherlands, Griffis		
☐ The Story of the Old North State, Connor		
☐ The Story of the Pilgrims, Stein		
☐ The Thanksgiving Story, Dagliesh		
☐ The World of William Penn, Foster		
☐ This Dear Bought Land, Latham		
☐ We Were There With the Mayflower Pilgrims, Webb		
☐ Who's Saying What in Jamestown?, Fritz		
☐ Who's That Stepping on Plymouth Rock?, Fritz		
☐ World & Play in Colonial Days, MacElroy		

Forgotten Classics:

- ☐ F2-1 Story of Pilgrims for Children
- ☐ F11-46 Stories of Early Virginia
- ☐ F11-57 Stories of Early Maryland
- ☐ F11-61 Stories of Early New England
- ☐ F11-76 Stories of Early New York
- ☐ F11-85 Stories of Early Pennsylvania
- ☐ F11-89 Stories of Georgia
- ☐ F11-92 Life in Early Colonial Days
- ☐ F12-6 A Fire to Light the Way
- ☐ F12-9 A Mother's Daring Rescue
- ☐ F12-11 William Penn
- ☐ S9-143 Story of Ezekiel Fuller
- ☐ S9-316 Virginia Wife Market
- ☐ S9-323 Prayer Answered

My Book House:

- ☐ 5-113 The First Thanksgiving Day
- ☐ 11-107 Wolfert Webber

Junior Classics:

- ☐ 1-82 American Rhymes
- ☐ 1-116 Pennsylvania Dutch Rhymes
- ☐ 6-332 The First Thanksiving
- ☐ 9-317 The Witch Trial

SETTLING THE 13 COLONIES		
ADDITIONAL BOOKS		
ELEMENTARY	MIDDLE SCHOOL	HIGH SCHOOL

NETHERLANDS

ELEMENTARY	MIDDLE SCHOOL	HIGH SCHOOL
☐ Belgium Fairy Tales, Haviland	☐ Anne Frank, Frank	☐ A Dutch Boy Fifty Years After, Bok
☐ Boxes for Katje, Fleming	☐ By Pike and Dyke, Henty	☐ Belgium, Morris
☐ Dutch Fairy Tales - Young People, Griffis	☐ Corrie Ten Boom, Wellman	☐ Belgium, Omond
☐ Hana In the Time of the Tulips, Noyes	☐ Golden Thread, Schrier	☐ Brave Little Holland, Griffis
☐ Hans Brinker or The Silver Skates, Dodge	☐ Holland, Finnemore	☐ Famous Days and Deeds in Holland
☐ Jounrey from Peppermint Street, deJong	☐ Holland, Jungman	and Belgium, Morris
☐ Little Philippe of Belgium, Brandeis	☐ Of Dikes and Windmills, Spier	☐ Hortense, Abbott
☐ Shadrach, deJong	☐ Stories from Dutch History, Dawsom	☐ Rembrandt, Breal
☐ Story of Little Jan, Campbell	☐ The Boy Travellers in N. Europe, Knox	☐ Rembrandt, Hurll
☐ Tales Told in Holland, Miller	☐ The Netherlands, MacGregor	☐ Story of Dutch Painting, Caffin
☐ The Belgian Twins, Perkins	☐ Young People's History of Holland, Griffis	☐ The Hiding Place, Ten Boom
☐ The Boy Who Held Back the Sea, Hort		☐ The Story of Holland, Rogers
☐ The Dutch Twins, Perkins		☐ The World's Story V7, Tappan
☐ The Gentleman and Kitchen Maid, Stanley	**Forgotten Classics:**	☐ William the Silent, Miall
☐ The Land of Pluck, Dodge	☐ G6-70 William the Silent	
☐ The Picture Story of Holland, DeJong	☐ G12-169 Mary Mapes Dodge	**Forgotten Classics:**
☐ The Wheel on the School, deJong	☐ S9-282 Siege of Leyden	☐ N9-309 The Van Eycks & Their Followe
☐ The Young Artist, Locker	☐ S11-358 The Counter-Reformation	☐ N9-315 Rubens
☐ When I Was a Boy in Belgium, Jonkheere	☐ W2-3 Peeps at History: Holland	☐ N9-327 Van Dyck & Other Followers o
☐ When the Dikes Broke, Seymour	☐ W12-30 Troublesome Burghers	Rubens
	☐ W12-77 William the Silent	☐ N9-338 Rembrandt
Forgotten Classics:		☐ N9-349 A Group of Dutch Painters
☐ G5-17 Laurence Coster		☐ N9-355 Landscape and Marine Painter
☐ N12-25 Lohengrin		
☐ S1-23, 25 Van Dyck		**Delphian Course:**
☐ S1-170 de Hooch		☐ 9:46-63 Flemish Dutch Art
☐ S1-174 van der Meer		☐ 9:137-141 Belgium Art Galleries
☐ S1-179, 182, 184 Rembrandt		☐ 9:142-146 Art Galleries of Holland
☐ S4-57 The Boy Hero of Haarlem		
☐ S12-143 The Christmas Porringer		

My Book House:
- ☐ 1-126 Dutch Nursery Rhymes
- ☐ 2-141 O Belgian Morning
- ☐ 2-143 How the Finch Got Her Colors
- ☐ 2-164 Little Hanswort

Junior Classics:
- ☐ 1-312 The Little Old Woman Who Uses Her Head
- ☐ 4-184 The Wheel on the School
- ☐ 10-394 Excerpt from Hans Brinker

NETHERLANDS		
ADDITIONAL BOOKS		
ELEMENTARY	**MIDDLE SCHOOL**	**HIGH SCHOOL**

SPAIN / SPANISH MAIN

ELEMENTARY	MIDDLE SCHOOL	HIGH SCHOOL
Carmen: The Story of Bizet's Opera, Bizet	Across the Spanish Main, Collingwood	Captain William Kidd, Abbott
Don Quixote, Cervantes (Baldwin)	Among Malay Pirates, Henty	Historical Tales: Spain, Morris
Don Quixote, Cervantes (Bogin)	Buccaneers and Pirates, Stockton	In the Track of the Moors, Fitzgerald
Don Quixote, Cervantes (Parry)	Famous Pirates of New World, Whipple	King Philip, Abbott
Don Quixote & Sancho Panchez, Hodges	Held Fast for England, Henty	Murillo, Calvert
El Cid, McCaughrean	Howard Pyle's Book of Pirates	Royal Palaces of Spain, Calvert
Fairy Tales from Spain, Escamez	I Juan de Pareja, de Trevino	Spain's Golden Queen Isabella, Noble
Favorite Fairy Tales Told in Spain, Haviland	Queen Elizabeth and the Spanish Armada, Winwar	Terror of the Spanish Main, Marrin
Getting to Know Spain, Day		The Adventures of Don Quixote, Cohe
In Sunny Spain with Pilarica and Rafael, Bates	Sir Henry Morgan Buccaneer, Syme	The Christian Recovery of Spain, Watts
	Spain, Browne	The History of Don Quixote, Dore
Look Out for Pirates!, Vinton	Stories of the Spanish Main, Stockton	The Prado, Calvert
Our Little Spanish Cousin, Nixon-Roulet	Tales of Enchantment from Spain, Eells	The Sea Rovers, Marrin
Peter Pan, Barrie	Teddy Roosevelt and His Rough Riders, Castor	The Story of Spain, Hale
Pirate's Promise, Bulla		The Story of Spanish Painting, Velasqu
Pirates and Privateers, McCall	Terror of the Spanish Main, Marrin	The Story of the Christians and Moors
Tales from the Alhambra, Brower	The Barbary Pirates, Forester	of Spain, Yonge
Tales from the Alhambra, Irving	The Bravest of the Brave, Henty	The Story of the Moors in Spain, Lane
Tales from Culture Near and Far: Renaissance Spain	The Cornet of Horse, Henty	The Life and Achievenements of Don
	The History of Spain for Young Persons, Bennett	Quixote, Cervantes
The Book of Pirates, Hague	The Three Golden Oranges, Bogge	The World's Story V5, Tappan
The Little Spanish Dancer, Brandeis	The True Story of Sir Francis Drake: Privateer, Holwood	Velasquez, Stevenson
The Queen's Pirate		West Indies and the Spanish Main, Rodway
The Story of Ferdinand, Leaf	The Young Buglers, Henty	
The Story of the Cid for Young People, Wilson	With the British Legion, Henty	**Forgotten Classics:**
		N9-276 Glimpse at Moorish Art
Treasure Island, Stevenson (Rhead)	**Forgotten Classics:**	N9-283 Early Spanish Painting
Treasure Island, Stevenson (Weiss)	S5-273 The Cid	N9-287 Velasquez
Treasure Island, Stevenson (Wyeth)	S9-304 Invincible Armada	N9-296 Murillo
Where the Flame Trees Bloom, Ada	W2-95 Child's History of Spain	
	W11-370 England and Spain	**Delphian Course:**
Forgotten Classics:	W12-106 Malibran the Great Singer	5:126-145 Spanish Literature-El Cid
G2-281 Murillo		6:222-268 Spanish Literature of the
S1-33 Velasquez		Renaissance
S1-99 Murillo		9:147-150 The Prado-Art Gallery of
S9-126 Story of Roger		Spain
S10-13 Don Quixote for Children		

My Book House:
- 1-64 Spanish Nursery Rhymes
- 6-92 The Three Wishes
- 8-35 Sea-Fever
- 10-108 The Story of the Cid
- 11-90 The Adventures of Don Quixote

Junior Classics:
- 2-137 Chick Chick Halfchick
- 2-143 Tonino and the Fairies
- 9-1 Head Winds and a Rough Sea
- 10-173 Excerpt from Don Quixote
- 10-229 Excerpt from Treasure Island

SPAIN / SPANISH MAIN		
ADDITIONAL BOOKS		
ELEMENTARY	MIDDLE SCHOOL	HIGH SCHOOL

OCEAN		
ELEMENTARY	**MIDDLE SCHOOL**	**HIGH SCHOOL**
☐ 20,000 Leagues Under the Sea, Verne	☐ 20,000 Leagues Under the Sea, Verne	☐ A Home in the Sea, Goodrich
☐ A Child's Treasury - Seaside Verse, Daniel	☐ Captains Courageous, Kipling	☐ Half Hours w/ Lower Animals, Holder
☐ A First Lesson in Natural History, Agassiz	☐ Carry On Mr. Bowditch, Latham	☐ The Sea and Its Wonders, Hall
☐ All About Undersea Exploration, Brindze	☐ Charting the Oceans, Brindze	☐ The Sea and Its Wonders, Kirby
☐ Along the Seashore, Buck	☐ Hurricanes: Monster Storms, Brindze	
☐ Carry On Mr. Bowditch	☐ River of the West, Sperry	
☐ Moby Dick, McCaughrean	☐ Sea-side Walks of a Naturalist, Houghton	
☐ One Morning in Maine, McCloskey	☐ West Coast Shells, Keep	
☐ Pagoo, Hollings		
☐ Rachel Carson Who Loved Sea, Latham		
☐ Shells and Sea-Life, Keep		
☐ Swimmy, Lionni		
☐ The Hall of Shells, Hardy		
☐ The Sea-Shore Book, Smith		
☐ The Water Babies, Kingsley		
☐ Tim and Ginger, Ardizzone		
☐ Time of Wonder, McCloskey		

Forgotten Classics:
☐ N2 Stories of the Ocean and Sea-Life

My Book House:
☐ 2-24 Wynken Blynken and Nod
☐ 2-105 The Bow That Bridges Heaven
☐ 2-139 Paper Boats
☐ 3-150 The Sea-Shelf
☐ 3-151 Clytie
☐ 3-170 The Mock Turtle's Song
☐ 3-210 Little Blue Apron
☐ 3-211 The Adventures of a Water Baby
☐ 4-183 Old Stormalong
☐ 8-134 The Enchanted Island
☐ 10-88 Excerpt 20,000 Leagues Under
     the Sea
☐ 10-365 Excerpt Captains Courageous

Junior Classics:
☐ 7-325 Stormalong
☐ 8-287 The Astrea to the Rescue

OCEAN		
ADDITIONAL BOOKS		
ELEMENTARY	MIDDLE SCHOOL	HIGH SCHOOL

MOVING TOWARDS INDEPENDENCE

ELEMENTARY	MIDDLE SCHOOL	HIGH SCHOOL
A Little Maid of Ticonderoga, Curtis	Abigail Adams: Witness to a Revolution, Bober	Benjamin Franklin, Abbott
Abigail Adams, Lakin	America's Paul Revere, Forbes	Biographical Sketichs of the Signers of the Declaration, Lossing
Abigail Adams Dear Partner, Peterson	Benjamin Franklin Inventor and Statesman, Stein	Dames and Daughters of Colonial Days, Brooks
Abigail Adams First Lady of Faith and Courage, Witter	Benjamin Franklin of Old Philadelphia	Early American History for Young Americans, Sabin
America's Paul Revere, Forbes	Calico Bush, Field	Jefferson, Padover
And Then What Happened Paul Revere?, Fritz	Carolina Gold, Best	John Adams and the American Revolution, Bowen
Ben and Me, Lawson	Carry on Mr. Bowditch, Lathan	Last of the Mohicans, Cooper
Ben Franklin and His First Kite, Krensky	Cromwell's Head, Coolidge	Our Country's Founders, Bennett
Ben Franklin and Magic Squares, Murphy	Early Thunder, Fritz	Sons of Liberty, Sutton
Benjamin Franklin, d'Aulaire	Ethan Allen and the Green Mtn Boys	Stepping Stones of American History
Benjamin Franklin Printer and Patriot, Weir	Give Me Liberty, Freedman	Struggle for a Continent, Marrin
	Give Me Liberty Speech of Patrick Henry	The Autobiography of Benjamin Frank
Bread and Butter Indian, Colver	Heroes of the Middle West, Catherwood	The Making of New England, Drake
Can't You Make Them Behave King George?, Fritz	Historic Americans, Brooks	The Making of the Ohio Valley States, Drake
Day of Glory, Spencer	Johnny Tremain, Forbes	
Founders of Our Country, Coe	Old Times in the Colonies, Coffin	The Real Benjamin Franklin, Allison
John Adams Speaks for Freedom, Hopkinson	Patsy Jefferson in Monticello, Vance	The Real Thomas Jefferson, Allison
	Paul Revere and the Minutemen, Fisher	The Works of Francis Parkman
Meet Thomas Jefferson, Barrett	Pioneer Histories of the Mississippi Valley, McMurry	Vol 1 Pioneers of France
Old Ben Franklin's Philadelphia, Rider	Poor Richard, Daugherty	Vol 2 Pioneers of France
Paul Revere's Ride, Corey	Roger Rangers and the French and Indian Wars, Smith	Vol 3 Jesuits in North America
Paul Revere's Ride, Parker		Vol 5 LaSalle
Paul Revere's Ride, Rand	The Boston Tea Party, Freedman	Vol 9 Half-Century of Conflict
Sam the Minuteman, Benchley	The Boys' Parkman, Hasbrouck	Vol 10 Half-Century of Conflict
Sons of Liberty, Sutton	The French and Indian War, Altsheler	Those Who Love, Stone
Slumps Grunts and Snickerdoodles, Perl	The Hunters of the Hills	
The Empire of Fur, Derleth	The Lords of the Wild	**Forgotten Classics:**
The Fourth of July, Phelan	The Masters of the Peaks	☐ G11-143 Abigail Adams
The Matchlock Gun, Edmonds	The Rulers of the Lakes	
The Mystery Candlestick, Bothwell	The Shadows of the North	
The Story of Benjamin Franklin, Davidson	The Sun of Quebec	
The Story of Lexington & Concord, Stein	The Signers, Fradin	
The Story of the Boston Tea Party	The Story of Benjamin Franklin, Meadowcraft	
The Story of Thomas Jefferson, Miers		
The Tales of Peter Parley About America, Goodrich	The Story of the Boston Massacre, Phelan	
	Thomas Paine, McKown	
The Whole History of Grandfather's Chair, Hawthorne	Ticonderoga The Story of a Fort, Lancaster	
	Tom Paine: Freedom's Apostle, Gurko	
Thomas Jefferson's America	Under the Liberty Tree, Otis	
Thomas Jefferson: Author of Independence, Colver	Young Nathan, Brown	
Thomas Jefferson: Champion of the People, Judson	**Forgotten Classics:**	
	☐ F12-78 Declaration of Independence	
We Were There at the Boston Tea Party, Webb	☐ F12-83 The Liberty Bell	
What's the Big Idea Ben Franklin?, Fritz	☐ G6-111 Benjamin Franklin	
Where Was Patrick Henry on the 29th of May?, Fritz	☐ G6-155 Sam Adams	
	☐ G6-168 John Adams	
Will You Sign Here John Hancock?, Fritz	☐ G6-182 Patrick Henry	
Why Don't You Get a Horse Sam Adams?, Fritz	☐ G6-195 Thomas Jefferson	
	☐ W11-455 American Independence	

MOVING TOWARDS INDEPENDENCE

ELEMENTARY	MIDDLE SCHOOL	HIGH SCHOOL

Forgotten Classics:

- [ ] F3-1 True Stories of the American Fathers
- [ ] F11-103 Father Marquette
- [ ] F11-107 Cavelier LaSalle
- [ ] F11-111 New Englanders and Indians
- [ ] F11-118 England and French in North America
- [ ] F11-132 Patrick Henry
- [ ] F11-141 Samuel Adams
- [ ] F11-151 War Begins Near Boston
- [ ] F12-21 Franklin Own Teacher
- [ ] F12-24 A Great Good Man
- [ ] F12-30 The Dark Day
- [ ] F12-33 Stories about Jefferson
- [ ] F12-38 Story of Ben Franklin
- [ ] F12-87 The Midnight Ride
- [ ] S6-24 Benjamin Franklin

Junior Classics:

- [ ] 6-232 Paul Revere's Ride
- [ ] 10-50 Excerpt from Last of the Mohicans

Junior Classics:

- [ ] 9-97 Johnny Tremain

ENGLAND		
ELEMENTARY	**MIDDLE SCHOOL**	**HIGH SCHOOL**
A Christmas Carol, Dickens	A Christmas Carol, Dickens	A Distant Mirror, Tuchman
A Christmas Carol, Innocenti	A Connecticut Yankee in King Arthur's	A History of England, Bright
A Medieval Feast, Aliki	Court, Dickens	Volume 1: 449-1485
A Nursery History of England, O'Neill	A March on London, Henty	Volume 2: 1485-1688
A Visit to William Blake's Inn, Willard	A Messenger for Parliament, Haugaard	Volume 3: 1689-1837
Adam of the Road, Gray	A Midsummer Night's Dream, Perkins	Volume 5: 1880-1901
Alice's Adventures in Wonderland, Carroll	Beric the Briton, Henty	A History of English Speaking, Churchil
Baden-Powell, Blassingame	Both Sides of the Border, Henty	Volume 1: The Birth of Britain
Beautiful Stories - Shakespeare, Nesbit	Canterbury, Grierson	Volume 2: The New World
Book of Dragons, Nesbit	Canterbury Chimes, Storr	Volume 3: The Age of Revolution
Brave Irene, Steig	Castle, Macaulay	Volume 4: The Great Democracies
Castle, Macaulay	Children's Stories in English Literature,	A History of Everday Things, Quennell
Chanticleer and the Fox, Cooney	Wright	Volume 1: 1066-1499
Chanticleer and the Fox, Roberts	Colonel Thorndyke's Secret, Henty	Volume 2: 1500-1799
Chaucer for Children, Haweis	Cromwell's Boy, Haugaard	Volume 3: 1733-1851
David Copperfield Retold for Children,	Dickens' Dream Children	Volume 4: 1851-1934
Jackson	Elizabeth Tudor Sovereign Lady, Vance	A Junior History of England, Oman
Days of the Knights, Maynard	England, Finnemore	A Short History of England, Cheyney
Dick Whittington and His Cat, Brown	English History Condensed and Simplified	Alfred the Great, Abbott
Dream Peddlar, Haley	for Children, Hyde	Alfred the Great, McKilliam
English Fairy Tales, Steele	Facing Death, Henty	An Introduction to the Industrial and
Excalibur, Heyer	Florence Nightingale, Hume	Social History of England, Cheyney
Favorite Fairy Tales - England, Haviland	Hamlet, McKeown	An Introduction to the Study of
Five Children and It, Nesbit	Hereford, Grierson	English Fiction, Simonds
Goldilocks, Spirin	Hero of Trafalgar, Whipple	Blood-Red the Roses, Alderman
Goldilocks, Sanderson	Heroes of Chivalry, Maitland	Britten, Young
Great Englishmen-Short Lives, Beale	In the Days of the Guild, Lamprey	Charles I, Abbott
Gulliver's Travels	John Keats a Portrait in Words, Peare	Charles I, McKilliam
Handel at the Court of Kings, Wheeler	King Arthur and His Knights, Robinson	Charles II, Abbott
Imps and Angels, Gilbert	King Arthur and His Knights of the Round	Charles and Emma, Heiligman
Jack and the Beanstalk, Spirin	Table, Green	Conqueror of Smallpox, Levine
John Bunyan's Dream Story, Baldwin	King Arthur's Knights: The Tales Retold for	Cranford, Gaskell
King Arthur & His Knights, Warren	Boys and Girls, Malory	David Copperfield, Dickens
King Arthur & His Noble Knights, Macleod	London, Mitten	Dr. Jenner & Speckled Monster, Marrir
King Arthur & the Knights of the Round	Made in the Middle Ages, Price	Emma, Austen
Table, Sterne	Master Cornhill, McGraw	Florence Nightingale, Nolan
Legends of King Arthur, Greene	Master Skylark, Bennett	Gilbert and Sullivan, Purdy
Little English Story-Book, Blaisdell	Masters of the Guild, Lamprey	Great Expectations, Dickens
Little Lord Fauntleroy, Burnett	Mor King Arthur's Page, Peare	Handel, Young
Little Stories of England, Dutton	Our Island Story, Marshall	Hawk That Dare Not Hunt by Day, O'De
Little Tom of England, Brandeis	Paige Squire and Knight, Lansing	Henry IV, Abbott
Merlin and Making of the King, Hodges	Prince and the Pauper, Dickens	Historical Tales: Great Britain, Morris
Newton-Galileo and the Stargazers	Queen Victoria, Streatfield	Historical Tales: King Arthur v1, Morris
Nothing is Impossible: The Story of	Romeo and Juliet, McKeown	Historical Tales: King Arthur v2, Morris
Beatrix Potter, Aldis	Royal Palaces of Great Britain, Home	Historical Tales: King Arthur v3, Morris
Our Little English Cousin, McManus	Shakespeare's Stories Simply Told,	History of the English People, Green
Perceval: King Arthur's Knight of the	Seymour	Isaac Newton, Sootin
Holy Grail, Spirin	St. Paul's, Grierson	Jane Eyre, Bronte
Peter Pan, Barrie	Stories and Legends of Travel and	Knighthood and Chivalry, Malone
Peter Pan Retold	History for Children, Greenwood	Lark Rise to Candleford, Johnson
Pilgrims Progress Told to Children,	Stories from English History, Creighton	Lord of the Rings, Tolkien
MacGregor	Stories from English History, Hack	Lorna Doone, Blackmore
Robin Hood, Wyeth	Stories from Shakespeare V 1, Pratt	Margaret of Anjou, Abbott
Robin Hood and His Merry Foresters,	Stories from Shakespeare V 2, Pratt	Masters of the English Novel, Burton
Cundall	Stories from the Faerie Queene, Macleod	Men of Iron, Pyle

ENGLAND

ELEMENTARY	MIDDLE SCHOOL	HIGH SCHOOL
Royal Children, Nesbit	Stories of King Arthur, Clay	Middlemarch Vol 1, Eliot
Royal Children of English History, Morris	Stories of King Arthur, Haydon	Middlemarch Vol 2, Eliot
Saint George and the Dragon, Hodges	Susanna Mother of the Wesleys, Harmon	Nicholas Nickleby, Dickens
Shakesperian Fairy Tales, Bitten	Susanna Wesley Servant of God, Dengler	Old English History for Children, Freem
Sherlock Holmes for Children	Tales from Shakespeare, Lamb	Oliver Cromwell, Levine
Sir Gawain and the Green Knight, Hieatt	Tales from Shakespeare, Lamb/Rhead	Oliver Twist, Dickens
Sir Gawain and the Loathly Lady, Hastings	The Chaucer Story Book, Tappan	Persuasion, Austen
Stories from English History, Skae	The Children of the New Forest, Marryat	Pride and Prejudice, Austen
Stories from English History, Warren	The Children of Westminster Abbey,	Queen Elizabeth, Abbott
Stories from English History, Williams	Kingsley	Richard I, Abbott
Stories of Beowulf Told to the Children,	The Children's Story of Westminster	Richard II, Abbott
Marshall	Abbey, Troutbeck	Richard III, Abbott
Stories of Guy Warwick Told to the	The Door in the Wall, d'Angeli	Sense and Sensibility, Austen
Children, Marshall	The Dragon and the Raven, Henty	Sherlock Holmes, Doyle
Stories of King Arthur	The Flight and Adventures of Charles II	Silas Marner, Eliot
Stories of King Arthur's Knights,	The Hidden Treasure of Glaston, Jewett	Sir Walter Raleigh, Marshall
MacGregor	The Hobbit, Tolkien	Source Book of English History, Kendal
Stories of Robin Hood Told to Children,	The Magna Charta, Daugherty	Tales from Chaucer for Young People,
Marshall	The Queen's Cup, Henty	Clarke
Stories of the King, Baldwin	The Queen's Smuggler, Jackson	Tales of True Knights, Krapp
Swallows and Amazons, Ransome	The Story of Scotland Yard, Thompson	The Adventurous Life of Winston
Sword in the Stone, Maccarone	The True Story of Lord Nelson, Houghton	Churchill, Bocca
Tales from Shakespeare, Lamb	The Young Douglas, Nolan	The Courage of Dr. Lister, Noble
Ten Drawings of Dickens' Children, Smith	Through the Fray, Henty	The Development of the English
The Beast of Lor, Bulla	Under Wellington's Command, Henty	Novel, Cross
The Borrowers Series	When Knights Were Bold, Tappan	The Discoverer of Oxygen, Crane
The Borrowers	Will Shakespeare & Globe Theater, White	The English Novel, Lanier
The Borrowers Afield	William the Conqueror, Costain	The First Woman Doctor, Baker
The Borrowers Afloat	With Moore at Corunna, Henty	The Golden Century, Alderman
The Borrowers Aloft	Wulf the Saxon, Henty	The Man Who Built a City, Weir
The Enchanted Castle, Nesbit		The Master Painters of Britain, White
The Happy Prince, Wilde	**Forgotten Classics:**	The Mill on the Floss, Eliot
The Happy Prince and Other Tales, Wilde	G4-357 Maud Ballington Booth	The Once and Future King, White
The Hound of the Baskervilles	G6-85 Queen Elizabeth	The Story of Champions of the Round
The Joy of the Court, Hieatt	G7-6 John Ruskin	Table, Pyle
The King With His Six Friends, Williams	G7-10 Metcalf: A Blind Boy	The Story of Early Britain, Church
The King's Highway, Fullmer	G10-50 Newton	The Story of King Arthur, Pyle
The Kitchen Knight, Hodges	G10-98 Rumford	The Story of Mediaeval England, Bates
The Little Lame Prince, Craik	G10-126 Davy	The Story of Religion in England, Herfo
The Lost Prince, Burnett	G10-258 Tyndall	The Story of the British Race, Corkran
The Merry Adventures of Robin Hood,	G12-122 Charles Dickens	Barons and Kings
Pyle	G12-234 Frances Hodgson	Birth of England
The Nightingale and the Rose, Wilde	G12-271 Robert Louis Stevenson	Conquest to Charter
The Peter Pan Alphabet	N11-7 Singing the Heart Open	Dawn of British History
The Phoenix and the Carpet, Nesbit	N11-20 Other Refuge	The Story of the Building of the British
The Pooh Cook Book, Elison	N11-164 Mrs. Alexander Hymns	Empire Vol 1, Story
The Prince and the Pauper, Twain	S5-210 Launcelot and Elaine	The Story of the Building of the British
The Queen's Progress, Mannis	S5-229 The Holy Grail	Empire Vol 2, Story
The Railway Children, Nesbit	S5-237 Sir Bors	The Story of the People of England of
The Reluctant Dragon	S5-238 Sir Launcelot	the 19th Century Vol 1, McCarthy
The River Bank, Leach	S5-240 Sir Percivale	The Story of the People of England of
The Selfish Giant, Wilde	S5-244 Guinevere	the 19th Century Vol 2, McCarthy
The Shakespeare Story-Book, Banks	S5-249 Passing of Arthur	The World's Story V 9, Tappan
The Story of Chaucer's Canterbury	S9-311 The Invincible Armada	The World's Story V 10, Tappan
Pilgrims, Bates	S10-288 Macbeth	William Shakespeare, Noble

ENGLAND		
ELEMENTARY	**MIDDLE SCHOOL**	**HIGH SCHOOL**
The Story of Florence Nightingale, Leighton	S10-318 Hamlet	William the Conqueror, Abbott
The Story of Nelson, Sellers	W3-1 Little Stories of England	**Forgotten Classics:**
The Story of the Amulet, Nesbit	W11-224 The Great Pope Hildebrand	G7-49 Sir Titus Salt
The Story of the Treasure Seekers, Nesbit	W11-286 The Black Death	G7-55 George Peabody
The Sword and the Grail, Hieatt	W11-382 The Seventeenth Century	G8-71 Handel
The Sword in the Tree, Bulla	W12-5 Queen Philippa and the Citizens	G11-25 The Good Protestant
The Wind in the Willows Country Cookbook, Boxer	of Calais	G11-64 Susanna Wesley
The Writing on the Hearth, Harnett	W12-37 Sad Story of a Boy King	G12-23 Charles Lamb
The Young Elizabeth, Plaidy	W12-83 Elizabeth Fry	G12-44 Jane Austen
The Young Faraday, Pringle	W12-334 Florence Nightingale	G12-134 Charlotte Bronte
The Young Jane Austen, Sisson		G12-144 George Eliot
Tolkien's World: Paintings Middle Earth	**Junior Classics:**	G12-172, 177 Lewis Carroll
Treasury of Wisdom-Beatrix Potter	10-208 Excerpt from Pride & Prejudice	G12-342 Ernest Thompson Seton
Twenty Beautiful Stories from Shakespeare, Nesbit	10-246 Excerpt from Pilgrim's Progress	N1-143 The Wesley Family
When We Were Very Young, Milne	10-324 Excerpt from Jane Eyre	N10-87 Early English Music
Wind in the Willows, Grahame	10-337 Excerpt from David Copperfield	N10-96 Madrigalian Era
Winnie the Pooh, Milne		N10-102 A Musical Medley
Young Arthur, Souci		N10-108 The Age of Handel
		N10-121 19th Century Music
		N10-126 Early English Painting
Forgotten Classics:		N10-129 Sir Joshua Reynolds
G2-288 Bewick		N10-139 Gainsborough & Constable
G2-333 Saint-Gaudens		N10-148 Turner
G4-76 Fry Elizabeth		N10-159 19th Century English Art
G8-59 Handel George Frederick		N11-186 Bishop Heber
N12-195 HMS Pinafore		N11-197 Sara Flower Adams
S1-36 Landseer		N11-214 Augustus Toplady
S1-70 Reynolds		N11-224 Charles Wesley Hymns
S1-94 Raeburn		N11-230 Isaac Watts Hymns
S1-96, G2-303 Millais		N11-236 William Cowper
S1-110 Gainsborough		N11-239 William Williams
S1-176 Herring		N11-251 Jemima Thompson
S1-198 Watts George		N11-256 Mary Baker
S1-202 Boughton		N11-259 Sweet Hour of Prayer
S3-279 Tattercoats		W12-174 William M. Hunt
S5-161 St. George and the Dragon		W12-357 Edith Cavell
S5-185 Coming of King Arthur		W12-385 Champion of 'The Cause'
S5-195 Gareth and Lynette		
S5-165 Robin Hood		**Junior Classics:**
S6-56, G4-137 Nightingale Florence		8-298 The Meeting: Elizabeth Barrett Browning
S6-117, G6-22 King Alfred		
S6-130 King Alfred and the Cakes		**Delphian Course:**
S6-132 King Alfred and the Beggar		5:61-90 Early English Literature
S6-137 Sons of William the Conqueror		5:117-125 Legends of King Arthur
S6-141 The White Ship		7:44-214 English Drama
S6-145 King John and the Abbot		8:2-48 English History
S6-152 The Miller and the Dee		8:49-349 English Prose
S6-173 Goldsmith		8:350-423 English Prose
S6-223 Tennyson Alfred		9:94-100 English Art and Artists
S10-51 Dorigen by Chaucer		9:169-185 British Art Galleries
S10-65 Emelia by Chaucer		9:186-374 British Writers
S10-78 Griselda by Chaucer		
S10-96 The Unknown Bride		

☐ S10-96 The Red Cross Knight
☐ S10-162 As You Like It by Shakespeare
☐ S10-190 Twelfth Night by Shakespeare
☐ S10-226 Midsummer Night's Dream by
       Shakespeare
☐ S10-354 Merchant of Venice by
       Shakespeare
☐ S11-23 Boy Who Could Not Be Bribed
☐ S11-53 Perseverance Wins
☐ S11-92 Fawcett Blind Postmaster
☐ S11-141 Stephenson George
☐ S11-295 Sidney Sir Philip
☐ S11-354 Edward the Black Prince

My Book House:

☐ 1-18 English Nursery Rhymes
☐ 1-118 Sweet and Low by Tennyson
☐ 1-148 Rhymes from Shakespeare
☐ 1-152 Verses of John Keats
☐ 1-154 Poems by Tennyson
☐ 2-13 Little Red Hen
☐ 2-42 The Magpie's Nest
☐ 3-20 Goldilocks and the Three Bears
☐ 3-70 King Hilary and the Beggerman
☐ 3-148 Master of Masters
☐ 3-176 Chanticleer and Partlet
☐ 3-198 The Birds' St. Valentine Day
☐ 4-50 The Selfish Giant
☐ 4-119 Little Diamond & the North Wind
☐ 4-143 Teeny-Tiny
☐ 5-11 The Story of Tom Thumb
☐ 5-33 Dick Whittington and His Cat
☐ 5-20 Jack and the Beanstalk
☐ 5-68 Winnie the Pooh
☐ 5-76 How Jack Sought the Golden Apples
☐ 6-40 Jack the Giant Killer
☐ 7-182 David Copperfield and Little Em'ly
☐ 8-189 Maggie Tulliver Goes to Live With
       the Gypsies
☐ 9-177 The Rose and the Ring
☐ 10-7 A Perfect Knight
☐ 10-8 Sir Beaumains the Kitchen Knight
☐ 10-54 Richard Feverel and the Hay-Rick
☐ 10-80 How Beowulf Delivered Heorot
☐ 10-89 The Last of the Dragons
☐ 11-8 Una and the Red Cross Knight
☐ 11-49 Ye Merry Doings of Robin Hood
☐ 12-11 Chaucer, Geoffrey
☐ 12-15 Shakespeare: Down by the River
       Anon
☐ 12-102 Dickens, Charles: London Streets
☐ 12-213 Mother Goose

Junior Classics:

☐ 1-2 Mother Goose Rhymes

ENGLAND		
ELEMENTARY	**MIDDLE SCHOOL**	**HIGH SCHOOL**
☐ 1-38 Mr. and Mrs. Vinegar		
☐ 2-36 History of Tom Thumb		
☐ 2-43 Jack and the Beanstalk		
☐ 2-53 The Three Sillies		
☐ 2-59 Dick Whittington and His Cat		
☐ 2-338 The Apple of Contentment		
☐ 3-20 Alice's Adventures in Wonderland		
☐ 3-117 The Borrowers		
☐ 3-148 Winnie-the-Pooh		
☐ 3-263 The King of the Golden River		
☐ 3-297 Mr. Toad from Wind in the Willows		
☐ 3-310 The Mermaid's Lagoon		
☐ 3-352 The Old Lady's Bedroom		
☐ 7-233 The Merry Adventures of Robin Hood		
☐ 7-277 The Beginning of King Arthur		
☐ 8-174 Nightingale, Florence		
☐ 8-298 Browning, Elizabeth Barrett		
☐ 9-213 Men of Iron		
☐ 9-284 The Adventure of the Blue Carbuncle from Sherlock Holmes		

SCOTLAND / IRELAND / WALES

ELEMENTARY	MIDDLE SCHOOL	HIGH SCHOOL
Alexander Graham Bell, Montgomery	A Land of Heroes, O'Byrne	Adventures of Sherlock Holmes, Doyle
Allan Pinkerton, Anderson	A Short History of Wales, Edwards	Bonnie Scotland, Palmer
Always Room for One More, Leodhas	Bonnie Scotland, Greenwood	Edinburgh, Stevenson
At the Back of the North Wind, McDonald	Bonnie Prince Charles, Henty	First Lady of the Theatre, Haycraft
Celtic Fairy Tales, Jacobs	Captain Kidd, Whipple	Gulliver's Travels, Swift
Celtic Treasures	In Freedom's Cause, Henty	Ivanhoe, Scott
Clancy's Coat, Bunting	Ireland, Home	Kidnapped, Stevenson
Favority Fairy Tales - Scotland, Haviland	Ireland, Tynana	Mary Queen of Scots, Abbott
Gulliver in Lilliput, Hodges	Ivanhoe Retold, Mayer	Robert Louis Stevenson, Cruse
Gulliver's Travels Told to Children, Lang	Ivanhoe Retold - Young People, Scott	Robinson Crusoe, DeFoe
Irish Fairy Tales, Leamy	Mary Queen of Scots, Hahn	Sir Gibbie, MacDonald
Irish Fairy Tales, Stephens	Muir of the Mountains, Douglas	The Black Arrow, Stevenson
Irish Fairy Tales, Yeats	Orange and Green	The Real Sherlock Holmes, Hoehling
Lassie Come Home, Jeffers	Scotland, Grierson	The Scottish Chiefs, Porter
Lassie Come Home, Knight	Scotland's Queen, Vance	The Story of Ireland, Lawless
Magic in the Margins, Nikola-Lisa	Scotland's Story, Marshall	The Story of Scotland, Mackintosh
More Celtic Fairy Tales, Jacobs	Sir Gibbie, McDonald	The Story of Wales, Edwards
Names Upon the Harp, Heaney	Stories from Scottish History, Edgar	The Wearing of the Green, Alderman
Our Little Irish Cousin, Wade	Tales of Irish History, Birkhead	The World's Story V 10, Tappan
Our Little Scotch Cousin, McManus	The Boy Travellers in Great Britain and	Trinity, Uris
Patrick Patron Saint of Ireland, dePaola	Ireland, Knox	True Stories from the History of
Robert Louis Stevenson, Peare	The Cottage at Bantry Bay, van Stockum	Ireland, McGregor
Robert Louis Stevenson, Wilkie	The Flying Scotsman, Magnusson	Unknown to History, Yonge
Robinson Crusoe for Boys/Girls, McMurry	The Life of Robert Louis Stevenson for	Victor Herbert, Purdy
Robinson Crusoe Retold, Stevenson	Boys and Girls, Overton	
Saint Patrick and the Peddler, Hodges	The Life of St. Patrick, Reynolds	**Forgotten Classics:**
Shaun O'Day of Ireland, Brandeis	The Names Upon the Harp, Heaney	G12-282 Robert Louis Stevenson
The Cottage at Gantry Bay, van Stockum	The Story of Robert Bruce, Lang	W3-369 Ancient Ireland
The Ink Garden of Brother Theophane,	Wales, Wilmot-Baxton	W12-302 Robert Bruce
Millen		
The Irish Twins, Perkins	**Forgotten Classics:**	
The Light Princess, MacDonald	G9-32 Robert Bruce	
The Man Who Loved Books, Fritz	G9-296 St. Patrick	
The Princess and Curdie, MacDonald	G10-142 Charles Lyell/Rocks	
The Princess and the Goblin, MacDonald	G10-196 John Muir	
The Scotch Twins, Perkins	G12-1 Sir Walter Scott	
The Scottish Fairy Book, Grierson	W12-86 Burning of Carlyle's Book	
The Wee Scotch Piper, Brandeis		
Under the Hawthorn Tree, McKenna		
Waverly Novels, Scott		
Welsh Fairy Tales, Griffis		
Welsh Fairy Tales/Other Stories, Emerson		
Wonder Tales Ancient Wales, Henderson		

Forgotten Classics:

- G5-70 James Watt
- G7-1 Andrew Carnegie
- S3-248 The Magic Wall
- S5-280 Brian Boru
- S6-150 Bruce and the Spider
- S6-209 Sir Walter Scott
- S9-241 At the Ford of the Tribute
- S11-129 Lesson of the Teakettle
- S11-257 John & Scots Gray

SCOTLAND / IRELAND / WALES		
ELEMENTARY	**MIDDLE SCHOOL**	**HIGH SCHOOL**

My Book House:

- [ ] 1-58 Welsh Rhymes
- [ ] 1-59 Rhymes from Ireland
- [ ] 1-158 Poems of Robert Louis Stevenson
- [ ] 2-155 The Bee the Mouse and the Bum-Clock
- [ ] 2-209 Wee Robin's Christmas Song
- [ ] 3-99 The Wee Wee Mannie and the Big Coo
- [ ] 5-45 Jamie Watt and the Giant in the Teakettle
- [ ] 5-90 The Red Ettin
- [ ] 6-18 Old Pipes and the Dryad
- [ ] 7-20 The Youth Who Wanted Some Fun
- [ ] 8-38 Gulliver's Travels to Lilliput
- [ ] 10-21 Robert Bruce Scotland's Hero
- [ ] 10-33 Excerpt from Ivanhoe
- [ ] 10-188 Cuculain the Irish Hound

Junior Classics:

- [ ] 2-28 Hudden and Dudden and Donald O'Neary
- [ ] 3-352 The Old Lady's Bedroom
- [ ] 4-348 A Picnic on and Island from the Cottage at Gantry Bay
- [ ] 6-82 Saint Patrick
- [ ] 10-117 Excerpt from Gulliver's Travels

SCOTLAND / IRELAND / WALES		
ADDITIONAL BOOKS		
ELEMENTARY	MIDDLE SCHOOL	HIGH SCHOOL

ROCKS		
ELEMENTARY	**MIDDLE SCHOOL**	**HIGH SCHOOL**
☐ All About Earthquakes, Pough	☐ Earth and Sky Every Child Should Know, Rogers	Brooks and Brook Basins, Frye
☐ King Midas and the Golden Touch, Craft		☐ Diggers in the Earth, Tappan
☐ Ming-Lo Moves the Mountain, Lobel	☐ Journey to the Center of the Earth, Verne	Geological Sketches, Agassiz
☐ My Side of the Mountain, Stone	☐ The Geographical Story Briefly Told, Dana	History of a Mountain, Reclus
☐ Rocks, Evans	☐ The Strange Adventures of a Pebble, Atkinson	☐ Talks About the Soil, Barnard
☐ Rocks All Around Us, White		☐ The Handbook of Nature Study, Comstock
☐ Stone Soup, Brown		
☐ Stories of Rocks and Minerals, Fairbanks		☐ The World's Foundations, Giberne
☐ Sylvester and the Magic Pebble, Steig		☐ Town Geology, Kingsley
☐ The How & Why Wonder Book of Rocks		☐ Water and Land, Abbott
☐ The Story of Gold, Brindze		
☐ There are Rocks in My Socks		
Forgotten Classics:		
☐ N3 Stories of Rocks		

GEORGE WASHINGTON

ELEMENTARY	MIDDLE SCHOOL	HIGH SCHOOL
☐ A Man Named Washington, Norman	☐ A Little Story of Washington's Crossing, Lee	☐ A History of the Life and Death, Virtue and Exploits of Gen. George Wash.
☐ General Washington and the General's Dog, Murphy	☐ George Washington, Camp	☐ George Washington, Abbott
☐ George Washington, d'Aulaire	☐ George Washington, Scudder	☐ George Washington, Russell
☐ George Washington, Graff	☐ George Washington Frontier Colonel, North	☐ George Washington and the Founding of a Nation, Marrin
☐ George Washington, Judson	☐ George Washington's World, Foster	☐ George Washington the Christian, Johnson
☐ George Washington, Stevenson	☐ Martha Daughter of Virginia, Vance	
☐ George Washington, Weiss	☐ The Story of George Washington, Meadowcroft	☐ The Heart of Washington, Whipple
☐ George Washington: A Picture Book Biography, Giblin		☐ The Life of George Washington, Weem
☐ George Washington First President, Albee	☐ The Story of Martha Washington, Nolan	☐ The Real George Washington, Allison
☐ George Washington's Breakfast, Fritz	☐ The Story of Washington, Seelye	☐ The Real George Washington, Parry
☐ George Washington's First Victory, Krensky	☐ The Years Between, Wilson	☐ The Story-Life of Washington, Whipple
	☐ Washington and the Revolution, Montross	☐ The Wonderful Story of Washington and the Meaning of His Life, Stevens
☐ The Bulletproof George Washington, Barton	☐ Washington's Rules of Civility, Toner	☐ Washington in Domestic Life, Rush
☐ The Story of George Washington, Walk	**Forgotten Classics:**	
☐ The Story of Martha Washington, Nolan	☐ F4-359 Recollections of George Washington	**Forgotten Classics:**
☐ The Story of Washington, Smith		☐ F4-123 History of Life and Death of General Washington
☐ The Story of Young George Washington, Whipple		☐ G11-111 Mary Washington
☐ The True Story of George Washington, Brooks		☐ G11-130 Martha Washington
☐ Washington at Valley Forge, Freedman		

Forgotten Classics:

☐ F4-1 True Story of George Washington

☐ F11-160 George Washington in the Revolution

☐ S6-68 A Rich Boy and What Became of Him

☐ S11-357 Hero of Valley Forge

My Book House:

☐ 5-118 George Washington and the First American Flag

Junior Classics:

☐ 6-60 Stories for Washington's Birthday

GEORGE WASHINGTON		
ADDITIONAL BOOKS		
ELEMENTARY	MIDDLE SCHOOL	HIGH SCHOOL

GREECE

ELEMENTARY	MIDDLE SCHOOL	HIGH SCHOOL
☐ Aesop's Fables, Santore	☐ A Knight of the White Cross, Henty	Aeschylus, Plumptre
☐ Aesop for Children, Winter	☐ A Wonder Book for Girls/Boys, Hawthorne	☐ Alexander the Great, Abbott
☐ Animal Tales from Aesop's Fables	☐ Alexander the Great, Gunther	☐ Alexander the Great, Russell
☐ Atlantis The Legend of a Lost City, Balit	☐ Archimedes & Door of Science, Bendick	☐ Ancient Greek Literature, Murray
☐ Aunt Charlotte's Stories of Greek History	☐ Black Ships Before Troy, Sutcliffe	☐ Aritosphanes, Frere
for the Little Ones, Yonge	☐ Caesar's Gallic War, Coolidge	☐ Caesar and Christ, Durant
☐ Children of the Fox, Walsh	☐ Children of the Dawn, Buckley	☐ Classic Mythology, D'Ooge
☐ Courage and a Clear Mind	☐ Famous Men of Greece, Haaren	☐ Classic Myths, Gayley
☐ Cupid and Psyche, Craft	☐ Greece, Browne	☐ Classic Myths in Art, Addison
☐ D'Aulaire's Greek Myths	☐ Hercules and Other Tales, Coolidge	☐ Euripides, Coleridge
☐ Famous Men of Greece, Haaren	☐ In Greek Waters, Henty	☐ Famous Men of Ancient Times, Goodri
☐ Favorite Fairy Tales - Greece, Haviland	☐ Men of Athens, Coolidge	☐ First History of Greece, Sewell
☐ Galileo and the Stargazers	☐ Old Greek Folk Stories, Peabody	☐ Gods and Heroes, Francillon
☐ Gods and Heroes, Francillon	☐ Our Young Folks' Plutarch, Kaufman	☐ Grammar of Greek Art, Gardner
☐ Greek Myths, Lock	☐ Plutarch's Lives for Boys and Girls, Weston	☐ Greece, M'Clymount
☐ Greek Myths, Weiss	☐ Stories from Greek Mythology, Wood	☐ Greek Gods Heroes and Men, Harding
☐ Heroes in Mythology, Weiss	Stories from the History of Greece, Groves	☐ Greek History, Zimmern
☐ In Myth-land, Beckwith	☐ Volume 1	☐ Greek Myths, Coolidge
☐ King Midas and the Golden Touch, Craft	☐ Volume 2	☐ Handbook of Greek Sculpture, Gardne
Myths of Old Greece, Pratt	☐ Stories of Old Greece and Rome, Baker	☐ Helmet and Spear, Church
☐ Volume 1	☐ Tales About Mythology of Greece and	☐ Historical Tales: Greece, Morris
☐ Volume 2	Rome, Parley	☐ History of Greek Art, Gardner
☐ Volume 3	☐ Tales of the Greek Heroes, Green	☐ History of Greek Literature, Fowler
☐ Pegasus, Mayer	☐ Tanglewood Tales, Hawthorne	☐ History of Greek Literature, Mahaffy
☐ Persephone, Clayton	☐ The Adventures of Odysseus, Colum	☐ History of Orient and Greece, Bostford
☐ Shakespeare for Children, Weiss	☐ The Adventures of Ulysses, Gottlieb	☐ History of Philosophy, Weber
☐ She and He: Adventures in Mythology	☐ The Exploits of Xenophan, Household	☐ Life of the Ancient Greeks, Gulick
☐ Stories from Greek History, Lemon	☐ The Golden Fleece, Baldwin	☐ Manual of Mythology, Murray
☐ Stories from Plato, Burt	☐ The Heroes, Kingsley	☐ Masterpieces of Greek Literature, Wrig
☐ Stories from the Iliad, Lang	☐ The Luck of Troy, Green	☐ Myths of Greece and Rome, Guerber
☐ Stories from the Odyssey, Lang	☐ The Maid of Artemis, Coolidge	☐ Oliver Cromwell, Ross
☐ Stories of Greek Gods, Harding	☐ The Odyssey, McCaughrean	☐ Outlines of Greek Philosophy, Zeller
☐ Stories of Long Ago in New Dress, Kupfer	☐ The Spartan, Snedeker	☐ Progress of Hellenism, Mahaffy
☐ Stories of Old Greece, Firth	☐ The Story of Greece Told to Boys and	☐ Pyrrhus, Abbott
☐ Tales of Christophilos, Nankivell	Girls, MacGregor	☐ Short History-Greek Philosophy, Marsh
☐ The Arrow and the Lamp, Hodges	☐ The Tale of Troy, Green	☐ Social Life in Greece, Mahaffy
☐ The Grasshopper and the Ants, Pinkney	☐ The Trojan War, Coolidge	☐ Sophocles, Coleridge
☐ The Iliad for Boys and Girls, Church	☐ Theras and His Town, Snedeker	☐ Source Book of Greek History, Fling
☐ The Librarian Who Measured the	☐ Wonder Tales from the Greek and	☐ Story of the Greeks, Guerber
Earth, Lasky	Roman Myths, Davidson	☐ Studies in Greek Poets, Symonds
☐ The Lion and the Mouse, Pinkney	☐ Young Folks' History of Greece, Yonge	☐ Tanglewood Tales, Hawthorne
☐ The Story of the Greek People, Tappan		☐ The Ancient Classical Drama, Moulton
☐ The Tortoise and the Hare, Pinkney	**Forgotten Classics:**	☐ The Echo of Greece, Hamilton
☐ The Trojan Horse, Little	☐ G10-3 Archimedes	☐ The Greek Philosophers, Benn
☐ Three Greek Children, Church	☐ G10-14 Galileo	☐ The Greek View of Life, Dickinson
☐ Treasury of Wisdom	☐ W4-1 Story of the Greeks	☐ The Greek Way, Hamilton
☐ Wonder Stories, Bailey	☐ W11-36 The Greeks	The History of Greece, Holm
	☐ W11-56 The Athens of Pericles/Socrates	☐ Volume 1
Forgotten Classics:	☐ W11-63 Greek Colonies in the West	☐ Volume 2
☐ G3-3 Children's Plutarch	☐ W11-68 The Peloponession War	☐ Volume 3
☐ S4-1 The Greeks	☐ W11-78 Last Days - Greek Independence	☐ Volume 4
☐ S4-9 Jupiter/His Mighty Company	☐ W11-88 Greece and Macedonia	☐ The King of Men, Coolidge
☐ S4-12 The Golden Age		☐ The Life of Greece, Durant
☐ S4-16 Prometheus		☐ The Lives of Noble Grecians and
☐ S4-27 The Flood		Romans, Dryden

GREECE		
ELEMENTARY	**MIDDLE SCHOOL**	**HIGH SCHOOL**

ELEMENTARY	HIGH SCHOOL
☐ S4-33 Story of Io	☐ The Mythology of Greece and Rome, Appleton
☐ S4-39 Lord of the Silver Bow	☐ The Story of Alexander's Empire, Mahaffy
☐ S4-55 Admetus and Alcestis	
☐ S4-65 Cadmus and Europa	☐ The Story of Greece, Harrison
☐ S4-77 Quest of Medusa's Head	☐ The World's Story V 4, Tappan
☐ S4-101 Wonderful Weaver	☐ The Youth's Plutarchs Lives for Boys and Girls, Ellis
☐ S4-106 Horse and the Oliver	
☐ S4-117 Pegasus Flying Horse	☐ Wonder Book, Hawthorne
☐ S4-123 Zeus King of Gods	
☐ S4-127 Poseidon God of Sea	**Forgotten Classics:**
☐ S4-130 How Minerva Built City	☐ G4-110 Samuel Howe
☐ S4-139 Hades King of Dead	☐ G4-334 E.D. Cushman
☐ S4-142 Hera Queen of Gods	☐ N9-24 Greek Music
☐ S4-142 Echo and Narcissus	☐ N9-38 A Storied Hill
☐ S4-149 Apollo God of Light	☐ N9-48 The Jupiter Olympus
☐ S4-153 Apollo God of Light	☐ N9-50 A Little Sculpture Gallery
☐ S4-156 How Vulcan Made Best of Things	☐ N9-55 Stories of Greek Painters
☐ S4-163 How Orion Found Sight	
☐ S4-170 Aphrodite Goddess of Beauty	
☐ S4-173 Wonders Venus Wrought	**Delphian Course:**
☐ S4-180 Hermes Messenger	☐ 2:69-226 Greek Mythology
☐ S4-184 When Proserpine Lost	☐ 2:227-374 Story of Greece
☐ S4-192 Hestia Goddess/Hearth	☐ 2:375-428 Greek Social Life
☐ S4-195 Pan God of Shepherds	☐ 2:429-480 Greek Literature
☐ S4-198 Phaeton's Chariot	☐ 3:1-86 Greek Drama
☐ S4-207 Psyche	☐ 3:87-377 Greek Philosophy/Poetry/ Literature/Art
☐ S4-218 Heracles	
☐ S4-224 Bee Man of Arcadia	☐ 5:49-60 Greek Fiction
☐ S4-233 Orpheus and Eurydice	
☐ S4-237 Golden Fleece	
☐ S4-245 Baucis and Philemon	
☐ S4-254 Wood-Folk	
☐ S4-259 Judgment of Midas	
☐ S4-263 Prometheus	
☐ S4-269 The Deluge	
☐ S4-274 Orpheus and Eurydice	
☐ S4-279 Icarus and Daedulies	
☐ S4-282 Phaeton	
☐ S4-288 Niobe	
☐ S4-292 Admetus and Shepherd	
☐ S4-296 Acestis	
☐ S5-1 The Iliad	
☐ S5-37 Ulysses Story of Patience	
☐ S6-167 Diogenes the Wise Man	
☐ S6-184 Aesop	
☐ S10-1 Memory & Her Beautiful Daughter	
☐ S11-63 Greek Slave Who Won Olive Crown	
☐ S11-216 Damon and Pythias	
☐ S11-304 A Modern Bayard	

My Book House:
☐ 1-204 Children's Songs of Ancient Greece
☐ 2-33 The Two Crabs

GREECE		
ELEMENTARY	**MIDDLE SCHOOL**	**HIGH SCHOOL**
☐ 2-35 Belling the Cat		
☐ 2-50 The Donkey and the Lap Dog		
☐ 2-84 The City Mouse and the Country Mouse		
☐ 2-92 The Dancing Monkeys		
☐ 2-106 The Hare and the Tortoise		
☐ 2-108 The Lion and the Mouse		
☐ 3-196 The Wind and the Sun		
☐ 3-197 Dog in the Manger		
☐ 6-38 A Midsummer Night's Dream		
☐ 7-90 Phaeton		
☐ 7-210 The Golden Touch		
☐ 9-140 The Adventures of Perseus		
☐ 9-151 The Labors of Hercules		
☐ 10-217 The Homecoming of Odysseus		
Junior Classics:		
☐ 2-3 Aesop's Fables		
☐ 4-301 Christophilos and the Pascal Lamb		
☐ 7-83 Pandora the First Woman		
☐ 7-86 The Golden Touch of King Midas		
☐ 7-101 The Flight of Icarus		
☐ 7-105 Pyramus and Thisbe		
☐ 7-107 Orpheus and Eurydice		
☐ 7-111 Pygmalion and Galatea		
☐ 7-114 The Miraculous Pitcher		
☐ 7-132 The Chimaera		
☐ 7-153 Phaeton		
☐ 7-188 Odysses at the Palace of King Alcinous		
☐ Perseus Slays the Gorgon		

GREECE		
ADDITIONAL BOOKS		
ELEMENTARY	MIDDLE SCHOOL	HIGH SCHOOL

ANCIENT ROME

ELEMENTARY	MIDDLE SCHOOL	HIGH SCHOOL
☐ Augustus Ceasar's World, Foster	☐ Buildings of Byzantium, Leacroft	☐ Ancient Rome, Lanciani
☐ Famous Men of Rome, Haaren	☐ Childhood of Rome, Lamprey	☐ Architectural History of Rome, Parker
☐ Julius Caesar and the Story of Rome	☐ City, Macalaulay	☐ Architecture of Greece/Rome, Anderso
☐ Little Arthur's History Rome, Butterworth	☐ Famous Men of Rome, Haaren	☐ Augustus, Francis
☐ Stories from Roman History, Dakleith	☐ Galen and the Gateway to Medicine,	☐ Ben-Hur, Wallace
☐ Stories from the History of Rome, Beesly	Bendick	☐ Caesar and Christ, Durant
☐ Stories of Old Rome, Pratt	☐ In Search of a Homeland, Lively	☐ Days Near Rome, Hare
☐ The Dancing Bear, Dickinson	☐ Lives of Famous Romans, Coolidge	☐ Destruction of Ancient Rome, Lanciani
☐ The Young Cicero, Barbary	☐ Our Young Folks' Plutarch, Kaufman	☐ Early Christian and Byzantine
	☐ Plutarch's Lives for Boys and Girls, Weston	Architecture, Browne
Forgotten Classics:	☐ Prisoners of Hannibal, Merrell	☐ Famous Men of Ancient Times, Goodri
☐ G3-187 Children's Plutarch	☐ The Aeneid for Boys and Girls, Church	Greatness and Decline of Rome, Ferrer
☐ S5-84 Perilous Voyage of Aeneas	☐ The Bronze Bow, Speare	☐ Volume 1: The Empire Builders
☐ S6-163 Story of Cincinnatus	☐ The Byzantines, Chubb	☐ Volume 2: Julius Caesar
☐ S9-60 Story of Horatius the Roman Boy	☐ The Child's First History of Rome, Sewell	☐ Volume 3: The Fall of and Aristocrac
☐ S11-20 Story of Regulus	☐ The City of the Seven Hills, Harding	☐ Volume 4: Rome and Egypt
☐ S11-341 Boy Who Loved Justice	☐ The Fall of Constantinople, Kielty	☐ Volume 5: The Republic of Augustus
	☐ The Standard Bearer, Whitehead	☐ Greek and Roman Sculpture, Perry
My Book House:	☐ The Story of Caesar, Clarke	☐ Helmet and Spear, Church
☐ 7-145 The Dog of Pompeii	☐ The Story of Rome, MacGregor	☐ Historical Tales: Rome, Morris
☐ 10-203 The Wanderings of Aeneas	☐ The Story of the Roman People, Tappan	☐ History of Roman Literature, Fowler
		☐ History of Rome, How
	Forgotten Classics:	History of Rome, Mommsen
	☐ G6-1 Julius Caesar	☐ Volume 1
	☐ W4-245 Story of the Romans	☐ Volume 2
	☐ W11-96 Rise of Rome	☐ Volume 3
	☐ W11-108 Rome and the Celts	☐ Volume 4
	☐ W11-115 Rome Mistress of Italy	☐ Volume 5
	☐ W11-136 Rome and the East	☐ Julius Caesar, Komroff
	☐ W11-142 Last Days of the Roman	☐ Latin Literature, Mackail
	Republic	☐ Latin Poetry, Tyrrell
	☐ W11-167 Early Days of Roman Empire	☐ Nero, Abbott
	☐ W11-180 The Barbarians & the Empire	☐ Pictures from Roman Life, Church
	☐ W11-193 The New Nation	☐ Pillar of Iron, Caldwell
	☐ W12-272 Cornelia's Jewels	☐ Pompeii Its Life and Art, Mau
		☐ Quo Vadis, Sienkiewica
		☐ Roman Life in Pliny's Time, Pellison
		☐ Roman Life Under the Caesars, Thomas
		☐ Roman People, Coolidge
		☐ Roman Sculpture, Strong
		☐ Rome, Tuker
		☐ Romulus, Abbott
		☐ Source Book of Roman History, Munro
		☐ Story of the Romans, Guerber
		☐ The City of the Sultans, Clement
		☐ The History of the Decline and Fall of
		the Roman Empire, Gibbon
		☐ The Lives of Noble Grecians and
		Romans, Dryden
		☐ The Private Life of the Romans, Presto
		☐ The Robe, Douglas
		☐ The Roman Way, Hamilton
		☐ The Story of Mediaeval Rome, Miller
		☐ The Story of Rome, Gilman
		☐ The Story of the Byzantine Empire, Om

ANCIENT ROME		
ELEMENTARY	**MIDDLE SCHOOL**	**HIGH SCHOOL**
		☐ The World's Story V 4, Tappan
		☐ The Youth's Plutarchs Lives for Boys and Girls, Ellis
		☐ Walks in Rome, hare
		☐ Young Folks History of Rome, Yonge
		Forgotten Classics:
		☐ G11-13 Cornelia Mother of the Graach
		☐ G11-15 Monica Mother of Augustine
		☐ N9-61 Roman Music
		☐ N9-67 Monuments of Ancient Rome
		☐ N9-74 Paintings Buried
		☐ N9-82 The First Church
		Delphian Course:
		☐ 3:387-486 Story of Rome
		☐ 4:1-58 Roman Principate
		☐ 4:59-129 Social Life in Rome
		☐ 4:130-379 Latin in Literature
		☐ 4:380-386 Roman Architectural Wonders

ITALY

ELEMENTARY	MIDDLE SCHOOL	HIGH SCHOOL
☐ A Treasure of Wisdom	☐ All About Leonardo da Vinci, Hahn	☐ Art of Italian Renaissance, Wolfflin
☐ Angelo, Macaulay	☐ Florence, Grierson	☐ Character of Renaissance Architecture
☐ Brother Francis and the Friendly	☐ Garibaldi, Davenport	Moore
Beasts, Hodges	☐ God's Troubadour, Jewitt	☐ Galileo: First Observer, Levinger
☐ Brother Sun Sister Moon, Mayo	☐ Italy, Finnemore	☐ Leonardo da Vinci: Who Followed the
☐ Five Sons of Italy, Acker	☐ Leonardo da Vinci, Hahn	Sinking Star, Levinger
☐ Galileo and the Stargazers	☐ Michelangelo, Ripley	☐ Life of Michel Angelo, Grimm
☐ Italian Twins, Perkins	☐ Out With Garibaldi, Henty	☐ Painters of the Renaissance, Berenson
☐ Legends and Stories of Italy for	☐ Red Sails to Capri, Wells	☐ Pictures and Their Painters, Bryant
Children, Steedman	☐ Secret in a Sealed Bottle, Epstein	☐ Romeo and Juliet, Shakespeare
☐ Leonardo da Vinci, D. Stanley	☐ Stories from Italian History Retold for	☐ The History of Painting Vol 1
☐ Leonardo da Vinci, G. Stanley	Children, Troutbeck	☐ The History of Painting Vol 2
☐ Little Tony of Italy, Madeline	☐ The Lion of St. Mark, Henty	☐ The Painters of Florence, Cartwright
☐ Masters of the Renaissance	☐ Truth on Trial, Cobb	☐ The Story of Italy, Manning
☐ Michelangelo's World, Ventura		☐ The Story of Modern Italy, Orsi
☐ Our Little Italian Cousin, Wade		☐ The Story of Sicily, Freeman
☐ Petrosinella, Stanley	**Forgotten Classics:**	☐ The Story of the Tuscan Republics, Duf
☐ Pinocchio, Collodi	☐ G2-125 Michel Angelo	☐ The Story of Venice, Wiel
☐ Pompeii: Buried Alive, Kunhardt	☐ G4-29 St. Francis of Assisi	☐ The World's Story V 5, Tappan
☐ Saint Francis and the Wolf, Eglielski	☐ G6-310 Guiseppi Garibaldi	
☐ Shakespeare for Children, Weiss	☐ G8-301 Guiseppe Verdi	**Forgotten Classics:**
☐ Short Stories Founded on European	☐ S9-261 Story of Venice	☐ G9-269 Had You Been Born a Roman
History: Italy	☐ W11-276 St. Dominic and St. Francis	Catholic
☐ Stories from Italy, Dolch	☐ W11-310 Beginnings of Modern Times	☐ N9-86 St. Sophia's and St. Mark's
☐ Starry Messenger, Sis	☐ W12-1 Petrarch	☐ N9-91 Two Gothic Cathedrals
☐ Strega Nona, dePaola		☐ N9-96 St. Ambrose/St. Gregory
☐ The Adventures of Pinocchio, Innocenti	**Junior Classics:**	☐ N9-106 Church Music/Medieval
☐ The Black Falcon, Wise	☐ 8-331 Years of Agony: Michelangelo	☐ N9-112 Palestrina
☐ The Clown of God, dePaola		☐ N9-120 Orotorio/Opera
☐ The Golden Book of the Renaissance		☐ N9-130 Il Cherubino
Shapiro		☐ N9-143 Spontini
☐ The House, Innocenti		☐ N9-147 Rossini
		☐ N9-157 Bellini
Forgotten Classics:		☐ N9-161 Verdi
☐ G2-3 Giotto		☐ N9-174 Leaning Tower of Pisa
☐ G2-27 Fra Angelico		☐ N9-178 Giotto's Tower
☐ G2-35 Botticelli		☐ N9-181 Ghiberti's Gates of Paradise
☐ G2-47 Perugino		☐ N9-183 Brunelleschi's Done
☐ G2-65 Leonardo da Vinci		☐ N9-187 Donatello
☐ G2-86 Lippi		☐ N9-191 Michael Angelo
☐ G2-119 Carpaccio		☐ N9-202 Cellini Blogna Bernuiri
☐ G2-173 Raphael		☐ N9-207 Canova
☐ G2-188 Del Sarto		☐ N9-211 Christ Child in Art
☐ G2-205 Del Sarto		☐ N9-213 Cimabue and Giotto
☐ G2-217 Titian		☐ N9-224 Fra Angelico
☐ G2-227 Corregio		☐ N9-231 Leonardo da Vinci
☐ G2-238 Tintoretto		☐ N9-240 Raphael
☐ G2-250 Reni		☐ N9-250 Correggio
☐ G4-21 Francis of Assisi		☐ N9-255 Titian
☐ G5-322 Gugliemo Marconi		☐ N9-265 Venetian Painters
☐ G8-3 Whittle of Cremona		☐ N9-271 17th Century Italian Art
☐ S1-196 Carfaccio		☐ N11-32 Hymns of Eastern Church
☐ S5-305 King Robert of Sicily		☐ N11-54 St. Ambrose/Augustine
☐ S6-1 Michelangelo		☐ N11-67 Mother of Augustine
☐ S6-182 Little Brothers in the Air		

ITALY		
ELEMENTARY	**MIDDLE SCHOOL**	**HIGH SCHOOL**
☐ S10-151 The Vision of Dante		☐ W12-159 Guiseppi Garibaldi
☐ S11-119 Boy Who Wanted to be a		☐ W12-321 Dante
Sculptor--Antonio Canova		
☐ S11-326 Garibaldi and the Lost Lamb		**Delphian Course:**
		☐ 4:387-397 Italy of Today
My Book House:		☐ 5:14-20 St. Francis of Assis
☐ 1-62 Italian Nursery Rhymes		☐ 6:1-29 Italian Renaissance
☐ 1-156 Poems by Christina Rossetti		☐ 6:30-144 Literature of the Renaissance
☐ 6-164 The Wonderful of an Artist's		☐ 6:145-169 Life During the Renaissance
Workshop		☐ 6:363-510 Modern Italian History/
☐ 7-119 Columbine and Her Playfellows		Literature
☐ 7-199 Gigi and the Magic Ring		☐ 7:39-43 Italian Drama
☐ 8-18 The Tempest by Shakespeare		☐ 7:283-296 Modern Italian Drama
☐ 11-152 The Man Who Lived in the		☐ 9:22-45 Early Italian Painters
World of Dreams: Dante		☐ 9:110-136 Art Galleries of Italy
Junior Classics:		
☐ 3-1 The Adventures of Pinocchio		
☐ 4-246 The Son of the Gondolier		
☐ 5-212 The Great Balloon Ascension		
☐ 6-110 Nino's Easter		
☐ 8-151 God's Troubadour		
☐ 8-331 Years of Agony: Michelangelo		

PLANTS / TREES

ELEMENTARY	MIDDLE SCHOOL	HIGH SCHOOL
☐ A Treasury of Flower Fairies, Barker	☐ A Bunch of Wildflowers for the Children, Whitcomb	☐ A Guide to the Trees, Lounsberry
☐ A Tree Is Nice, Udry		☐ Myths and Legends of Flowers, Skinne
☐ Alison's Zinnias, Lobel	☐ The Garden of Earth, Giberne	☐ The Apple Tree, Bailey
☐ Blueberries for Sal, McCloskey	☐ Trees that Every Child Should Know, Rogers	☐ The Handbook of Nature Study, Comstock
☐ Flower Children, Gordon		
☐ Flower Fairies of the Garden, Barker		
☐ Flower Fairies of the Trees, Barker		
☐ Flowers and Their Friends, Morley		
☐ Forest of Dreams, Wells		
☐ In Woods and Fields, Buck		
☐ Linnea in Monet's Garden, Buck		
☐ Miss Rumphius, Cooney		
☐ Nature's Stories for Young Readers: Plant Life, Bass		
☐ Over Under in the Garden, Schories		
☐ Plants and Their Children, Parsons		
☐ Pond and Marsh Plants, Earle		
☐ State Trees, Earle		
☐ The Burgess Flower Book, Burgess		
☐ The Carrot Seed, Knauss		
☐ The Flower Hunter, Ray		
☐ The Gift of the Tree, Tresselt		
☐ The Giving Tree, Silverstein		
☐ The Rose Family, Earle		
☐ The Rose in my Garden, Lobel		
☐ The Secret Garden, Burnett		
☐ The Story of the Forest, Dorrance		
☐ The Strangler Fig, Earle		
☐ The Study of Trees, Weed		
☐ The Tale of the Three Trees, Hunt		
☐ The Trellis and the Seed, Karon		
☐ The Wonder Garden, Olcott		
☐ Weeds, Hogner		
☐ Wild Flower Children, Gordon		

Forgotten Classics:
☐ N4 Stories of Plants and Trees

My Book House:
☐ 2-78 Spring Songs from the Bible
☐ 2-223 The Sugar-Plum Tree
☐ 3-104 A Quick-Running Squash
☐ 3-128 Rosy Posy
☐ 3-146 The Shaking of the Pear Tree

Junior Classics:
☐ 6-133 Stories for Arbor Day

PLANTS / TREES		
ADDITIONAL BOOKS		
ELEMENTARY	MIDDLE SCHOOL	HIGH SCHOOL

AMERICAN REVOLUTION

ELEMENTARY	MIDDLE SCHOOL	HIGH SCHOOL
☐ Betsy Ross, Weil	☐ Alexander Hamilton and Aaron Burr	A Pictorial Field Book, Lossing
☐ Building the Nation, Wade	☐ Benedict Arnold, Syme	☐ Volume 1
☐ Francis Marion Swamp Fox	☐ Benedict Arnold: Hero/Traitor, deLeeuw	Volume 2
☐ George the Drummer Boy, Benchley	☐ Captain John Paul Jones, Syme	☐ Benedict Arnold: Traitor to his Country
☐ I Have Not Yet Begun to Fight, Alphin	☐ Drummer of Vincennes, Sentman	Nolan
☐ If You Lived at the Time of the	☐ Guns for General Washington, Reit	Cast for a Revolution, Fritz
American Revolution, Moore	☐ He Went With John Paul Jones, Kent	Drums of Monmouth, Sterne
☐ John Paul Jones, Worcester	☐ Hero Stories from American History for	John Paul Jones, Abbott
☐ Molly Pitcher, Stevenson	Elementary Schools, Blaisdell	Sword of Liberty, Hutchins
☐ Patriots in Petticoats, Clyne	☐ Heroes of Our Revolution, Hall	The Boys of '76, Commager
☐ Pioneers and Patriots, Dickson	☐ John Paul Jones: Fighting Sailor	The War for Independence, Fiske
☐ Pioneers of the Revolution for Young	☐ Lafayette in America, Maurois	☐ The War for Independence, Marrin
People, Pratt	☐ Lafayette the Friend of American	
☐ Silver for General Washington,	Liberty, Burton	**Forgotten Classics:**
Meadowcraft	☐ Powder Keg, del Rey	☐ F3-261 Grace Barclay's Diary
☐ The Century Book of the American	☐ Retreat to Victory, Alderman	☐ F5-223 Lafayette's Letters to His Wife
Revolution, Brooks	☐ The American Revolution	☐ G7-228 Stephen Girard
☐ The Secret Soldier, McGovern	☐ The Knight of Liberty, Butterworth	
☐ The Story of John Paul Jones, Vinton	☐ The Marquis de Lafayette	
☐ The Story of Lafayette, Wilson	☐ The Story of the Revolution, Lilly	
☐ The Story of Mad Anthony Wayne, Wilson	☐ The Swamp Fox of the American	
☐ The Story of Valley Forge, Stein	Revolution	
☐ The True Story of Lafayette, Brooks	☐ The Watch Fires of '76, Drake	
☐ Toliver's Secret, Brady	☐ The Winter at Valley Forge	
☐ Why Not Lafayette?, Fritz	☐ Three Little Daughters of the	
	Revolution, Perry	
Forgotten Classics:	☐ Traitor: The Case of Benedict Arnold,	
☐ F5-1 True Story of Lafayette	Fritz	
☐ F11-177 Nathaneal Greene	☐ Tree of Freedom, Caudill	
☐ F11-187 John Paul Jones		
☐ F12-92 The Truth Speaker	**Forgotten Classics:**	
☐ F12-114 A Patriot Mother's Prayer	☐ F12-98 Liberty or Loyalty	
☐ F12-127 Lydia Darrah	☐ F12-106 Israel Israel with the Tories	
☐ F12-130 Washington's Christmas Gift	☐ F12-117 Green Mountain Boys	
☐ F12-141 Captain Molly Pritcher	☐ F12-119 Martyr Patriot	
☐ F12-167 Washington's Last Battle	☐ F12-136 A Winter at Valley Forge	
☐ G11-314 A Mother's Faith	☐ F12-143 'Mad Anthony'	
☐ S6-88 Robert and the Spy	☐ F12-150 Francis Marion	
☐ S6-97 The Drummer Boy	☐ F12-153 Another of Marion's Men	
☐ S6-109 Betty Zane	☐ F12-158 A Hero of the Sea	
☐ S6-126 An American Army of Two	☐ G11-153 Molly Pitcher	
☐ S9-155 Story of Jonathan Yankee Boy	☐ W12-67 Two Obscure Heroes	
My Book House:		
☐ 1-101 Yankee Doodle		
☐ 8-8 A Boy on the High Seas		
☐ 8-82 John Paul Jones		
☐ 9-78 Princess Nelly and the Seneca Chief		

AMERICAN REVOLUTION		
ADDITIONAL BOOKS		
ELEMENTARY	MIDDLE SCHOOL	HIGH SCHOOL

FRANCE

ELEMENTARY	MIDDLE SCHOOL	HIGH SCHOOL
Abroad, Crane	A History of France, Marshall	A History of French Painting, Stranahan
Beauty and the Beast, Craft	A Roving Commission, Henty	A Scientist of Two Worlds, Peare
Beauty and the Beast, Hague	A Tale of Two Cities, Dickens	A Tale of Two Cities, Dickens
Beauty and the Beast, Heyer	A Woman of the Commune, Henty	Bolero, Goss
Beauty and the Beast, Sanderson	Around the World in Eighty Days, Verne	Charlemagne, Komroff
Cinderella, Jeffers	At Agincourt, Henty	Cyrano, McCaughrean
Cinderella, Sanderson	By Conduct and Courage, Henty	French Art, Brownell
Discovery in the Cave, Dubowski	Cartier, Syme	French Explorers of North America,
Favorite Fairy Tales - France, Haviland	Cathedral, Macaulay	Abodaher
Favourite French Fairy Tales, Douglas	Champlain of the St. Lawrence, Syme	French Pictures & Their Painters, Bryan
French Fairy Tales, Cary	France, Finnemore	Hero Stories of France, Tappan
Huguenot Garden, Jones	French History for English Children,	Historical Tales: French, Morris
Joan of Arc, Corey	Stephen	History of French Literature, Dowden
Joan of Arc, Poole	Heroes of Chivalry, Maitland	Jean Francois Millet, Tomson
Joan of Arc, Stanley	In the Irish Brigade, Henty	Jeanne d/Arc, Wilmot-Buxton
Joan of Arc the Lily Maid, Hodges	In the Reign of Terror, Henty	Joseph Bonaparte, Abbott
Little Jeanne of France, Brandeis	Joan of Arc, Hodges	Josephine, Abbott
Louis Braille, Davidson	Joan of Arc, Ross	Judith of France, Leighton
Madeline, Bemelmans	Journey for a Princess, Leighton	La Salle and the Great Enterprise, Nola
Madeline's Rescue	LaSalle of the Mississippi, Syme	Les Miserables, Hugo
Millet Tilled the Soil, Wheeler	Marie Antoinette, Kielty	Liberty! Equality! Fraternity!, Alderma
Mirette on the High Wire, McCully	Marie Curie, McKown	Louis XIV, Abbott
Now You Can Read Sleeping Beauty	Marquette and Joliet, Syme	Louis Philippe, Abbott
Old French Fairy Tales, Segur	Napoleon and the Battle of Waterloo	Madame Curie, Curie
Our Little French Cousin, McManus	No Surrender!, Henty	Madame Roland, Abbott
Page Esquire and Knight, Lansing	One of the 28th, Henty	Man in the Iron Mask, Dumas
Puss 'n Boots, Pinkney	Out of Darkness, Freedman	Marie Antoinette, Abbott
Rosa Bonheur, Peare	Paris, Williams	Marie Antoinette, Birkhead
Saint Joan of Arc, Twain	She Lived for Science, McKown	Modern French Masters, Von Vorst
Sleeping Beauty, Craft	St. George for England, Henty	Paintings of the Louvre, Mahler
The Clown of God, dePaola	Stories from French History, Dalkeith	Peasant and Prince, Martineau
The Fairy Tales of Charles Perrault	Stories from French History, Price	Personal Recollections of Joan of Arc,
The Family Under the Bridge, Carlson	Stories of Roland Told to the Children,	Twain
The French Twins, Perkins	Marshall	Stories of Charlemagne, Church
The Happy Orpheline, Carlson	The Bayeaux Tapestry, Denny	Studies in Mediaeval Life, McLaughlin
The King's Day, Aliki	The Boy Travellers in Central Europe,	The Coming of the Friars, Jessopp
The Little Prince, de St. Exupery	Knox	The Count of Monte Cristo, Dumas
The Sleeping Beauty, Quiller-Couch	The French Foreign Legion, Blassingame	The Great Invasion, Alderman
The Sleeping Beauty, Sanderson	The King's Shadow, Alder	The Scarlet Pimpernel, Orczy
The Story of Babar, de Brunhoff	The Journal of Madame Royale, Powers	The Seine River of Paris, Wilson
The Story of Louis Pasteur, Malkus	The Little Marquise, Wilson	The Story of Mediaeval France, Masson
The Story of Madame Curie, Thorne	The Marquis de Lafayette, Carter	The Story of Modern France, LeBon
The Three Musketeers	The Story History of France, Bonner	The Story of the Normans, Jewett
Twenty-One Balloons, du Bois	The Story of France Told to Boys and	The Story of Roland, Baldwin
	Girls, MacGregor	The Three Musketeers, Dumas
	The Striped Ships, McGraw	The World's Story V 5, Tappan
Forgotten Classics:	The Young Franc-Tireurs, Henty	
G2-267 Claude Lorraine	Through Europe with Napoleon, Marsha	**Forgotten Classics:**
G2-313 Bonheur		G4-46 St. Vincent de Paule
G2-321 Bonheur		G11-50 Rachel Lady Russell
S1-11 Julius Adam	**Forgotten Classics:**	G11-159 Marie Antoinette
S1-101 Madame LeBrun	G4-70 Isaac Jogues	G11-178 Wife of Lafayette
S1-103 Ronner	G5-51 Palissy	G11-212 Mary Murray
S1-114 Rosa Bonheur	G6-49 Jeanne D'Arc	G11-296 Marie Curie
S1-137 Bouguereau	G6-294 Napoleon Bonaparte	N10-1 Church and the King
S1-140 Millet	G10-110 Cuvier and Animals of the Past	

FRANCE

ELEMENTARY	MIDDLE SCHOOL	HIGH SCHOOL
☐ S1-200 Le Page	☐ G10-159 Agassiz and the Animal Kingdon	☐ N10-6 Song and the Singer
☐ S1-207 Emily Renouf	☐ G10-272 Louis Pasteur	☐ N10-14 Lully and Rameau
☐ S1-212 Corot	☐ G10-341 Marie Curie	☐ N10-22 Revolutionary Song
☐ S3-1 French Fairy Tales	☐ S9-296 French Revolution	☐ N10-30 Grand Opera
☐ S5-259 Roland	☐ S11-218 A Loyal Worker: Louis Pasteur	☐ N10-36 Hector Berlioz
☐ S6-29 Bonheur	☐ W5-1 Little Stories of France	☐ N10-43 French Music of Today
☐ S6-93 Roland and the Jewel	☐ W5-151 Joan of Arc	☐ N10-48 Early French Art
☐ S6-243 Jean Francois Millet	☐ W11-210 Charles the Great and the	☐ N10-56 18th Century Art
☐ S6-251 The Little Corporal	Holy Roman Empire	☐ N10-64 Rousseau Diaz Troyon Jacque
☐ S9-101 The Story of Gilbert the Page	☐ W11-297 End of the Middle Ages	Corot
☐ S11-109 Lampblack	☐ W11-401 Age of Louis XIV	☐ N10-74 Jean Francois Millet
☐ S11-175 Boy Who Conquered Fire	☐ W11-466 French Revolution	☐ N10-81 Modern French Painting
☐ S11-211 Boy Who Could Give Up	☐ W11-479 Story of Napoleon	☐ N11-69 Charlemagne: Hymn Writer
☐ S11-349 The Good Bishop fom Les	☐ W11-505 Remaking of Europe	☐ N11-78 Robert II of France
Miserables	☐ W12-19 Boy Commander of the	☐ N11-85 The Bernards
	Camisards	☐ S11-205 Napoleon's Love for Josephir
My Book House:	☐ W12-49 Emperor Napoleon	☐ W12-186 Joseph Marie Jacquard
☐ 1-124 French Nursery Rhymes	☐ W12-53 Back from Exile	
☐ 3-114 The Honest Woodman	☐ W12-57 Little King of Rome	**Delphian Course:**
☐ 4-12 Cinderella	☐ W12-73 Genevieve	☐ 5:91-116 Early French Literature
☐ 6-11 The Sleeping Beauty		☐ 5:201-217 Aucassin and Nicolete
☐ 6-184 The Fairyland of Science		☐ 5:333-350 French Opera
☐ 7-173 The Knights of the Silver Shield		☐ 6:170-221 French Literature of the
☐ 10-38 The Song of Roland		Renaissance
☐ 10-98 Joan of Arc		☐ 7:215-282 French Drama
☐ 10-165 As You Like It		☐ 8:431-465 History of France
		☐ 9:79-93 French Art
Junior Classics:		☐ 9:158-168 Art in the Louvre
☐ 1-54 Cinderella		☐ 9:375-460 French Fiction
☐ 1-287 Susanna's Auction		
☐ 2-120 Sleeping Beauty in the Wood		
☐ 2-130 Puss in Boots		
☐ 3-330 Twenty-One Balloons		
☐ 7-219 The Death of Roland		
☐ 8-251 The Discovery of Radium:		
Madame Curie		

FRANCE		
ADDITIONAL BOOKS		
ELEMENTARY	MIDDLE SCHOOL	HIGH SCHOOL

CANADA

ELEMENTARY	MIDDLE SCHOOL	HIGH SCHOOL
☐ A Prairie Boy's Summer, Kurelek	☐ A Child's History of Canada, McIlraith	☐ Acadian Reminiscences
☐ A Prairie Boy's Winter	☐ Alexander MacKenzie, Syme	☐ Canada, Bourinot
Anne of Green Gables, Montgomery	☐ Canadian Summer, Stockum	☐ Canada: History of the Dominion,
☐ Anne of Green Gables	☐ Captured by Mohawks, North	Hopkins
☐ Anne of Avonlea	☐ General Brock and Niagara Falls	☐ Evangeline, Longfellow
☐ Anne of the Island	☐ James Jerome Hill, Judson	☐ Mrs. Mike, Freedman
☐ Anne of Windy Poplars	☐ Little Giant of the North, Malkus	☐ Tears Love and Laughter, Daigle
☐ Anne's House of Dreams	☐ Saint Lawrence Seaway, Judson	☐ The Discoverer of Insulin, Levine
☐ Anne of Ingleside	☐ Stories of New France, Marquis	☐ The Doctor Who Dared, Noble
☐ Rainbow Valley	☐ The First Northwest Crossing, O'Meara	☐ The World's Story V 11, Tappan
☐ Rilla of Ingleside	☐ The Royal Canadian Mounted Police	
☐ Applesauce Needs Sugar, Case	☐ With Wolfe in Canada, Henty	**Forgotten Classics:**
☐ Evangeline, Moore		☐ G12-346 Lucy Laud Montgomery
☐ Ida and the Wool Smugglers, Alderson	**Forgotten Classics:**	
☐ Lumberjack, Kurelek	☐ G4-364 Wilfred Grenfell	
☐ Mary of Mile 18, Blades	☐ W5-241 Our Empire Story	
☐ Owls in the Family, Mowat	☐ W11-442 Story of Canada	
☐ The Golden Phoenix, Hornyansky		
☐ The Talking Cat, Carlson		
☐ Wilfred's Hospital Ship, Ready		

Forgotten Classics:
☐ N11-4 Mother Recognized by a Hymn
☐ S6-121 Noel Duval
☐ S6-190 Heroic Madelon

My Book House:
☐ 1-130 Canadian Songs
☐ 4-161 The Story of Big Paul Bunyan
☐ 4-180 A Song of the Canadian
    Lumberjack
☐ 6-71 The Strong Boy

Junior Classics:
☐ 2-275 The Golden Phoenix
☐ 4-99 Anne's Confession

CANADA		
ADDITIONAL BOOKS		
ELEMENTARY	MIDDLE SCHOOL	HIGH SCHOOL

SWITZERLAND		
ELEMENTARY	**MIDDLE SCHOOL**	**HIGH SCHOOL**
☐ A Bell for Ursli, Chong	☐ Stories of William Tell, Marshall	☐ Switzerland, Hug
☐ Heidi, Classic	☐ Switzerland, Finnemore	
☐ Heidi, Spyri	☐ Switzerland, MacKenzie	
☐ Heidi, Spyri/Stork	☐ Switzerland, Taylor	
☐ Heidi, Spyri/White	☐ The Apple and the Arrow, Buff	
☐ Moni the Goat-Boy, Spyri	☐ The Story of Albert Schweitzer, Daniel	
☐ Our Little Swiss Cousin, Wade	☐ Treasures of the Snow, St. John	
☐ Swiss Family Robinson, Wyss		
☐ Swiss Family Robinson, Wyss/Mitton	**Junior Classics:**	
☐ The Swiss Twins, Perkins	☐ 9-253 Men of the Forest Cantons	
☐ The Legend of William Tell, Small		
Forgotten Classics:		
☐ S6-161 Arnold Winkelreid		
My Book House:		
☐ 1-66 Swiss Nursery Rhymes		
☐ 5-146 Heidi in the Alpine Pasture		
☐ 10-44 Legend of William Tell		
Junior Classics:		
☐ 4-268 The Sesemann House is Haunted		
☐ 10-97 Swiss Family Robinson		

GARDENING		
ELEMENTARY	**MIDDLE SCHOOL**	**HIGH SCHOOL**
☐ Gardens Shown to the Children, Kelman	☐ A Few Familiar Flowers, Morley	☐ A Child's Garden, Dannenmaier
☐ Linnea's Almanac, Bjork	☐ The Garden Book for Young People, Lounsberry	☐ A Simple Flower Garden for Country Homes, Barnard
☐ Linnea's Windowsill Garden, Bjork		☐ Joy in Your Garden, Bossi
☐ Little Gardens for Boys and Girls, Higgins		☐ Little Gardens, Skinner
☐ Mary's Garden and How it Grew, Duncan		☐ My Handkerchief Garden, Barnard
☐ Planting a Rainbow, Ehlert		☐ Planting a Bible Garden, Hepper
☐ The Children's Book of Gardening, Sidgwick		☐ Square Foot Gardening, Bartholomew
☐ The Tiny Seed, Carle		☐ The Joyous Art of Gardening, Duncan
☐ When Mother Lets Us Garden, Duncan		☐ The Shakespeare Garden, Singleton
Forgotten Classics:		
☐ N5 Stories from Gardening		

A NEW NATION

ELEMENTARY	MIDDLE SCHOOL	HIGH SCHOOL
☐ Alexander Hamilton, Albee	☐ A Herald of the West, Altsheler	☐ 1812: The War Nobody Won, Marrin
☐ Alexander Hamilton, Kulling	☐ Beacon Lights of Patriotism, Carrington	☐ 1984, Orwell
☐ American Patriotic Prose/Verse, Stevens	☐ Betsy Ross and the Flag, Mayer	☐ A Brief Enquiry, Upshur
☐ American Patriotism in Prose and	☐ Birthdays of Freedom, Foster	☐ A Loyal Traitor, Barnes
Verse, Gathany	☐ Bugle Calls of Liberty, Southworth	☐ Alas Babylon, Frank
☐ Celebrating America, Whipple	☐ Elementary Catechism of the Constitution	☐ America Land That We Love, Miller
☐ Century Book of Famous Americans,	of the United States, Stansbury	American War Ballads/Lyrics, Egglesto
Brooks	☐ Flat-Tops: The Story of Aircraft Carriers	☐ Volume 1
☐ Dolly Madison, Monsell	☐ In the Wasp's Nest, Brady	☐ Volume 2
☐ Dolly Madison Famous First Lady,	☐ Medal of Honor Heroes, Reeder	☐ Animal Farm, Orwell
Davidson	☐ Mr. Justice Holmes, Judson	☐ Atlas Shrugged, Rand
☐ Francis Scott Key's Star Spangled	☐ My Country, Turkington	☐ Brave New World, Huxley
Banner, Kulling	☐ Old Ironsides	☐ Dames and Daughters of the Young
☐ James Madison: Statesman and	☐ Our Independence and Constitution	Republic, Brooke
President, Kelly	☐ Patriots and Tyrants, Lansing	☐ Democracy in America 1, Toqueville
☐ Katharine Lee Bates, Myers	☐ Places Young Americans Want to Know,	☐ Democracy in America 2, Toqueville
☐ James Madison: Statesman and	Tomlinson	☐ Discovey of Freedom, Lane
President, Kelly	☐ The Battle of Lake Erie, Mason	☐ Dolley Madison, Nolan
☐ My Country 'Tis of Thee, Dunn	☐ The Burning of Washington 1814, Phelan	☐ Farenheit 451, Bradbury
☐ My Country 'Tis of Thee, Smith	☐ The F.B.I. Reynolds	☐ Father of the Constitution, Moseley
☐ Poems of American Patriotism, Matthews	☐ The Founders, Fradin	☐ Fighters and Martyrs for the Freedom
☐ Red White and Blue, Herman	☐ The Giver, Lowry	of Faith, Walmsley
☐ Shhh! We're Writing the Constitution,	☐ The Pirate Lafitte & Battle of New Orleans	☐ Heroes of Annapolis, Hatch
Fritz	☐ The Story of Liberty, Baldwin	☐ Historic Buildings of America, Singleto
☐ Sing for America, Wheeler	☐ The Story of Liberty Part 1, Coffin	☐ How to Win Friends and Influence
☐ Statue of Liberty, Bauer	☐ The Story of Liberty Part 2, Coffin	People Carnegie
☐ The Fourth of July Story, Dalgliesh	☐ The Story of Our Constitution, Tappan	☐ In God We Trust, Cousins
☐ The Great Little Madison, Fritz	☐ The Story of Submarines	☐ John Jay, Faber
☐ The Powers of Congress, Stein	☐ The Story of the Air Force	☐ Miracle at Philadelphia, Bowen
☐ The Star-Spangled Banner, Spier	☐ The Story of the Liberty Bell, Shipple	☐ Our National Government, Willhauck
☐ The Statue of Liberty, Penner	☐ The Story of the Naval Academy	☐ Our Old World Background, Beard
☐ The Story of Old Glory, Mayer	☐ The Story of the US Border Patrol	☐ Our Sacred Honor, Bennett
☐ The Story of the Bill of Rights, Stein	☐ The Story of the US Coast Guard	☐ Profiles in Courage, Kennedy
☐ The Story of the Capitol, Prolman	☐ The Story of the US Marines	☐ Stories of National Songs, Smith
☐ The Story of the Constitution, Prolman	☐ The Story of West Point	☐ Sylvanus Thayer of West Point, Eliot
☐ The Story of the Statue of Liberty, Miller	☐ The War of 1812, Tomlinson	☐ The 5000 Year Leap, Skousen
☐ The Story of the Powers of the Supreme		☐ The Amazing Alexander Hamilton,
Court, Stein	**Forgotten Classics:**	Orrmont
☐ The Story of Presidential Elections,	☐ F6-211 Story of the Constituion	☐ The Dawn's Early Light, Lord
Hargrove	☐ F6-278 Franklin's Call to Prayer	☐ The Federalist, Jay
☐ The Story of the Star-Spangled Banner,	☐ F6-281 Civics for Young Americans	☐ The Law, Bastiat
Miller	☐ F12-194 Star-Spangled Banner	☐ The Presidents in American History,
☐ The Story of the Supreme Court, Richards	☐ G6-233 James Madison	Beard
☐ The Story of the White House, Miller	☐ G6-246 John Marshall	☐ The Story of the World, Elson
☐ The Tuttle Twins Learn About the Law,	☐ G6-260 Alexander Hamilton	☐ Those Who Love, Stone
Boyack	☐ N11-9 A Prisoner Singing Himself Into	
☐ We the People, Spier	Liberty	**Forgotten Classics:**
☐ Whatever Happened to Justice?	☐ S11-221 Patriotism of Senator Foelker	☐ F6-368 Thoughts from Founding Fathe
☐ Whatever Happened to Penny Candy?,		☐ G11-201 Dolly Madison
Maybury		☐ G12-150 Edward Everett Hale
		☐ N11-260 Star-Spangled Banner
Forgotten Classics:		☐ N11-268 America
☐ F6-1 Stories of the Government		
☐ F11-233 A New Republic		
☐ F12-35 The Landlord's Mistake		

A NEW NATION		
ELEMENTARY	**MIDDLE SCHOOL**	**HIGH SCHOOL**
☐ F12-185 The Surly Guest		
☐ F12-188 Why He Carried the Turkey		
☐ F12-191 The Star-Spangled Banner		
My Book House:		
☐ 5-129 The 4th of July		
☐ 8-84 Young Midshipman David Farragut		
☐ 11-172 The New Colussus		
Junior Classics:		
☐ 6-178 Betsy Ross and the Flag		
☐ 6-184 Star-Spangled Girl		
☐ 8-266 A Lawyer's Oath: Oliver Wendell Holmes Jr.		

HOLY LAND

ELEMENTARY	MIDDLE SCHOOL	HIGH SCHOOL
A Book of Little Bible Boys, Spalding	Adventures of Two Younths in Egypt	Ben-Hur, Wallace
A Child's Life of Christ, Lathbury	and the Holy Land, Knox	Chaim Weizmann, Baker
A Picture Book of Hanukkah, Adler	Ben-Gurion and the Birth of Israel, Comay	Christ and the Fine Arts, Maus
A Treasury of Wisdom, Weiss	Flight to the Promised Land, Hamori	Dear and Glorious Physician, Caldwell
All-of-a-Kind Family, Taylor	For the Temple, Henty	Exodus, Uris
All-of-a-Kind Family Downtown	Hebrew Heroes	Fantastic Victory, Skousen
All-of-a-Kind Family Uptown	Hero Stories from the Old Testament,	Hebrew Religion to the Establishment
More All-of-a-Kind Family	Loveland	of Judaism, Addis
Bible Pictures and Stories, Donaldson	Jesus of Nazareth, Fosdick	Historical Geography - Holy Land, Smit
Bible Stories, Comstock	Old Stories of the East, Baldwin	History of Apostolic Church, Thatcher
Bible Stories for Children, Hill	On Holy Ground Vol 1, Worcester	History of the Hebrew People, Kent
Chronicles of Narnia, Lewis	On Holy Ground Vol 2, Worcester	Volume 1
Prince Caspian	Our Young Folks Josephus, Walsh	Volume 2
The Horse and His Boy	Slave Boy in Judea, Lau	History of the People of Israel, Cornill
The Last Battle	Song of Deborah, Jenkins	Home Life in All Lands, Morris
The Lion the Witch and the Wardrobe	The Antiquities of the Jews	In His Steps, Sheldon
The Magician's Nephew	The Bronze Bow, Speare	Joshua, Ebers
The Silver Chair	The Child's Life of Jesus, Steedman	Life and Literature of the Ancient
The Voyage of the Dawn Treader	The Christ Story, Tappan	Hebrews, Abbott
Catherine Marshall's Story Bible	The Game of Doeg, Harris	Literary Study of the Bible, Moulton
David, Petersham	The Gospel Story for Young People,	Magnificent Obsession, Douglas
Great Stories of the Bible, Miles	Stretton	Modern Reader's Bible: Old, Moulton
It Could Always be Worse, Zemach	The Life of St. Paul, Fosdick	Modern Reader's Bible: New, Moulton
Jewish Fairy Tales/Fables, Landa	The Story of Stories, Gillie	Out-of-Doors in the Holy Land, van Dyl
Jewish Fairy Tales/Stores, Friedlander	The Story of the Bible, van Loon	People in Palestine, Coolidge
Jewish Holiday Stories	The Story of the Chosen People, Guerber	Semitic Origins, Barton
Jonah and the Big Fish, Bulla	Vinegar Boy, Hawse	Short History of the Hebrews, Ottley
Joseph the Dreamer, Bulla		Short Introduction to Literature of
Just Enough is Plenty, Goldin	**Forgotten Classics:**	the Bible, Moulton
Life When Jesus was a Boy, Maxwell	G4-9 St. Paul	Social Life of the Hebrews, Day
Moses, Petersham	G4-141 William Ambrose Shedd	Study of Child Life, Washburne
My Mother's Bible Story	G9-162 Abraham and Lot	The Big Fisherman, Douglas
Noah's Ark, Pinkney	W6-286 Stories from Jewish History	The Chosen, Potok
Noah's Ark, Spier	W11-19 The Jews and Phoenecians	The Holy Land, Kelman
Nursery Book of Bible Stories, Steedman		The Natural History of the Ten
Playmates in Egypt, Levinger	**Junior Classics:**	Commandments, Seton
Saint Jerome and the Lion, Hodges	8-314 The Pillar of Cloud and the	The Old Testament & the Fine Arts, Ma
Silent Night, Jefers	Pillar of Fire	The Religion of the Old Testament, Ma
Snow in Jerusalem, da Costa		The Robe, Douglas
Something from Nothing, Gilman		The Story of the Jews Ancient Medieva
Stories from the Life of Christ, Kelman		and Modern Times, Hosmer
Stories from the Old Testament, Chisholm		The Story of the Jews Under Roman
Stories from the Old Testament, Kellogg		Rule, Morrison
Stories of the Kings of Judah and Israel		The World's Story V 2, Tappan
Tales and Customs of the Ancient		What is Christianity?, Harnack
Hebrews, Herbst		Zion Chronicles Series, Thoene
Tales from the Old Testament		Zion Covenant Series, Thoene
The Always Prayer Shawl, Oberman		
The Golden City, Waldman		**Forgotten Classics:**
The Jewish Fairy Book, Friedlander		G4-92 Henry Martyn
The Peddler's Gift, Schur		G9-172 Had You Been Born a Jew
The Story of Christ and His Apostles, Rusk		N9-17 Hebrew Music
The Story of Noah and the Ark, Spirin		N9-76 Early Christian Music
When the King Came, Hodges		N11-21 Hymns of Jewish Origin

HOLY LAND		
ELEMENTARY	**MIDDLE SCHOOL**	**HIGH SCHOOL**

Forgotten Classics:
- [ ] G9-249 The King is Come
- [ ] S6-102 David the Brave Shepherd Boy
- [ ] S8-3 Old Testament for Young People
- [ ] S8-139 Child's Story of the Life of Christ
- [ ] W6-96 Story of the Chosen People

My Book House:
- [ ] 1-216 Songs of Joy From the Bible
- [ ] 1-218 Mary and the Christ Child
- [ ] 2-101 Noah's Ark
- [ ] 3-156 The Babe Moses
- [ ] 4-80 The Boy Samuel
- [ ] 7-73 David the Shepherd Boy
- [ ] 9-134 Gideon the Warrior
- [ ] 10-48 Joseph and His Brethren

Junior Classics:
- [ ] 5-58 A Friend in Need
- [ ] 6-109 Stories for Easter
- [ ] 6-308 The Library Lady
- [ ] 6-346 The Hanukkah Story
- [ ] 6-353 Festival of Lights
- [ ] 6-402 So Hallowed and So Gracious is the Time
- [ ] 8-314 The Pillar of Cloud: Moses

High School — Delphian Course:
- [ ] 1:372-483 Hebrew History/Neighbors
- [ ] 2:1-68 Hebrew Literature

HOLY LAND		
ADDITIONAL BOOKS		
ELEMENTARY	MIDDLE SCHOOL	HIGH SCHOOL

ANCIENT CIVILIZATIONS

ELEMENTARY	MIDDLE SCHOOL	HIGH SCHOOL
☐ Afghan Dreams, Sullivan	☐ For the Right to Learn, Langston-George	☐ A King of Tyre, Ludlow
☐ Alia's Mimssion, Stamaty	☐ I am Malala, Yousafsai	☐ A Student's Study Guide in Ancient History, Southworth
☐ Ancient History Told to Children, Lane	☐ Iqbal, d'Adamo	
☐ Gilgamesh the King, Zeman	☐ Stories of East from Herodotus, Church	☐ Acres of Diamonds
☐ Listen to the Wind, Mortenson	☐ The Golden Bull, Crowley	☐ Ancient Chaldea, Maspero
☐ Malala Yousafzai, Abouraya	☐ Three Cups of Tea, Thomson	☐ Assyria Its Prices Priests & People, Say
☐ Silent Music, Rumford	☐ When I Was a Boy in Persia, Mirza	☐ Babylonian and Assyrian Laws, Scribne
☐ The King's Fountain, Alexander	☐ Young People's History of the Ancient World, Hillyer	☐ Babylonians and Assyrians, Sayce
☐ The Last Quest of Gilgamesh, Zeman		☐ Cyrus the Great, Abbott
☐ The Legend of Persian Carpet, dePaola		☐ Darius the Great, Abbott
☐ The Librarian of Basra, Winter	**Forgotten Classics:**	☐ History of Ancient Peoples, Boughton
☐ The Revenge of Ishtar, Zeman	☐ W6-1 Ancient History Told to Children	☐ History of Babylonia/Assyria, Rogers
☐ Three Cups of Tea, Thomson		☐ History of Babylonians and Assyrians, Goodspeed
		☐ History Prophecy and the Monuments, McCurdy
Forgotten Classics:		☐ Life in Ancient Egypt/Assyria, Masperc
☐ S6-178 The Young Cupbearer		☐ Stories of Ancient Peoples, Arnold
☐ S9-19 Story of Darius the Persian Boy		☐ The Great Cities of Ancient World, Smi
☐ S11-28 Truth is Mighty and Will Prevail		☐ The Hittites, Sayce
☐ S11-240 The Little Persian		☐ The Story of Assyria, Ragozin
☐ S11-245 Dama's Jewels		☐ The Story of Chaldea, Ragozin
☐ S11-308 The Persian and His Three Sons		☐ The Story of Media Babylon and Persia, Ragozin
		☐ The Story of Persia
My Book House:		☐ The Story of Phoenicia, Rawlinson
☐ 10-228 A Story of Rustem the Hero of Persia		☐ The Story of Queen Esther, Seymour
		☐ The Story of the Persian Wars from Herodotus, Church
		☐ The World's Story V 2, Tappan
		☐ The Epic of Gilgamesh, Sandars
		☐ Three Cups of Tea, Mortenson
		☐ Xerxes, Abbott
		Forgotten Classics:
		☐ G4-92 Henry Martyn
		☐ G4-141 William Ambrose Shedd
		☐ G9-35 Had You Been Born a Parsi
		☐ G11-4 Mothers of Antiquity
		☐ N9-3 Ancient Music
		Delphian Course:
		☐ 1:193-371 Babylon Assyria Persia

ANCIENT CIVILIZATIONS		
ADDITIONAL BOOKS		
ELEMENTARY	MIDDLE SCHOOL	HIGH SCHOOL

INSECTS / BUGS		
ELEMENTARY	**MIDDLE SCHOOL**	**HIGH SCHOOL**
☐ A Little Gateway to Science: Patch	☐ Butterflies and Moths Shown to Children, Kelman	☐ A Year Among the Bees, Miller
☐ Anansi the Spider		☐ American Butterflies and Moths, Matschat
☐ Apricot ABC, Miles	☐ Spiders, Kurata	
☐ Buz, Noel	☐ The Children's Life of the Bee, Maeterlinck	☐ Insect Biographies with Pen and Camera, Ward
☐ Cecil's Book of Insects, Peabody	☐ The Handbook of Nature Study, Comstock	
☐ Charlotte's Web, White		☐ Nature Biographies, Weed
☐ Cricket in Times Square, Selden		☐ Scenes of Industry, Johnstone
☐ Cricket on the Hearth, Dickens		☐ The Bee-Keeper's Manual, Taylor
☐ Crickets, Earle		☐ The Population of an Old Pear Tree, Van Bruyssel
☐ Fabre's Book of Insects, Fabre		
☐ Green Darner, McClung		☐ The Wonders of Instinct, Fabre
☐ I Like Caterpillars, Conklin		
☐ I Watch Flies, Conklin		
☐ Insect Adventures, Fabre		
☐ Insect Lives, Ballard		
☐ Little Black Ant, Gall		
☐ Little Busybodies, Marks		
☐ Look About Club, Bamford		
☐ Mosquitoes, Ripper		
☐ Moths, Hogner		
☐ Praying Mantis, Conklin		
☐ Scavengers, Earle		
☐ Short Stories of Our Shy Neighbors, Kelly		
☐ Someone Saw a Spider, Como		
☐ Spiders, Hogner		
☐ Sphinx, McClung		
☐ Summer Birds, Engle		
☐ The Butterfly Hunters, Conant		
☐ The Very Hungry Caterpillar, Carle		
☐ We Like Bugs, Conklin		
☐ When Insects are Babies, Conklin		
☐ Where Butterflies Grow, Ryder		
☐ Why Mosquito Buzzes in People's Ears		
☐ Wonderful Little Lives, Schwartz		
☐ Yonder, Johnston		

Forgotten Classics:
☐ N6 Stories of Insects and Other Bugs

My Book House:
☐ 2-76 Grasshopper Green
☐ 2-163 The Song of the Bee
☐ 2-185 The Song of the Flea
☐ 3-162 The Butterfly's Ball
☐ 5-54 Wilbur's Boast--Charlotte's Web

INSECTS / BUGS		
ADDITIONAL BOOKS		
ELEMENTARY	MIDDLE SCHOOL	HIGH SCHOOL

WESTWARD EXPANSION		
ELEMENTARY	**MIDDLE SCHOOL**	**HIGH SCHOOL**
A Picture Story of Daniel Boone, Garst	A Dime for Romance, Maher	Alaska's Railroad Builder, Herron
A Pioneer Sampler, Greenwood	A Gathering of Days, Blos	America's First Trained Nurse, Baker
Adventures of Tom Sawyer, Twain	A Girl of the Limberlost, Porter-Stratton	Angel of Mercy, Baker
Adventures of Tom Sawyer, Weiss	A Lantern in Her Hand, Aldrich	Benjamin Bonneville, Miller
Aleck Bell, Widdemer	Adventures of Huckleberry Finn, Twain	Bill Williams, Johnson
America's Mark Twain, McNeer	Andrew Carnegie and the Age of Steel,	Bride of Glory, Leight
American Tall Tales, Weiss	Shippen	Buffalo Bill, Garst
Andrew Jackson, Stanley	Around the World with Nellie Bly, Hahn	Cancer Cocaine and Courage, Crane
Andy Jackson and the Long Road to the	Boy Settlers, Brooks	Christopher ('Kit') Carson, Abbott
White House, Angell	Buffalo Bill's Wild West Show, Havighurst	Cowboy Artist, Garst
Antoine of Oregon, Otis	Building of the First Transcontinental	Daniel Boone, Abbott
Away Goes Sally, Coatsworth	Railroad	Dick Wootton, Garst
Besty-Tacy Series, Lovelace	Calamity Jane, Faber	Dr. Morton, Baker
Bird-Woman of the Lewis and Clark	Captains Courageous, Kipling	First Woman Ambulance Surgeon, Nob
Expedition, Chandler	Continent for Sale, Groom	First Woman Editor, Burt
Boat Builder, Judson	Daniel Boone, Brown	Frederick Law Olmstead, Noble
Buffalo Bill, Beals	Daniel Boone, Daugherty	Frontier Hero, Garst
Buffalo Bill, d'Aulaire	Daniel Boone the Pioneer of Kentucky,	Gene Rhodes, Day
Buffalo Bill, Stevenson	Abbott	In My Youth, Dudley
Buffalo Bill and the Pony Express, Coerr	Dawn, Porter	Inventive Wizard, Levine
Caddie Woodlawn, Brink	Disaster at Johnstown, Hildegarde	James Fenimore Cooper, Proudfit
Cherokee Strip, Fisher	Donald McKay & the Clipper Ships, Chase	Joseph Pulitzer, Noble
Child of the Silent Night, Hunger	Down the Colorado with Major Powell,	Lewis and Clark: Partners in Diversity,
Children of the Covered Wagon, Carr	Ulman	Bakeless
Cowboy, Walker	Dr. Beaumont and the Man with the	Love Comes Softly, Oke
Cowboys and Cattle Trails, Garst	Hole in His Stomach, Epstein	Man of Courage, Harrod
Dan Beard, Seibert	Educating for Democracy, Treichler	Master Bridge Builders, Harrod
Daniel Boone, Mason	Freckles, Porter-Stratton	Memoirs of John R. Young: Utah Pionee
Daniel Boone, Stevenson	Frontier Living, Tuni	Men to Match my Mountains, Stone
Daniel Boone Taming the Wild, Wilkie	Henry David Thoreau, Daugherty	Nellie Bly, Noble
Desert Harvest, Oakes	Heroines of the Early West, Ross	O. Henry, Nolan
Eli Whitney: Great Inventor, Latham	Hobnailed Boots, Nolan	Old Hickory, Marrin
Eli Whitney: Master Craftsman, Gilbert	Holding the Fort with Daniel Boone,	Patterns on the Wall, Yates
Elizabeth Blackwell, Latham	Meadowcroft	Petticoats West, Burt
Gone West, Weiss	Hunter's Stew and Hangtown Fry, Perl	Rails Across the Continent, Johnson
Green Grows the Prairie, Simon	In the Heart of the Rockies, Henty	Roy Rogers, Rasky
Henner's Lydia, de Angeli	Jacob Hamblin	Son of the Smoky Sea, Hatch
Henry Wadsworth Longfellow, Peare	John James Audobon, Kieran	The Autobiography of Mark Twain
Heroes of the Western Outposts, McCall	Just David, Porter	The Log of a Cowboy, Adams
Hitty Her First Hundred Years, Field	Kit Carson and the Wild Frontier, Moody	The Sound of Trumpets, Daugherty
Hunters Blaze the Trails, McCall	Letters of a Woman Homesteader, Pruitt	The Virginian, Wister
In Those Days, Hallock	Little Britches, Moody	The Way to the West, Hough
Jim Bridger, Luce	Mill, Macaulay	Walt Whitman, Deutsch
John Wanamaker, Burt	Mr. Bell Invents the Telephone, Shippen	Will Rogers, Garst
John Wesley Powell, Place	Nelly Bly Reporter, Baker	William Clayton's Journal
Johnny Appleseed, Harrison	Nickels and Dimes, Baker	
Johnny Appleseed, Kurtz	Of Courage Undaunted, Daugherty	**Forgotten Classics:**
Johnny Appleseed, Lindbergh	Old Johnny Appleseed, Miller	F7-247 First Bride of Seattle
Johnny Appleseed, Norman	On the Way Home, Wilder	G4-205 Father Damien
Journey of a Pioneer, Murphy	Pacific History Stories, Harriman	G7-183 Leland Stanford
Juliette Low, Radford	Pike of Pike's Peak, Baker	G7-258 Charles Pratt
Katharine Lee Bates, Myers	Pioneers of the Rocky Mountains and the	G7-280 Employers and Employees
Keep the Lights Burning Abbie, Roop	West, McMurry	G9-365 The Mormons
King of the Clippers, Collier	Race to the Golden Spike, Wellman	G11-195 Jemima Johnson
Kit Carson: Mountain Scout, Worcester	Redskin and Cowboy, Henty	G11-225 Mother of Garfield

WESTWARD EXPANSION		
ELEMENTARY	**MIDDLE SCHOOL**	**HIGH SCHOOL**
Laddie, Porter-Stratton	Riders of the Pony Express, Moody	G11-254 Jean Lathrop Stanford
Land of Gray Gold, Derieth	Robert Fulton and His Steamboat, Hill	G11-279 'The Princess' of Wellesley
Laura Ingalls Wilder, Wadsworth	Sailing the Seven Seas, Chase	G12-54 Washington Irving
Lewis and Clark, Montgomery	The Adventures of Lewis & Clark, Bakeless	G12-223 Glimpses of Mark Twain
Little Giant of Schenectady, Markey	The Alaska Gold Rush, McNeer	G12-264 Orison Swett Marden
Little Engine that Could	The Blowing Wand, Ziegler	G12-269 Laura Richards
Mail Riders, McCall	The Boy's Life of Mark Twain, Paine	G12-305 Henry VanDyke
Mark Twain: His Life, Peare	The California Gold Rush, McNeer	G12-317 Kate Douglas Wiggin
Martha Berry, Phelan	The Coming of the Mormons, Kjelgaard	N11-210 God Be With You
Men on Iron Horses, McCall	The Erie Canal, Adams	N11-246 Phoebe Cary
Oh Lizzie!, Faber	The First Overland Mail, Pinkerton	W12-194 Ezra Cornell
Old Settler Stories, Fletcher	The Gift of Magic Sleep, Shapiro	W12-207 Charles Goodyear
Over the Hills to the Nugget, Fisher	The Golden Ages of Railroads, Holbrook	W12-424 A Campfire Interpreter
Ox-Cart Man, Hall	The Greatest Cattle Drive, Wellman	
P.T. Barnum, Groh	The Lewis & Clark Expedition, Hitchcock	**Delphian Course:**
Picture Story of Alaska, O'Neill	The Lewis & Clark Expedition, Neuberger	10:466-511 American Life in American
Pioneering on Early Waterways, McCall	The Louisiana Purchase, Tallant	Fiction
Race for the Prairie, Fisher	The Mississippi Bubble, Costain	
Reaper Man, Judson	The Oregon Trail, Daugherty	
Rebecca of Sunnybrook Farm, Wiggin	The Pony Express, Adams	
Riding the Pony Express, Bulla	The Santa Fe Trail, Adams	
Ringling Brothers, Glendinning	The Sign of the Beaver, Speare	
Rip Van Winkle, Weiss	The Story of Thomas Alva Edison, Cousins	
Robert Fulton, Henry	The Trail Blazers, Evans	
Sarah Plain and Tall, MacLachlan	The World's Greates Showman, Bryan	
Simon Kenton, Wilkie	The Young Trailers Series, Altsheler	
Sky High, Kulling	The Border Watch	
Sons of the Big Muddy, Granberg	The Eyes of the Woods	
Stone Fox, Gardiner	The Forest Runners	
Stories of Pioneer Life, Bass	The Free Rangers	
The Biography of a Prairie Girl, Gates	The Keepers of the Trail	
The Cabin Faced West, Fritz	The Rifleman of the Ohio	
The Challengers, Lundy	The Scouts of the Valley	
The Cowman's Kingdom, Collier	The Young Trailers	
The Greatest Adventure, Lane	Tidewater Valley, Lundy	
The Josefina Story Quilt, Coerr	To California by Covered Wagon, Stewart	
The Little House Cookbook, Walker	Trappers and Traders of the Far West,	
The Little House on the Prairie, Wilder	Daugherty	
By the Shores of Silver Lake	Waterway West, Phelan	
Farmer Boy	Wells Fargo, Moody	
Little House in the Big Woods	Westward Adventures, Steele	
Little House on the Prairie	Wild Bill Hickock Tames West, Hobrook	
Little Town on the Prairie	Writing About the Frontier, Rickhoff	
On the Banks of Plum Creek	Wyatt Earp, Holbrook	
The First Four Years	Year of the Horseless Carriage, Foster	
The Long Winter	Young Mark Twain and the Mississippi,	
These Happy Golden Years	Kane	
The Long Way to a New Land, Sandin	Young Wayfarers of the Early West, Burt	
The Oak's Long Shadow, Burt		
The Peterkin Papers, Hale	**Forgotten Classics:**	
The Story of Daniel Boone, Steele	F7-37 Crossing the Plains	
The Story of Laura Ingalls Wilder, Stine	F7-263 Letters of a Woman Homesteader	
The Story of the Lewis and Clark	F12-214 David Crockett	
Expedition, Stein	F12-234 May Lyon	
The Story of Opal, Whiteley	F12-241 Samuel Howe	

WESTWARD EXPANSION		
ELEMENTARY	**MIDDLE SCHOOL**	**HIGH SCHOOL**
☐ The Story of the Pony Express, Stein	☐ F12-249 Dorothea Dix	
☐ The Story of the Transcontinental	☐ F12-352 James Hill	
Railroad, Stein	☐ F12-369 A Daring Rescue Across the	
☐ The True Tale of Johnny Appleseed,	Rocky Mountain	
Hodges	☐ G7-88 Peter Cooper	
☐ Timber! Logging in Michigan, Fisher	☐ G7-99 Johns Hopkins	
☐ Toby Tyler, Otis	☐ G7-111 Lawrence Brothers	
☐ Trails of Apple Blossoms, Hunt	☐ G10-136 John James Audobon	
☐ Wagon Wheels, Brenner	☐ G10-336 Luther Burbank	
☐ Washington Irving, Peare	☐ G12-85 Henry Wadworth Longfellow	
☐ We Were There at the Oklahoma	☐ G12-97 Going to the Theater with	
Land Run, Kjelgaard	Longfellow	
☐ We Were There on the Oregon Trail,	☐ G12-103 Boyhood of John Greenleaf	
Steele	Whittier	
☐ We Were There with the Pony Express,	☐ G12-259 Eugene Field	
Steele	☐ G12-321 A Child's Journey with Dickens	
☐ What Katy Did, Coolidge	☐ G12-356 Eleanor Gates	
☐ Clover	☐ W12-112 Edward Everett Hale	
☐ In the High Valley	☐ W12-140 Samuel Pierpont Langley	
☐ What Katy Did at School	☐ W12-365 Prophet and Pioneer	
☐ What Katy Did Next		
☐ Wheat Won't Wait, Nathan		
☐ When I was Young in the Mountains,		
Rylant		
☐ When Chicago was Young, McCague		
☐ When Clipper Ships Ruled the Seas,		
McCague		
☐ Yonie Wondernose, de Angeli		
Forgotten Classics:		
☐ F7-1 Stories of Pioneer Life		
☐ F7-153 Death Strikes the Handcart		
Company		
☐ F11-192 Daniel Boone		
☐ F11-202 James Robertson		
☐ F11-213 George Rogers Clark		
☐ F11-241 Increasing Size of the New		
Republic		
☐ F11-256 Internal Improvements		
☐ F11-269 Republic Grows Larger		
☐ F12-169 Moving West		
☐ F12-178 The Young Scout		
☐ F12-181 The Whisperers		
☐ F12-209 Longfellow as Boy		
☐ F12-211 Indian Rubber Man		
☐ F12-219 Webster and the Poor Woman		
☐ F12-255 Horace Greeley as a Boy		
☐ F12-262 Daniel Webster		
☐ F12-365 A Lonely Life on the Frontier		
☐ G4-105 Horace Mann		
☐ G5-77 Eli Whitney		
☐ G5-130 Samuel Morse		
☐ G5-192 Charles Goodyear		
☐ G5-211 Cyrus McCormick		
☐ G5-226 Elias Howe		

WESTWARD EXPANSION		
ELEMENTARY	**MIDDLE SCHOOL**	**HIGH SCHOOL**
☐ G5-241 George Westinghouse		
☐ G5-253 Alexander Graham Bell		
☐ G5-267 Thomas Edison		
☐ G5-293 Henry Ford		
☐ G5-306 The Wright Brothers		
☐ G7-200 Marshall Field		
☐ G9-343 Joseph Smith		
☐ N11-182 O Little Town of Bethlehem		
☐ S6-158 Grace Darling		
☐ S9-171 Frank Wilson Boy of 1885		
☐ S11-68 There is Room Enough at the Top		
☐ S11-147 Fulfilled		
☐ S11-124 Mill Boy of the Slashes		
☐ S11-164 The Boy Who Said 'I Must'		
☐ S11-236 Ezekiel and Daniel		
☐ S11-250 A Tribune of the People		

My Book House:

☐ 2-58 Gingerbread Man		
☐ 2-200 The Little Engine that Could		
☐ 4-193 The Cowboy's Life		
☐ 4-195 Pecos Bill the Cowboy		
☐ 4-213 Old Johnny Appleseed		
☐ 5-64 Casey Jones		
☐ 5-96 The Steamboat and the Locomotive		
☐ 5-130 The Yankee Peddlar		
☐ 5-139 John Henry the Big Steel-Driven Man		
☐ 8-144 The Circus Man: PT Barnum		
☐ 9-9 Exploring the Wilderness		
☐ 9-25 Pushing Westward With Lewis and Clark		
☐ 9-72 The Rough Rider		
☐ 9-119 Little House in the Big Woods		
☐ 9-127 How Peary Reached the North Pole		
☐ 12-99 A Rover in the Catskills		
☐ 12-122 Life in Concord		
☐ 12-135 The Harvard Professor		
☐ 12-141 The Hoosier Poet		
☐ 12-143 The Poet of the Sierras		
☐ 12-147 A Tramp of the Middle West		

Junior Classics:

☐ 1-380 Jonathan's Lucky Money		
☐ 2-338 The Apple of Contentment		
☐ 5-1 The Wold Pack		
☐ 5-17 Away Goes Sally		
☐ 5-35 Waiting for Jeptha		
☐ 5-85 The Covered Bridge		
☐ 6-10 A Disastrous New Year's		
☐ 6-216 Fourth of July		
☐ 7-295 The Black Duck Dinner		
☐ 7-314 Joe Magarac		
☐ 7-331 Johnny Appleseed		

WESTWARD EXPANSION		
ELEMENTARY	MIDDLE SCHOOL	HIGH SCHOOL
☐ 7-346 Pecos Bill Invents Modern Cowpunching		
☐ 7-361 Tony Beaver		
☐ 8-55 The First Tom Sawyer		
☐ 8-212 Growing Pains: Edgar Allen Poe		
☐ 10-1 Excerpt from Tom Sawyer		
☐ 10-1 Excerpt from Rip Van Winkle		
☐ 10-285 Poe's The Gold Bug		

NATIVE AMERICANS		
ELEMENTARY	**MIDDLE SCHOOL**	**HIGH SCHOOL**
Adventures of Tom Sawyer	American Indians, Starr	A Century of Dishonor, Jackson
American Indian Fairy Tales, Compton	Book of Indian Braves, Sweetser	A Delaware Indian Legend, Adam
American Indian Fairy Tales, Larned	Custer's Last Stand, Reynolds	Black Hawk, Beckhard
Brother Eagle Sister Sky, Jeffers	Esther Wheelwright, Vance	Chief Joseph of the Nez Perces, Garst
Captured Words, Browin	Famous Indian Chiefs I Have Known	Crazy Horse, Garst
Cherokee Chief, Clark	Geronimo, Syme	Forty Years Among the Indians, Hubba
Chief Seattle, Montgomery	Geronimo: Wolf of the Warpath, Moody	Indian Heroes and Great Chieftains,
Eagle Feather, Bulla	Homeward the Arrow's Flight, Brown	Eastman
Four American Indians, Whitney	Indian Brother, Wilson	Ishi: In Two Worlds, Kroeber
Friday the Arapaho Indian, Anderson	Indian Wars and Warriors, Wellman	Jim Beckwourth, Burt
Grandmother Spider Brings the Sun,	Indians, Tunis	Ouray the Arrow, Burt
Keams	Ishi Last of His Tribe, Kroeber	Sitting Bull and His World, Marrin
Hiawatha, Jeffers	Maria Tallchief, Tobias	Sitting Bull Champion of His People, G
Hiawatha's Childhood, Longfellow	Moccasin Trail, McGraw	The Boy's Catlin, Catlin
Hope the Cliff Dweller, Jewett	Nay Nuke, Thomasma	The Gospel of the Redman, Seton
If You Lived With the Sioux Indians,	Prince in Buckskin, Widdemer	The Soul of the Indian, Eastman
McGovern	Runner in the Sun, McNickle	The Story of the American Indian, Broc
In My Mother's House, Clark	Sacajawea, Burt	War Clouds in the West, Marrin
Indian Fairy Tales as Told to Children	Sequoyah: Leader of Cherokees, Marriot	Winged Moccasins, Farnsworth
in the Wigwam, Wade	The Great Pine's Son, Widdemer	
Indian Folk Tales, Nixon-Roulet	The Great West Series, Altsheler	**Forgotten Classics:**
Island of the Blue Dolphins, O'Dell	War Chief of the Seminoles, McNeer	F7-177 Speech of a Flat-Head Chief
Jared's Island, de Angeli	With the Indians in the Rockies, Schultz	
King Philip, Edwards		
Knots on a Counting Rope, Martin	**Forgotten Classics:**	
Maria Tallchief, de Leeuw	F7-195 Indian Stories	
Massasoit Friend of the Pilgrims, Voight		
North American Legends, Haviland		
Osceola, Blassingame		
Our Little Indian Cousin, Wade		
Paddle-to-the-Sea, Hollings		
Picture Story of Red Cloud, Garst		
Pontiac, Hays		
Pontiac Mighty Ottawa Chief, Voight		
Portugee Phillips and the Fighting		
Sioux, Anderson		
Red Cloud Sioux War Chief, Voight		
Rip Van Winkle, Weiss		
Sacagawea, Seymour		
Sacajawea, Seibert		
Sacajawea Guide to Lewis/Clark, Seibert		
Sitting Bull, Stevenson		
Sitting Bull Great Sioux Chief, Anderson		
Stories of Indian Chieftains, Husted		
Stories of Indian Children, Husted		
Tales from Cultures, Weiss		
Tecumseh, McCague		
Ten Little Rabbits, Grossman		
The Story of Geronimo, Kjelgaard		
The Story of Little Bighorn, Stein		
The Story of the Trail of Tears, Stein		
The True Story of Pocahontas, Penner		
Totem Tales, Phillips		
Trail of Tears, Bruchae		

NATIVE AMERICANS		
ELEMENTARY	**MIDDLE SCHOOL**	**HIGH SCHOOL**
Wewa the Child of the Pueblos, Campbell		
White Swallow, Sterne		
Wildcat the Seminole, Clark		

Forgotten Classics:
- F7-179 Stories About Indians
- F11-13 American Indians
- S5-310 Story of Hiawatha
- S11-364 The Forgiving Indian

My Book House:
- 1-80 American Indian Songs
- 2-94 Ten Little Indians
- 2-96 Shingebiss
- 3-94 Indian Children
- 6-102 How Yehl the Hero Freed the Beaming Maiden
- 6-127 The Man Who Loved Hai Quai
- 6-198 The Fisherman Who Caught the Sun (Hawaiian)
- 9-89 Hiawatha's Fasting

Junior Classics:
- 2-227 Scarface
- 2-241 How Glosskap Made the Birds
- 2-249 The Bad Wishers
- 5-120 Little Navajo Bluebird

NATIVE AMERICANS		
ADDITIONAL BOOKS		
ELEMENTARY	MIDDLE SCHOOL	HIGH SCHOOL

ARABIA / ISLAM / CRUSADES

ELEMENTARY	MIDDLE SCHOOL	HIGH SCHOOL
☐ Ali Baba, Latham	☐ Big John's Secret, Jewett	☐ A Muslim Sir Galahad, Dwight
☐ Arabian Nights, Weiss	☐ Buildings of Early Islam, Leacroft	☐ Among the Turks, Hamlin
☐ How Many Donkeys?, MacDonald	☐ For Name and Fame, Henty	☐ Hero of Modern Turkey, Heller
☐ Olcott's The Arabian Nights, Jenkins	☐ Jerusalem and the Crusades, Blyth	☐ Khaled a Tale of Arabia, Crawford
☐ Our Little Crusader Cousin, Stein	☐ Knights of the Crusades, Williams	☐ Moors in Spain, Florian
☐ Our Little Turkish Cousin, Wade	☐ Lawrence of Arabia, McLean	☐ Ottoman Turks, Sell
☐ Saladin, Stanley	☐ Mosque, Macaulay	☐ Pilgrimage to Al-Madinah and Meccah,
☐ Sindbad from One Thousand and One	☐ One Thousand and One Arabian Nights,	Burton
Arabian Nights, Zeman	McCaughrean	☐ Ring of Fate, Bothwell
☐ Stories from Arabian Nights, Housman	☐ Star of Light, St. John	☐ Story of the Crusades, Boyd
☐ The Arabian Nights Entertainments, Lane	☐ Tales of the Crusades, Coolidge	☐ The Arabian Nights, Colum
☐ The Arabian Nights Their Best Known	☐ The Crusades, West	☐ The Boy Crusaders, Edgar
Tales, Wiggin	☐ The Lance of Kanana, French	☐ The Crusades, Archer
☐ The Flying Carpet, Brown	☐ The Quest of the Four-leaved Clover,	☐ The Crusades Through Arab Eyes
☐ This is a Tale of Djinns	Laboulage	☐ The People of Turkey, Blunt
	☐ The True Story of Lawrence of Arabia,	☐ The Prince and the Page, Yonge
Forgotten Classics:	Thomas	☐ The Story of Islam, Lunt
☐ S3-311 Aladdin or the Magic Lamp	☐ To Herat and Cabul, Henty	☐ The Story of Mohammed and the Rise
	☐ Turkey, Van Millingen	of Islam, Margoliouth
My Book House:	☐ Winning His Spurs, Henty	☐ The Story of the Saracens, Gilman
☐ 8-92 The Magic Horse from Arabian		☐ The World's Story V 3, Tappan
Nights	**Forgotten Classics:**	☐ The World's Story V 6, Tappan
☐ 8-109 The Story of the Talking Bird	☐ G9-296 Mohammed	☐ Turkey, Lane-Poole
from Arabian Nights	☐ W7-115 Jerusalem and the Crusades	
☐ 10-30 The Children's Crusade	☐ W11-203 Beginnings of Mohammedism	**Forgotten Classics:**
	☐ W11-233 The Crusades	☐ G4-80 Abdallah and Sabat
Junior Classics:	☐ W11-245 The Monks and the People in	☐ G9-212 Had You Been Born a Moslem
☐ 2-207 The Bear in the Pear Tree	the Time of the Crusades	☐ W7-1 The Story of Islam
☐ 3-175 Mischief in Fez	☐ W11-261 The Thirteenth Century	☐ W7-87 Hand of Providence
☐ 7-3 Aladdin and theMagic Lamp		
☐ 7-57 Ali Baba and the Forty Thieves	**Junior Classics:**	
	☐ 9-118 The Lance of Kanana	

ARABIA / ISLAM / CRUSADES		
ADDITIONAL BOOKS		
ELEMENTARY	MIDDLE SCHOOL	HIGH SCHOOL

BIRDS		
ELEMENTARY	**MIDDLE SCHOOL**	**HIGH SCHOOL**
☐ All About Birds, Lemmons	☐ Audobons' Drawing of American Birds	☐ Bird-Life, Thompson
☐ Angus and the Ducks, Flack	☐ Birds That Every Child Should Know, Blanchan	☐ Birds of Song and Story, Grinnell
☐ Bird Children, Gordon		☐ How to Study Birds, Job
☐ Bird Songs	☐ Citizen Bird, Wright	☐ Knowing Birds Through Stories, Brallia
☐ Bird Stories, Patch	☐ Gray Lady and the Birds, Wright	☐ The Handbook of Nature Study, Comstock
☐ Bird World, Stickney	☐ In the Days of Audobon, Butterworth	
☐ Birds and Their Nests, Earle	☐ Second Book of Birds, Miller	
☐ Birds from the Crow Family, Earle	☐ Stories About Birds of Land and Water, Kirby	
Fairy Tales	☐ Tenants of the Trees, Hawkes	
☐ The Happy Place		
☐ The Nightingale		
☐ The Ugly Duckling		
☐ Ground Birds, Ripper		
☐ Hawks, Ripper		
☐ Make Way for Ducklings, McCloskey		
☐ John James Audobon: His Life, Peare		
☐ John James Audobon Bird Artist, Ayars		
☐ Mamma's Stories About Birds, Leathley		
☐ Mr. Popper's Penguins, Atwater		
☐ Our Birds and Their Nestlings, Walker		
☐ Owl Moon, Yolen		
☐ Owls in the Family		
☐ State Birds and Flowers, Earle		
The Firebird		
☐ Demi's The Firebird		
☐ Gennady Spirin illustrated		
☐ The Firebird, Yolen		
☐ The Firebird/Other Russian Tales		
☐ The Golden Mare The Firebird		
☐ The Painter and the Wild Swans, Clement		
☐ The Silver Swan, Morpugo		
☐ The Swans of Willow Pond, Earle		
☐ Tico and the Golden Wings, Lionni		
☐ Thunder Wings, Earle		
☐ Thy Friend Obadiah, Turkle		
☐ Trumpet of the Swan, White		
☐ Vulcan, McClun		
☐ White Patch, Earle		
☐ Whooping Crane, McClung		

My Book House:

☐ 2-41 The Twilight		
☐ 2-42 The Magpie's Nest		
☐ 2-45 The Goldfinch		
☐ 2-143 How the Finch Got Her Colors		
☐ 2-152 Nurse's Song		
☐ 3-28 The Owl		
☐ 3-29 The Ow's Answer to Tommy		
☐ 3-62 Duck's Ditty		
☐ 4-83 The Nutcracker and Sugardolly Stories		
☐ 5-103 Little Gulliver		
☐ 5-111 The Sea Gull		
☐ 9-106 Excerpt from The Trumpet of the Swan		

BIRDS		
ELEMENTARY	MIDDLE SCHOOL	HIGH SCHOOL

Junior Classics:

☐ 1-166 The Wide-Awake Owl

☐ 1-191 The Box with Red Wheels

ABRAHAM LINCOLN

ELEMENTARY	MIDDLE SCHOOL	HIGH SCHOOL
☐ A Man Named Lincoln, Norman	☐ A Life of Lincoln for Boys, Spearhawk	☐ Abe Lincoln's Other Mother, Bailey
☐ Abe Lincoln, Stevenson	☐ Abe Lincoln: Log Cabin to White House, North	☐ Abe Lincoln's Yarns and Stories, McClu
☐ Abe Lincoln's Hat, Brenner		☐ Abraham Lincoln, Elias
☐ Abraham Lincoln	☐ Abe Lincoln Grows Up, Sandburg	☐ Abraham Lincoln: The Prairie Years an
☐ Abraham Lincoln, d'Aulaire	☐ Abraham Lincoln, Collins	the War Years, Sandburg
☐ Abraham Lincoln, Gordy	☐ Abraham Lincoln: A True life, Baldwin	☐ Commander in Chief, Marrin
☐ Abraham Lincoln & the Heart of America	☐ Abraham Lincoln's World, Foster	☐ In Lincoln's Chair, Tarbell
☐ Abraham Lincoln for the People, Colver	☐ Abraham Lincoln Friend of the People, Judson	☐ Latest Light on Lincoln, Chapman
☐ America's Abraham Lincoln, McNeer		☐ Lincoln's Love Story, Atkinson
☐ Boys' and Girls' Biography of Abraham Lincoln, Shaw	☐ Life of Abraham Lincoln for Boys and Girls, Moores	☐ Lincoln's Secret Weapon, Wise
		☐ Lincoln in Story, Pratt
☐ Gettysburg Address	☐ Lincoln: A Photobiography, Freedman	☐ Lincoln the Unknown, Cargnegie
☐ If You Grew Up with Abraham Lincoln, McGovern	☐ Lincoln and Douglas, Kelly	☐ New World Heroes, Farmingham
	☐ Lincoln and the Sleeping Sentinel, Chittenden	☐ Personal Recollections, Rankin
☐ Just a Few Words Mr. Lincoln, Fritz		☐ Stories from Lincoln's Life
☐ Long Tall Lincoln, Dossling	☐ Mr. Lincoln Speaks at Gettysburg, Phelan	☐ The Early Pioneers and Pioneer Events
☐ Mary Todd Lincoln, Wilkie	☐ The Boyhood of Abraham Lincoln, Gore	of the State of Illinois, Ross
☐ Mr. Lincoln's Whiskers, Winnick	☐ The Children's Life of Abraham Lincoln, Putnam	☐ The Great Proclamation, Commager
☐ Robert Todd Lincoln, Anderson		☐ The Heart of Lincoln, Whipple
☐ Story of Abraham Lincoln, Hamilton	☐ The Little Life Story of Lincoln, Whipple	☐ The Little Giant, Nolan
☐ Story of Abraham Lincoln, McSpadden	☐ The Story of Young Abraham Lincoln, Whipple	☐ The Statesmanship of Abraham Lincol Coolidge
☐ Story of Lincoln, Husted		
☐ Tad Lincoln Abe's Son, Anderson		☐ The Story Life of Lincoln, Whipple
☐ The Story of Abraham Lincoln, Baker	**Forgotten Classics:**	☐ The Story of Abraham Lincoln, Gridley
☐ The Story of Abraham Lincoln for Young Readers, Baldwin	☐ F8-66 Abraham Lincoln: A True Life	☐ What Abraham Lincoln Read
	☐ F12-308 Lincoln's First Reading	
☐ The Story of Ford's Theather and Death of Lincoln, Kent		**Forgotten Classics:**
		☐ F8-315 Lincoln: His Story
☐ The Story of Lincoln for Children, Craven		☐ F8-357 Wisdom of Lincoln
☐ The Story of the Gettysburg Address, Richards		☐ G11-218 Abraham Lincoln's Mother
		☐ S11-197 Lincoln's Proposal
☐ The Story of the Lincoln Memorial, Miller		
☐ The True Story of Abraham Lincoln, Brooks		
☐ When Abraham Talked to the Trees, van Steenwyk		

Forgotten Classics:

☐ F8-1 Story of Lincoln for Children
☐ F12-325 Kindness of a Great Soul
☐ F12-326 A Beautiful Story
☐ S6-60 A Poor Boy and What Became of Him
☐ S11-347 A Soldier's Pardon

My Book House:

☐ 11-170a Lincoln's Gettysburg Address
☐ 5-133 A Story About Abe Lincoln

Junior Classics:

☐ 6-24 d'Aulaire's Abraham Lincoln

ABRAHAM LINCOLN		
ADDITIONAL BOOKS		
ELEMENTARY	**MIDDLE SCHOOL**	**HIGH SCHOOL**

AFRICAN AMERICANS / SLAVERY

ELEMENTARY	MIDDLE SCHOOL	HIGH SCHOOL
Benjamin Banneker: Astronomer and Scientist, Clark	A Boys' Life of Booker T. Washington, Jackson	African and the American Flag, Foote
Benjamin Banneker: Genuis of Early American, Patterson	Amos Fortune Free Man, Yates	Amazing Grace, Metaxas
Booker T. Washington, Patterson	Booker T. Washington, Graham	Angry Abolitionist, Arhcer
Bright April, de Angeli	By Secret Railway, Meadowcroft	Booker T. Washington, Drinker
Clara and the Freedom Quilt, Hopkinson	Come By Here, Coolidge	Booker T. Washington: Builder of a Civilization, Scott
Dream March, Nelson	Escape by Night, Wells	Booker T. Washington: Educator of Han Head and Heart, Graham
Escape North!, Kulling	George Carver, Stevenson	Booker T. Washingtons' Own Story, Washington
Follow the Drinking Gourd, Winter	George Washington Carver, Terry	Dr. George Washington Carver, Graham
Frederick Douglass Fights for Freedom, Davidson	Gifted Hands, Carson	Fighter Against Slavery, Orrmont
Harriet Beecher Stowe, Widdemer	Harriet Beecher Stowe, Wise	Fighting Journalist, Archer
Harriet Tubman: Flame of Freedom, Humphreville	Harriet Beecher Stowe and the Beecher Preachers, Fritz	Finding a Way Out, Moton
I Have a Dream, Davidson	Harriet the Moses of Her People, Bradford	Frederick Douglass, Holland
I Too Sing America, Weiss	His Was the Voice, Sterne	George Washington Carver, Holt
Jim Beckwourth, Blassingame	I Will Be Heard, Faber	Gifted Hands, Carson
Jump on Over!, Harris	Mary McLeod Bethune, Sterns	Harriet Beecher Stowe, Stowe
Ladycake Farm, Hunt	Singing for the World, Stevenson	Jim Beckwourth, Burt
Mary McLeod Bethune, Anderson	Sounder, Armstrong	Joel Chandler Harris, Harlow
Minty, Schroeder	Spokesman for Freedom, Stevenson	Narrative of the Life of Frederick Douglass, Douglass
Sojourner Truth, Merchant	The Juvenile Unlce Tom's Cabin, Crowe	Negroes in the Early West, Burt
Sure Hands Strong Heart, Patterson	The Slave Ship, Sterne	Paul Robeson, Graham
Sweet Clara and the Freedom Quilt, Hopkinson	The Slave Who Freed Haiti, Sherman	The Battle of Principles, Hillis
Tar Baby, Harris	Toussaint: The Black Liberator, Syme	The Little Professor of Piney Woods, D
The Classic Tales of Brer Rabbit, Borgenicht	Uncle Tom's Cabin Arranged for Young Readers, Stowe	The Negro in Our History, Woodson
The Snowy Day, Keats	Uncle Tom's Cabin Young Folks' Edition, Stowe	The Story of John Greenleaf Whitter, Cooke
The Story of African-Americans in the Thirteen Colonies, Kent	Underground to Canada, Smucker	The Story of Phillis Wheatley, Graham
The Story of George Washington Carver, Bontemps	Up From Slavery, Washington	There Was Once a Slave, Graham
The Story of Harriet Beecher Stowe, Ash		They Took Their Stand, Sterne
The Story of Harriet Beecher Stowe, MacArthur	**Forgotten Classics:**	To Kill a Mockingbird, Lee
The Story of the Assassination of Martin Luther King, Stein	F12-336 Samuel Armstrong	Twelve Years a Slave, Northup
The Story of the Underground Railroad, Stein	F12-343 Booker T. Washington	Uncle Tom's Cabin, Stowe
The Upward Path, Pritchard	G1-30 How I Escaped	Up From Slavery, Washington
Thee Hannah, de Angeli	G1-39 Paul Dunbar	Your Most Humble Servant, Graham
Uncle Remus, Harris	G1-95 Up From Slavery	
Unspoken, Cole	G1-101 Harriet Tubman	**Forgotten Classics:**
Unsung Heroes, Haynes	G1-117 Blanche Bruce	F12-313 Scenes from the Life of Harriet Tubman
Wanted Dead or Alive, McGovern	G1-137 Benjamin Banneker	G1-205 Paul Cuffe
Treasury of Wisdom: Satchel Paige	G1-140 Phyllis Wheatley	G1-250 The Colored Cadet at West Point
	G1-151 Josiah Henson	G1-256 A Negro Explorer at the North Pole
Forgotten Classics:	G1-168 Sojourner Truth	G1-264 Music that Stirred a Nation
G1-1 Frederick Douglass	G1-187 Crispus Attucks	G1-272 How Two Colored Captains Fe
G1-59 The Boy and the Bayonet	G1-194 Paul Cuffe	G1-274 Ira Aldridge
G1-73 Booker T. Washington	G1-212 Alexander Cummel	G1-293 A Mere Matter of the Feelings
G1-125 Benjamin Banneker	G1-216 John Langston	G12-110 Harriet Beecher Stowe
	G1-231 Going to School Under Difficulties	N11-154, 161 John Newton
	G1-239 My First School--DuBois	W12-60 Abolition of British Slavery
	G1-279 Out of Africa	

AFRICAN AMERICANS / SLAVERY		
ELEMENTARY	MIDDLE SCHOOL	HIGH SCHOOL
☐ S11-134 The Uplift of a Slave's Boy Ideal		
☐ S11-138 The Boy Who Wanted to Learn		
My Book House:		
☐ 2-87 The Little Rabbit Who Wanted Red Wings		
☐ 3-116 Lil Hannibal		
☐ 3-123 A Story About Little Rabbits		
☐ 4-130 How Brer Rabbit Met Brer Tar-Baby		
☐ 6-108 Jasper the Drummin' Boy		
☐ 12-79 The Loneliest Battler		
☐ 12-104 The man Who Made Adolf Hitler Run: Jesse Owen		
☐ 12-138 Way Down South in Dixie		
☐ 12-154 Pioneer in Surgery		
☐ 12-188 The Negro Speaks of Rivers		
☐ 12-198 Learning to Be Free		
Junior Classics:		
☐ 5-278 Bright April		
☐ 8-72 Greek and a Toothbrush		
☐ 8-231 The Boy with the Horn		

AFRICAN AMERICANS / SLAVERY		
ADDITIONAL BOOKS		
ELEMENTARY	MIDDLE SCHOOL	HIGH SCHOOL

AFRICA		
ELEMENTARY	**MIDDLE SCHOOL**	**HIGH SCHOOL**
14 Cows for American, Deedy	An Empire Story, Marshall	African Adventure, Price
A Story! A Story!, Haley	At Aboukir and Acre, Henty	Africa Trek I and II, Poussin
Albert Schweitzer, Montgomery	Born Free, Adamson	African Firebrand, Archer
Black Tales for White Children, Stigand	By Sheer Pluck, Henty	Alexander Mackay
Bringing the Rain to Kapiti Plain, Aardema	David Livingstone, Wellman	Beau Geste, Wren
Cunnie Rabbit Mr. Spider, Cronise	Exploration of Africa, Sterling	Cry the Beloved Country, Paton
From Ashanti to Zulu, Musgrove	Livingstone the Pathfinder, Matthews	Elephant Adventure, Price
Gift of the Sun, Stewart	My Life With the Chimpanzees, Goodall	From the Darkness of Africa to the
Henry Morton Stanley, Graves	Nigerian Pioneer, Syme	Light of American, Beolow
Jambo Means Hello, Feelings	Seven Grandmothers, Mirsky	Hannibal, Abbott
Kintu, Enright	Tarzan of the Apes, Burroughs	History of Hannibal the Carthiginian,
Lala Salama, MacLachan	The Boy Travellers on the Congo	Abbott
Mama Miti, Napoli	The Boys' Book of Explorations, Jenks	Incredible Africa, Price
Mama Panya's Pancakes, Chamberlin	The Cow-Tail Switch, Coulander	Kisses From Katie, Davis
Misoso, Aardema	The Curse of Carne's Hold, Henty	Life Out of Death
Moja Means One, Feelings	The Dash for Khartoum, Henty	Lion Adventure, Price
Mufaro's Beautiful Daughter, Steptoe	The Kidnapped Prince, Cameron	Livingstone, Dawson
Nelson Mandela, Van Wyk	The March to Magdala, Henty	My African Journey, Churchill
Nomusa and the New Magic, Mirsky	The Story-Teller's Beads, Kurtz	My Life and Thought, Schweitzer
Seven Grandmothers, Mirsky	The Story of David Livingstone, Golding	Safari Adventure, Price
Shaka King of the Zulus, Stanley	The Story of H.M. Stanley, Golding	The Hill of Good-bye, Currie
South African Folk Tales, Honeij	The True Story of Cecil Rhodes, Gibbs	The Missionary Heroes, Morrison
The Adventure of Spider, Arkhurst	The True Story of David Livingstone,	The Return, Levitin
The Beast of Lor, Bulla	Arnold	The Story of Carthage, Church
The Cow-Tail Switch, Courlander	The Young Carthaginian, Henty	The Story of MacKay in Uganda
The Fire on the Mountain, Coulander	The Young Colonists, Henty	The Story of South Africa, Theal
The Hat-Shaking Dance, Coulander	The Young Midshipman, Henty	The Story of South Africa, Worsfold
The King's Drum, Arno	The Young People's Story of Africa	The White Horse, Coatsworth
The Long Black Schooner, Sterne	and Asia, Hillyer	The World's Story, Tappan
The Value of Dedication, Johnson	Through Three Campaigns, Henty	Unbowed, Maathai
Thirty-one Brothers and Sisters, Mirsky	With Buller in Natal, Henty	
Told by Uncle Remus, Harris	With Kitchener in the Soudan, Henty	**Forgotten Classics:**
Wangari's Trees of Peace, Winter	With Roberts to Pretoria, Henty	G4-347 Archibald Forder
West African Folk Tales, Barker	Views in Africa, Badlam	W8-125 Exploration of Africa
When the Drum Sang, Rockwell		
Why Mosquitos Buzz, Aardema	**Forgotten Classics:**	
Why the Sun and the Moon Live in the	G4-192 Khama	
Sky, Dayrell	G4-244 Mary Slessor	
	G4-265 Alexander McKay	
Forgotten Classics:	G6-26 Toissant L'Ouverture	
G4-116 David Livingstone	S11-228 General Gordon	
N12-51 The Flying Dutchman	W11-124 Rome and Carthage	
S11-300 Dutch Boer and His Horse	W11-523 Africa-Land of Mystery	
My Book House:		
1-146 African Child Rhymes		
6-132 The Lost Spear		
8-36 Afar in the Desert		
6-159 Snowflake the Gorilla		
12-70 Jane and the Wild Chimps		
Junior Classics:		
2-214 The Fire on the Mountain		
2-220 Ansige Karambe the Glutton		
4-38 Damasi's Party from Thirty		

AFRICA		
ADDITIONAL BOOKS		
ELEMENTARY	MIDDLE SCHOOL	HIGH SCHOOL

ANCIENT EGYPT

ELEMENTARY	MIDDLE SCHOOL	HIGH SCHOOL
☐ Cleopatra, Stanley	☐ A Cry from Egypt, Auer	☐ A History of Egypt, Breasted
☐ How Djadja-Em-Ankh Saved the Day, Manniche	☐ Adventures of Two Youth in an Adventure to Egypt and the Holy Land	☐ A History of Egypt, Petrie
☐ Egyptian Treasures: Mummis & Myths	☐ Ancient Egypt, Baikie	☐ A Thousand Miles up the Nile, Ward
☐ Ikhnaton of Egypt, Meadowcroft	☐ Ancient History Told to Children, Lane	☐ An Egyptian Princess, Ebers
☐ Mummies Made in Egypt, Aliki	☐ Buildings of Ancient Egypt, Leacraft	☐ Ancient Egypt, Rawlinson
☐ Pharaoh's Boat, Weitzman	☐ Cleopatra of Egypt, Hornblow	☐ Cleopatra, Abbott
☐ Pharaohs and Pyramids, Allan	☐ Egypt, Kelly	☐ Egypt, Waters
☐ Pharaohs and Queens of Egypt	☐ God King, Williamson	☐ History of Egypt, Maspero
☐ The Day of Ahmed's Secret, Heide	☐ Legends of Ancient Egypt, Brooksbank	☐ Life in Ancient Egypt, Erman
☐ The Egyptian Cinderella, Climo	☐ Mara Daughter of the Nile, McGraw	☐ Manual of Egyptian Archaeology, Maspero
☐ Tut's Mummy, Donnelly	☐ Peeps at Many Lands: Ancient Egypt	☐ Pharaoh, McGraw
	☐ Peeps at Many Lands: Egypt	☐ Pyramids and Progress, Ward
Forgotten Classics:	☐ Pyramid, Macaulay	☐ The Boys' and Girls' Herodotus, White
☐ N12-273 The Magic Flute	☐ The Cat of Bubastes, Henty	☐ The Civilization of the Ancient Egyptia Gosse
☐ N12-303 Aida	☐ The Golden Goblet, McGraw	
	☐ The Lost Queen of Egypt, Morrison	☐ The Story of Ancient Egypt, Rawlinson
My Book House:	☐ The Pharaohs of Ancient Egypt, Payne	☐ The World's Story V 3, Tappan
☐ 7-84 Rhodopis and Her Gilded Sandals		
	Forgotten Classics:	**Forgotten Classics:**
	☐ W8-1 Stories of Ancient Egypt	☐ N9-6 Glimpse into Egyptian Art
		Delphian Course:
		☐ 1:13-192 History and Social Life
		☐ 5:31-48 Egyptian Literature

ANCIENT EGYPT		
ADDITIONAL BOOKS		
ELEMENTARY	MIDDLE SCHOOL	HIGH SCHOOL

ANIMALS

ELEMENTARY	MIDDLE SCHOOL	HIGH SCHOOL
A Child's Treasury of Animal Verse, Danie	A Dog of Flanders, Ouida	Call of the Wild, London
All the Pretty Horses, Jeffers	Albert Pasyon Terhune Books	
Andy and the Lion, Daugherty	Further Adventures of Lad	
Animal Secrets Told, Brearley	Lad: A Dog	
Animal Stories for Children, Newton	All Creatures Great and Small, Heriott	
April's Kittens, Newberry	Animal Heroes, Seton	
Bambi, Dusikova	Bambi, Salten	
Bats, Ripper	Because of Winn-Dixie, deCamillo	
Billy and Blaze Series, Anderson	Black Stallion Series, Farley	
Black Beauty, Sewell	Son of the Black Stallion	
Black Beauty's Early Days in Meadows	The Black Stallion	
Child's Version, Jeffers	The Black Stallion Returns	
Blaze, McClung	The Black Stallion Revolts	
Book of Cats and Dogs, Johonnot	Jonathan and David, Phelps	
Buzztail, McClung	Lad: A Dog, Terhune	
Camels and Llamas, Earle	Old Yeller, Gipson	
Carl's Afternoon in the Park, Day	Summer of the Monkeys, Rawls	
Carl's Christmas, Day	The Animal Story Book, Lang	
Carl's Summer Vacation, Day	The Handbook of Nature Study, Comstock	
Chipmunks on the Doorstep, Tunis	The Story of Scotch, Mills	
Clara Dillingham Pierson Books	The Wonder Book of Horses, Baldwin	
Among the Farmyard People	The Yearling, Rawlins	
Among the Forest People	Where the Red Fern Grows, Rawls	
Among the Meadow People		
Among the Night People		
Among the Pond People		
Dooryard Stories		
Dogger, Hughes		
Flat Tail, Gall		
Four-Handed Folk, Miller		
Fox Eyes, Brown		
Foxes and Wolves, Ripper		
Fritz and the Beautiful Horses, Brett		
Frogs and Polliwogs, Hogner		
Going to Sleep on the Farm, Lewison		
Lassie Come Home, Knight		
Lassie Come Home, Wells		
Little Folks in Feathers and Furs, Miller		
Lions in the Barn, Voight		
Lost Wild America, McClung		
Marguerite Henry Books		
Album of Horses		
Brighty of the Grand Canyon		
Gaudenzio Pride of the Palio		
Justin Morgan Had a Horse		
King of the Wind		
Misty of Chincoteague		
Sea Star Orphan of Chicoteague		
Stormy Misty's Foal		
White Stallion of Lippiza		
Millions of Cats, Gag		
Moles and Shrews, Ripper		
Mousekin Books, Miller		
Mr. Rabbit & the Lovely Present, Zolotow		
My Pony, Jeffers		

ANIMALS		
ELEMENTARY	MIDDLE SCHOOL	HIGH SCHOOL
Nature Stories for Young Readers, Bass		
Nature's Children, Hawkes		
Ringtail, Crew		
Small Pets from Woods and Fields, Buck		
Spike, McClung		
Squirrels in the Garden, Earle		
Stone Fox, Gardiner		
Strange Companions in Nature, Earle		
Strange Lizards, Earle		
Stuart Little, White		
The Adventures of Buster Bear, Burgess		
The Adventures of Jimmy Skunk, Burgess		
The Adventures of Johnny Chuck, Burgess		
The Adventures of Paddy Beaver, Burgess		
The Adventures of Reddy Fox, Burgess		
The Burgess Animal Book, Burgess		
The Mare on the Hill, Locker		
The Valentine Cat, Bulla		
The Weasel Family, Ripper		
Voyages of Dr. Doolittle, Lofting		
Wagtail, Crew		
Where They Go in Winter, Buck		
Woodchucks and Their Kin, Ripper		

Forgotten Classics:

N8 Stories About Animals

My Book House:

1-160 First Adventures

1-162 The Little Turtle Animal Crackers

1-163 Conversation

1-198 The Little Pig

2-17 The Little Gray Pony

2-57 The Teddy Bear's Picnic

2-82 Whisky Frisky

2-112 The Tale of Peter Rabbit

2-172 Krazy Kat

2-180 The Owl and the Pussycat

2-188 Dame Wiggins of the Lee

2-192 The Cock the Mouse and the
    Little Red Hen

3-39 The Elf and the Doormouse

3-49 Peter Rabbit Decides to Change
    His Name

3-63 The Mad Dog

3-85 Bucky the Big Bold Faun

3-129 Mrs. Tabby Gray

3-133 The Kitten and Falling Leaves

3-134 Of a Tailor and a Bear

4-113 The Rarest Animal of All

4-145 Tippity Witchit's Halloween

9-98 Old Yeller

Junior Classics:

1-71 Three Little Pigs

ANIMALS		
ELEMENTARY	**MIDDLE SCHOOL**	**HIGH SCHOOL**
☐ 1-160 Scaredy Cat		
☐ 1-177 The Circus Baby		
☐ 1-182 Angus and the Cat		
☐ 1-197 The Velveteen Rabbit		
☐ 1-221 Sneakers the Rapscallion Cat		
☐ 1-227 Evie and the Wonderful Kangaroo		
☐ 1-251 Billy and Blaze		
☐ 1-257 Peter Churchmouse		
☐ 1-357 The Good Horse Kristie		
☐ 3-131 Miss Hickory		
☐ 3-158 A Crime Wave in the Barnyard		
☐ 5-247 Pony Penning Day		
☐ 6-120 The Country Bunny and the Little Gold Shoes		
☐ 9-189 Lassie Come Home		
☐ 9-227 Black Beauty		

CIVIL WAR

ELEMENTARY

- [ ] Brave Clara Barton, Murphy
- [ ] Civil War Sub, Jerome
- [ ] Clara Barton, Stevenson
- [ ] Clara Barton Soldier of Mercy, Rose
- [ ] Fort Sumter, January
- [ ] From Slave to Soldier, Hopinkson
- [ ] Gettysburg: Tad Lincoln's Story, Monjo
- [ ] Henry Clay Leader in Congress, Peterson
- [ ] If You Lived Time of the Civil War, Moore
- [ ] Just a Few Words Mr. Lincoln, Fritz
- Louisa May Alcott
  - [ ] An Old Fashioned Girl
  - [ ] Eight Cousins
  - [ ] Jack and Jill
  - [ ] Jo's Boys
  - [ ] Little Men
  - [ ] Little Women
  - [ ] Rose in Bloom
  - [ ] Under the Lilacs
- [ ] Our Hero: General Grant, Pollard
- [ ] Robert E. Lee A Play and a Story, Hill
- [ ] Robert E. Lee Hero of the South, Graves
- [ ] The Civil War Through the Camera, Elson
- [ ] The Last Brother, Noble
- [ ] The Life of Robert E. Lee, Williamson
- [ ] The Perilous Road, Steele
- [ ] The Romance of Civil War, Hart
- [ ] The Son of Light Horse Harry, Barnes
- [ ] The Story of a Great General, Elson
- [ ] The Story of Robert E. Lee, Vinton
- [ ] The Story of Ulysses S. Grant, Nolan
- [ ] The Story of Ulysses S. Grant for Young Readers, Burton
- [ ] The True Story of U.S. Grant, Brooks
- [ ] We Were There at the Battle of Gettysburg, Malkus
- [ ] Women in Blue or Gray, Weiss
- [ ] Young Folks' History - Civil War, Cheney

Forgotten Classics:
- [ ] F9-1 Story of Ulysses S. Grant
- [ ] F9-239 Robert E. Lee
- [ ] F11-280 Three Great Statesmen
- [ ] F11-293 The Civil War
- [ ] G4-156 Clara Barton
- [ ] S6-43 Louisa May Alcott
- [ ] S7-72 U.S. Grant
- [ ] S11-313 The Girl Who Was Loving Sister

My Book House:
- [ ] 11-170c Robert E. Lee

Junior Classics:
- [ ] 6-162 Light Bread and Apple Butter
- [ ] 10-76 Excerpt from Little Women

MIDDLE SCHOOL

- [ ] Across Five Aprils, Hunt
- [ ] America's Robert E. Lee, Commager
- [ ] Andrew Johnson: Defender of the Constitution, Green
- [ ] Blow Bugles Blow, Allen
- [ ] Johnny Reb
- [ ] Brady, Fritz
- [ ] Clara Barton Founder of the American Red Cross, Boylston
- [ ] Gettysburg, Kantor
- [ ] Invincible Louisa, Meigs
- [ ] JEB Stuart, de Grummond
- [ ] Ladd of the Big Swamp, Matschat
- [ ] Lee and Grant at Appomattox, Kantor
- [ ] On the Plantation, Harris
- [ ] On the Trail of Grant and Lee, Hill
- [ ] On Wheels and How I Came Here, Smith
- [ ] Photographing History, Komroff
- [ ] Rifles for Watie, Keith
- [ ] Robert E. Lee, Gilman
- [ ] Robert E. Lee & the Road of Honor, Carter
- [ ] Stonewall Jackson, Daniels
- [ ] Strange Stories of Civil War, Shackleton
- The Civil War Series, Altsheler
  - [ ] The Guns of Bull Run
  - [ ] The Guns of Shiloh
  - [ ] The Rock of Chickamauga
  - [ ] The Scouts of Stonewall
  - [ ] The Shades of the Wilderness
  - [ ] The Star of Gettysburg
  - [ ] The Sword of Antietam
  - [ ] The Tree of Appomattox
- [ ] The Golden Book of the Civil War
- [ ] The Life of Robert E. Lee, Hamilton
- [ ] The Monitor and the Merrimac, Pratt
- [ ] The Stolen Train, Ashley
- [ ] The Story of Robert E. Lee, Vinton
- [ ] Two Boys in the Civil War and After, Houghton
- [ ] Unconditional Surrender, Marrin
- [ ] Virginia's General, Marrin
- [ ] War Stories and School-Day Incidents for the Children, Zettler
- [ ] With Lee in Virginia, Henty

Forgotten Classics:
- [ ] F12-327 Clara Barton
- [ ] G4-163 The Red Cross
- [ ] N11-191 How Firm a Foundation
- [ ] S11-366 Robert E. Lee and the Union Soldier

Junior Classics:
- [ ] 8-1 A Soldier is Made
- [ ] 8-344 Running in the Wind

HIGH SCHOOL

- [ ] A Short History of the Civil War, Pratt
- [ ] All Around the Civil War, Hawn
- [ ] Andrew Johnson
- [ ] Angel of Mercy, Baker
- [ ] Behind the Blue and Gray, Ray
- [ ] Belle Boyd: Secret Agent, Nolan
- [ ] Boys' Life of General Grant, Knox
- [ ] Daring Sea Warrior, Eliot
- [ ] David Farragut: Sea Fighter, Mudra
- [ ] Deeds and Daring of Both Blue and Gray, Kelsey
- [ ] Fighting Journalist, Archer
- [ ] Gone With the Wind, Mitchell
- [ ] Life of Andrew Johnson, Sawyer
- Personal Memoirs of U.S. Grant, Grant
  - [ ] Volume 1
  - Volume 2
- [ ] Southern Heroes, Trueblood
- [ ] Sparks from the Camp Fire, Greene
- [ ] The Many Faces of Civil War, Werstein
- [ ] Under the Guns, Wittenmeyer
- [ ] When Life Was Young at the Old Farm in Maine, Stephens

Forgotten Classics:
- [ ] F9-173 Grant: The Man
- [ ] F9-193 Selections from Grant's Memo
- [ ] F9-257 Lee's Character
- [ ] F9-275 Personal Recollections from Letters of Robert E. Lee
- [ ] G11-232 Julia Ward Howe
- [ ] G12-156 General Lew Wallace
- [ ] G12-192 Louisa May Alcott
- [ ] N11-204 Civil War Hymn
- [ ] N11-275 Battle Hymn of the Republic

CIVIL WAR		
ADDITIONAL BOOKS		
ELEMENTARY	MIDDLE SCHOOL	HIGH SCHOOL

LATIN AMERICA		
ELEMENTARY	**MIDDLE SCHOOL**	**HIGH SCHOOL**
Abuela's Weave, Castaneda	A Long Vacation, Verne	A Time to Stand, Lord
Arroz con Leche, Delacre	Ashes of Empire, Vance	An Unknown People in an Unknown
Benito, Bulla	Black Rainbow, Bierhorst	Land, Grubb
Biblioburro, Winter	Bolivar the Liberator, Syme	Aztecs and Spaniards, Marrin
Borreguita and the Coyote, Aardema	By Right of Conquest, Henty	Big Foot Wallace of the Texas Rangers,
Cortez and Montezuma, Pratt	Captain Baylay's Heir, Henty	Garst
Cowboys and Cattle Drives, McCall	Captain Cortez Conquers Mexico, Johnson	Carlota: American Empress, Barnes
Davy Crockett, Beals	De Soto: Child of the Sun, Steele	David Crockett, Abbott
Davy Crockett, Krensky	Francisco Coronado and the Seven Cities	Drift O' Dreams, McRoskey
Elena, Stanley	of Gold, Syme	Empire Builder: Sam Brannan, Young
Fairy Tales from Brazil, Eels	Francisco Pizarro, Syme	End of the Spear, Saint
Francisco Pizarro, Pratt	George Goethals, Latham	Fray Junipero Serra and the Conquest
George Goethals, Latham	Gold in California, Wellman	of Mexico, Wise
Gold Rush Adventures, McCall	In the Hand of the Cave Dwellers, Henty	From Empire to Republic, Noll
In Mexico They Say, Ross	Inside the Alamo, Murphy	Goethals and the Panama Canal, Fast
Lost City, Lewin	Jessie Benton Fremont, Higgins	Green Mansions, Hudson
Mexico, Wharton	Juarez Hero of Mexico, Baker	Hernando Cortez, Abbott
New Shoes for Silvia, Hurwitz	Make Way for Sam Houston, Fritz	Historical Tales: Spanish America, Mor
Nine Days to Christmas, Ets	Makers of South America, Daniels	In and Out of the Old Missions of
Our Little Argentine Cousin, Brooks	Martha of California, Otis	California, James
Our Little Brazilian Cousin, Nixon-Roulet	Mexico, Coxhead	Inca and Spaniard, Marrin
Our Little Mexican Cousin, Butler	Montezuma and the Conquest of Mexico,	James Bowie and His Famous Knife, Ga
Our Little Panama Cousin, Pike	Eggleston	Junipero Serra, Fitch
Papa and Me, Dorros	Out of Many Waters, Greene	Makers of Latin America, Worcester
Ranch of a Thousand Horns, Bothwell	Out on the Pampas, Henty	South America, Bryce
Stalwart Men of Early Texas, McCall	Pacific History Stories, Wagner	South America: A Popular Illustrated
Stories of El Dorado, Wait	Secret of the Andes, Clark	History, Butterworth
Tales of Enchantment from Spain, Eels	Siege, Hays	Stories of Old New Spain, Janvier
Tales of Giants from Brazil, Eells	Simon Bolivar, Whitridge	The Expedition of the Donner Party an
Tales of the Gauchos, Hudson	South America, Browne	Its Tragic Fate, Houghton
The Gold Coin, Ada	Stories of South America, Brooks	The Royal Highway, Corle
The Golden Book of California, Shapiro	Story of Davy Crockett, Meadowcroft	The Story of Mexico, Hale
The Legend of the Poinsettia, dePaola	Tales of Silver Lands, Finger	The Story of Mexico: The Mexican
The Mexican Twins, Perkins	The Birth of Texas, Johnson	Revolution, Stein
The Mission Bell, Politi	The Boy Travellers in Mexico, Knox	The Story of South American Republics
The Moon Was at a Fiesta, Gollub	The Boy Travellers in South America, Knox	Part One, Dawson
The Rush for Gold, Beals	The Conquest of Montezuma's	Part Two, Dawson
The Story of Davy Crockett, Meadowcroft	Empire, Lang	The World's Story V 11, Tappan
The Story of Junipero Serra, White	The Corn Grows Ripe, Rhoads	Three Conquistadors, Garst
The Story of the California Gold Rush,	The King of the Mountains, Jagendorf	Walter Reed: Doctor in Uniform, Wood
Stein	The King's Fifth, O'Dell	Young Folks' History of Mexico, Ober
The Two Uncles of Pablo, Behn	The Listening One, Karney	
The Umbrella, Brett	The Lost Lakes, Peare	**Forgotten Classics:**
The Village that Learned to Read, Tarshis	The Missions of California, McRoskey	G6-331 George Goethals
Tonight is Carnaval, Dorros	The Treasure of the Incas, Henty	W9-203 Makers of South America
We Were There at the Alamo, Cousins	The White Conquerors, Munroe	
	The Youngest Conquistador, Mantel	
	Their Shining Hour, Maher	
Forgotten Classics:	Walk the World's Rim, Baker	
F11-24 Hernando Cortez	With Cochrane the Dauntless, Henty	
F11-28 Francisco Pizarro	Young Inca Prince, Malkus	
F12-221 Samuel Houston		
F12-229 John Sutter		
S12-221 Why the Chimes Rang	**Forgotten Classics:**	
	W9-1 Cortez and Montezuma	
	W9-107 Pizarro & the Conquest of Peru	

LATIN AMERICA		
ELEMENTARY	**MIDDLE SCHOOL**	**HIGH SCHOOL**

My Book House:

☐ 1-68 South American Rhymes

☐ 1-70 Mexican Rhymes

☐ 1-224 A Rhyme from Santo Domingo

☐ 2-37 Reen-Reen-Reeny-Croak Frog

☐ 2-68 The Poor Old Lady

☐ 3-172 How the Brazilian Beetles Got
   Their Gorgeous Coats

☐ 4-103 A Child in a Mexican Garden

☐ 8-172 Mr Hampden's Shipwreck

☐ 9-41 Adventures of Alexander Selkirk

☐ 12-45 Senor Kon-Tiki: Thor Heyerdahl

Junior Classics:

☐ 1-243 Rosa-too-Little

☐ 2-257 How the Brazilian Beetles Got
   Their Gorgeous Coats

☐ 2-263 Million Dollar Somersaults

☐ 4-71 Tomas is Lost from the Village

☐ 5-134 And Now Miguel

☐ 4-117 Chucaro

☐ 9-332 Outside from Secret of the Andes

WORLD WARS

ELEMENTARY	MIDDLE SCHOOL	HIGH SCHOOL
☐ All Those Secrets of the World, Yolen	☐ Battle of the Bulge, Toland	☐ And They Thought We Would Never Fight, Gibbons
☐ Anne Frank's Chestnut Tree, Kohuth	☐ Combat Nurses of WWII, Blassingame	☐ Bold Leaders of World War I, Reeder
☐ Boxes for Katje, Fleming	☐ Edith Cavell, de Leeuw	☐ Commander of the Flying Tigers, Archibald
☐ Casey Over There, Rabin	☐ Edith Cavell, Vinton	☐ Day of Infamy, Lord
☐ Luba: The Angel of Bergen-Belsen	☐ Essays for Boys and Girls, Paget	☐ Heroes and Heroic Deeds of the Great War, Mackenzie
☐ Miracles on Maple Hill, Sorensen	☐ Falcons of France, Nordhoff	☐ Incredible Victory, Lord
☐ Primrose Days, Haywood	☐ Friend Within the Gates, Grey	☐ Overlord, Marrin
☐ Shooting at the Stars, Hendrix	☐ From Casablanca to Berlin, Bliven	☐ Pen Pictures of the Great World War, Smyth
☐ Swallows and Amazons, Ransome	☐ From Pearl Harbor to Okinawa, Bliven	☐ The Airman's War, Marrin
☐ Coot Club	☐ Great American Fighter Pilots of WWI, Blassingame	☐ The Fighting Mascot, Kehoe
☐ Great Northern?	☐ Guadalcanal Diary, Tregaskis	☐ The Little Book of the War, Tappan
☐ Missee Lee	☐ John F. Kennedy and PT 109, Tregaskis	☐ The Miracle of Dunkirk, Lord
☐ Peter Duck	☐ Journey Home, Uchida	☐ The Story of the Great War, Braithwaite
☐ Pigeon Post	☐ Journey to Topaz, Uchida	☐ The Story of the Great War, Usher
☐ Secret Water	☐ Medical Corps Heroes WWII, Blassingame	☐ The Yanks are Coming, Marrin
☐ Swallowdale	☐ Midway: Battle for the Pacific, Castillo	☐ Winston Churchill and the Story of Two World Wars, Coolidge
☐ The Big Six	☐ Omar Nelson Bradley, Reeder	
☐ The Picts and the Martyrs	☐ Radar Commandos, Glemser	**Forgotten Classics:**
☐ We Didn't Mean to Go to Sea	☐ Story of the World War for Young People, Nida	☐ F10-112 Cardinal Mercier
☐ Winter Holiday	☐ Surrender, White	☐ F10-114 Killing the Soul
☐ The Story of D-Day, Stein	☐ The Avion My Uncle Flew, Fisher	☐ F10-119 Why Belgium Fought
☐ The Story of the Battle for Iwo Jima, Stein	☐ The Battle for Iwo Jima, Leckie	☐ F10-120 Victors
☐ The Story of the Battle of the Bulge, Stein	☐ The Battle of Britain, Reynolds	☐ F10-121 German Proclamation
☐ The Story of the USS Arizona, Stein	☐ The Battle of the Atlantic, Williams	☐ F10-185 America's Standard
☐ The Little Ships, Borden	☐ The Children's Story of the War, Parrot	☐ F10-193 How Our Boys Go to Battle
☐ Waiting for the Evening Star, Wells	☐ The Commandos of World War II, Carter	☐ F10-201 Quality of Mercy
☐ We Were There at the Battle of Britain, Knight	☐ The Flying Aces of WWI, Gurney	☐ F10-204 When the Tide Turned
☐ We Were There at the Normandy Invasion, Knight	☐ The Flying Tigers, Toland	☐ F10-233 James Clark
☐ We Were There with the Lafayette Escadrille, Knight	☐ The Seabees of World War II, Blassingame	☐ F10-280 Second Line of Defense
☐ Yellow Star, Deedy	☐ The Sinking of the Bismarck, Shirer	☐ F10-285 The Unseen Host
	☐ The Story of Admiral Dewey, Beebe	
Forgotten Classics:	☐ The Story of D-Day, Bliven	
☐ F10-3 I Am an American	☐ The Story of Our War With Spain, Brooks	
☐ F10-110 Saving a Soldier's Life	☐ The Story of the Paratroops, Weller	
☐ F10-232 I Knew You Would Come	☐ The U.S. Frogmen of WWII, Blassingame	
	☐ The Winged Watchman, van Stockum	
Junior Classics:	☐ The World War I Series, Althsheier	
☐ 6-306 In Flander's Fields	☐ The Forest of Swords	
☐ 9-87 Adventure in Sheridan Square	☐ The Guns of Europe	
	☐ The Hosts of the Air	
	☐ Thirty Seconds Over Tokyo, Considine	
	☐ Twenty and Ten, Bishop	
	☐ We Were There at the Normandy Invasion, Knight	
	☐ We Were There at the Battle of Britain, Knight	
	☐ Winston Churchill, Reynolds	
	Forgotten Classics:	
	☐ F10-67 King Albert	
	☐ F10-125 Joseph Joffe	
	☐ F10-138 An Alsatian Boy	
	☐ F10-145 Marie the Courageous	

WORLD WARS		
ELEMENTARY	MIDDLE SCHOOL	HIGH SCHOOL
	☐ F10-163 John Pershing	
	☐ F10-176 Let us Save the Kiddies	
	☐ F10-186 The Last Flight	
	☐ F10-196 Joyce Kilmer	
	☐ F10-218 Sir Douglas Haig	
	☐ F10-245 The Truce	
	☐ F10-253 Ferdinand Foch	

1900s AMERICA

ELEMENTARY	MIDDLE SCHOOL	HIGH SCHOOL
A Tree for Peter, Seredy	A Jar of Dreams, Uchida	A Night to Remember, Lord
Aaron Copland His Life, Peare	Americans in Space, Dille	A Tree Grows in Brooklyn, Smith
All the Places to Love, MacLachlan	Andrew Carnegie, Judson	Albert Einstein, Levinger
Bully for You Teddy Roosevelt, Fritz	Blue Willow, Gates	American and Vietman, Marrin
Charles Lindbergh: Hero Pilot, Collins	Eleanor Roosevelt, Faber	Angel Island, Bamford
Cheaper by the Dozen, Gilbreth	Enrico Fermi, Faber	Cancer Cocaine and Courage, Beckhard
City Neighbor, Judson	Entertaining the World, Cook	Clarence Darrow, Noble
Come on Seabiscuit, Moody	Harry Truman, Faber	Daddy Long-Legs, Webster
David Sarnoff, Myers	Henry Ford, Kelly	Edna St. Vincent Millay, Shafter
Drawn from New England, Tudor	Jane Addams of Hull House, Wise	Electronics Pioneer, Levine
Eleanor Roosevelt, Graves	Light a Little Lamp, Ziegler	First Woman Ambulance Surgeon, Nob
Five Little Peppers Series, Sidney	Little Britches Series, Moody	First Woman in Congress, White
Five Little Peppers and How They Grow	Father and I Were Ranchers	Genius with a Scalpel, Denzel
Five Little Peppers at School	Living Architecture, Ransohoff	Geraldine Ferraro, Lawson
Five Little Peppers Grown Up	Making Music, Bernstein	Gifford Pinchot, White
Five Little Peppers in LittleBrownHouse	Making Poems for America, Munson	Helen Keller: The Story of My Life
Five Little Peppers Midway	Mama's Bank Account, Forbes	Henry Ford's Own Story, Lane
Phronsie Pepper	Master of Ballyhoo, Sutton	Joseph Pulitzer, Noble
The Stories Polly Pepper Told	Petticoat Politics, Faber	Lillian Wald, Epstein
Franklin D. Roosevelt, Blassingame	Putting Electrons to Work, Tebbel	Nellie Bly, Noble
Gone Away Lake, Enright	Rallying a Free People, Cook	Nurse Around the Wolrd, Noble
Return to Gone Away Lake	Roller Skates, Sawyer	Our Home, Sargent
Helen Keler, Davidson	Ronald Reagan, Doherty	Physician to the World, Burt
Helen Keller, Wilkie	Shaping a New World, Moss	President from Missouri, Martin
Helen Keller: Toward the Light, Stewart	Story of Dwight D. Eisenhower, Beckhard	The Good Years, Lord
I Said I Could and I Did, Weiss	Striving to be Champion, Miller	The Healing Heart, Ruggles
Mother Carey's Chickens, Wiggin	That Touch of Magic, Hickok	The Man Who Dropped from the Sky,
Mrs. Wiggs of the Cabbage Patch, Rice	The Boys Life of Edison, Meadowcroft	Shyne
Pollyanna, Porter	The Conquest of the North and South	The Many Worlds of Herbert Hoover,
Pollyanna Grows Up	Poles, Reynolds	Terzian
Return of the Alaskan, Herron	The Doctors Who Conquered Yellow	The Ringlings, Harlow
Robert H. Goddard, Lomask	Fever, Hill	The World Was His Laboratory,
Streets to Gold, Wells	The Early Days of Automobiles, Janeway	Westervelt
Susan B. Anthony, Hopkinson	The Helen Keller Story, Peare	Theodore Roosevelt, Harlow
Take a Hike Teddy Roosevelt, Murphy	The Kid from Tomkinsville, Tunis	Thomas Alva Edison, Garbedian
The First Flight, Shea	The Mayo Brothers, Clapesattle	World Citizen, Archer
The House that Jane Built, Stone	The Story of Oklahoma, Tinkle	Young 'Ike', Hatch
The Hundred Dresses, Estes	The Story of San Francisco, Jackson	Young Man in the White House, Levins
The Little House, Burton	The Story of Thomas Alva Edison, Cousins	
The Moffats, Estes	The True Story of Albert Einstein, Oldfie	**Forgotten Classics:**
Rufus M.	The United Nations in War and Peace,	F12-376 Case of Mr. Tweed
The Middle Moffat	Fehrenback	G7-67 Herbert Hoover
The Moffat Museum	The Woodrow Wilson Story, Peare	G7-209 John D. Rockefeller
The One Bad Things About Father, Negri	The Wright Brothers, Reynolds	G12-344 Alice Hegan Rice
The Story of Apollo 11, Stein	The Wright Brothers: How They Invented	S11-185 Almost Home
The Story of Chuck Yeager Breaks the	the Airplane, Freedman	S11-193 The Telephone A Memory
Sound Barrier, Stein	Thimble Summer, Enright	S11-200 It Will Mend
The Story of Dwight D. Eisenhower,	Underground, Macaulay	S11-201 They Two
Beckhard	Walt Disney, Montgomery	S11-203 Because You Love Me
The Story of Ellis Island, Stein	Women of Courage, Nathan	S11-204 I Am Your Wife
The Story of Helen Keller, Hickock	Young People's Story of the Modern	
The Story of the Flight Kitty Hawk, Stein	World, Hillyer	
The Story of the Great Depression, Stein	Young Thomas Edison, North	

1900s AMERICA

ELEMENTARY	MIDDLE SCHOOL	HIGH SCHOOL

ELEMENTARY

- [ ] The Story of the Nineteenth Amendment, Stein
- [ ] The Story of the Spirit of St. Louis, Stein
- [ ] Theodore Roosevelt, Foster
- [ ] Theodore Roosevelt: Man of Action, Beach
- [ ] Thomas Alva Edison, Kaufman
- [ ] Understood Betsy, Canfield
- [ ] Wilfred Gordon McDonald Partridge, Fox
- [ ] Wright Brothers Kings of the Air, Kaufman

Forgotten Classics:
- [ ] G4-317 Jane Addams
- [ ] S6-18 Thomas Edison
- [ ] S6-37 Helen Keller
- [ ] S6-83 Teddy Roosevelt
- [ ] S6-200 Partners
- [ ] S11-57 Jack Binns Hero
- [ ] S11-77 The Golden Windows
- [ ] S11-84 The Discontented Pendulum
- [ ] S11-277 The Newsboy of Gary
- [ ] S11-278 Wanted: A Real Mother
- [ ] S11-289 Margaret of New Orleans
- [ ] S11-323 The Lame Boy
- [ ] S12-1 Birds' Christmas Carol
- [ ] S12-229 This Way to Christmas

My Book House:
- [ ] 2-23 An American Miners' Song
- [ ] 3-181 A Happy Day in the City
- [ ] 4-218 The Pert Fire Engine
- [ ] 5-66 Wilbur and Orville Wright
- [ ] 7-144a Babe Ruth
- [ ] 11-216 Your America
- [ ] 12-31 The First Moon Landing
- [ ] 12-60 Telegraph Boy: Andrew Carnegie
- [ ] 12-170 The Lone Star Team of Texas
- [ ] 12-218 The Gentle Genius

Junior Classics:
- [ ] 1-278 Any Old Junk Today?
- [ ] 1-305 The Funny Thing
- [ ] 5-66 The Yellow Shop
- [ ] 5-152 Experiment 13
- [ ] 5-184 The Hundred Dresses
- [ ] 5-232 The Girl in Pink
- [ ] 5-263 A Different World
- [ ] 5-335 Henry and the Paper Route
- [ ] 5-354 Jane and the Chief of Police
- [ ] 6-196 The Night When Mother was Away
- [ ] 6-202 Mr. Chairman
- [ ] 6-302 The Singing Tree
- [ ] 8-94 The Traveling Newspaper Office
- [ ] 8-123 Boy of Wrigley Field
- [ ] 9-46 The Kid from Tomkinsville

MIDDLE SCHOOL

Forgotten Classics:
- [ ] F12-333 Frances E. Willard
- [ ] F12-359 Jane Addams
- [ ] G4-295 Peter Rowe
- [ ] S6-205 Are You There My Lad?
- [ ] S11-188 What the Spirit of Sunshine Means
- [ ] W11-548 Our World Today

Junior Classics:
- [ ] 5-311 The Fair from Thimble Summer
- [ ] 8-15 Out of Darkness from The Story of My Life

1900s AMERICA		
ADDITIONAL BOOKS		
ELEMENTARY	MIDDLE SCHOOL	HIGH SCHOOL

GERMANY

ELEMENTARY	MIDDLE SCHOOL	HIGH SCHOOL
☐ Beethoven, Mirsky	☐ A History of Germany, Marshall	☐ Beethoven, Young
☐ Beethoven Lives Upstairs, Nichol	☐ Brahms the Master, Goss	☐ Beethoven and the World of Music, Komroff
☐ Child Stories of the Masters, Menefee	☐ Martin Luther, Fosdick	☐ Bonhoeffer: Pastor Martyr Prophet Spy, Metaxas
☐ Favorite Fairy Tales - Germany, Haviland	☐ Martin Luther: Hero of Faith, Nohl	☐ Defender of Human Rights: Carl Schurz
☐ Grimm's Fairy Tales, Pratt	☐ Number the Stars, Lawry	☐ Discoverer of X-Rays, Esterer
☐ Grimm's Fairy Tales, Turpin	☐ Stories from German History, Aston	☐ Historical Tales: Germany, Morris
☐ Hansel and Gretel, Jeffers	☐ The Ark, Margot-Benary-Isbert	☐ House Life in Germany, Sidgwick
☐ Hansel and Gretel, Zelinsky	☐ The Boy Travellers in N. Europe, Knox	☐ Iron Chancellor, Apsler
☐ Johann Gutenberg, Smith	☐ The Cuckoo Clock, Stolz	☐ The Story of Germany, Baring-Gould
☐ Little Red Riding Hood, Pinkney	☐ The Diary of a Young Girl, Frank	☐ The Story of the Goths, Bradley
☐ Little Red Riding Hood, Spirin	☐ The Rise and Fall of Adolf Hitler, Shirer	☐ The Story of the Hansa Towns, Zimmer
☐ Ludwig Beethoven and the Chiming Tower Bells, Wheeler	☐ The Silver Sword, Serraillier	☐ The World's Story V 7, Tappan
☐ Martin Luther, Maier	☐ The Story of Siegfried, Baldwin	☐ Young Folks' History of Germany, Yonge
☐ Mitz and Fritz of Germany, Brandeis	☐ With Frederick the Great, Henty	
☐ Nibble Nibble Mousekin, Anglund		
☐ Olcott's Grimm's Fairy Tales, Jenkins	**Forgotten Classics:**	**Forgotten Classics:**
☐ Our Little German Cousin, Wade	☐ G2-92 Albrecht Durer	☐ G7-130 Frederch Perthes
☐ Rapunzel, Berenzy	☐ G5-61 Bottgher	☐ G8-138 Beethoven
☐ Rapunzel, Zelinsky	☐ G6-140 Frederick the Great	☐ G8-193 Franz Joseph Hyde
☐ Rose Red and Snow White, Sanderson	☐ G6-321 Otto von Bismarck	☐ G9-319 Had You Been Born a Protestant
☐ Rumpelstiltskin, Zelinsky	☐ G7-34 Nathan Straus	☐ G10-39 Kepler
☐ Sebastian Bach, Wheeler	☐ G8-11 Johann Bach	☐ G11-123 The Mother of Goethe
☐ Snow White, Santore	☐ G8-251 Mendelssohn	☐ N10-167 Early German Songs
☐ Snow White and Other Stories, Cappe	☐ G8-280 Robert Schumann	☐ N10-174 German Church Music
☐ Stories from Old Germany, Pratt	☐ G8-292 Richard Wagner	☐ N10-179 Johann Sebastian Bach
☐ Stories of Siegfried, MacGregor	☐ G9-306 Martin Luther	☐ N10-189 Christoph Wilbald Gluck
☐ The Borrowed House, van Stockum	☐ G10-80 Herschel and the Story of Stars	☐ N10-198 Franz Josef Haydn
☐ The Butterfly, Polacco	☐ N11-116 Martin Rinkart	☐ N10-223 Ludwig von Beethoven
☐ The Cuckoo Clock, Stolz	☐ N11-127 Paul Gerhardt	☐ N10-239 Carl von Weber
☐ The Elves and the Shoemaker	☐ N11-136 Gerhard Tersteegen the Weaver	☐ N10-248 Franz Schubert
☐ The Frog Prince, Berenzy	☐ N11-174 Martin Luther	☐ N10-255 Robert Schumann
☐ The Pied Piper of Hamelin, Dunlap	☐ W10-243 A History of Germany	☐ N10-261 Mendelssohn
☐ The Story of Beethoven, Kaufmann	☐ W11-334 The Reformation	☐ N10-273 Richard Wagner
☐ The Traveling Musicians, Fischer	☐ W11-419 The Eighteenth Century	☐ N10-285 Johannes Brahms
☐ The Twelve Dancing Princesses, Craft		☐ N10-287 German Art: Nuremberg
☐ The Twelve Dancing Princesses, Sanderson		☐ N10-294 Albrecht Durer
☐ The Young Brahms, Deucher		☐ N10-305 Hans Holbein
		☐ N10-312 Later German Art
		☐ N10-317 Familiar German Pictures
Forgotten Classics:		☐ N11-98 German Hymns
☐ G5-24 John Gutenberg		☐ N11-123 Now Thank We All Our God
☐ G5-31 John Gutenberg		☐ N11-179 A Mighty Fortress is Our God
☐ G8-28 Bach		
☐ G8-122 Beethoven		**Delphian Course:**
☐ N12-7 Haensel and Gretel		☐ 5:146-176 Early German Literature/ Minnesingers
☐ N12-65 Tannhauser		☐ 5:351-356 German Opera
☐ N12-87 Wagner's Opera		☐ 5:357-383 Wagner/Ring of Nibelung
☐ S1-16 Ludwig Knaus		☐ 7:317-392 German Drama
☐ S1-18, 21 von Bremen		☐ 8:466-473 German Unity
☐ S3-81 German Fairy Tales		☐ 8:474-500 Modern German Literature
☐ S5-122 Siegfried: Hero of Germany		☐ 9:64-78 Paintings in Germany
☐ S6-175 The Kingdoms		☐ 9:151-157 German Art Galleries
☐ S6-187 The King and the Page		
☐ S11-3 The Golden Pears		

GERMANY		
ELEMENTARY	**MIDDLE SCHOOL**	**HIGH SCHOOL**

ELEMENTARY:

- [ ] S11-13 Sweet Rice Porridge
- [ ] S11-26 The Honest Farmer
- [ ] S11-32 Hans the Shepherd Boy
- [ ] S11-104 The Little Loaf
- [ ] S11-319 The Magic Mask
- [ ] S11-328 The Golden River
- [ ] S12-345 The Legend of the Christ Child

My Book House:

- [ ] 1-122 German Nursery Rhymes
- [ ] 2-140 A German Evening
- [ ] 2-182 The Story Adventure of Baron Muchausen
- [ ] 3-95 The Shoemaker and the Elves
- [ ] 3-111 The Little Girls and the Hare
- [ ] 4-28 The Twelve Dancing Princesses
- [ ] 4-34 Snow White and Rose Red
- [ ] 4-73 Hansel and Grethel
- [ ] 4-159 The Blacksmith by Brahms
- [ ] 5-162 The Nuremberg Stove
- [ ] 6-59 A Musical Visit to Fairyland
- [ ] 7-126 The Six Swans
- [ ] 7-134 The Golden Bird
- [ ] 11-73 The Tale of the Rhine-Gold

Junior Classics:

- [ ] 1-48 Little Red Riding Hood
- [ ] 2-70 Rapunzel
- [ ] 2-76 The Elves and the Shoemaker
- [ ] 2-79 Hansel and Grethel
- [ ] 2-91 Bremen Town Musicians
- [ ] 2-96 The Fisherman and His Wife
- [ ] 2-106 The Goose Girl
- [ ] 2-114 The Golden Goose
- [ ] 6-390 A Star for Hansi

GERMANY		
ADDITIONAL BOOKS		
ELEMENTARY	**MIDDLE SCHOOL**	**HIGH SCHOOL**

RUSSIA

ELEMENTARY	MIDDLE SCHOOL	HIGH SCHOOL
Baba Yaga and Vasilisa the Brave, Mayer	A Brief History of Russia, Shaw	A Literary History, Bruckner
Baboushka and the Three Kings, Robbins	A Jacobite Exile, Henty	Beloved Friend, Bowen
Byliny Book, Harrison	Boy Travellers in Russian Empire, Knox	Crime and Punishment, Dostoyevsky
Caps for Sale, Slobodkin	Chief of the Cossacks, Lamb	Empress of All Russia, Noble
Favorite Fairy Tales - Russia, Haviland	Catherine the Great, Scherman	Historical Tales: Russian, Morris
Folk Tales from the Russian, Blumenthal	Condemned as a Nihilist, Henty	Lenin, Levine
Foma the Terrible, Daniels	Dancing Star, Malvern	Michael Strogoff, Verne
I Dreamed I Was a Ballerina	Dvora's Journey, Blaine	Nicholas and Alexandra, Massie
Katrinka, Haskell	Jack Archer, Henty	One Day in the Life of Ivan Denisovich,
My Mother is the Most Beautiful Woman	Joseph Stalin and Communist Russia,	Solzhenitsyn
In the World, Reyker	Blassingame	Peter the Great, Abbott
Old Peter's Russian Tales, Ransome	Old Peter's Russian Tales, Ransome	Peter the Great, Baker
Our Little Russian Cousin, Wade	Russia, Walter	Recollections of Pre-Revolutionary
Peter and the Wolf	Struggle is Our Brother, Felsen	Russia, Alboo
Illustrated Version	Swan Lake, van Allsburg	Russia, Wallace
Peter the Great, Stanley	The Endless Steppe, Hautzig	Russia: Story of the Nations, Morfill
Salt: A Russian Tale, Zemach	The Promised Land, Antin	Russia and Turkey in Nineteenth
Seven Simeons, Artzybasheff	The Story of Russia, Benson	Century, Latimer
Swan Lake, Diamond	The Story of Russia, VanBergen	Russian Literature, Waliszewki
Tale of the Firebird, Spirin	The Wild Children, Holman	Stalin: Russia's Man of Steel, Marrin
Tales the People Tell in Russia, Wyndham	Through Russian Snows, Henty	Stormy Victory, Purdy
The Fool of World & Flying Ship, Ransome		Story of the Nations Russia and Poland
The Frog Princess, Spirin	**Forgotten Classics:**	Lodge
The House on Walenska Street, Herman	G6-99 Peter the Great	Stravinsky, Young
The Littlest Matryoshka, Bliss	S9-274 The Charge of the Light Brigade	Tchaikovsky, Young
The Nutcracker, Innocenti	W10-1 Story of Russia	The Gulag Archipelago, Solzhenitsyn
The Peasants Pea Patch, Daniels	W11-43 17th Century East of Europe	The Story of Russia, Morfill
The Russian Garland, Steele	W12-12 Vladimir the Great	The World's Story V 6, Tappan
The Sea King's Daughter, Spirin	W12-42 Story of Catherine	Trotsky: World Revolutionary, Archer
The Snow Princess, Sanderson	W12-407 Making of a Patriot: Mary Antin	
The Story of Prince Ivan, Whitney		**Forgotten Classics:**
The Tale of Tsar Saltan, Spirin		G12-164 Leo Tolstoy
The Three Questions, Muth		N10-31 Russian Music
Vasilisa the Beautiful, Morgunova		W12-344 Catherine Breshkovsky
When I Was a Boy in Russia, Debogorii		
		Delphian Course:
Forgotten Classics:		9:477-521 Russian Fiction/Writers
S3-285 Baba Yaga		
S3-296 Salt		
S11-37 The Girl Who Saved Her Father		
S11-267 Where Love Is There God Is		

My Book House:

- 1-132 Russian Rhymes
- 2-46 Uncle Mitya's Horse
- 2-149 Building the Bridge
- 4-63 Christening the Baby in Russia
- 7-112 The Little Man is Big As Your Thumb
- 8-105 Dancing Star: Anna Pavlova
- 10-119 The Word of Igor's Armament
- 12-190 A Boy in Russia: Leo Tolstoy

Junior Classics:

- 6-148 My Mother is the Most
  Beautiful Woman in the World

RUSSIA		
ADDITIONAL BOOKS		
ELEMENTARY	**MIDDLE SCHOOL**	**HIGH SCHOOL**

EASTERN EUROPE

ELEMENTARY	MIDDLE SCHOOL	HIGH SCHOOL
Busy Monday Morning, Domanska	A Day of Pleasure, Singer	Copernicus, Thomas
Curtain Calls for Franz Schubert, Wheeler	Dangerous Journey, Hamoir	Electrical Genius, Beckhard
Czechoslovak Fairy Tales, Fillmore	Joseph Haydn, Wheeler	Flight of the Wildling, Vance
Favorite Fairy Tales - Czech, Haviland	Patriot of the Underground, McKown	Haydn, Young
Favorite Fairy Tales - Poland, Haviland	Petar's Treasure, Judson	Life in a Jar, Mayer
Harry Houdini, Kraske	The Chestry Oak, Seredy	Physician Rebel, Archer
Hayden, Mirsky	The Good Master, Seredy	Red Rebel, Archer
Irena Sendler and the Children of the Warsaw Ghetto, Rubin	The Singing Tree, Seredy	The Great Houdini, Epstein
Joseph Haydn, Wheeler	The Story of the von Trapp Family Singers, von Trapp	The Story of Austria, Whitman
Mozart the Wonder Boy, Deucher	The Trumpeter of Krakow, Kelly	The Story of Bohemia, Maurice
Mozart the Wonder Child, Stanley	The Wall, Sis	The Story of Marco, Porter
Polish Fairy Tales, Biggs		
Slavonic Fairy Tales, Naake	**Forgotten Classics:**	**Forgotten Classics:**
The Boy Who Loved Music, Lasker	G7-14 Edward Alfred Steiner	N10-210 Wolfgang Amadeus Mozart
The Cats in Krasinski Square, Hesse	G8-216 Mozart	N10-322 Franz Liszt
The Champion of Children, Begacki	G8-226 Wolfgang Mozart	N10-329 Antonin Dvorak
The Gypsies' Tale, Pochocki	G8-244 Franz Schubert	W12-310 St. Elizabeth of Hungary
The Jolly Tailor, Barski		
The Man Who Kept His Heart in a Bucket, Levitin	**Junior Classics:**	**Delphian Course:**
The Mitten, Brett	9-62 The Great Tarnov Crystal	9:461-476 Polish Fiction/ Writers
The Shepherd's Nosegay, Fillmore	9-205 The Riding Lesson	
The Treasure, Shulevitz		
Up the Hill, de Angeli		
Zlateh the Goat, Singer		

Forgotten Classics:
- G8-212 Wolfgang Mozart
- G8-267 Chopin
- S3-221 Prince Kindhearted
- S3-253 The Two Brothers
- S3-257 The Golden Duck
- S3-271 The Golden Grandmother
- S6-52 Mozart

My Book House:
- 1-73 Polish Rhymes
- 1-128 Czechoslovakian Rhymes
- 1-136 Hungarian Rhymes
- 1-137 A Roumanian Lullaby
- 1-145 Estonian Rhyme
- 2-52 The Rooster and the Sultan
- 2-71 The Little Rooster & the Little Hen
- 2-150 The Little Dog Waltz
- 7-11 Miksa & the Man w/ the Iron Head
- 7-40 The Maiden the Knight & Waterfall
- 7-96 The Prince Who Rode Through a Mousehole
- 7-102 Vladimir's Adventure in Search of Fortune
- 11-29 Marko the Champion of Serbian Liberty

EASTERN EUROPE		
ELEMENTARY	**MIDDLE SCHOOL**	**HIGH SCHOOL**
Junior Classics:		
☐ 1-214 Poppy Seed Cakes		
☐ 2-170 Budulinek		
☐ 8-161 Dream of Freedom: Mozart		

AMERICA - OVERVIEW		
ELEMENTARY	**MIDDLE SCHOOL**	**HIGH SCHOOL**
☐ A First Book in American History, Eggleston	☐ Children's Stories of American Progress, Wright	☐ A First Book in American History with European Beginnings, Southworth
☐ American First: One Hundred Stories from Our Own History, Evans	Real Stories From Our History, Faris	☐ A Student's History of the United States, Channing
☐ American Histroy Story Book, Blaisdell	☐ The Makers of the Nation, Coe	☐ America is Born, Johnson
☐ Broad Strips and Bright Stars, Bailey	The Story of Our Country Every Child	☐ America Grows Up, Johnson
☐ Primary History of the United States for Young Folks, Morris	Can Read, Hurlbut	☐ America Moves Forward, Johnson
☐ Stories of American History, Dodge	This Country of Ours, Marshall	American History Told Contemporarie:
☐ Stories of American History, Gordy	☐ Volume 1	☐ Volume I
☐ The Child's Story of Our Country, Morris	☐ Volume 2	☐ Volume II
☐ The Child's Pictorial History of the United	☐ Volume 3	Our Country, Lossing
States, Goodrich	☐ Volume 4	☐ Volume 1
The Golden Book History of the U.S.	☐ Volume 5	☐ Volume 2
☐ Vol 1 The Explorers	☐ Volume 6	☐ Volume 3
☐ Vol 2 The Indian Wars	☐ Volume 7	☐ Volume 4
☐ Vol 3 The Age of Revolution		☐ Volume 5
☐ Vol 4 Building the Nation		☐ Volume 6
☐ Vol 5 The Civil War		☐ Volume 7
☐ Vol 7 The Age of Steel		☐ Volume 8
☐ Vol 10 The Age of the Atom		Settlement to the Present Time, Hart
☐ Vol 11 Famous Americans A-L		☐ Volume I
		☐ Volume II
		☐ Volume III
		☐ Volume IV
		☐ Volume V
		☐ Source Book of American History, Hart
		☐ The Story of American Painting, Caffin
		☐ Told in Story: American History Stories
		From American History
		☐ True Stories of American History for O
		Young People, Bright
		Delphian Course:
		☐ X:2-82 American History Overview

AMERICA - OVERVIEW		
ADDITIONAL BOOKS		
ELEMENTARY	MIDDLE SCHOOL	HIGH SCHOOL

WORLD - OVERVIEW		
ELEMENTARY	**MIDDLE SCHOOL**	**HIGH SCHOOL**
☐ A Child's Geography of the World, Hillyer	Around the World in 80 Minutes, Walsh	An Outline of World History, Tappan
☐ A Child's History of the World, Hillyer	☐ Stories of Heroic Deeds for Boys and Girls, Johonnot	☐ Barbarian and Noble, Lansing
☐ Favorite Tales of Long Ago, Baldwin	Story of the World, Syne	Beacon Lights of History, Lord
☐ Fifty Famous Stories Retold, Baldwin	☐ Growth of the British Empire	☐ Volume 1
☐ Number Stories of Long Ago, Smith	☐ On the Shores of the Great Sea	☐ Volume 2
☐ Old World Hero Stories, Tappan	☐ The Awakening of Europe	☐ Volume 3
☐ Seven Historic Ages, Gilman	☐ The Discovery of the New World	☐ Volume 4
☐ Tales from Far and Near, Terry	☐ The Struggle for Sea Power	☐ Volume 5
☐ Ten Boys of History, Sweetser	Story of the World: A European Background, Elson	☐ Volume 6
☐ Ten Boys Who Lived on the Road to Long Ago, Andrews	☐ The Story of the Middle Ages, Harding	☐ Volume 7
☐ The Book of Brave Adventures, Calhoun	True Stories from Ancient History, Budden	☐ Volume 8
☐ The Seven Little Sisters that Live on the Round Ball That Floats in the Air, Andrews	Wonders of History, Parley	☐ Volume 9
☐ The Story of the World, Bauer	Young People's History of the Medieval World, Hillyer	☐ Volume 10
		☐ Volume 11
		☐ Volume 12
		☐ Volume 13
		☐ Volume 14
		☐ Volume 15
		☐ Modern Times and the Living Past, Elso
		☐ Patriots and Tyrants, Lansing
		☐ Recent European History, Fellows
		☐ Social Evenings, Lee
		☐ Strange Stories from History for Young People, Eggleston
		☐ Ten Great Events in History, Johonnot
		☐ The Story of Mankind, van Loon
		☐ The Story of the Nineteenth Century of the Christian Era, Brooks
		☐ The True Story Book, Lang
		☐ The Young Folk's Story of the World, Chapin
		☐ Time Telling Through the Ages, Brearly
		☐ Torch Bearers of History, Stirling
		☐ World Pictures, Menpes
		☐ Young People's History of the World fo One Hundred Years, Morris
		Delphian Course:
		☐ Volume 1
		☐ Volume 2
		☐ Volume 3
		☐ Volume 4
		☐ Volume 5
		☐ Volume 6
		☐ Volume 7
		☐ Volume 8
		☐ Volume 9
		☐ Volume 10
		☐ 1:xiv-xxxi Prehistoric Man
		☐ 4:408-484 Middle Ages Overview
		☐ 5:1-13 Chivalry
		☐ 7-1-38 Survey of Drama
		☐ 8:424-430 General Survey of Western Europe History

WORLD - OVERVIEW		
ADDITIONAL BOOKS		
ELEMENTARY	MIDDLE SCHOOL	HIGH SCHOOL

AMERICA - BIOGRAPHIES

ELEMENTARY	MIDDLE SCHOOL	HIGH SCHOOL
☐ American Hero Stories, Tappan	☐ American Hero Stories from History, McFee	☐ American Authors for Young Folks, Har
☐ American History Stories, Pratt	☐ Extraordinary Women Scientists, Stille	☐ American Leaders and Heroes, Gordy
☐ An American Book of Golden Deeds, Baldwin	☐ Famous Americans, Uhrbrock	☐ Crusaders for Freedom, Commager
☐ Days and Deeds a Hundred Years Ago, Stone	☐ Hear the Distant Applause, Vance	☐ Famous Leaders of Character in America, Wildman
☐ The Child's Book of American Biography, Stimpson	☐ Heroes of History	☐ Great American Nurses, Collins
☐ They Led the Way, Johnston	☐ Historic Americans, Brooks	☐ Group of Famous Women, Horton
☐ Watchtowers and Drums, Sterne	☐ Stories About Famous Men and Women of Our Great Country, Hadley	☐ Hero Tales, Roosevelt
	☐ Stories of Great Americans for Little Americans, Eggleston	☐ Heroes of History and Their Grand Achievements, Northrup
	☐ Ten American Girls from History, Sweetser	☐ In Search of Peace, Feuerlicht
	☐ Ten Brave Men, Daugherty	☐ Noble Living and Grand Achievements Mabie
	☐ Women in American History, Humphrey	☐ Our Famous Women
		☐ Portraits of American Women, Bradfor
		☐ Some Forgotten Heroes and Their Plac in American History, Powell
		☐ Splendid Deeds of American Heroes o Sea and Land, Fallows
		☐ The Men Who Made the Nation, Spark
		☐ The Rocket Pioneers, Beryl
		☐ The Triumph of Discovery, Dash
		☐ The Twelve Stars of Our Republic
		☐ True Stories of Famous Men and Wom of American for Young People
		☐ Youth of Famous Americans, Banks

AMERICA - BIOGRAPHIES		
ADDITIONAL BOOKS		
ELEMENTARY	MIDDLE SCHOOL	HIGH SCHOOL

WORLD - BIOGRAPHIES

ELEMENTARY	MIDDLE SCHOOL	HIGH SCHOOL
☐ A Treasury of Heroes and Heroines, Edwards	☐ Heroes Every Child Should Know, Mabie	A Group of Famous Women, Horton
☐ Boy and Girl Heroes, Farmer	☐ Heroines That Every Child Should Know, Mabie	Anecdotes of Kings, Gertrude
☐ Boyhood Stories of Famous Men, Cather	Historic Boyhoods, Holland	Famous Types of Womanhood, Bolton
☐ Fifty Famous People, Baldwin	☐ Lives of Girls Who Became Famous, Bolton	Heroes of Modern Europe, Birkhead
☐ Heroes of the Middle Ages, Tappan		Heroines of Service, Parkman
☐ Historical Tales of Illustrious Children, Strickland	Lives of Poor Boys Who Became Famous, Bolton	Lives of Celebrated Women, Goodrich
☐ Little People Who Became Great, Large	Ten Boys From History, Sweetser	Readers Digest Family Treasury
☐ When Great Folks Were Little Folks, Calhoun	Ten Girls From History, Sweetser	☐ Volume 1
☐ When They Were Children, Steedman	☐ Ten Great Adventurers, Sweetser	☐ Volume 2
		☐ Volume 3
		☐ Volume 4
		☐ Volume 5
		☐ Volume 6
		☐ Volume 7
		☐ Volume 8
		☐ Volume 9
		☐ Volume 10
		☐ Volume 11
		☐ Volume 12
		☐ Servants of the King, Speer
		☐ Some Famous Women, Creighton
		☐ Some Remarkable Women, Wise

WORLD - BIOGRAPHIES		
ADDITIONAL BOOKS		
ELEMENTARY	MIDDLE SCHOOL	HIGH SCHOOL